New York State
FOLKTALES, LEGENDS AND BALLADS

Harold W. Thompson

DOVER PUBLICATIONS, INC.
NEW YORK

Published in Canada by General Publishing Company,
Ltd., 30 Lesmill Road, Don Mills, Toronto, Ontario.
Published in the United Kingdom by Constable and Com-
pany, Ltd., 3 The Lanchesters, 162-164 Fulham Palace Road,
London W6 9ER.

This Dover edition, first published in 1962, is an unabridged
and unaltered republication of the work originally published
in 1939 under the title *Body, Boots and Britches; Folktales,
Ballads and Speech from Country New York.* This work is
reprinted by special arrangement with J. B. Lippincott
Company, publisher of the original edition.

International Standard Book Number: 0-486-26563-3
Library of Congress Catalog Card Number: 65-7559/CD

Manufactured in the United States of America
Dover Publications, Inc.
31 East 2nd Street
Mineola, N.Y. 11501

To Art and Kate, Yorkers

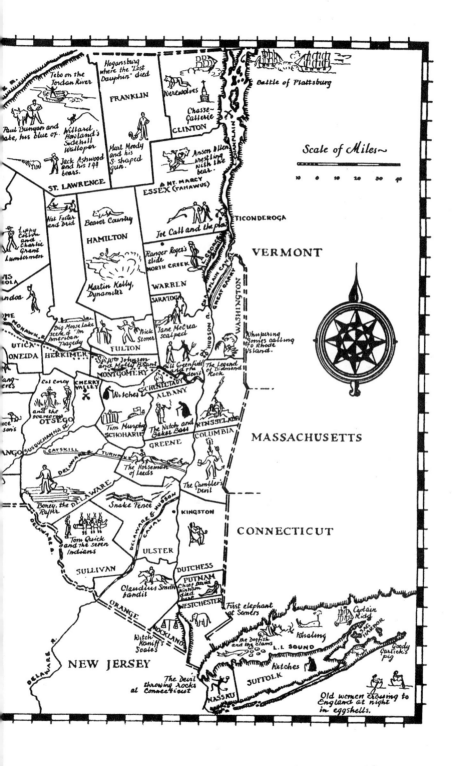

CONTENTS

I	PRELIMINARY CHIRK	9
II	PIRATES	20
III	INJUN-FIGHTERS	45
IV	SONS OF ROBIN HOOD	72
V	UNCANNY CRITTERS	101
VI	HEROES OF TALL TALES	128
VII	TRICKSTERS AND RETORTS	155
VIII	WHALERS	182
IX	PLAIN SAILORS	201
X	CANAWLERS	220
XI	LUMBERMEN AND RAFTERS	255
XII	MOUNTAINEERS	284
XIII	WARRIORS, COLONIAL AND REVOLUTIONARY	311
XIV	WARRIORS OF THE NEW NATION	341
XV	BALLAD LOVERS: TRIALS AND TRAGEDY	367
XVI	BALLAD LOVERS: COMEDY	401
XVII	MURDERERS	427
XVIII	PLACE-NAMES	449
XIX	PROVERBS	481
XX	APPENDIX: WHO TOLD YOU?	505

CONTENTS

I.
II.
III.
IV.
V.
VI.
VII.
VIII.
IX.
X.
XI.
XII.
XIII.
XIV.
XV.
XVI.
XVII.
XVIII.
XIX.
XX.

New York State
FOLKTALES, LEGENDS
AND BALLADS

I: Preliminary Chirk

IT WAS a wet British week-end—wet in the English sense—we were drinking tea. One of the ladies began to fizz.

"Tell me, Mr. Thompson," she said. "What history do you study in America? You have no history of your own."

"We study the wars of George the Third."

I fear that the reply was churlish by intent, and as stupid as the question. It had no effect whatever except to make a Scottish Herald swallow his tea the wrong way. I wish now that I had answered by telling the anecdote I had from Miss Nell Adams about the Risley shawl and the Marquis.

It happened in 1825 at the frontier village of Fredonia near Lake Erie. New York State was furiously playing host to the venerable Marquis de Lafayette—towing him up and down the Grand Canal, letting him shake the hand of every surviving veteran of the Revolution, and giving him a sight of Red Jacket, Niagara Falls, and all the other natural wonders. At Fredonia the citizens had prepared something special. A French explorer had named their creek *La Terre Puante*, "Stinking Shore,"— not without cause; now the village could and did boast that it was the first in America to be illuminated by natural gas. In honor of the Marquis, additional lights had been installed about a platform on the village green, to shine on the bright red hue of the only "boughten" carpet in the region, generously and anxiously lent by the Episcopal minister's wife. Her anxiety was well founded, for on that memorable night the carpet was damaged beyond repair by the stomp of hobnailed boots.

The expectation was that the General would arrive in the early evening. Long before dark, the five hundred citizens were assembled, their numbers augmented by other hundreds who had come from out-lying farms to tread upon the store-carpet. Night fell, and the wonder-ful lights were turned on, but no Lafayette appeared. Nine, ten, eleven, twelve o'clock struck, and still the crowd waited. Then up to the com-mon raced yelling boys with the news that the General's carriage was at the bridge. The great Reception began.

Now there was one lady in Fredonia who was expected to shine with special glory when she curtseyed to Lafayette. Mrs. Laurens Risley was the owner of a handsome Paisley shawl, presumably imported from Scotland, certainly the fairest article of feminine apparel in the county. Tradition derives the name Fredonia from an Indian one meaning Free Woman; that night Mrs. Risley proved herself free in the noble sense of generous. No sooner had she greeted the French hero on the platform than she slipped back into the shadows and handed her shawl to a friend—and then to another, and to another, until the General's eyes were more dazzled by bright Paisley tints than by the illumination. Afterward he said: "Fredonia! It is a village of beautiful women, beautifully dressed. You would scarcely believe it of a frontier settlement, but I give you my word that in none of the large cities of America have I ever seen so many handsome shawls."

The Sprague piano shares a place in story with the Risley shawl. The first instrument of its sort in the county, it attracted as much attention as the circus of a later era, particularly among the numerous citizens who had no idea what a piano was. One farmer left his oxen at the mill, and with his son at heel started afoot across country to satisfy his curiosity. When the visitors arrived at the kitchen door, Mrs. Sprague had just taken biscuits from another new contraption, a tin bake-oven whose fame was not yet abroad. As he entered, the boy pointed toward the oven and whispered hoarsely, "Paw, paw, what is that?" Not to be overawed by the grandeur of the Spragues, his father answered, "Piano, you damn fool!"

These two anecdotes—aren't they history? If there is anything worth hearing in the corridor of time, it is the courageous laughter of our ancestors; if there is anything in the past worth preserving, it is the generosity of the frontier. To me the laughter and generosity seem contemporary, and not merely because, like all the poets, I "believe in the continuing present". When the Centenary of Chautauqua County was celebrated in 1902, my grandfather Thompson, his white pow covered with a silk hat, raised his ebony stick to the gold-headed cane of the oldest college graduate in America, explaining to me that "Squire" Austin Smith of Westfield, first Principal of the Fredonia Academy, was an object of special interest today, because he had married a daughter of the County's first white settler. So these eyes have blinked at one of "old Hamilton's" early graduates, the son-in-law of my County's founder. Of course, not all of York State is so comically young as Chautauqua County. For twenty-five years, I have lived in Albany, which claims to be the second-oldest city in the United States; founded earlier than Boston, its easy dignity rests upon more than three centuries of prosperous tradition. This book concerns the pioneer Yorkers as I have followed their legend from the founding of Albany in the early seventeenth century to the beginnings of Buffalo, Westfield, and a hundred other frontier communities in the nineteenth.

Probably the most diverting songs and stories you know are those you *heard* and did not read. That was certainly my experience. I liked my mother's ballads and hymns, my Scotch-Irish grandfather's reminiscences, the spirituals of the Negroes who worked for my father when we lived in a suburb of New York City, the fairy-tales of our German nurse-girl. Later, when we moved back to Chautauqua County, I revelled in the droll anecdotes of my pastor, his wife, and our organist—three wits who knew the town from A to Izzard. Then I had the luck to attend the college which believes most firmly in the spoken word; the Hamilton which I knew required what was called Public Speaking through every term of the four years, and regarded singing as equally important though properly more spontaneous. I think that more than one college then was a depot of American folksong; our curiously varied collection included a sniffing chorus which John Lomax later identified for me as a cocaine-song from a southern Negro dive.

The President at Hamilton was Melancthon Woolsey Stryker, the most electrifying orator I have heard and, with the exception of Caruso, the possessor of the loudest "beller". Only once was he surpassed, when he commissioned me, as college organist, to have a classmate introduce a pair of Turkish war-cymbals into the Easter service. We contrived to conceal these notable engines until Prex started a hymn, "Lion of Judah, hail!" Then Jack West—now an innocent Professor of Mathematics—spread both arms to full length, brought the cymbals together above his head, and drowned Prex with a brazen clangor the like of which I shall not hear again. All the faculty wives and half the students reeled back and sat down hard. (Alec Woollcott will deny that he fainted; I did not see him.) Nobody but Prex, now with God, and myself knows what his gentle wife said directly after the service; I will reveal this much—that he and I were forbidden so much as to store that Obscene Tinware in the Presidential barn.

Somehow Prex convinced us that literature is what is said out loud —often very loud—or sung, not what is written down *in litteris*. This idea he applied even to Latin; he conducted Commencement in the ancient tongue, greatly to the confusion of a brass band which could never learn that his "Musica sit!" meant "Let there be music!" but only cowered down into their seats when his order was given. A considerable number of us have tried to apply his theory. Not to mention the brilliant lawyers, clergymen, and teachers that he trained, there were within a decade Alec Drummond, who founded the folk-drama of New York and directs the Cornell Theatre; Alec Woollcott, First Gentleman of the radio and the lecture-platform; Johnny Weaver, who wrote for stage and screen and put American slang into verse; and Carl Carmer, who records the spoken lore of Alabama and New York. At the founding of the New York Folklore Society, four of the seven officers were Hamilton graduates.

My own love for folksong and the folktale, reinforced by Professor Kittredge at Harvard, remained a demure hobby for years, because I could make plenty of noise playing a four-manual church-organ.

Once a year, John Lomax, the first collector of cowboy songs, came up from Texas to keep my enthusiasm warm. Though I was a plain teacher of English, I was asked to reorganize a department of music at the State College in Albany; I had the big chorus sing a great deal of folk-music, and Musical Appreciation became a course in Folksong and Bach. Finally I had to decide whether I was a musician or what, and decided on the second; but I was unregenerate—we roared ballads in Scottish Literature and hummed madrigals in Shakespeare class. After three or four years of ineffective blandishment I was permitted to relapse into Prexism so far as to give a course in the Folk-Literature of America, which, it was feared with reason, was going to be extremely noisy, and which, as was not foreseen, was to produce the present volume. Pretty soon I began to ask why seventy to two hundred students should sing the ballads of Texas or South Carolina or Kentucky, when they might be gathering the lore of their own State. A learned lady had told Lomax that New York has no folklore, but we started to collect it anyhow.

The time was at least ripe, perhaps over-ripe. No matter when you start, you are always told that you are ten years late. At first I succeeded in getting songs, then tall tales, then all the kinds of traditional material concerned with pioneering farmers, and with such romantic occupations as whaling, lumbering, rafting, guiding, and canawling. As all this lore poured into a big filing cabinet, my lectures improved because they were no longer mine; the folk had taken charge. I began to say: "Suppose that anyone wanted to know the history of New York outside the big city—know it *body, boots, and britches*—what better could he do than to read this lore collected by a group of native Yorkers of superior intelligence, many of whom belong to families which pioneered our counties?" To be frank, I said this only in rare moments of solemnity; oftener I used another proverbial expression and just said, "I haven't had so much fun since Grandpa sat in the hornets' nest!"

What I am about to print in the following chapters should speak for itself, but it is only decent to hint where I got it and who brought it. A few examples will suffice. Perhaps the handsomest county in the State is Essex, which borders on Lake Champlain and has most of the highest Adirondack peaks. Miss Edith Cutting of that "up-histed" land brought me more than a hundred typed pages of ballads and other songs, tall tales, legends, proverbs, weather-rhymes, beliefs in the supernatural, games, retorts, and assorted lore of the lumber-jacks. Her grandfather, her father, and a number of uncles have all worked in the "wildwoods". A grandmother's uncle was a whaler who left to the family a fascinating log, a model ship, and some "pints" about the weather. A great-great-grandmother was a Quaker lady so skilled at spinning and weaving that at one time she had in her house two thousand yards of material of her own manufacture. One great-grandfather was the Adirondack guide who built the first road around the Cascade lakes; that pioneer's son, Grandfather White, was also a guide. Edith's family live on a hill-farm half way between the vil-lages of Lewis and Elizabethtown, but her mother, who was once a teacher, "keeps up" by attending teachers' conventions. Back-a-ways, you can find a strain of Dutch and another of Scotch, but for the most part the family—Cuttings, Whites, Coucheys—are English of the sort whose inheritance will always be our pride. I have accepted their gracious and numerous contributions to this book—folklore of-fered with the same hospitality which I have enjoyed at table in that mountain home.

Take another example of my indebtedness—from President Roose-velt's county of Dutchess. At about the time when his family came from Holland in the seventeenth century, old "Tristum" (Tristram) Coffin migrated from Devonshire, England, to become the chief magistrate of the wind-blown island of Nantucket, and to sire the most famous family of American whalers—not to mention poets, preachers, and other small deer. In the late eighteenth century more than one branch of the family moved to York State. Doris Coffin's people have preserved the proverbs and sea-faring terms of ancestors—as you are to find later. She brought to me one day *The Last of the "Logan"*, an unpublished manuscript by a Robert Coffin who went awhaling in the era of Melville's *Moby Dick*, was wrecked in the South Seas, lived among cannibals at Fiji, hunted gold in Australia, and came home because he heard there was to be a war. I am quoting from this manuscript; sometime I hope to publish it all.

The finest single collection of old ballads came unsolicited because Principal Harry S. Douglass of Arcade saw a little essay of mine and thought that I might like to copy songs which his family had written down in the two decades preceding the Civil War. When I had typed them, I found that I had seventy-nine songs, filling ninety-four pages. Most of them were about war and love; in age they range from very old English and Scottish ballads ("Child ballads" we call them after a Harvard Professor who made the most important collection and classification) to campaign songs of American Presidential elections.

Most of the ballads which you are to read were taken down from memory. (I almost used the pedantic expression, "oral transmission", which once brought upon me the resonant ridicule of Carl Sandburg.) There was Mr. Peleg W. Andrew of C'rinth in Saratoga County, who was born in 1853 on the 26th of December; he explained to his grand-daughter Jane that he would have been a Christmas present to someone if the 25th hadn't fallen on Wash-Day (Monday). This sprightly grandfather learned many songs from his own Yankee father, memorized more of them in the lumberwoods, picked up several at singing school, and became a prince of balladeers. From time to time, Jane brought me a sheaf of ditties until I had thirty-five of his best songs. Finally I was permitted to pay a visit. The fine old man's voice was still as true and moving a tenor as I have heard anywhere among folk-singers, but nothing would induce him to sing me more than one ballad. Some other time, perhaps. He was taken sick with pneumonia, and sang himself out of delirium into something like health; but he was sure now that he would never let me hear those tunes—he had a frog in his throat. He died in the winter of 1938-9. He used to listen to my monthly broadcasts on folklore; it is grief to me that he will not read his ballads in this book, and that while I was writing, both Blind Sam and old Mr. Mack slipped out of the nineties into a life where I hope there is balladry.

I have collections larger than the ones I have mentioned; in fact, several of my students have completed under my direction at Albany and Cornell long dissertations for the Master's degree, usually on the folklore of a single county. Some of these are listed in the Appendix. I won't divulge further the collector's pride, except to say thank-you to the scores of people whose names are listed in the proper place. To show how such a book as this is really built, I have left up the scaffolding on a chapter concerned with the Tall Tales, where I let you

know how the stories were obtained and how one folk-hero led to another. I could have secured a more artistic unity there and in the entire
volume by pretending that I went around getting all these tales myself. The fact is that I had a job no less exacting, training hundreds of
young people how to collect, and what and where. Those hundreds
had their fun and will now feel pride in a book which no one person
could have made.

After I had filled a big case with lore collected from students,
members of my radio audience, and other generous friends, Christopher Morley and Frank Henry, with whom I've roared ballads until
every survivor except Chris was hoarse, decided that I'd better start
printing. My brother "Speed" had some ideas about the typography.
When President Brubacher of the State College gave me sabbatical
leave and the Rockefeller Foundation presented a grant-in-aid, I had
to write the book. It has been composed just as the clipper-captains
claimed that the clumsy whaling ships were built—"made by the mile
and cut off in len'ths". The trouble is that I made too many miles
and the lengths exceed that of an ordinary chapter; you will be comforted to know that the book once was nearly twice as long. I had
"cute" titles for the chapters and other fixin's, but they seemed inap-
propriate to the homespun ballads, and anyhow I share Morris
Bishop's hatred of elves.

Let's have it out here and now about the accuracy of this book
or of any book about folklore. In an Appendix I have told where I
got my material; that is expected of anyone with a proper feeling
of gratitude and a willingness to have his work appraised by experts.
As if you were sitting in with me on a little poker-game and—how
did the question go?—you said, "Gentleman's game, Dry, but what
in Sam Hill did you open with?" I have the openers and, to tell the
truth, not much more; but some poet or novelist or playwright may
come along and play the hand with great success. I don't want any
onlooker to say, as I heard one declare about a good book: "This fellow is a fake; that incident belongs in Malone, not Watertown."
The story belongs wherever the folk choose to put it; they keep moving it around and changing it a little. What you have a right to ask
is that I shan't do any of the moving and changing. In spite of all my
care, I am bound to make scores of mistakes; that is the penalty of

anyone who breaks new ground. I remember what happened to Dr. Hedrick, whose *History of Agriculture in New York State* is one of the half dozen best books about Upstate ever written—a book which demonstrates how a man who knows one subject thoroughly can illuminate a hundred other matters. Well, Dr. Hedrick wrote his noble book but was prevented from reading part of the proofs. When he got the bound volume, he discovered that the name of the prime hoss in the history of New York and the Milky Way was spelled Hamiltonian instead of Hambletonian. If you don't live in New York or Kentucky, you cannot realize the full horror of that moment. I expect to shudder often at my own ignorance, imbecility, and bad luck, but I shall comfort myself that Dr. Hedrick survived *his* ill fortune and that even he did not make a perfect book.

It would have been easier to inflate each chapter into a little volume than to diminish it to its present proportions. I tell in curt, anecdotal form a story which Alec Woollcott could have made into something rare and strange, holding an audience for fifteen minutes. Even if I didn't have the need for compression, I do not possess any of his gift at upholstering. I do believe, however, that brevity is a characteristic of my State's lore. I was talking about this with the official collector of folklore for Eire, Mr. O'Delargy. When he says *folktale*, he means something that lasts from breakfast to the going down of the sun; a Yorker means by the same word something that lasts about as long as the interval between the first and second drinks at a tenth college reunion. My book is deliberately intended to be taken as a series of "quick ones"—not too many at a time.

As happened in the case of a book by Carl Carmer, some cities or sections may think that I have scanted them. I wasn't writing about sections; that has been done by Carmer in *Listen for a Lonesome Drum* and *The Hudson*, and by Hungerford in *Pathway of Empire*. Deliberately I have slighted the cities except Buffalo, which happens to have a wealth of racy frontier lore; the others will contribute to a book in which I shall show the contributions of Irish, Italian, Polish, Russian, and Jews to our legends and songs. I have tried not to duplicate Carmer, Hungerford, or any of the other writers whom I admire, but I hope that I have shown the real people and true stories back of the fiction of Irving, Cooper, Melville, Westcott,

Bacheller, Edmonds, Roberts, Burlingame, and all the others who have tried to interpret our State's romance.

I didn't desire to glorify any little region, nor even New York except as it is the most typical and varied of all States in its folklore. Vermont is the home of the pawky anecdote—as all readers of Walter Hard's unique poetry know; yet I am constantly getting retorts and trickster tales identical with some of Hard's, brought me by people of New York who have never read a line of the Vermont poet's. At luncheon recently, two colleagues, "raised" west of the Mississippi, told me tall tales for fifteen or twenty minutes; with a single exception —a story about grasshoppers—I had heard every one of the tales in my own State. When I was a boy, I loved to read about Dan'l Boone of Kentucky; if you try my chapter about our Injun-fighters, you will see that we have known the same type of frontiersman. The Virginians have charming stories about the owners of great estates and their Negroes. Well, I know of four Negro families in Albany who claim descent from slaves of Dutch patroons in the seventeenth century, and who have never condescended to marry into colored families from the South. As for baronial estates—the late James Fenimore Cooper of "Fynmere", grandson of the novelist, told me that old Judge Cooper of Cooperstown had three-quarters of a million acres in land and forty thousand tenants, and that the last patroon Van Rensselaer had an estate almost identical in size.

If you write well about other States, you will probably be describing something in New York. I enjoy the pictures of rural life found in the books of Mrs. Della Lutes, partly because, though she is narrating a girlhood in Michigan, she is depicting York State manners as truly as if her father had never migrated from us. If you wish to get a humorously delightful account of rural life in Georgia before the Civil War, you will certainly read W. T. Thompson's sketches of "Major Jones"; but the manners revealed seem to me almost identical with those that could have been found in New York about thirty years earlier, and even the Major's dialect strongly resembles ours in that era.

There is one other word of apologetic explanation to be said, about that lack of tunes in this book which my friend John Lomax and other important collectors will condemn. This isn't a book of ballads; it is

a book of Yorkers, whose balladry does happen to express well some
of their favorite stories and strongest emotions. I hope to publish a
book of tunes later; for the present I beg that readers will be content
to accept a more inclusive collection of folklore, in verse and prose,
than any other State has published in a single volume. Almost as
much as the tunes I regret the holiday lore, weather-rhymes, folk-
medicine, omens, balladry of married life, songs about accidents, and
a dozen other chapters which I have had to leave in dock until the
time comes to try the "delight and danger of blue water".

Body, boots, and britches*is a proverbial expression collected in
Dutchess County; it means "the whole thing". A hundred volumes
would not tell the whole thing about Upstate New York, but in this
book I have at least tried, without smirk or caper, to let the folk say
their own piece. This isn't what I think about them, spun out of a
dull fancy; this isn't an individual traveling up and down as a "star
reporter". This, as I want Carl Sandburg to say, is *The People, Yes.*
At the beginning of each topic I have had trouble shifting from my
own style—that of a fat person feebly waving a pointer—to the livelier
speech and narrative of the folk. If you don't like the opening of a
chapter, skip three pages and see what happens. Pleasant skipping!

*This expression was used as the title for previous editions of this book.

II: Pirates

PIECES of eight to doits, you were introduced to Captain Kidd in that blessed year when you read *Treasure Island* for the first time. It was at his Anchorage on Skeleton Island that you and Jim Hawkins landed for the great adventure. A little later you found the Captain's treasure in Poe's prize story, *The Gold Bug*. If you were lucky, it was not long after when you came upon Irving's *Tales of a Traveller* and its juicy section called *The Money Diggers*, in which is inset that short, romantic account of the Captain which is still the inspiration of a hundred folktales.

There are three Captain Kidds, but to the folklorist the best of them is Irving's—really the creation of the folk and the balladeers. The *romantic* Kidd still sails Long Island Sound in his sash of velvet orange; he is wearing heavy gold ear-rings set with yellow sapphires, a bandoleer of cloth of gold, King Charles boots with gold buckles. There are more than fifteen on that dead man's chest; the Earl of Hell himself has taken charge and all the powers of Night. Not a County on Hudson's River, not an islet in the Sound but has its whispers and hopes of buried treasure, all planted by Kidd on those few nights when he hovered between Block Island and Gardiner's, swithering whether to trust a Royal Governor or to let his long, low, black sloop, the *Antonio*, slip away to Hispaniola where the *Quedah Merchant* and a greater trove awaited the master who never returned.

The Terror of the Malabar Coast, for two centuries the Captain has been the pride of that island which he called Nassau (Long Island). I wonder how many people bought that map published in Sag Harbor, port of the whalers—the map which infallibly showed the location of Kidd's treasure. One of my students from Long Island has something even more authentic to report:

My uncle has in his possession now a map copied from an "original" which probably was not one of those printed at Sag Harbor, for it locates the treasure at a spot on the mainland of Long Island, not on Gardiner's Island. With this map comes a most interesting story which accounts for its being in America in this way:

Before Captain Kidd was hung back in England on the banks of the Thames, he gave a map of buried treasure to a young cabin boy of his— that member of the crew most likely to be set free. After several years, the boy got passage to America. For some unknown reason he landed in Ellsworth, Maine. He planned, of course, to come to Long Island, but before he could ever gather enough money to complete his trip, he was taken very ill. When he knew that he would die, he gave the map to his landlady in payment for his room and board, for he was quite penniless. In course of time, this map came into the possession of a certain Captain Smith in Maine who had a brother living in Sayville, L. I. Also living in Sayville was an architect, a friend of Smith's. When Smith and he learned about the treasure, they set out for Amagansett by train, and went from there by bicycle. They spent several days digging, but found no trace of the treasure.

According to the map, the treasure is buried on the north side of the narrow strip of land at Montauk, just east of Great Pond. The way you find the spot is by "sighting"; find the spot where you can see all three of these places: New Haven, Connecticut; Stonington, Connecticut; and ————.* The exact location, after you have determined the general area, is in the shape of a triangle whose angles are marked with a piece of Connecticut brown stone and two pieces of Long Island stone respectively. My uncle obtained his copy from the architect, who made this copy from the original.

* Just for fun I omit the name of the third place.

Even if you had that superlative map, you would need to remember to preserve strict silence when you were digging. Of course you would take care to use only a brand-new spade, upon which it would be wise to fix your stare with hypnotic calm. If, at the sight of an iron ring on an oaken plank, you should utter the slightest exclamation, your trove would disappear under extremely unpleasant circumstances. You might observe these precautions in vain, because at least one of the chests is guarded by a sailor who was put into the hole, made to swear to guard the chest, and then slain where his ghost would do most service. The greatest peril of all is that the Earl of Hell himself, at whose command Kidd "buried his Bible in the sand", might appear as he did to those seeking Kidd's treasure at Point of Pines, Massachusetts, in the form of a hatless giant riding a charger with flaming nostrils.

Like Poe and Stevenson, I regard a map as indispensable, but a good word is to be said for the Mineral-Rod. This valuable apparatus is a fork of witch-hazel, such as our *dowsers* upstate use in finding water-wells; into its straight part is inserted a pure white goose-quill filled with quicksilver and covered tightly with kid. For some days before using this occult instrument the operator should carry a lucky bone; he should also keep his errand as secret as the hidden rod. When the proper time arrives, remember that the tighter you hold the rod, the better it works.

While there are thousands who still think wistfully of the treasure and cherish its lore, I have found nobody who knows more than a stanza or two from tradition of that doleful ballad which was hawked about Execution Dock, London, for tuppence on that May day when Captain Kidd was "turned off" and "left drying". Washington Irving knew part of it, and there is plenty of other evidence that it was once popular in America. I will give you a few stanzas from a little volume which for a century or so has been in the possession of a North-Country family; it is entitled *The Forget Me Not Songster, containing a choice collection of old ballad songs as sung by our grandmothers.* Curiously enough, the ballad always gives Kidd's name as Robert, though it was indubitably William; there is an artistic appropriateness in calling the blue-eyed Scottish-American by the name of the Bruce. The poet seems to have been aware that Kidd's father was a minister,

and that his first trial was for murdering his gunner, William Moore
—next day he was tried for piracy. Kidd did *not* capture any Spanish
ships, but most Englishmen from Drake's day forward liked to see
that done. I omit stanzas in which the Captain, moved by a dying
mate's warning and by his own sickness, has a fit of repentance.

> You captains bold and brave, hear our cries, hear our cries,
>> You captains bold and brave, hear our cries,
> You captains bold and brave, tho' you seem uncontrolled,
>> Don't for the sake of gold lose your souls, lose your souls,
>> Don't for the sake of gold lose your souls.

> My name was Robert Kidd, when I sailed, when I sailed,
>> My name was Robert Kidd when I sailed,
> My name was Robert Kidd, God's laws I did forbid,
>> And so wickedly I did when I sailed.

> My parents taught me well when I sailed, when I sailed,
>> My parents taught me well when I sailed,
> My parents taught me well, to shun the gates of hell,
>> But against them I rebell'd, when I sailed.

> I cursed my father dear, when I sailed, when I sailed,
>> I cursed my father dear when I sailed,
> I cursed my father dear, and her that did me bear,
>> And so wickedly did swear, when I sailed.

> I made a solemn vow, when I sailed, when I sailed,
>> I made a solemn vow when I sailed,
> I made a solemn vow, to God I would not bow,
>> Nor myself one prayer allow, as I sailed.

> I'd a Bible in my hand when I sailed, when I sailed,
>> I'd a Bible in my hand when I sailed,
> I'd a Bible in my hand by my father's great command:
>> And sunk it in the sand when I sailed.

> I murdered William Moore, as I sailed, as I sailed,
>> I murdered William Moore as I sailed,
> I murdered William Moore, and left him in his gore,
>> Not many leagues from shore, as I sailed . . .

I steered from sound to sound, as I sailed, as I sailed,
I steered from sound to sound as I sailed,
I steered from sound to sound and many ships I found,
And most of them I burned, as I sailed.

I spy'd three ships from France, as I sailed, as I sailed,
I spy'd three ships from France, as I sailed,
I spy'd three ships from France, to them I did advance,
And took them all by chance, as I sailed.

I spy'd three ships of Spain, as I sailed, as I sailed,
I spy'd three ships of Spain, as I sailed,
I spy'd three ships of Spain, I fired on them amain,
Till most of them were slain, as I sailed.

I'd ninety bars of gold, as I sailed, as I sailed,
I'd ninety bars of gold, as I sailed,
I'd ninety bars of gold, and dollars manifold,
With riches uncontrolled, as I sailed.

Then fourteen ships I saw, as I sailed, as I sailed,
Then fourteen ships I saw, as I sailed,
Then fourteen ships I saw, and brave men they are,
Ah! they were too much for me, as I sailed.

Thus being o'ertaken at last, I must die, I must die,
Thus being o'ertaken at last, I must die;
Thus being o'ertaken at last, and into prison cast,
And sentence being passed, I must die.

Farewell, the raging sea, I must die, I must die,
Farewell, the raging main, I must die,
Farewell, the raging main, in Turkey, France, and Spain,
I ne'er shall see you again, I must die.

To Newgate now I'm cast, and must die, and must die,
To Newgate now I'm cast, and must die,
To Newgate I am cast, with a sad and heavy heart,
To receive my just desert, I must die.

To Execution Dock, I must go, I must go,
  To Execution Dock I must go,
To Execution Dock will many thousands flock,
  But I must bear the shock, I must die.

Come all you young and old, see me die, see me die,
  Come all you young and old, see me die,
Come all you young and old, you're welcome to my gold,
  For by it I've lost my soul, and must die.

Take warning now by me, for I must die, I must die,
  Take warning now by me, for I must die,
Take warning now by me, and shun bad company,
  Lest you come to hell with me, for I must die,
  Lest you come to hell with me, for I must die.

Of the thousands who saw Kidd "turned off" at Execution Dock, *infra fluxum et refluxum maris,* we may be pretty sure that none found themselves welcome to his gold. The most spacious estimate of it is mentioned in the diary of a certain Luttrell who reported on August 1, 1699, that the Captain was said to have taken four hundred thousand pounds from subjects of the Great Mogul. Just before the execution it was rumored that he had offered one hundred thousand pounds for a pardon. The fact seems to be—and I am unaware of the ultimate destination of Kidd's loot—that the property and effects forfeited to the Crown amounted to exactly six thousand, four hundred and seventy-one pounds; at any rate, that is what Queen Anne gave with her compliments (and Kidd's) toward the founding of Greenwich Hospital. That sum represents the more or less honestly earned fortune of a New York shipmaster and owner. Regarding the loot, some of which was returned to England by Governor Bellomont, I cannot certify; it is extremely unlikely that it reached its original owners, the subjects of the Great Mogul and others unknown. It is quite possible that some of it is buried in New York State.

During the past twenty-five or thirty years, a new interpretation of Captain Kidd has grown up, presenting him as the innocent and puzzled victim of a group of hi-jackers, leaders in English official life, men who hired him to rob for their own benefit from the King's enemies, the French, and from the pirates whom a greedy colonial policy had engendered. This interpretation is almost as serviceable for the films as the older one—though it has not produced entertaining folklore—and it is probably true to some extent, because it was invented by men who did consult some of the records, though they had not the scholarship or the caution to go far enough in their researches. In 1911 we had an early example of this new interpretation in a *Book of Hidden Treasure* by R. D. Paine, who was excited to discover in the Public Records Office at London the two French passes for captured vessels which Kidd asserted would establish his innocence. If those two vessels were sailing under passes from the English King's enemies, Kidd, as a commissioned privateer, had some justification for seizing the ships, though he had still to explain why they were not properly condemned in a court—and he did attempt to explain by asserting that his men mutinied and deserted.

Kidd's new defenders build up their case somewhat as follows: Here was an able Scot, the son of a clergyman and himself a shipmaster and owner of repute in the colony of New York. His naval services against the French in the West Indies in 1689-90 were highly regarded by his English commander; the Governor of the Leeward Islands in 1690 rewarded him for the loss of a ship by presenting a barkentine, the *Antigua*. In 1691 Kidd married at New York the respectable widow of a prosperous merchant, a "lovely and accomplished woman"—though she could not write her name. By her he seems to have had at least one daughter. So he was a settled married man with a family and a flourishing business. Toward the government his loyalty had been so conspicuous that the Provincial Council of New York in April, 1691, put on record his "many good services done to the Province in his attending here with his vessels before His Excellency's arrival"—that is, during the semi-anarchy preceding the administration of Governor Sloughter. In May, the House of Representatives recommended a reward of £150. Later in the year, the Government of Massachusetts commissioned him to chase an enemy privateer off the coast. This does not sound like the "notorious pyrate" who was hanged ten years later.

In the autumn of 1695, while he was in London on his own proper affairs, Kidd was persuaded to undertake an expedition under two commissions: to exterminate piracy, and to act as a privateer in capturing vessels of the French against whom William III was still waging war. In his statement to the House of Commons before which he was to be tried in 1701, Kidd said:

I hope I have not offended against the Law, but if I have, it was the fault of others who knew better, and made me the Tool of their Ambition and Avarice, and who now perhaps think it their interest that I should be removed out of the world.

I did not seek the Commission I undertook, but was partly Cajold, and partly menac'd into it by the Lord Bellomont, and one Robert Livingston of New York, who was the projector, promoter, and Chief Manager of that designe, and who only can give your House a satisfactory account of all the Transactions of my Owners. He was the man admitted into their Closets, and received their private Instructions, which he kept in his own hands, and who encouraged me in their names to do more than I ever did, and to act without regard to my Commission.

Now who were the sinister persons whose Ambition and Avarice caused the overthrow of our innocent pirate? First of all, there was Robert Livingston (1654-1728), first lord of a famous manor on the Hudson, probably the ablest man in the Province of New York and pretty certainly the most acquisitive. He was born in Roxburghshire, Scotland, of a cadet branch of the noble Earls of Linlithgow; like Kidd, he was the son of a Presbyterian minister who suffered for his religion at the time of the Restoration. Livingston came to Albany in 1674 after a residence of several years with his father in Holland. At the end of one year he was Town Clerk and Secretary of the Board of Commissioners for Indian Affairs. He married a sister of Peter Schuyler, the widow of a Van Rensselaer, and within a remarkably short time was able to make her the mistress of a manorial estate of 160,000 acres in what we now call Columbia and Dutchess Counties. He acquired money out of trade with the Indians, out of government contracts, out of interest from sums advanced to a royal governor in anticipation of the collection of taxes, and in sundry other ways. The two Governors who were concerned with Kidd have left their opinions of Livingston: Fletcher said, "He has made a considerable fortune . . . never disbursing sixpence but with the expectation of twelve pence, his beginning being a little Book keeper, he has screwed himself into one of the most considerable estates in the province . . . he had rather be called knave Livingston than poor Livingston." Bellomont, in a moment of exasperation against one with whom he usually got along fairly well, said that Livingston had "pinched an estate out of the poor soldiers' bellies". While I am sure that the Livingstons were and are one of the ablest and most useful families in the history of the State, it is evident that when Kidd charged Robert with sharp practice, he could have got others to agree.

Livingston's noble partners included the first Earl of Bellomont of the Irish Peerage, one of Dutch William's Earls, appointed Governor of New York in 1695 with the express desire of his King that he clean up piracy. Supposedly he was to pay four-fifths of the cost of a ship for the expedition; Livingston and Kidd were to pay the other fifth. The crew was to be hired on the contract of *No purchase, no pay*—the word *purchase* being an euphemism for *loot*. The crew's share was to be not more than one-fourth, and less "in case the same may reasonably and conveniently be agreed upon". If Kidd hadn't taken enough by March 20, 1697, to repay Bellomont, he and Livingston were to reimburse the noble lord for what he had put out, "the Danger of the Seas, and of the King's Enemies, and Mortality of the said Captain Kid always excepted". If the Captain were lucky in looting and were still alive at the end of the voyage, the crew was to get its one-fourth; the other three-fourths were to be divided into five parts, of which Bellomont was to have four, and the other fifth was to be split between Kidd and Livingston. If Kidd should be so fortunate as to bring to Boston one hundred thousand pounds or upward, the ship was to be his.

This sounds as if Kidd were to do all the work, run all the risk, and get a small proportion of the reward. It must be remembered, however, that Bellomont was to secure the two royal commissions for seizing pirates and for acting as a privateer against the King's enemies; moreover—and this took some finesse—Bellomont was to get from the King a Grant (to "some indifferent and trusty person") of all merchandise and treasure which should be taken from the pirates; in this manner, the original owners of the loot would be checkmated if they tried to recover.

While a "prety frigate built ship" called the *Adventure Galley*—two hundred and eighty-seven tons and thirty-four guns—was being secured, Bellomont evidently decided to let in some of his friends on the venture. This may have been an example of that sheer good-nature which the American historian, Bancroft, attributed to him, but it may have been a desire to protect himself politically as well as financially. At any rate, the £4,800 for which he was supposedly responsible was largely if not entirely subscribed by six persons whose identity was not revealed in the Grant, but whose names were not hard to discover. They included Sir John Somers, most noted lawyer in the Kingdom and from 1697 Lord Chancellor. (That was like bringing in our American Chief Justice.) Then there was Henry Sidney, Earl of Romney, who had helped to enthrone William and Mary and who had been richly rewarded; he was made Secretary of State in 1690-91, Master-General of Ordinance in 1693, and a Lord Justice four years later. Edward Russell, Earl of Orford, another favorite of William, was First Lord of Admiralty. Charles Talbot, Duke of Shrewsbury, called by William his King of Hearts, was Secretary of State, a Lord Justice, and in 1695 practically head of the administration. Anyone who attacked what these noble lords did would need courage. They had in the cozy little party one London man of business, Edward Harrison, a City merchant, director of the new East India Company—the organization most anxious to see piracy ended. For the crew, whose selection he supervised, he rejected all Scots and all colonists, because he thought that their sympathies would be with smugglers and pirates.

The creators of the legend of the innocent Kidd point out that a considerable number of his hand-picked crew were taken off by press-officers as the *Adventure Galley* reached the Nore, and that consequently he had to shark up a contingent in New York that must have included a good many who were not indisposed to piracy. They also point out that on the way to New York the Captain seized a little French fishing vessel or "banker", and had her properly condemned when he reached the Province on July 4, 1696.

After making up his crew and seeing that King William got his tenth of the loot of the French banker, Kidd put to sea from New York on the sixth of September. From that time it is fairly easy to trace his general movement, though he asserted that his mutinous crew later stole his log—so that even he was not quite sure of what happened. His story was that he sailed around the Cape of Good Hope, proceeded to Madagascar (which was supposed to be the head-quarters of the pirates he was seeking, though he found none), thence to Mohilla, where he lost fifty in a week from cholera; and, a year out from London, with no loot to show, found his crew getting out of control, demanding that he turn pirate. He asserted that he increased discontent by refusing to attack a Dutch ship called the *Loyal Captain*, and that he met further peril when he was attacked by two Portuguese ships, which he bravely repelled. One mutinous gunner he accidentally killed by hitting him with a bucket. Finally he did take two ships, each one sailing with a French pass though not French in ownership—each one legally his prey by commission as a privateer. The smaller of these, called the *Maiden*, was not worth much, but the larger, the *Quedah Merchant*, was a truly rich prize of 400-500 tons.

In May of 1698 he arrived in Madagascar at St. Marie, an islet off the coast, headquarters for some pirates, as he soon discovered. The head of this gang was one Robert Culliford. Not only did Kidd's men refuse to capture the pirates, but some ninety-seven of them deserted to the other commander, leaving only thirteen to navigate Kidd's ship and her prizes. Moreover, according to Kidd, his mutinous men stole his papers and much of his loot, burned the *Adventure Galley* after transferring her treasures to the *Quedah Merchant*, and sailed off with Culliford. Kidd waited in Madagascar five months to recruit his crew and get a fair wind; then he sailed for Boston to surrender to Bellomont what he had saved from the mutineers and deserters. In the West Indies he got news that he had been proclaimed a pirate, and also realized that the *Quedah Merchant* was no longer seaworthy; whereupon he bought a fast sloop called the *Antonio* or *St. Anthony*, put part of his treasure in her, left the rest to be guarded by a man from whom he had bought the *Antonio*, and sailed for home with about ten thousand pounds of treasure.

In June of 1699 he was in Long Island Sound, where he consulted with his friend John Emmott, an Admiralty lawyer of New York, who undertook to present his case to Governor Bellomont at Boston. The Governor accepted the two French passes and replied:

I am apt to believe they will be a good Article to justify you, if the late Peace were not, by the Treaty between England and France, to operate in that Part of the World at the time the Hostility was committed, as I am almost confident it was not to do. [He was right; the Peace provided for six months' leeway.] And this I have to say in your defence that several persons at New York who I can bring to evidence it, if there be occasion, did tell me that by several advices from Madagascar and that part of the world, they were informed of your men revolting from you in that place, which I am pretty sure they said was at Madagascar; and that others of them compelled you much against your will to take and rifle two ships. [The testimony of these persons was not used at the trials. Why?]

I have advised with his Majesty's council and showed them this letter this afternoon, and they are of the opinion that if your case be as clear as you (or Mr. Emmott for you) have said, then you may safely come hither and be equipped and fitted out, to go fetch the other ship; and I make no manner of Doubt but to obtain the King's Pardon for you and those few Men you have left, who, as I understand, have been faithful to you, and refused, as well as you, to dishonour the Commission you had from England.

If Kidd buried any pirate hoards, it must have been during the days while he was in the Sound. He had his wife and children come aboard his sloop at Block Island, and spent a few days between there and Gardiner's Island, where he left some treasure which the Lord of the manor later returned to Governor Bellomont. Then the Captain went to Boston and had a conference with Livingston, who had hurried over from Albany to see whether Bellomont would release him from some sort of bond that he had given for Kidd—his request was refused. Kidd was finally arrested on July sixth, and the question now arose what to do with him. He could not be hanged for piracy in Massachusetts, where a bill enforcing that penalty had recently been rejected. Samuel Sewall, one of the ablest of the council, was of opinion that it was not legal to send him to England for trial, but he was sent anyway. There he languished in Newgate from April, 1700, until May of 1701; so he was in jail in America and England for nearly two years before his case was decided.

When his trial was finally held, he was convicted first of murdering a gunner, William Moore, and then was arraigned for piracy. Though nine of his men stood with him in the dock, all were reprieved except Kidd and a boy with an Irish name, Darby Mullins. Kidd was not permitted to give direct evidence in his own defence, he could not have the aid of counsel except in some question of law, he could not use the men indicted with him; all that he could do was to question two of his deserters who had turned King's evidence. His two French passes, which the House of Commons had ordered to be returned to him and which were obviously his chief means of defence, had disappeared. So they hanged Captain Kidd, the innocent victim of a greedy crew of noble hi-jackers who wouldn't even have the rogues' virtue of standing by a member of their gang.

By carefully suppressing a number of cardinal facts I have now given you another hero, Captain Kidd number Two, *sentimental* style. The hero of the old ballad was Bad but Romantic; the new hero is Good and Pitiful. If space were available, I should present a Third Captain Kidd, the man revealed in his trials as neither very good nor very bad, the fool of fortune and the tool of politicians, a pirate in spite of himself. That he did commit acts of piracy, and not merely against ships with French passes, there seems no doubt after the trials and other documents have been read; yet the people you are likely to despise are the rats who turned King's evidence, the partners who wouldn't guarantee even a fair trial, and the scandalously prejudiced judges. The folk may not have been far wrong in supposing that Kidd had sold his soul to the devil. The legend goes that the Earl of Hell kept his bargain to the extent of snapping the hangman's rope—once. If his lordship was indeed responsible for that ineffectual gesture, he kept faith better than others of the nobility.

That our interest in the pirates does not derive solely from a hope of discovering their treasure is proved by the currency of ballads about freebooters who, unlike Kidd, did not approach our shores. There is, for example, the song about Captain Ward, who flourished in the first quarter of the seventeenth century. Legend asserts that he was a fisherman who became a petty officer on the British ship called *Lion's Whelp*. At about the time when Queen Bess died, he stole a small bark of twenty-five tons, captured a French ship in the

Channel, and began a gaudy career which finally brought him to lucrative cruising under the Turkish or Tunisian colors, especially in raids upon the shipping of Venice and the Knights of St. John. He achieved lordly wealth and even built himself a palace at Tunisia. He lives in a ballad which I was happy to find in the Douglass MS., as follows:

> Come all ye jolly sailors bold
>   That live by tuck of drum;
> I'll tell you of a rank robber
>   Now on the seas is come.
>
> His name is called Captain Ward,
>   As you the truth shall hear,
> For there's not been such a robber
>   This hundred and fifty year.
>
> He wrote a letter to our King
>   On the fifth of January,
> To see if he would take him in
>   And all his company;
>
> To see if he would accept of him
>   And all his jolly sailors bold,
> And for a ransom he would give
>   Two thousand pounds in gold.
>
> First he beguiled the wild Turks
>   And then the King of Spain.
> Pray, how can he prove true to us
>   When he proves false to them?
>
> "O no, O no," then said the King,
>   "For no such thing can be,
> For he has been a rank robber
>   And a robber on the seas."
>
> "O then," says Captain Ward, "my boys,
>   Let's put to sea again,
> And see what prizes we can find
>   On the coast of France and Spain."

Then we espied a lofty ship
A-sailing from the west;
She was loaded with silks and satins
And cambrics of the best.

Then we bore up to her straightway,
They thinking no such thing.
We robbed them of their merchandize,
Then bade them tell their King.

And when their King did hear of this,
His heart was grived full score [sic],
To think his ships could not get past
As they had done before.

Then he caused a worthy ship
And a worthy ship of fame,
The *Rainbow* she was called
And the *Rainbow* was her name,—

He rigged her and freighted her
And sent her to the sea,
With five hundred bold mariners
To bear her company.

They sailed east, they sailed west,
But nothing could espy,
Until they came to the very spot
Where Captain Ward did lie.

"Who is the owner of this ship?"
The *Rainbow* then did cry.
"Here I am," says Captain Ward.
"Let no man me deny."—

"What brought you here, you cowardly dogs,
You ugly, wanton thief?
What makes you lie at anchor
And keep your King in grief?"—

"You lie, you lie," says Captain Ward,
  "As ever I heard you lie!
I never robbed an Englishman,
  An Englishman but three.

"As for the worthy Scotchmen,
  I love them as my own.
My chief delight is for to pull
  The French and Spaniards down."—

"Why curse thou, so bold a robber?
  We'll soon humble your pride."
With that, the gallant *Rainbow*
  She shot out of her side

Full fifty good brass cannons,
  Well charged on every side,
And then they fired their great guns
  And gave Ward a broadside.

"Fire on, fire on!" says Captain Ward.
  "I value you not a pin.
If you are brass on the outside,
  I am good steel within."

They fought, eight o'clock in the morn
  Till eight o'clock at night.
At length the gallant *Rainbow*
  Began to take her flight.

"Go home, go home!" says Captain Ward,
  "And tell your King for me:
If he reigns King upon dry land,
  I will reign King at sea."

With that the gallant *Rainbow*
  She shot and shot in vain,
And left the rover's company
  And home returned again.

"Tell our royal King of England
  His ship is returned again,
For Captain Ward he is too strong,
  He never will be taken [ta'en]."—

"O shame, O shame!" said the King,
  "For no such thing can be,
For I have lost two thousand pounds
  Besides lost jewels three:

"The first was brave Lord Clifford,
  Great Earl of Cumberland;
The second was brave Lord Mountjoy,
  As you shall understand;

"The third was brave Lord Essex,
  From field would never flee;
Who would have gone unto the sea
  And brought proud Ward to me."

Captain Ward's compliment to the Scots is a crafty method of
recommending himself to James I of England, who was James VI
of Scotland and as such received a number of similar compliments,
including a play called *Macbeth* written by one of his Grooms of the
Chamber. It was not long before Jamie's reign that Andrew Barton,
who died in 1511, had made the fame of Scotland's tars so disagreeable
that he was classed south of the Border as a rank pirate. In 1506,
James IV of Scotland built Barton a great and costly ship in which
he cleared the Scottish coast of Flemish pirates; in his grim Scots
way he sent three barrels of their heads to his royal master. He had
letters of marque against the Portuguese—the old prelude to piracy,
you see; it was said in England that he seized *English* vessels engaged
in the Portuguese trade. Henry VIII of England, who understood
the modern art of undeclared warfare against neighbors, "permitted"
Sir Thomas and Sir Edward Howard to fit out two ships against the
alleged pirate. Barton was cruising in the Downs in his *Lion* on
August 2, 1511, when he was shot through the heart by an English
arrow. King James protested, of course, but Henry remarked to his
brother of Scotland that "the fate of pirates was never an object of

dispute among princes". It is said that he followed this silken remark
by freeing Barton's sailors, giving them sufficient money to take
them home to Scotland. There is undoubtedly a good deal of political
folklore mixed with all this; the fact emerges that Scotland's ablest
commander at sea was out of the way.

Andrew Barton is the best guess that can be made for *Elder Bardee*
of ballad-fame. To be sure, the name of the Young Pretender, Charles
Stuart, is substituted for that of the noble English family of Howard,
but stranger things have happened in a ballad. From an Anglican
point of view, an adherent of the Church of Scotland might well be
called in derision *Elder*, and *Bardee* carries a more satirical ring
than *Barton*.

There was three brothers in Scotland did dwell,
    Three loving brothers were they;
They all did cast lots to see which of them
    Should go robbing all round the salt sea.

The lot it fell on Elder Bardee,
    The youngest of the three,
And for to maintain those other two
    He went robbing all round the salt sea.

He had not sailed but one day, two, or three,
    Before three vessels he spied,
Sailing far off, and sailing far off,
    Till at length came sailing close by.

"Who there? Who there?" cried Elder Bardee,
    "Who there that sails so nigh?"—
"We are three merchant vessels from old England shore;
    And if no offence, let us pass by."—

"O no, O no!" cried Elder Bardee,
    "O no, that can never be.
I'll have your ships, your cargoes, my boys,
    And your bodies I'll cast in the sea."

The news it reached King Henry's ears,
　　The man that wears the crown.
To think he had lost three of his ships,
　　And his merry men they were all drowned!

"Go build a ship both strong and secure,
　　As you shall understand,
And on board place Captain Charles Stewart
　　To take that bold command."

They built a ship both strong and secure,
　　As you shall understand,
And on board placed Captain Charles Stewart
　　To take that bold command.

He had not sailed but one day, two, or three,
　　Before a vessel he spied,
Sailing far off, and sailing far off,
　　Till at length came sailing close by.

"Who there? Who there?" cried Captain Charles Stewart,
　　"Who there that sails so nigh?"—
"We are the bold robbers from Merry Scotland,
　　And if no offence, let us pass by."—

"O no, O no," cried Captain Charles Stewart,
　　"O no, that never can be.
I'll have your ship, your cargo, my boys,
　　And your bodies I'll carry with me."

Broadside, broadside, those ships they did come;
　　The cannon loud did roar.
They took Elder Bardee and his whole company
　　To the land of old England's shore.

With the two ballads just given I should rank *The Bold Pirates*, which, if it does not concern so famous a personage, has the advantage of refrains that swing the capstan merrily:

Two lofty ships from England they came,
　　Blow high, blow low, so sailed we.

One was the *Prince of Luther* and other *Prince of Wales,*
Cruising down on the coast of Barbary.

"Aloft, aloft!" our jolly bo'sun cried,
  "Look astern, look astern, look aweather, look alee,
  Look down on the coast of Barbary."—

"I see nothing astern, I see nothing alee,
But I see a ship at windward, and a lofty ship is she."—

"Hi-O, hi-o!" our jolly bo'sun cried.
"Are you a man-of-war or a privateer?" says he.

"I am no man-of-war, no privateer," says she,
"But I am a bold pirate seeking for my fee."

Then broadside and broadside for a long time we lay,
And the broadside we gave them, we cut their mast and away.

"O quarters, O quarters!" these pirates did say;
But the quarters that we gave them—we sunk them in the sea!

There is one ballad called *The Flying Cloud* about a pirate who
was a slaver:

My name is Edward Howland, I would have you understand;
I was born in the town of Waterford, in Erin's happy land.
I being young and boyish and beauty on me smiled;
My parents daunted [doted] on me, I being their only child.

They bound me in a trade there, in Waterford's fair town,
They bound me to a trader by the name of William Brown.
I served my master faithfully for eighteen months or more,
Then I shipped on board of *Ocean Queen* bound for Bellefraisure's
    [Valparaiso's?] shore.

When we landed on Bellefraisure's shore, I met with Captain Moore,
Commander of the *Flying Cloud* and belonging to Trimore.
He asked me if I'd sail with him, on a slaving voyage to go,
To the burning shores of Africa where the sugar-cane doth grow.

Now the *Flying Cloud* was as fine a ship as ever sailed the sea
Or ever hoisted a maintop sail to a brisk and lively breeze;
Her sails were as white as the driven snow, on them there was no specks,
And eighteen hundred brass four-powder [sic] guns she carried all on
    her deck.

Now the *Flying Cloud* was a Spanish ship, five hundred tons or more;
She could easily sail round any ship sails out from Baltimore.
I have often seen our gallant ship when the winds were aft her beam,
With her royal and main topsail going forth like an African eel.

It was but a few days after, we landed on an African shore,
Where one thousand of these poor slaves from their native land we tore.
We marched them in upon a plank and stowed them down below,
And eighteen inches to a man was all we could allow.

The very next day we put to sea with our cargo of slaves.
It would have been better far for their poor souls had they been in
    their graves,
For the fever and plague it came on board, swept half of them away.
We carried their dead bodies on board and threw them in the sea.

It was but a few days after that we landed on Cubea's shore,
Where we sold them to the planters to be slaves forevermore,
With rice and coffee fields to plant beneath a burning sun,
To lead along a wretched life till their career was done.

And when our money was all gone, we put to sea again;
Captain Moore he came on board, and he said to us, his men,
"There is gold and plenty to be had if you'll remain with me;
We'll hoist aloft a pirate-flag and scour the Southern Sea."

They all agreed but five young men, and them we left on land;
Two of them being Boston boys, two more from Newfoundland,
The other was an Irish lad belonging to Trimore.
I wish to God I'd joined those lads and went with them ashore!

We robbed and plundered many a ship down on the Spanish Main,
Left many a mother and little child in sorrow to remain,

For the men we made to walk the plank, gave them a watery grave,
For the saying of our Captain was, "Dead men tell no tales."

We were chased by many a ship, both liner and brigade [frigate] too,
Until at length a Spanish ship, the *Dungeon*, hove in view.
She fired a shot across our bows, a signal to heave to,
But we paid to her no attention but sailed before the wind.

We cleared our decks for action as she hove up alongside,
And soon across our quarterdeck there ran a crimson tide.
We fought till Captain Moore was slain and eighty of his men,
When a boom-shell set our ship on fire—we were forced to surrender
   then.

Then to Newport we were sent, bound down in irons strong,
For we had sailed a pirate sea and done full many a wrong;
And robbing and plundering of ships has made a wreck of me;
So boys, beware of my sad fate, and a curse to the pirate sea!

So fare ye well, my shady grove, and the girl I do adore;
Her voice like music in my ears will never charm me more,
I never shall kiss her ruby lips or press her lily-white hand,
For now I must lead a scornful life down in some foreign land.

A recent movie has reminded us of Jean Lafitte, who flourished
from about 1809 till 1821—the man whom the *Dictionary of American
Biography* calls the "last of the great freebooters". There is a
ballad about him which seems to have fallen out of use in York State,
but there was brought to me from Columbia County a version in an
old chapbook which has lost covers and title-page; I think it is not
presumptuous to assume that this was once well known in our state.

THE BRAVE LAFITTE

Each young land bird I'm sure has heard
   Of the ocean lamb and wolf,
For by both names he's often famed,
   This pirate of the gulf.

A home held he by rock and sea,
   Proof 'gainst each searching fleet,

And far and near, all hearts did fear,
   This island king Lafitte.

He roved the main, great wealth to gain,
   Won treasures rich and rare,
'Mongst prizes bright, he took one night
   A treasure passing fair.

This treasure gay he bore away,
   Unto his rock retreat,
She soon with pride became the bride
   Of the island king Lafitte.

Her love and smiles all care beguiles,
   And lights his cavern home,
And thus enrich'd Lafitte scarce wished
   Upon the seas to roam.

Ere months had run, a cruiser's gun
   Was heard near his retreat,
With ships and guards and high rewards,
   They roused the bold Lafitte.

"Up, up, my boys!" the pirate cries,
   "Let our proud bark be mann'd.
These hunters bold, shall soon behold
   My 'vengeful pirate band."

He clasps his bride, then hastes with pride,
   His ship's firm decks to greet;
His bark rides out, his comrades shout,
   "Revenge, and brave Lafitte!"—

"Boys, to your guns," each pirate runs
   His port-fire to apply,
The foe draws near, their broadsides glare,
   And quick the hot balls fly!

Now side by side 'mid smoke they ride,
   Quick death the pirates meet;

With gun and sword the cruisers board,
And rush at bold Lafitte.

He speaks no word, but with his sword
Deals wounds and death to all,
Their guns they raise, but as they blaze,
Some strange breast meets each ball.

He drives them from the deck, then bends
This stranger form to greet.
'Tis she, alas! in pirate dress,
The bold bride of Lafitte.

"Up, comrades, turn, their fleet we'll burn,
From hence they ne'er shall ride;
I'll make their blood one crimson flood,
But I'll avenge my bride!"

The last of these pirate ballads I include for the light which it throws upon the origin of *Mademoiselle from Armentières*—that favorite of the A. E. F. and its legionnaires. I have seen statements to the effect that the American song derived from an older one of the Tommies but had no proof from my own experience as collector until the following ditty was brought to me from Oneida County:

Three pirates came to London town—Yo-ho, yo-ho!
Three pirates came to London town—Yo-ho, yo-ho!
Three pirates came to London town
To see the King put on his crown.
Yo-ho, ye lubbers, yo-ho, ye lubbers; yo-ho, yo-ho, yo-ho!

At first they came to a wayside inn,
And said, "Good landlord, let us in!"

"O landlord, have you good red wine
Enough to fill this cask of mine?"

"O landlord, have you bags of gold
Enough to fill the after-hold?"

"O landlord, have you daughter fair
With laughing eyes and curly hair?

"O landlord, will she marry me,
And sail with me across the sea?"

The "old, bold mate of Henry Morgan" would probably call such songs as these last two "fit only for a wench", but they prove that the lore of the pirates, from the day of Henry VIII to this pupil age, has something oaken about it. "Blow high, blow low, so sailed we."

III: Injun-Fighters

"THE spirit of Leatherstocking is not dead." With that sentence a French statesman greeted the entrance of the United States into the World War. If he was right, if Natty Bumpo represents to Europe the spirit of American freedom and valor, it would be a poor book about York State which did not throw some light upon the creation of Cooper's hero. Rip Van Winkle is a genuine American character, but—he is the universal type of the indolent, henpecked man, his legend is borrowed from Germany, his background reminds you that Irving's father was a countryman of Sir Walter Scott. Natty is indigenous. Though he is the universal and immortal hunter, his native haunts are vividly York State, and striking elements from his story and character are to be found in the legends about our Injun-fighters of the eighteenth and early nineteenth century.

Unfortunately it is impossible to be fair either to the Injuns or to their enemies without making a deeper study than anyone has yet put between the covers of a single book. When men with guns arrived at the hunting grounds of men still in the stone age, the event, as the elegant old authors say, might have been foreseen. There are now some five thousand Indians on the Reservations of New York

State; when the *Half Moon* sailed up Hudson's river, there may have been five or six times that number, roaming over a territory which now supports (so to speak) some thirteen millions. Agriculture of a primitive sort the Iroquois had, and the most remarkable political organization to be found among primitive men north of Mexico. They had brave warriors, supple athletes, mighty hunters, unselfish statesmen, and at least one orator (Red Jacket) who mastered the noblest American eloquence before Abraham Lincoln's. And they were doomed: doomed because they were anachronisms, because they claimed a land which they could not populate and exploit; doomed because they were sunset men against the men of a new dawn; doomed because at the first they did not know the use of fire-arms and at the last could learn only the abuse of alcohol.

We hear in legend about the cruelty of the Indians. They did torture some of their male captives; others they made to run the gauntlet, selecting for adoption those who ran swiftly, fearlessly, and in silence. The folk of western New York remember the Torture Tree where Little Beard and his Senecas tied Lieutenant Boyd of Sullivan's army. Tomahawks were hurled as near his head as possible without hitting him. His finger-nails were pulled out, his nose was cut off, one eye was plucked out, his tongue was cut, he was stabbed in various places. Then a small incision was made in his abdomen, his intestines were tied to the tree, he was driven around and around the trunk, and finally his head was struck from his body. This is the story told by the American commander, and vouched for by Mary Jemison, the white woman of the Senecas, who claimed to be an eye-witness. Colonel Butler denied the story; he declared that Boyd was tomahawked by an old woman. Both sides knew that the Senecas were maddened by a campaign of ruthless destruction which wiped out every Indian village in its path and even cut down orchards, burned all grain in the fields, and destroyed the winter's provisions buried in pits.

The other most memorable example of individual torture is that of the Jesuit Father, Isaac Jogues, the "Saint of the Wilderness", whose short apostleship and two captivities ended in martyrdom for a man whom his Canadian converts among the Hurons named Ondesonk, "The Heroic". Unfortunately the Hurons were the deadliest enemies of the Mohawks of eastern New York, to whom Father Jogues wished to preach the Gospel. It was in the company of a party of Hurons—who fled—that the Jesuit was first captured. His captors beat him, tore out his nails, chewed his forefingers till the bones of the last joint were completely crushed. Staked down at night, he had his hair and beard pulled out. After surviving the gauntlet, he fell and could not rise; then one finger was burned and another crushed between a Mohawk's teeth. Again he ran the gauntlet, was knocked unconscious by an iron ball, and had his last three nails torn out. A captured Christian woman of the Algonquins was compelled to cut off his thumb with a clam-shell. At nightfall he was staked out for insects to torture; children opened his wounds and laid hot coals on them. Again he ran the gauntlet; again children made a night horrid with torture. For a quarter-hour he was suspended by the arms, then cut down nearly dead. Escaping with the aid of the Dutch at Rensselaerswick (Albany), he was tenderly visited by a Protestant minister who accompanied him to New Amsterdam. Father Jogues arrived in France in time to celebrate the Christmas of 1643.

Given a special dispensation by Pope Urban VIII to celebrate Mass with his mangled hands, he returned to Canada, hoping to make peace between Algonquin and Mohawk. His end came when he was captured by Mohawks whose medicine men had convinced them that the Jesuit had brought them pestilence. One Indian sliced flesh from his arm and back, and ate it. The Wolf clan would have spared him, but as he entered a cabin of a member of the Bear clan to eat, an Indian behind him split his skull with a tomahawk, and in the twilight of October 18, 1646, he went to God.

These are two of the most appalling stories of the tragic struggle between white and red. In the days of the Injun-haters such tales were remembered, together with the massacres of Revolutionary days at Wyoming and Cherry Valley. If any excuse was made for the Indian, it was usually to recall that at Cherry Valley, when Little Aaron protected the aged minister, Samuel Dunlop, it was a Tory white who boasted that he had killed Robert Wells at prayer.

What I have told is to explain the hatred felt by the Injun-killers. I should add that I have never found a single charge of an Indian raping a white woman. (At times, white women were apparently compelled to marry Indians, doubtless against their will, and to do labor too severe for their strength.) I should add that in the wars between French and English both sides used Indian allies and—unpardonably—paid for scalps. We shy away from the last charge, but the facts are spread in the sixth and seventh volumes of Dr. E. B. O'Callaghan's *Documents Relating to the Colonial History of the State of New York* (1855-6). For example, on November 25, 1745, "the Govr. laid before the Assembly several papers . . . relating to the Damages done by the Enemy at Saraghtoga and to their further proceedings. Whereupon the Assembly [came] to several Resolutions, vizt. To allow rewards for Scalps". Indians were cheap help: in the following year a bounty of six pounds was offered to any *white* volunteer, but the Assembly thought that "the presents of cloathing arms and ammunition were always deemd by the Indians to be in lieu of Pay and bounty money". When Indians were asked to assist against the French and Indian allies in December, 1755—the service to be in Pennsylvania—Governor Shirley of New York decided that there should be a "reward for every prisoner or scalp taken from the enemy and every other reasonable encouragement". I am quoting here from instructions which the Governor gave to Major General Johnson, the Yorker who understood Indians best.

By the time of the Revolution, most colonists had learned better than to offer money for scalps. They tried to get the Six Nations to promise neutrality, but Sir William Johnson was no longer alive to control his Mohawks. The valleys of the Mohawk, the Schoharie, and the Delaware became the scene of those horrors of which Mr. Walter Edmonds has recently given so memorable an account. The whites paid for their tragic blunders, and the Indians—except Dominie Kirkland's Oneidas and the Tuscaroras—made the final mistake of killing for the wrong side.

The earliest of the very famous Injun-haters, and the most single-minded of whom legend tells, was the man whose monument at Milford, Pennsylvania, bears the inscription:

> Tom Quick, the Indian Slayer;
> or
> The Avenger of the Delaware.

On the north side another inscription tells us that "Thomas Quick, Sr., father of Tom Quick, his oldest child, emigrated from Holland to America, and settled on this spot in 1733". It is likely that this was the same Thomas Quick who took the oath of allegiance in Ulster County, New York, on September first, 1689, the same person who, on July 20, 1684, bought from an Indian for eight hundred schepels of wheat a piece of land at Mombaccus. Tom's father, therefore, was originally a Yorker. Certainly many of Tom's exploits were performed in the upper reaches of the Delaware River in New York State, and the antiquary who did more than anyone else to preserve tales about the Indian-Slayer was G. E. Quinlan, the historian of Sullivan County, who, in 1851 published at Monticello, New York, a fascinating little book about a man whose deeds are part of our goriest legend.

Tom was born in 1734 in a region long the favorite hunting ground of the Delaware (Leni-Lenape) Indians. The folk say that he cut his teeth on an arrowhead and in childhood chewed lead slugs; that he was one of the first settlers in that section to speak with Indians in their own tongue; that he hunted with the red brothers, learned their woodcraft, and adopted their ways of life. When his white brothers were attending school and assisting on the farm, Tom was providing the family with fish and game. He grew to be the tall, gaunt frontiersman of legend, with high cheekbones that resembled an Indian's; his eyes were gray and piercing, his beard was dark, his body was clothed in deerskin.

In his youth began what we still call in York State the French and Indian wars. While Sir William Johnson was keeping his Mohawks true to the British Crown, the Delawares south of them were restless. They had long hated the Mengwe (Iroquois), who, regarding them as a defeated and subject race, called them "The Women". They needed little prompting from the French to recall that Dutch and British settlers on their river had cheated them abominably in the purchase of land. Before they were pushed back into the sunset, they would strike a blow that would prove them not women. Some of them had eaten the bread of the Quicks, but if there was to be war, it should begin with the family whose mills and farm were best worth

looting. After the English General Braddock's defeat, in July of
1755, the Lenape "dug up the hatchet".

One evening Tom, with his father and a brother-in-law, had
crossed the Delaware to cut hoop-poles. From ambush a volley was
poured from Indian rifles, and the elder Quick fell mortally wounded.
The two younger men seized him and attempted to drag him toward
the river, but he gallantly and sternly commanded them to leave a
dying man, to spread the alarm at Milford. When Tom reached the
river, the Indians opened fire again. He fell, tripped by a ball that
had struck the heel of his shoe; but directly he was on his feet again,
zigzagging across the ice to safety. Then and there he swore eternal
vengeance upon the murderers of his father. Too much of an individualist to join the colonial militia, he would bide his time like an
Indian; one hatchet would never be buried.

Some two years after the termination of the French and Indian
war, Tom entered the Decker tavern on the Neversink—a dark, silent
man under a coonskin cap. At the bar an Indian named Muskwink,
bold with rum, invited him to drink. For answer Tom returned a
curt insult. Muskwink began to recount his exploits in the recent war,
soon reaching the story of how he had shot the elder Quick; he
grimaced, he imitated the death-agonies of his victim, he exhibited
a set of silver buttons. Snatching a French musket from the wall,
Tom drove Muskwink out of the door. For a mile the Avenger and
his victim marched up the road leading from Wurtsboro to Car-
penter's Point. Then Tom spoke, "Indian dog, you'll kill no more
white men." A heavy charge of slugs struck the Indian in the back
between the shoulders; he pitched onto his face. Putting the silver
buttons into his own pouch, Tom dragged the body of Muskwink to
an uprooted tree, kicked some dead leaves and dirt upon it, returned
the musket to the tavern, and left the neighborhood.

Tom's next exploit was so bloody that he never told it until shortly
before his own death, when he confessed to Jacob Quick of Callicoon
that once he had carried his vengeance beyond the killing of warriors
to the extermination of an entire family. Probably it was not long
after the Muskwink affair that he was hunting at Butler's Rift, when,
from a hiding place in the reeds he saw a canoe approaching filled with
an Indian brave, a woman, and three children. Rising from the reeds,

Tom ordered the Indian to shore in a tone so grim and with a gesture so unmistakable that the Delaware cried out, "The hatchet is buried!" Tom remembered that this was one who had eaten at his father's board, one who was thought to have taken part in several outrages upon the frontier. The Avenger's rifle cracked, the Indian leaped from his canoe and "after a few convulsive throes" died in the river. Tom then despatched the woman and killed the two older children, who, he remembered, "squauked like crows". The third child, an infant, smiled up at him so sweetly that his heart wavered until the memory returned of a ravished frontier, and he dashed out the child's brains. When asked how he could bring himself to such a deed, he answered in a proverb still used in our countryside, "Nits make lice".

Among the folk the favorite tale about Tom concerns the railsplitting. The same story is related about Tim Murphy and other heroes of our frontier; it is even told of Daniel Boone in Kentucky and has claim to being the classic trickster-story of the American frontier. One spring Tom was splitting rails in the Mamakating Valley for a man named Westbrook. Temporarily off guard, he had left his rifle standing against a tree and was driving a wedge into an unusually tough log when he looked up to see seven armed Indians grinning at his predicament. That might have been the end of his railsplitting, but the Indians always made the mistake of wishing to share their fun with an entire village by taking their captive to a place of torture. The secret of Tom's own success was that he was an individualist who hunted redskins alone and shot on sight. In this case, he agreed to go with them quietly if they would help him finish splitting his log. The proposal appealed to two traits which you still find in our Indians—their curiosity and their ironic sense of humor. Dropping their rifles, they ranged themselves as directed, three on one side of the log, four on the other, each with his hands in the split. At Tom's word of command they pulled manfully, but instead of driving the wedge in farther, Tom knocked it out and beheld the pleasing sight of seven enemies caught by the hands in his log. Without wasting powder he swung his ax; he was nearer by seven to his goal of one hundred slain Indians.

Another contribution of the folk to the saga of Tom is the tale of the Buck with Seven Skins. Tom was about to winter at the cabin of a friend who was happy to have so mighty a hunter provide food through the harsh months of snow. An agreement was made between Tom and an Indian who drifted into the neighborhood that they should go hunting together; Tom should have the venison, the Indian should have the skins, which, of course, could be traded for firewater and other coveted goods. Deer were plentiful: at the close of the first afternoon the Indian declared that he was quite satisfied with seven skins, which he proceeded to pack on his back. When Tom returned to the settlements next day with the promised venison plus skins, his friends asked how he happened to come by the hides. "O," responded Tom, "I killed a buck with seven skins on his back." Sure enough, there was a single bullet-hole through each of the pelts. The grim reply is matched by another which he made when asked how he managed to keep in such fine condition two guns which he pulled from concealment in a hollow tree: "Every critter, two legged or four, has grease under its hide somewhere." If you are ever trudging through the Shawangunk region and find an old gun or two hidden in a decayed tree-trunk, you can guess who put them there.

Of all the stories which Quinlan gathered about Tom, the most poetical concerns a conversation between Quick and one of his victims who, stopping at Quick's winter-quarters, invited him to go hunting next day. Convinced that the Indian meant no good, Tom got up stealthily in the night, unloaded the redskin's rifle, substituted ashes for most of the powder, and put back the ball. Let Quinlan tell the tale—it is his masterpiece of narrative:

The next morning the savage slyly inserted the ram-rod in the chamber of the rifle, examined the priming, &c., and seemed satisfied that all was right. This and some other circumstances confirmed Tom in the belief that mischief was brewing.

There was considerable snow on the ground, and the hunters found it quite inconvenient to tread through it, and apparently to render the walking easier, the Indian proposed that one of them should go ahead to break the path. To this Tom readily agreed, and the Indian was greatly pleased when Tom made no objection to be the first to go in advance.

After they had proceeded in this way a mile or two, and had come to a very lonely place, Tom heard the Indian's gun snap, and the powder flash in the pan. Tom looked back and asked what the Indian had seen.

"A fine buck," was the reply.

The Indian reprimed his gun, and they went on. Pretty soon Tom heard another snap and flash.

"Well, brother Indian," inquired he, "what did you see this time?"

"An eagle swept over the forest," replied the other as he again primed the gun.

"Brother Indian," said Tom, "the snow is deep. I am tired. You go ahead."

"Brother Yankee speaks well," said the savage gloomily, and took his station in advance.

Tom levelled his rifle.

"Lying Indian dog!" exclaimed he, "what do you see now?"

"The spirit land," was the reply, as the Indian hung his head and drew over it his blanket.

There was that time when two Indians seized him while he was sleeping in a cabin near Port Jervis. One Delaware loaded himself with Tom's deerskins and walked in advance; the other, carrying the two Indians' rifles—one ready cocked, marched in the rear. With his hands bound behind him, Tom was quietly obedient until they reached a dizzy ledge far above the river. The first Indian, laden with the furs, trudged on stolidly; but Tom, pretending to be giddy, advanced only under the compulsion of blows from the man behind him. Finally, at the narrowest place in the path, he backed against the cliff, giving signs of the most craven fear. Taunting him, the second Indian administered a beating and attempted to seize hold of Tom to push him along, when by an "adroit movement" the Indian-Slayer put a foot to his captor's stomach and the savage toppled over the brink. Fifty feet below, the brave landed with a broken back in the crotch of a button-ball tree, the guns dropping farther to the river. Tom was away.

At another time, in the autumn of 1788 or 1789, he escaped from a party of Indians because his youthful guard was so inexperienced as to drink a horn of firewater that Tom had managed to secrete under his shirt. But his closest call came when he was a man of fifty, making his headquarters at a lonely cabin on the Lackawaxen. Creeping up in a rainstorm when a heavy fog was on the hills, a party of twenty warriors surprised Tom near nightfall when he was unarmed and unsuspecting the red brothers of the mist. Tired by a long journey and elated by the discovery of a keg of firewater, the Indians decided to remain at the cabin till morning. Tom was bound round and round and taken to the garret or loft; then, as extra precaution, a long piece of deerskin was attached to his bonds and to a rafter. As the evening wore on, he could hear from below the drunken shouts of his captors and the ingenious plans for the torture of their hated foe. By midnight the shouts died down; in the dark above, Tom felt for the first time the poison of despair.

Suddenly he heard the pad of unsteady moccasins on the ladder leading to his loft. A cruel face appeared, lit by a brand of fire; in the Indian's other hand was a knife. One enemy had decided not to wait for the ceremonial torture. There was triumph in his snake-eyes as he whispered, "My knife shall drink the blood of the panther who has slain my kindred." As the Indian lurched forward drunkenly for the death-blow, Tom fell on his face; the knife passed over his head; the Indian lost his balance, fell over Tom's body, struck his brow on a rafter, and lost consciousness. The brand fell to the wet floor, sputtered out. Death was deferred.

Rising to his feet again, Tom listened for signs that the sleeping Indians below had heard the impact of his foe's body. All was still. If only Quick could reach the unconscious Indian—or was he unconscious?—and get that knife . . . Tom lowered himself and began to crawl softly on his belly. Alas, the Indian had rolled too far away—with a jerk the thong brought up the creeping frontiersman. For a second time that night he felt despair. Death had been deferred that it might be more terrible. As he crawled miserably back to his first position at the wall, his bare foot touched something colder than the floor. It was the knife.

Taking the handle between his teeth. Tom cut the thong that bound him to the rafter and the bonds which held his ankles; but his arms were still pinioned behind him. It seemed ages while he found a crevice in the side of the cabin, and, after attempts which left him bleeding and spent, managed to thrust the knife into a position which permitted him to back up and sever the strips which held his arms. To descend the ladder and pass the sleeping braves was too dangerous.

Slowly and quietly he cut a hole in the bark roof, lowered himself, and ran naked through the forest to the settlement of Minisink, where he was clothed and revived.

You might suppose that even a valorous man would have abandoned that cabin. Tom returned a week later. When he found that thirty dollars' worth of skins had been stolen—not to mention the firewater—he was, as a neighbor said, "tearing mad".

The folk like two other tales of escape whose plots I must give only briefly. There was the evening when an Indian slipped into the pig-pen, where he was pretty well protected by a rampart of logs, and squeezed a pig in the hope of making Tom run out unarmed to investigate. But Tom waited, gun in hand, at a crevice of his door to see what was causing the alarm. Just as Quick opened the crack a little, the unhappy pig bounced up; its rider's head appeared over the topmost log. When the scalplock appeared for a second time, the pig was released from his burden.

A similar stratagem was tried when Tom was living in a cabin near Handsome Eddy. Three Indians, studying his domestic habits, discovered that he always brought home a cow at evening. So they skirmished up a hill behind the cabin, removed the bell, and drove the cow farther away. Tom was on his way to bring home Bossy, when he paused, puzzled. That ringing was too violent, too continuous. (It must be explained that Indians were not cow-keepers; to this day, many Indians will not drink milk.) Tom made a long circle, passing the cow, and slipped from tree to tree till he was behind the Indians. One brave had dropped his rifle and was devoting all his energies to the bell; the other two had their rifles pointed toward the direction from which they hoped to see their foe emerge.

You can realize that the Indian-Slayer's position was still one of great danger: there were three armed Indians, and Tom had only one shot. If only he could— A twig snapped under his foot; the Indians came to startled attention, but providentially Bossy appeared, furnishing an explanation for the sound. Providence had done its share; marksmanship must do the rest. At last Tom was in the position which he had sought: two coppery forms were in line. He fired his one shot, bringing down two Indians and slightly wounding the bell-ringer, who abandoned his rifle and sped through the forest.

Once and perhaps only once, Tom spared an Indian who was in his power. Hunting with a cousin one day on the Pennsylvania side of the Delaware, Quick saw an Indian in a canoe and sternly ordered him to land. The cousin, however, had a prejudice against murder. Tom relented, but he was morose all day, murmuring, in the only example of this dialect which I have found: "Ho could ich, de dunder! out de cano tumbly!" ("By thunder, how I could have tumbled him out of his canoe!")

On his deathbed in 1795 or 1796, Tom grieved to think that he had not fulfilled his ambition to slay one hundred Indians. Quinlan was assured, by a gentleman who was present at Quick's death and his funeral, that Tom died of old age, but the folk have a better story. They say that the Indians, hearing of the demise of their foe, exhumed his body, cut it into pieces, and sent it to several villages. Then Tom had his hundred—for he had died of smallpox. At any rate, when a descendant of Tom—one who helped found the Chicago *Tribune* and reached the honor of being Lieutenant Governor of Illinois—erected in 1889 a monument to the old Indian-Slayer, he didn't have a complete skeleton to bury. Says Frederick W. Crumb, who has written the best recent account of Tom:

Buried under the shaft is a chestnut coffin which contains the few mortal remains of this early American. The coffin contains a glass jar which in turn holds fragments of the original coffin, the tibia of the right leg, a piece of the skull that overhung the socket of the eye, and a phalanx bone from his right hand—perhaps it was his trigger-finger.

For tales of the second of our famed Injun-fighters it is necessary to move from Orange, Ulster, and Sullivan Counties, northwest to Delaware, Schoharie, and Otsego Counties—nearer to the baronial estates of Cooper. On the hillside slope of the cemetery of Middleburg (Schoharie) you find a monument bearing in relief the handsome figure of a man dressed in a fringed hunter's costume of the Revolutionary period. His left hand grasps a knife; his right, a rifle. Above the bold features is the inevitable coonskin cap. Under his left foot is a hatchet or tomahawk; an arrow has just missed striking his right foot. The inscription tells us that this is Timothy Murphy (1751-1818), "patriot, soldier, scout, citizen, who served in Morgan's Rifle

Corps, fought at Saratoga and Monmouth, and whose bravery repelled the attack of the British and their Indian allies upon Middlefort, October 17, 1780, and saved the colonists of Schoharie Valley". At the old Schoharie fort, now a museum, you may see a painting of Tim. His story is in the memory of our folk. Sometime it will be checked by competent historians; for the present I can write only that mixture of history and folklore which, however inaccurate, certainly gives a portrait of the man who seems to me the most interesting private soldier of the Revolution and in some respects the greatest Injun-fighter of York State.

Tim Murphy is said to have been born in 1751 at the town of Minisink, New Jersey, the child of immigrants from Ireland. An old pamphlet declares that he moved in 1757 to Pennsylvania, where he had very little education "except such as was obtained from the pure study of nature". His inability to read and write has been given as the reason why he never accepted an officer's commission; it is just as likely that the spirit of a great frontiersman preferred the danger-ous, prowling duties of sharpshooter and scout. Though history first records his name as enlisting in a Pennsylvania regiment, there is a tradition that he came to York State earlier with a company of lusty rafters who were returning from a journey down the Delaware. Legend also says that he lived at Stamford and Harpersfield; that he married a girl about whom the early pamphlet is silent; and that he swore eternal vengeance upon the Indians when he returned with supplies bought in Middleburg to discover his cabin in ashes, his girl-wife and babes lying slaughtered.

At any rate, he enlisted in July, 1775, with the First Pennsylvania Regiment of the Continental Line, and after proving his mettle was sent north under Captain Long with one of the two companies of Morgan's Riflemen, arriving in September, 1777, at the place where General Gates was preparing for the battle of Saratoga. Daniel Morgan (1736-1802) was a man after Tim's heart, born near the Delaware River either in New Jersey or in Pennsylvania, migrating to Virginia, serving with Braddock in the French and Indian wars, when he received five hundred lashes for striking a British subaltern. Gates told Washington that Morgan's corps was "the one the army of Gen. Burgoyne are most afraid of", and he spoke moderately. Thanks to men like Tim Murphy, Gates always knew exactly where Burgoyne's army was; for lack of such a corps Burgoyne sometimes did not know the position of his American opponent until he heard his drums.

Two deeds of Tim in that campaign are memorable. Early in October, he slipped into the British lines, surprised an officer in his tent, and marched him into the American camp at the point of a hunting-knife. On October seventh, it was Tim's rifle that brought the Scottish General Simon Fraser from his black charger, robbing a Scottish clan of a gallant representative and General Burgoyne of perhaps his ablest commander. The places where Fraser fell and where Morgan's Rifles were stationed are marked on the battlefield; for a time the markers were so placed that, as a colleague of mine remarked, Tim must have been compelled to shoot over a hill with the bent rifle-barrel of legend.

For the rest of the Revolution, Tim seems to have served with New York militia—on the Schoharie, along the Mohawk, with Sullivan and Clinton in the terrible raid to the western counties, and again at Schoharie. In those years he is reputed to have killed forty Indians, some of whom he scalped. Like the Tory guerillas, he occasionally assumed the disguise of an Indian; the Tories enjoyed this imitation so little that they set a price upon his head. The Morgan Rifles were famed for their "Kentucky" guns; but Tim was equipped with a double-barrelled weapon which was the death of many an unsuspecting redskin. After he had fired once, they naturally supposed he was harmless until he had reloaded, and they would step gaily forth to finish him off, only to receive a second bullet which convinced some of them that a spirit kept his rifle perpetually loaded. At least once in that Sullivan expedition Tim was captured, when his party of twenty was surrounded by Brant and his Indians, and all but five were killed. Tim escaped, of course, but it was touch and go; he was hidden behind a brush fence while an Indian stood above him without seeing him—which will give some idea of Tim's woodcraft.

The rage of Indians and Tories after Sullivan's raid inspired Sir John Johnson and eight hundred men to sweep down the valley of the Schoharie in the autumn of 1780, vowing to wipe out the settlements of High and Low Dutch. Before they started attack upon the Middle Fort, Tim had shot two more Indians from an ambush; he must have realized that for him surrender meant death by torture. The fort's garrison of one hundred and fifty regular troops and one hundred militia was commanded by a cowardly Major named Wolsey, who was quite willing to strike his colors, especially after a cannon-ball had spoiled a perfectly good mattress where another not very valiant person was hiding. A white flag of truce was approaching, greatly to the relief of the Major and much to the unease of Tim and the valiant Dutch settler, Colonel Vroman.

As usual, Tim made a quick decision and acted upon it immediately —regardless of the rules of civilized warfare. (After all, the rules had not been observed by his enemies at Cherry Valley and a dozen other ravaged settlements; he was fighting Indians and a dispossessed Tory.) Murphy fired toward the flag of truce. When his Major ordered his arrest, nobody stirred. Again the enemy sent a flag of truce; again Tim fired. After this symbolical rejection of surrender had been repeated a third time, two angry men faced each other in the little beleaguered fort: the Major with a pistol pointed at Tim's heart, Tim with a rifle which slowly rose to cover an officer unworthy of obedience. Tim's eyes didn't waver; the Major's did. In fact, Wolsey went to bed, Colonel Vroman took over the command, and there was no surrender at Schoharie that day—or on any other day. Sir John Johnson marched off, burning crops and cursing Tim Murphy; to keep the score even, Tim burned the houses of several Tories.*

Unlike Tom Quick, Murphy was a marrying man. During the Revolution he found time for a whirlwind courtship of Peggy Feeck, whose Dutch parents objected to the attentions of a "wild Irishman". Nothing daunted, Tim "took her through the window", and the couple were married by Dominie Johnson of Duanesburgh. By this wife Tim had nine children; by another whom he married about 1812 he had four more. (Direct descendants of the Injun-fighter served in France with the American Expeditionary Force.) His housing of the family was rather casual: I am told that after the Revolution he settled down on a farm at the confluence of the Susquehannah and

---

* Simms, the historian of Schoharie County, has a different version of this incident, and of Tim's marriage.

the Charlotte, where he cleared the land and lived comfortably until it was discovered that he had never troubled to obtain any sort of deed to the property. An historical marker is on another farm, near South Worcester, several miles from the place of his first choice.

Folktales about Tim are numerous, though some of them are attributed to other heroes. The spider-web across a hollow log protected the hiding-place of Robert the Bruce also—and King David of the Jews. To Tim are attributed those stories of the Indians caught by their hands and of the Indians ringing a cowbell already told about Tom Quick. Despairing of attempts to sort out the legends, I finally appealed to my colleague, Dean Milton G. Nelson of the State College at Albany, whose ancestors lived in Delaware County before the Revolution; from his store I select three favorite tales of his father which the Dean learned in childhood.

Tim was returning from a search for Indians down the Chemung Valley, when a party of redskins pursued him until he had outrun all except a single brave. As Murphy and his enemy reached a high glacial boulder shaped like an inverted teacup, the game became Ring-around-the-Boulder. The Indian had no weapon except a tomahawk; Tim had only a rifle. The sun was low. After dark the Indian would have an overwhelming advantage. Two or three shots had convinced Murphy that even he could not shoot in a curve; so he grasped his rifle-barrel and with his mighty hands pressed it against the rondure of the boulder till it was properly bent; then he shot his Indian "as slick as a mink". (There is hardly a self-respecting guide in the Adirondacks who has not appropriated this feat.)

At another time Tim was again "scouting down toward the Chemung"—the proper opening formula in Delaware County for all Murphy tales—when he found his leggings torn to shreds by the August growth of blackberry briars. Conveniently he sighted an Indian, killed him, and skinned him from knee to ankle, making himself a useful pair of leggings. The summer heat was so torrid that by the time the frontiersman reached home the Indian's shrunken skin was "removed with the greatest difficulty" and poor Tim was "laid up for quite a spell". (Sometimes this is said to have occurred after the decisive battle of Newtown in the Clinton-Sullivan raid; sometimes we are told that Tim cut off the bizarre leggings while running at full speed before a band of avenging Indians.)

The Dean's third story concerns Tim's famous Leap. Again Murphy was returning from "down toward the Chemung" with a pack of Indians behind him. As usual, he made for Rattlesnake Hill (South Hill); with the Susquehannah behind him, Charlotte Creek on the right, and Schenevus Creek on the left, he could traverse a long tongue of high land without fear of a flanking attack. The trouble was that this tongue did not extend indefinitely; at its end was the lofty cliff on the Schoharie called Vroman's Nose. There was only one thing to do, and he did it: leaping over the cliff he struck far below on slippery shale and slid on his deerskin trousers the rest of the way. No Indian dared follow.

This mighty leap, rivalled only by that which Ranger Rogers did *not* take at Lake George, has been adorned by the folk-imagination. In one version, Tim jumped a hundred feet with a basket of seed-grain on his back, landing so hard that his feet were driven into the rock up to his knees. The hero hurried home, deposited his grain, borrowed a pick and shovel, returned to Vroman's Nose, and dug himself out of the rock. In another version he carried a pail of milk throughout the adventure without spilling a drop.

Not far from Vroman's Nose, near the confluence of the Charlotte and the Susquehannah, is the only place where Tim would cook his dinner out-of-doors. In the middle of a group of glacial cones called *hah-dee-dah-dahs*—and who will explain that word?—he could kindle a fire whose smoke was screened from Indian eyes by the lofty cones.

If you are a hunter, you may wish to know how expert the best shot in Morgan's Rifles was. Well, General Fraser didn't have a chance. In 1781, after he had brought in a fine lot of deerskins and cured them, Tim conducted a competition for marksmen who were to receive a hide as prize. In the shooting for the skins Tim was barred—he had already been paid by the competitors. Afterwards he proposed an additional competition for a gallon of rum, a super-extra-shoot in which the Old Master could compete. A small piece of paper was affixed by a brass nail to a blazed tree. Pacing off one hundred yards, he rested his rifle on his hat, as he always did when he took pains, and at the first shot drove the nail right into the tree.

Then there was the day in 1799 when the four best marksmen in Schoharie County, including Tim's old scouting partner, David Elerson, took turns holding between their knees a target made of a little piece of white paper fastened to a board two feet long. At one hundred yards the other three champions cut the edge of the paper; when Tim fired, the paper fell from the board—his bullet had driven the *pin* through the wood.

Tim came through the Revolution without a scratch and grew so peaceable that he couldn't recall more than two or three Indians shot thereafter. He even took to saving lives: in the March freshet of 1784 he rescued two sons of a neighbor, John Adam Brown. His kindness may have cost him dear; people said that the injury he received then caused the first growth of a cancer which finally ended his career; but others claimed that the cancer resulted from the recoil of his old rifle on his cheek. You may be sure that nothing terrified the old lion whose watchword in the war had been, "My boys, every ball was not moulded to hit." He lasted till a June day of 1818; meanwhile he made stump speeches for his friends, helped elect one Governor, and enjoyed raising a big family, especially one daughter for whom he used to buy five or six dresses at a time whenever he visited Albany. Tim Murphy was Tom Quick plus an Irish heart; he is the Dan'l Boone of York State.

Continuing our journey north, we must now cross the Mohawk to reach the homes of two more worthies, Nat Foster and Nick Stoner, the Yorkers fittest to sit down or shoot for a turkey with Tom and Tim. There is plenty of information regarding both—thanks to Jeptha R. Simms, whose *Trappers of New York* (1850) has been richly supplemented (1897) by the Rev. A. L. Byron-Curtiss in his enchanting *Life and Adventures of Nat Foster, Trapper and Hunter of the Adirondacks*.

About 1760, Nat's father migrated from Rhode Island to New Hampshire, only to find within a year that Indians had stolen all of his cows and twenty-four of his thirty sheep. He discovered that the settlers had a practice of shooting Indians, because the Tory grandee from whom they had a right to expect protection, a person interested in Indian trading, ignored complaints from white men. Into this air of hostile fear Nat was born on June 30, 1766, to learn the lesson of that frontier so well that when his father enlisted for the Revolution, the boy said, "Yes, Dad, you go, and brother Lish and me'll stay here and shoot Indians." For eight years Mrs. Foster and her six children did not see the patriot father; perforce Nat, the second son, did a man's work in his early 'teens, hunting and trapping. Once a party of Indians came to the Foster cabin, demanded a drink from young Nat, and when he brought them stagnant water, tied him to a tree. That day he swore that no Indian would ever lay hands upon him again and live.

Meanwhile the father fought at Lexington, Bunker Hill, Trenton, Saratoga, lived through Valley Forge, and saw the horrors of Wyoming and the Mohawk Valley. On his way from the battle of Oriskany to Saratoga, marching through the bloody valley, he saw many a slaughtered white. Once he saved a woman and her children from a burning, barricaded cabin around which Indians were dancing in gleeful triumph. (This was near Canajoharie.) After the battle of Saratoga he met the woman's husband and asked him to swear to kill every Indian that chance threw in his way. He told of finding a dead pregnant woman ripped open and her infant mutilated. "I and my children," said he, "are forever enemies of the Indians." After Valley Forge, where he drank soup made from horse-hide, he was sent with a detachment of four hundred to Wyoming, arriving after the massacre to find burned women and children lying in the ruins.

When the soldier returned to New Hampshire in 1782, sick and bent, he told sixteen-year-old Nat: "Make shooting Indians your life's work. You can't be peaceable with them nohow." Nat must have remembered that advice as they trundled west with an ox-cart and one cow, building a raft at Lansingburg to cross the Hudson, waking after midnight upon the river's west bank to fire at skulking redskins. That was the first time that Nat drew Indian blood. Trudging westward again toward Johnstown, they built a cabin near Sir William Johnson's old fish-house, a cabin with a real chimney and a door, though there was but a single room on the ground floor and only a little loft above. Less than two months after they arrived, raiding Indians appeared at the cabin when only Nat and his sister Zilpha were at home. Although the girl was seized and hurried away after the Indians had fired the loft, Nat escaped detection, hidden under a trap-door in the floor. Zilpha was rescued and all but five of her captors killed, but Nat was not avenged—he took an oath of his own: "Here is my life's work. I'll hate the red devils worse'n Dad, and I'll shoot 'em every chance I get." The Foster family was not molested again, but in August of the year when he was twenty-one, Nat had to rescue a neighbor's little daughter who had been captured while picking blackberries.

That year (1787), he appeared at St. Johnsville on the Mohawk to celebrate Independence Day. Clad in buckskin, he answered inquiries by saying that he had come a long distance and that his name was Leatherstocking. (This was twenty-six years before the first of Cooper's *Leatherstocking Tales* appeared.) That day Nat showed his quality: he won a race at the end of which he "lepped" over a pole held five feet in the air by Nick Stoner and another frontiersman. Six feet in height and weighing one hundred and eighty pounds, Nat wrestled and thrice threw a man two inches taller and thirty-six pounds heavier. On the same day he rescued a girl from drowning. Mr. Byron-Curtiss has reason to believe that Cooper knew this Leatherstocking and transferred to *The Deerslayer* an exploit of Nat's in rescuing two girls from a panther.

Two or three years after his appearance at St. Johnsville, Nat married Jemima Streeter, daughter of a St. Lawrence County Justice, and with her settled on a farm of one hundred and fifty acres at Salisbury, Herkimer County, where he lived for thirty years, hunting and trapping in autumn and winter. As for the hunting, I fear that today Nat would be called a game-hog: it is said that he killed more deer, bear, wolves, and panthers than any other white man in the history of the State. Bounties were paid on bears' tails, wolves' heads, and panthers' ears; these were "varmints" that must be exterminated to make safe human life on the frontier. Nat killed as many as twenty-five wolves in a single season; his traps for them were set from Salisbury to the St. Lawrence River. In three seasons he killed ninety-six bears. When he set three or four hundred muskrat traps in a season, he found it necessary to employ several assistants.

The modern hunter, permitted to shoot only one buck, will be shocked to learn that Nat's record for a season was either seventy-five or seventy-six—accounts differ. He did not hesitate to fire upon a doe and her two fawns—the little chaps' runnets would bring fifty cents each; yet he condemned the practice called *fleating*—firing from a canoe covered by green boughs at wondering deer who lifted their heads at the glare of a torchlight in the bow, flaring in the Adirondack night. He had his code—*his*.

Much of Nat's prowess he attributed to his remarkable "double-shotter" of which he boasted, "When you hear him speak, he always tells the truth." These "double-shotters" owned by Foster and Stoner were rifles, says Simms, "made with a single barrel but two locks, one placed above the other far enough to admit of two charges, and have the upper charge of powder rest upon the lower bullet". Nat could load an old flintlock with such rapidity that he could fire six times in one minute—partly because he carried three balls between the fingers of each hand. In time, the balls made convenient little pouches in the flesh.

While slaughtering all the game in sight, Nat did not forget his vow regarding the Indians, who were all the more obnoxious to him because they were competitors in hunting; they sometimes stole from his traps, and frequently were from Canada. I cannot feel much sympathy for an Indian named Hess who exhibited in a barroom at Little Falls a tobacco-pouch which, he boasted, was made from the skin of a white infant; his tally of murdered whites, he announced, was forty-two. Nat met Hess in the forest of northern Herkimer County—heard him cry, "Now, Foster, me get you!"—shot the Indian and stamped his carcase into the mud. At Little Falls one day Nat remarked that he had met Hess once, and "only once after that time".

Similar grim euphemisms hinted the death of other Indians. Nat said, "The best shot I ever made, I got two beaver, one otter, and fifteen marten skins; but I took the filling out of a blanket to do it," or, "I was once in the woods, and saw an Indian lay down to drink at a brook; something was the matter; he dropped his face into the water and drowned; I thought I might as well take his fur, gun, blanket, &c., as leave them to spoil."

In 1832, when he was sixty-six, "Uncle Nat" leased the Herreshoff place at Old Forge, then a part of "Brown's Tract". Brown was a short man weighing about three hundred—he drove about in a specially constructed low gig. He had bought 210,000 acres which he subdivided into eight townships named for his business mottoes: Industry, Enterprise, Perseverance, Unanimity, Frugality, Sobriety, Economy, and Regularity. It is thought that he saw his vast estate only once; but before he died in 1813, he opened up the region by building a twenty-five-mile road from Remsen to Old Forge. His son-in-law, Charles F. Herreshoff, built the famous forge, manufactured one ton of iron at a cost of one dollar a pound, lived at the scene of his smelting efforts two years, and shot himself.

Nat didn't shoot himself there, but he did polish off his last Indian; indeed, so far as I know, "Drid" was the last New York State Indian purged in the nonchalant manner of the frontiersman. Drid was an ugly person, twenty-eight years old, married to a woman who seems not to have regretted his passing. His theory, freely expressed to Nat, was, "There h'aint no law in woods here." What the true origin of his dislike for the old trapper may have been is not clear unless it was rum-born and nourished by Nat's attempt to collect seventeen shillings for goods which Drid preferred to regard as a gift. Drid certainly professed to be kindly disposed toward all the Fosters except Nat; to avoid murdering a friend, he investigated the white family's domestic arrangements and then warned Nat's wife to be sure to "keep her own side of the bed". He further made his bloody intent clear to several white men, one of whom gravely warned him that he might be put "where the dogs wouldn't bite him". Nat observed that he still owned a rifle that never told a lie, but for once the trapper was uneasy. He even asked a Justice for protection, and he might have changed his residence if his wife and daughter-in-law had been in good health.

Matters came to a crisis on a September morning of 1833, when, in the presence of a white hunting-party, Drid attacked Nat, cut him, and was with difficulty prevented from murdering or being murdered. "You no live till Christmas," said the Indian. Foster, once more stirred to his ancient wrath, replied, "You'll do damned well if you see another moon."

With the white hunting and fishing party Drid proceeded to a point where the waters of First Lake expand into a mile-broad surface and where you will now be shown a projection known as Indian's

Point. It was really Nat's Point—he was lurking there with the rifle that never told a lie. Spying his foe, Drid tried to save himself by paddling his canoe into a position between the whites, but Nat's old rifle spoke twice. Both bullets entered at the same spot on the left side near the armpit, passed through the heart, and went out below the right arm. When Drid's white employers returned to Nat's house to announce the Indian's death, the old trapper inquired, "Did he die in a fit?"

The days of Indian-shooting as a recognized sport were past in the Adirondacks. At Herkimer a year later, on September 3-4, 1834, Uncle Nat was tried before a presiding judge, Hiram Denio, who certainly did not show the defendant any favor. There were plenty of witnesses who were permitted to testify regarding Drid's threats; there was nobody who admitted that he saw the rifle in Nat's hands at the Point, though several testified to seeing him there. When the jury came in with their verdict of *Not Guilty*, Nat was insensible; when he was aroused and made to understand that he was free, he rose up, stretched out both hands wide over the heads of the crowd, and exclaimed: "God bless you all! God bless the people!" Then he rushed out of court and rode home on his pony. With the possible exception of Judge Denio, who would have preferred to have Drid shot when he made his murderous attack upon Nat, everyone was satisfied. The Indian widow had smiled when she saw her late husband's body, then had snipped off a piece of his shirt showing the bullet-hole. A chief of the St. Regis Indians came down from the St. Lawrence River to take away his sister. He said that Drid was a bad Indian who had been expelled from the tribe—that he had even threatened the life of his chief—that Foster had done right.

Some said that Uncle Nat was so disgusted at all the fuss made over an Indian's death that he resolved to flit; others thought that he wished to remove his family from vengeance. For a time he visited Boonville, then tried Wilkesbarre in Pennsylvania, and finally came home to York State to die near Ava. When his eyes closed, on March 16, 1840, he was smiling at a grandchild.

You have now heard so much about our Injun-fighters that you may sympathize with the man at Ava who, annoyed by hearing stories about Uncle Nat, partly destroyed his grave-stone. With considerable regret I pass over the names of Nathaniel Shipman, David Elerson, Moses Van Campen, Green White, John Trim, and several others to conclude this chapter with a brief account of Nicholas (Nick) Stoner, fifer of the Revolution and trapper extraordinary in Fulton and Hamilton Counties, who lived to correct his own biography.

Nick's father, Henry Stoner, was an immigrant from Germany who arrived on these shores some twenty years before the Revolution, married a wife in Maryland, gave his two sons a little schooling in New York City, and then settled at Fonda's Bush, some ten miles northeast of Sir William's Johnstown.

In the summer of 1777, at the age of fourteen or fifteen, Nick enlisted as fifer in the same New York regiment in which his father and brother served. At Saratoga, following Arnold, he was knocked senseless by a flying piece of skull from a comrade whose brains spattered the young fifer. He remembered also a later experience, when, at the feet of Major André's gallows, he bought a pie for one hundred dollars—Continental money and a bargain. He saw much service and played boyish pranks in Rhode Island, the Mohawk Valley, and Yorktown. Returning to New York City, he blew a clarinet at the British evacuation and "played off" General Washington's departure.

In the summer of 1782, while Nick was still with the Army at King's Ferry, a small party of Indians had surprised and tomahawked on his farm at Albany Bush the father, Henry Stoner, then had set fire to his dwelling and retired without injuring Mrs. Stoner. So, when he returned to Johnson's former domain, Nick found a widowed mother waiting. He also found another widow, pretty young Anna Mason; his courtship of her has been told in *Little Red Foot*, by R. W. Chambers. He lived with Anna happily some forty years; then he made an extra-legal alliance with a hay-widow, Mrs. Polly Phye, who was not sure that her wandering husband might not return. After fifteen or twenty years, Polly died. In 1840 Nick took unto himself his third widow, Hannah Houghtaling Frank. He had done as well as most of our early fathers of New England, who, it seems, invariably married thrice.

Once again, in 1813, Nick went to war, this time in the 29th New York Regiment, officially as Drum or Fife Major but often unofficially as Chief of Scouts or Sergeant of the Line. He was present at that victory of Plattsburg whose balladry will be found in another chapter. Ever after, on solemn occasions, he was called Major Stoner.

If tradition be correct, the novelist Cooper knew Major Stoner; certainly he could have drawn traits from him for his study of Leatherstocking. Even when he was an old man and slightly stooped, Nick was five feet, eleven inches in height. He kept the light brown hair of his German ancestry, but his face, described as "extraordinary likely", was as swarthy as an Indian's, and his striking appearance was rendered more romantic by two gold rings which he wore in his ears from boyhood. His only peer as a trapper in that section was Nat Foster, his intimate companion.

The most famous incident in Nick's life is the vengeance he took upon his father's murderer. He probably killed not more than a half dozen Indians, but the manner of this particular feat was notable. The scene takes us to Fon Claire's (De Fonclaiere's) inn at Johnstown, later called Union Hall. Deputy Sheriff Nick dropped in peaceably but perhaps warmed by kill-care, and addressed a member of an Indian party of hunters. Another Indian inquired insolently what business Nick had to interrogate his comrade. "Out, you black booger!" said the Major. A brawl followed, in the course of which Nick flung the surly Indian into a platter of fried pork, swimming in hot fat, standing on the hearth. His antagonist was burned severely, perhaps mortally. The landlord rushed out of the kitchen to find lawyer Amaziah Rust and get a writ against Nick; but, as a friend of Nick's, the Squire explained gravely that "Captain Stoner was apt to be deranged with the changes of the moon"—that he would make reparation and the morning's "frolic" would soon be forgotten, no harm resulting to the reputation of the inn.

The Squire was too sanguine of prophecy. Leaving the tavern's kitchen, Stoner had come upon an Indian called Captain John, lying dead drunk and, unfortunately, exhibiting in one ear a "heavy leaden jewel". Perhaps Nick resented anyone else wearing a decoration which burlesqued his own ear-rings. At any rate, he put one foot upon the Indian's neck, thrust his finger into the split in the Indian's ear, and tore out the adornment. The victim merely turned over with a grunt, while Nick proceeded to the bar-room, ready for further combat.

He found there another Indian, only half-drunk, brandishing a

scalping knife, boasting that its nine marks represented white American scalps taken in war. "This," he crowed, pointing to the deepest
notch, "was the scalp of old Stoner!" Nick's answering cry was terrible, "You never will scalp another one!" Seizing from the fireplace
a red-hot andiron, which burned his own hand to a blister, he hurled
it at his father's murderer, knocking him flat with a great burn across
the throat.

The Indians made for Canada, carrying a companion who, a physician assured them, could not possibly survive the "seared jugular".
Nick was jailed, but a mob stove in the door and bore him in triumph
to Throop's tavern. Taking Stoner to one side, the jailer got his consent to return to imprisonment; but the hero was soon missed, the
mob made a second rescue, and Nick was persuaded to go home to his
family and forget his inconveniences.

Nick killed one or two other Indians—poachers—but even a folklorist grows weary of slaughter, and I must bring his career to its
uneventful close. The old trapper spent his last years at Newkirks,
pensioned by a grateful government. When he died in 1853, the
funeral procession at Johnstown to the Kingsborough cemetery brought
out the largest procession Fulton County had ever seen. The students
of Gloversville High School have a song to Nick—"to the naughty
Indians he didn't do a thing". On August 21, 1929, there was unveiled at Caroga Lake a handsome monument only a few rods from
the hotel built upon the site of Nick's old farmhouse. Two young
descendants of Nick—of the sixth generation—drew the curtain and
let us see the idealized features of that "likely" trapper, soldier, and
citizen who made his country safe from marauders and joined the
Big Four of our Injun-fighters.

They are so much alike—aren't they?—that they guarantee the
type which Cooper knew and immortalized. I do not find them
monotonous, perhaps because I remember my grandfather's remark.
He was particularly fond of our evening ceremony: we played Five-
Fingers; I read aloud a psalm; then he had his whiskey, said his prayer
in a stage-whisper, and drew the curtains of his bed. Our favorite battles, because *he* liked them, were the Boyne and Waterloo; we had
good talks about them before his whiskey. Sometimes he was drowsy
enough to confuse the two events. I had been reading him a bit from

the late G. A. Henty's *Orange and Green* to give him a taste of Boyne-water.

"Ay, ay," he said sleepily, "and there he was praying for night or Blucher."

"But, Grandpa," I said, "that wasn't King William—I think that was Wellington who prayed for night or Blucher."

"O ay," said Grandfather. "Wellington, was it? What does it matter? They were both brave men."

IV: Sons of Robin Hood

H E TOOK from the rich and gave to the poor." That is the old
formula for a sort of criminal to whom the folk have always
been romantically inclined. The fact that the outlaw was giving away money not his own has never been an obstacle in the way of
admiration; he was, at any rate, presenting an object-lesson in distribu-
tion, and his legend afforded an opportunity for the expression of how
the poor folk feel regarding economic inequality. For the rest—he was
usually a striking figure of a man, at least in popular report, always
strong, bold, and defiant. The admiration of the primary virtue of
courage is older than economic theory.

York State has had a number of outlaws whose legend resembles
Robin Hood's, but only two bands seem likely to survive in popular
imagination. I refer, of course, to Claudius Smith and his sons in
the eighteenth century, and to George Washington Loomis and his
sons in the nineteenth. There is a considerable amount of verified
fact about each hero and his followers, but for the most part I shall
be following, not unwillingly, stories told at the hearth.

Time was when children were frightened into obedience, particularly in Orange County, by tales of the Scourge of the Highlands.

It is said that one unfortunate mechanic of adult years was actually driven insane by a punkinhead-lantern which appeared at his bedroom window and which to his drowsy terror resembled Claudius Smith. Smith was of English parentage and Tory inclinations. He is said to have been born at Brookhaven, Long Island; another legend connects him with Southhold. His father encouraged latent proclivities by showing how to grind out the owner's initials from two iron wedges which the lad had stolen. According to the same testimony—that of Mistress Abigail Letts—the father's natural cussedness increased with age. After he had become blind, he would strike out with his cane at his wife whenever she came near him, and would even amuse himself by chasing her about, locating her by the meek voice pleading for mercy. It was this long-suffering woman who prophesied to her son, "Claudius, you will die like a trooper's horse, with your shoes on". As will be seen, the son's last act deprived her of the slender pleasure of fulfilled prophecy.

At some time before the Revolution, the family moved to what is now Orange County, to a place later known as McKnight's Mills in the town of Monroe; for them was named Smith's Clove, a cleft in the mountains, sometimes called the Kitchen of the County. A Dutch Justice in Warwick made what may have been the only joke in a placid life when he ordered a tramp to leave his village. "Where shall I go?" asked the wanderer. "To Smith's Clove, the Kitchen of the County," was the reply.

By the time that the Revolution broke out, Claudius Smith had three sons old enough to join his gang of "Cowboys"—so called because they stole cattle and drove them to be sold to the British army at Suffern. (Later that region near Suffern was famous for the Jackson Whites, who live in the Ramapo hills, and who may have been recruited partly from the Cowboys.) Beside cattle, Smith stole horses, muskets, and silver. Just why the Tory and British government at New York City permitted this sort of freebooting is evident in the confession of one William Cole, a member of the gang captured a short time after Smith's execution. When, under the direction of a certain John Mason, a Mrs. Sidman was robbed, her gold watch was presented to the Mayor of New York; when Mr. Erskine was robbed, Mason gave his fine rifle to Lord Cathcart; when the gang robbed

Muster-Master General Ward, Lord Cathcart gave them one hundred guineas. Cole names sixteen men who have harbored the outlaws, including Edward Roblin and Benjamin Kelley in the Clove—two of Smith's lieutenants; he is evidently speaking of the organization recently headed by Claudius. He says that they have three different caves, each of which will "contain" eight persons. He adds that there is a similar gang across the Hudson, on the east side.

With this farflung organization, protected and abetted by the British authorities, pretending to be on the side of order against the rebels, Claudius Smith felt so secure that he said to J. Harvey Bull of the Clove: "Here I stand like a pillar of old St. Paul's Church and defy any man to move me." The "rebels" were not slow to accept this challenge. In July, 1777, he is on the records as a prisoner in Kingston jail, "charged with stealing oxen belonging to the continent". According to one tradition, he escaped on the way to the Goshen jail, or at the Goshen jail; according to another, he was on the road to Kingston from Goshen when he was rescued by his band. In either case, he had one foretaste of what punishment awaited him.

So far as his personality was concerned, he seemed to live up to some of the qualifications for a Robin Hood. He was slippery when caught; he was bold, wily, "of large stature and powerful nerve (muscle), of keen penetration". But the stories of his kindness are dubious, to say the least. The one incident oftenest told is his gallantry to Mistress McClaughry. Her husband, a colonel in the Patriot army, was taken prisoner by the British after the capture of Fort Montgomery. From New York he wrote to ask his wife for money, perhaps for comforts and necessities, perhaps, as another version says, for ransom. Having no "hard money", she tried to borrow from rich Abimal Youngs, who lived up to a reputation for careful management by answering that he had none to lend. Even after the poor lady had pawned her silver shoe-buckles, she could not raise the sum requested. Hearing of this piteous situation, Robin Hood Smith made a nocturnal visit to Youngs, hung him to his own well-pole, and asked where his money could be found. When the miser showed a disagreeable willingness to die rather than tell, Smith appropriated bonds and other valuable papers and rode away with his gang. I am not sure that Mistress McClaughry profited by this act of alleged gallantry.

The other favorite story of Smith's generosity is also a sequel to the fall of Fort Montgomery. Judge Bodle, later of Tompkins County, was wearily trudging away from the disaster when he met Smith, who addressed him heartily: "Good day, Mr. Bodle. You are weary with walking. Go to my dwelling yonder and ask my wife to give you breakfast. Tell her I sent you." Bodle thanked him, proceeded toward the house till Smith was out of sight, then walked rapidly in another direction.

Those who have difficulty in illustrating Smith's bounty are likely to cite his lieutenant, Edward Roblin of the Clove, whose story, as told by C. E. Stickney in 1867, certainly has romantic elements. This hopeful youth can be made a figure of sentiment by stressing his elopement with the daughter of his employer, an old man named Price, a person who thought (quite rightly, I believe) that young Roblin was a dubious bargain. The old gentleman came up with the young couple just as a parson was about to marry them. As a precautionary measure Roblin was jailed for debt, though he claimed that the sum mentioned was not money advanced as a loan but his just due for labor. During the months of Roblin's incarceration, Miss Price consented to marry her father's choice, whereat her former lover eloped with the jailor's daughter and the jailor's gelding, leaving the limb of a tree with the note, "As yours was a chestnut horse, the exchange is fair, for this is a horse-chestnut." It was Roblin who headed that part of Smith's gang which stole muskets and pewter plates from American army-wagons. The folk remembered that one robber shot during the foray was never buried by his companions.

As time passed and his thieving prospered, Smith seems to have grown less and less urbane; he even swore to kill certain eminent Patriots—Colonel Jesse Woodhull, Mathew Strong, Samuel Strong, and Cole Curtis. When, as a preliminary to more drastic measures, he announced that he would steal the Colonel's mare, the prudent Patriot had her stabled in the cellar. While the family and guests were at tea, they were startled to hear Smith's whoop, and realized that somehow he had got the mare out of the cellar and was riding away on her. When a guest pointed his ready rifle at Smith, the

Colonel knocked it up, exclaiming: "For heaven's sake, don't fire! If you miss him, he will kill me."

If Smith knew how he had been saved, he was nevertheless implacable: he decided to kill the Colonel anyway because he was "such a darned rebel". When the outlaw next visited, on October 6, 1777, the Colonel was away with his regiment, and his shrewd wife had hidden the silver under her child in the cradle. After the gang had broken open the door and while they were searching the house, she sat by the cradle soothing the child, who prettily asked whether the bad men were going to steal her calico dress. Disappointed of body and booty, the gang soon departed, taking a horse left at the Colonel's by a neighbor.

Other events of that night were not in the vein of comedy. About midnight the Cowboys arrived at Major Nathaniel Strong's, where the family was sleeping soundly. Unfortunately this "darned rebel" was at home. As the outside door crashed inward and a panel was smashed into the Major's bedroom, he armed himself with pistols and gun. As he entered the "inside room", unharmed by a shot fired through the window, he looked so formidable that a parley ensued. Smith's gang promised that if Strong would lay down his arms, he would not be injured. Putting down his gun, he advanced toward the door as if to open it, when two bullets fired through a broken panel pierced his heart. It was sheer murder, without even the usual justification of booty, for all that was found to take away was a saddle and bridle.

This stupid outrage, which must have been a little too overt even for the ruffians who protected and abetted Smith, unloosed the fury of a long-suffering countryside. The State Assembly (Continental) took up the case. On October 31, 1777, Governor George Clinton offered $1200 for the capture of Claudius, and $600 each for his sons Richard and James. A son William and another member of the gang were shot in the mountains that autumn, perhaps before the Governor's proclamation. Even the cranky old grandfather had a horse shot under him as he was returning from taking provisions to a hideout. (This, by the way, disposes of the story that he was blind, but not of the charge that he caned his wife.) Claudius evidently realized that the Highlands and the Ramapos were getting too hot; at any rate, he decamped to Long Island.

Unfortunately for his peaceful residence, a Major John Brush recognized him at his new abode, slipped over to Connecticut, collected four assistants, and caught Smith sleeping upstairs in a tavern. After a struggle the party crossed the Sound and took their prisoner to Fishkill Landing, New York, where the Sheriff of Orange County met the outlaw and escorted him to Goshen, attended by a troop of light-horse commanded, appropriately, by a Woodhull. At the Goshen jail Claudius was manacled, and guarded night and day until his execution.

Smith's trial on January 13, 1779, was not for murder, a charge hard to prove and complicated by the Cowboy's military status—if any. He was indicted "for burglary at the house of John Earle; for robbery at the house of Ebenezer Woodhull; for robbery of the dwelling and stillhouse of William Bell". Asked whether he had anything to say about the verdict, he replied: "No. If God Almighty cannot change your hearts, I cannot." It was decided that he should be hanged on January 22nd with a horse-thief and a burglar; another account says that no less than five associates were hanged with him, including a woman. There is no doubt that the principal character played his rôle to the satisfaction of a large audience. Dressed in a handsome suit of broadcloth with silver buttons, the tall outlaw had made his last graceful bows to former neighbors when he was addressed by an elderly person who elbowed his way to the scaffold. "Mr. Smith, Mr. Smith," he called, "where shall I find those deeds and other papers that you-er—*had* from me?" Smith turned his gaze from the hills from whence his help did not come—to Abimal Youngs, the miser. "Mr. Youngs," he said, "this is no time to talk about papers. Meet me in the next world, and I'll tell you about them."

His final jest was better remembered but less suave. Looking off toward the empty hills again, he must have remembered his mother's warning, *"Claudius, you will die like a trooper's horse, with your shoes on."* He kicked off his shoes. "This," he said, "is to prove my mother a false prophetess and a liar." Then they hanged him.

No doubt there were people present who immediately spoke of

him as a Robin Hood. As a principal historian of Orange County was to say in his stately manner: "It is believed that much of what he extracted from the wealthy he bestowed upon the indigent." I have little evidence of his generosity, as I have said, but I have more of the generosity of the folk toward a ruffian. His capture while snoring in a tavern was too ignoble for a hero; the folk, therefore, have a more "gallus" version, as follows: Driven by hostile hordes up onto Sugar Loaf Mountain, Claudius was finally forced out of a crevice in which he had hidden. "Surrender or we'll shoot!" shouted his bloodthirsty pursuers. Stepping grandly up onto a log, he replied, "Shoot and be damned!" They took the first part of his advice, shot him in the legs, and bore him off to the Goshen gallows. Too bad it isn't true.

The gang still menaced. Claudius and his son William were dead, the son James and two others are said to have been executed shortly after, but Richard lived to avenge his father. Says the *Fishkill Packet* of April 28, 1779: "We hear from Goshen that a horrible murder was committed near the Stirling iron works on the night of Saturday, the 27th of March, by a party of villains, 5 or 6 in number, the principal of whom was Richard Smith, eldest surviving son of the late Claudius Smith, of infamous memory, his eldest son having been shot last fall at Smith's Clove." Having coldly planned the murder of two men, the gang went to the house of John W. Clark, dragged him out of doors, and shot him. One said, "He is not dead enough yet", then shot him again—through the arm—and left him. Clark lived long enough to give the names of his murderers, who by this time had proceeded to the house of a second intended victim whose name is withheld by the newspaper. Hearing a noise, this intrepid man stood on defence in the corner of his little log cabin, his bayonet fixed and his gun cocked. When the door was broken in, he presented so formidable an appearance that the gang "thought proper to march off". At Clark's house, pinned to the victim's coat, was found the following:

A Warning to the Rebels. You are hereby warned at your peril to desist from hanging any more friends to government as you did Claudius Smith. You are warned likewise to use James Smith, James Flewwelling,

and William Cole well, and ease their irons, for we are determined to
hang six for one, for the blood of the innocent cries aloud for vengeance.
Your noted friend, Capt. Williams, and his crew of robbers and murderers, we have got in our power, and the blood of Claudius Smith shall
be repaid. There are particular companies of us who belong to Col.
Butler's army, Indians as well as white men, and particularly numbers
from New York, that are resolved to be avenged on you for your cruelty
and murder. We are to remind you that you are the beginners and
aggressors, for by your cruel oppressions and bloody actions you drive
us to it. This is the first, and we are determined to pursue it on your
heads and leaders to the last, till the whole of you are murdered.

What happened to "Flewwelling" I do not know. Apparently
James Smith was executed; and while the ruffians were demanding
tenderness for William Cole, he was turning State's evidence in a
confession which must have made red faces in the city of New York.
Richard Smith seems to have stayed in New York State until the end
of the Revolution, when he transferred his talents to Nova Scotia.
Accounts of Clark's death continued to inflame the patriots, one being
that he had been led out of doors, stripped of outer garments, told
to go back into the house, and then shot in the back.

To me the most memorable of all the Smith stories is yet to be
told—that which recounts the gallantry of Miss Phebe Reynolds of
Monroe, aged twelve, one of the real heroines of the Revolution.
The avengers of Claudius Smith came to her father's house, but
found the doors so sturdy that they crawled up onto the roof with
the evident intention of climbing down the great chimney. One of
the ladies had the presence of mind to rip the cover off a pillow and
throw the feathers onto the fire. Breathing suffocating smoke and
vengeance, the Cowboys retired.

The second attempt was made in July of 1782, when a gang led
by Benjamin Kelley and Philip Roblin, and pretending to be a detachment sent by Washington in search of deserters, appeared at
the same home. As soon as he opened the door and realized who his
visitors were, Reynolds attempted to escape. The resultant noise
aroused his wife, his seven children, and a lad who lived with them.
In the presence of these innocents, the gang cut Reynolds with knives
and swords, then hung him by the neck on the trammel-pole of the

fireplace. While the ruffians were searching for valuables, little Phebe cut the rope and got her father upon a bed. Discovering what she had done, the gang whipped her with the rope until they supposed her to be "disabled", then hung up Reynolds for a second time. Again she rescued him; whereupon the outlaws went at him with their knives and swords until they were sure he was dead. After destroying his papers and taking whatever valuables he had, they departed, fastening the door on the outside and setting the house on fire. Incredible as it seems, Phebe managed to put out the fire and to staunch her father's wounds. In the morning she alarmed the neighborhood so early that shortly after sunrise an avenging band was off to the mountains in pursuit of the gang. A neighbor named June had the fortune to shoot Benjamin Kelley, whose body was later recovered and identified by a suit of Quaker clothes which he had stolen from Reynolds. Meanwhile a surgeon was at work on the thirty wounds of Reynolds and was sewing on an ear that healed in such a way that he was "disfigured"; one hand was so badly cut that he never recovered its use. It is pleasant to add that he lived to see his eighty-fifth year; and that little Phebe, after the family's removal to Sullivan County, married a man named Jeremiah Drake and failed by only a year of enjoying as long a life as her sturdy sire's.

In 1804 or 1805, some of Smith's descendants came from Canada to search for what they called his treasure, and are said to have recovered the muskets but no pewter plates and no silver. About 1824, two descendants of Edward Roblin came across the border with what they believed to be better information but departed unsatisfied. So Claudius Smith's treasure, like Kidd's, still allures those who like to dig for ill-got gains.

There is a final story about the Scourge of the Highlands. His body is said to have been buried in the grounds of the Presbyterian Church at Goshen. One day a lame man penetrated the grave with his crutch, leaving it indecorously exposed. The bones were removed to a shop to be reinterred, but evidently were neglected. Some time later, a blacksmith, when asked to make a carving knife, found that he had no buckhorn for the handle but contrived a substitute; so somebody in Orange County may still have a knife whose handle was made from a thighbone of Claudius.

For an introduction to our other gang of famous bandits let me quote from a report transmitted shortly before the close of the Civil War to the State Legislature from the Prison Association of New York:

There is a family residing in Oneida County, who, according to common fame, have followed the profession of thieving for nearly twenty years. They have grown rich by their unlawful practices. Their children are educated in the best and most expensive seminaries. They dress genteelly, their manners are somewhat polished, and they appear tolerably well in society. Their operations are carried on through the counties of Oneida, Oswego, Otsego, Madison, Chenango, Schoharie, Delaware and Sullivan. They have numerous well trained confederates in all those counties, who are ready by day or by night, at a moment's warning, to ride off in any direction for the sake of plunder, or for the concealment or protection of associates who are in danger of falling into the meshes of the law. These men have been indicted times without number in the above mentioned counties, but none of them have ever been convicted, nor have any of them ever been in jail for a longer time than was sufficient for a bondsman to arrive at the prison. It is generally believed that there are farmers, apparently respectable, who belong to the gang and share in its profits. Whether this be so or not, it is certain that whenever bail is needed, any required number of substantial farmers will come forward and sign their bonds, without regard to the amount of the penalty. These men, as might be supposed, exert a great political influence, and it is well understood that they are always ready to reward their friends and punish their enemies, both in primary conventions and at the polls. Although, as we have said, they have been repeatedly indicted, yet the number of their indictments bears but a small ratio to the number of their depredations. It usually happens that any one who is particularly active in bringing any of the gang to justice has his barn or dwelling soon after burned, or his horses are missing from the stable, or his sheep or cattle from the pasture. These things have happened so often that people are careful how they intermeddle in the matter of seeking to bring them to justice. If a person so intermeddling happens to have a mortgage on his property, it is apt to be very soon foreclosed. If he has political aspirations, thousands of unseen obstacles interpose to prevent the fulfillment of his hopes. If he is a trader, his custom falls off. If he is a physician, malpractice is imputed to him, or other malicious stories are circulated to his discredit; and at length matters come to such a pass that his only recourse is to leave the county. All who make themselves conspicuous as their opponents, are in some way made to feel the effect of a thousand blighting and malign influences, which paralyze their energies and blast their hopes of success. Although the law has been powerless when exerted against the gang, they have been in the habit of using its energies with great effect against those who stood in their path. We are told, with great circumstantiality, by men worthy of all confidence, of numerous instances where the forms of law were used to punish innocence and shield robbery under their skilful manipulations. We content ourselves with a single example, which may be taken as a specimen of the rest, and which we select from the mass, because some of the facts belonging to it came under our personal observation.

We found in the jail at Pulaski, the half-shire town of Oswego county, a man and his wife who had been confined there for eighteen months, on a charge of grand larceny. The man was evidently a quite inoffensive person, a member of the Methodist church, and a class leader in it. He was in good repute among his neighbors, and no one of them gave any credence to the story of his guilt. The wife was a more energetic person, and although there is no proof that she was ever actually connected with the gang, yet it is believed that she was quite willing to conceal their secrets, so far as they might have been entrusted to her. Some time before her arrest, one of the gang ran off with her daughter, and neither he nor his associates would let her know where her child was concealed. This greatly enraged her, and she began to let out the secrets of the organization, and to threaten vengeance against them. She was repeatedly warned to desist, and menaced with punishment if she continued to operate against them; but she paid no attention to their threats, and continued her hostile action. One evening, just at dusk, a Jew peddler came in with his pack and requested her to let him stay all night. She assented, proposing to him to leave his pack in the front room, while they went into a rear apartment to get supper. They sat in the room until bedtime, and the peddler, in his affidavit, distinctly declares that she was never once out of his sight. When he was ready to retire, she lighted a candle for him, but before going to bed, he went into the front room to look at his pack, when, to his consternation, he found that it was gone. The next morning he entered a complaint before a justice, who was himself generally believed to be connected with the gang, against the couple at whose house he had lodged; and, although the complainant swore that the woman was never out of his sight from the time he left the pack in the front room until he discovered that it was lost, and the husband proved, or offered to prove, that he was at a Methodist meeting during the whole time that the peddler was in his house, yet the justice committed them for trial. A respectable farmer now came forward and offered to be their bail, and was accepted by the magistrate. He told the woman, at the same time, that if she would say no more about the gang and their affairs, she would hear no more about the larceny charge. But she was smarting so severely about the loss of her daughter that she could not restrain her propensity to talk, and frequently gave information which was adverse to the interests of the parties who she believed were keeping her daughter in concealment. When the bondsman found that she would not keep quiet, he surrendered both her and her husband, and they were then committed to jail, where they had remained up to the time of our visit. Their cases had been put over from court to court on account, it was alleged, of the absence of material witnesses for the prosecution. It was generally believed in the neighborhood that they would be kept there, on one pretense or another, just as long as it suited the interests of their prosecutors.

Last summer, one of the constables of Madison county had been very active in tracing out their operations, and they determined to give him a lesson. They procured a warrant from a justice, supposed to be devoted to their interests, who deputed two of the gang to convey him to jail, as special constables. It was not convenient for them (such at least was the pretense) to convey him to the prison immediately; so they were taking him to their own home, to be kept there until it should suit their purpose to carry him to the jail. Their route lay through the village of Hamilton, where the constable was well known, and when the citizens saw him in the custody of two members of the rogues' gang, instead of their being in his, it awakened a very lively curiosity in their minds. On being interrogated, they produced the warrant, which appeared regular on its face, and the citizens did not attempt to resist it; but they insisted that the prisoner should be taken directly to the jail, or otherwise they would forcibly release him. Finding that they were in earnest, the special constables finally yielded the point, and carried him to the jail. Five citizens of Hamilton made themselves especially conspicuous in the matter. Before a month had elapsed, the barns of all of them were burned, and two of them lost valuable horses, which were stolen in the night. This last outrage roused the people of the vicinity into action. They knew, from long experience, that they could obtain no redress through the tardy processes of the law, against the men who had for so long a time successfully resisted its action, and they resolved to take the law into their own hands, and administer punishment to the offenders. Disguising themselves effectually, they went at night to the house of the ringleaders; set fire to the barns; killed one of them outright; wounded another severely; and finally, set fire to the dwelling house, which, however, was extinguished before any serious damage had been done.

The facts here narrated, have not, it is true, been judicially verified; but we were visiting the county of Madison at the time when this instance of retributive vengeance occurred, and inquired minutely into all the circumstances, of the county officers and of the principal inhabitants, and we entertain no doubt that they are substantially true, as above stated. If there is any doubt about the matter, it will be easy for the Legislature to establish their truth or falsity by a commission or committee of their own body, duly authorized to investigate them.

Those who know the Loomis saga—and who in Oneida and Madison Counties does not know part of it?—will not be surprised to learn that the State Legislative Library has no record of our lawgivers making the suggested investigation; nevertheless there is plenty of material for an entire book about the "Lummises". From the year 1879, when the New York *Weekly Sun* published an account of the gang, printed materials have been piling up. Collecting oral traditions about the "Lummises" has become a recognized sport in Central New York. I am specially indebted to four collectors really learned in the subject: Mr. Thomas L. Hall, County Historian of Madison County; Mr. George W. Walter, who is writing a book on the subject; my colleague, Prof. G. M. York, who introduced me to the subject with tales learned in his Madison County boyhood; and Mr. L. A. Dapson, who has reported on his investigations to the State Historical Association. Thanks to them, I am able to supplement the legends with a more accurate background of fact than my own research had discerned; without their authority I should hesitate to disagree with numerous printed articles.

Loomis is an honored name both in New England and in New York, and I wish to be emphatic in stating that among the descendants of the gang are to be found highly respected citizens of our commonwealth. The bandits are merely an example of a malicious (and entertaining) "sport" in an admirable family which happened to number, in two generations, people who were all the more dangerous because they were superior in physique and mentality. One who has acknowledged with zest his relationship is the brilliant (and politically mistaken) poet, Ezra Loomis Pound. Members of the family will remind you that two hundred Loomises fought for American independence, including—as most of them do not know—Daniel, father of the gang's founder. "Old Lummis" himself served in the War of 1812 and was probably born at Windsor, the charming Connecticut village where a famous school for boys bears worthily an honored Yankee name.

The founding father was George Washington Loomis (1779-1851), who came from Vermont about 1802 and built a farmhouse on the old road along the west side of the Nine Mile Swamp near Sangerfield, Oneida County, about a half mile from the Madison-Oneida County line. On his farm of three hundred and eighty-five acres he cleared the land and made a reputation as a friendly neighbor and a fine horseman. The house stood on a high knoll overlooking ten miles of the Chenango River, which, a short distance in front of the house, watered a cedar swamp so treacherous that it is said that today "not more than ten men can penetrate its depth with confidence".

Loomis took for wife a schoolmistress named Rhoda Mallett, whose father, an officer of the French Revolutionary army, was said to be an embezzler. One day the sheriff of Oneida County tried to crawl into Mallett's window to arrest him for debt, but was promptly knocked down by a fire-shovel in the hands of Rhoda. Loomis was impressed. "A girl who will fight for her father will fight for her husband," he remarked. "I am going to marry her." In 1812 her father was convicted of perjury and jailed.

Meanwhile Loomis was himself in trouble. In 1810 he was one of five arrested on a charge of passing counterfeit money. Three were sent to State's Prison. Before the Grand Jury had met, Loomis got out of the difficulty by paying back one hundred dollars to Captain Leonard for the return of a counterfeit bill. There was also a story of a peddler visiting the Loomis farm about 1820 and never being seen thereafter. While there is hardly a county which hasn't some such tale, in this case there is the unusual circumstance of the big boulder covering a perfectly good well.

Shady as Loomis was, the folk tell most of their tales about his

six sons and one of his six daughters, two of whom died in infancy.
The outstanding boy, who had the unswerving obedience of his
brothers after their father's death, was George Washington ("Wash").
He was a handsome man resembling John Wilkes Booth—with dark
blue eyes, a full, black, curly beard and mustache, and a jaunty
carriage. Those who liked him called him affable, generous, a good
story-teller, a man of his word; in short he was the Robin Hood. The
other sons were named William W. (Bill), Grove L., Wheeler T.,
Amos Plumb (always called Plum), and Hiram Denio. Of these,
Grove seems to have been second in importance. According to Mr.
Hall, he was a lover of the chase:

He owned several foxhounds. He started one at a time, beginning with
an old and sure trailer and tracker. If Grove failed to get the fox the
first time, he let loose a faster dog. Then, if he failed in the second
attempt, his faithful old Hathaway slut, part greyhound, would be
whining. Grove would say, "Just a minute, just a minute." Then he
would slip her collar. Away she would bound and most often catch
Mr. Fox ahead of the hounds.

Grove was also a famous fisherman and a fine horseman. At one time
he owned the black stallion *Flying Cloud*, whose market price reached
six thousand dollars. Of the others I am interested in Denio, who, Mr.
Hall says, looked like a professor but was called "the Judge".
     Of the girls who grew up—Calista, Cornelia, Lucia, and Charlotte—
all except Cornelia (the smartest) were married, two of them to respected persons, though you hear tales of their shoplifting and stealing
muffs. One story is that they would go to a store, try on several
dresses, and walk out with one or two concealed under their hoops.
The favorite anecdote about the "gals", told usually of the unmarried
one, describes the consternation at the end of a dance when it was
found that a number of expensive little muffs were missing. Some of
the bereft just cried; one of them accidentally-on-purpose knocked
over Cornelia, and there, "like doughnuts on a frying fork" were the
missing muffs, visible under her hoops, strung up her legs.
     Another ballad-like story about a "Lummis gal" tells how she
dressed up in Wash's clothes when a cow-dealer appeared, and made
him believe that she *was* Wash. She gave him about one hundred

dollars for cows—only twenty-five dollars being in authentic money. When the dealer reached Waterville, he discovered the counterfeits and rode back to the Loomis farm, accompanied by officers of the law. Wash was able to establish the fact that he was not present at the sale, and there seemed no way of proving that a girl had dressed in his clothes. The cows were hidden in the swamp. There is a similar story about how two of the girls, Cornelia and Charlotte, drove up and paid Russell Crumb near North Brookfield his asking price of three hundred and sixty dollars for a pair of oxen. When he demanded two dollars for a yoke to use in driving the animals to their new home, Cornelia laughed and tossed over a two-dollar bill. Next morning, the bank at Waterville informed the astonished farmer that all the money he had been paid except that one bill was counterfeit. He traced the oxen by their mud-prints, but he didn't get the critters back.

The folk do not spare the old mother. She is said to have exhorted the young men who became members of the gang—technically hired men on the farm—in this manner: "Now don't you come back till you have stolen me something, even if it's only a jack-knife." She had her standards; she boasted of the times she had read the Bible through. When Wash's wife died leaving the wish that her son might not be brought up under Loomis influence, the old lady was scandalized. The child was given to another woman to "raise," but Rhoda kidnapped him and almost succeeded in getting him to Canada.*

The first serious conflict of the "Lummis" boys with the law seems to have occurred in 1848, when Wash and Grove drove up, in a wagon stocked with clubs, to a hop-pickers' dance at Brookfield. They refused to pay for admission, and in a brief time were busily at work with their clubs. In the fight their unwilling host, Mr. Abbey, was almost killed and several were injured. Indicted for assault with intent to kill, Wash was brought before a County Judge (who later became

* "Wash's woman", Hannah Wright, was killed in 1861 by a member of the gang called Tom Mott—his real name was Jones. The coroner's inquest accepted his story that he didn't know that the gun which he was cleaning was loaded, but it is claimed that years later Tom confessed that two of the Loomis brothers, jealous of Hannah's influence with Wash, had offered fifty dollars to have her shot. There is also a tale about a servant-girl who was shot by a gun "accidentally" laid upon a hot stove.

a Senator from a western state), was admitted to bail, and contrived to have the trial deferred again and again. All might have been forgotten cozily if Dan Douglass of Sangerfield Center hadn't sworn out a warrant for Wash for stealing a saddle and bridle. "Things got too hot"; Wash skipped bail and went to California for a couple years (1849-51). Vague reports came of his being hanged out there, but he was just biding his time. One story is that he treacherously shot a man in a duel not conducted according to gold-rush codes; another is that he rode all the way home on a splendid animal thenceforth known as the California Mare.

Perhaps the absence of Wash emboldened the neighbors to what is known as the Big Search of 1849. Citizens from Waterville and along the swamp drove up one cold night to recover a considerable amount of stolen goods. Some of the things were immediately packed into the sleighs, a guard was stationed, and most of the neighbors drove off. What happened to the guard is matter of debate—I favor the story that the Lummises locked them into a room. Anyway, the gang returned from hiding and spent most of the night in burning whatever stolen goods had not been taken away. There was a trial, of course, but the net result was only a short sentence in jail for the eldest brother, William.

Except for the death of old Wash, the father, nothing very drastic happened to the Lummises between 1849 and 1865; therefore this is the place to tell about some of their methods and exploits. They were specialists in horse-stealing; to realize the heinousness of that, you must remember that Yorkers then loved horses as the Arabs do, or the Texans, or the Kentuckians. The great harness horses are nearly all descended from Orange County sires, including Hambletonian himself, who begat a world of racers. (From Vermont came the Morgan breed which shared affection with the Orange County hosses.) In our men's clubs today the conversation keeps returning to President Roosevelt, sports, and automobiles; in the nineteenth century the hoss was at least as important as automobiles are now. Furthermore, a farmer spent large sums on expensive harness; so when the Lummises stole horse and harness, they took the most precious of possessions.

The success of these bandits depended not alone upon the ability to hide animals in their swamp; nor upon a system of confederates reaching up into Canada and west to the Finger Lakes, south to Pennsylvania, and east to Albany; nor upon the dugout back of headquarters, the ravine in which fifty horses could be pastured, the underground tunnel, the hollow haystacks. Of equal importance probably was the remarkable ability of one brother to disguise horses. A gentleman in Clinton has heard that one of the most effective tricks—and the cruelest—was to make a white star on a horse's forehead by binding a hot baked potato on the place to be bleached, repeating the process until satisfied; nitrate of silver, he says, was used to color white markings. The result was that the owner himself could not identify his horse. There was the famous case of the Dygart mare, bred on a farm near Verona. Bill Lummis had been seen with the animal, and search revealed on his farm a mare which Dygart felt positive in identifying. On the day of the trial two identical mares were produced; even Dygart could not tell them apart! Later it came out that Grove had sold the real horse in Pennsylvania and had marked one like it to keep; before the trial he had found time to get into Pennsylvania and bring back the original mare. The Lummises sued the crestfallen Dygart; it is said that he was so nearly ruined financially by the litigation that he went west.

A similar tale tells of a man losing a roan horse and buying a black one from a reputable person in Chenango County. When the purchaser went into the "new" horse's stall, the animal whinnied joyfully—back home in changed costume. A third variant of the stolen-horse tale, told me about a Mr. Wagert (probably Dygart), asserts that the Loomises prepared the two horses to look identical, then sent notice to Mr. Wagert to come and get his lost property. Wagert and several neighbors all identified the same horse, and the joyful owner departed with what he supposed to be his recovered animal. Next day, a Loomis brother drove past Wagert's; as he neared the place, he loosened the reins, and the horse turned into the driveway. Wagert and the neighbors had selected an inferior counterfeit; Loomis laughed and drove on with the really valuable mare.

My favorite story of this type is one brought from Vernon Center. A farmer whom we shall call Green lost his horse, suspected the

Loomises. As if to buy a new horse, he priced the one which had been his, and then claimed it. He pretty much proved his point when the animal answered to its name, but one of the Loomises said: "Are you sure that this horse is identical with yours in every respect?"

"No," said Mr. Green, "my mare had a different colored tail."

"Well," said Loomis, "we can cut the tail completely off."

"Stop!" said the tender-hearted Green. "You mustn't do that."

"In that case," said Loomis, "the mare's price is still a hundred dollars."

Green paid.

There are many other trickster tales not connected with disguising a horse. A favorite tells about how Grove escaped a charge of counterfeiting in 1858, after he and a certain Jane Barber had successfully "worked" the city of Utica. When Jane was arrested, she "unbuttoned her mouth"; three or four weeks later, Grove was arrested in Oriskany Falls and taken to jail. In the evening, Wash came to see him, and suddenly interrupted the conversation to cry out angrily: "What are you doing with my best boots on? Take them right off and put on these old ones." Wash was so indignant that Grove consented to exchange boots in the presence of an officer. Later, when Grove was searched and no counterfeit was found, it dawned on the authorities that Wash had carried off the damning evidence in those best boots. This same story is told in various forms; sometimes the Lummis girls are heroines.

Then there is the anecdote which illustrates what happened to a certain member of the gang who got restless because he saw no sign of being paid sixty dollars which the Loomises owed him. When he wanted to go to Clinton on some business, he was told not to waste money on fare but to take a horse from the Loomis stable. Upon his arrival at Clinton, he was arrested for stealing the animal. At the trial in Deansboro he swore that the horse had been a loan, but he couldn't prove it. My informant, who was present at the trial, says that he heard Plum tell an attorney where to find the answer to a knotty legal point. Finally Plum suggested to his hired man that if *he* would forget about the alleged debt of sixty dollars, *they* would drop the matter of the horse.

At another time, one of the employees, during an argument about wages, threatened to have the whole gang arrested, and set out for Utica to execute his intention; but when he arrived, he was immediately brought before a Justice for stealing a watch which was found on his person, just where it had been "planted".

These last three stories represent the usual successful termination of Lummis tricks. I like the story of Mr. Hall about how Wash was tripped up. Mr. Hall's father came down to breakfast at a country inn to find Wash storming about what a "damn pretty place it was where a man couldn't spend a night without being robbed of a pair of boots worth fourteen dollars". The proprietor, named Foote, was just about to hand over the money when a simple-minded fellow who "hung out" at the inn asked Foote to come to his sleeping-place in the barn. There in the hay were the boots, just where Wash had hidden them. Foote returned full of wrath. "Here are your boots," he said. "Phin saw where you hid them. Now get out and don't come near my place again." He slapped Wash with the boots and assisted him out *a tergo* with his own footwear. Wash left, carrying the boots, but it is not certain that the inn-keeper, in his wrath, did not forget to collect his bill from the unwelcome guest.

As might be expected, there are Robin Hood stories of the generosity of the gang, usually confined to near neighbors with whom it paid to remain on good terms. There was the testimony of a Mrs. C., member of a good family, who lived near the headquarters. When Loomis cows got into her meadow, she told Wash. He not only drove the beasts out himself but assured her that she would never have a minute's trouble with his family—and she never did. She was luckier than the other woman whose line-fence was moved in the night.

A neighbor had sold his hops for a considerable sum, too late in the day to deposit the money in a bank. Until midnight he sat jittering on his bed, shotgun in hand, hoping that he would not be robbed, for he wanted to pay an installment on his home and buy a new horse and fine harness. Plum Loomis walked in saying, "I know you've got that money there under the bed. I need it for tonight; so you might just as well give it to me". Plum took the money, but promised that since the neighbor had been so peaceable, he would be reimbursed.

Next day the money was returned—it was supposed that the Loomises had needed it to get out of some scrape—and Plum said, "Don't say a word about this; but if you ever have any trouble with my family, just let me know." Not long after, the farmer bought the coveted harness, only to have it stolen. He went to Plum immediately. Two weeks later, the harness was found hanging in its owner's barn; it had been brought back all the way from "Canady".

I have a similar story of how one of the Lummis boys felt his social obligations so strongly that he helped to recover a horse and "rig" stolen at a dance:

The next morning, after the dance, this Loomis boy started out with the owner of the horse, having furnished him with one for the occasion. They went down across New York State towards Pennsylvania. As they were traveling, they stopped at every woods they passed, and Loomis got off his horse and looked around under brush piles, etc. When they had gotten down towards the border, he began to find parts of a carriage in wooded spots which they passed. In one place he found the thills hidden, in another the wheels, in another the carriage-top, in another the body, and so forth until he had found all the parts of the carriage which had been stolen. Finally he found the horse hidden somewhere in a dense wood in northern Pennsylvania. He gave the horse back to his friend, left the one there which he had ridden down on, and turned back towards home. He had "gotten wind" of where one of his brothers had gone, and had decided to help out a friend.

Another neighbor says:

Plum was always good to me, and I never had any trouble with any of them. He was always telling me to help myself to any of the horses any time I wanted a good one, but I never did 'cause I didn't want to get mixed up with them. I only went over to Plum's house once; that was one afternoon when I found him and a lot of tough-looking fellows sitting on the porch talking. I stayed about an hour, and they asked me to have supper with them; but I told Plum I had come over to see if he would sell me some turkey eggs. He called his wife and asked her how many eggs they had. She came back with six; but Plum said, "You'll need about eleven if you're going to set a hen on them"; so he went out and found me five more. I tried to pay him for them, but he wouldn't take the money. My wife and I figured maybe there was something tricky about the eggs since he gave them away so freely; but do you know, ten of them hatched out just fine! Funny how we never trust a man with a reputation like theirs, isn't it?

That it paid to be on good terms with near neighbors, and that the Loomises kept close account of a neighbor's attitude is proved by another story from the same informant:

Yes, it was exciting to live so near such a notorious outfit, and many nights did I hear goings-on over there. To reach this barn where they stored things, they had to go by my back door. I don't know how true it is that they muffled the horses' feet with burlap when they were transferring some of them to their brother's in Oneida or to customers. I always kept a great fierce shepherd dog when I lived there as a young man; this dog used to growl when a stranger was around—he barked right out for a friend. One night, he woke me with his growling at my elbow, and, in spite of my wife's protests, I went to the front door. There, standing at the foot of the steps, was a man with a gun in each hand. He said he was going over to shoot up the Loomis gang and wanted me to come along. He offered to pay me twenty-five dollars before we went and to give me one of the pistols. I said no, they always treated me fine—why should I want to shoot them? Well, he said they had done so-and-so; I said I knew that, but they had never harmed me. He finally went away—I really think if it hadn't been for my wife who begged me not to go, I would have gone just to see what he'd do!—and I found out later that he was one of the gang himself, sent to test me out.

You must remember that again and again the Loomises, in spite of all their cleverness, were caught almost red-handed. I like a story of an incident near Woodstock where there was a bee-farm. One night in the autumn the owner saw something white on the hill back of his house, and strolling up found a piece of paper. At the same time that he was puzzling over the paper, he noticed that his hives were missing. The gang had smoked out the bees with burning paper, and on the scrap left behind was the name of one of the Loomises. On that evidence arrests were made.

Until the time of the Civil War, however, the gang avoided serious penalties. Then the tide turned. For one thing, they committed outrageous depredations upon *public* property; for another thing, their Nemesis arrived in the person of a pock-marked, sandy-haired black-

smith who in 1858 was selected constable of North Brookfield, across
the county line from Sangerfield, in Madison County. He swore that
he would get the Loomises, and ultimately he did, but he had a
stirring time in the meanwhile. The Loomises had him arrested for
assault and battery and taken to Waterville, Oneida County; he was
permitted to go home, was arrested again and spirited away to
Oneida, where he was bailed out and never brought to trial. (Evidently he knew some Loomis tricks.) Then he moved to Waterville
in Oneida County, was elected constable there in 1862, or early in
1863, and continued his attempts. By July of 1863 things had grown
very hot indeed for the Loomises.

At midnight of July 22nd something happened about which I have
detailed accounts; of course, they may not be completely correct.
Mrs. Filkins was attending a sick child; the constable was in his usual
state of expecting trouble from the Loomises. There came a rapping
at the door. Taking a revolver, he approached the kitchen window,
and asked what was wanted. A voice said: "I'm Mr. Clark's hired
man. Last evening he came by VanDee's and saw Jack VanDee at
home; and he asked me to come here and let you know." Now Van-
Dee was accused of being one of the Loomis gang—a person whom
Filkins had vainly tried to arrest; but the constable thought that this
was a ruse—in fact, the voice he had just heard sounded like that
of Plum Loomis. As Filkins stood cocking his revolver and wondering
what to do, a double barrelled shotgun discharged slugs and pieces
of nails through the window. He started for the bedroom, and two
more shots were fired through the bedroom window. The blinds were
shattered and the lower part of the sash torn out; the bedroom door
was filled with buckshot, and there were fourteen shot-holes in the
mantle; seven buckshot and forty small shot had riddled the bed-
curtains. Wounded in the right arm and left hand, Filkins was fainting
from loss of blood when the aroused neighbors scared his assailant or
assailants away. Next day the constable exhibited a letter which he
said had been received two months before:

J. Filkins—Dear Sir: As a friend to you and all mankind I set down
to write you to forewarn you of danger. That gang has offered one of
their associates a good sum of money to kill you at some convenient

time, and he says he doubts whether they will pay him if he should do so. He is a daring and bold robber. I dare not sign my name.

Filkins dug out enough evidence to get an indictment against Plum, Wash, and three others, but, according to his own story, he found out in May of 1865 that the indictment has been *nolle prossed* by the District Attorney at the request of the Sheriff, who "came in the December term of court, saying that it was his last term, and he had an agreement with the Loomises to see them clear of everything before he went out of office". The District Attorney added simply, "The Sheriff wanted to make his word good and asked me to help him."

The people who finally arose in indignation in that year of 1865 were doubtless remembering also another incident even more shocking. A member of the gang outraged a girl fourteen years old. The girl's father took the accused before a justice in South Brookfield. That night, the justice-docket in which the accused had posted bail was stolen; the thieves had not been aware that the bonds had been mailed to the county courthouse. A plan was laid by the gang to kidnap the girl before she could come before the Grand Jury to get an indictment; but in spite of her absence the indictment was obtained through the testimony of her father, her mother, and her family physician. The gang then released her, but the poor girl was so scared that she remained in the family of the Sheriff, in jail, for two years. Her assailant disappeared, but two other Loomises came to court and pled not guilty on another charge. During their trial, they ran out of court, were recaptured, and got a *habeas corpus* writ to a Syracuse judge who let them go again on bail. The farmer who went bail for them is said to have committed suicide when they did not appear. Meanwhile the girl's assailant escaped to Canada.

The contempt of law increased. In September, 1864, the gang was suspected of firing the courthouse at Morrisville to destroy indictments—after cutting the firehose at which Wash is said to have made noble gestures as a volunteer-fireman. The Loomises must have been peevish when they learned that the indictments had not been in the burned courthouse; at any rate, someone then broke into the safe at the office of the County Clerk and burned the records in the Clerk's stove. In Oneida County someone also rifled the District Attorney's office, and that harassed gentleman subsequently paid $250 for the return of papers not connected with the Loomises but inadvertently taken along. Strangely enough, the papers for which he paid were found mixed with leaves in a Loomis yard.

When a protective association was formed at the North Brookfield Baptist Church, in 1864, with dues of one dollar a year, Wash and Grove Lummis attended, expressed their approval, and planked down their dollar bills as members.

Such jokes had grown stale. Besides, there were soldiers returning from the Civil War, men who may have ridden horses stolen by the Lummises and sold to the government—men, at any rate, who were not afraid of ruffians and who were determined to correct abuses which had multiplied during their absence. On the night of October 29-30, 1865, a posse as ruthless as the Loomises killed Wash in his own back woodshed with a blow on the head delivered by a long-barrelled .44 pistol. (Did you ever see one?) Grove was ferociously kicked, and beaten by an iron "slungshot" or "billy"; then someone threw two coats over him, poured on "camphene" (kerosene oil), and applied a match. He came to with a yell that brought Wash's mistress and Cornelia intrepidly to the rescue. The Lummises had opportunity to tell this story in court later, but the other side—well, the assailants had sworn to reveal nothing so long as two of them remained alive. (Mr. Walter, whose account of that savage night I have just condensed, saw the last survivor before that Waterville gentleman's death.) Wash was certainly killed, anyway, and the barn burned. Next morning, one neighbor shot horses staggering about the fields in agony, blinded with smoke.

Who had struck these blows? The Loomises had Filkins indicted— he had recently been let out on bail from another of their charges. In fact, there were five indictments, including ones for murder and arson. The great Roscoe Conkling was secured as counsel for a defence conducted successfully through trials in lower courts. It was a new era; when bail of $10,000 was demanded, twenty-eight of the county's leading men stepped forward to endorse it. It is even said that some of them had previously been allied with the Loomises.

On June 9, 1866, the implacable Deputy Sheriff Filkins appeared at Loomis headquarters again, with a Sheriff, two constables, and a number of aides to make arrests of men in hiding. When they attacked the house about daybreak, old Mother Lummis was out feeding her chickens. She screamed a warning in which the name of Filkins was not omitted. There was a battle for the wanted men on the attic stair; Filkins was wounded and several of his men. Arrests were made, but when the scene of combat changed to a wood near the swamp, the arrested men escaped.

The last fight occurred on June 17, 1866. A crowd estimated at from sixty men to four hundred vigilantes decided to end the power of the gang forever. The Legislature had been given the Prison Association's report a year and a half before; every law-enforcing agency had shirked its task. There are a few of those vigilantes still alive. One of my students has a Colt's pistol that her grandfather carried that night. He had had a horse stolen, had threatened to shoot if the animal were not returned, and had got back the horse, but a few nights later his barn had been burned.

At daybreak the vigilantes closed in on the house. Every inmate surrendered. Stolen silks, satins, and furs were quickly removed and the house burned. (Cornelia later charged that she had been robbed of more than eight hundred dollars.) Then the barns were cleared of loot and set afire. All that was saved was Grove's prize horse, and beds for Cornelia and her mother. What happened thereafter is not so clear. Mr. Dapson reported to our State Historical Association that Plum was half-hanged twice and then confessed; that he was sentenced to jail for ninety days and fined only one hundred dollars; that he later sued the county for twenty-two thousand and got one thousand; that the indictments were never brought against Filkins. Mr. Walter believes that Plum and a "Dutchman" named John Stone were hanged—Plum twice—on a maple tree in front of the house. A limb from the tree was exhibited in a Waterville saloon. Miss Finen, who has gathered more data than any other of my students, has the story that Plum was hung up by his two thumbs; this torture was tried *five* times. Another story she found was that he was snaked up over a limb on which there was a *know* which lacerated his jaw and marked him for some time. She was also told that *Grove* was hung up five times by the neck, and there are tales of a Loomis who always had a twisted neck thereafter. Another story recently reached me of a small boy who learned from Plum how he escaped death.

"There," said Plum, "is the tree I was hanged on. I tightened my muscles and swung like a leaf in the breeze. They thought I was done for and rode away, but my wife cut me down and I'm here to tell the story."

Another detail comes from a Middlebury College Professor whose great-grandfather's store at East Hamilton was cleaned out by the Lummises. His grandfather was one of the vigilantes who broke up the gang. Years later, while buying hop-poles in Canada, he met the "Loomis with the crooked neck" and had a visit about Madison County. If Plum did stay on the old place, this sounds like evidence that Grove *was* given the rope-treatment, as well as Plum.

There are many more stories, but I conclude this saga of the Lummises with a letter from the grandfather of one of my students, a gentleman now living on Long Island, but formerly of Brookfield, a short distance from the Loomis headquarters. It seems to me as vivid a picture of the organization as we are likely to get:

My Dad, Dr. A. D. Fitch, Registered Veterinary, was called many times to doctor their horses and cattle. One night about 9 o'clock my mother and I were in the kitchen. Dad had been out on a trip doctoring someone's cow or horse; was at the table eating when we heard someone pounding on the front door. My mother went and opened the door and asked who was there and what was wanted. It was quite dark outside and raining.

A man on horseback replied: "It's me, Plumb Loomis, by God. I want Dr. Fitch and damn quick."

My Dad went to the door.

Loomis said, "Doc, come to my place. Have a very sick horse. Don't let any grass grow under your feet either—understand?"

Dad said, "All right—soon as I can get there."

I think he had been to their place a great many times. Mother said to him often: "I wish you did not have to go tonight. I always worry when you go across that swamp; it is so dark and rainy tonight, you had better take Charles with you for company."

Finally Dad said, "All right, if it will make you feel any better."

Dad had three horses at the time. One was lame for some reason. Mollie had been out all afternoon. So Dad said, "Harness up General."

In a few minutes we were on our way. On the dash of the wagon hung a bull's-eye lantern which when lit threw out a good light ahead. After driving six miles we came to the swamp. About half-way across the swamp someone grabbed the horse by the bit and tried to stop us. Dad did something I never knew him to do before—pulled the whip out of the holder and struck the horse. He stood up nearly straight, jumped to one side, threw the man, and we went on and left him cursing by the side of the road, and [we] arrived at the Loomis place in due time, drove in on the barn-floor, and Grove, the other son, said, "Well, you made good time."

He had a lantern in his hand, did not notice me at first. When he did, he said to Dad, "What's the kid doing here?"

Dad told him Mother wanted me to go along for company. He said "Well, all right."

We were both blindfolded and taken some distance from the barn to a cave, down several stone steps to a room where the sick horse was, along with several others. After Dad had given medicine to the horse and left some to be given later, we were taken back to the barn and to the house where the family lived, and asked to have something to eat.

I was more interested in looking around the kitchen and at the mother and daughter than anything else. Dad told me: "Eat what I do, also drink the same. Keep your eyes open and don't say anything."

Well, we got away after a time; went to the barn where we left the horse. When I went up to take the blanket off General, as I supposed, I said, "Hello, old pard," and rubbed my hand along his back. I noticed he did not whinner as he always had before. The light was dim and I could not see very good. When Dad came in, I said to him, "This is not your horse."

Dad lit the lantern on the dashboard and found I was right. Grove came in while we were talking. Dad said: "What is the meaning of this? This is not my horse."

Then Grove began to rare at the man who took care of the horses in that stable; called him all kind of names, and kicked him out of the barn; said he knew nothing about the shift. Well, we got straightened out after'while, and when Dad got his horse back in the shafts, we started back home, and believe me, I was glad to [get] home and to bed.

The Loomises had a good match for General in color, size, etc.—had

offered Dad good money for him but Dad could not and would not sell
or trade.

I was fifteen years old when I was with Dad that night in the year of
1877; about the middle of September or October, I don't just remember
which. There was six in the gang at that time.

Unless Mr. Fitch's memory for dates is not quite reliable, this
shows how hard the old ways died in the Loomis family, for this
occurred eleven years after the gang is supposed to have discon-
tinued depredations. Some of the old love of swagger was there; perhaps some of the old talent for juggling horses. Suppose that young
Fitch had not gone along that night? Suppose that the Doc had not
noticed until after reaching home that the horses had been switched?
Where were his proofs? For the matter of that, where were the suave
manners that the Prison Association mentioned? And what price
Robin Hoods?

V: Uncanny Critters

L
ONG time ago, when this country was new, when there were all
sorts of hideous beasts and monsters to be found in the great
woods or forest, in those days many things used to happen that
would scare the people." So Jesse Cornplanter of the Senecas begins
his tale about the Stone Giants. If you would like to know about the
"wanchancy" things that haunted our forests, you cannot do better than
to read Jesse's *Legends of the Longhouse* (1938), wherein a New
York Indian of patrician family and poetic memory tells of the Sky-
Woman and her two sons, Evil-Minded and Good-Minded; of the
Great Little People, Indian fairies who are divided into hunters,
stone-throwers, and plant-tenders; of the Stone Giants, Great Horned
Serpent, Flying Heads, and Giant Leech; of the Indian equivalents
of our devils, vampires, spectres, and witches. Having "edited" this
book by leaving it exactly as Jesse wrote it—except for trifling
matters like punctuation—I shall not now have the imprudence to
retell these master-tales; paraphrase by white men is almost sure to
spoil the myths and legends of the Iroquois, and moreover I am
trying to give a picture not of the Red Brother, but of the pioneering
White Man. Jesse begins one of his best stories by remarking:

According to the Pale-face superstition, this is Friday the 13th. I hold
no faith in this idea; so I am writing you today. If I did believe in Jinx
or what not, I would not write at all. It only shows that we, as Indians,
are not the only ones that believe in the super-natural things.

Being a commercial, sensible, and tolerant people, the Dutch were
much less given than most of their European neighbors to the fear
of witches. It will be remembered to the credit of Leyden University's
faculty that when they were queried on the occasion of a trial for
witchcraft in 1593 whether the water-ordeal could properly be used—
the test which assumed that if an alleged witch sank, she was innocent—they replied that this notion had no validity whatever. In the
seventeenth century there are a few cases of witches being strangled
and afterwards burnt in the Low Countries, but these seem to have
been chiefly in what is now Belgium. I have found no case of a witch
being tried during the Dutch rule of New York, but there are one
or two stories which seem to show that even the Hollanders were not
free from such fears.

The most interesting of these stories sounds suspiciously like some-
thing invented in the nineteenth century, but it is still told in Eastern
New York and deserves preservation. It concerns a baker named
Volckert Jan Pietersen Van Amsterdam, commonly called Baas
(Master), who, in the days when Albany was named Beverwyck,
kept a snug little shop off what we now call Broadway. In the year
1655 on December's last day, Baas was working late, selling the
New Year's cookies which had carried his fame far down the Hudson
River. He afterward admitted that he had taken an extra horn of
rum in honor of St. Nicholas, who then presided over our entire
holiday season; but the baker was sure that his judgment and sight
were unimpaired. As trade grew less, he was about to shut up shop,
when an uncommonly ugly old woman thrust her way in, demanding
a dozen of the special cookies bearing an effigy of St. Nick.

When the baker had handed her the fragrant bag, she said crossly,
"One more cookie: I said a dozen."

"You have a dozen," said Baas. "I counted them carefully—twelve
of my finest cookies."

"One more cookie," said the old woman. "One more than twelve makes a dozen."

Now Baas had been working from dawn, and his temper snapped. "Of all the crazy ideas!" he cried. "Everyone knows that twelve make a dozen. Where have you been living?"

"One more cookie for a dozen," said the old woman.

Baas grabbed her by the shoulder and pushed her to the door. "You may go to the devil for another cookie!" he shouted. "You won't get another here." Then he slammed the door and locked it. When he told the story to his wife, she suggested that perhaps on the eve of a holiday he should have given the extra cookie, but Baas reminded her that business was business up to the very moment that a shop was locked for the night.

In the days that followed, mysterious bad luck came to the little bakery off Broadway. Money and cookies seemed to be taken by invisible hands. Bread rose to the ceiling or fell flat as a pancake. A handsome brick oven collapsed. Finally the baker's wife gave proof of approaching deafness. Three times the ugly old woman appeared to demand her thirteenth cookie—always appeared to Baas, never to his afflicted wife. When thrice she had been angrily refused, the stubborn Dutchman began to wonder whether supernatural powers were not at work. On New Year's Eve the memory of the old woman's first appearance was so vivid that Baas exclaimed: "Holy St. Nicholas, suppose that the witch comes again! Holy St. Nicholas, what shall I do?"

As the baker spoke these words, there appeared before him the benignant saint, smiling with holiday kindness beneath the tall bishop's hat which featured his appearance to Dutch children. Taking a quick glance out of a window, Baas could see the pure white horse on which the Saint rides.

"Well, Baas," said his Saintship, "you were speaking to me; so I thought I would drop in. You are a good baker, and you make uncommonly fine likenesses of me on your cookies. This whole trouble can be solved if you have the spirit which my holidays demand. Give the old woman what she requests, and see what will happen."

"I will, sir," said Baas obediently.

As he spoke, the figure of the Saint vanished; in its place stood the ugly old woman demanding a dozen cookies. Rapidly Baas counted thirteen of them, presenting the bag to her with a bow and a "Happy New Year!"

"The spell is broken, Baas," said the witch. "Now swear to me on the likeness of St. Nicholas that hereafter in Beverwyck and all the patroonship of Van Rensselaer thirteen will make a baker's dozen."

Baas took the oath, and from that day to this when you say a baker's dozen, you mean thirteen. (I am sorry to say that most Albany bakers have forgotten the legend.) Before she left the shop, the witch prophesied that some day thirteen mighty states should unite to remind the world of her magic number.

The last trial for witchcraft among the whites of New York State was an impromptu affair in 1816, held in a Rockland County hamlet called Clarksville (Mount Moor).* Dutch settlers had built a church there more than a score of years before the Revolution, but it was 1834 before the hamlet was to be large enough to claim a post office. Everyone was related to everyone else, and practically all were Dutch. Into this closed community at some time before 1816 there entered an eccentric widow, Mrs. Jane Kanniff, relict of a Scotch physician, to occupy a cottage a few rods west of the old church on the New City road, and to devote herself to an only child, her son by a former marriage.

Probably any outsider would have been suspect, but "Naut" Kanniff gave special occasion for gossip. To begin with—and this would be a serious matter still—she wore scandalously gay, parti-colored dresses and arranged her hair in a fashion unknown to Clarksville. Moreover, she was unsocial and sometimes actually morose—which may not have been her fault entirely. Last of all and most sinister, she had a remarkable knowledge of medicinal herbs which really acted with devilish promptness. Soon the children showed signs of fear when passing her house. Several women had trouble at churning. One worthy male member of the church lay awake all night listening to the strange lowing of his herd; in the morning he found his best

---

* A trial at Ludlowville, Tompkins County, occurred at some time "after 1806". A Deacon B, from New England demanded that a "Dutch woman" be tried for making his daughter ill. Judge Townley finally conducted a trial which resulted in an acquittal. Nobody but the Dutch woman and the Deacon took the case seriously.

cow standing in a farm-wagon. Thereafter Bossy refused to give milk.

Frontier communities are always more interested in justice than in law. No recourse was had to duly constituted authorities in court or church; in fact, considerable care seems to have been taken to keep the whole matter from the Dominie's attention. Selecting the resident physician for judge—and we can understand how the position may have given him professional satisfaction as an opponent of "socialized medicine"—the citizens appeared at Naut's cot one evening and proceeded to an old mill near Pye's Corner for the unusual but picturesque "trial by balance". She was seated in one pan of the millscale, strong hands supporting her so that the balance should be even. Then a board-covered, brass-bound Dutch Bible was put into the other pan and support was removed from the supposed witch. If the Bible outweighed the woman, she was obviously in league with the devil. It is a pleasure to relate that the pan in which Naut was seated hit the floor, the big Bible struck the ceiling, and Mistress Kanniff was vindicated as an innocent child of God.

As might be expected, the Yankees from Connecticut who settled in Long Island and Westchester furnish our cases of *legal* trials for witchcraft. All three of them took place within five years as a backwash of the Connecticut trials which precede those at Salem. In October, 1665, a certain Ralph Hall and his wife Mary were put on trial in the Court of Assize at New York. They came from "Seatallcott", Long Island, in what was then known as the East Riding of Yorkshire. Indictments stated that on the 25th day of December, "being Christmas day last, was Twelve Months", and several times since, "by some detestable and wicked Arts" the Halls had practised on the person of George Wood, who "most dangerously and mortally sickened and languished, and not long after by the aforesaid wicked and detestable Arts, the said George Wood (as is likewise suspected) dyed". It was claimed, moreover, that similar Arts had killed the infant child of Wood's widow, whose distraction and accusations can perhaps be pardoned because of her double loss.

Only written depositions were used at the trial—surely a dubious legal procedure—and I have been unable to discover their contents, but the verdict was as follows:

We finde that there are some Suspitions by the Evidence, of what the woman is charged with, but nothing considerable of value to take away her life. But in reference to the man wee finde nothing considerable to charge him with.

This sounds like a Scottish verdict of Not Proven, which, of course, was not legal in the New World; the verdict certainly should have been acquittal. The court, however, assumed to require a recognizance for Mary Hall's future good behavior. After the unfortunate pair had been held in jail for some time, the husband was bound, body and goods, for his wife's appearance "at the next Sessions; and so on from Sessions to Sessions as long as they stay within this Government". The periodic reports must have proved satisfactory: in August, 1668, Governor Nicolls released the Halls from the recognizance, and I find no further record.

A second Long Island case is that of "Goody" Garlick of East Hampton. When in 1657 Elizabeth Garlick and her spouse Joshua moved to that village from the amiable Lionel Gardiner's Island, where the couple had been servants, malicious tongues started awagging. Goody Davis had said that she "hoped Goody Garlick would not come to Easthampton, because, she said, Goody Garlick was naughty, and there had many sad things befallen them at the Island, as about the child, and the ox . . . as also a negro child she said was taken away, as I understand by her words, in a strange manner, and also of a ram that was dead, and this fell out quickly one after another, and also of a sow that was fat and lustie and died. She said they did burn some of the sow's tale and presently Goody Garlick did come in".

Then there was Goodwife Howell, whose illness hastened the arrest of the supposed witch. This afflicted woman "tuned a psalm and screked out several times together very grievously", crying, "A witch! a witch! Now are you come to torter me because I spoke two or three words against you." This was just such skimble-skamble stuff as Cotton Mather was shortly to report from Massachusetts. A town meeting took the case seriously enough to send the accused to "Keniticut", which had just received jurisdiction over East Hampton. Goody Garlick was tried by a General Court and acquitted.

The third and last of these legal trials of New York witches has a prologue in Connecticut. Katharine Harrison, born in England, migrated to America in 1651, settled in Wethersfield, and in 1653 married. On May 25, 1669, this woman, now a widow, was indicted for witchcraft and given a partial trial, adjourned till October and not finally decided until May of the following year; so she "languished" in jail about a year. Thomas Bracy had been threatened by her for calling her a witch; her apparition had pinched him and attempted to strangle him in bed; he had seen "a red calfes head, the eares standing peart up", going into the Harrison barn and vanishing. Joane Francis had had a vision of Katharine just before her own child sickened and died. Mary Hale, lying in bed, had thrice been oppressed by a dog with the head of the witch.

The jury at Hartford found her guilty, but the magistrates were so unconvinced that they sent a set of questions to clergymen, who were specialists in the occult. While she languished, she filed a petition of grievance which declared that her townsmen had attacked her oxen, cows, and swine. Finally, on May 20, 1670, the Connecticut Court of Assistants dismissed her with the charge that she leave Wethersfield—which she was doubtless glad to do.

She went to Westchester, New York, hoping to live with her sixteen year old daughter, "Rebeckah", and her son-in-law, Josiah Hunt. Unfortunately Rebeckah thought that she had a grievance against her mother regarding the disposal of some property left by her father. Soon Hunt's father, a local magnate, and another person named Waters, appeared before Governor Lovelace, declaring that they represented the town of Westchester in requesting that the widow Harrison, "suspected for a Witch", be ordered to leave that place. The Governor obligingly ruled on July 7, 1670 that she was to return to her former abode—from which, of course, she had been banished; she was to depart "in some short tyme after notice given". Of two evils, she sensibly chose New York. Again the people of Westchester complained to their Governor; she appeared before His Excellency on August 20th, and he rendered a cautious decision on the 25th, to the effect that she and her children could remain where she was until the meeting of the next Court of Assize. Just in case she should be found guilty of witchcraft and her goods be forfeit to the Crown, he ordered an inventory of her chattels. As a matter of fact, no charge of practicing witchcraft since her arrival in New York had been laid. In October, 1670, the Court released her from her recognizances and gave her full liberty to live in Westchester. The unfortunate widow had further legal troubles, but she was not again subjected to charges of witchcraft.

These three cases seem to have been the only epidemic of witchcraft that troubled the legal record of our colony. To be sure, Governor Bellomont reported to his Lords of Trade in 1700 that Aquandero, chief sachem of the Onondagas, had fled to Col. Schuyler's near Albany because his son was supposed to be bewitched. Perhaps the sachem was being punished in a subtle way for a treaty he had recently sponsored. One of our antiquaries tells of an Indian named Buckinjehillish who angered the Indian Council by remarking tartly that only the ignorant make war, whereas the wise and the warriors have to do the fighting. He was accused of witchcraft for living so long, and was sentenced to be tomahawked by a boy.

Meanwhile, though there were no further legal trials, the traditions of our Yankees on Long Island continued to be rich in witchlore. In Sag Harbor you could see ships with horse-shoes nailed to the mast and cabin-door to ward off witches; in the Hamptons many a farmer kept a horse-shoe nailed to his hog-trough. Stories were muttered of old women crossing the Atlantic in an egg-shell at night for a grand frolic in England. At Brookhaven they told with bated breath the tale of Aunty Greenleaf and the White Deer. Hunters in the early eighteenth century reported this phantom creature to be impervious to bullets. When a numerous party was organized to pursue the deer, the usual lack of success discouraged all except one man. Unrelenting as Ahab in *Moby Dick*, he continued the hunt until one day when his quarry appeared within range. Ripping the silver buttons from his coat, the hunter loaded his gun and fired. This was the final test—if the creature were really supernatural, only a silver bullet would avail. The deer stumbled, jerked upright, and took flight, disappearing in the unlikely neighborhood of a shack belonging to a queer old woman who lived alone among the pines and catbriars. Convinced that once again he had failed, the hunter returned to his home; but a few days later, some of his townsmen

chancing near Aunty Greenleaf's, entered her cottage to find the old
woman groaning in bed. The doctor who was summoned found the
three silver bullets in her spine.

The Yankee Yorkers carried their witch-tales with them right
across the State. I like the following one, which comes from Stamford,
Delaware County, in the Catskills:

There is a wooded area near South Gilboa called Spook Woods. It was
commonly believed that cattle, driven through these woods, would
scatter and run wild before the spooks. The road was quite likely to close
in upon a traveller.

A Mr. Williams had been hired to work on the Cornelius Mayham
farm. He had heard tales of Spook Woods which he hardly believed; yet
when he entered the woods on his way home one moonlight night, he
felt some trepidation. All went well until he was into the middle, when
he saw something moving over the snow beside the road ahead. On
reaching the object, he found two cats dragging between them a third
which was dead. Although he hurried along, the cats kept up with him,
and to his horror one called out his name. Mr. Williams had not the
slightest desire to enter into conversation, and hurried on. Just before
he left the woods, one of the cats called out again, "Mr. Williams, tell
Molly Meyers she can come home now; old Hawkins is dead."

Mr. Williams was soon home. He was hesitant about revealing his
experience, but finally when the family was seated about the fireplace,
he told what had happened. As he came to the passage, "Tell Molly
Meyers she can come home," the old family cat jumped from Mrs.
Mayham's lap, ran to the open fireplace, leaped up the chimney, and
was never seen again.

If there is any group in our colonial history more interested in
witchcraft than the Connecticut Yankees and the Indians, it is the
Germans. When we speak of Germans or "High Dutch", we think
first of the Palatines who migrated in large numbers to the province
of New York in the early eighteenth century, at the close of Queen
Anne's reign; but as a matter of fact these dwellers on the Hudson,
Mohawk, and Schoharie had been preceded by a considerable number of their countrymen who came in the seventeenth century. Killian
Van Rensselaer, for example, brought settlers from Germany and
from Scandinavia; by 1655 one-third of the population of what is

now Albany was probably Lutheran—not of the Dutch Reformed
faith. It is therefore certain that the rather tepid interest of the
Dutch in witchcraft was reinforced during the seventeenth century
by the belief of settlers coming from a country notorious for witch-
trials.

In her valuable study called *Folklore from the Schoharie Hills*
(1937), Miss E. E. Gardner devotes an entire chapter to about sixty
cases of witchcraft, collected in six summers (beginning in 1912) from
various persons, most of whom had German names. She found traditions of witch-doctors, the most respected of whom seems to have
been Dr. Jake Brink, who during the last years of his life lived at
Lake Katrine near Saugerties. The fact that Miss Gardner was able
to locate a son of Dr. Jake living in Kingston shows how recently a
large number of Schoharians believed themselves threatened by the
supernatural terrors of witchcraft.

Instead of quoting from her learned and valuable book, I think
it will be sufficient to show a case or two among German people outside the Schoharie valley. There is, for example, a witch-tale from
Taberton in the Berlin Mountains of Rensselaer County, across the
Hudson from Albany. A farmer there named Hohausen* noticed on
several mornings that one of his horses had its tail and mane braided
in a fashion that Mercutio described in his speech about the queen of
the fairies:

> This is that very Mab
> That plats the manes of horses in the night.

There were indications also in the stiffened hair of the horse that
it had been driven all night, hints borne out by the creature's evident
fatigue during the day's work.

One night, chancing to go to his stable at twelve o'clock, Mr. Hohausen discovered a large, black cat sitting on the horse's back. Again
the horse's mane and tail were braided. Grabbing a three-tined pitch-
fork, the farmer stuck it into the cat's back. Next morning old Dame
Hohausen, the farmer's mother, failed to appear at breakfast, and
though she refused to have a physician called, her suffering was so
obvious during the next three days that her son finally summoned

---

* At the suggestion of my informant I have changed the name.

medical aid. Examination showed three deep wounds in her back, which remained as running sores until her death. From the time that the old woman took to her bed, the horse's mane and tail were unbraided, and he regained his usual vigor.

Another tale about this alleged witch concerns her interest in a boy and girl employed by their parents in taking a cow to pasture. Mrs. Hohausen urged them not to wash their faces and hands until after they had performed this chore. Each morning she would ask them some question about the cow: how much milk it gave, or when they milked it.

Soon the children's parents discovered that they were unable to churn their cream. They also learned that Mrs. Hohausen was selling an unusual amount of butter, and taking away some of their customers. As their suspicion grew, they decided to appeal to an old man known to be the seventh son of a seventh son. He informed them that Mrs. Hohausen was the cause of their trouble, and he advised them to caution the children not to answer the witch's questions truthfully. I dare say that the children also took care to wash themselves before seeing the witch. At any rate, their parents found results entirely satisfactory.

This seventh son of a seventh son was the venerable great-grandfather of a student of mine, Miss Dolores Leffler. A sort of "white witch" or wizard himself, he never used his powers except to do good, and usually with great reluctance because he was a pious Christian and evidently felt that the supernatural held dangers which could be avoided only by rare use, followed by penance. When he tried to cure the sick—and the lack of a physician in that neighborhood made him frequently consulted—he would look toward the sun, his silky white hair gleaming, and would recite the Lord's Prayer, followed by other petitions read from a worn book which disappeared after his death. Quite typical was the case of a man whose leg was badly cut at wood-chopping. A brother hastened to Mr. Leffler to ask his prayers. The request was immediately granted; and when the brother reached home, he found that the cut leg had stopped bleeding and had started to heal at the same hour when the prayers began. The pious old gentleman had no hesitation in the case just mentioned, but in another, when a woman came to beg that he use his powers to open a sealed door, he refused his services until she had persuaded him that the family needed badly articles shut behind the door. In that case he laid severe penance upon himself for using, on what might be called a trivial case, power which he believed he derived from the Lord. His is the clearest case of the beneficent employment of supernatural power which has come to me from our German tradition.

From another student, I have a number of stories about witchcraft in the Mohawk Valley at Fort Plain, Sprakers, and Canajoharie. These are all quite recent, remembered by a grandmother and an aunt, both of whom have German names. One tale is of pigs bewitched at Sprakers so that they would not eat. Dr. X of Canajoharie was summoned and ordered a certain number of pails of river-water to be poured over each animal. "He made good with the Lord" to such an extent that two of three pigs were saved. When he left next morning, he refused even a cup of coffee, saying, "I saw something last night I never want to see again." At another time the Doctor was summoned to save the life of a dying child. "He straddled the cradle and talked over that baby for hours till it was cured." The aunt has also three stories about a witch of Fort Plain, now dead. In one case, she bewitched a horse, but a Doctor (perhaps X) was sent for; "he pulled some hairs out of the horse's tail and it jumped up and was all right again." On another occasion, a rooster was bewitched and died; when his carcase was burnt, the witch took to her bed. In the third case, jealousy on the part of the same witch caused her to afflict a young man at a party so severely that he not only was kept from dancing—he "couldn't even get up".

From Schenectady I have the recipe for becoming a witch: "Stand on the manure heap at midnight and wave a red lantern behind your back with your left hand while looking at the moon over your right shoulder." Another method from the same city is this: "Say the Lord's Prayer backwards very fast three times with feet and hands crossed." Evidently it is easier to become a witch than to cure her victims.

Suppose that you discovered, as Mr. Hohausen thought he did, that you had a witch in the family. What could you do about it? One of my students from Washington County had a great-great-uncle, Richard Thomas, who faced that delicate problem. He hadn't been long settled near Hoosac Falls when he began to suspect that the woman whom he had brought over from England as his wife was one of the devil's ladies. During the night he had visions of crowds around his bed, dancing and singing as at a witch's *sabbat* (convention), with a large black cat at the center of all this hilarity. His neighbors, also aware of the presence of this cat appearing to their waking senses, melted a silver coin into a bullet, shot the cat in the paw one night, and next morning found upon inquiry that Mrs. Thomas had taken to her bed with an infected hand. The neighbors' tale convinced Thomas, who, knowing that a body of water is pretty sure protection against evil spirits, took his witch-wife back to England and left her there. Returning alone to America, he settled down peacefully with relatives near Warrensburg and in due time married respectably.*

The witch's master, the Earl of Hell, alias the devil, appears in plenty of Dutch folklore, especially such as is connected with place-names. In my chapter on such names you will find comment on Hellgate, Spuyten Duyvel, and De Duyvels Dans Kammer. You may have wondered why Long Island is so sandy while, just across the Sound, Connecticut is rocky. One explanation is that the devil was unceremoniously ejected from the New England state—some say by the Indians; he retreated by skipping from stone to stone. To express his disgust at the way he had been treated, he gathered a great pile of rocks at Cold Spring and hurled them across the Sound into the green fields of Connecticut. Indians used to be able to show you just where he left his hoof-prints. There is another Indian story about how the Red Men drove the devil back across the Sound. In one severe winter, disease broke out of a sort which the medicine-men could not master. So the Indians ranged the island, found the Evil Shadow lurking in a forest, and with yells of hatred drove it to the water's edge. For a moment the devil poised himself on a huge

* According to another version given me by a descendant of Thomas, Mrs. H. F. Stark, the witch-wife was Dutch or German. Thomas believed that she turned him into a horse which she rode to her nocturnal revels. He swam the river and never returned. Though she did not attempt to follow, she cursed him and his descendants. The curse did not operate.

boulder off Orient Point; it is said that to this day you can see his print on Devil's Rock.

The devil is not always in such unpleasant dilemmas. In Rensselaer County there is a story of a group of men playing cards in a hilltown. Late in the evening, a stranger who knocked at the door was hospitably invited to join in the game. Toward morning, when he had won every penny in the house, he departed, leaving behind an unspoken question as to his identity which was answered when one of the discomfited players noticed beneath the card-table the dirty mark of a cloven hoof. A similar story from Columbia County was told by an old lady whose great-uncle was returning late at night from Kinderhook to Valatie, cursing his heavy gambling losses. Suddenly from the ditch beside the road there skipped out a little man bearing on his head a candle which remained lighted in spite of the high wind blowing. "Play your game! Show your game!" shouted the little man, brandishing a pack of cards. The gambler took to his heels, pursued by the candle-light and the voice squeaking, "Play your game! Show your game!" At length Valatie was reached, where the great-uncle fell exhausted across his doorstep while the candle flickered out. "And who do you think the little man with the candle was?" asks the old lady.

The devil is not dead in York State; indeed he is said to have had a new birth about forty years ago at Johnstown when a strange baby appeared in the cradle of an immigrant family. Its eyes were wide open always; from its long hair protruded a pair of horns; and a long, muscular tail was not lacking. When it was three hours old, the baby jumped from the cradle and ran around the room, its scarlet body hunched up like a frog's. Next day the thing disappeared and the family soon moved away, leaving the belief among some residents that the parents had been so evil that the mother had given birth to the devil, who had tarried only long enough to get his breath and have a good laugh at his trick.

There are many other stories of monstrous births. One of the most striking is known in Troy where they tell of a rich, proud woman who in the days before her confinement used to ride with maid, coachman, and footman past miserable dwellings called the Barracks. One day, passing a poor woman and children, the rich lady observed to her maid, "Doesn't she look like a sow with her five pigs?" When the little heir was born, he had instead of one hand a pig's foot, which was amputated and an artificial hand substituted.

In the village of Cattaraugus it is said that a farming family contrived to send a peddler into the cellar while they stole his wares. Hearing suspicious sounds, he attempted to climb back into the kitchen, but the thieves trampled on his fingers and finally slashed them off. As he fell back dying, he cursed the family till the end of their days, praying that their hands might turn to claws. For generations every child born into the family had thin, clawlike hands. Finally nobody would "marry into the curse", and the family disappeared.

Some of the most potent curses are commanded by the mendicants feared and respected by the French of our northern border. I was told of a family which refused alms to one of these strollers, usually so welcome as bearers of gossip and tellers of folktales. As the beggar turned cursing from the inhospitable door, the only child of the family, a little girl, started to rise from the floor and continued this terrifying levitation until her head struck the ceiling; then she dropped and again began to rise. The father rushed in pursuit of the mendicant, and with the aid of a stout stick persuaded him to remove the curse.

By all odds the most interesting of the French Canadian tales concern the *loup-garou*, the man-wolf so feared by the Continental French in the seventeenth century. Why a man should be transformed into a beast's shape, or should run about in man's shape acting like a beast, is variously explained; one common theory is that this is a punishment for the neglect of Easter duty during seven consecutive years. Other beast-forms beside that of the wolf are not unknown: the red bull or the white horse occur, even the devil-dog, though that is usually a form chosen only by Charlot (the devil) himself. I have heard also of a *loup-garou* having the head and tail of a wolf but otherwise retaining the form of a man. Frequently the afflicted person may be freed from his wolf-form and nature by being cut, preferably in the forehead with a cross. To kill such a beast you may use bullets with incised crosses and wadding of four-leafed clover; or a score of beads from a rosary will be potent.

The pleasantest tale of the *loup-garou* that I have collected was

brought me by Miss Pearl Hamelin, whose family once lived at
Mooers on the border. She has been singularly fortunate in ancestors:
one great-grandmother was confident of living to the age of ninety
because she had seen a potato-hill bearing that number of tubers;
another great-grandmother saw a *chasse-galerie*, shortly to be explained; but the most delightful of great-grandparents was Joseph
Hamelin, who often talked with ghosts and who once met a man-wolf.
He was born about 1820, and by the time of his marriage he prided
himself on what he called his strong will—his wife soon had another
name for it. His story, just about as told me, runs thus:

When old Henry, a neighbor, died owing him two dollars, Mr.
Hamelin declared that Henry's soul could not enter heaven until it
had first come to him begging for the gift of this sum. The declaration
was made confidently: an old French belief of Clinton County held that
if you die owing money, you cannot enter heaven until your creditor
generously informs the Powers Above that he makes your soul a gift of
the debt. For several long nights Mr. Hamelin stayed up, grimly awaiting
Henry's ghost, but greatly to his annoyance no ghost appeared.

One clear winter night in that same year, Mr. Hamelin was driving
his sleigh home to Mooers through a wood under a bright, hard moon.
Suddenly he saw a shaggy creature trotting along the road behind his
"rig". The first thing that he noticed was the wolf's eyes, gleaming like
frozen fire; next he observed with a start that the animal's legs scarcely
brushed the snow as he ran.

Reaching for his whip, Mr. Hamelin forced his already trembling
horse into a gallop, but the wolf easily kept pace. When the plunging
horse slowed to a walk, the strange companion slowed to the same speed.
Then it flashed upon Mr. Hamelin that this was a *loup-garou*, Henry's
soul prowling the night.

At the edge of the wood the animal spoke: "Joe, Joe, are you going to
give me those two dollars?"

Remembering his boasts, Joe roared, "No, I am not!"

Three times the request was repeated, thrice refused. When the barn
was reached, the *loup-garou* trotted in and leaped into a manger while
Joe unhitched his frightened horse. A stubborn man glared at a stubborn
wolf. Then Joe Hamelin did the bravest deed of his life: contemptuously
he turned his back upon the supernatural eyes and moved toward the
barn-door. With a sudden rush of air a huge body struck his back,

bearing him down to the lintel. Hot, furry jaws were at his neck, and a hoarse, furry voice cried, "For the last time—will you give me those two dollars?"

Joe did not take long to decide. "Yes," he said. "I give you the two dollars. Take them with you to a place where they will melt."

At these words the *loup-garou* vanished. With great dignity Joe picked himself up and stalked into the house.

"See, Delphine," he said to his wife. "I give in to no woman' and to no man. Tonight for once I have given in, but not until the *loup-garou* had me by the neck."

Delphine looked and shuddered. On the collar of his coat was a savage rent and the white froth from a wolf's jaws.

Old Madame Delphine Hamelin had a story which illustrates one method of rescuing a man bewitched into the form of a beast—in this case not a *loup-garou* paying the penalty of sin. It concerns a Clinton County neighbor of hers, a spinster of unblemished reputation but unattractive appearance. In managing the farm for her father this lady carried about a set of heavy keys suspended from a cord under her apron. One early morning, as she was leaning on the railing of a pen, she noticed a pig which she had never seen before—larger than the rest and grunting more loudly than any swine she had ever heard. When she threw food into the trough, he crowded out the other pigs and ate with more than hoggish speed. Irritated by these manners, the spinster grabbed her key-ring and struck the animal on the snout. As the blood spurted forth, the pig disappeared; in its place stood a tall, handsome young man.

I wish that I could tell you that the lady was rewarded by an offer of marriage, but that is not how Madame Delphine Hamelin ended the tale. Perhaps life with the strong-minded Joe had made her prefer irony to sentiment; she would close the tale by saying, "The handsome young man tipped his hat, said '*merci*', and walked away—*voila!*"

Madame Hamelin got the fright of her life one day when she was in the fields near Mooers. Dashing into the house she exclaimed that she had looked above the woodlot and had a sudden sight of a *chasse-galerie*, a hunting boat flying through the sky. When questioned she averred that she had heard quite plainly the music of a *chanson* and

the sound of oar-locks. The accepted theory was that a number of
men from Clinton County had gone north to Hudson's Bay in Canada,
signing up for a period of two or three years during which they
were to trade with the Indians. They had been paid in advance a
considerable sum, which had been left with their families. The wives
had been philosophical about this long absence, but the lonely men
had chanced a ride in the devil's boat for one sight of their homes.
If you read a book published at Montreal in 1900, M. Beaugrand's
La Chasse-Galerie, you will find that this sky-ride is a bet with
Charlot: a set time for the return must be agreed upon; during the
trip nobody must mention the name of *le bon Dieu*; and under no
circumstances must the crosses on church-steeples be touched. If any
part of this covenant be broken, the *voyageurs* lose their souls to the
devil. The surprising fact is, according to the lore of the St. Lawrence
and the lumbercamps, that men will undertake the rash journey
merely to attend a dance. As you might expect, they are usually men
very lax in attendance upon religious duties.

Frequently I am asked whether the supernatural element in the
stories of Washington Irving was obtained from the folk in America
or was borrowed from European legend. There is never time for a
proper answer—the subject deserves a doctoral dissertation or two;
but I can suggest to the layman a few facts. You have to remember
that Irving was the son of a Scot, and that in childhood he was priv-
ileged to hear the ballads and tales of a Scotch maid. When he came to
man's estate, and before he wrote his *Sketch Book*, he numbered
among his British friends two of the chief romantic writers of Cale-
donia, Thomas Campbell and Sir Walter Scott. So Scottish folklore
was his native inheritance and inspiration; undoubtedly he wished
to do for the Hudson what Scott had done for the Tweed. (He also
tried to do in the sentimental tale what Mackenzie and Goldsmith
had accomplished in periodicals; it happens that our taste runs to
romance rather than sentiment—we prefer *Rip Van Winkle* to *The
Broken Heart*—both in the *Sketch Book*.)

You must remember also that the scenery of the Hudson obviously
demands a phantom ship and a headless horseman. As the Scottish
author of *Dreamthorp* would say: "Here time has fallen asleep in
the afternoon sunshine." No German folktale fully explains *The*

Legend of Sleepy Hollow; you must see Kinderhook as it is and imagine Tarrytown as it was. We can show you the Van Tassel house, built in 1736; if you are not convinced by the iron figures in a brick wall, you can fall asleep in the afternoon sunshine while the fair prospect dims, and you will hear in dream the thundering hooves of Irving's horseman. As to *Rip Van Winkle,* the author smilingly admits a foreign suggestion for the plot; an appended Note says:

The foregoing Tale, one would suspect, had been suggested to Mr. Knickerbocker by a little German superstition about the Emperor Frederick *der Rothbart,* and the Kypphauser mountain: the subjoined note, however, which he had appended to the tale, shows that it is an absolute fact, narrated with his usual fidelity:
"The story of Rip Van Winkle may seem incredible to many, but nevertheless I give it my full belief, for I know the vicinity of our old Dutch settlements to have been very subject to marvellous events and appearances. Indeed, I have heard many stranger stories than this, in the villages along the Hudson!"

Irving did not need to visit Germany—which he did two years after writing the *Sketch Book*—nor must we suppose that he was just introduced to German legends in Sir Walter Scott's library. He could have heard plenty of German as well as Dutch legends along the Hudson. There is in European tradition the story of the Flying Dutchman, and on the Hudson the story of a phantom ship and a phantom oarsman; but on our *western* border we have the story of a phantom French ship, the *Griffon,* which was built by La Salle in 1679 and sailed away on Lake Erie, never to return. As for the phantom horseman, recently I was given the story of a mysterious ghost who gallops near Sharon, New York. The spectre rides bareback, Indian fashion; the horse has only four burning hooves and a powerful red-eyed head and throat; the man sits astride where the horse's body should be. Whenever this phantom appears, usually to someone "doing an evil thing", it leaves on the earth or on the wooden floor the deeply burned hoofprint of its passing. In *Tales of a Traveller* by Irving you do find stories of hidden treasure similar to *European* types; but you find among these very stories the best romantic account of Captain Kidd, an *American,* and in *Dolph Heyliger* the best picture of old Albany. So without detracting a bit from such studies as Professor Pochmann's investigation into the possible German sources of the *Sketch Book*, I should answer all inquiries by declaring that Irving is true to character, landscape, and lore of the Hudson, adding such romantic elements as he got from his Scottish inheritance and taste, with a certain amount of German lore which he could have picked up in America from oral source or from his reading. Not to labor the obvious point further, let me tell two or three legends of the Hudson and the Catskills still current among the folk.

Take the story of the horseman of Leeds. In 1801, when Irving was 18 years old, there died a man named Ralph Sutherland. When he had come from Scotland many years before, he had brought as "bound servant" a poor lass whom he treated with such severity that she ran away. Before she had gone far, he overtook her, tied her hands together, leaped on his horse, and dragged her behind him—some say that she was tied to his horse's tail. Sutherland later pled in his defence that the horse became frightened and bolted, throwing its master to the road and flinging the girl against a boulder; neighbors thought that he might have killed her deliberately by driving his horse at a gallop.

It sounds like a plain case of murder, or at least manslaughter; but for some reason the man's sentence was postponed, to be carried out when he reached the age of ninety-nine; meanwhile he was to wear a hangman's noose around his neck and once a year was to exhibit himself to the judges at Catskill. The effect of this symbol upon his community was even stronger than that of the minister's black veil in Hawthorne's story. Folk-imagination came into play: it was said that nightly a shrieking woman passed Sutherland's stone house, tied to the tail of a giant horse with fiery eyes; that a curious phantom in woman's shape sat on his garden wall, uttering unearthly laughter, lights shining from her finger tips; that "domestic animals reproached the man by groaning and howling beneath his windows". This is the version chosen by a student of mine, Mr. Charles F. Wilde, for his *Ghost Legends of the Hudson Valley*.

To show what a variation there is even in a story so recent as one born in the late eighteenth century, let me give the same story as written by another careful student, Miss Ruth Bedell, after studying the case in such *written* versions as those of Vedder's *Historic Catskills* and De Lisser's *Picturesque Catskills.* Here the villain is a certain William Salisbury of Leeds, and the girl is an *American* bound out by her parents to a man who was unable to control her wayward actions. In spite of all that her master could say, the girl insisted on visiting at the home of a family which had a bad reputation. When she ran away, he did pursue her and capture her. Binding a cord around her waist, he tied the other end to his saddle. As in the other version, the horse was frightened, the girl was dashed to her death; Salisbury himself narrowly escaped a similar fate. At the inquest he was acquitted of criminal intent and honorably discharged.

Miss Bedell adds what she considers fictional details: the conviction and sentence to be hanged at the age of ninety, the requirement of wearing a red silk cord around the neck. She is convinced that Salisbury died at the age of eighty-seven of natural causes, and that the story of the cord originated in his habit of wearing a red string around the neck as a supposed prophylaxis for nosebleed.

After giving this matter-of-fact explanation, she goes on to tell of a Spook Rock at the scene of the girl's death, visited on the anniversaries of her death by a huge gray horse and its rider; of a female figure on a rock, with a lighted candle on each finger; of a wild, shaggy white dog howling at Salisbury's house and then disappearing upon your approach. The variations in the two versions, even in the name of the villain, will give some idea of the vagaries of folk-imagination and memory among Irving's Yorkers. It is amusing to imagine Irving listening to the story, rejecting the plot as too grim, and remembering this as one of a number of phantom riders. It is even more amusing to speculate on what Hawthorne might have done if he had chanced upon the tale—say, in his visit to a Williams College Commencement, when he was able to study types of our Yorkers who had drifted across the State border.

For an example of the Hudson legends of haunted mansions let me give a single version of the story of Forbes Manor, the one which Mr. Wilde prefers. The house still stands on high ground at Rensselaer, overlooking the Hudson, though the figures that now walk its paths are members of the Franciscan order of St. Anthony, quite

unrelated to the fashionable ladies and gentlemen who once knew
the wealthy family of Forbes, tea-merchants of New York City,
who had bought the Georgian house from a member of the patroon
family of Van Rensselaer.

Since the earliest day of the Dutch, the principal holiday of the
Albany region had been the New Year. It was a gay party in 1799
which drove up in sleighs and entered the marble-pillared hall to
enjoy a New Year's Eve dance given by Richard Forbes and Alice,
his beautiful wife. The one gloomy face was that of Ronald Dunshon,
who, rumor said, had been rejected by the lovely Alice in favor of
young Forbes. Evidently the mistress of the house felt that Ronald's
mere presence was a pledge of reconciliation, and when she paused
to ask him why he was not dancing, she readily granted his request
for the midnight minuet.

Having given her gracious consent, the mistress of the house
crossed the great hall and ascended the winding marble stairway
to visit her little son. She was kissing the sleeping babe when swift
tragedy began in the movement of her former lover. Dunshon passed
through the dancing throng to begin the ascent of the stairway, almost
immediately followed by the watchful Forbes. Reaching the top of
the stairs, Dunshon turned to find himself within "bloody distance"
of his former sweethcart's husband. A moment later a silent and
terrified crowd in the hall below was watching the glitter of two
narrow blades. Then a third figure appeared at the top of the stairs
—the young wife carrying her golden-haired child. As she cried out
and moved to separate the men who loved her, Richard attempted
to thrust her back, and in that moment Ronald's sword went home.
Richard's body toppled and fell, slithered down the marble stairs;
his sword clattered on till it lay at the feet of a lovely lady in the
hall below. Above, another sword pierced the mother and babe. In
the silence the great hall-clock struck midnight. Then with a cry
the murderer sped down the backstairs and into the cold New Year
without. Several days later he was found frozen to death in a snowdrift.

Years after, when the great house was deserted, a belated traveler,
lost on the way to a New Year's party at Albany, came through a
wooded stretch to see lights gleaming from Forbes Manor. A

stranger to the region, he advanced to the house to ask for shelter or guidance. Just as he reached the open door, every candle-flame was extinguished and at the same instant the music of violins began. Crouching behind a pillar, he beheld a lady in the costume of a former age pass up the stairs, to be followed shortly by the figures of two hasting men. The tragedy of the century's turn was re-enacted; the traveler staggered out and ran until he reached the village opposite Albany, and the legend of Forbes Manor had become a legend of the haunted house. For years lights were seen annually in the old mansion at New Year's Eve; the wail of violins was heard. Then came the Brothers of the black robe, and the peace of Mother Church.

For comparison with this tale of glittering swords on a marble stair, let me give you one of those romantic Indian legends which the whites love to tell in the Catskill region. This is the story of Manaho as it has drifted down through generations in the Mountains of the Sky, as a boy learned it long ago sitting at the base of a cliff that rises two hundred feet above Manaho Gorge, watching a quiet pool and listening to his grandfather's dreamy voice.

Schenevus was an Indian chieftain who lived half a mile from that gorge; his name was proud along the Susquehanna and the Delaware; but for him the brightness of life was not in the chase nor on the warpath but in the countenance of his beautiful daughter, Manaho, last of his proud line. Yet not the last in *hope*—for she had many suitors and one loved above the rest, the gallant Manetee.

A winding trail led from the village of the chief, across the valley and past the mouth of the gorge. To that dusky place the lovers would stray in the warm twilight, to spend a quiet hour by the pool at the foot of the falls. One evening, gazing into that mirror, Manaho said: "Look! We are there, in the water—together." And Manetee answered: "It is the Great Spirit, telling us that thus it shall be always; where I am, there shall you be, and our nation shall be the Happy People."

But there was one of the hill people who was not happy. Changu had loved Manaho; and as he brooded over her beauty, a hate rose in his breast against Manetee. "I will kill him," he swore to the wind.

It was a clear morning in summer; the braves went forth to hunt with light hearts, for the Squaw of the Sky Mountains was bountiful that day. Light of foot and light of heart Manetee took the trail which led along the brink of the gorge until he reached a place directly above the Pool of the Joined Faces. He would spare a little while to lean forward and dream the faces back into the pool.

He did not hear the panther tread of Changu. One wailing cry rose to a wheeling eagle as Manetee fell; the scarp of the gorge was bruised a little, soon to heal; the quiet waters of the pool rose for an instant and fell back. Toward the west a panther in human form sped into exile, his hate appeased.

When the summer day drew toward dark, all the hunters returned save two. "Manetee will be at the pool," said the daughter of the chieftain. As she entered the gorge, the thrush was singing farewell to the "indolent sun". Manaho listened, her face upturned. Then smiling she remembered the omen of the Joined Faces, and turned to look into the pool. She brushed her eyes, stooped forward, and lo —there *were* two faces in the pool, but one face was cold and drowned.

The thrush stopped singing. The two faces were still there, the face of the living talking to the face of the dead: "Where you are— it is the will of the Great Spirit—where you are"— There were two faces in the pool, both turned toward the sky. Schenevus found them next day and knew that his name was ended. Perhaps not quite ended. Lovers still hear at twilight the pool's voice and see two white faces turned upward; "Where you are"—

I used to think that all these romantic and sentimental legends about Indian lovers—particularly the ones about innumerable Lovers' Leaps* where some Red Juliet or Romeo plunged to death rather than endure separation from a beloved of a hostile tribe—I thought that all these were the invention of white men, inspired by Chateaubriand and other writers of the romantic period. I am not so sure now; I find that occasionally an Indian will tell a story of sentiment.

* On the west side of Canandaigua Lake is a cliff from which a Seneca maiden and her wounded Huron lover leaped when pursued by her people. Across the lake is Bare Hill, where the serpent lived who ate all the Senecas except two, a boy and girl who destroyed him. Rolling down the hill, the creature vomited out the heads of his victims, now round stones. The two legends afford an interesting contrast in types of tale.

Let me give as example a tender little myth which "Old Norm" told to white children, first in broken English and then in sign language. Old Norm came from somewhere in the north, established himself in Schenectady with a Scotch housekeeper, told stories and sang songs to the children of the Dorp, and died. A little girl learned this story when she was seven and told it to me when she was a senior in college. Like the Saranac tale of the origin of the water-lily, it is a myth of sacrifice, with a touch of the supernatural.

Many moons ago, before you were born, or I was born, or anyone who lives, there was a brave chieftain of our tribe named Gomac; he was a good chief and had killed many wolves. He had a beautiful daughter, so beautiful that all the young men of the tribe wanted to marry her, but Nawisga would not. Only one did she love, Nokgan, and him she married.

Years passed and to Nawisga and Nokgan came a little Nokgan. Now at the time when Nokgan was a small boy came a great famine, for the Great Spirit sent no rain. The medicine men prayed for rain; the people prayed for rain; the Great Spirit gave no rain. A sacrifice must be made to the Great Spirit, they said. Gomac ordered blankets and furs to be brought for a burning.

Now Nokgan the father went hunting on this day, but Little Nokgan and Nawisga stayed at home. Nawisga took Little Nokgan in her arms and walked to the edge of the cliff.

"A sacrifice to the Great Spirit for rain—I, daughter of a chieftain and my son!" she said, and leaped. At that very moment a black cloud rolled up and lightnings flashed; rain fell.

Returning from the hunt, Nokgan found his wife and son gone; but when the rain stopped, at the foot of the cliff ran two rivers, one large and the other a little river running into it.

And Gomac said to Nokgan: "My son, the large one we will call Nawisga; the small one, Little Nokgan, for in his fright at the storm he ran to his mother."

Equally touching, I think, is the better known legend about Diamond Rock, a glittering mass of crystals atop the cliffs that follow the Hudson River's east bank and come to abrupt end back of Lansingburg (Rensselaer County). Here is the story as told by a man of Mohawk ancestry who guides in the Raquette Lake region; I have condensed it a little:

Long ago the Mohawks lived in Canada, in warfare with the Algonquins. Weary of that land, my people journeyed south down the Champlain valley till they came to the Hudson and the Mohawk rivers, where they drove out the Mohicans and made their home. Often the Mohawks sent raids north against their old enemies; on one of these parties were the great chief and his handsome son. Many days passed and the raiding party returned, saying that the chief and his son had been left behind as captives.

The chief's younger son made a vow that when he grew up he would go to the north and not return without his father and brother, dead or living. When he was old enough to depart, his mother promised to watch always for his return and to keep a fire every night on a rock of the high cliff near their village. Years went by, and the beautiful young mother grew old, but every night she crossed the swampy trail and lit a fire for her son's guidance. When she grew crippled, the braves carried her to the rock, leaving her there all night on watch.

One night of wind and storm, she lay alone on the rock weeping. Her son climbed to her look-out, threw at her feet the bones of his father and brother, and took her in his arms. As they were weeping together, Manitou, the Great Spirit, sent for them his lightning and bore them away. The same flash of lightning changed to crystal the many tears that she had wept through frosty moons of loneliness.

You see how our Indian tales of the supernatural, as known to white men, merge into sentimental romance or preserve traces of genuine myth. We have at least one plain Indian ghost, with no romance or mythology about him; and of all apparitions in York State he is my favorite. I heard about him from the late James Fenimore Cooper, whose *Legends and Traditions of a Northern County* includes a chapter called *Ghosts—Ours and Others*. Mr. Cooper was a man whose portrait I should like to possess; he was the type of our great gentleman—handsome, literate, gracious, and, in spite of a sharp sense of irony, devoted to tradition. It would be easy to apply to him Sir Walter Scott's description of his grandfather, the novelist, "Cooper—a castle of a man". He had a smiling belief in the ghosts that a Cooper could see—he couldn't speak for others; he assured me that after his first ghost he had felt no perturbation. Imagine him sitting in a magnificent Chippendale chair at "Fynmere", Cooperstown, sipping Amontillado and chatting about the ghosts he had known:

The oldest of them is the Indian chief who for nearly a century and a half is known to have sat behind the old stone wall on River Street, and with his sturdy, if bony legs, many a time kicked it down. For five generations, from father to son, has the tradition been handed down, how, back of this wall, with chin on knees and hands clasped around shin bones, sat, amidst his weapons and scanty pots and pipes, the skeleton of a great Mohawk Chief.*

Well I remember the terrors of the spot on dark and rainy nights. I suppose because he was an Indian was the reason why one's scalp had that queer feeling and the scalp lock seemed to rise and pull! I never heard that he was seen to leave his grave, but I was told, as have been all the family, that no wall ever had stood, or ever would stand, at that place. It was the despair of successive owners, wall after wall was built and kicked down, until the present heavy one was put up, thick and strong enough, it was hoped, to withstand the feet of the old chief; but even it is yielding, as all may see. When its predecessor fell, in my youth, there, glaring at the fallen wall, sat the triumphant old chief, with bony chin on knees, cavernous eyes, and skinny legs; there he was left; and there he sits to-day.

* This is only one of many Indian ghosts. In Putnam County the ghost of Chief David Nimham of the Wappingers haunts the spot near Indian Bridge where he fell in 1778, fighting against the British. A mountain is named for him.

VI: Heroes of Tall Tales

I T IS thought that Americans have a special talent for drawing the long bow. Far back in 1765 our Dr. Franklin satirized the ignorance of Englishmen regarding America by a grave series of tall tales:

The very Tails of the American Sheep are so laden with Wooll, that each has a little Car or Waggon on four little Wheels, to support & keep it from trailing on the Ground . . . Cod, like other Fish when attack'd by their Enemies, fly into any Waters where they can be safest; . . . Whales, when they have a mind to eat Cod, pursue them wherever they fly; and . . . the grand Leap of the Whale in that Chase up the Fall of Niagara is esteemed, by all who have seen it, as one of the finest Spectacles in Nature.

The first important book by a citizen of New York State is, of course, Washington Irving's *A History of New York* (1809), alleged to be the work of Diedrich Knickerbocker, in which the spirit of burlesque produced such memorable portraits as that of Governor Wouter Van Twiller who was "exactly five feet six inches in height, and six feet five inches in circumference".

As time went on, our folk enjoyed cycles of tales about local heroes.

Sometimes these tall stories were created by the admiring friends and neighbors of some man possessing prodigious strength or sagacity; oftener an individual created his own legend for the amusement of his neighbors and the inflation of his ego, frequently borrowing from Baron Munchausen and his imitators. We should have a scholarly study of *Munchausen in America* to explain how the adventures of that mendacious noble, as published in England by a German adventurer (1785), were spread over York State and claimed by a number of rustic and sylvan liars. The story of a stag shot with cherry-pits, growing a tree from his antlers; the story of the wolf turned inside out by a valiant hunter who thrust his arm down the creature's throat; the story of the fox flogged out of his skin; the merry tale of a bear blown up by flints which entered his mouth and "rear door", meeting in the stomach with disastrous results—these tall tales of the Baron naturally appealed to a people who were still hunters, and inspired even mightier lies in the same manner. Naturally the tall tales are found oftenest in the mountains, among lumbermen and guides and descendants of the Injun-fighters. In three other chapters I am giving such stories in their proper settings, but the form is so universally popular in Eastern New York and in the North Country that something will be gained by subordinating the setting in order to focus upon the heroes, and in order to show how my students have led me from one heroic cycle to another. This is the chapter on which I have left the scaffolding.

As you might expect, our pursuit was inspired by those tales of Paul Bunyan the Woodsman which are now the common heritage of the United States and Canada. I was quite aware of the fact that the wide dispersion of this saga within the past twenty years has made it almost impossible to separate the oral tradition from the written. I would read a few stories from Esther Shephard's *Paul Bunyan* (1924), stories collected for the most part in Oregon, Washington, and British Columbia, and told without that attempt at fine writing which is so irritating to those who love the "wild woods". Then I would suggest that the students try to collect tales of Paul in the Adirondack and Catskill counties, preferably from old men who did not own radios or read books; thus we might discover whether such legends were known before the printing-press captured them. One reply gives such a vivid picture of the sort of man who preserved the legends that I shall give it to you in Miss Agnes S. Holsapple's own words:

Mr. C. is a young-old man of nearly eighty, but he can still out-saw any young man in the neighborhood. He is a little over average height with very broad shoulders. His face is a dark brown and deeply wrinkled. His hair and beard are a scraggly gray and look bristly. In fact, he looks bristly all over. When he laughs—and that is often, with a terrific, ear-splitting "Haw—haw, haw"—his little black eyes disappear completely from view behind his shaggy brows. But one has the feeling that from somewhere behind those quantites of brows, whiskers, and wrinkles, those eyes aren't missing much. He still dresses in typical lumberman fashion—heavy woolen trousers, quantites of shirts topped by a green and black lumberjacket, high boots laced with hide-strings, with heavy woolen socks folded over the top.

His wife was a little wizened woman who was never without her pipe. She could handle a saw and ax with the best of them. Unfortunately she died, and Mr. C. was heard to say, "By Gar, the old woman she didn't die from overwork." They lived in a one-room hut in the Adirondacks until Mr. C. set fire to it by sleeping with his pipe, and was only rescued from a fiery death by his neighbors just before the hut collapsed.

On this particular day the old gentleman sat in his son's kitchen, shaping the curve of an ax-handle with a piece of window-glass; a foul-smelling pipe clenched between his teeth, a jug of cider at his side, shavings all over the floor. He calls me the City Girl with the utmost scorn and disgust. He told me he wouldn't live in the city because it choked him, and he attempted to show me—and I quite feared for the safety of his throat as he still held the broken glass in his hand. He said that he had to have room to move about, and he flung out his arms as though to push back the walls. I was quite speechless and overcome.

He shouted, "Say something, City Girl—say something!"

I stammered out a weak "no" .

He bellowed: "My God, the Girl says no. You say *yes*."

I speedily gasped "yes" and subsided.

When I had recovered sufficiently, I asked him if there was a Paul Bunyan in Canada. He took a firmer clutch on his pipe and told this story:

"*Oui*, there was a Paul Bunyan. He big like hell, fight like hell, and lie like hell. He lived a long time ago. He was so big that he would lift a man with his thumb and forefinger to have him so he could see him without bending. So strong was he! By Gar, he lived in a cave bigger than ten caves together. He often picked up as many as ten of his loggers and put them in his pocket. Then he would forget them for maybe ten weeks. By Gar, he was some man! But he didn't like women. No sir! He had no use for women. He had no use for lumbermen who washed and recited poetry—he thought they were—how do you say?—flowers."

Being assured that the Paul Bunyan legends were known of old among our lumbermen, I was hopeful of finding his name attached to some place in the Adirondacks. Sure enough, I soon received the following communication from Mrs. Mary Barnett Burke, whose family is well known among the lumbermen of the North Country:

Mamie B. and her husband Sam were in charge of Huggard's Farm, a sort of supply station for the A. Sherman Lumber Company, located between South Colton and Stark in St. Lawrence County . . . She told me the only story of Paul Bunyan which I heard in a childhood spent near logging country. This is the story, as accurately as I can remember it, told me about 1912:

Mamie was telling us about an Indian who, returning to camp before a spree had run its course, caused a good deal of trouble for her and Sam, and was finally, after he had drunk a bottle of bluing, shut up in a smoke-house. According to Mamie, he was a big Indian and pretty tough. "I guess he thought he was Paul Bunyan," Mamie said. When we asked who Paul Bunyan was, she replied: "O, he was the big lumberjack who had a big ox, and his camps were so big that when the cook made pancakes, the cookie had to go around the griddle on roller skates to drop the batter." Gratified by our incredulous laughter, Mamie warmed to her tale and said: "Why, once Huggard's Pond here was dry for a long time on account of him. He came through here with some tote-teams on the way to some camps he had, and it got too dark to go farther that night. They was all hungry; so he dumped all the loads of beans he had and a load of salt-pork right into the pond, and built fires all around the banks, and made the whole pond into bean soup. They ate the pond dry, and it was quite a while before it filled up again."

Having now sufficient evidence that Paul Bunyan was known in the Adirondacks before the Great War, I awaited proof that Yorkers had created their own legends of a similar type. In 1934 Miss Mildred

Tyler, of a family long domiciled in Sullivan County, brought me a cycle of tales about a certain John Darling, of whom she knew few biographical facts except that he died a long time ago, yet in the memory of some now living; that he had a farm on the banks of Sand Pond, that he probably had rafted on the Delaware, and that he certainly was the champion liar of her county. In order to recover more of the legend, I broadcast in February, 1935, some stories of which I shall proceed to give samples.

"You know, boys," John would say, "you know I never shave nor have my hair cut oftener than once a year. Yessir, every May I figure on going down to the barber in Roscoe and getting my whiskers cut off. 'Taint worth while to go oftener than that. Well, last spring I went down, and when the barber cut off my beard, I decided to take it home. Seemed as if there was quite a bit of weight to it; so I took it along, and my old woman poured a little water on it and put it on the stove; and darned if she didn't get seven gallons of maple syrup out of them whiskers! You see, boys, we'd had an extra lot of pancakes that winter.

"I remember a colder winter, though. One day it was so cold that the fire in my chimley wouldn't draw, and the smoke kept coming into the room. Well, I couldn't stand that; so finally I figured a way to get the smoke up. I whittled a paddle out of a piece of wood, and I fastened it onto the end of a bit of rope. I hung the rope over a nail, and then I stuck the paddle into the fireplace under the smoke. I sat down by the fire and began to pull the rope, like ringing a bell. The paddle kept jerking up and down every time I pulled the rope, and pushed the smoke up the chimley. Well, I sat there a spell, working the paddle and singing songs. (You know, boys, I was born with a clarion lung.) Pretty soon I noticed that the paddle wasn't working so good. It was getting awful heavy and hard to lift, and the smoke seemed harder to push up. Finally I went outside and looked at the chimley. The weather was so cold that the smoke I had paddled had frozen as it came out, and had made a solid column ninety-six feet high in the air. Yessir—that was a real pretty sight all the rest of the winter; and in the spring, when the smoke began to melt, coming out of the air I heard the songs I had sung while I was paddling.

"I remember another day when it was pretty cold. That was when I had that old tomcat that I was so fond of. Well, my old woman, she used to set the jug of pancake-batter behind the stove so it would get light. One day, the cat got into the pancakes, and the old woman took a notion that they was spoilt. She seemed to be pretty mad, and she grabbed a dipperful of boiling water off the stove and went after the cat. I didn't want to see him hurt just for liking pancakes; so I opened the door, and he run for it. Just as he flopped through the door, the old woman let loose with her boiling water. Well, sir, it was so cold that day that the water froze the minute it left the dipper, and when it hit the cat on the head, it was such a heavy chunk of ice that it killed him.

"Speaking of pancakes and syrup—I worked out in California for a man who had some of them tremendous big sugar-bushes. They boiled down so much sap, that the man had to have big pans that weighed one ton each. About that time, mosquitoes out in California used to be pretty brisk, and they was big too. My boss told me that if I ever heard a sort of thundering sound coming from the sky, I'd better hide quick, because it wouldn't do no good to run.

"Well, I was out in the woods working one day when I heard a sort of *roar, roar, roar* up in the sky that made me look for a place to hide. There wasn't any place except under the big sap-pan, laying bottom-side up on the ground; so I picked up one corner of it and jumped under. Less than a minute later, there was a *crash*; a swarm of mosquitoes had hit that pan so hard that they drove their bills into it. There was some big stones on the ground under the pan where I was; so I picked up a stone and went around clinching all the bills of those mosquitoes onto the inside of the pan. The next thing I knew, they begun to clap their wings and make a sound like as if a big storm was coming. Then the sap-pan begun to lift up slow. It riz up graceful from the ground and over the tree-tops, and the last thing I saw of that sap-pan, it looked no bigger'n a baseball, on the way to China.

"Did I ever have any pets after the old Tom was killed? Well, I got kind of attached to an old sow once, though she caused me some trouble by always snooping around under the barn and getting into the feed-box. One day when I caught her at her tricks, I grabbed up a broom-stick and hit her on the back. I guess I hit harder than I meant to, and it seemed like I broke her back—I never know my own stren'th. Anyway, she couldn't use her hind legs, and I thought for a while I might have to kill her. But I managed to build a nice two-wheeled truck for her to pull around under her hind-quarters. One day I missed this particular sow and finally decided that she had gone off somewhere to die. But a few months later, up in our grove of oaks I found her, grunting around, picking up acorns, and as nice and fat and friendly as could be. There was thirteen little pigs running around beside her under the trees, and every one of them had a nice little two-wheeled truck under his hind-quarters."

In February of 1935, Miss Tyler printed some of the Darling tales in a short-lived but admirable magazine called *The Half-Moon*; she therefore deserves full credit, I believe, for being the first one to bring Sullivan County's hero into print. Not content with her first collection—of which I have given some of the best samples—she enlisted the aid of a college friend, Miss Josephine Barrile, and the two girls scoured the county for more stories of which they found a plenty, including Munchausen's tale of the deer and the cherry-tree and several more very tall tales, including two which follow:

"Some of the most re-markable things," said John Darling, "have happened to me right here to home. I'll never forget that foggy day in early fall when I was shingling the barn. I ain't one to let the weather stop me; so I started good and early and worked hard till noon, encouraging myself with my clarion lung. I knocked off at noon, and when I came back from dinner I had one of the surprises of my life. While I was eating, the sun had come out. Imagine my surprise when I discovered that I had laid the shingles onto the fog forty foot above the roof!

"The most unexpected and beautiful things have happened to me right here on Sand Pond. In summertime I'm a great hand to go swimming, and one day I was feeling specially strong; so I thought I'd see whether I could dive right down to the floor of the Pond out in the middle. Well, by Jeepers, I dove like a fish and landed at the bottom right in an Indian graveyard. I stayed down an hour, walking up and down, reading the names and inscriptions on all them stones. It was one of the prettiest sights I ever saw, and I hated like sin to come up and go back to work."

Was there a real John Darling? Mr. William Lieb of the *Sullivan County Record*, commenting editorially on Miss Tyler's article and my broadcast, was ready to answer in the affirmative:

While only a lad of less than a dozen years, the writer remembers Darling when he walked from his home at Sand Pond (now known as Shandalee, and the Darling place the property of Anthony Westfall). He looked like a Rip Van Winkle as he sauntered along in ragged attire, sandy straggling hair and beard, and a crooked cane cut from the woods. He was known as John Cicero Caesar Augustus Darling, as that was the name he applied to himself. . . . Darling lived to an old age and died at Sand Pond before that locality began to develop into the popular summer resort it is today.

For readers in Livingston Manor, Mr. Leigh R. Hawley printed a long and interesting article, in which he pointed out that in Quinlan's History of Sullivan County there is reference to a youthful revivalist of Monticello named John C. C. Darling, a prominent member of the sect known as the Protestant Methodists who established a circuit in the county in 1832. For some obscure reason, Darling was refused a license to preach, and the refusal "turned the young man into a cynic". Possibly this is the famous teller of tales; at any rate, it was some fifty years ago that the Westfall family bought John Darling's farm. Judge William H. McGrath, now of Livingston Manor, remembers Darling flourishing a mysteriously carved cane which he claimed to have cut upon a mountain 20,000 feet high back of Valparaiso, Chile. Darling told the Judge of living among Eskimos in the Arctic regions where the snows were more than a mile deep and the natives got their firewood by chopping off the tops of gigantic pines. Returning from the Arctic, the hero stopped off to visit the Queen of Spain in whose palace he enjoyed a dinner that required seven hours for its consumption. How true these reports might be, the Judge would not say, but he added that Darling did teach school for a while at Thumansville, now Callicoon Center, and, like most schoolteachers, died poor. The Judge describes him as a "small, wiry man with yellow hair and beard, whose quizzical face was distinguished by two protruding upper teeth". This de-

scription tallies well with one given by Editor A. M. Scriber of
Monticello, who remembers also a "tumor in the cheek" made by
an ever-present chaw of tobacco.

While the good people of Sullivan County were recalling the
exploits of John Darling and while my friend Carl Carmer was putting him into two books and a broadcast, we were on the hunt for more
cycles of tall tales. Our next strike landed the biggest fish of this
sort that ever twitched on my line. Hearing about Paul and John,
Miss Maud Post recalled that her uncle George Darling had a
favorite story about a certain Bill Greenfield who once worked in
her grandfather William Darling's lumber-camp at Conklingville,
Saratoga County. She wrote out for me a tale which proved to be
a variant of one of the Paul Bunyan legends but so amusing a variant
that I shall give it in shortened form:

Bill was annoyed to find that he was not getting enough griddle-
cakes for breakfast because, although the cook got up twenty-six hours
before breakfast, all that he managed to cook was sixty-four dripping-
pans full of sour biscuits at one time; to provide the required number
of griddle-cakes was out of the question. So one day Bill went to a
plow-works with an order for a proper griddle. Enough steel was
used to make two hundred and sixty plows. When the work was
achieved, the griddle measured two hundred and thirty-five feet
across, and the difficult question arose as to how this vast structure
was to be carried to camp. Bill himself solved the problem by putting
the griddle on edge, hitching it to his blue ox, and starting it rolling.
When he was five miles from camp, he unhitched the ox and let the
griddle spin on alone. As it reached the spot where it was to be
used, it spun around like a top until it dug a hole large enough for the
fire. Several men were shod with slabs of bacon with which they
greased the griddle while they skated gracefully over its surface.
When the batter was too thick, they climbed up on chicken-wire which
Bill had thoughtfully strung around the griddle.

Encouraged by her luck in finding this introduction to the mighty
Bill, Miss Post continued her search, enlisting the aid of another
uncle, Mr. Truman Darling of Saratoga, who proved a rich source
of further tales. The hunt was now in full cry, and three under-
graduates volunteered to join in the fun, not to return from Saratoga

County until they could bring back Bill's brush. At Batchellerville, not far from the site of camps where Greenfield had worked, they were lucky enough to find Mr. Floweram Redmond, a gentleman of seventy-six years who had known Bill well and was prepared to tell his stories as long as anyone would listen. While the college students sat in awe, Mr. Redmond's tales poured forth, justifying the remark of Mr. William Redmond (aged eighty-one and too busy building a house to add his own recollections) that "Bill Greenfield was the goldarndest, most unreasonable liar you ever saw, though he meant no harm to anyone". To make sure that these stories were not confined to one family or to one town, the three young people then proceeded to the home of Mr. Clarence Wheeler, aged eighty-three, near Beecher's Hollow, where Mrs. Wheeler recalled whoppers heard from Bill and his father Abner.

A chance remark that Bill's son Frank was still living led Miss Janet Lewis to dragoon her father into a search which ended at Gloversville. Mr. Frank Greenfield said that his great-grandfather, John Greenfield, was born in Scotland and came to America about the year 1800, dying in 1847 at the age of about seventy. This pioneer's son, Abner, was the one who "used to get off some remarks", and Bill did little more than tell his father's stories. Bill was born in 1833 in the town of Edinburg, N. Y., and died seventy years later in the town of Hope; he is buried in Clark Cemetery, not far from Gloversville. Mr. Frank Greenfield told two stories to explain his father's particular talent:

My father said he had a pair of four-year-old steers that could draw anything in Day. Once by Sand Lake he was driving them along when he heard some noises; a wind-storm had upset a crooked birch tree, and it was rocking in the earth. He hitched the oxen to it, and the first draw set the tree and straightened out the crook. Someone said Father was lying. He said: "Why, I told it for a lie; I supposed it's what you are all doing."

Once when my father was going up to the lakes, he saw a flock of pigeons on a limb. He waited a minute to look at them, and then he decided to catch them. He didn't have any bullets; so he put his jack-knife in the muzzle of his gun. The knife split the limb open and then snapped back, catching ninety-nine pigeons by their toes. Someone asked him why he didn't make it a hundred and be done with it. He just grinned and said he wouldn't lie for one pigeon.

After consulting with Mr. Peleg W. Andrew of Corinth, Saratoga County, whose memory for ballads has enriched this book, I had at my disposal enough tales of Bill Greenfield to while away a winter's night, and I proceeded to select some of the best for a broadcast, part of which I shall now quote just as it was written—at a time when the stories were fresh in memory:

Everything that Bill experienced was remarkable, especially the weather. One time when he was hunting it got so cold that every morning he had to pound up the air so he could breathe it. Outside the camp he had a saw with twenty-one teeth to the inch—and that should have been fine enough to escape destruction—but the wintry wind blew all the teeth out of the saw. One day Bill froze his feet and hastened to plunge them into a bucket of water to thaw them out. This should have been effective, but he hadn't realized how far the frost had gone. "Well, sir," said Bill, "my feet was so cold, a inch of ice come on top of that water quicker'n you could count two." But Bill recovered in time to go hunting soon after with Abner, his father. They didn't want any more frozen feet; so they set a stump afire to warm themselves, but the cold was still so intense that the blaze, forty feet high, froze in a column. Abner went into a cave to get warm. He tried to talk, but no words came; so, after a pull at a bottle, he and Bill went home. On the next Fourth of July, Bill happened to go into that same cave again, when he was startled to hear Abner's words, just thawing out of the air, saying, "Here, Bill, have a drink."

There were big rains in those days too. Mrs. Wheeler once saw Bill driving past in a downpour, taking a pig home. Later he reported to her that he had driven so fast that he hadn't got a mite wet, but it was a close call, for the pig in the back of the wagon had got drowned. At another time it rained so hard that it took seven men each with a ten-quart pail, working one entire week, to dip up the water that came into camp through a six-inch stove-pipe. The *worst* rain that he reported occurred one day when he took a trip to Saratoga. Standing in a doorway, he observed in front of the store a pork-barrel with both ends knocked out. It rained so hard that the water went into the bunghole faster than it could run out at both ends.

Some of his friends used to say that Bill beat the devil; one day he told them how true that remark was. He was walking in a field of his father's when he suddenly met that Enemy of Mankind whom Bill's Scottish ancestors named respectfully the Earl of Hell.

"Bill," said the devil, "I need a liar of your talents; you must come with me."

Bill sat down on a stone and began to cry—probably for the first time in his life. Somewhat softened by the spectacle of so great a genius at a loss, Auld Clootie made a concession.

"Bill," he said, "you may ask me to do three things; if you find just one that I cannot manage, you may stay on earth and entertain the County of Saratoga."

At these words Bill grew thoughtful. Pulling up a small sapling he said, "Let me see you pull up that large elm over there."

The devil did it easily.

Picking up a small pebble, Bill turned it around in his hands several times. "Now," he said, "you take that ten-ton boulder over there and do with it just as I've done with this pebble."

"That is easy too," said the devil, performing the feat with nonchalance. "Now, Bill, you have just one more chance."

"I know it," replied Bill, "but I wasn't brought up in the woods to be scared by owls. Those first two jobs would have been easy for me; now here is a hard one for anybody: you go find a bigger liar than Bill Greenfield."

The devil sat down and cried. Then he arose, shook his head, and said, "Bill, you can go."

A man who could get the better of the devil had an easy time beating ordinary Yorkers, but I admire the way Bill would sit back and wait before smiting his rivals. One day in Conklingville some fellows were boasting about their parents while Bill listened in cold contempt.

One man said: "I don't see why people can't raise stuff like they used to. I remember my father growing a cucumber four foot long."

"Humph!" said another. "My father growed an ear of corn as long as your arm."

A third boaster sighed with pity. "Poor farming," he said, "poor farming! My father raised a head of cabbage as big as a washtub."

"The trouble with you boys," said Bill, "the trouble is that you ain't traveled. Five or six years ago I spent some time looking around out west. On my way home I stopped off to see a big kittle being made; I'd been hearing about it. There was ten men building it in sections, and it was so big that when they were riveting they were that far apart that they couldn't hear the fellow next to them."

"Now, Bill," someone interrupted, "that is unreasonable. What could anybody do with a kittle that size?"

Bill moved toward the door, spat, and turned. "I suppose," he said, "they were aiming to bile that cabbage your father raised."

At least once Bill was embarassed—when a boy believed his tales. The Old Master had dropped into a store in Huntsville with the remark that he was proud of three possessions. The boy asked what they were.

"I've got an ox," said Bill, "that could travel to Boston and back in one day. I've got some hens that can pick corn off the big beams of my barn. I've got a dog smart enough to teach school."

Next day the Greenfields saw the boy trudging up the road toward their house. Immediately guessing the cause of this visit, Bill hid after instructing his wife what to say.

"I've come," said the boy, "to see the ox that can go to Boston and back in a day."

"I'm sorry," said Mrs. Greenfield, "but we were all out of corn and other feed; so Bill has taken the ox and gone to Boston."

"That's too bad," said the boy, "but maybe I can see those hens that can eat off the highest beams in the barn."

"I'm sorry," said Mrs. Greenfield, "but seeing as there was no corn, Bill has turned those hens into the woods to eat nuts off the trees."

"That's too bad," said the boy, "but what I want to see most is that dog who is so smart that he can teach school!"

"Well, there!" said Mrs. Greenfield. "It does beat all how I have to disappoint you. The teacher took sick, and they sent for the dog to teach in her place till she is well."

Bill was embarassed that time. Mrs. Greenfield gave the boy a danger-ous number of cookies.

Being a man of imagination himself, a lover of poetry and a master of the ballads, Mr. Andrew remembered a couple of Bill's stories that prove him to have been a person of poetical as well as tricksy imag-ination:

Yes, this is a good scythe, but not so good a one as I once had. On a clear day the *shadow* of that scythe would cut off the blades of grass.

While I was passing through the woods one day, I heard a funny sound, and getting nearer I heard a man say, "He-O-He—tuck under!"

Soon I come to a small clearing where there was four men and a five-gallon keg. Two of the men with levers were trying to turn over a beechnut; the third man had a big wooden wedge, and when they raised the beechnut with the levers and when the fourth man gave the order to tuck under, he pushed the wedge under to hold what they had gained. At last they had the beechnut turned over, and just then a shower came; so the four men all went into the bunghole of the keg.

Miss Margaret Mattison confirms the statement that Bill and his father, Abner, must both be considered when we assemble the tales of this cycle. She has heard that when the Greenfields lived near Stony Creek they were such wonderful shots that they used to pace off a considerable distance, turn, and shoot. The marksmanship was so perfect that their bullets would meet and fall flattened to the ground. Once Bill's gun held fire; Abner's bullet entered the barrel of Bill's rifle and plugged it.

One of the family's boasts was that Abner had the best team of oxen in the country, and he would add loyally that the mother made the best fullcloth. Both claims were fully substantiated one day when Bill was plowing. His team of oxen suddenly ran away, plunging on either side of a white-oak stump. The plow split the stump in two; and as Bill flew along, the halves of the stump closed on his pants. But the pants, made of his mother's cloth, held without splitting, the oxen drove ahead, and in a trice—oxen, man, and pants had pulled up the stump.

It would be interesting to know how many towns now claim the Greenfields. Miss Ina Young of Northville says that Abner lived up there; she has stories with the true ring:

One day Abner started to hunt without loading his gun. On the way through the woods to his favorite hunting-ground he suddenly met up with a big black bear. Having no time to load, he dropped the weapon at the foot of the nearest tree and shinnied up to what he hoped was a position of safety. Then, according to Abner, the bear lumbered over to the foot of the tree, picked up the shotgun with its two front paws, looked it over carefully, reared back on its hind legs, gazed up playfully at Abner, and stuck out a paw for the treed man to drop a shotgun-shell into. There aren't many bears as smart as that in the Adirondacks now, but it is still cold in the Northville winters. Abner remarked that he had to lean a broom-handle up under the thermometer so that the mercury could fall far enough to tell the truth.

There are other tales of the Greenfields, many of them variants of stories which I am telling in another chapter about the Adirondack guides and hunters. Enough have been given to indicate the richness of the cycle. If you are tempted to be a disbeliever, remember the retort of Bill. He had been hunting in a forest so thick that he had to pass sideways among the trees. All at once he saw a buck, full-antlered, running with speed through the forest. "Hold on, Bill!" someone said. "How could that buck run through the woods that way if you had to turn sideways to get through?" Bill stared contemptuously. "Well," he said, "the buck had to pull in his horns, the way some of you have to do sometimes."

In the cases of John Darling and the Greenfields you have cycles of tales started by the heroes themselves, drawing upon Munchausen and various folktales of foreign origin, enthusiastically adopted by Yorkers and increased from the common stock of such stories drifting among lumbermen, hunters, and guides. In the case of Joe Call of Essex County you find the other type of hero—a man of prodigious physical strength, not given to lying about himself but erected by the folk into a figure of legend. Though he died in 1834 and consequently antedates Darling and the Greenfields, his reputation has continued before the winter fires of Lewis, Elizabethtown, Ticonderoga, and other villages and towns of Essex. I first heard of him from my friends the Cuttings of Elizabethtown and their relatives the Coucheys; I gathered more from Mr. Thomas Cooke of Ticonderoga, whose grandfather (born in 1813) remembered seeing Call, and I have added here and there to my stories of the Lewis Giant. The folktales may well be preceded by a few biographical facts, some of which appear in a History of Essex County edited by H. P. Smith and published in 1885 at Syracuse:

It was in these early years, from about 1820 to 1830, that Joseph Call, the Lewis Giant, was in the zenith of his physical power. He was a mill-wright by trade, and did a good deal of lumbering here. It is related that he was double-jointed and had a double set of teeth. He was not more than six feet in height, but was thickset.

He was particularly noted as a wrestler, and was at different times engaged in matches in many parts of the world. The writer has seen a watch formerly worn by Judge Henry H. Ross of Essex, which Call won in a wrestling match in Scotland nearly fifty years ago. The writer has also seen a stick of timber fifty feet long and ten inches square, now forming the plate of one of the stone stores in Essex, which it is said Call had dragged with one end on his shoulder a distance of twenty rods, then up an inclined staging to the top of the wall in its present position.

Mrs. Caroline Halstead Royce, in her charming book called *Bessboro* (1902), says that Joe came from Britain, where he gained fame in the army as a wrestler, his most famous match taking place in Scotland. He migrated, took the American side and fought in the War of 1812, settled at Lewis as a farmer, and died in 1834 at Westport on Lake Champlain. Now for some of the tales:

One day there arrived at the farm a wrestler who had come all the way to Lewis from England to have a match with Joe. Seeing a man plowing, he asked him to give directions to Mr. Call's residence. Without saying a word, Joe lifted the plow in one hand, held it at arm's length, and pointed toward the nearest house. The English wrestler turned around—also without a word—and headed for the Atlantic Ocean. At another time, Joe was asked for direction to a neighbor's. Again a gesture from the silent plowman sufficed. He lifted one of his oxen by the tail, straightened his arm, and pointed up the road. The stranger started on the run. Mr. Alex. Couchey, who told me this story, estimated that the ox weighed between six and ten hundredweight.

Just as Paul Bunyan's wife was a giantess, Joe's sister was a strong girl. One time a man came to Joe's looking for a wrestling match— apparently Joe did more wrestling than farming, though the stories may be misleading. Joe wasn't at home, but his sister suggested that if the stranger would care to wrestle her, they could decide whether he deserved a match with her brother. Then she picked the visitor up and threw him into the pig-pen. (I heard a similar story from Mr. Van Dyke, one of the officers of the General Electric Company, about his eighteenth-century ancestor, the powerful Dutch Yorker, Ross Bogardus: The champion wrestler of Vermont knocked at the door and asked for Ross. While he told his errand, Miss Bogardus looked him over; then she said, "Ross Bogardus is out, young man; and besides, we can't be bothered with Vermonters". Thereupon, she threw the visiting champion over the fence.)

To get back to Essex County—Joe Call was dangerous when angry. It is said that at Plattsburg he crushed between his hands a big British grenadier who refused to wrestle according to Joe's rules. Again at Plattsburg he killed a man, unintentionally breaking his back; Joe had been induced to come up there to wrestle for a prize without being told that his opponent was a Negro. Less unfortunate were two rough fellows who walked down the middle of a narrow road boasting that they would turn out for nobody. Tossing them into the ditch like straws with a single gesture to left and right, the Lewis giant said, "If anyone asks you who did it, tell them you saw Joe Call". When you hear such stories, your informant is likely to add: "Joe wasn't a tall man—short and thickset—about six feet tall". I wonder how tall they used to grow in "them thar hills".

Apparently Joe's fame drifted to neighboring counties. Miss Margaret Mattison of Saratoga County recently obtained from Mr. Carlton Young a story of Joe working as a blacksmith. A powerful stranger entered the smithy with a swagger, picked up a horse-shoe, and straightened it out. Joe gravely picked up the stranger's horse and lifted it across the shop. The stranger nodded and requested a light for his pipe. Still silent, Joe put a live coal on his anvil and carried the anvil across the smithy. The stranger accepted the anvil, held it in one hand, and lit his pipe. After he had smoked a while, he observed, "I believe you must be Joe Call". Joe nodded. "Well," said the stranger, "I came here aiming to have a fight, but I guess we are both too strong." Joe nodded. Here, of course, we see the myth-making folk at work, as you do in a Couchey legend that Joe chopped up frozen fog and used it next year to smoke his hams.

The Lewis giant's feats seem to have inspired tales in Clinton County on the Canadian border, where the Hamelin family tell of a powerful Frenchman, known merely as Joe, who had a habit of pointing with his plow. This French Joe used turkey-gobbler for bait: he would dangle the turkey's goatee in the fair waters of Lake Champlain, and the pike would come a-tearing.

In European tradition, and particularly among the Italians, there are cycles of tales about boobs, regarded as inferior mentally or even deranged but often able to get the better of their neighbors. These boobs are usually tricksters rather than heroes of tall tales, but in Otsego County we have a cross between the two types in the legend of Cal Corey. I learned about him from Miss Thelma Shatzel, whose father is a native of Edmeston.

Along about 1880, Calvin Corey, better known as Cal, was working in the Chapin Hotel at Edmeston. He was reported to be slightly *tetched*; some people said that he had been that way ever since he was hit on the head by a stone not intended to injure him. Cal claimed, indeed, that the missile didn't hurt him, but that he had been left in the mud too darned long after he received the blow, and that at the end of two weeks, when he came to what we may call his senses and got up, his mind had got "sort of soaked up".

Apparently, up to that date he hadn't realized his own strength, but soon made the discovery in a manner which I shall try to give in his own words:

I was unloading logs one day when they drove up with an oak log thirty feet long and four feet through the butt. As they unloaded, they asked me to take the butt and ease her down. Maybe they was just joking, but I took holt and everybody else let go; and there I was, holding it all alone. That made me so darn mad that I give the log a heave to one side. Then to show how I felt I picked up a stone and squeezed it till the juice ran out. After that they knew what kind of feller I was.

Cal always dressed informally, so that people who didn't know him supposed him to be a tramp. When he needed clothes, he used to select a scarecrow in the field and make a trade. He was always polite about the transaction. He would say: "Now, Mister, how will you trade? Even? All right—we'll swap." The clothes always suited him perfectly. There was that time when he was caught in the woods by a big storm; everybody was thinking that poor Cal would get miserably wet in his rags. He waited till the storm was over and then breezed into the mill smiling, apparently as dry as those who had been under shelter. Someone said: "Jeepers, Cal, how come you didn't get soaking wet?" Cal replied: "Well, I figgered that the devil was up to one of his tricks, trying to get me all wet out there. So I fooled him. I hid my clothes under a pile of bark and danced naked in the rain till the devil saw I'd won."

Although it is doubtful whether Cal had ever been outside the county which nourished James Fenimore Cooper and gave the nation our game of baseball, he claimed that he had once visited California. (California apparently had a fascination for a number of our master liars, including John Darling and Bill Greenfield.) Cal discovered that one of the boasts about the Golden State was true—that they did have some mighty big trees. His envy was aroused when he heard that one spry Californian had actually run the length of a redwood while it was falling. "So," said Cal, "I waited till a gang was cutting one of them big trees, and I ketched myself a good holt on the bark. When the tree commenced to fall, I started running on its trunk. I run and I run, night and day, and jumped off just as the tree struck the ground; in fact, the tip-top of the tree brushed the seat of my pants. And where do you suppose me and the top of that tree had landed? Right smack in the center of the state of Alabama!"

Probably it was in California that Cal worked as a stage-driver; at any rate, he said that a gang of western bandits announced that they intended to make a haul from his stage. "Sure enough," he would add, "one day I was driving along as slick as a mink when a feller about seven feet high on a hoss to match held me up with one of them old muzzle-loading rifles. I used to be mighty quick in my youth; just as the feller started to shoot, I picked up a hatchet from the seat aside of me and threw it at the cuss. It flew straight and true towards the bullet and split it in two. No, it didn't hurt me none, that bullet—just cut off the two ends of my mustache."

He said that back in 1876 they had a spell of cold that beat anything he had ever seen. It was so cold that all the skunks in his neighborhood holed up together to keep warm. One day when Cal and Russ Perkins started to dig out the big skunk-hole, they found that the cold had been so intense that the hole stuck right out of the ground about two feet. So they brought up a team, hooked it onto the projecting part, drew the hole all the way out of the ground, and bagged fourteen skunks.

It was in the same winter of 1876 that the folk of Otsego County had such a time with Butternut Creek. When it was frozen right through, naturally a lot of people thought that they would make some money cutting ice. By and by, Cal pointed out that if they chopped up the entire stream for ice, there wouldn't be any creek left for fishing. The cutters were sufficiently impressed to throw back a good many chunks of ice, but they must have thrown them in carelessly—the wrong way around—because in the following spring, when the ice thawed, the creek ran up-hill and was never properly straightened out until along in the month of May.

The caution exhibited in this tale appears again. Mr. Shatzel says that Cal never did a stroke of carpentering in his life but declared himself an excellent shingler and had for proof a hammer by which he set great store. "One day," said Cal, "I was on a high scaffold, shingling the tallest building I ever put up. All at once I slipped and began to take a header. When I was about half-way down, I happened to think of my hammer and went right back for it. Yes, sir, that hammer is all that kept me from an awful dirty fall."

You have some samples of our cycles of tall tales and will find others in various chapters devoted to special occupations; now I should like to take a little whirl around the State, picking a sunflower of exaggeration here and there. The natural place to begin is on Long Island, where Mr. Birdsall Jackson has made a varied collection presented in his *Stories of Old Long Island* (1934). I enjoy most his tales of Captain Tom, who filled in idle hours by making wonderfully realistic duck *stool*, as decoys are called in that happy region. The trouble was that the Captain made the decoys too natural: one night a neighbor's cat crept in and ate the heads off two of them. An even worse catastrophe followed:

"I fergot an' left the boat-house door open, an' a strange dog run in here this morning an' barked at 'em an' the hull blank flock got scared an' jumped up an' flew right out of the boat-house, an' I ain't seen 'em since."

The Captain had a pet dog-fish named Fido whose affection he had won by throwing out a couple of dog-biscuit from his boat. Difficulties arose when a couple of pet catfish belonging to a family of spinsters came at night to the Captain's boat-house and quarreled noisily with Fido. For the most part, Fido stayed out of trouble and was decidedly useful:

"I had all my money invested in my clam-herds down in the Bay, an'

once when I was away for a few days, they started to wander off from
the feedin' range, an' I would have lost 'em all. But Fido was watchin',
an' he herded 'em up an' brought 'em back an' kept 'em safe. He must
'a' been part shepherd."

It is sorrowful to relate that at length Fido took sick, refused his
biscuits, died, and was buried under a big tree at High Hill Beach—
which is part of Jones Beach, our most scrumptious place for bathing.

Not all the tales regarding Long Island Cap'ns are so jolly. Cap'n
Albert Tuthill of Sayville told one of my students that she could
gather how inadequate the pay of fishermen used to be if she heard a
farflung tale of that region. When the fishing-boat came in, its captain
would sell the cargo and proceed to distribute their share to the
crew. Standing above the open hatch, the captain (not, of course,
Cap'n Tuthill) would throw the money he had received into the
bottom of the boat. The coins that landed on the bottom of the boat
were the cap'n's share; the coins that landed on the rungs of the ladder
and stuck there were the share of the crew. Hence the Long Island
rhyme:

> Naught to naught,
> Two to two,
> All for the captain,
> None for the crew.

Coming up the Hudson, we might stop off at Ulster County, visit
the Service family in their fine old stone house at Stone Ridge, and
hear great-aunt Kitty's story about the time when one of her neighbors built a Virginia rail-fence. In the spring when he went out to
survey his winter's handiwork, he found that his rails were crawling
away: he had built the fence with frozen blacksnakes. (Lots of snakes
then in Old Ulster, and lots of cider.)

If you come up to Albany County, we can let you know about a
man of eighty who had the strongest grip in York State. One day
while he was hauling hickory wood, his wagon got a hot wheel which
he was able to take off from the axle after it cooled but couldn't grease
until his brain came to his aid. Picking in the waste of an old pine
fence, he found a pine-knot harder than Pharaoh's heart—something
that the average man couldn't dent if he had it in a vise. But the hero

of this tale scraped the knot, held the axle between his knees, and then squeezed the knot until the sap ran right out over the axle. Mr. Merrihew of Slingerlands has no explanation for this prodigious squeeze except that his hero came from Rotterdam Junction, and the Dutch were said to be a grasping lot of folks.

As a matter of fact, the Albany County "Dutch"—whether they came from Holland or from the Palatine, Germany—have their own stock of tall tales. For instance—one of my students named Myndert Crounse told me about a farmer near Guilderland who had a barn full of popcorn. One hot July day, the corn all popped, burst the barn, and cascaded out in glittering whiteness. Thereupon a near-sighted old horse in the barnyard became bewildered, lay down beside what looked like a pile of snow, began to shiver, and froze to death.

If you go north of Albany on the east side of the Hudson, you will reach Washington County and will do well to visit the pretty village of Greenwich where the local historian, Mrs. Sharpe, can tell you about the Yorker who had the loudest voice ever heard across our hills. This was Whispering Somes, who came to Greenwich in the eighteenth century, liked its soil, ascended Bald Mountain, and called back to his pal in Rhode Island, "Come up, Captain Foster—there is good land here." The Captain heard quite well, and in that year of 1767 "came up" to found a numerous family in Greenwich.

Heading west toward the Adirondacks, you are bound to hear a mort of tall tales from the guides, but those must wait for another chapter. We might stop just long enough in Essex County to collect the story of its one miser. He was leaning over the bridge looking into the river when his glass eye fell out. He searched for two hours without success until a friend appeared with a helpful suggestion. Someone took a penny, tied it on the end of a string, and dragged it through the river. In less than a minute, the miser's glass eye came out glued to the penny. At Elizabethtown you can get name and place. I believe every detail of the story except that Essex County has a miser.

Striking westward across the Adirondacks you will reach St. Lawrence, the County of Big John Kingston. "Things he told me wouldn't be any good for a book—all lies," said one of his neighbors, but Ray Belanger got me two stories that belong here. Big John, hurrying home, reached Kingston Brook to find it tremendously swollen. "I takes a long run and just as I reached the edge I lept hard. About half-way across I sees I wouldn't make it: so I lept again and just barely reached the other side." Big John shared my own astonishment at the snowstorms of the North Country: "I went out to the barn one night to milk. Not a bit of snow on the ground when I left the house. Milked just the four cows. When I started for the house, I had a terrible time plowing through six foot of snow."

Dropping down into the plains of Oneida County, we find this elegiac little tale of the Cat-Hard-to-Kill: as told by Mr. Hubert Root:

My neighbor Jones had a cat he wanted to kill or give away. First he carried it in a bag to a friend a great distance away; next morning when Mr. Jones went out to milk, he met the cat in the barn. Next he tried to drown the critter by putting it in a bag loaded with stones and flinging the bag into the Oriskany Creek. Almost before Mr. Jones reached home the cat was in the barn. Then he took the cat into the back woods and cut off her head. He walked sadly home—he couldn't help feeling sorry for a beast with so much character. As he came in at the gate, he turned around to take a last look at the woods. There was the old cat trailing after him with its head in its mouth.

If you move as far west as possible in York State, you will come to the home of the muskallunge and grape-juice, and my own branch of the Thompson family. We ought to know the county legends, but I confess that I had never heard about Cornelius Cole until one of my students named David Nelson collected from the White family at Frewsburg stories that evidently belong in a cycle, two incidents of which follow, much as they were brought to me:

Among other vocations Cornelius was a pretty good blacksmith. Occasionally he would move his shop to another location and had devised a simple way of doing this. Being an extraordinary man of an extraordinary family, he would slip two long poles under the shop, and then he and his mother would carry it as if on a stretcher. One morning they carried the shop to its new location, but when it was put down, the mother was somewhat out of breath. She said the shop seemed heavier than usual. The explanation was found when they opened the doors: an early rising farmer had brought two teams of oxen to be shod, had hitched them at the end of the shop which Mrs. Cole had to carry, and—there you are.

In the days of wild-pigeon flights, Cornelius used to require a large amount of bird-shot. Whenever a neighbor went to Jamestown, more would be procured, but Cole never seemed to have a sufficient supply. One day he decided to make a special trip and get a real supply in a large bed-tick. In Brooklyn Square, then unpaved, the weight of the tickful of shot caused him to sink in the mud up to his hips. He shouted for help, but the hungry people hurrying home for lunch wouldn't stop to help him. This unfriendly behavior made him so mad that he hurried back to the hardware store himself, got a shovel, came back, and dug himself out.

As a matter of fact—and it is high time that we spoke of facts—the Empire State does things in a big way, whether the job happens to be the digging of a canal or the making of a cheese. Black shame fall upon us when we forget Colonel Thomas S. Meacham of Sandy Creek, Oswego County—the year 1835—and the Great Cheese. That autumn all the milk of one hundred and fifty cows was turned into curd and for five successive days piled into a great hoop until a noble cheese was formed weighing fourteen hundred pounds. Forty-eight gray horses drew it in procession to Pulaski, where the hoop was removed and the cheese proceeded to Oswego. On November fifteenth, amid the booming of cannon, Ontario's port bid farewell to the Colonel's masterpiece, which advanced via canal and river to Syracuse—Albany—New York. At Washington the gallant Colonel presented it, in the name of the Governor and the People of the Empire State, to Old Hickory, the President, who had sufficient respect for cheese to preserve it until Washington's birthday, when he ordered it cut into pieces and invited all the men, women, and children of the Capital City to partake of the Colonel's bounty. Congress adjourned; the White House was thrown open. Led by Van Buren of New York, Webster, the foreign ambassadors, and other dignitaries, the crowd advanced. Let an eye-witness describe the scene:

It was cheese, cheese, cheese. Streams of cheese were going up the avenue in everybody's fists. Balls of cheese were in a hundred pockets.

Every handkerchief smelled of cheese. The whole atmosphere for half a mile around was infected with cheese.

For the Colonel all the rest of life was anti-climax. He made and sent several little cheeses of seven hundred pounds apiece—to Vice-President Van Buren, to Governor Marcy, to the Mayor of New York City. For these he received only thanks and reputation. But when he sent a similar gift to the Mayor of Rochester, the magistrate of the Flour City sent back an immense barrel of his product weighing nearly a ton. Several years later, when the flour was all used, the Colonel built a vast Agricultural Hall for fairs—a frame building much too large for any possible use in that section but not too big for the Colonel's purpose: into the front of the hall was built the head of the Mayor of Rochester's barrel. And the Colonel rested from his labors.

I have wondered what the feelings of the Colonel must have been when he gazed on Niagara Falls. Perhaps he merely murmured, as a friend of mine did, "Exaggerated". There has been at least one sort of Yorker who could take the Falls in his stride and look for something bigger—the sort who sold "oil-boiled stockwhips" at the County Fairs of my youth, the sort who wrote the advertisements for patent medicines and sold remedies in the flare of coal-ile torches. Do you know the old advertisements? Here is one which I came upon at the Kirkland Town Library in Clinton, New York, where I was indulging my passion for old almanacs. It is in *Phinney's Calendar, or Western Almanac* for 1839, published at Cooperstown:

THE MATCHLESS SANATIVE. Invented by the immortal Louis Offon Goelicke, M.D. of Germany, Europe, is astonishing the World with its mighty victories over many fearful diseases, which have been pronounced incurable by physicians in every age, being the most VALUABLE MEDICINE and the most unaccountable in its operations of any ever prepared by human hands! a medicine obtained equally from the ANIMAL, MINERAL & VEGETABLE KINGDOMS, thus possessing a three-fold power; a medicine of more value to mankind than the united treasures of our globe, and for which we have abundant cause to bless the beneficent hand of a kind Providence; a medicine which begins to be valued by physicians, who have heretofore opposed it, who are daily witnessing its astonishing cures of many whom they had resigned to the grasp of the INSATIABLE GRAVE!! A precious and powerful medicine, which has thoroughly filled the great vacuum in the materia medica, and thereby proved itself to be CONQUEROR OF PHYSICIANS. Dose of the Sanative.—For adults, one drop; for children, half a drop; and for infants, a quarter drop.

This Conqueror of Physicians sold at $2.50 per half-ounce at the bookstore of I. Tiffany in Utica "and in most of the towns in America".

It would be strange if a folk so fond of the tall tale and the long bow had no ballads of imaginative inflation. We have them—some brought over from the British Isles, some of our own pure invention. The most popular is the song of *The Derby Ram*: the following version is one which Miss Marjorie G. Thomas's grandfather used to sing at Newark, New York, in Wayne County:

As I went down to Darby Town all on a market-day,
I saw the biggest ram, Sir, that ever was fed on hay.
He had four feet to walk, Sir, and he had four feet to stand,
And every foot he had, Sir, would cover an acre of land.
      You, Sir, and I, Sir—and if you think I lie, Sir,
      You can go down to Darby Town and see the same as I, Sir.

The wool upon his back, Sir, reached into the sky;
Eagles built their nests there—I heard the young 'uns cry.
The horns upon his head, Sir, reached up into the moon;
A man went up in January and never got back till June.

Of nostrils he had two, Sir, were thirty cubic (sic) each;
The devil built a pulpit there, 'n Satan went up to preach.
The wool upon his belly, Sir, dragged upon the ground;
The man that sheared it off, Sir, was lost and never found.

The wool upon his tail, Sir, so the weavers say,
Made five hundred yards of cloth, Sir, and they wove it all in a day.
The man that butchered this ram, Sir, was drowned in the blood,
And many thousand people, Sir, were washed away in the flood.

For a song of farewell here is *As I Rode Out*, as it was preserved in Saratoga County by Mr. Peleg William Andrew of Corinth, some of whose tales of Bill Greenfield you have been reading:

As I rode out a-hunting
All on one summer day,
The fields were all in blossom
With flowers fresh and gay and gay,
With flowers fresh and gay.

I took my gun upon my back
And into the woods did go.
I followed a herd of deer all day,
I tracked them through the snow, the snow,
I tracked them through the snow.

I crooked my gun in circle
And fired around a hill,
And out of five and twenty
Ten thousand I did kill, did kill,
Ten thousand I did kill.

As I ascended yonder hill,
Just as the sun drew nigh,
I bundled up my venison,
Jumped on as she passed by, passed by,
Jumped on as she passed by.

All round the world she carried me,
Quite over the swelling tide.
The stars they bought my venison,
So merrily I did ride, did ride,
So merrily I did ride.

Just as the sun was going down,
She took a sudden whirl;
I could no longer sit on her,
I fell into the world, the world,
I fell into the world.

Come, all good people far and near,
And try and do your best;
And see if you can all tell
A bigger lie than this, than this,
Tell a bigger lie than this.

VII: Tricksters and Retorts

IF ANYONE acquainted with our folkways were asked to name the most famous and most typical Yorker in American fiction, he might pass over Natty Bumpo to mention David Harum—banker, hoss-trader, and philosopher, whose motto was, "Do unto others as they would like to do unto you—and do it first". One reason why Westcott's immortal character is so convincing is because he has drawn from an affectionate study of a real hoss-trader, David Hannum of Homer, who, among his other rôles, was part-owner and general manager of the Cardiff Giant.

When, in the autumn of 1869, a figure weighing about a ton and a half was discovered buried at Cardiff in the Onondaga Hollow, the most spectacular hoax in our history was launched. Petrified fish and reptiles had been found aplenty in that region—why not a petrified man? Here, said the clergy who hated Darwin, was proof of that passage in *Genesis* VI, 4, "There were giants in those days"; this would establish the infallible scientific accuracy of Scripture. Here, said David Hannum, was something more remunerative than hoss-trading and country banking. With five other gentlemen, including the father of that E. N. Westcott who was to be the author of *David*

Harum, the sage of Homer was able to buy for $30,000 a three-fourths interest. To be sure, Captain George, chief of the Onondagas, was enough of a hoss-trader himself, though an Injun, to claim the giant as a sacred personification of the Great Spirit, buried six or seven centuries earlier, when the Red Man was temporarily driven from the Onondaga Valley. This was good authentication, but Indian writs did not run with David.

The financial value of the Giant had not been overestimated. Everyone wanted to look at him, even the hard-boiled reporters who saw through the hoax. One of them writing in the Utica *Morning Herald* eleven days after the unearthing said, "He laid down to rest (how many years ago!) with his pockets full of specie". A letter in the Syracuse *Journal* reported a visit made by "Tom, Dick, and Harry":

> "Let us at least give him one—just one—kiss for his mother."
> "He never had no mother," responded the inexorable valet.

But not everyone in Syracuse was so callously sceptical. A veterinary of that city picked up at the side of the giant's pit a coin issued in 1091 by "Jestyn, Prince of Glamorgan"—possibly to establish a claim for the Welsh. Clearly this was a time to consult the learned. David Hannum invited a Rochester anatomist, an ethnologist, the Secretary of the Board of Regents of the State Department of Education, and —most important—the State Geologist. The last named gentleman, Dr. James Hall, wrote to the Albany *Argus* as cannily as David himself might have done:

> Altogether, it is the most remarkable object yet brought to light in this country, and although, perhaps, not dating back to the *stone age*, is, nevertheless, deserving of the attention of archaeologists.

That was enough for the country's chief showman. Mr. P. T. Barnum of New York and elsewhere offered $60,000 for the use of the Giant for three months. The offer was refused. The Giant was moved to Syracuse, where passenger trains on the New York Central Railroad stopped ten minutes to permit a view of David's "curiosity". The original of John Lenox in *David Harum*, former Mayor John Rankin of Binghamton, said that on the day when he viewed the marvel at Syracuse, more than 4,000 people paid a half-dollar each. Barnum offered $50,000 for a half-interest; then he suggested that he would lease, and pay one-half of the receipts to Hannum and company. Refused in this third offer, Barnum hired a German named Otto in Syracuse to make a duplicate giant.

The marvel moved to the Geological Hall at Albany, where an important scientist decided that the stone in the giant was different from any found in New York State. (He was right; it was Iowa gypsum.) And so to New York's Apollo Hall, only two blocks from the place where Barnum was exhibiting his copy as the genuine Cardiff Giant and offering one thousand dollars if Hannum could prove that *his* was the original. At Boston, Ralph Waldo Emerson and Oliver Wendell Holmes were ushered into the solemn presence and had a hard time persuading Hannum to let them bore a hole in the giant's head. Ambiguously they were able to report it gypsum of genuine antiquity. Finally David sold the statue to a Syracuse photographer who was to pay $20,000 but who, failing to make a success as a showman, broke his contract. When David died, his papers revealed that the Cardiff Giant was stored in a vault in Massachusetts.

Just how much Hannum was fooled himself will never be known, but it is a fact that he was always proud of his connection with the hoax. One day he was riding on the D.L. & W.R.R. ("Delay, Linger, and Wait") when a dapper young man ordered him to move over on the seat. David continued to sprawl silently.

"See here," said the young man, "do you know who I am? My name is Sloan, and my father is President of this road."

"See here, young man," answered David, "do you know who I am? My name is David Hannum, and I'm the father of the Cardiff Giant."

The connection between banking, showmanship, and love of hosses is told in another York State story. Hachaliah Bailey, who imported a famous elephant into the United States in 1815, had a bank at Somers. Whenever there was a hoss-race, he declared a holiday. One day he received an irate note from Washington charging that an examiner had been unable to do his duty because he could not obtain access to the Somers bank. Hachaliah replied: "Any fool who expects me to keep the bank open when there are horse-races has no right to be employed at Washington."

If such a retort could come from a banker, we may pardon the dignitaries of the church for their interest in horseflesh. When Lucius Turner was ordained a Deacon in 1865 at Summer Hill Church (Cayuga), he was made to promise that he would never again trade hosses. At Catskill there was a scandal when Brother William Layman early one Sunday morning so far forgot his Methodist principles as to race his horse down Main Street—and made good his boast that his animal was one of the fastest in the County of Greene. Impenitent when rebuked, Layman was tried in an ecclesiastical court which acquitted him by a single vote of Benjamin Wiltse, who admitted that he was a lover of nags himself and declared that "even the trustee of a church wasn't to blame if his horse chirked up a bit when some old plug tried to pass him".

Out in Erie County in the early days a tender-hearted minister called "Father" Spencer was derided when seen leading his horse over a bad road. "See here, old gentleman," said a smart young frontiersman, "you ought to trade that horse off for a handsled; you could draw it a great deal easier." The good Father had different ambitions from those of a parson about whom Dr. Lester of Seneca Falls tells a story. The Reverend Mr. Josephus Krum liked a real "stepper" and promised to buy a horse from Dan Christopher if the critter would go a mile in three minutes. Tried on the track, the horse made the distance in the slow time of four minutes. Mr. Christopher remarked plaintively, "It's a queer business when a Reverend can't wait a minute". That reminds me of the story, told in various forms throughout the State, of the horse who dropped dead. The man who had just sold him remarked: "I dunno what to make of it: he never done that before."

In Otsego County they like to talk about the tricks of the pious but shrewd Quakers who were early settlers. The hero of one tale owned a horse which looked very handsome as it drove up to a crossroads store. The men around the cracker-barrel had heard a rumor that the Quaker's bay was for sale at a modest price. One of them stepped out to inquire.

"Is that the hoss you are selling?"

"He is, friend."

"Is he sound?"

"Is thee a horseman? Yes? Well, there is the horse. Look him over for thyself."

A hasty examination followed.

"Does thee see any fault in him?" asked the Quaker. "No? Well, then the horse will never see any fault in thee. The price is eighty dollars."

The money was paid immediately, and both parties went on their way rejoicing. The horse was delivered that day; next morning, the purchaser discovered that the handsome bay was blind, and realized the full meaning of the words, "Then he will never see any fault in thee." Ordinarily in York State the matter would have ended there, but in this case the rigor of the game was forgotten. The dupe threatened to report the Quaker to the Meeting of Friends, and got his money back. Not proper hoss-trading.

David Harum's opponent, the Deacon, had a counterpart in a North-Country *Ballad of the Deacon's Ox*:

> A truthful man was Deacon Slocum,
> Honest as the day was long;
> He would never let you catch him
> Telling anything that was wrong.
>
> The Deacon had a pair of oxen,
> And he could not make them work;
> The nigh-one was an awful good one,
> But the off-one was a shirk.
>
> The Deacon tried all sorts of projects,
> And that head of his was full;
> He said it did beat all creation
> When that critter didn't pull.
>
> A man called around to see the Deacon
> For to git a pair to work.
> The Deacon said, "I've been a thinkin'
> I would sell old Bright and Turk".—

"Can you recommend these oxen?"
Said the man who came to buy.
" 'Seems to me as if that off-one
Holds his head a little high."—

"Tell the truth and shame the devil,"
Popped into the Deacon's head;
So, stepping alongside the oxen,
He placed his hand on Bright and said:

"There, Sir, is an awful good one,
Better worker never stood;
And I cannot see why the off-one
Isn't equally good."

So the Deacon sold his oxen,
Got his greenbacks for the pair,
Shoved the roll into his pocket,
And went in and offered prayer.

When the fellow tried to work them,
People said he swore like sin,
Drove them back and told the Deacon
He must pay him back his tin.

"You told me that those oxen
Was perfection and 'ware,"
Said the man in tones of language
That would fairly curl your hair.

"My dear Sir," replied the Deacon,
"I think you misunderstood,
For I surely never told you
That off-ox was any good.

"I told you that the nigh-one
Was just as good as ever stood,
And I said I could not tell you
Why old Turk was not as good.

"And I surely cannot tell you,
For I never knew the cause,
But what prompted me to sell him
Was just because he never was."

Now ever since this little incident
That happened in my boyhood youth,
I always hold a high regard
For the man that always speaks the truth.

Then there was that Schoharie County man whose name began with
M. He had a horse but no harness. One day a neighbor came to him
with a harness which he was ready to trade or sell. Elated at the
prospect of realizing his ambition, Mr. M. traded his horse for the
harness. It was this same M. who always used a wooden poker for
his fireplace. He sharpened his forks to spear with—you mustn't use
them for anything else or you would cut your lip; the knives were
for "eating purposes".

A favorite song in eastern New York, crooned to the melody of
Reuben Reuben, was *Napoleon*:

I had a horse and his name was Napoleon,
All on account of his *bony part*;
He was raised by old Hambletonian,
Damned by all who him tried to start.

He was so thin you could peek right through him,
And his coat was as fine as silk.
I drove him around on my old milk-wagon;
When I wanted him to stop, I called out, "Milk!"

One fine day as I was out riding,
Along came a fellow with a rig so neat.
Says he to me, "Come on, my hearty,
Let's try a race right down this street."

Off we started, helter skelter;
I had a smile all o'er my face.
As sure as a sinner, I was coming out a winner
When he called out, "Milk!"—and I lost the race.

Down near the place where Hambletonian was raised, the people in the Newburgh region have a story about "Doc" Higby, who was as proud of his fruit as most Orange County men were of their hosses. One day he came tearing out of his house to rebuke a neighbor who had stopped his "rig" on the road to pull a few cherries.

"Nate, what are you doing there?" roared the Doc. "Don't you know those are my cherries?"

"Well—don't know but I have 's much right to 'em as you," answered Nate. "I've always heard that nobody in particular owns what is found on the high-road."

"Maybe that's so," said Doc. "There's some fine ones on that limb that hangs over the road. Why don't you climb up and pick 'em?"

Nate had just reached the coveted limb, when he saw Doc pick up the lines and drive off in Nate's rig. He roared for Doc to stop.

"That's my rig, and I want it. What are you doin'?"

Doc pulled up.

"You're mistaken, Nate," he said. "This is my rig. I found it in the road. Nobody in particular owned it, and *finders, keepers.*"

For those who drove hosses a century ago, there was the irritation of paying at the toll-gates on the high-roads. An old farmer in Oneida County objected so strongly to "shelling out" at one station on the Deansboro-Clinton road that in order to get to a village two miles away he would go round-about some eight miles. In Chenango County a more vigorous measure was taken by one of the citizens. The old turnpike to Catskill and Kingston had toll-gates every few miles and toll-bridges; it is still remembered that it cost thirty-two cents for a "rig" to go about ten miles. Mr. Samuel Lyon had two farms, one on either side of a toll-gate, and though by 1835 that part of the turnpike had fallen into disrepair, the keeper not only refused to improve the road but also refused to make a yearly rate. One morning, Lyon sent his son Seth with a team of oxen from one farm to the other, with firm instructions: "If you find the gate locked, hitch the oxen to a gate-post and pull it out." As a result of the lawsuit which ensued, the gate was removed.

The best of these toll-gate stories is told by an Englishman who visited York State in 1833-4. An unlettered man named Judge Sterling was appointed to arbitrate between settlers and squatters from the East. He put a chain across the road in front of his house on Sunday, and exacted toll for Sabbath travelling. One westbound Yankee demanded a receipt so that he would not have to pay another toll in that Central New York district. The almost illiterate Judge let him write the acknowledgment, and then painfully added a signature. At a store in the next village the Yankee traveller cashed his "receipt" which read, "Please to pay the bearer the sum of 100 dollars."

There is a favorite ballad of *The Kennebec Bite* (trick) which tells how a young Yankee outwitted another sort of foe on the highway:

> Near Boston there lived a mason by trade.
> He had for his servants a man and a maid.
> A Kennebec boy he had for his man
> And for to do his work—his name it was John.
>
> 'Twas early one morning he calléd to John;
> John hearing his master, he quickly did come.
> "Go take that cow and drive her to fair,
> For she's in good order and all I have to spare."
>
> John takes the cow out of the barn
> And drives her to the fair, as you shall larn.
> In a little time he met with a man
> And sold him the cow for a six pound-ten.
>
> He stepped to the tavern to take him a drink;
> 'Twas there the old merchant he paid him all his chink.
> He stepped to the landlady and unto her did say,
> "What shall I do with my money, I do pray?"—
>
> "Sew it up in your coat-lining, I think it the best way,
> For fear that you be robbed all on the highway."
> There sets a highwayman a-drinking of his wine;
> He says to himself, "That money is all mine."
>
> In a little time John started for to go.
> The highwayman followed after also;
> In a little time he overtakes John.
> "You are welcome overtaken," says he, "young man."

They rode till they came to a long, dark lane.
The highwayman says, "I will tell you in plain:
Deliver up your money without fear or strife
Or here I will end your sweet, precious life."

John seeing now no time to dispute,
He jumped off the horse without fear or doubt,
And from the coat-lining he pulled the money out,
And among the tall grass he strewed it all about.

The highwayman coming down from his horse,
But little did he think it would be to his loss.
Whilst he was picking the money that was strewed,
John jumped upon the horse and away did ride.

The highwayman called to John for to stop,
But little did he mind,—but away he did trot
Home to his master, and thus he did bring
A horse and a saddle and many a fine thing.

The maid stepped to the door to see John return.
She went to 'quaint her master that was in the other room.
He stepped to the door and says to him thus:
"The devil! Has my cow turned into a horse?"—

"O no—your cow I very well sold,
But, robbed on the way by a highwayman bold,
And whilst he was putting your money in his purse,
To make your amends I came off with his horse."

The bags were taken out, and out of them were told
Five hundred pounds in silver and in gold,
Besides a pair of pistols. He says, Jack, "I vow
I think, my good old master, I very well sold."—

"As for a lad, you have done very [rare],
Three quarters of the money you shall have for your share;
As for the villain, you served him just right,
I think you tucked upon him a Kennebec bite."

It is not an easy matter to get the better of a York State farmer. There was "Wit" (William) Cook of Hague, whose memory is cherished in Warren and Essex Counties. Shortly after a pack-peddler had got the better of "Wit" in what was thought an unethical manner, Cook's cat died. He skinned her and waited until the peddler called again one evening.

"Do you buy mink-skins?" asked "Wit".

"Yes," said the peddler, "I'll give you ten dollars for one."

Such was the reputation of the Cook family for honesty that the skin was bought at once and tossed into the peddler's cart. Next day the itinerant drove into the yard.

"Say," he called, "that fur you sold me wa'nt a mink-skin, it was cat."

"I didn't say it was mink-skin," answered "Wit". "All I did was to ask whether you bought mink-skins. Anybody will tell you that my old cat that just died was named Mink. I guess we are even."

"Wit's" reputation for honesty was well earned. One day he dropped into Orlando Ralph's store in Ticonderoga and asked how much they paid for hides. Fifty cents was named as the price, and the deal was closed. Then "Wit", moved by his conscientious desire to tell the truth, asked: "How much do you generally take off from the price for a hole in a hide? The hired man did the skinning, and he wasn't very careful." Mr. Ralph named ten cents as the usual discount. When six holes were found, "Wit" took out his purse and paid the storekeeper ten cents instead of accepting the half-dollar.

Long before America was settled there were stories about millers who got the better of their customers. In Chenango County they tell how a farmer tried to turn the tables. At Chenango Forks he went to the grist-mill to get a sack of flour; and while the miller's back was turned, he dipped a few scoops from an open bag into his own. Next day the farmer returned.

"Say," he said, "that flour you sold me was no good: my wife tried to make some bread with it, and the dum stuff wouldn't rise."

"I'm not surprised," said the miller mildly. "I didn't think the bread would rise when I saw you putting in that lime."

Sophronie wasn't too bright but bright enough. Through the streets of Watertown she wore all the clothes she could find handy, man's or woman's, adorned in summertime with dandelions and daisies. One day she entered a store to buy some blue calico. Not having cloth of the desired color, the clerk measured off the required length in red material. When it was wrapped up, Sophronie protested.

"I asked for blue."

"That's all right, Sophronie," said the clerk. "You can imagine it's blue."

Sophronie picked up the package and headed for the door.

"Say," called the clerk, "you haven't paid for that calico."

"That's all right," was the reply, "you can imagine I've paid."

The courts of pioneer days were schools of wit. There was Counsellor John Root, who brought his formidable talents to Buffalo in 1810, at a time when its inhabitants, as Timothy Dwight had recently remarked, were a "casual collection of adventurers". A Judge had decided a case against Root.

"This," said the Counsellor, "is equalled only by the memorable decision made by Pontius Pilate on a well-known occasion."

"Mr. Root," thundered the Judge, "sit down, Sir! You are drunk."

"That," retorted the lawyer, "is the only correct decision Your Honor has made the whole term."

A temporary presiding judge had demonstrated his thorough incompetence, and in characteristic fashion had covered his embarassment by an attack upon the lawyers.

"I wish," said His Honor, "that some way could be devised for shortening the lawyers' tongues."

"Perhaps, Your Honor," suggested the silken Counsellor, "the same object could be effected by shortening the Judge's ears."

At an old-fashioned "horning" or "shivaree", the father and brothers of the tormented bride had fired at the crowd guns loaded with peas, an act which prompted two or three to bring in a charge of wounding honest citizens. One rough and dirty fellow testified that he had been hit in the calf of the leg. Root insisted that he show the place.

"And that," asked the Counsellor, "is the place where the peas went in?"

"Yes, Sir."

"And when did the shooting occur?"

"About six weeks ago."

"O nonsense! If there had been any peas planted in that soil six weeks ago, they would have been four inches high by this time."

The old Justices of the Peace were a rich lot. Among the memorable characters of Chenango County was Justice Thompson of Kings Settlement, before whom a plea was brought that a citizen of that hamlet had shot a neighbor's dog. There were witnesses to swear that the defendant was seen with a gun that day, and everybody knew that the dog was dead. The plaintiff grew impatient while the Justice seemed lost in thought. Finally Thompson arose and announced his decision: "I do fine the plaintiff. I shot the dog myself. It needed doing."

Once at the height of a dispute over a hoss-trade Thompson pulled a farmer's beard, and soon found himself before another Justice to answer for an assault. When asked to state his side of the case, he looked at the farmer and said: "Was it your whiskers I pulled? I thought I had hold of the horse's tail."

On the other hand, some of those Justices must have been rather dull. At Springville (Erie) the droll Wales Emmons, counsel for the *defendant*, told His Honor that his client had decided to withdraw the case and pay costs. It was so ordered.

The lawyers were always ready to enliven a case with vituperation. In Columbia County two of the chief ornaments of the Bar were aroused to a high pitch which called for personalities.

"You, Sir," roared Elisha Williams of Hudson, "have enough brass to make a copper kettle!"

"And you, Sir," retorted Ambrose Jordan of Hillsdale, "have enough sap to fill it!"

Even betwen a lawyer and his client there might be a matching of wits. 'Rastus Hopkins of Otsego County agreed with lawyer Pomeroy that if he would collect a bill for him, 'Rastus would pay by cutting wood. The bill was collected, and 'Rastus split wood for about an hour. Then he appeared at Mr. Pomeroy's office door and said, "Well, boss, I've worked as long as you did; so we will call it quits."

Out in my County of Chautauqua, stories are told of the powers of vituperation possessed by William Newton of Jamestown. In summing up the Hidecker case in the town of Conewango, he spent an hour in denouncing Mr. Hidecker. Then he turned toward Mrs. Hidecker, who had been a witness. Shaking out his long black locks and pulling himself up as if for a supreme effort, Mr. Newton said: "Now, gentlemen of the jury, there is Mrs. Hidecker. God knows I wouldn't say a word against Mrs. Hidecker, but *God pity Hidecker.*" The speech was at an end.

Another story in the late Charles M. Dow's delightful reminiscences, *The Lawyers and Pettifoggers of Chautauqua County,* may end this account of lawyers' tricks and retorts. Oscar Johnson of Fredonia had a cow killed on the tracks of the D.A.V. & P.R.R. He put in a bill, which in due time reached himself as attorney for the railroad. He examined the law carefully, advised the company that it was not legally liable, and then sent in a bill for services large enough to cover the value of the cow. The honor of Bar and County was maintained, just as it was in an old court in Schoharie when Lawyer Nate pled with tears in his eyes that "Old Schoharie may not be disgraced by having a citizen sent to the State Prison"—and won.

There is a thin line between stories of the Bar and stories of the early church, because the Congregationalists and Presbyterians set great store by canon law, and cases of ecclesiastical discipline were frequent. I like an anecdote told me by a descendant of "Black" Sessions of Oneida County, a member of the Continental Congress as well as a Deacon in the Congregational Church:

In a time when provisions were very scarce, when they had little to eat but potatoes and salt, the good deacon saw a deer come out of the woods near his house late Sunday afternoon; he seized his gun and shot the deer. For this the church summoned him. He pleaded that it was both a work of necessity and a work of mercy, and that he was justified in killing game so providentially brought within range of his trusty gun, even if it were before sunset on Sunday. The church, however, instructed the pastor to read the sentence of excommunication on the following Sabbath. The deacon was asked to rise in his pew while the sentence should be read severing his relation to the church on account of Sabbath-breaking. He arose, and as the pastor was about to read, reaching behind him he took his gun, levelled it at the minister's head, and in the most deter-

mined tone commanded, "I forbid this paper being read from the pulpit."
The pastor quietly remarked, " 'All things are lawful unto me, but all
things are not expedient'; and I do not think it expedient to read this
paper." "Black" Sessions lived and died a member and deacon.

In Orange County they tell how love found a way to circumvent
canon law. At the age of sixteen, in the year 1700, Miss Sarah Wells
had come to the region in the care of three Indians to whom her
foster father somewhat rashly had entrusted her, together with his
livestock and his household goods. (The fact seems to be that he didn't
want his creditors to discover his plan to move from Staten Island up
the Hudson.) In a fine old stone house still standing this brave girl
was wed to an Englishman, the father of a numerous stock, William
Bull. Inasmuch as there was no church, no clergyman could proclaim
the banns of matrimony properly on three successive Sundays; but
when the wedding guests had arrived, a local magistrate, prayer-book
in hand, proceeded to the front door of the cabin and "proclaimed
the banns to the listening forest", then went to the back door where
he proclaimed to the cattle and outbuildings, and finally, returning to
the front door, proclaimed the banns once more to the forest. Canon
law had been fulfilled, and the issue of William and Sarah Bull was
blest.

Another of Mr. Moffat's tales of Orange County gives a picture of
folkways and presents a variant of a type of trick frequent in our
lore. It concerns the great dispute in the Goodwill Presbyterian
Church of Montgomery:

When the building was first erected there was no provision for heating
it, though two services were held in it every Sunday, both summer and
winter, and many of the congregation rode from ten to twenty miles to
attend them. Every woman who came was provided with a foot-stove in
cold weather, a box of perforated tin, enclosed in a wooden frame in
which was an iron saucer filled with live hickory coals. On their arrival
they would report first at the tavern on the opposite side of the road, and
when the men were thawing out in front of the huge fire-place, the women
would replenish their foot-stoves. As the services were separated by an
hour's intermission, the entire congregation would again adjourn to the
tavern where each woman and child was provided with a glass of "flip"
while the minister was given a separate room and a glass of "toddy". In

the pastorate between 1776 and 1815, someone suggested that it would
be a good plan to install a stove to mitigate the temperature of the church
as stoves were then quite a novelty and just coming into use. Forthwith
two parties arose. The pro-stove party won. The next Sunday after the
stove was installed was bitterly cold. The anti-stove party upon entering
the church snuffed the hot air the w,omen loosened their wraps, some
laying them aside altogether, while the men removed their overcoats. One
man sat through the services in his shirt-sleeves. One woman overcome
by the terrific heat fainted and had to be carried over to the tavern to be
served with a glass of "toddy". At intermission it developed that the pro-
stove faction had not built a fire in the stove, as they were afraid of
setting the building afire with the new-fangled thing.

A special type of tale concerns the Baptists, whose rite of immersion
has always provided amusement to a population which respects
deeply the denomination that founded Colgate, the University of
Rochester, and Keuka College. A story is told in Otsego County of
a "contrary" citizen of Roseboom named Charlie who was converted
at a revival and wished to be baptized. In those days the church had
no baptistry; the rite had to be performed down by the bridge in
the Cherry Valley Creek. When Charlie's turn came, his son elec-
trified the congregation by shouting to the minister: "Don't let loose
of him; but if you do happen to let him go, look for him upstream—
he's too damn contrary to go down."

The clergy were almost always respected, not only for their piety
but also for their learning. Now and then, however, you come upon
some such *fabliau* as the following, from Otsego County:

A farmer whom we shall rename James Sharpe had a big lot of hay
down, all cured and ready to set in the barn. In the morning it looked
as though there would be rain before night. Sharpe's wife had gone to
pick berries in the upper lot near the woods. About nine o'clock in the
morning came a minister who stopped and asked if he could get permission to pick berries in the upper lot.

"Well, Elder," Jim drawled, "I don't believe there are enough berries
up there to pay for your time. Now I am short of help, and I want to
get this hay in before it rains. If you don't mind, I'll give you five dollars
to help with the hay."

Being a thrifty man, the "Elder" accepted the offer, and they worked
hard and steadily, getting the last load into the barn just before the rain

commenced. Jim gave the Elder his five dollars—with many thanks. Not long afterwards, some of Sharpe's neighbors asked him if he wasn't rather liberal with his money, to pay the Elder five dollars.

"Wal," he said, "I would rather have paid him *ten* dollars than have him up in that berry-lot all day with my wife."

The wily ambiguity of the Quaker hoss-trader has already been exhibited, but while we are in Otsego County let me tell another brief tale—of how the Quaker got rid of a balky horse. He was able to assure the purchaser that the horse was sound, but when he was asked whether the animal was "good to pull", he stood on one leg and then on the other and finally devised an answer which sold the horse: "O, thee would be pleased to see him pull at a load!"

Other retorts and sayings of the religious are cherished by the folk. There was that earnest believer at West Kortright (Delaware) who urged his friend to attend Meeting: "You know, Sammie me man, if a person don't go to church, what the hell does he amount to?" It was a man in the same village who excused a neighbor's swearing, "Lizzy, we must remember that he could never have got to heaven with all those cusses *in* him". Then there was the remark of Spraker of Spraker's Basin who, when lightning struck the church, refused to rebuild: "If God chooses to strike His own house, why should I build it up again for Him?" And there was the macabre request of an ex-minister in Westchester County, that he be buried in a pine coffin. When his friends asked the reason for this desire, he replied, "So I can go through hell a-snappin' and a-crackin' ".

This anecdote is told about others. A somewhat similar request was made by the jovial eccentric, Dr. John Jakway, pioneer of Cato Village (Cayuga). He asked that he be buried under a nut-tree in an upright position, with his skull sticking out of the ground so that boys could crack the nuts on it. He was buried standing up, but entirely underneath the ground.

War too has had tricks and retorts cherished by a citizenry which endured more than its share of the fighting which founded and preserved the nation. That was an excellent stratagem of Aunt Sally Gee of what is now Highland Falls (Orange). When news came of the burning of Fort Montgomery, she began to fear for the loss of her most cherished possession—a half-pound of tea. To frustrate the haughty invaders she brewed the entire half-pound in her old pot, only to discover that the resultant beverage was too strong even for such a sturdy patriot as Aunt Sally. With her belongs Goodwife Osborne of East Hampton on Long Island, who was baking a noble berry pudding one day when redcoats from Bridgehampton started on a foraging expedition. Bent over her work, the Goodwife heard a British sergeant's voice at her door, "Hurrah, boys—just in time— come on!" A charming ballad by Miss Fannie Elkins asserts that the Goodwife retorted briefly, "O no, you're not!" She ran through the open door and, to the consternation of a hungry file of soldiers, hurled boiling pot, pudding, and all down a steep hill into the sand.

> And all East Hampton villagers
> Are proud of Pudding Hill.

Even the solemn dignity of George Washington was lightened when he came to York State. "Stopping" in the Davis house at Tarrytown, he was delighted by the innocent blunder of a boy who called him Mr. Washtubs. A lady in Croton has a letter from the General to one of his commanders who had complained that he was troubled by desertions. Washington replied: "Be sure that any soldier who deserts dismounts. We cannot afford to lose the horses."

In western New York, for tricks of battle we have to be content with stories of the War of 1812, such as two which Mr. C. P. Turner told in *The Pioneer Period of Western New York*. One of these concerns the "easiest victory of the war"—an incident in the defence of the arsenal at Petit's Run, two miles below Tonawanda. The "arsenal" was just an old log house defended by a few volunteers. Hearing horses and men coming up the river, they got out a dilapidated, one-horse lumber-wagon and trundled it over a corduroy bridge, making a thundering noise like artillery, and roaring such commands as "Bring up the cannon!" Again and again the wagon was brought back noiselessly through the mud, to bounce again over the bridge. The approaching troops halted and sent out scouts. When the outlooks from the two parties tremblingly approached one another, they discovered by the uniforms that they were both on the same side.

Then there is the story about Dr. and Col. Cyrenius Chapin, who ranks with Joe Ellicott, Red Jacket, and Counsellor Root as one of the four most colorful figures in the frontier village of Buffalo. Volunteering to lead a few men in reconnaissance, he and his companions were captured by Indians, taken to prison at Niagara, and after three weeks put into two rowboats for transportation to Little York (Toronto) in Canada. Their British captors made the Americans provide a "white-ash breeze" by doing all the rowing. After a few miles of hard pulling the American leader requested that the other boat be brought alongside and all refresh—Americans and British—from a five-gallon keg he had been courteously permitted to bring with him into exile. Again and again the ceremony was repeated, while Colonel Chapin anxiously wondered whether he had not underestimated the ability of British troops to drink American whiskey.

The sun was low. Chapin, feigning fatigue from rowing, inquired how much farther he had to go. Handed a spy-glass, he could make out the village of Little York which, even if he rowed slowly, was only a few hours off. He suggested another drink. Just as the two rowboats met for the refreshment, the American prisoners suddenly arose and conquered their guards, who were immediately put to the oars and ordered to head for Fort Niagara on the American side. At daylight Colonel Chapin found himself within sight of his destination. Quite naturally the British Lieutenant who had been tricked felt disgraced, but the Colonel assured him that he should have the same privileges promised the Americans the day before—the freedom of the yard to play ball and pitch quoits. Nothing was said about American whiskey.

That reminds me of Red Jacket's farewell to the American Colonel Snelling: "May you be a Governor and have one thousand children. And above all, wherever you go, I hope you may never find whiskey above two shillings a quart".

The rigors of that war were increased by the appallingly bad roads of a time when passengers on coaches really "went on foot and carried a rail". It was in the New York State of that date that a favorite American tale perhaps originated—at any rate, a historian of Erie County claims it as belonging originally to Evans. Floundering along the boggy road, a traveler picks up a hat, only to be rebuked by its owner who has been invisible underneath in the mud.

"My dear Sir," says the first traveler, "won't you permit me to help you out?"

"Thanks, no," is the reply. "I don't feel that I should leave my horse, who is underneath me, traveling on hard ground."

Allied to the tales about war's tricks are the stories about the mimic war of local politics, and particularly about the long-drawn-out campaigns to determine the location of *county-seats*, as we call the shire-towns when we are not showing off. Of these stories I like the account I had from Mr. J. B. Achilles of Albion of how his town triumphed over its neighbor, Gaines. When in 1824 the new County of Orleans was cut off from Genesee County, rivalry came to a boil. Gaines was larger and older; it was on the famous Ridge Road and consequently accessible by land. Albion was nearer to the geographical center of the County, on the Oak Orchard Road and the Canal. Gaines had no water-power. Albion had two sawmills on the west bank of Sandy Creek; in spring when snow melted there was water enough to operate, but in summer, when the Commissioners were coming to determine the county-seat's location, the creek was almost dry. Yet water-power might turn the decision to Albion.

Philetus Bumpus, Nehemiah Ingersoll, and other Yankee fathers of Albion decided to try guile. For days before the Commissioners arrived, water was held back behind two dams, whose flumes and gates had been carefully repaired. As a successful inn-keeper, Philetus prepared a noble feast to be drenched in all manner of spirited liquors. The Commissioners arrived, were wined and dined, and in misty felicity headed for the creek, where teams had been set to hauling logs just before the banquet ended. The mills were started, and when the Commissioners arrived, no busier scene could have been observed west of Rochester. Fortunately the Commissioners did not linger; before the water was drained, they had returned to the inn to vote Albion the County-Seat.

That war had a sequel. In October of 1838 the village of Gaines declared its financial independence from its old rival by opening the Farmer's Bank of Orleans, complete with vault. By December of 1840 its circulating notes amounted to the total of $106,626 in "red-backs"—currency issued by these so-called "free banks". It was decided by the older Bank of Orleans at Albion to declare war upon an institution which was draining its profits. Luck decided that in 1841 the State of Indiana, in whose bonds the Gaines' bank had invested, defaulted payment of interest, forcing the Farmer's Bank to call in its "red-backs" in the face of the depreciated value of its reserve. Deliberately the Albion bank began a run upon its competitor, forcing it to close. Meanwhile the citizens of Gaines had joined in the war; enraged farmers brought in their notes of the Bank of Orleans, agents collected others throughout the county, and then the lot would be presented with a demand for specie at the Albion bank. During the run, the institution daily received thousand-dollar boxes of silver half-dollars; these with great piles of "cartwheels" (silver dollars) were piled up behind the counter in plain sight, only to melt before the assault of the embattled farmers of Gaines, who hurried back home to exchange the silver for more notes on the Albion bank. Batavia and Rochester were intimidated from giving full aid to Albion by citizens of Gaines who demanded that such assistance be withheld, giving as convincing argument the sight of thousands of dollars of Batavia and Rochester notes which might be used to demand specie-payment. "But all would not do." Banks farther east sustained Albion, and the war was lost by Gaines after one of the most stirring battles in the annals of our counties.

That love too has its tricks our folk know well. There is the story of a venerable political leader of Westchester County who was unfortunate enough to outstay the welcome of his girl's parents; the mother even stalked downstairs and stated plainly that she was not going to have Jim burning her midnight oil. Next night, Jim appeared with a lamp in one hand and an oil-can in the other, to announce defiantly at the besieged door, "Now, by gosh, I can burn my own midnight oil and stay all night if I have a mind to." It was probably in the pursuit of the same gal that Jim went to a revival meeting and was kneeling with one eye open when a male acquaintance prodded him *a tergo* with a hatpin.

"O my God!" cried Jim in anguish.

"Halallujah!" answered the evangelist. "Another soul proclaimed for glory!"

Quite another type of swain is described in a story from the other side of the Hudson at Warwick (Orange):

A Miss H., the hard-working daughter of a local farmer, had a most persistent beau who wanted to make every night beau-night. He was a farm-boy who worked hard too; so as soon as he got Miss H. on the parlor sofa, he would put his arms around her, whisper sweet nothings for a while, and finally go to sleep. The young lady soon wearied of this behavior; and one night when her faithful swain fell asleep, she stealthily disengaged herself from his embrace, put the churn in his arms, and went to bed.

Frequently I come upon the story of an apparently scurvy trick played by a husband who traded his wife for a gun. At Oneonta the tale is told about a certain Hugh Houghtailing of long ago. When asked about his "dicker", Hugh replied: "It's a fact, and I'm pleased to say that the shotgun kicks less'n my wife did." This belongs in the cycle with the observation of a farmer near Downsville (Delaware) who said: "Before I married Louisa I loved 'er so much I used to tell 'er I could eat 'er, and now, b' God, I wish't I had!"

In an older and simpler day the purchase of a wife may not always have seemed funny; and the fact is that in this very pupil age there is at least one matrimonial agent in Oneida County who will provide for ten dollars a mate for any lonely and respectable Adirondack guide. One of the customers paid high compliment to this arrangement. Said he, in his grave, untroubled manner: "I've traded with the man twice, and both times the woman was perfectly satisfactory. My first wife was all right, but she happened to die the first winter; so what did the honest feller do but let me have another for only five dollars."

Life plays few tricks upon the serene folk of the mountains. Neighbors like to remember that a certain woman at Horicon called her husband Amasa to breakfast one morning, and then observed mildly, "Why, you're dead!" When for the first time she saw a deer-head mounted, she remarked: "If I'd knowed about it, I'd a had Amasy fixed that way."

After reading this collection of tricks and retorts from the lore of hoss-traders, tollgate-tenders, farmers, lawyers, churchmen, revolutionary dames, warriors, politicians, bankers, and lovers—after all these examples you might say: "That is the sharp Yankee strain." As a matter of fact, however, the Trickster tale is a staple in the folklore of practically all races and peoples. Before a white man walked our woodland paths the Indians were telling such tales; in Professor Stith Thompson's great collection called *Tales of the North American Indians* (1929) the third chapter is devoted entirely to Tricksters. In York State, in addition to the gory tricks of the Injun-fighters and their foes, we have a number of stories of less sanguine combat, of which the most widely known has been connected with the name of nearly every famous Iroquoian chieftain in the eighteenth century. Because it is the earliest appearance of this popular tale which I have been able to find, I give the version found in *Funny Stories: or the American Jester*, published in 1804 at the shop of Christian Brown, New York:

Soon after Sir William Johnson had been appointed superintendent of Indian affairs in America he wrote to England for some suits of clothes richly laced. When they arrived Hendrick, king of the Mohawk nation, was present and particularly admired them. In a few succeeding days, Hendrick called on Sir William and acquainted him that he had had a dream. On Sir William's enquiring what it was, he told him that he had dreamed that he had given him one of those fine suits he had lately received. Sir William took the hint and immediately presented him with one of the richest suits. The Indian chief, highly pleased with the generosity of Sir William, retired. Some time after this, Sir William happening to be in company with Hendrick, told him, that he had also had a dream. Hendrick being very solicitous to know what it was, Sir William informed him, that he had dreamed that he (Hendrick) had made him a present of a particular tract of land (the most valuable on the Mohawk river, of about five thousand acres). Hendrick presented him with the land immediately, but not without making this shrewd remark: "Now, Sir William, I will never dream with you again, you dream too hard for me."

For explanation of this tale it must be understood that among our Indians the dream is sacred and often prophetic; Sir William would know this, of course, and would not act contrary to Indian folkways. The late James Fenimore Cooper, grandson of the novelist, in telling me this tale about Johnson and Red Jacket (instead of Hendrick) expressed his belief that the story is based upon some real occurrence, for he had seen on an old map what was listed as a Dream-Tract. When the story is told of Conrad Weiser, the Palatine who acted as interpreter and liaison officer with Indians, it is said that the chief Shekallamy dreamed that Weiser gave him a rifle, which was given; that Weiser dreamed that the Indian gave him an island in the Susquehanna (Que); and that the chief in presenting the island said, "But Conrad, let us never dream again!"

Another tale concerns a white man sitting on a log. In our favorite version of western New York the white man is Joseph Ellicott, surveyor of Buffalo, and the Indian who sits down beside him is the wily orator and civil chief of the Senecas, Red Jacket. Three times the Indian says, "Move along, Joe," and each time Ellicott complies, until he is at the end of the log. When the request is made for the fourth time, Ellicott says, "Why, man, I can't move any farther without getting off the log into the water." Red Jacket replies: "Ugh! Just so white man. Want Indian move along—move along. Can't go farther, but he say move along." The tale is particularly appropriate when applied to these two heroes, for Joe was the representative of that Holland Land Company which coveted the territory of the Senecas. The story is told of other pairs: in one version the Indian is Chief Oun-di-a-ga of the Onondagas arguing with an unnamed white land-agent; in another version Conrad Weiser is the hero and the Indian is not named. The tale has even migrated from the State: recently I found it in *The Christian Almanac for the Western District*, 1830, where it is told about General Lincoln and a Creek Indian.

King Hendrick was not the only Mohawk who tried the trick of dreaming. It is said that when Molly Brant of that nation was living at Fort Niagara during the Revolution, she attempted to have a prisoner executed. She announced to the British commandant, Colonel Butler, that she had dreamed that she had Colonel Stacia's head, and that she and her Indian friends were kicking it about the fort. Butler ordered a small keg of rum to be painted with a man's head on it and given to her. Soon she returned with the same dream, except that this time the Yankee's head had a hat on it. Butler gave her another keg of rum but warned her that no dream would permit him to surrender Stacia to the Indians.

Molly's brother, Joseph Brant, is the hero of a tale sometimes given to Red Jacket—whom Brant described as a coward and a "Cow-Killer". The famous Jemima Wilkinson, who claimed to be an incarnation of the Spirit of Life from God, came with great pomp to a treaty-making convention. Brant addressed her in three Indian dialects and, of course, received no reply. "Madam," he said to her in English, "you are not the person you pretend to be. Jesus Christ can understand one language as well as another."

Of course, the way in which Indians were tricked into selling lands for almost nothing is the chief scandal of our annals. When citizens of Rochester tell you the history of their handsome city, they sometimes recall that after the Revolution a Massachussetts Yankee named Phelps, who got an incredible bargain in real estate, asked and received from the Indians as a gift enough extra land for a "mill and mill-yard" at those falls of the Genesee which made Rochester the "Flour City". Accustomed as they were to Yankee bargains, the Indians must have been surprised to learn that the "mill-yard" extended from Avon to the mouth of the river—a strip which our older antiquaries estimate as twelve miles wide by twenty or more miles long. The whole transaction was fantastic. By the Hartford agreement of 1786, Massachussetts was admitted to have a "pre-emption right" to a large part of western New York, by which was meant the first right to purchase from the Indians. Two years later, Massachussetts sold these rights to Oliver Phelps and Nathaniel Gorham for a million dollars. Gorham proceeded to buy from the Indians some 2,600,000 acres for five thousand dollars cash and five hundred dollars annually forever.

Now and again you hear of the Indians trying to over-reach the Yankee traders. Captain Pratt, store-keeper in frontier Buffalo, was respected by the Senecas so much that he was given the name of *Hodanidach*, "Merciful Man"; but at a time when beaver-skins were bought by weight the red brothers would sometimes manage to put a little lead into the dead animals' claws. Finally the Captain clipped off the claws with his hatchet before weighing, saying that he would make proper allowance for them. If the Indian objected, the Captain picked up the claws and offered to weigh them separately. Only once was the Merciful Man in danger—when he flogged Peter Gimlet for stealing meat. Some three hundred Indians drifted into a semi-circle before the store; their chief, Farmer's Brother, asked for explanation of the indignity; all listened gravely to the testimony of the Merciful Man and his little daughter; then Farmer's Brother rendered the tribal decision—that Gimlet was a bad Indian, that the Captain might flog him again, and that the thief was banished by the Senecas.

A recent trickster tale comes from Cattaraugus County regarding King Tandy (Tahadondeh), a Seneca Indian, wise in folklore and woodcraft, who died a little before the Great War.

It was reported to officials that the King had been dynamiting fish in the Allegheny River, a practice of which the game wardens disapproved. Consequently, one of them, a Mr. X., hoping to prove the charges, set out to learn the truth. Late in the autumn, he went to Tandy, telling him that he was a stranger from Buffalo and begging to be taken fishing on the river. However, the Indian was on guard and assured his visitor there would be no fish at that time of year. Pleadingly, X. reasserted that he had come all the way from Buffalo and couldn't bear the disappointment of returning without at least making an attempt. At last he prevailed, and King Tandy condescended to take him out in the boat.

For a long time they angled unsuccessfully, until finally the Indian said, "I know how to catch 'em!" Bringing forth a small stick of dynamite, he asserted, "That'll kill 'em!"

Then he struck a match several times on the oar, but he couldn't seem to light it. "You try," he suggested, handing X. a match. Obligingly, the unsuspecting warden tried; and, surprisingly enough, he was at once successful. Next, King Tandy handed him the dynamite, and the warden lighted the fuse.

But King Tandy's next remark proved he was nobody's fool. "X.," he said shrewdly, "you can now do whatever you're a mind to with that stick. If you hold on to it, you'll be blown up. I can jump in and swim ashore."

It didn't take the warden long to decide to throw the dynamite into the water. King Tandy then calmly gathered in the fish which the chagrined X. had killed.

When the Indian and the white start calling each other tricksters, they might remember the retort of an old Indian woman in that same County of Cattaraugus: "What for you call me Humpy? Humpy yourself! I'm just the way the Lord performed me."

The arts and wiles of David Harum have not perished. Out in Almond, almost on the county line between Allegany and Steuben Counties, the last days of August see a famous meeting of old-time

hoss-traders. There you can count three hundred or more horses attended by men in boots laced to the knees, corduroy trousers, flannel
shirts, and slouch hats. In 1936 posters sent out through New York
and Pennsylvania offered "free parking, free pasturage, free shade".
Most of the "swaps" involve no money, sometimes five or ten dollars.
In 1937 the officials decided that auto-swapping should be barred
as "not good ethics". The first President of this group told a reporter
that he was "dang near the best horse swapper in New York State";
after his re-election he announced that if David Harum should arise
from the grave and attend, "someone would have to lead him around
by the hand". The watchword, we may guess, is David's: "Do unto
others as they would like to do unto you—and do it first."

VIII: Whalers

"No sea, but what is vexed with their fisheries—no climate that is not witness of their toils." Edmund Burke's tribute to the American whalemen should be remembered specially by Yorkers. Governor Dongan, who gave our first two cities their charters, said in 1686: "New York and Albany live wholly on trade with the Indians, the English, and the West Indies. We send to England mostly beaver, whale oil and some tobacco." At the height of Sag Harbor's glory it was said for that famous port on Long Island that she had only three kinds of men: "those who were away on a whaling voyage, those who were just returning from one, those preparing to start on one." A homespun poet wrote a string of verses that tell the story; here are a few of them, quoted from that golden book called *Whale Off*, written by two members of the famous Edwards family in whom the traditions of harpoon and lance still live:

> This chosen retreat
>   Was the home and the seat
>   Of the bold and adventurous whaler;
> And for years had supplied
>   To the world far and wide
>   The model American sailor.

For no maiden would look
  On a young man who took
    To a land life of torpor and stupor,
When the scene was here laid
  Of the *Sea Lion's* raid
    Of our national novelist, Cooper.

In these prosperous years
  It had shipyards and piers
    And coopers and riggers and caulkers,
Ship chandlers, sail makers,
  And ship biscuit bakers,
    And the whalemen then known as Montaukers.

Herman Melville says in *Moby Dick* that "islanders seem to make the best whale-men". It was certainly Paumanok, Isle of Shells, and the far eastern stretches of its one hundred and twenty miles that turned hardy English farmers into men renowned in song and legend. The Yorkshiremen who founded Southampton in 1640 and the Kentishmen who settled East Hampton in 1649 certainly came to Long Island with no thought of whale-oil and baleen; but the storms on the "south fluke" of the great eastern tail washed up leviathan, and the Shinnecock Indians could show the art of the wooden harpoons in off-shore fishery. When the Red Men sold East Hampton in 1648 for twenty coats, twenty-four hoes, and other goods, they specified that they were to have the "fynnes and tayles of all such whales as shall be cast up, and desire that they may be friendly dealt with in the other parte". I hope that they had their wish. It is evident that their skill was used to profit the whites, just as the Mohawks' craft in hunting was the source of Albany's wealth.

The settlers kept a sea-watch that lasted for more than two centuries. In March, 1644, the Town of Southampton was divided into four wards, with eleven persons in each to watch for stranded whales. When a carcase was discovered, the whole community profited. After the white men had learned to follow the example of the Indians and engage in off-shore whaling from boats, stations were set up along the coast, some miles apart, with boats, harpoons, lances, and furnaces for trying out the blubber. Hence arose the practice of raising a *weft* whenever a whale was sighted, followed by the stirring cry of *Whale Off!* In earlier times, the weft seems to have been a man's coat waved from a pole; later it was a flag, sometimes the Stars and Stripes. Even Mr. Lion Gardiner, first lord of the manor on his little isle where Captain Kidd buried treasure, joined in with the minister of East Hampton in watching for whales, but their gentility saved them from the noisome task of "cutting-in", and presumably from taking turn-about at the trying-vats, which, as Melville later remarked, "smelled like the left wing of the day of judgment". In return for this recognition of their superior station the two gentlemen agreed in 1662 that they would "give a quart of licker apeece to the cutters of every whale, and be free from cutinge". This community interest was carried so far that even the school-children realized that from December to April, in the whaling season, they would have a holiday so that everyone could concentrate upon the chief occupation of East Hampton. The holiday is specified in a contract of 1675, where the teacher's salary is put at "fortie Shilling a month and his Dyet". There was a time in that town's history when the salaries of minister and schoolmaster were paid in whale-oil and bone.

Long Islanders like to remember that when the people of Nantucket wished to learn the true art of whaling, they made an agreement, dated June 5, 1672, to bring to their assistance as instructor one James Loper of East Hampton, where whaling had been an organized industry for some twelve years. Loper was a member of prominent Dutch families: his father was a councilman at New Amsterdam, and his mother was a daughter of the patroon, Cornelius Melyn, who owned most of Staten Island. For some reason Loper did not venture to that other famous island of whalers, perhaps, as is suggested in *Whale Off*, because he was busy in his deliberate Dutch assault upon the heart of the first Lion Gardiner's grand-daughter, Mistress Elizabeth Howell, who succumbed to his importunity two years later. Mistress Elizabeth deserves well of folklorists in her own right: it was shortly after her birth that her mother died exclaiming that she had been bewitched. Suspicion fastened upon Goody Garlick of East Hampton, who, as I have told in another chapter, was taken to Connecticut for a trial in which she was acquitted. As for Nantucket, bereft of Loper's direction it managed to achieve such reputation that even Yorkers now think of it as the headquarters of whaling—thanks partly to a Yorker named Melville. As a matter of fact, we have some right to claim both the whaling islands of chief renown; for several years Nantucket was supervised by the Governor of New York.

Until the early part of the eighteenth century, Long Island was content with shore-whaling, her output of whale-oil rising to 4,000 barrels by 1707; but in the early part of that century short voyages were attempted into blue water, preference being still given to the so-called right whales—the sort that came close to shore. Here it had better be said that the right whale is the one who has the "Venetian blinds" in his mouth, the whale-bone or baleen. He is toothless and comparatively slow, though monstrously large; unlike the great sperm whale, the cachalot of *Moby Dick*, he cannot take a mariner or boat between his crunching jaws, but he can smash it to kindling wood with a flip of his mighty *flukes*, his tail.

One personality of that first century of whaling from Long Island remains in the folk-memory. Samuel Mulford (1645-1725) was a forerunner of the American Revolution; he revolted against the mismanagement and corruption of the Royal Governors. The whale was a Royal Fish—he happens to be a mammal—and the Kings were within shadowy rights in disposing of these creatures wherever found. I have read—and doubt a little—that at one time old Trinity Church was given supposed rights to all whales washed up in the Province of New York. At any rate, the Governors attempted to license and tax the industry, and the Long Islanders objected. In 1711, Governor Hunter—whose name for other reasons is still a stench among descendants of the German Palatines—decided that whale-oil should pay a royal tax and that all whalemen should be licensed. Mulford fought in the Assembly, tooth and nail, and even published his remarks. He was expelled from the legislature in 1715 and immediately reëlected, only to be expelled again in 1720. In that latter year, however, Governor Burnet remitted the tax on whale-fishing, and Mulford's visits to London had probably been the chief reason why even the fuming Hunter had backed down. The old Mulford house in East Hampton, built in the 1660s, still stands beside the one sacred to *There's No Place Like Home*, the Payne house. As I said, there remains in the folk-memory something of the forerunner of John

Wilkes the protester, though he seems to be known now chiefly for his nickname, "Fish-Hook Mulford".

One of my students has had the privilege of living in East Hampton with Miss Hannah Mulford, from whom was obtained what amounts to an official statement about the fish-hooks:

When I was a little girl, my grandfather used to take me on his knee and tell me the story about "Fish-Hook" Mulford. His real name was Captain Samuel Mulford, and he was a great-great-uncle of mine. He was one of East Hampton's earliest whalers. Grandfather said that he was also one of Long Island's earliest political reformers, but I don't believe a Mulford would stoop so low as to follow that profession. Anyway, I do know he pleaded the cause of Long Island whaling because he thought it was a custom that would be important to the third and fourth generation. And so it was.

Why they called him Fish-Hook Mulford? Well, grandfather always said that he was an awful cautious man. One year he took a trip to England, and he was so afraid of pickpockets there that he had his pockets sewn with fish-hooks so they wouldn't get picked.

The belligerent spirit of Captain Mulford continued to the Revolution, when Patriots used whaleboats with swivel-guns to cut off supplies from the British ensconced in New York City. There is the story of what was known as the Battle of Long Island. On May 21, 1771, Lieutenant-Colonel Return Jonathan Meigs set out from New Haven with two hundred and thirty-four men in fifteen whaleboats, and I have never understood how he packed them in either, for a whaleboat is intended for six men. Anyway, he went ninety miles by land and by water within twenty-four hours, and in that time killed five and captured fifty-three of General Delancy's Brigade, then destroyed eleven sloops with supplies for New York, killed a Captain and captured forty sailors—and so home to New Haven with his prisoners, having lost not a single man himself. Believe it or not.

From the close of the Revolution, the name of Sag Harbor became more and more important in the saga of whaling. It was a port of entry from 1788, and it is said by Long Islanders that in 1790 it actually had more tons of square-rigged vessels in foreign commerce than New York. The towns famous for off-shore whaling lacked harbors for larger vessels, but Sag Harbor could accommodate the ships of 500 tons that were being used by those who went round the Horn to hunt in Pacific waters for Moby Dick. It is said that the first Sag Harbor whaling vessel that made this trip was appropriately named *Argonaut*; in 1817 Captain Eliphalet Halsey sailed in her, returning in twenty months with 1700 barrels of sperm-oil. Thereafter the term of deep-sea voyages lengthened until men signed on for as long as four years.

In its Golden Era, Sag Harbor had sixty-three vessels engaged in whaling, though meanwhile New Bedford had pulled far ahead of the other whaling ports. It has been estimated by Dr. E. P. Hohman that in 1847 there were about 900 whaling vessels in the entire world, of which the United States owned some 722, ships or barks, ranging from 200 to 500 tons. In that year New Bedford claimed 254; Nantucket, 75; New London, Connecticut, 70; and Sag Harbor, 62. Whale-oil was used for illumination and in the curing of leather; whale-bone was used in women's clothing (corsets, basques, hoop skirts, bodices, and hats), for the ribs of umbrellas, for carriage whips, and even (when scraped) for the stuffing of furniture. There was money in the business for the owners of ships and their captains; the people of Sag Harbor like to remember that Cooper not only saw the romance of whaling but was part-owner of the ship *Union*, whose captain, Jonathan Osborn of Wainscott, sat for the portrait of Long Tom Coffin, and whose sailors inspired the story of the *Sea Lions*.

Whether the whaling was from a vessel—as it usually was in the Golden Era—or from shore, the method was practically identical for two centuries. The whaleboats, now found only in such museums as the ones at Sag Harbor, East Hampton, and New Bedford, were beautifully shaped, ordinarily twenty-eight feet long and six feet wide, sharp at both ends. Each was equipped with a mast, sprit, and sail. In the front sat the so-called Boatsteerer or Harpooner, pulling the harpooneer oar of fourteen feet, with his back to the whale until his Boatheader "called him up" to fasten to the whale. After he had hurled his harpoon, sometimes two of them,[*] he went aft to tend the

---

[*] Captain E. J. Edwards, who revised this paragraph, explained that the first iron is on the main towline; the second iron is on a running bowline attached to the main towline.

towline round the loggerhead and to man the steering-oar, while his Boatheader went forward to give the whale the *coup de grâce* with a lance. Next to the Boatsteerer in the front was the Bow-oarsman, with an oar sixteen feet long; his duty was to furl the sail and unship the mast when commanded to do so. Third was the Midship-oarsman, with a seventeen-foot oar. Fourth was the Tub-oarsman, with an oar seventeen (or sixteen) feet long; he had the duty of coiling the line. Fifth was the Stroke or Leading-oar, with an oar fifteen or sixteen feet long. Last was the Boat header, usually a Captain or Mate, managing the great steering oar of twenty-three or twenty-four feet until the whale had been struck by the harpoon, when he went forward to dart his lance—sometimes as far as fifty or sixty feet. The harpoon was eleven feet long, including a three-foot shaft and an eight-foot pole; the lance was fifteen feet long, including the five-foot double-edged shank which a good whaler could sink, all five feet, into the whale.

It is no wonder that the lore of the "Montaukers" still, like Moby Dick, "sheds off enticings". The far, high cry of the watchers aloft, "Thar she blows, and sparm at that!" The rush of preparation and the order of the Boatheader, "Spring ahead!" The approach of six men over a tumultuous sea to a vast creature two or three times as long as their boat. The order for reverse, "Hold water!" The glitter of the harpoon. Then perhaps a "Nantucket Sleigh-ride" behind the creature at thirty miles an hour, or the descent of the whale to the depths below as he "sounded". The danger from a huge rising bulk, or from a line that smoked as it ran from the tub around the loggerhead and out through the chuck in the bow. The crashing oars, the high smudder of foam! We shall always remember these as long as men love the contest of skill with force, of courageous intelligence with blind bulk and power.

Even off-shore whaling for the toothless right whale had its thrill and its legends. One of the best recent adventures in the telling is the accident to Cap'n Gabe Edwards, now hale and active at ninety-three. When Cap'n Gabe was ninety, a student went to see him for me, to get an account of this experience. It is similar to the story told in *Whale Off* from a nephew's point of view, and yet it differs sufficiently to be interesting:

When he was forty-one years old, he had a frightening experience. The surf was heavy, and a northwest wind was blowing. Only one boat went to meet the whale, with six men aboard. "Spring ahead!" was the command to row toward it. "Hold water!" meant *halt*. The surf was so rough that when the latter command was given the boat did not stop, but continued to move until it was right on top of the whale. Uncle Gabe said: "Well, the master told me to go ahead, so I put two harpoons into him while we were still on him. Now there's where I made a mistake. If I had to do it now, I'd put only one in him, orders or no. You see, the whale doesn't get sore at the first one, but boy! at the second he begins a-fighting! This one thrashed his tail something fierce. Before we had time to stern off, he broke two oars.* We thought by the cracking and the snapping the boat was in pieces. When the smudder cleared away, they found the boat all right. But I didn't. I was stiff as a mackerel, laying on the water, thirty feet away. The whale had struck both sides of the boat, broke two oars, knocked me out, without scratching the boat! When they hauled me in, they thought I was dead; and probably I would be if a sea hadn't broken right on my chest, staved my lungs in. As it was, I was unconscious for two days. They tell me the first thing I said then was, 'Where's that whale?' And they had to disappoint me: they'd let him go. By Cod!"

Not all of the adventurous escaped. In the Oakland Cemetery at Sag Harbor is a shaft representing a ship's mast, shattered at the top; at the bottom is a coiled hawser. On the face of the stone below the mast are a harpoon and a lance, and beneath them the representation of a sperm whale who has just struck a boatload of men, some of whom are clinging to part of their smashed and overturned boat. An inscription contains the names of half a dozen shipmasters, with their age at death—not one older than twenty-nine. On the east side is the legend:

To commemorate that noble enterprise, the whale fishery; and a tribute of lasting respect to those bold and enterprising shipmasters, sons of Southampton, who periled their lives in a daring profession, and perished in actual encounter with the monsters of the deep. Entombed in the ocean, they live in our memory.

* He also knocked two other oars out into the water, but Captain Gabe didn't see that part.

One of the gallant lads here commemorated is Captain R. S. Topping, twenty-eight-year-old master of the *Thorn*, who "died in the Atlantic ocean"—how spacious that is!—with all the crew of the boat which he headed. One version of his mysterious legend is that he stayed in his craft beside a supposedly dead whale while the rest of the boats returned to his ship. When they returned to where they thought he had been, the sea was blank. Then some of them remembered that several miles away they had noticed white water about his boat but had assumed that it must be the whale's death-flurry. The other version is that Captain Topping fastened to the whale before the other boats got near, and the whale sped away in the fog; stubborn as he was brave, Topping refused to cut his line, and followed his prey to his own doom. His position was not so picturesque as that of Uncle Rance (Rensselaer) Conkling, last seen in 1845 bound out to sea on the back of a whale. You begin to edge over into fantasy here, I suppose; Mrs. Rattray reminds us that in 1818 there was a sworn statement made about a fight between a sperm whale and a sea-serpent.

It is hard to draw the line between fact and folklore when you are dealing with such large critters. One of the whalers who scorned inaccuracy was Robert Coffin of Dutchess County, whose *Last of the "Logan"* is a vivid account of deep-sea whaling in the era of Melville's *Moby Dick*. Here is one incident which has puzzled me:

One day we lowered the boats for quite a large one [a school of whales], but in some way they became alarmed; so we chased them, and the mate's boat struck and fastened to a calf. He bellowed with fright, but immediately the whole school gathered around him, and the boats all pulled hard to catch up and get one. Suddenly a large whale, (old whalemen said it was a young bull), reared its head above water and made straight for the line of the mate's boat fast to the calf, with its enormous jaws open. When he reached it, he bit it right in two. Then we tried an old whaling trick: we all began to yell and pull hard to catch up at the same time. The effect was singular. It did gally (frighten) them, for they all stuck their heads out of water and swam slowly just ahead of us, but they didn't let us get near enough to strike. Pulling at such a rate, we soon tired out, and they got away. It was a singular sight to see those big heads bobbing up and down, and the action and feat of that young bull was remarkable, showing that aquatic animals have some kind of a thinking apparatus.

This much of the marvelous a landsman is willing to accept, but there was Joe Burke's story which flies in the face of the pretty well established fact that no whale can "breach" or jump entirely out of water. Joe claimed that he saw a whale breach up in the air and over a boatload of men with oars a-peak. His audience took this for a moment in silence and then sent for a Long Island specialist in cussing to tell him just how colossal a liar he was. That story was surpassed by one which apparently started with Prentice Mulford of Sag Harbor, scion of a great race of whalers, himself once a popular humorist writing under the pen-name of Dogberry and later a founder of what is now called New Thought. Mulford was in a boat ripping through the ocean after a whale, on the fastest Nantucket sleighride he had ever enjoyed. Looking behind him, he saw a shadowy craft following at practically the same speed, though he was aware that no other boat had been near when the whale was harpooned. Looking more closely, he realized that the critter had pulled Mulford's boat so fast that it had slipped out of its own coat of green paint; the paint was the phantom. In confirmation it was gravely stated that the hair had been blown off three of the boatmen, and a fourth had lost his eye-lashes. I fear that this is to be classified with the common as-surance of whalemen that off Cape Horn it blows so hard that it takes two men to hold one man's hair on. That anonymous author of *The Wonderful Whalers* was right when he said:

> Strong are those daring fellows,
> Doubtless, the harpoon to throw;
>   And—to judge from what they tell us—
>   Stronger still to draw the bow.

Few whalers had the inclination or the talent to write out the story of their adventures, true or fanciful; Robert Coffin, who wrote for his family fifty years after his wreck on Rapid Reef, was an excep-tion. But if you are patient, the scenes unroll in numerous logs pre-served in museums and attics. Usually these are devoted chiefly to giving the bearings, prevailing winds, and account of whales caught— the latter frequently indicated by conventional inked illustrations

made with stencils which distinguished between types of whale. It is
a great day when *two* pictures are drawn. Every now and then, you
come upon drama. Here are some entries from the log of the *Nimrod*,
Captain Erastus Barns:

Sunday, July 15th, 1833. Saw 2 black fish lored and Chased with out
Success. People Employed in taking Care of our vegetables. So ends all
well.

Friday, 16th August. Portuguese fell over board out of the Chains.
All hands was Called on boat directly, and with the Smiles of the All-
mighty Saved him.

Saturday, 9th November. Saw severall whales and chased hard. Struck
2, in the course of the day but lost boath of them drew from one and
the other staved the boat.

It was a voyage without "greasy luck"—little oil being taken. We
can imagine the Captain's feelings as he reached home waters at Ram
Head.

When I saw the Pilot and Agent Approaching the Ship I observed to
my first officer that the worst of the voyag was yet to come. Po The
devil Said he Carry a Stiff upperlip.

What a difference there was between this master's feelings and those
of Captain Maltby Cartwright of Shelter Island, who planned a
voyage of three years beginning in 1844, and at the end of six months
was so heavily laden with his lucky catch that he decided to return
home. Coming past Montauk he killed two more whales. The barrels
were filled with oil—what was to be done? He sailed proudly into
Sag Harbor with huge pieces of blubber from his last catch hanging
in the rigging.

Now and then the logs show that mates and masters were not so
hard-boiled as novelists have stated. To be sure, the Long Island
ships were probably luckier in obtaining decent crews than the ones
from New Bedford which, unable to find Yankee boys of Massachusetts in the era 1840-60, sharked up a lawless and inexperienced
crew that would hardly appeal to the pride of any officer. Here is an
entry from the log of the *Washington* of Greenport, Robert N.
Wilbur, Master:

Thursday, 26th October, 1837. Awful to relate . . . At 11 o c one of our crew while in the Act of furling the jib was plunged into the water no more to return on board the ship was laboring very hard at the time and passed directly over him A boat was lowered instantly but before she arrived at the fatal spot he sank to rise no more his name was Thomas Hudson a Sprightly lad 16 Years of age and well beloved by the whole ships company

This is the tender side. You are not to suppose that the stronger emotions were never expressed. I like the disgust with which George Edward Dean, mate of the *Caleb Eaton*, records the bad luck which he had on Sunday, July 18, 1880:

Commences fine wind from the East and pleasant weather at 8 a.m. saw spirm whales lowered two Larboard Boats. The L.B. [larboard boat] struck Boatsteerer got hurt broke Three Oars took line and let out to windward for God sake it was good bye whale

These logs are so numerous that I sometimes wish that we could trade them at the rate of ten logs for one good chantey. To be sure it is somewhat unreasonable to expect to collect whalers' songs at this late date, because the few whalers left alive are almost all men who engaged in *off-shore* whaling in the winter months, and, as Charlie Baker remarked, "The fishermen at Newfoundland used to sing while they unloaded their boats, but we didn't—it was too damn cold". Now and again a Long Islander keeping the log of a deep-sea cruise would include a favorite ballad. For example, the log of the bark *Timor*, 1849-1852, has an excellent version of *The Burning of Schenectady*; the log of the *Tuscarora*, out of Cold Harbor, 1839-40, has *Gaily the Troubadour* and a fair version of *The Wreck of the Albion*— a favorite among sailors of all sorts. Except in books I have been able to get very few chanteys (work-songs) and other songs about whaling.
Here is a chantey which Sally Logan of Sag Harbor got from "Old Man Cuffee", a man of Indian blood who died last year (1938) at the age of eighty-two.

> Oh Sally Brown of New York City,
> *Ay, Sally—Sally Brown,*
> Of pretty Sal this is a ditty.
> *I'll spend my money on Sally Brown.*

Oh Sally Brown is a white man's daughter,
   Ay, Sally—Sally Brown,
And Sally isn't what she orter.
   I'll spend my money on Sally Brown.

Miss Logan says that her father recited to her this fo'castle song of *The Coast of Peru*:

Come, all ye bold seamen who are scarsting [cruising] for sperm,
Come, all ye jolly, bold seamen who have rounded Cape Horn,
For our Captain has told us, and we hope he says true,
That there's plenty of sperm whale on the coast of Peru.

The first whale that we raised, it was late in the day,
Which caused our bold captain these kind words to say,
"Get ye down to your hammocks and there quietly lay;
We'll raise him in the morning at break of the day."

'Twas early next morning, just as the sun rose,
That a man at the masthead sang out, "There she blows!"—
"Where away?" cries the skipper, and the answer from aloft,
"Three points on the lee bow and about two miles off."—

"Then call up all hands and be of good cheer;
Get your lines in your boats, and your tackle-falls clear.
Hoist and swing fore and aft; stand by, each boat's crew.
Lower away, lower away, when the mainyard swings to."

Now the captain is fast and the whale has gone down,
And the chief mate lies waiting his line to bend on.
Now the whale has come up, like a log he did lay,
It can never be said that he gave us fair play.

While the sailors were weighing anchor, they sometimes sang *The Sailors' Alphabet* as a capstan chantey. Unfortunately, Mr. Mortimer Corwin could remember only part of the song:

A is the anchor that ships from the bow,
B is the bowsprit that puts from the prow,
C is the capstan we merrily go round, and
D is the derrick that throws us all down.

Sing hi-derry, ho-derry, hi-derry dong;
Give sailors their grog, and there's nothing goes wrong.
E is the ensign that floats from the forepeak,
F is the foretop
G is the gasket we merrily pass round, and
D is the derrick that throws us all down.
Refrain.

Mr. Corwin, who used to live in Bellport, often heard the old captains on the South Shore sing *Round Cape Horn*:

I asked a maiden by my side
Who sighed and looked at me forlorn,
"Where is your heart?" She quick replied,
    " 'Round Cape Horn".

I said, "I'll let your fathers know",
To boys in mischief on the lawn.
They all replied, "Then you must go
    'Round Cape Horn".

In fact, I asked a little boy
If he could tell where he was born.
He answered with a mark of joy,
    " 'Round Cape Horn".

There is a chapter to be written some day about the maidens and wives whose men went 'round Cape Horn. It is remarkable how many of the adventurous men survived two or more spouses. At Oakland Cemetery, Sag Harbor, the grave of Captain David Hand, surrounded by those of five wives, is ennobled by this epitaph:

Stranger, perceive as you pass by
How thick the partners of one husband lie.

Often the unmarried girls must have wished for some such object of worship as the bust of Hercules, an old ship's figurehead, now at Hampton Bays. On its pedestal is this legend:

This is the strong god Hercules
His mighty tasks he did with ease
One yet remains

Womankind to please.
The maid who kisses his mighty cheek
Will meet her fate within a week.
The one who presses his forehead
In less than a year will wed.
No maid nor matron ever taunted Him
With refusing what she wanted.
Though hewn of wood and patched with tin
To all the Gods he is akin
And the spirits of them all
Hover over his pedestal.
So whisper what you wish the most
Fair maid, it's yours, and ——

　　　　　　　　　　　　the cost.

There is one old song about the ladies and Cape Horn which I found at the Grosvenor Library in Buffalo. It is in *The American Songster*, published at Providence in 1807; so it is a little difficult for me to claim it for the York State whalers. The best I can do is to remind you that Providence was near Long Island, and that the songster turned up in a York State library. In the last stanza, you find a reference to the old joke about married men growing horns when their wives are unfaithful.

CAPE HORN

As you mean to set sail for the land of delight,
And in wedlock's soft hammock to swing ev'ry night—
If you hope that your voyage successful should prove,
Fill your sails with affection, and your cabin with love.

Let your heart, like the main-mast, be ever upright,
And the union you boast, like our tackle, be tight.
Of the shoals of indiff'rence be sure to keep clear
And the quicksands of jealousy never come near.

If husbands e'er hope to live peaceable lives,
They must reckon themselves, give the helm to their wives;
For the evener we go, the better we sail,
And on shipboard, the helm is still ruled by the tail.

> Then list to your pilot, my boy, and be wise;
> If my precepts you scorn, and my maxims despise,
> A brace of broad antlers your brows may adorn,
> And a hundred to one that you double Cape Horn.

Up to this point, I have been speaking as if all the York State whaling had been done from Long Island, where it began and ended; but as a matter of record it should be said that many a cachalot was harpooned by men whose vessels sailed from the Hudson River towns. The city of Hudson—the first one chartered (1785) after Albany and New York—though it is one hundred and fifteen miles from the ocean, has upon its seal a man with a harpoon astride a whale's back. At one time, the entire jaw of a whale used to stand on the principal street (Warren); it is said that a favorite way for a naughty child to escape its mother's vengeance was to slip into this hidie-hole. When the English traveler Winterbotham reported his American travels in four volumes published in London in 1795, he said that Hudson could boast the most rapid growth in the United States except Baltimore—the city was planned in 1783, some houses were built in 1784, and within three years the town had 1500 souls.

The principal Yankee settlers of Hudson were Quakers, mostly whalers, driven from Nantucket by the British destruction of their industry during the Revolution. Perhaps the "first family" of old Hudson was the Coffins, descendants of "Old Tristum" Coffin, founder and first chief magistrate of Nantucket. I like specially the stories told about Cap'n Alexander Coffin, who arrived at Hudson in 1784 and rose to be the new city's mayor. It has been claimed that he commanded the ship which brought to America the news of our treaty of alliance with France; at any rate, he was an able, honored, and belligerent person who seems a perfect type of the great race of whalemen. He believed in direct methods, even in politics. When party strife began to agitate his little city, he stated that since the Federalists had begun it, his own party, the Democrats, should end it. He therefore made the serious offer to be one of twenty Democrats to meet twenty picked Federalists and fight the matter out, once and for all. Nobody seemed to accept the challenge except a dog—of which party we cannot know—who darted between the Cap'n's legs just as he was about to vote. Unable to locate his assailant, the Cap'n leaped to his feet and roared, "Come on, I can whip the whole damn lot of you!" Upon another occasion, when some matter was in hot dispute, a young man laid his hand upon Coffin's shoulder and asked him to step to the door. Misunderstanding the object of this request, the Çap'n cried, "Yes, sir—fist or pistols—don't care a damn which!"

Under the direction of the Coffins and other seafaring folk, Hudson became a port noted for shipping; in 1786 its citizens already owned twenty-five vessels. Some of these were used for the seal-fishery, some for general traffic, a few for whaling. In 1829, an association decided to make a real bid for oil: with anxious hearts they despatched the *Alexander Mansfield* in June of 1830, hoping that she might prove a lucky forerunner of a new fleet of whaling vessels. Nine months later she returned; even though it was Sunday when she dropped anchor, she was received with a discharge of cannon. The enthusiasm was justified: her lading consisted of 2,020 barrels of whale-oil, 180 of sperm, and 14,000 pounds of whale-bone—alleged to be the best cargo brought in by an American whaler during that year. So the fleet was built, and the people of Hudson developed the plan of having a "mother ship" attended by smaller ones. When this mother ship was filled, she was sent back to Hudson; the others remained until they also had a full cargo. Success continued for several years, but, for reasons which I cannot guess, the last whaler left the dock at Hudson in 1845—fifteen years before the golden era of Moby Dick closed.

Similar accounts might be given of whaling from Poughkeepsie and Newburgh, though Hudson will always have the reputation of being the chief river-port for our whalers. Even Long Island whaling was doomed. The gold-fields of California called the adventurous; within two years, 1849-51, no less than 250 men left the little whaling town of Southampton, Long Island, for the new lure in the west. Many returned disappointed, but the days of whaling were drawing to a close. In 1859 oil was drilled in Pennsylvania, then in Allegany County, New York. In 1860 there were a half-million barrels of petroleum; next year, two million barrels. The chief use of whale-oil, for illumination, was over. To be sure, a few vessels still headed round the Horn after the last whaler, the *Myra,* sailed away from Sag Harbor (1871); off-shore whaling continued and dwindled until 1918, when the last right whale was captured at Long Island. Whaling today is pretty much in the hands of Scandinavians who sail to Antarctic waters in steamships as large as Atlantic liners, drop steam hunting boats which carry cannon shooting a harpoon weighing 150 pounds, and slaughter whales by the hundred. One vessel in 1929 killed 1,306 whales which yielded a cargo valued at more than three million dollars.

What is left of the adventure which is one of America's chief legends? Stories and songs, logs and museums; a few valiant old men, and a salty dish of words. The authors of *Whale Off* have preserved and used part of this vocabulary. A man who is wild to go, not afraid of anything, is *rank*; if he loves his work and seems born to it, he is *fishy*. A *mug-up* is a snack to eat. *Waking* a whale preserves an old English meaning—watching; in this case, you watch his *slick*, which is the slight ooze of oil he leaves behind on the surface of the water. The old-time Long Islander speaks of *lines*, not reins (but so do many Yorkers inland); he *makes fast* instead of hitching; he *heads* or *steers* even when on land. When the watcher for whales waved his coat as signal, he was *making a weft*; upstate we should not recognize that phrase. The beautiful hand-carving in the ivory of a sperm whale's teeth is *skimshaw*; elsewhere, particularly on Nantucket, you would be more likely to hear it called *skrimshaw*.

It is curious how these old phrases and words remain in whaling families. In Dutchess County, the family which gave us the memoirs of Robert Coffin (*Last of the "Logan"*) left Nantucket before the Revolution and for the most part have not been seafarers since that date. Yet they will ask you hospitably to "scull up your chair to the table"; and if they are brought up shortly, they will observe that they have "fetched up with a wet sail". If they are tardy, they are "behind the lighthouse". If they are "all in", they are "all stove up"; on Nantucket they would probably have said that they were "fin out"—referring to the dying gesture of the whale rather than to the state of the whale-boat. The Coffins advise you "not to look a gift-cask in the bunghole". If they inquire after a friend, they say, "How is Jim carrying sail?" Their *hurricane deck* is a high shelf.

How brightly this driftwood of the whaling days still burns! That is my comfort when I admit how little at first hand I know about the subject of this chapter. I like to recall a story that I found in an old Sag Harbor newspaper: Shortly after the War of 1812, Colonel Huntting bought the *Octavia*, a whale-ship "about as shapely as a fish-box", with no copper on her bottom and nothing else to help her slip through green water except her barnacles. She didn't cut the sea; she pushed old ocean ahead in a heap. People on the South Shore of the Island knew for a week when she was coming: the water that she shoved caused a high tide and a pounding surf. Yet she had greasy luck, and she made so many v'yages that she learned the way to Brazil Banks and back. All the crew ever did was to get her outside Montauk Point, put on what sail was thought needful, make the helm fast, and go below. Three months later, by Cod! she was right in among the whales off Brazil! On one voyage outbound she picked up a piece of driftwood, pushed it down to her favorite hunting-ground, and brought it back under her bow. There has been some clumsy pushing in this chapter, but we are back at the Island—a good place to be.

IX: *Plain Sailors*

And a fine day it is," said Blind Sam. "I can see well enough to
know that. I remember you well enough, and your grandfather, old John Thompson. He had the prettiest cart I ever
saw, but he would neither give nor sell it. It would have been just the
thing for my fish. I couldn't buy it now, even if he was alive, and I
suppose he is not, unless he is a hundred and ten. I'm ninety myself
and was just making a piece about it in case they should give me a
stone." Sam stood up and cleared his throat:

> Here lies the bones of Samuel Taylor.
> In early life he was a sailor.
> He sailed the world three times around
> And fortunately has not been drowned.
>   (*But damn near.*)
> But his sight got dim, he could sail no more;
> He finally landed safe on shore.
> He's growing old and the end is nigh,
> He's on the county farm to die.

"As you say, there is no hurry. Old John Thompson, cart and all,
was in no hurry. You don't know where the cart is? It makes no odds.

I've seen many changes, most of all in myself. You may remember
that I would sometimes take a little too much? Well, sir, seventeen
years ago on the twelfth of May—and I was only seventy-three—I
says to myself one morning, 'Sam, here it is nine o'clock and you
haven't had a drink'. So I dropped into a place at Dunkirk where they
ignored the Prohibition Law, and I had one. It tasted bad. I stepped
down the street and tried another. It tasted worse. Says I, 'Sam, I
believe you've lost your taste for it.' I haven't had a drink since, that
you could call a drink—a bottle of beer now and then. I made a piece
about it, like one I heard long ago after I saw Lincoln lying at Buffalo. (I tried sailing the Lakes after that.) Well, here's the piece—
some of it mine and some of it somebody else's, like all the songs we
made at sea; this is Samuel Taylor up-to-date:

> "Samuel, you look healthy now,
>   Your dress is neat and clean,
> You're never drunk about the streets.
>   Tell us where you've been.
>
> "Something must have happened;
>   You used to look so strange.
> Has MacClelland preached a sermon
>   Has brought about this change?"
>
> No, it was a voice, a warning voice
>   That Heaven sent to me,
> To take away the slavish curse
>   From want and misery.
>
> My money all was spent for drink,
>   I was a wretched view,
> I'd almost tired all my friends
>   And tired their patience too.
>
> For when I'd get arrested,
>   And in drunken stupor lay,
> And brought before Jim Prendergast
>   Without a word to say,

And when he read the sentence,
　And would take no fine or bail,
The only thing was left for me
　Was *ninety days in jail.*

My friends with me grew weary,
　I was unhappy then;
I tired all their patience
　By getting drunk again.

Had this have been misfortune's end,
　How happy I'd have been!
But health with wealth declining,
　Dr. Seymour was called in.

He looked at me so serious,
　And answered me so plain,
"You've wrecked your constitution, Sam,
　By getting drunk again."

So in every heart there's some good
　Hidden in the dark,
If man would only take the pains
　To fan that vital spark.

So let this be a warning,
　Reflect while you have time:
It's folly to be jolly
　In drinking too much wine.

Sam stopped and looked thirsty; I felt that I should say something.
"You fool them all, Sam. They are all gone: Judge Prendergast
and Doc Seymour and the Dominie."

"They are," Sam agreed. "Maybe responsibility is what killed them.
I used to say to Dr. MacClelland, 'Reverend, you preached a grand
sermon on Sunday; I can give you all the headings of it. It ain't your
fault, but it didn't do me a damn bit of good.' He would say, '*How
do you know, Sam?*' He hadn't gone to sea at twelve as I did.

"Was I ever wrecked? Why did you boys always ask that? To hear

the song, eh? Well, yes, I remember one song about a wreck. I heard
it in a Scotch port, but it's about an American ship; I wasn't in her, but
I think this song is fact." Sam stood up again and clasped his hands.

> "Come all you jovial seamen
>> And listen to me,
> Till a dreadful story I relate
>> That happened at the sea.

> The wreck of the *Albion* ship, my lads,
>> Upon the Irish coast,
> And all her passengers and crew
>> Were most completely lost.

> It was on the first of April
>> When from New York we sailed;
> Kind Providence protected her
>> With a sweet and pleasant gale,

> Till along about the twentieth
>> A storm there did rise,
> When the raging billows loud did roar
>> And dismal were the skies.

> 'Twas on a Sunday afternoon
>> The land we chanced to spy.
> At two o'clock we made Cape Clear,
>> And the sea run mountains high.

> The outward winds began to blow,
>> And heavy squalls came on,
> Which made our passengers to weep
>> And seamen to mourn.

> All prudent sail we carried then
>> To keep her clear from land,
> Expecting every moment
>> Our vessel she would strand.

Our foresail it was split, my boys,
   And foreyard took away,
Our mainmast by the deck was broke
   And mizzen swept away.

Our captain was washed overboard
   Into that boundless deep,
Which made all hands which were on board
   For to lament and weep.

We lashed ourselves then to our pumps,
   Most dreadful to know,
And many a gallant soul, my lads,
   They overboard did go.

We had a lady fair on board,
   Miss Powell was her name,
Whose name deserves to be engraved
   Upon that list of fame.

She wished to take a turn at the pumps,
   Her precious life to save;
No sooner was her wish denied
   Than she met with a watery grave.

All night in this condition
   We were tossing to and fro;
Till three o'clock next morning
   We were in the midst of woe.

Full twenty-seven men on deck,
   Each with a broken heart,
When the *Albion* struck against a rock,
   And amidships she did part.
      (*Oooooh my Gooooood! It split her right in two.*)

Our passengers were twenty-nine
   When from New York we sailed,
With twenty-five brave seamen
   As ever crossed the main.

Full fifty-four we had on board
When first we did set sail,
And only one escaped that wreck
To tell that dreadful tale.

So now that noble vessel,
The *Albion*, she is lost,
Through that tremendous ocean
She so oft-times had crossed.

Our noble captain, he was lost,
A man and a seaman bold,
And many a gallant life was lost,
And many a heart made cold."

This ballad and the one about *James Bird* always made Sam's eyes wet. He blew his nose and accepted congratulations. Bill Welch was trying to pick out the modal melody, but Sam assured him that any one of four tunes would do and not to bother.

"The fact is, boys," he said, "I never advised you to go to sea. And you didn't go. But I wasn't thinking of the wrecks. I was thinking of shipmasters like old Bully Host* and the way he used to treat us lads. A nice man on shore, mind you, but a black devil at sea. That time out of San Francisco ——

"I was steering—though I wasn't an able seamen. We had known from the minute we came on board that there would be hell to pay. The Old Man made every member of the crew lay his bag down on the deck, and then Host, he runs up and down on the bags with his heavy boots. That was to prevent our bringing drink aboard, he says, grinning. Well, as I say, I was steering. The Old Man swaggers up, and just as he comes beside me, he sees the young Swede. There's always one like the young Swede aboard. A fine-looking lad but mouthy. He had been complaining that he wasn't getting his pint and his pound—that's the way we called the legal rations. Somebody was making money on us.

" 'You, Swede,' says the captain, 'I hear you have been complaining that you haven't been getting your pint and your pound.'

* I have changed the name.

" 'Yes, sir,' says the Swede, knowing in his heart that the old devil Host was the one who made the money by starving us.

"The captain looks at him long and slow.

" 'Is your watch up?' says the captain.

" 'It is not, sir,' says the Swede.

" 'Then up to the mizzen top gaffs'l,' says the captain, 'and see what you can see.' (I think that was what he said; I don't remember the old names for things well, but he was sending him a hundred feet in the air.) Host stood there grinning till the Swede was aloft. Then he turned on me.

" 'Sam, you raynick!' he bellers. 'Where are you heading for?'

"I answered polite, giving my direction. We were headed for China.

" 'Why, damn you for a raynick,' says he, 'you're headed for San Francisco! Put her up in the wind!'

"I saw what he was about then; and he saw that I saw, and pulled out his revolver. I put her up as he said. The ship swung sharp and heeled as she turned. The Swede spun from a hundred feet aloft into the sea.

" 'Sam, you raynick,' says the Old Man, 'where are you headed? Do you want to take us to San Francisco?'

" 'Man overboard, Sir,' says I.

"He grinned and pointed his revolver. 'Put her back,' says he, 'or I'll be short *two* hands.'

"I swung her back—and we left the Swede alone in the sea."

We were quiet for a while. Then Bill said, "Sam, what is a raynick?"

"It's an expression," said Sam.*

"What happened to Captain Host?" I asked.

"We said nothing till we came home that voyage. Just outside San Francisco a feller came on that always asked whether the crew had any complaints. We had a committee ready for him. They kept us shut up for a long time till they could try Host. Oooooh my Goooooood, I wish I had some of the food they gave us! That's all of that story."

"No, it isn't," said Bill. "What happened to Host?"

"Oh, Host," said Sam. "They gave him a fine berth ashore with bigger pay than ever. A very nice man ashore was Host, though I've

---

* Possibly the Dutch slang-word *roinek*, "red neck."

asked myself whether he said his prayers. He did things he ought not to have done."

"That sounds Episcopalian, Sam," I said.

"I don't claim to be an Episcopalian," said Sam. "Just a Christian that sings songs to people. But I have got a prayer. I made it up for myself, in a manner of speaking—like the piece about my drinking. (Queer how thirsty I used to get when I sang to people.)"

Sam stood up again. His shoulders were rounded a little, but he gave the impression of being undefeated. His accent was refined, with a true cadence and love of words. He didn't shut his eyes.

"O Lord," he said, "teach me that sixty minutes make one hour. Teach me that sixteen ounces make one pound. Teach me that one hundred cents make one dollar. (Sailors never learn that.) Grant that I may lie down with a clear conscience, unhaunted by the faces of those to whom I have brought pain. Grant that I may do as I would be done by. *Deefen me to the jingle of tainted money and the rustle of unholy skirts.* (I haven't heard the jingle often, but I know about the other.) Blind me to the faults of others but reveal to me my own. And when I have done with this unfriendly world—not always unfriendly—let the ceremony be brief and the epitaph simple: *Here lies a man.* Amen."

We went through Sam's dormitory, very clean, with old men staring like silent penguins. Bill went to get the car. I kept thinking about Sam blowing the fish-horn; Sam selling shoestrings in summer, pretending to be stone-blind; Sam in that mine-explosion; Sam looking at the dead face of Lincoln; Sam treading the decks—*Sam, you raynick!* We were outside in the early autumn haze of the Chautauqua hills. You could almost smell the Westfield grapes over the ridge.

"Thanks for the pipe," said Sam. "Tell Mrs. Douglas I liked the peaches; she is a lady. They take care of us here all right. I used to slip away in summer, and they always let me come back. There's no disgrace in poverty, they say, but it's damn inconvenient. Next time I'll sing you *The Cumberland's Crew.* That cart of John Thompson's was the prettiest I ever saw, but he wouldn't part with it. We all have something we won't part with."

Bill was ready. I hated to leave Sam.

It is not only from such old tars as Sam that I have been able to collect songs of the sailors. Just recently two chanteys came from one of the Adirondack Counties, Jefferson. How those two work-songs drifted up to the mountains I cannot say:

>As I was a-walking down Paradise Street,
> *Hey, hey! Blow the man down!*
>A pretty young damsel I chanced for to meet.
> *Give me some time to blow the man down.*
>
>Says she to me, "Will you stand treat?"
> *Hey, hey! Blow the man down!*
>"Delighted," says I, "for a charmer so sweet!"
> *Give me some time to blow the man down.*
>
>Blow, my bullies, I long to hear you,
> *Blow, boys, blow!*
>Blow, my bullies, I come to cheer you.
> *Blow, my bully boys, blow!*
>
>Yankee ship's gone down the river,
> *Blow, boys, blow!*
>And what do you think they got for dinner?
> *Blow, my bully boys, blow!*
>
>A dandy-funk and donkey's liver,
> *Blow, boys, blow!*
>Then blow, my boys, for better weather,
> *Blow, my bully boys, blow!*

In the little songsters sold throughout the state a century ago and more, ditties about the sailors were numerous. One such book whose covers and title-page are missing contains the "doleful perjury" of *Handsome Harry*, who "delighted pretty maidens to betray". He ruined Ruth and took to the sea.

>So wretchedly with her own garters
>She hung herself upon a tree.

Her ghost followed Harry to his ship, where, in spite of the Captain's desire to shield him, the specter had her revenge:

> Then she took him by the shoulders,
>   And plung'd him down into the main,
> Into the midst of the foaming sea,
>   Where he never rose again.

The ballad is skimble-skamble stuff not worth mentioning if it were not for the parody of this theme that inspired another song: *The Ghost of Polly Rock and Her Two Bantlings:*

> When I was but a tiny boy,
>   And sailed on board a privateer,
> Three dreadful ghosts did me annoy,
>   And to my sight did oft appear!
> A woman tall, who, on each arm,
>   A little, pale-faced bantling bore,
> And cried, "O Sam, we'll do no harm,
>   For we alas! are no more!"
>
> "The Captain of your ship," she cried,
>   "My love and truth did sore betray;
> And these poor babes with me have died,
>   Who might have lived another day!"
> "Dear ghost," I said, "all this is hard,
>   If Captain Rock be such an elf;
> While I am watching on my guard,
>   I think you'd better tell himself."
>
> She took the hint—down slid the ghosts
>   To where the Captain slept below;
> She drew his curtains to the posts,
>   And pale she gazed as drifted snow!
> "I'm come," she cried, "bold Captain Rock,
>   To plague thy heart our ghosts are come;
> Full cold I am as marble block,
>   And eke the young ones, Sal and Tom."
>
> "Dear Polly Rock," the Captain said,
>   And trembled much as he thus spoke;

"I never heard that you were dead,
　And fear, my love that you but joke."
To prove her truth they vanished straight,
　And at their heels a fiery flame;
The Captain roared out for his mate,
　Drank off his grog—and slept again.

We landsmen have all been told that maids should beware sailors, who have sweethearts in every port. When you begin to collect chanteys and fo'castle songs, you find the other side of that story: that girls like sailors only for the money they spend and only for as long as they will spend it. The favorite ballad on this subject is usually called *Green Beds*; in the version which I give the title will need to be changed to *The Down Bed*.

Young Johnny came from Ireland,
　Young Johnny came on shore,
Young Johnny came from Ireland
　Where he had been before.

"You're welcome home, young Johnny,
　You're welcome home from sea;
Last night my daughter Polly
　Was dreaming of thee.

"What luck, John, what luck?"—
　"O very bad," says he,
"My ship and cargo's lost
　All in the raging sea.

"Call down your daughter Polly,
　And married we will be."

"My daughter Polly's absent
　And won't be home today,
And if she were at home, John,
　She would not let you stay.

"For she is very rich, John,
　While you are very poor;

And if she was at home, John,
  She'd turn you out of door."

Young Johnny being weary,
  He hung down his head,
He called for a candle
  To light him to bed.

"My beds are full of strangers
  And have been so this week.
Now for your lodging, John,
  Somewhere else you must seek."

He looked upon the people,
  He looked upon them all,
He looked upon the landlady,
  And for a reckoning called.

Saying, "Twenty shillings of the new
  And thirty of the old."
Young Johnny he pulled out
  His two hands full of gold.

The sight of the money
  Made the old woman rue,
Saying, "My daughter Polly
  Will soon be down to you.

"For I was not in earnest, John,—
  I was only in jest;
Without any cash, John,
  She likes you the best."

Then down came Madame Polly
  With a sweet, pleasant smile.
She hugged him, she kissed him,
  She called him her child,

Saying, "Mother dear is weary,
  And has been so this year.

The down bed is empty;
   Young Johnny shall lie there."—

"Before I would lie there,
   I would lie within the streets,
For when I had no money,
   No lodging I could seek.

"Now I have money a-plenty,
   I will make the taverns whirl,
With a bottle of good brandy,
   And on each knee a girl."

Come all ye jolly sailor-boys
   Who plow the raging main,
Who now doth earn their living
   Through hard storms of rain,

Be sure and take good use of it,
   And lay it up in store,
For without this companion
   You're turned out of door.

In Mr. James Mack's version, which he sang me with great spirit and a good deal of improvised freedom, I got glimpses of an earlier and less decorous form of the song. After Johnny pulls out two purses of gold with the significant remark, "I am not as poor as that I was told," Molly bounces in; the lines which follow explain the song's earlier title:

In come beautiful Molly
   With a shining face;
She hugged him, she kissed him,
   She did to him embrace.

"You're welcome home, dear Johnny,
   Welcome home from sea,
For the green beds are empty
   For both you and me."

A somewhat similar theme—the poor, scorned sailor—combined
with the trickster motive, disguise, and the male Cinderella, made a
dainty dish for an English ballad preserved in two northeastern
counties, where it is entitled *The Sailor Boy*:

There was a young sailor boy with courage stout and bold,
Who courted a lady worth thousands of gold,
Whose father said, "Dear daughter, if it is your intent
To marry with yon sailor boy, I'll never give consent.

"Here is twelve thousand pounds and to you I do give,
And it shall be your fortune as long as you do live.
My blessing you shall have, and your fortune I will make,
Provided that young sailor boy you ever will forsake."

She wrote a long line, to her sailor boy did send,
All for to let him know of her father's intend (sic).
He said, "I'll be sincere, and my heart will be true;
There's nothing in this wide world I fancy but you."

He said, "My noble Molly, if you I can't obtain,
I'll cross the wide ocean, I'll go into Spain."
This crafty bold project did set out to try!
To deceive her old father, or else he would die.

He bought him a suit and apparelled did appear,
And disguised like a Prince to Morocco did steer;
With a star upon his breast went to see his love again,
And the old man was well pleased with the young Prince from Spain.

He said, "My young Prince, if you will agree
To marry my daughter, your bride she shall be."—
"O yes, with all my heart," the young sailor boy did say,
"If she will be my bride, we'll be married today."

Then off to the church they were hurried with speed.
The old man bid off his daughter, his daughter indeed,
Which caused the old father to jump and to dance
To think that his daughter had married a Prince.

Then up steps the Prince, saying: "Don't you know me?
I am the little sailor boy you drove away to sea;
But since I have outwitted you at the risk of my life,
I've twelve thousand pounds and a beautiful wife."

"O go to the devil!" the old man did cry.
"You've robbed me of my daughter, my money besides;
But if I had once mistrusted you or thought of your plot,
Not one single farthing would you have ever got."

The favorite subject of the disguised lover's return, of which I
have given a sample in the chapter on Love's Comedies, appears in
ballads about sailors, the most popular in York State probably being
Jack Riley, otherwise known as *George Reily*.

On one bright summer's morning, the weather being clear,
I strolled for recreation down by the river fair.
I overheard a damsel most gracious-like complain
All for an absent lover who plowed the raging main.

I, being unperceiving, did unto her draw near;
I lay me down in ambush, the better for to hear.
While she was thus lamenting and grieving for her dear,
I saw a gallant sailor boy who unto her drew near,

With eloquence and compliments he did address the fair,
Saying, "Sweet and lovely fair maid, why do you wander here?"—
"All for an absent lover," the maiden did reply,
"Who has left me here to wander, and to lament and cry.

" 'Tis three long years and more his absence I have mourned,
And now the wars are at an end, he has not yet returned."—
"Fair lady," then the sailor said, "what was your true-love's name?
Both that and his description, I'd like to know the same."—

"Jack Riley they did call him, a lad both slick and trim,
Both manly in deportment—if you can excel him!"—
"Fair maid, I had a messmate, Jack Riley was his name.
I'm sure from your description that he must be the same.

"Three years we spent together on board the old *Bell Flew*,
And such a royal messmate before I never knew.

"It was on the 22nd day of April, down by Port Royal Bay,
We had a tight engagement just at the break of day.
It was betwixt Rodney and the Degrade grave, where many a man
    did fall.
Your true-love he was shot by a French cannon-ball."

O with doleful lamentation and melancholy cries,
While sparkling tears, like crystals, were streaming from her eyes,
Saying, "Now my joys are at an end, if what you say be true,
For instead of having pleasure I have naught but grief in view."

On hearing this, his person no longer could conceal,
He threw off his disguise and his person did reveal,
Saying, "O my dearest Nancy, with you I'll ever stay;
I never more shall leave you till my main-mast is cut away."

Now these two constant lovers each other did embrace;
He wiped the bright tears from her cheeks and kissed her lovely face.

    The absent sailors were in real danger from "murmaids", as the
Douglass MS. calls them:

      On Friday morning we set sail.
        Not being far from land,
    It was there we espied a fair murmaid
      With a comb and a glass in her hand.

      Our boatsman bo'sun at the helm stood
        And in steering his course right well
    With a tear standing in his ere (sic),
      Saying, "O how the seas they do swell, swell!"

      Then up spoke the boy out of our gallant ship,
        And a well spoken lad was he,
    Saying, "I have a mother in fair New York town,
      And this night she will weep for me."

Then spoke the mate out of our gallant ship,
    And a well spoken man was he,
Saying, "I have a wife in fair Boston town,
    And this night she will a widow be."

Then spoke the captain out of our gallant ship,
    And a vallant man was he,
Saying, "For the want of a long-boat
    We all shall be drown and sink to the bottom of the sea."

The moon gave light and the stars shone bright,
    And my mother was looking for me.
She may look, she may weep with a watery eye,
    And blame the endless sea.

Then once around went our gallant ship,
    And twice around went she,
And the third time around went our gallant ship,
    And she sank to the bottom of the sea.

I think that the most touching song of separation which I have collected from the tradition of sailors is *The Sailor and His Bride*, a favorite of the late Captain Hiram Beldin, who for years was master of a tug-boat on Lake Champlain, where his father had been a cap'n before him. Cap'n Hiram's sailors sang at their work; when he specially liked a song, he would write it down. The one which I am about to give you was found by his daughter, Mrs. Dodge, written out on a paper yellowed with time and dated August 1, [18]58. I like it so well that I want to preface it with a description of the Cap'n, to show you that we have had the true sailor type on our northern waters:

Mr. Beldin died about ten years ago, but I can remember seeing him come down the street with his sailor's swing, his head held high, and his big shoulders erect. He was a tall man—about six feet and three inches—and his shoulders were massive with muscles that had been trained to hold the wheel of a tugboat steady, for the winds sweep down Lake Champlain from the north, rocking even the heaviest boats, and making navigation difficult. His cheeks retained their ruddy hue, and his blue eyes sparkled with mirth. His hair had turned white, and he threw it

back upon his neck, as he wore it rather long. A corncob pipe usually
protruded from his mouth, and in winter his beaver cap marked him as
different from the rest of the people in the town. To a child he gave the
general impression of massiveness, which made you rather afraid until
you were close enough to see his twinkling eyes and charming grin, and
the fear vanished—you could tell that he loved children. He was restless
in Hudson Falls, for he missed hearing the Lake pound upon the rocks
beneath his home in Dresden. Every summer he returned to fish and
while away the hours talking to his tugboat pals of former days.

And now here is Cap'n Beldin's favorite song, with the addition of
two stanzas that I found in the Douglass MS.:

'Twas early spring, and the flowers were young,
The flowers had bloomed and the birds had sung;
    Never was a bird happier than I,
    For my sailor love was ever nigh.

The morning star was shining still,
The twilight peeped o'er the eastern hill;
    The sailor and his lonely bride
    Were weeping by the ocean's side.

" 'Tis just three months since we were wed,
And O how sweetly have the moments fled!
    But we must part at the dawning of the day,
    And the proud ship bear my love away."

Months passed by, but he came no more
To his weeping bride on the ocean's shore;
    The ship's gone down 'mid the howling of the storm,
    And the waves roll o'er my sailor's form.

It is Autumn now and I am alone;
The flowers are dead, the birds have flown,
    And all is sad, but none so sad as I,
    For my love the sailor no more is nigh.

My sailor sleeps beneath the waves,
And the mermaids sing o'er his ocean grave;

The mermaids are at the bottom of the sea,
A-weeping there sad tears for me.

I would I were a-sleeping too
Beneath the silent waves of the ocean blue,
My soul to God and my body in the sea
And the wild waves rolling over me.

To end on that lovely note of elegy might be artistic but it would hardly be fair to the sturdy characters of Blind Sam, Cap'n Beldin, and the other mariners who have sailed our fresh and salt waves. I prefer to close with a rousing ditty that I found in an old songster in Buffalo, *The American Vocalist*. I hope someday to find the tune for it, so that I may roar it with Cap'n Christopher Morley of the *Quercus*, the only person I know who likes chanteys as well as I do.

A Yankee ship, and a Yankee crew
    Tally hi ho! you know!
O'er the bright blue waves like a sea bird flew,
    Singing hey! aloft and alow!
Her sails are spread in the fairy breeze,
The spray sparkling as thrown from her prow.
Her flag is the proudest that floats on the seas
When homeward she's steering now.

X: Canawlers

IN THE year which gave us the Federal Constitution, an American poet named Joel Barlow produced his *Vision of Columbus*. A graduate of Yale College, a citizen of Connecticut, and (strangely enough) a radical in politics, the poet made a true prophecy for the Empire State:

> He saw, as widely spreads the unchannell'd plain
> Where inland realms for ages bloom'd in vain,
> Canals, long winding, ope a watery flight,
> And distant streams, and seas and lakes unite.
> From fair Albania, tow'rd the falling sun,
> Back through the midland lengthening channels run;
> Meet the far lake, the beauteous towns that lave,
> And Hudson joined to broad Ohio's wave.

Jefferson was less sanguine; he thought that to "talk of making a canal three hundred and fifty miles through a wilderness is little short of madness at this day". Madison vetoed a bill that would have assisted the State to construct it. The Holland Land Company, which had for sale a considerable portion of Western New York, hesitantly granted a hundred thousand acres upon condition that by 1842 the Canal should be completed. So the Yorkers built the Ditch themselves—extemporizing engineers, inventing tools, importing bog-men from Ireland to cut through the swamps. On Independence Day of 1817 the first spadeful of earth was turned at Rome, New York. On October 26, 1825, cannon boomed across the State, from the port of Buffalo to the port of New York, the news that Governor Clinton's Ditch was built, that New York had become the Empire State, that America was ready to march west to continental glory.

Buffalo should never forget that October day. After the singing of an ode composed by a journeyman mechanic, the little frontier settlement heard its cannon roar while DeWitt Clinton boarded the *Seneca Chief* for the first trip through the entire length of the Grand Canal. The name *Seneca* was symbolic of the Indian Keepers of the Western Gate. The cannon were symbolic: many of them had been brought from Presque Isle's Navy Yard—from the ships of Commodore Perry and his defeated foes, in memory of another autumn day, thirteen years before, when the United States had won the mastery of the Great Lakes. Following the Governor's boat came several others with symbolic names: *Superior, Commodore Perry, Buffalo, Lion of the West*. On the last named of these boats were more symbols, of a day that was passing: two Indian boys, a bear, two eagles, two fawns, and many birds and fish. In the cabin of the *Seneca Chief* lay "two elegant kegs", painted with patriotic designs and filled with water from Lake Erie. Within about eighty minutes the cannon, placed eight to twelve miles apart, brought to New York, nearly five hundred miles away, the news that the Governor's four gray horses had begun a journey that was to continue through villages soon to be great cities—a journey that was to end at the metropolis which DeWitt Clinton had assured the commercial supremacy of the Western Hemisphere.

The final ceremonies took place at Sandy Hook in New York harbor. The waters of Lake Erie were mingled with the Atlantic; vials were emptied containing a few drops from the Mississippi, the Columbia, the Thames, the Seine, the Rhine, the Danube, the Amazon, the La Plata, the Orinoco, the Ganges, the Indus, the Gambia, and the Nile. Said the Governor:

This solemnity, at this place, . . . is intended to indicate and commemorate the navigable communication which has been accomplished between our Mediterranean Seas and the Atlantic Ocean, in about eight years, to the extent of more than four hundred and twenty-five miles, by the wisdom, public spirit, and energy of the people of New York; and may the God of heavens and the earth smile most propitiously on this work, and render it subservient to the best interests of the human race.

So far as America was concerned, and the incredible hordes of her immigrants, the prayer was answered. I have been told that when the nation saw *The Farmer Takes a Wife*, Mr. Edmonds' moving-picture portraying life on the old canal, the peak of interest was reached not in New York State and in the East, but in those western states where the people remembered that it was the canal which set their destiny. In 1810 the State of Ohio ranked thirteenth in population; in 1840 it was third. In 1810 there were four settlements in Michigan, with less than five thousand people; in 1840 the population was 212,000—largely of immigrants from New York and New England. It is no wonder that the state song of the Wolverines said:

> Then there's the state of New York, where some are very rich,
> Themselves and a few others have dug a mighty ditch,
> To render it more easy for us to find the way,
> And sail upon the waters to Michigania;
>   Yea, yea, yea, to Michigania.

As for the Yorkers, all of them who saw the canal built realized the new importance of the Irish, sturdy folk who did most of the hard work in constructing the Ditch and the early railroads. Dr. O. P. Hubbard, who lived at Rome, New York, where the digging started, wrote to a friend years later:

Wild Irish bog trotters from West Ireland, cutting out the trees the width of the canal track, were set to work knee deep in the wet muck; they could wear no clothing but a flannel shirt and a slouch cap, and there were no tools that could be used. Shovels and spades were out of the question and a rectangular side-board wheelbarrow equally useless . . . It was a weird sight to see on a long line, both sides of the canal, hundreds of these wild Irish men at work. Saturday nights in their board shanties, "fighting drunk", and contractors had to go in and club them right and left to quiet them . . . I have seen teacher Mathews . . . without a hat, long hair flying, screaming "Murder!" and running up

James Street from the old canal bridge to get out of the way of a half dozen of those fellows, each with a paving stone or a shillelah in hand.

I dare say that there is another side to that story; the wild Irish probably endured many insults from the Yankees. There is the tale of how one bog-trotter answered Peter Colt, superintendent of construction on the Black River Canal. It is almost unbelievable that the Black River ever was built, even in nineteen years; thirty-five miles in length, it had to carry between Rome and High Falls no less than one hundred and nine locks for a total rise and fall of 1,082 feet. No wonder they named it the Mountain Climbing Canal! Here is the story:

Then, as now, canals were mainly constructed by Irish laborers. As Mr. Colt was passing through a company of these laborers one day, for some real or supposed offence or delinquency he gave one of them a smart kick on his rear exposure. The man instantly let go his barrow, and while with his left hand rubbing the seat of attack, with his right very respectfully raised his hat, and rolling the quid in his mouth, and with a peculiar knowing twinkle of the eye, said, in the richest Irish brogue: " 'Faith and by J——, if yer honor kicks so hard while ye're a *coult*, what'll ye do when ye get to be a horse?"

In the Grosvenor Library at Buffalo they have an old broadside ballad of six stanzas called *Paddy on the Canal*. Three of its stanzas give the picture of our Irish building the Ditch:

When I landed in sweet Philadelphia, the weather was pleasant & clear.
I did not stay long in the city, so quickly I shall let you hear.
I did not stay long in the city, for it happened to be in the fall.
I never reefed a sail in my rigging, till I anchored out on the canal.

> So fare you well, father and mother,
>   Likewise to old Ireland too,
> So fare you well, sister and brother,
>   So kindly I'll bid you adieu.

When I came to this wonderful rampire, it filled me with the greatest surprise
To see such a great undertaking, on the like I never opened my eye[s].

To see full a thousand brave fellows at work among mountains so tall.
To dig through the valleys so level, through rocks for to cut a canal . . .

I being an entire stranger, be sure I had not much to say,
The Boss came round in a hurry, says, boys, it is grog time a-day.
We all marched up in good order, he was father now unto us all.
Sure I wished myself from that moment to be working upon the canal.*

If you ask an old canaller about those heroic fights which Mr.
Edmonds has made so vivid, the reply will usually be: "Oh, there
wasn't much fightin' in my time," or, "All the fightin' was at Buffalo
and West Troy, when the men had nothin' else to do". But once in
a while you may meet someone like Mr. George Denniston of Waterloo, who can remember the decade of 1860-70 when as a lad he drove
for his father, the tall, brown man with white beard whom the Erie
knew as "Uncle Billy". Here is Mr. Denniston's story:

In my day we had mostly slow, heavy boats, ninety-six feet long,
carrying heavy loads of coal or lumber or salt. Most of the fighting was
before that, when the packets were running. They were light passenger
boats, built for speed. It used to be that if one canal boat got within
two hundred yards of a lock, another boat couldn't pass it; but the
packets wouldn't do that waiting for two or maybe three hours—time
was important to them. So all the packets carried fighters. Sometimes
they were men who didn't do anything but just sit around till they came
to a lock, then they'd fight to see who'd go through first.

Chippy Connolly was known as Champion of the Erie Canal; he
wouldn't hire a man that wasn't a fighter. He challenged any man be-
ween Buffalo and Albany, but nobody would fight him if it could be
helped. One time I saw his boat near Montezuma. Connolly's driver
wculdn't let another boat pass him. The driver of the other boat started
calling names, and pretty soon the two of them got to fighting. The other
fellow ran away, and Connolly's driver threw stones after him.

The champion before Connolly was John McMan [McMahon?]. I saw
him once when he was an old man at Troy—tall and broad-shouldered,
with a great big head on him. One time his driver got into a fight—his
name was Bill Stewart—it was up at Centerport, and the other driver
licked him. John said: "Bill, I didn't think you'd let him roll you around

* It is generally assumed that we got the pronunciation *canawl* from the Irish.
Mr. Joel Munsell, the antiquary-printer, maintained that it was of Dutch origin.

in the dust like that." Bill said: "well, Captain, you know, before breakfast I can't seem to fight right." So John took him over to a canal-store and bought him some beer and bread and cheese—all he wanted. When he'd finished eating, Bill called the other driver off his boat and licked him easy.

Jerry McCarthy was known as the Champion of the Chemung Canal, a branch going down from Seneca Lake to Elmira—it's closed now. I seen this Jerry fight a nigger at Geneva—a fellow named George Taylor. McCarthy's boat with a load of lumber on it was tied up at the dock. The colored fellow had his towline out and his team drawing; the towline caught in the lumber and threw some of it into the canal. McCarthy wanted the coon to get the boards out of the water; he wouldn't do it; McCarthy hit him, and they began punching around. First one would be on top and then the other; neither one could get the best of it. Finally some men standing around watching separated them—they generally did this after a fight had lasted some time. The coon said: "If I'd knowed you was a champion, I don't believe I'd have started; but as long as I did, I'd just as soon finish it."

The biggest fight I ever heard of was at Memphis, a little town about thirteen miles from Syracuse. I was two-three miles away, near Peru, when I heard there was a big fight going on. The way it started was, there was this bran-new boat, and this old boat came alongside and scratched the paint. This made the captain of the new boat pretty mad, and he said to the captain of the other boat: "Say, I'd like to punch your jaw for that!"

The other captain says: "Why, I got a driver that kin lick you!" This was an insult, because the drivers were generally young boys.

The first captain says: "Where is he? I'd like to see the driver that can lick me."

The driver spoke up from the towpath and says: "Here I am; come on out, and I'll show you."

The captain jumped off his boat, and they went to fighting on the grass. Then a man jumped off and joined them, then one off the other boat, until both crews were out there, mixing in. There's generally five men on a crew—the captain, two steersmen, and two drivers—so pretty soon here was the whole ten of them, fightin' to beat the deuce. After they fit for a long time, they was all knocked out except one man on one side and two on the other. The two of them couldn't knock this one man down; so after a while one of the two went over to the boat and asked the cook to give him a heavy stick or something. She handed him a heavy iron bar. He went back with it, watched his chance, and gave the fellow a crack on the head along by his jaw, and it killed him. There wasn't any jail at Memphis; so they locked the men up in a barn till they could take them to Syracuse to be tried. I never heard what happened to that fellow that killed the man.

They used to have races without fights, too. There was two towing lines on the canal: the Liverpool, and the Western Towing Company or W. T., originally called the Conbo. The W. T. had red hames for the harness, and the Liverpool had blue ones. I wish't I could remember that long piece that tells about a race:

> Yonder goes the *Sea Gull*, five miles ahead:
> Up comes the Conbo, hames painted red.
> Then the Captain hollered, "I'll give you half a dollar
> If you can overhaul the boat up ahead."
> The driver says, "Captain, half a dollar's pretty small;
> You give me a dollar, and I'll let the team haul."

The plain fact is that the canallers enjoyed fighting from sheer high spirits. Mr. Tommy Collins of Waterford on the Champlain branch of the canal remembers the heyday of an innocent sport which he describes:

Just as much as boxing and wrestling nowadays, a great sport of the canallers was knocking off hats. They'd buy these wide-brimmed straw hats and wet the crown, then stick their fist up 'em, and stretch 'em 'way up till they'd be about a foot high.

I remember seeing these fellows, with these big, yellow straw hats and their pants rolled up above their knees and prancin' around in their bare feet, tryin' to knock off the other fellow's hat. It was great sport. The one who knocked off the other fellow's hat most times in a certain length of time won. Then the loser bought a drink. They were a happy lot. In them days instead of a-goin' to the Foreign Legion they'd get jobs as drivers on the canal.

If you wanted something lively, you should have seen Election Day. The State boats used to start comin' early in the mornin'. They'd be loaded with men bought by some party or other, and they'd start right in Albany to vote, then they'd go to Watervliet—then here—Mechanicville—then Stillwater and right up the line. They'd stop at every single place along the way, and every last one of 'em would vote. By the time they'd stopped in two or three places—well, they'd be noisy. All of us kids used to ride on the boats too, and then parade in every town for whatever party wanted us to. And politicians runnin' around buyin' votes. There was one man in Stillwater that they said would sell his vote for a barrel of flour. Useful stuff, flour, but you know, nobody that *was* anybody would sell their vote. On Election Day you could tell those who were anybody and those who weren't. Sing? I can't remember what they sang, except one verse:

> Never tickle a mule when he's reposing.
> If you disturb his slumbers, you're a fool.
> Take my advice—don't do it twice.
> Don't bother 'round the hind-end of a mule.

The reputation earned on the canal for fighting might be embarrassing. For instance, there was a certain driver who settled down in Mechanicville, only to be summoned to the door one night by a drunken railroader who wished to revive the ancient feud of railroad vs. canawl.

"You think you're the best damn fighter in Mechanicville, doncha?" says this guy to Bill.

"Well, now," says Bill peaceable, "I don't dispute another's right to the claim."

"You think you're the best damn fighter in Mechanicville, doncha?" says the feller, madder'n hell and squarin' off to paste one on Bill.

Bill's wife's been standin' there too, and she runs and gets the broom, and comes back wavin' it. But Bill grabs the broom and says to her, "Wait a minute, wait a minute!"

Then he says to the feller, "Now, if ye think ye're the best of them in Mechanicville, then so ye are."

"O no, you don't," says the railroader, "I gonna prove it."

"Well then, come on," says Bill, grabbin' his coat; and they go up 'side the High School and they goes to it.

Bill was a bucker. Have ye met any? He didn't hit with his fists; he banged with his head, very hard. He bucked the railroader all to hell. He knocks him out and stamps on him two or three times. Then he carries him about three blocks all the way up to the drugstore and gets him all fixed up before he goes back to his own peaceful home again. It's a terrible thing, a reputation.

Another driver who left the canal had a nice little "place" up at Schuylerville, where, just to keep himself in form, he "used to clean up his bartenders just before he let them go and got a new one". The one exception was a lad with a good Irish name, a stutterer; either it was not in the master's code to strike one who stuttered, or no convenient excuse occurred for starting the shindig when the lad departed. Two years later he returned for a jolly visit with his former employer. As he was leaving, well fed and happy, he said:

"Do y-y-you know, I'm the only b-b-bartender you ever let g-g-go without a c-c-cleaning up?"

"Well," cried the master, dragging back his first, "thank God, it ain't too late now!"

Across the river from Waterford, at Cohoes, the easiest and politest way to start a fight among the canallers was to drop into any "power-house" or tavern on Saturday and mention with disrespect any of the counties of Ireland. This would insure a fine time for everyone, because so great was the local pride of the Irish canaller that a man from Limerick was only too happy at any time to accommodate a "Tip" with the back of his hand. I wish that I could have seen an evening at "Pole" Berry's place near the Falls at Cohoes, as it lives in the memory of a few old men. Having only one leg, Berry scorned a crutch; the pole which he used could be employed to string a whole row of empty steins or to disqualify anyone creating a nuisance. Perhaps he could have given me full versions of the many songs which I possess only in fragments. Here are two stanzas from a ditty about one of the cheap Cohoes hotels for canallers:

> It's one cent for coffee,
>   Two cents for bread,
> Three for mince pie,
>   And five for a bed.

> There's eighty-three boarders
>   All packed at my door,
> And they paid their five cents
>   For to sleep on the floor.

Another song says:

> The breeze from the gutter
>   Is the salt-water smell

> On the European plan
> At the bummers' hotel.

If obstreperous enough, the canaller might find accommodation in the old Cohoes jail, which, for some obscure reason, is called in a ballad the *Albany Jail*:

> Oh, one gets arrested,
>   The other goes bail,
> That's what you get
>   At the Albany jail.

> The coffee's like tobacco-juice,
>   The bread is hard and stale;
> That's what you get
>   At the Albany jail.

"Yep," they would say, "when I die, I'm not going to stop at Heaven. I'm going fifteen miles beyond, to Fiddler's Green. We'll never be dry there, and there'll be fun on Saturday nights." Pending their approach to Fiddler's Green, most canawlers of convivial habit after the Civil War were content to spend their money along the old Sidecut at the east end of the Erie. The map of what is now the city of Watervliet has changed, but if you stroll down Second Avenue there, between 22nd and 24th Streets, you can imagine the Lower Sidecut, Erie Street, Whitehall Street, and what the newspaper boys call the "Barbary Coast of the East", a name which the lads of the Buffalo *News* and *Courier-Express* will steal for the Buffalo waterfront any time that you aren't looking. The Sidecut, in the memory of "Footy" Gilboy (once the best dancer on the canal and hero of a gallant rescue) lives on,* though the Tub of Blood closed long ago, and you look in vain for the Black Rag, The Pig's Ear, Peg Leg House, The Right Bower of Oswego, Free and Easy, Limpy George's, The Gamecock House, The Newark Goose, and about fifty other places of liquid refreshment and sanguinary encounter. What could you expect? If you permitted locktenders—notoriously crazy—and canawlers to meet, fists must fly, though the general rule held that if two were fighting and a third intervened, the original combatants

---

* As this book goes to press, word reaches me of "Footy's" demise.

both turned upon the interloper, whether he happened to be a lock-tender or a true son of the towpath.

To be sure, at Paddy Ryan's there was a sign reading, "All the fighting done here I do", but Paddy was not only a handsome, soft-spoken host, he was that truly heroic pugilist from whom in 1882 the great John L. Sullivan won the heavyweight boxing champion-ship of the world. Next to Governor Clinton, who liked to call him-self Hibernicus, Ryan seems to me the most memorable personality of our romantic Ditch. Let me give an unlaquered story of his career as told me by his only living child and her stalwart son.

Patrick Henry Ryan was born in 1853 on the March day sacred to his Saint. Like many another canawler he was a real "Tip" from Tip-perary. In the years of his might he wore green stockings, black trunks ornamented with green shamrocks, and a red-white-and-blue belt. He arrived in America at the age of eight, just as the Civil War was beginning. Four years later, at old West Troy (Watervliet), he saved little Judy McGraw from drowning in the canal. His leap from the bank to a raft from which he dove resulted in a rupture which com-pelled him to wear a truss even in his formal fights; but he was so little handicapped by the injury that he could do a man's hard work in the shops of the D. and H. R. R., and a little later could win the combats required of a locktender on the Erie. About 1874 he opened his famous bar at the old Sidecut, where his ability to dis-cipline unruly patrons impressed Jimmy Killoran, athletic director at the Rensselaer Polytechnic Institute. By 1877, Killoran's training had prepared his protégé for professional boxing.

Ryan's earliest fight remembered in legend was the one for a purse of twenty-five dollars at Green Island. His opponent, a certain "Blue-skin", came into the ring so heavily greased that Paddy's knuckles kept slipping off until Killoran had the happy idea of rubbing them in the dirt. In another early bout against a man named Myers in the Gaiety Theatre at Albany, the strenuous Killoran went at Ryan with a chair-leg between rounds for not exerting his full strength. "He says he's sick," was Paddy's respectful excuse. In the next round, Myers was knocked out.

Probably the fight with "Professor" Miller of Australia was one of these early encounters. The Professor was introducing at Boston his scientific method of scoring: The boxers smeared their knuckles with lamp-black; between rounds, the officials counted the marks made by the blows; then the smudges were washed off, and a new round began. When it was announced that Ryan had won by a score of 29-9, the Professor so far lost his temper and caution as to start wrestling, an art at which he claimed to be the Australian champion. But Paddy, trained in a hundred tussles on the canal, accomplished a cross-buttock throw. The next moment, the Professor went crashing over the footlights into the orchestra pit, doing such damage to the piano that he was compelled to pay for a new instrument.

It was the code of the Sidecut that anyone pretending to skill as a fighter should be compelled to demonstrate his talents to any number who cared to lock him into a bar-room. At the old Collins House, W. Troy, a dozen earnest experimenters secured the door and announced to Ryan that they intended to "kick him apart". At the end of the affair, those who unlocked the door (from the outside) found twelve recumbent forms, an incredible number of smashed bottles, and a bent stove-shaker. Though it involved only four opponents, I prefer the fracas described by Paddy's veracious trainer, Mr. Killoran:

I had been over to see Ryan that day, and he had not been in his place. So I kept along the street until I came to a saloon kept by a man named Sullivan. This was in what was then called Durhamville. I thought Paddy might have stopped in there. Sure enough, there was Ryan sitting on the little wooden stoop, his face in his hands. And he was a sight. He was cut all over the face and head and his clothes were hanging to him. Said I: "What's the matter, Paddy?" "Matter!" said he. "Look inside." I didn't have to go in the place to look. There wasn't a light of glass in the windows or the top of the door, and the floor was covered with broken bottles that used to be on the back bar. It looked as if there had been a riot there. I found out from Paddy that four had set on him and had locked the door while they went at him. And it wasn't him all that time that wanted that door open—it was the four of them. Ryan told me he had fired one fellow through the window. It looked it.

"Come on home," I says, starting away, but Ryan didn't get up to go. I said, "What are you waitin' for?"

And Paddy said, looking up the street: "I'm waitin' for them to come back."

After some three years of desultory boxing, with Troy as head-quarters, Ryan's great day arrived. A certain Johnny Dwyer, claiming to be the American heavyweight champion, fought an exhibition bout at Troy with the English and European champion, Joe Goss. That night, Paddy challenged Dwyer. The Englishman helped the young aspirant to train at Sand Lake. When Dwyer failed to keep his appointment, Goss challenged Ryan, who could now claim the American title by default.

The epic Ryan-Goss fight took place on June 1, 1880, at Colliers Station, West Virginia. It was a contest with bare knuckles by the old Marquis of Queensberry rules: A round ended when either man "fell", even if he only dropped to one knee, as was discreetly done when need was felt for an intermission. If you struck a kneeling opponent, you forfeited the bout. Long before those eighty-six rounds were finished, Goss was repeatedly trying the wily trick of snarling, "Paddy, you Irish son-of-a-bitch!"—just before falling to his knee. But Killoran's warnings were heeded; Ryan did not foul, and the fight went on until both faces were "beaten to a jelly". When the bell rang for the opening of the eighty-seventh round, Goss did not come out of his corner; Ryan had won in one hour and twenty-eight minutes. The King of the Erie Canal was the Champion of the World. His triumph was sung by the American folk in *Paddy Ryan's Victory*, a ballad of ten double stanzas containing these fervid lines:

> From round seventy-eight to eighty-six,
>   Left room for to believe
> No Englishman could ever stand
>   The weight of Paddy's sleeve;
> For his well trained hundred pounder
>   It lighted with free will
> In the very corner that Joe choose
>   His flood did freely spill.
>
> Round eighty-seven you would swear
>   The heavens burst out in war,
> The word of victory freely went
>   From every ancient craw;

> The referee the time did call,
> But Joe could not reply,
> And the fight was freely given
> To our bold Tipperary boy.

Not all those who had bet their shirts could enjoy the ballad. Some disgruntled patrons explained that Goss had been handicapped from the moment when Paddy had knocked his front teeth down his throat. (As a matter of fact, Goss had prudently removed a set of false teeth.) Feeling ran so high on one train returning from West Virginia that the conductor locked the doors of a car in the hope of limiting a free-for-all massacre. Apparently Ryan left the train. Somewhere in Virginia a gang mobbed him and left him, feigning death, with a knife-wound in the abdomen. It will always be remembered that a little later, rather than disappoint a crowd of canallers and other neighbors, Ryan and his wife removed the stitches from his gash so that he might spar a few exhibition rounds at Rensselaer Park in Troy.

It is a pity that Ryan had to live in the same era with the Strong Boy of Boston; he should have worn his crown more than two years. On February 7, 1882, at Mississippi City he was knocked out in the ninth by the peerless John L. Sullivan—in the presence of another ballad-hero, Jesse James the bandit, who a few months later was shot by a "dirty little coward". Beside the championship of the world, the diamond belt (fresh from the jeweller), and the side-bet of $1,000 posted by each contender, Ryan lost forever the affection of some men who would never admit that their neighbor could have been defeated unless he had "thrown" the fight, though, as the faithful Killoran truly said, "If the devil was to come out of the pit this moment, he couldn't lick Sullivan." There was a return bout at Madison Square Garden, but prize-fights were illegal, and the New York police stopped the contest in its third round.

The rest of Ryan's story is the familiar one of the defeated champion, except that Paddy never was dissipated—though he did add forty pounds to the two hundred and twenty of his best days. Everyone with whom I have talked says that he remained the quiet, generous gentleman. For a time he traveled with Sullivan the uproarious, acting and sparring and trying to keep his friend sober. When the

Strong Boy of Boston fell off a rear platform, it was Paddy who stopped the train and hastened back to find his pal, "orry-eyed" but uninjured. It was not Ryan's practice to go behind the bar in his "places" at Albany, New York, Chicago, and San Francisco, but indirectly he was responsible for a famous American drink. On the bar of his saloon in Chicago stood a steaming bowl of Tom and Jerry, served free, named for two brothers-in-law who assisted Ryan's hospitality, Tom and Jerry Gettings. Perhaps Paddy was too generous with his free drinks. When he died at Green Island, most of his money had gone with the old fighting days of the canawl, leaving faithful Killoran to tell over past glories and to help bear a coffin containing six-feet-two of courage fallen quiet, Patrick Henry Ryan.

To return to the Sidecut—there was plenty of entertainment in addition to boxing and brawling. It is said that a certain Davie would allow himself to be knocked downstairs five times in succession with a hammer-blow on the head. I have not learned the reason for his prejudice against a sixth blow. "Jumpy" Burke's favorite exhibition was to leap clear across a lock with a pair of heavy dumb-bells in his hands. Nelse Carter ambitiously introduced a variety show for his patrons; he is said to have been the first and only one of the old-time hosts to try dancing girls. His patrons preferred a tightrope artist who every night walked from Nelse's place, across the canal and to the top of a tree, pushing a wheelbarrow and at times (by some cantrip which I have not clearly in mind) frying an egg in transit. Jimmy Wood is said to have installed the first telephone in West Troy, as it was called, and insisted upon a large gong in place of the sissy bell usually provided. When someone called him up, the canallers for three blocks would rush up to hear the critter talk.

Toward the end of the century, a favorite song at the east end of the canal was *The Edison Machine*, a vigorous expression of Irish prejudice against England and the A. P. A. (American Protective Association, an anti-Catholic group):

> Mike Murphy owned a fine saloon,
> He never knew grief nor care;
> It mattered not to Murphy
> Whether the day was dark or fair.

An Irish gang hung 'round his place
That better days had seen,
When Murphy caused his troubles
With an Edison talking-machine.

The picture that was in the place,
The anxious look on each man's face!
Beside the great machine Murphy could be seen
Explaining all the great things done by Edison.

A neighbor called Dan Brady called—
Dan was an awful pest;
He looked upon the new machine
And was delighted like the rest.

Said Brady, "Can you make it play
The Wearing of the Green?"
But Murphy by mistake put on
The song known as *God Save the Queen.*

Dan Brady he went out and soon came back;
Poor Murphy still lay on the floor,
And "Bull" McCarthy shouted out,
"Let's try the thing once more!"

Poor Murphy from the floor got up
And fainted dead away,
For by mistake the thing got mixed
With the speech of an A. P. A.

Dan Brady's mug was white
When he threw some dynamite.
Now Murphy's dead and buried—
    All through Edison.

Now and again a shindig would lead to an entertaining day in
court, though justice was usually lenient. One unfortunate parrot
lost his life by screeching too often a sentence learned from his
mistress, the wife of a West Troy judge: "The Judge is drunk again."
One beloved but formidable canal-captain always took to court, when

summoned, his wife and thirteen children, to create unfailing sympathy of one sort or another.

It is not to be supposed that fighting was confined to ancient times or to the east end of the canal. Mr. Oviatt McConnell of Buffalo likes to tell of the late Captain Ed Scouten, who died in 1922 at the ripe age of ninety-three. Cap'n Ed was a Civil War veteran who knew the canal intimately for half a century, and who lived to command one of the modern "hoodledashers", powered boats which surge along with a barge in front and a couple behind. The Cap'n used to *stop* fights by stepping in and thrashing the combatants one at a time or, if they preferred, together. When he was about seventy-five, he decided to follow a general custom by hiring a fighter. On the first voyage out, it occurred to him that he hadn't tried his slugger to see whether he was up to canal-standards; so he picked a fight and knocked out the professional. It is told of him that in the 'seventies he was walking through a canal town, his luxuriant whiskers waving. Approaching some loungers, he predicted, "One of these fellows is going to say *Baa* to me on account of my whiskers, and I am going to pop him". The prediction was immediately fulfilled.

The classic tale at Buffalo is of the big battle between Charley and Jack. Jack bit off a piece of Charley's ear and spat it on the deck; whereupon there followed the following curt dialogue:

"There's your ear, Charley."

"You bit it off, you cuss. Now eat it!"

Fighting and even the biting off of ears is a part of the frontier tradition and waterfront etiquette. Most of our canallers, of course, led quiet and, on the first Ditch, idyllic lives. Some of the old-timers tell you that fighting stopped after the Civil War; others say that it started then with the "hoggies", floating laborers. Mr. Allen Walsh, who has made a more careful study of canal-life than anyone else I know at Buffalo, told me that it is the floating laborer who still gives trouble: one large company has had to bail out of jail as many as fifty men in a week. Such stories have elements of pathos, but the most poignant ones concern the boy drivers on Clinton's Ditch.

There is a thin volume published in 1845 and entitled *Five Years on the Erie Canal*. It was written by a puritanical but compassionate and obviously sincere layman missionary sent out by the American

Bethel Society—a certain Deacon M. Eaton. Convicted of sin when an "old and very wicked man", he says that he was the first missionary concerned with improving the morals of the canallers. He estimates that in 1845 there were some 4,000 boats employing 25,000 men, women, and boys. Of these, about 5,000 were boy drivers, often only thirteen or fourteen years of age, hired for ten dollars a month and board. Some unscrupulous captains employed tactics familiar to whaling masters: toward the end of the season they became so brutal that the boys left without collecting their pay. Some captains were brutal all the time.

One of the Deacon's stories concerns a sick orphan—and half of the boys were orphans—who was so ill that he fell off his horse at a lock, cut his head severely, and lay senseless. Throwing him into a board shanty, the captain ordered his other boy to drive on. The lock-tender, when asked whether he didn't intend to do something for the lad, replied: "No. I wish he *was* dead. He is the wickedest boy on the canal." It was a hot day in July; the sun beat down on the unconscious driver—the boards were off one side of the shanty. Finally a good Samaritan passed, took him home, and called a doctor. Four days later, the boy returned to consciousness. Asked if he was really the worst boy on the canal, he replied that he supposed he was; for five years he had been treated like a slave; cheated out of his wages, he had taken to lying, stealing, and getting drunk. Restored to health, he got a job with a decent captain and within five years was a captain himself.

Another story is of a boy thrown off a boat in a big swamp between Rome and New London. The captain had two defenses: that the child had cholera, and that "he is no more sick than you are—he is a lazy villain". Next day a dog found the lad lying upon logs in the swamp. He never spoke—died within an hour and a half. It is no wonder that the Chaplain at Auburn State's Prison reported to Deacon Eaton that he found on the prison records four hundred and eighty names of those who had worked on the canals and the lakes.

The one song about these boy drivers which I have collected shows a merrier side of their life. Mrs. A. H. Shearer of Buffalo got it from Mrs. Broadbeck of Tonawanda, who used to live on canal-boats:

When I was young and about sixteen, none was more light and gay;
I gamboled nimbly on the green or sported in the hay;
The bloom of youth was on my cheeks, my heart was full of joy.
How happy were those days to me, a merry boatman's boy!

For I was a boatman's boy, for I was a boatman's boy.
Johnny, get your mules fed; Johnny, get your mules fed,
   For I was a boatman's boy.

I loved to use a pocket-knife before I went to school,
And soon I learned the mysteries of that wasteful, magic tool.
I hoarded cents I prized so high—I gladly gave to own—
And soon I learned the magic art to whet it on a stone.

On the whole, the old Ditch bore a merry crew whose chief trials
were of a burlesque variety. The one canal ballad which you are
likely to find in any songster printed before the Civil War is *The
Raging Canal*, the nub of whose long-winded humor is that boatmen
were in peril on a ditch originally four feet in depth. As a matter of
fact, there was some danger of shipwreck on Lake Oneida, where
storms come up suddenly and ports were few; but the whole ballad
is simply an elaboration of the canal's favorite joke, its tall tale. I give
the version printed in *The American Vocalist* (1853).

Come, list to me, ye nobles, ye heroes and ye braves,
For I've been at the mercy of the winds and the waves,
I'll tell you of the hardships to me that did befall
While going on a voyage up the Erie can-all [canawl].

From out of this famed harbor we sailed without fear,
Our helm we put hard up, and for Albany did steer,
We spoke full fifty craft, without any accident at all
Until we passed into that 'are raging can-all.

We left old Albany harbor, just at the close of day,
If rightly I remember 'twas the second day of May;
We trusted to our driver, although he was but small,
Yet he knew all the windings of that raging can-all.

It seemed as if the devil had work in hands that night,
For our oil was all out, and our lamps they gave no light;

The clouds began to gather, and the rain began to fall,
And I wished myself off and safe from the raging can-all.

With hearts chock-full of love, we thought of our sweethearts dear,
And straight for Utica our gallant bark did steer,
When in sight of that 'ere town, there came on a *white squall*,
Which carried away our mizen mast, on the raging can-all.

The winds came roaring on, just like a wild cat scream,
Our little vessel pitched and tost, straining every beam,
The cook she dropt the bucket, and let the ladle fall,
And the waves ran mountains high, on the raging can-all.

Our boat did mind the helm, just like a thing of life,
Our mate he offered prayers for the safety of his wife;
We threw our provisions overboard, Butter, Cheese, and all,
And was put on short allowance, on the raging can-all.

Now the weather being foggy we couldn't see the track,
We made our driver come on board, and hitched a lantern on his back.
We told him to be fearless, and when it blew a gale,
To jump *up* and knock *down* a horse, that's taking in a sail.

The captain bid the driver to hurry with all speed,
His orders were obeyed, for he soon cracked up his lead;
With that 'ere kind of towing, he allowed by twelve o'clock
We should have the old critter right bang agin the dock.

But sad was the fate of our poor devoted bark,
For the rain kept growing faster, and the night it grew dark,
The horses gave a stumble, and the driver gave a squall,
And they tumbled head and heels into the raging can-all.

The captain cried out, with a voice so clear and sound,
"Cut them horses loose, my boys, or else we will be drowned!"
The driver paddled to the shore, although he was but small,
While the horses sank to rise no more in the raging can-all.

The cook she wrung her hands, and then she came on deck,
Saying, "Alas! what will become of us, our vessel is a wreck."

The steersman knocked her over, for he was a man of sense,
And the helmsman jumped ashore, and lashed her to a fence.

We had a load of Dutch, and stowed 'em in the hole,
And the varmint wer'nt the least concerned for the welfare of their souls:
The captain he went down to them, implored them for to pray,
But all the answer that he got was "Due deutsch sproken, nex come
   arouse, ex for shtae".

The captain trembled for his money, likewise for his wife,
But to muster courage up, he whittled with a knife,
He said to us with a faltering voice, while tears began to fall,
"Prepare to meet your death this night, on the raging can-all."

The passengers to save their souls would part with any money,
The bar-keeper went on his knees, then took some peach and honey;
A lady took some brandy, she'd have it neat or not at all,
Kase there was lots of water in the raging can-all.

The captain came on deck, with spy glass in his hand,
But the fog it was 'tarnel thick, he couldn't spy the land;
He put his trumpet to his mouth, as loud as he could bawl
He hailed for assistance from the raging can-all.

The sky was rent asunder, the lightening it did flash,
The thunder rattled above, just like eternal smash;
The clouds were all upsot, and the rigging it did fall,
And we scudded under bare poles on that raging can-all.

A mighty sea rolled on astern, and then it swept our deck,
And soon our gallant little craft was but a floating wreck;
All hands sprang forward, aft the main-sheet for to haul,
When slap dash! went our chicken coop into the raging can-all.

We took the old cook's petticoat, for want of a better dress,
And rigged it out upon a pole, a signal of distress;
We pledged ourselves hand to hand, aboard the boat to bide,
And not to quit the deck while a plank hung to her side.

At length that horrid night cut dirt from the sky,
The storm it did abate, and a boat came passing by,
She soon espied our signal, while each on his knees did fall,
Thankful we escaped a grave on the raging can-all.

We each of us took a nip, and signed the pledge anew,
And wonderful, as danger ceased, how up our courage grew;
The craft in sight bore down on us, and quickly was 'long side,
And we all jumped aboard, and for Buffalo did ride.

And if I live a thousand years, the horrors of that night
Will ever in my memory be, a spot most burning bright;
There's not in this varsal world can ever raise my gall
As the thoughts of my voyage on that raging can-all.

And now, my boys, I'll tell you how to manage wind and weather:
In a storm hug the towpath, and lay feather to feather,
And when the weather gets bad, and rain begins to fall,
Jump right ashore, and streak it from the raging can-all.

The yarn is rather long, my boys, so I will let it drop,
You can get the whole particulars in comic Elton's shop,
At eighteen in Division Street you've only got to call,
And you'll get an extra dose of the raging can-all.

It may be supposed that no further particulars would be required,
even when the ballad was sung to the enchanting tune of *Caroline of
Edinburgh Town*. I shall therefore proceed to a better ballad about
one real danger present on the canal—the menace of the low bridge.
Boatin' on a Bull-Head was found by Mr. Alex. Stearns of Syracuse,
written out in an old copy-book left in his father's hair-trunk, long
ago used on the canal; a copy was given to Mr. Walsh, who kindly
furnished me with the following note:

A Bull-Head boat was built flush up to the cabin. The mule-cabin was
away up in the bow, and the stern-cabin left no room for a stern-deck.
The steersman had to stand on the cabin-roof to steer. Between the top
of the cabin and the bridges there was very little clearance; therefore,
if the steersman didn't see a bridge in time, in a very little space he was

swept off by the bridge-timbers. Many a canaller was killed or crippled
by this type of boat.

> I was sleepin' in a Line-barn
>   And eatin' beans and hay,
> While the boss was kickin' my starn
>   Ev'ry night and ev'ry day.
>
> So I hired out canawlin'
>   As a horny hand of toil,
> Drivin' mules that kept a-bawlin'
>   'Long the towpath's smelly soil.
>
> But my feet raised corns and blisters
>   While the mules but raised a stink,
> Roped my feet and threw some twisters
>   Plump into the dirty drink.
>
> So I thought I'd give up drivin',
>   For the captain thought so too,
> He said, "Hire out at divin'
>   Or go bowin' a canoe."
>
> I was dryin' on the heel-path,
>   Watchin' boats haul up and down,
> A-shiverin' from the first bath
>   I'd got since I left town,
>
> When a boat tied in the basin
>   At the wood-dock for the night,
> And I lost no time to hasten
>   'Round the bridge to ask a bite.
>
> They filled me up with beans and shote
>   And lighted me a cob.
> They asked me if I could steer a boat
>   And offered me a job.
>
> The next mornin' I was boosted
>   To the stern-cabin's roof;

With the tiller there I roosted
 And watched the driver hoof.

Now the boat she was a Bull-Head,
 Decked up to the cabin's top;
Many canawlers now are dead
 Who had no place to drop.

(When the bowsman he forgot to yell,
 "Low bridge, ducker down!"
The Bull-Head steersman went to hell
 With a bridge-string for a crown.)

We were loaded with Star Brand Salt;
 The Cap, he was loaded too.
I wouldn't say it was his fault,
 But what was a man to do?

The bridge was only a heave away
 When I saw it 'round the bend.
To the Cap a word I didn't say
 While turning end over end.

So canawlers, take my warning:
 Never steer a Bull-Head boat
Or they'll find you some fair mornin'
 In the E-ri-e afloat.

Do all your fine navigatin'
 In the Line-barn full of hay,
And *Low Bridge* you won't be hatin'
 And you'll live to Judgement Day.

Other varieties of tribulation are told in *Black Rock Pork*. Mr. Walsh says that this pork, alias Black Rock turkey, was sold about 1840 by Elijah Leonard in his grocery at Black Rock, now a part of Buffalo.

I shipped aboard of a lumber-boat,
 Her name was *Charles O'Rourke*.

The very first thing they rolled aboard
  Was a barrel of Black Rock pork.

They fried a chunk for breakfast
  And a chunk for luncheon too.
It didn't taste so goody-good,
  And it was hard to chew.

From Buffalo to old New York
  They fed it to dear-old-me;
They boiled the barrel and the rest of the pork,
  And we had it all for tea.

About three days out, we struck a rock
  Of Lackawanna coal.
It gave the boat quite a shock,
  And stove in quite a hole.

So I hollered at the driver
  Who was off a-treadin' dirt;
He jumped aboard and stopped the leak
  With his crumby [lousy] undershirt.

Now the cook upon this canal-boat
  Stood six feet in her socks;
She had a bosom like a box-car,
  And her breath would open the locks.

Now the cook is in the poor-house,
  And the crew is all in jail,
And I'm the only canaller
  That is left to tell the tale.

There are numerous variants of this very popular song. I like one
which Johnny Bartley used to sing at the "Alhambra Varieties" on
Commercial Street, Buffalo, in the eighteen-eighties:

I've travelled all around this world and Tonawanda too,
I've been cast on desert island and beaten black and blue,
I fought and bled at Bull's Run, and wandered as a boy,
But I'll never forget the trip I took from Buffalo to Troy.

Whoa! Back! Get up!—Forget it I never shall,
When I drove a team of spavin mules on the E-ri-e Canal.

The cook we had on board the deck stood six feet in her socks;
Her hand was like an elephant's ear, and her breath would open the locks.
A maid of fifty summers was she, the most of her body was on the floor,
And when at night she went to bed, Oh sufferin'! how she'd snore!

Whoa! Back! Get up! and tighten up your lines,
And watch the playful flies as on the mules they climb.
Whoa! Back! Duck your nut!—Forget it I never shall,
When I drove a team of spavin mules on the E-ri-e Canal.

"Kip" Conway gave Mr. Walsh a version in which he himself
appears honorably for the refrain:

Hit 'er, shove 'er, go up in the juber-ju;
Give her a line and let her go, ol' Kip'll pull her through.

Later in the song, after the coal has done its damage and the cook
has been described, we get this satisfactory close: .

One night on the Erie I couldn't sleep a wink,
The crew they all bore down on me because I refused to drink.
Fearful storms and heavy fogs, forget it I never shall,
For I'm every inch a sailor-boy upon the Erie Canal.

When we arrived at Buffalo with Sally, Jack, and Hank,
We greased ourselves in tallow-fat and slid off on a plank;
Sally's in the poor-house, the rest of the crew's in jail,
And I'm the only bugger afloat that's left to tell the tale.

Some of the cooks were inartistic in their mystery. Captain Wimett
of Port Byron remembered a dismal rune beginning:

Hash is fried, hash is tried, hash is come in with the tide.
[Good for] drunks, cut in chunks, made of hinges of old trunks.

Certainly the cooks added to the romance as well as to the comfort
of the old Ditch. There were agencies where they could be hired,
at Rome, Baldwinsville, Utica, Lockport, and elsewhere. Often the
captain took his wife as cook. In at least one of the songs she is
being wooed.

So pull in your towline,
    And haul in the slack,
Take a reef in your britches,
    And straighten your back.

But, whatever you do,
    Don't never forget
For to touch the mules gently
    When the cook's on the deck.

The cook, she's a daisy,
    She's dead-gone on me;
She's got fiery red hair,
    And she's sweet twenty-three.

A less romantic version runs as follows:

You yacht on the Hudson, you ride on the Lake,
    But a trip on the Erie you bet takes the cake,
Where the beefsteak is tough as a fighting dog's neck,
    And the cook she plays tag with the flies on the deck.

Our cook is a daisy and dead stuck on me,
    Has fiery red hair and she's sweet sixty-three.
Though sunburned and freckled, a daisy, you bet,
    And we use her at night for a headlight on deck.

So haul in your towline and take in your slack,
    Take a reef in your breeches and straighten your back.
Through sunshine and storm down the towpath we'll walk,
    And we'll touch up the mules when they kick and they balk.

Whatever his feelings about the cook, the boatman was likely to be fond of his horses or mules. Captain Wimett has a sort of *Canalman's Farewell*:

Lay me on the hoss-bridge
    With my feet toward the bow;
Let it be a Laker
    Or a Tonawanda scow.

> See that my mules are well cared for
> With salve upon their breasts.
> Give me a chunk of Black Rock pork
> And lay me down to rest.

Perhaps it should be explained that the Laker is a pointed boat, and a Tonawanda scow is rounded. The hoss-bridge was run from the boat to the bank when the animals were being changed.

A less elegiac version, whose vocabulary is charming, I had from Mr. Walsh; he put it together from versions given by Captain Jake·Oatman and Captain Wesley Thomas:

> Lay me on the horse-bridge
> With my feet toward the bow;
> And let it be a Lockport Laker
> Or a Tonawanda scow.

> For the Erie, it is ragin',
>   And our gin is gettin' low;
> Oh, I hardly think we'll get a drink
>   Till we get to Buffalo.

> For Nell has got blind staggers,
>   And Maude has got the heaves;
> Black Tom has thrown his off-shoe,
>   Our driver's got the weaves.

> And as we got into Buffalo
>   It was but four o'clock.
> The very first man we chanced to meet
>   Was Gilson on the dock.

> Says he, "What's all the noise?"
>   Says he, "What team is that?"—
> "It's Yorker Min, and Goose-Neck Tim,
>   And we're both a-gettin' fat."

At least one canal-horse has an epitaph. Miss Myrtle Ray of Port Byron says that her grandmother composed the following lines for a favorite who had given many years of faithful service towing barges:

Here lies the bones of my old hoss.
    He's none the better and none the wuss.
From Senecy Falls to here he towed,
    And now he lies beside the road.

There is one spirited piece about a team of horses. The speaker is supposed to be a Dan Smith, canal grocer at Smith's Basin, who may have been at some time captain of a packet.

Attend all ye drivers, I sing of my team;
They're the fleetest and strongest that ever was seen.
There is none will toll with such speed down the crick
Or start at the word of the driver so quick.

There's Dandy, my leader, looks boldly ahead
With his tail raised aloft, and majestic his tread.
He has a bright, shining coat of a beautiful bay;
His eyes sparkle bright as the sun at noon-day.

He's a roarer, no doubt, there's few can match him;
Once let him loose, and the devil may catch him.

The next in procession is my Charlie, a buster.
Gen. Pluck might feel proud on his back at a muster.
So graceful he moves in the midst of his team,
So strong, you would think he traveled by steam!

And lastly my Jimmie, my saddle-horse true,
It's hard to tell how much this horse cannot do.
He has the pride of an emperor, the wisdom of kings;
He moves o'er the ground like a bird on its wings.

At the call he is ready like a reindeer to jump;
Obedient, when ordered he stands like a stump.

The three altogether in motion outdo
Any team of their age, the whole canal through.
Should any company try to go by us,
We'll show them our steam whenever they try us.

> While Baker and Walbridge their packets run daily,
> Proud Dandy and Jimmie and Charlie so gaily
> Will waft all the passengers through the canal
> In spite of all others, and in style, so they shall.

The classic tribute to the canal mule is *Low Bridge, Everybody Down*, alias *I've got a mule, her name is Sal*, which Carl Sandburg calls the *Volga Boat Song* of America. You may have heard the rich voice of the poet chanting it to the strumming of his guitar, "movingly, meditatively, so that the Erie Canal took on the character of a symbol of life as a highway to be taken ploddingly with steady pulse". The history of the song adds to my own enjoyment, for this is the canaller's farewell to his companion: when Mr. Thomas S. Allen published it in 1913, we were already in sight of the day when the Barge was to replace the Erie—the Barge which has no towpath for Sal. The stanzas have a minor tune that resembles a folk-melody; the refrain shifts to major with rhythmic suggestion of the age of "coon-song". I have never heard a canal-man sing the song, but my students rank it in favor with another collected by Sandburg entitled *The E-ri-e*. Here is part of Mr. Allen's ballad as originally published:

> I've got an old mule and her name is Sal,
> Fifteen years on the Erie Canal,
> She's a good old worker and a good old pal,
> Fifteen years on the Erie Canal.
> We've hauled some barges in our day,
> Filled with lumber, coal and hay—
> And every inch of the way I know
> From Albany to Buffalo.
>
>   Low bridge, everybody down,
>   Low bridge! We're coming to a town!
>   You can always tell your neighbor, you can always tell your pal,
>   If you've ever navigated on the Erie Canal.
>
> Oh! where would I be if I lost my pal?
> Fifteen years on the Erie Canal,
> Oh, I'd like to see a mule as good as Sal,

Fifteen years on the Erie Canal.
A friend of mine once got her sore,
Now he's got a broken jaw,
'Cause she let fly with her iron toe
And kicked him in to Buffalo.

When Walter Edmonds used this song in *Rome Haul* (1929), he
borrowed from Sandburg a stanza in which Sal is the name of a cook,
and it is as a cook that Sal appears in Carl Carmer's *Hurricane's
Children* (1937). Carmer has taken John Darling from his farm and
rafts in Sullivan County, has put him on the Erie, and has had him
fall in love with the heroine whose hands were as big as elephant's
ears—a daring example of what the folklorists might call "accretion".
Here is the stanza used in *Rome Haul*:

> Drop a tear for big-foot Sal,
> The best damn cook on the Erie Canal;
> She aimed for Heaven but she went to Hell—
> Fifteen years on the Erie Canal.
> The missioner said she died in sin;
> Hennery said it was too much gin;
> There weren't no bar where she hadn't been,
> 　　From Albany to Buffalo.

The other song which Edmonds borrowed from Sandburg's *American Songbag* for *Rome Haul* is the one which I mentioned as a
favorite with students. Part of the success of the *E-ri-e* is due to the
limited range of its tune.

> We were forty miles from Albany,
> 　　Forget it I never shall,
> What a terrible storm we had one night
> 　　On the E-ri-e Canal.
>
> Oh the E-ri-e was a-rising,
> 　　The gin was getting low;
> 　　And I scarcely think we'll get a drink
> Till we get to Buffalo.
>
> We were loaded down with barley,
> 　　We were chuck up full of rye;

And the captain he looked down at me
With his goddam wicked eye.

Oh the girls are in the *Police Gazette*,
The crew are all in jail;
I'm the only living sea-cook's son
That's left to tell the tale.

You now have some idea of the lore of the canal in its three eras—the Ditch, the Erie, and the Barge—its songs, fighting men, boy drivers, cooks, horses, and mules; but I have told you nothing about the passengers who, in the days before the Civil War, sweated in the packets that sometimes exceeded the legal speed-limit of four miles an hour while the sleek horses kicked dirt into Clinton's Ditch. That is a whole subject in itself; Mr. A. F. Harlow has presented it vividly in his *Old Towpaths* (1926), particularly in a chapter (XXXII) called *Travelling by Canal*. He says that by 1829 there was such competition that various lines had "runners" at Schenectady who contended so vigorously for business that one strip of canalbank was long known as the Battleground.

You are to imagine a boat seventy-five or eighty feet long by eleven feet in width, and with a height from keel to roof that seldom exceeded eight feet. Charles Dickens found that it was hard for a man of middle stature to walk to and fro in the cabin "without making bald places on his head by scraping it on the roof". In the bow would be a little cuddy for the crew; then the ladies' dressing room or sleeping cabin, sometimes separated from the men's cabin only by a red curtain. The main cabin, used for dining room and for the men's dormitory, was thirty-six to forty-five feet long, with a bar in the rear. Finally, in the extreme rear was the kitchen, presided over by a Negro man who also acted as a bartender and must have spent fifteen to eighteen hours a day at work. The crew was the standard one of a captain, two drivers, and two steersmen. On the Erie packets the horses were usually kept in barns along the route, not on the boat.

All went fairly well in the daytime, but night brought trials far in excess of anything found on the modern American railroad. The berths were narrow frames topped by a strip of canvas; at the rear they were attached to holes in the wall by two iron rods; at the front they were suspended from the ceiling. You found at least three beds in a tier, sometimes four, instead of the lower and upper of the modern Pullman. Imagine forty people—and there might be twice that number—crowded onto these shelves. Again Dickens has the right word: "Three long tiers of hanging book shelves designed apparently for volumes of the small octavo size." Sometimes additional accommodations—so to speak—were provided in the middle of the cabin. When Bernhard, Duke of Saxe-Weimar-Eisenach, visited the State in 1825-6, he was quartered in the exact center of the men's cabin on a bench supplemented by a chair. The acidulous Miss Harriet Martineau, a Unitarian, in addition to "the heat and noise, the known vicinity of a compressed crowd packed like herrings in a barrel", suffered also "under an additional annoyance in the presence of sixteen Presbyterian clergymen—some of the most unprepossessing of their class". A passenger assured the English lady that these gentlemen were so strict that they wouldn't drink water out of the Brandywine River. What irritated her most was that instead of trudging along the towpath from time to time, to air out the cabin, these godly men shut up the cabin for prayers before dinner, for missionary conversation in the afternoon, and for Scripture reading and prayers late into the night. Good Deacon Eaton, who loved the boy drivers, could not have complained about these devout persons, as he did about other clergymen, that they refrained from "testifying" on the packets. It is hard to please everybody; it was very hard to please Miss Martineau.

A German tourist, Frederick Gerstaecker, managed to find humor; it was in the 1830's, when packets were flourishing.

I awoke with a dreadful feeling of suffocation; cold perspiration stood on my forehead and I could hardly draw my breath; there was a weight like lead on my stomach and chest. I attempted to cry out—in vain; I lay almost without consciousness. The weight remained immovable; above me was a noise like distant thunder; it was my companion of the upper story, who lay snoring over my head; and that the weight which pressed on my chest was caused by his body no longer remained a doubtful point. I endeavored to move the Colossus—impossible. I tried to push, to cry out—in vain. He lay like a rock on my chest and seemed to have no more feeling. I bethought me of my breastpin, which luckily I had not taken out of my cravat the night before; with great difficulty I succeeded in reaching the pin, which I pressed with a firm hand into the mass above me. There was a sudden movement, which procured me momentarily relief; but the movement soon subsided, the weight was growing more insupportable, and to prevent being utterly crushed, I was obliged to reapply the pin. "What's that? Murder! Help!" cried a deep bass voice above me. Feeling myself free, I slipped like an eel from under the weight and saw by the dim light of the lamp a sight of no common occurrence. A stout, heavy man who slept in the upper frame without mattress was too much for the well-worn canvas; during his sleep it had given way under the weightiest part of his form, which descended till it found support on my chest. The thrust of my breastpin caused his body to jerk upward, allowing me to escape. As he returned to his former position with greater force, the support being gone, the canvas split still wider, and more than half asleep, he was sitting on my bed, while his head and feet remained in his own. He continued calling out, "Help! Murder!" Everybody started up to see what was the matter and to laugh heartily at the extraordinary attitude of this stout gentleman.

If a visitor from afar could find such humor in distress, it is no wonder that the old Ditch continues to wind its sluggish way through the hearts of Yorkers. Almost the first words that I can recall were shouted by my jovial father—a man as tall as Paddy Ryan—when he passed through a doorway with me on his shoulder: "Low bridge!" I was remembering that call the other day at the bachelor home of Mr. John Helt who lives near Verona now after spending forty-seven years on the canal. He said:

We didn't need any of these horns you've read about. When we got near a lock, we'd just holler, "Hurrah, lock!" Lots of good hollering on the canal. Captain Guest had a boat that he named the Uno. If someone called out in the dark to ask her name, he'd holler, "Uno!" It sounded kind of impolite . . . Yes, sir, I had a good time on the Erie from the day when I started out to drive—a boy of thirteen—for eight dollars a month and board. When you got to be a steersman, you might get as much as thirty-five; and if you saved your money, some day you'd own a boat worth three thousand dollars. You moved fast enough: in six hours on duty, driving or steering, you'd go nine or ten miles with a loaded boat, and with a light one you could hit 'er up to fifteen or

eighteen. We had a pretty good time. By May first we were always ready
to go back onto the canal.

Someone like Mr. Helt must have made up the parody called *A
Life on the Raging Canawl*:

> A life on the raging canawl,
>   A home on its muddy deep,
> Where through summer, spring, and fall,
>   The frogs their vigils keep.
> Like a fish on the hook I pine,
>   On this dull, unchanging shore—
> Oh give me the packet line,
>   And the muddy canawl's dull roar.
>
> Once more on the deck I stand
>   Of my own swift gliding craft—
> The horses trot off on the land,
>   And the boat follows close abaft.
> We shoot through the turbid foam
>   Like a bull frog in a squall—
> And, like the frogs, our home
>   We'll find in the muddy canawl.
>
> The sun is no longer in view,
>   The clouds have begun to frown,
> But, with a bumper or two,
>   We'll say, let the storm come down.
> And the song we'll sing, one and all,
>   While the storm around us pelts,
> A life on the muddy canawl,
>   Oh, we don't want nothin' else.

XI: Lumbermen and Rafters

I T WAS a land of noble pines, tall and straight, masts for the Royal
Navy, for the whaling vessels, for the Yankee clippers. It was a
land of hemlocks, whose bark was peeled and carried to a thousand little tanneries. Every pioneer must swing an ax to clear his land,
though often he burnt trees as they stood and took them to asheries
to receive the only money he saw in the first year. Mighty rafts
lunged down the Delaware to Philadelphia. Lumbering on a grand
scale moved west from Maine, assailed the Adirondack forest, moved
on to Michigan and Wisconsin. At night the lumberjacks upon the
"deacon-seat" sang their ballads, told tall tales, played tricks, remembered perils past, invented a new vocabulary, and scorned a softer
life. To make you see it, I suppose I shall have to start with "Uncle
John" Nichols.

"Did you know it was my eighty-fourth birthday?" he said, leaning his ax against the house. "You caught me chopping. The year I
was seventy, I cracked rocks all one summer. 'Twasn't as hard as
choppin' wood—I didn't have to pull out an ax. That's my grandson
diggin' potatoes, a smart lad but he aches for a lickin' some days.
Come right in. Jenny, here's that girl again, and the Professor, and
a couple other boys."

The daughter-in-law welcomed us with the serene grace that you find in the hills. Uncle John had himself some coffee and got his wind. We were in no hurry. He has the sort of eyes I like to look into, and I knew that, in spite of Eleanor Waterbury's introduction, a Professor is a dubious critter to one who has led a rich life unpuzzled by books. We talked casually and with long pauses.

"Yes, they had tiers of bunks in the shanties, just the way you've heard. The food wasn't what you'd call good, but we had enough . . . I was twelve when my father went to the Civil War, but before he went, he taught me a song about his dinnerpail. I'll chirp it for you."

It wasn't a lumberman's song, but it proved that he had a true voice, one of the rare ones you want to record. The trouble was that there was no electricity nearer than the hospitable little inn at Stratford. I nodded to Eleanor, and she asked straight out without any fuss.

There was another long pause. "Well, now," said Uncle John, "I haven't shaved today. No, I don't suppose it will spoil the singing. I really ain't dressed for town, though. O well, Jenny, I guess I look as well as I ever will. Jenny, I don't know where they are taking me, but I'll be back when I get back."

We had a nice room to ourselves at the hotel, and it didn't take Bill Hardy long to rig up the machine.

"Well, what'll you have, girl, *Shanty-Boy* or *Shanty-Girl*? I guess you'll be more interested in the boy, and that one will give you an idea of how we made out in lumbercamps sixty or seventy years ago." His hands were shaking a little, but he started in manfully:

O, a shantyman leads a wearisome life,
  Some think him free from care,
With the swinging of his ax from morning until night
  In the middle of the forest so bare.

In the shanty we lie—it is bleak and cold,
  And the cold stormy winds they do blow,
And in broken slumbers we do pass
  Those cold winter nights away.

At four o'clock our noisy old cook
    Cries out, "It's the breaking of day!"
And as soon as the daylight-star it does appear,
    To the wildwoods we must flee.

Had we ale, wine, or beer, our courage for to cheer,
    While we're here in the desert so wild!
Not the smile of any lass, nor the tip of any glass,
    But the thoughts of old Erin's isle.

Transported I am from a handsome maid
    To the banks of the Hudson stream,
Where the wolves and the owls and the panther's ugly growls
    It disturbs our nightless [nightly] dreams.

Then springtime comes in, double hardship then begins,
    With its waters so piercing and cold;
Dripping wet were our clothes, and our limbs were almost froze
    And our hand-spikes we scarcely can hold.

Over rocks, shores, and dams, gives employment to all hands,
    Our well-bounded raft for to steer;
Those rapids we do run, fierce—to us but merely fun,
    To avoid all slavish fears.

O, the shantyman is the lad that I love best,
    And I never will deny the same;
My heart it does despise those foolish city-boys
    Who think it a disgraceful name.

You can boast of your farms; give a shantyman his charms,
    For he fairly surpasses them all;
We will join each other's heart until death it does us part,
    Let our riches be great or small.

While we played back the record of what he had just sung, Uncle
John formed every word with his lips. Then beaming upon our
applause, he said: "That's fine—they got every word. It means more
to you when you know the words and can follow it along." He was
ready now to sing as long as his voice held out—which proved

to be a long time. He thought the *Shanty-Girl* should be performed next:

As I rode out one evening and the sun was a-going down,
I carelessly did wander to a place called Plymouth town.
I heard two maids conversing as slowly I rode by;
One said she loved her farmer's son, and the other a shanty-boy.

"I own I love my shanty-boy that goes out in the fall;
He is both stout and hearty, and fit to stand each fall.
With pleasure I'll receive him, in the spring when he comes home;
His money free he will share with me where the farmer's son has none."

"I own I love my farmer's son," those words I heard her say,
"And the reason why I love him, for it's home with me he'll stay;
He'll stay at home all winter, to the wildwoods will not go,
And when the springtime does come in, his lands he'll plow and sow."

  "All for to plow and to sow his ground!" the shanty-girl did say.
  "If the crops would prove a failure, your debts you could not pay;
  While my shanty-boy doeth work each day all through the rain and
      snow,
  Oft-times the bail would sell you out to pay the debts you owe."

"All for the bailiff selling me out, it does not me alarm.
What is the sense of running into debt when you live on a good farm?
How easy and contented my farmer's son will lie,
And tell some tales of love to me as the stormy winds pass by!"

  "O, how I hate such silly talk!" the shanty-girl did say.
  "Those farmer boys they are so green the cows might eat for hay.
  How easy you can tell them when they drive into town:
  The small boys comes up to them, says, 'Nick, how—air you down?'

"Now what I said of the shanty-boy, I hope you'll excuse me;
And for a silly farmer's son—I hope I can get free;
And if ever I get free from him, for a shanty-boy I'll go—
I'll leave *him* broken-hearted, his land to plow and sow."

Sooner or later we were sure to get *The Jam on Gerry's Rock*, most popular of all lumbermen's ballads. Mr. Nichols was glad to oblige with his version of what he called *Garian's Rock*:

Come all you true-born shanty-boys, wherever you may be;
I will have you give a-tention and listen unto me,
Concerning six brave shanty-boys, so manful and so brave,
Who broke the jam on Garian's rock, met with a watery grave.

It was all in the summer—in the springtime of the year:
Our logs were piled up mountains high, we could not keep them clear,
Until aloud our boss cried out with a voice avoiding fear,
"We'll break the jam on Garian's Rock, for Saginaw we'll steer."

Some of them are ready, whilst others they held back,
"To work upon a Sunday, I hardly think it's right."
Till six of those Carnadian [Canadian] boys to volunteer did go,
To break the jam on Garian's Rock and follow young Monroe.

They had not rolled off many logs when the boss to them did say,
"I would have you on your guard, my boys; this jam will soon give way."
He scarcely had those few words spoke when the jam did break and go
And carried away those six brave youths and their foreman, young Monroe.

When the rest of those brave shanty-boys those tidings came to hear,
To search for their dead bodies to the river did propare [repair].
One of those headless bodies—to their sad grief and woe—
On the beach lay cut and mangled, [and] the head of young Monroe.

They took him from the water, smoothed down his curly hair.
There was a fair among them whose cries would rang [rend] the air,
There was a fair among them, a maid from Saginaw town,
Whose mourns and cries would roam the skies for her lover that was drowned.

They buried him quite decently, all on the fourth of May.
Down by the river-bend there stands a tall pine tree;
O, the shanty-boys cut the woods all round in letters plain to show
The name and age and drownding of the foreman, young Monroe.

Young Clara was a widow's daughter, lived down by the river-bend,
Young Clara was a fine young girl, likewise the raftsman's friend;
And the wages of her own true-love the boss to her did pay,
And a liberal subscription received from the shanty-boys next day.

Young Clara did not serve life long with her sad grief and woe,
And in less than six months after, death brought to her relief:
And in less than six months after, when she was called to go,
Her last request was granted by being buried by young Monroe.

Now come all ye true-born shanty-boys who chance to pass that way.
Down by the river-bend there stands a tall pine tree;
O, the shanty-boys cut the woods all round: "True lovers here lie low."
One's name was Clary Benson, and the other was James Monroe.

Our singer was in full voice now, and he showed us that he knew
plenty of songs not specially connected with lumbering: he even gave
us two that seem to have drifted into the lower Adirondacks from
Australia—*Johnny Troy* and *The Wild Kerlonial Boy*, not to mention such a favorite of American sailors as *The Cumberland's Crew*.
I will give one that he sang with roguish emphasis for Eleanor:

> "I'm deep in love, my mind is troubled,
> I know not where to wander to
> Since my own true love has turned from me.
> Come, sit you down by the side of me
> And tell to me the very reason
> That I've been slighted so by she."—

> "Now you have asked a leading question,
> I will answer this reply:
> If you expect a fair young lady,
> You must lay your whiskey by."—

> "If I must leave off all my drinkin'
> And settle down in married life,
> I'll bid adieu to all fair maidens,
> And I'll never take a wife.

"I'll lay my head on a cask of brandy,
It's my fancy, I do declare;
But while I'm drinkin', I'm always thinkin'
How I might gain some lady fair.

"The oceans 're wide, I cannot wade them,
Nor neither had I wings to fly,
But must I hire some jolly boatswain
To ferry o'er my love and I.

"I wish my love was a bunch of roses
Planted down by yonder fall,
And that I myself was a pretty dewdrop
That on her bosom I might fall.

"I wish I was in Cold Castle's garden
Where the marble stones are black as ink,
And all those pretty girls adore me—
I'll sing no more until I drink!"

We had a very mild drink and started for Uncle John's after two hours of solid pleasure. Before we left, he asked us to play off a couple records to the people in the kitchen and in the bar; they congratulated him properly. On the road he started to hum another song, perhaps to show us that he knew lots more. He was getting a little sad.

"Some of the young ones," he said, "don't seem interested in the old songs, but Jed offered me five dollars last winter if I'd sing in his theatre. I'd a done many things different if I'd gone to school."

"Well," I said, "you've had a good time and you've given pleasure to a lot of people."

"Yes, lots of them tell me to come and see them—I don't notice they come after me."

"We came," said Eleanor, "and it was all fine."

He got out of the car slowly. This is the part I always dislike; they always remind me of Grandfather Thompson.

"I don't suppose I'll ever see you again," he said, fumbling for the birthday present Eleanor had brought him.

"O, sure," she said, "I'm coming up with some magazines and get your picture."

"My package," he mumbled, and went into the house.

"He's a beautiful old man," Eleanor said. The rest of us weren't saying anything.

Like the sailors, our lumbermen have a rhymed alphabet, which, so far as I know, is never *sung* in York State but merely recited. Here is a version from Essex County:

> A is for axes, you very well know,
> B for the boys who can swing it also,
> C is for chopping so early begun,
> D is the danger we oft-times do run.

> Chorus: So merry, so merry, so merry are we,
>   No mortals on earth are so happy as we.
>   Hi derry, lo derry, lo derry down;
>   The shanty-boy's merry when nothing goes wrong.

> E is for echo that through the woods rang,
> F is the foreman who headeth our gang,
> G is for grindstone, so swift it did turn,
> H is the handle so smooth it was worn.

> I is for iron that marketh our pine,
> J is for joker that's never behind,
> K is for keen edge our axes doth keep,
> L is for logs our harvesting reaps, [or]
> L is for lice that keeps us from sleep.

> M is for moss that we stick in our camps,
> N is the needle that mendeth our pants,
> O for the owl that hooteth by night,
> P is the pine that always fell right.

> Q is for quarreling we do not allow,
> R is for river we run our logs through,
> S is the sled so stout and so strong,
> T is the team that hauls them along.

U is the use that we put our teams to,
V is the valley we draw our logs through,
W is the wildwood we leave in the spring,
X, Y, and Z find us all home again.

In a version from Saranac Lake, the last line of the refrain for some stanzas runs:

The shanty-boy's well when the cook flies around.

In this version I like better also the line for the letter H:

H is for helves, how smooth they were worn!

A favorite song describes the lumberjacks' social forays:

One Monday morning
In eighteen-eighty-five,
I thought myself quite lucky
To find myself alive.

I harnessed up my horses
My business to pursue,
A-drawin' logs to E.-Town [Elizabethtown]
As my Daddy used to do.

The ale-house bein' open,
The whiskey bein' free,
Soon as one glass was empty
Another was filled for me.

Instead of goin' eight loads,
I didn't have but four;
I got so drunk on Fisher Hill
I couldn't draw no more.

I met an old acquaintance
As if it were by chance,
And he told me that night
There was goin' to be a dance.

I was hard to persuade,
But at last I did agree,

And we were to meet
Where the fiddlin' was to be.

My father followed after,
As I have heard them say;
He must have had a pilot
Or he never'd have found the way.

He peeked in every key-hole
Where he could see a light,
Till his old gray locks were wet
With the dew of the night.

There was four of us big Irish lads
Got on the floor to dance
With four as pretty French girls
As ever came from France.

The fiddler bein' willin',
His elbow bein' strong,
We danced *The Wrongs of Ireland*
For four hours long.

You old women, don't tell any lies,
'Twill only raise a fuss.
You're guilty of the same yourself,
Perhaps a damn sight wuss.

We'll go home to our plow, boys,
We'll whistle and we'll sing.
I never will be caught in such
A drunken scrape again.

In a version containing a number of local references, and entitled
The Dance at Clintonville, we get a glimpse of a colored musician:

Now daylight is breaking,
And we have danced enough;
We will spend a half an hour
In gathering cash for Cuff.

In a similar bouncing rhythm is a *Lumberman's Song* which describes the life in a camp at Newcomb (Essex), about the year 1870; it illustrates the frequent touches of satire found in this type of composition:

> Winter it has come again,
> And to the woods we go,
> To chop and skid and draw the logs
> Through the cold and drifted snow.
>
> It is work and work, from three till nine,
> Shiver and ready to freeze;
> But when we're in the shanty,
> We smoke and chew at ease.
>
> There was the leading teamster,
> He is full of funny tricks;
> His name I mean to mention,
> Was Huey Mallinix.
>
> He drove a fine, excited team;
> He'd have us up at three,
> Saying, "Go and harness your horses, boys,
> You have to follow me".
>
> There was the three McFarley boys,
> There's Tom, there's Bob, and Jim;
> Besides, there was John Cummings
> To roll the timber in.
>
> They loaded our horses to the ground
> With ten logs every time;
> And we would think it early
> If we got in at nine.
>
> And at the "double-header"
> Or an overhanging cliff,
> We had to be quite careful
> But we all had to just lift.

We rolled the logs and loaded the sleighs
And chained them on with care;
And if we had to leave a log,
They all commenced to swear.

The cook got up at two o'clock,
And breakfast soon was on;
The Boss crawled out of bed,
And his clothes he soon would don.

He'd grab the fire-poker,
And on the stove-pipe he would drum;
You would hear us boys a-tumbling out
While the Boss shouts, "Come, boys, come!"

Cold winter it is over,
And the spring is coming on,
And by the help of God, brave boys,
We'll all get home again.

We'll kiss the girls and squeeze them,
And play with them for fun;
And so lovingly they will say to us,
"You've all got home—well done!"

Miss Gertrude A. Jenks, of Schroon Lake, who brought me this song, had a few explanatory notes:

The real Boss came to camp only on payday, bringing money in a sheepskin bag. The Shanty Boss kept order as much as he could. They used to have two teams and drivers to take the lead—to start first in the morning. They tried to beat the others to the job. Their harnesses were all trimmed up with ribbons and tassels. Sometimes another teamster would want to get started ahead of the lead; he would sneak out early in the morning. A favorite trick was to pour water around the sleighs so they would freeze to the barn-floor. A "double-header" was a big skidway in a dangerous place; they took these logs first. Drumming on the stove-pipe, by the cook or the shanty boss, was called "ringing the gong". There were no funny names in the older lumber camps.

There are plenty of funny names now. At Mill Stream Camp on

Tug Hill in 1926 the *swamper* or *brush-rabbit* was the man who cut
trails through the fine brush for horse and driver or sledder. The
tailer was the one who ran logs down through loaders. The *cook's
swamper* did the dirty work for the cook; the *lobby hog* cleaned up
and made beds. The *road-monkey* patched holes in roads; the *whistle
punk* was the handy man for the tractor. The men in this camp made,
on a standard model used elsewhere, a song composed bit by bit and
tried out at night. Anyone was permitted to invent a stanza, but it
must pass muster with the rest; as clear a case of "communal composition", whatever that means, as you could find. Most of the stanzas
were satirical, all intended in fun; the opening and closing stanzas
are more or less standard. I give also the second stanza as a sample of
how the song was "filled in":

> Come all you old-timers, wherever you may be,
> Come sit yourselves down and listen to me;
> And I'll tell you a story that will make you all sad
> Of the scrub bunch of lumberjacks Lard Clemens had.
>   Derry down, down; down, derry down.

> Here's to Lard Clemens, the fat, greasy slob,
> Went way up on Mill Stream and took a log job
> To cut, skid, and haul to the Harvester Mill,
> But he couldn't have done much without Windy Bill . . .

> Come all you good people, adieu to you all,
> For Christmas is coming and I'm off to the Falls;
> And when I get there, I'm off on a spree,
> For when I've got money, the devil's in me.

In the same form and with practically identical opening and close
is *Blue Mountain Lake*, which has stanzas like this:

> One morning before daylight, Jim Lou got mad,
> Knocked hell out of Michael; the boys were all glad.
> His wife she stood by, and truth for to tell,
> She was tickled to death to see Michael catch hell.

George Colon, who knows the Blue Mountain song, has a store of
other ballads, including a very long one about a gang of lumberjacks

.from Plattsburg who were afflicted with lice. The guilt of their introduction was laid upon a certain Bill; the boss ordered a general search
by Henry.

> Now Henry's eye must have been keen,
> Because he found them all.
> "On me you found a few," said Bill,
> *"But then, I say they're small."*

To make matters worse, the cook was accused of making sour bread.
When she was banished, Ben drove her away:

> With blankets warm they wrapped her up,
> And a smile at him she tossed,
> And in the operations
> The team and crew got lost.

Pedicular difficulties could be turned to amusement, if we are to
accept the word of a Lake Placid resident whose parents were both
camp-cooks. One of my students had told him Walter Edmonds'
tale of the racing caterpillars on the canawls.

"I can tell you one better than that," and he proceeded to tell me a
tale that he swore was absolute truth: At night when the lumberjacks
were around the fire talking and singing, all of a sudden one would
challenge the other to a fight. The two men would then sit on a bench
and reach inside their flannel shirts that hadn't been off all winter, and
each would pull out a "bedbug". They would just touch the bugs to
each other and then put them on the bench real close. Soon the bugs
were touching each other of their own accord, and then the real fight
would begin. They would always fight until one had killed the other.
One winter a man had a favorite fighter that he kept on his chest where
the hair was thickest. That was the champion; it killed more than a
hundred bugs that season.

You will see that with this story we have reached the verge of
the region of tall tales. In the chapters on *Heroes of Tall Tales*, *The
Injun-Fighters*, and *Mountaineers*, I have told some of the cycles
familiar to the lumbermen. After all, Bunyan and Greenfield were
lumberjacks; John Darling was a rafter. But it was not merely the
saga-hero of the cycles about whom tall tales were told; a favorite

story might be attributed to anyone in camp—it might be claimed for yourself.

Probably the best liked of all the tall tales is the one about a harness that stretched and then contracted: that story always appears in the Paul Bunyan saga—Robert Frost has put it into a poem, and so has Walter Hard. Here is a plain version from Essex County:

A young lumberman had just made a new set of harnesses. He went into the woods one day to get a load of logs. He didn't get home till late. It was dark 'n' he couldn't see very well. All of a sudden he realized he'd lost his load somewhere. He couldn't see a thing of his wagon, even. Well, he thought 'twas funny, o' course, but 'twas too dark to go back for it then; so he just took care of his team and left the ends of the harness hangin' over the stump there. The next mornin' he went out, and the load was snubbed right up against the stump. You see, it was cold durin' the night 'n' the new leather had contracted.

This version is a combination of two types of tall tale: the shrunken harness—which is made to contract for various reasons—and the powerful cold. Just how much a harness can contract, and just how valuable a knowledge of the folk-tale might be, were borne in upon my ignorance by Mr. E. J. Grant, who worked in 1925 for Old Charlie, a "jobber" on the southern slope of Tug Hill:

The largest load of logs that season was drawn by one of the Dean boys; he drove the boss's big blacks and had a webb harness. The road was all the way downhill until they reached the landing where there was a hard pull. The day was cold, and the road was like glass. He had extra large logs, so therefore had a big scale, and as he neared the landing, he noticed that the webbing in the traces was stretching, and the team was past the landing when the bobs took a sudden drive from the road, and he found himself in a bad fix. The team would do just as he ordered; so he threw a block behind them so they couldn't slip back. The snow was piled high above the bobs, and he realized it would be some job to shovel them out. After careful planning and making sure he had the team well placed, he ran to the creek and threw a pail of water on the traces. This caused them to shrink back to their original length, and brought the load to the team. It was Dean's clever act that brought that load to the landing; and when the scalers totalled that load it measured 5,957 feet.

Ignorant man that I am, I should have had some difficulty believing all of Mr. Grant's stories if I had not been a student of folklore. I am perfectly willing, however, to accept the tale about one Christmastide of 1903 when Mr. Grant's father—the Charlie of the lumbercamp—decided on the second evening before the holiday to surprise his family by coming home across the snow. It is a plain tale of strength and courage:

He left Twenty-two at four a. m. and rode to Number Four camp, where he and a friend put on snow-shoes and started on an eight mile trip south on a blazed trail for Osceola. It was snowing hard and the trail was hard to follow. About dusk in the afternoon, they realized they had lost the trail. They started to back-track, but night overtook them, and they were prepared to build a fire, but everything was so damp that their efforts were futile. They lay out, and by morning every sign of their tracks was gone. They had no idea how far they were off the trail. They tramped all day, and along in the afternoon Charlie while crossing a creek got his feet wet. At dark they gathered wood for a fire; got birch curles and made great preparations, and then they hovered over their only match, which only sputtered and went out. They took turns running a circle that night, for it was thirty below zero, and they realized that they both couldn't lie down. The third morning broke bright, and they followed their southern direction and came out about noon after forty hours.

Charlie was frosted to his knees, and after letting a local doctor take his toes off at first joint without giving him a bit to deaden the pain, went to the hospital and had them removed, leaving him club-footed on both feet.

Call it what you may, a neighbor near where Charlie came out, awakened her husband on that Christmas night and claimed that she had heard Charlie call. The family had a dog which sat looking up toward the woods for the three days that Charlie was lost. Charlie had sent a letter saying that he would not be home, but the dog's actions began to cause the wife to worry.

More curious and harder to believe, if you are not a folklorist, is another of Mr. Grant's tales:

I think the boss had one of the meanest horses in the camp that season that ever lived. In fact, he didn't; he died. He was hurt with a falling tree and only lived a short time after. His teamster got along with him real well, receiving no injury from him until after he had been dead six hours, when he kicked Jack in the mouth and knocked out three teeth. It is true, for I saw it happen.

Did you ever hear about the time Old Mike, who was working for Little John, pulled the stub out of the ox's foot? Jim McCaw helped throw the ox and actually saw him bite on the piece and pull it out. It was eight inches long and had entered the foot just in front of the doclaws.

Another type of the true tall tale is illustrated by one about Martin Kelly, jam dynamiter on the West River in Hamilton County; the lumbermen say this happened "years ago":

His dynamite was frozen, as it often is in the spring of the year. Martin had a tent on the bank of the river with a stove in it to thaw out the dynamite. When he had it thawed, he put on the caps and fuses, and started out to blow the jam. The caps must have hit together and exploded. The explosion blew Martin out of the tent and into the river, leaving him unconscious. It is said that no live man could have floated down that wild river. Anyway, he washed up on the bank at a bend. The boys carried him to camp and brought him to. He hadn't a scratch on him; he was as well as ever. He died only recently.

Of course, some of the lumbermen like to draw a longer bow. Mr. Alec Couchey astonished his niece up in Essex County with the following remarks:

Gosh, the lice were awful in that camp. They were so darn big we had to nail the stove down to keep them from walking off with it. The mosquitoes was awful one time when we were choppin' wood in a swamp. We got one big tree—must 'a' been three foot through on the stump. We'd chopped it pretty near through, but it still didn't fall over. By the time we got it chopped 'way through, we begun to wonder *why* it didn't tumble over. Well, sir, we looked up, and there was the awfullest cloud of mosquitoes up there you ever see. Great big fellows. And they were hangin' onto that tree and holdin' it right up straight. I took my axe and clim' up there to drive 'em off. I hit at one of 'em, but the darn animal bit a chunk out of my ax . . .

It isn't only in the North Country that such stories are told. Wherever there are lumbermen, there are tall tales. In the hilly region around Hartwick, Otsego County, Mr. Ralph Potter did lumbering. He says that in one place the land was so hilly that they tied weights to the horses' heads to keep them from falling over backward. It was so cold in winter that when their cook tried to call them to dinner, they could see her come out and put the horn to her lips, but they heard no sound. In the spring, when things thawed out, they heard the horn blowing steadily for six months. Disconcerting and amazing things were always happening; one of the lumbermen, longing for domestic joy, built himself a house. Working on a foggy day, he shingled three times the length of the house into the fog.

The 'jacks like to tell stories about those French-Canadians who make up an important part of the help in every northern lumbercamp. They say that the Frenchmen love pea-soup above everything in the world; as the rhyme goes:

> Pea-soup and johnny-cake
> Make the Frenchman's belly ache.

The lumberjacks say that the "Canucks" bore holes in their peavey-handles and fill the holes with pea-soup so that they can lunch when rolling logs.

There was one mild old "Canuck" named Charlie living at Forestport (Oneida). Like nearly all lumbermen, he could kill a lot of liquor; in his own opinion he never got "soused", but once was terribly "bitten" after a period of refreshment. He paid to a fellow-lumberjack the sum of two hundred and fifty dollars for a parrot which, it was claimed, had such superlative powers of speech that she had a remark for any occasion.

After Charlie had handed over the money, he said to the parrot, "Are you worth two hundred and fifty?"

"No doubt," said the parrot.

Charlie took the bird home, and for two weeks it never uttered a word. Finally the disgusted owner exclaimed, "I was a damn fool to pay two hundred and fifty for you."

"No doubt," said the parrot.

Wherever you find a group of men living as intimately as lumbermen must, you find trickster tales and practical jokes. I give a sample, from Essex County, that shows how practical the effects of a joke can be:

Jim liked to put phosphorus on his face. Sometimes he would fill his mouth full of kerosene, then light a match and blow a flame clear across the room. One day a man came to camp who had left his wife and children without telling them where he was going. Earlier that fall, a fire had burned over a hill, and often a flame would flash up from the duff. When the newcomer saw one of these flashes, he told the others that he had had a warning and ought to go back to his wife. Later he went down to the barn to look after his horses. While he was gone, Jim dressed up in a blanket, took a mouthful of kerosene, and went toward the barn. When the worried husband came out of the barn, Jim lighted a match and blew; it looked as if a ghost were spouting a column of fire ten feet long. The man jumped back into the barn and held the door until the others came to rescue him. He went home the next day.

It is the newcomer who is likely to be tricked, especially if he is unlearned in the ways of the woods. In one camp on Tug Hill they sent young Dick down to town to buy them a pair of Sky Hooks, which, not knowing the lore of Paul Bunyan, he gravely ordered. Day after day he hunted the Side-Hill Jinx, which, he was assured, looks much like a fox except that nature has provided it with left legs shorter than the right so that it can walk or run on side-hills.

A lumbercamp is a good school of character, and part of the lore is concerned with funny people. George Colvin of Osceola (Lewis), named "Lippy" for his entertaining eloquence and ability as a songster, likes to tell about a 'jack nicknamed the "Bank-Beaver" because he was afraid to drive logs on the river, preferred to poke at them from the bank—hard work—and then yelp about what a driver he was. He had a favorite boast that he was going to "shoot the sun down". He would give away everything one day and ask for it all back on the next. One time he craved a pocket-book but had no money to pay for it; he told the sales-girl he guessed he'd charge it.

As is the case aboard ships, the cook is sometimes the most amusing person in the crowd. There was a couple, oldish, who hired out to cook at a Brandreth (Herkimer) camp; I shall call them Whoop, because they caused a good deal of amusement and created considerable noise. One night Whoop came back from Tupper Lake, not *quite* "orry-eyed", and started arguing with his wife.

All the while she was cooking, he sat in the corner in a high-backed rocking chair, calling her names and making nasty remarks. Finally, goaded beyond endurance and having thrown all the missiles in sight, Mrs. Whoop picked up a five-gallon coffee-pot, half full of coffee and grounds, whirled it around her head three or four times, and let go. It hit her husband square in the chest, and upset him backwards in the corner with the chair on top of him.

Finally he gained enough courage to crawl from under the chair, along the wall, to his room. After sticking his head three or four times from the blankets which served as a door, he decided to apologize and said humbly, "Well, you ain't what I called you, but you are a bitch".

Down in Sullivan County they claimed that Old Dan Tucker, hero of an early minstrel and play-party song, was really one of their local characters, a lumberjack; one old sawyer would scrape a three-stringed fiddle and shrill out these stanzas:

> Old Dan Tucker he went to the store;
> A string and a bag and not a thing more,
> A little piece of pork and a little flour too.
> Tucker went to work for the Tylertown crew.
>
> Old Dan Tucker was a fine old man;
> He washed his face in the frying pan,
> Combed his hair with a wagon-wheel,
> And died with the tooth-ache in his heel.
>
> Old Mis' Tucker, she got drunk,
> She fell in the fire, and she kicked out a chunk:
> And when a coal got in her shoe,
> O my gosh, how the fire flew!

Miss Mildred Tyler, from whom I first learned about John Darling and the other tales of Sullivan County, says that a collection of lumbering lore (or any other sort) might well take its name from that song: "A little piece of pork and a little flour too."

For all their jesting and their delight in amusing character, the men of the lumbercamp know death and its truths. The most famous tragic ballad, *The Jam at Gerry's Rock*, I have already presented in Mr. Nichols's version. I shall now give two which, so far as I know, have never been printed and certainly have not been made available in well-known collections. The first was sung by a lady of ninety-three, living at Sidney; her husband was a lumberman. She didn't know its title; perhaps we may call it simply *Frank Farrow*:

I am a lad seen trouble and sorrow, many accidents occur.
I will sing to you the latest—no doubt you all have heard.
It was out in Sullivan County where scores of men are found;
Known to all throughout other lands is that famous lumber-town.

The robins they were singing in the merry month of May.
Frank Farrow left his father's home so happy and so gay,
Little dreaming of the danger in that forest tall and sound,
Which has swept away many a loving son in that famous lumber-town.

It was on one Monday morning he began his daily toil;
Little did he know that morrow he would lie beneath the soil.
Parting from a living father, and laid beside his mother's mound,
Never more to hear those hemlocks falling, in that famous lumber-town.

His brothers a tree was cutting, and toward the earth did fall;
It caught on a limb of maple, and Jerry to his brother did call.
It shot down like an arrow, and crushed Frank to the ground;
He was killed there, [beside] his brothers, in that lumber-town.

Now Frank in his grave is sleeping, where the hemlocks creep and wave
Little do we know which one of us will next go to our grave.
Whenever we visit the cemetery, let us stroll by Frank's mound,
Who met his death in Sweenup Camp, in that famous lumber-town.

This naïve ballad would probably have been lost completely if a student had not chanced upon it, but the song about *Tebo* (Thibault) is still known to a considerable number of people. I first heard about it from Mrs. Mary Barnett Burke, who got a fine version with tune from Mrs. Margery Sisson White, whose father is a member of the A. Sherman Lumber Company, with headquarters in Potsdam. When Mr. Sisson sang it to his daughter, he said that Tebo was a "Canuck" working on a drive in the Jordan River. The man who composed the ballad made other songs popular in lumbercamps, including one which I covet, *Bedbugs, go back in your holes*; Mrs. Burke's father knew him, and I wish that I had. The tune is about the same as *The*

Jam on Gerry's Rock, and a few of the words show the inspiration of the better known ballad:

It was on the sixth of May, my boys, as you will understand,
When Sherman ordered out his men all for to break a jam.
The logs were piled up mountains high, the water so dreadful strong
That it washed away poor Tebo and the logs that he was on.

He nobly faced the water and manly swam away,
He tried his best to save himself in every shape and way,
The jam soon overtook him, towards sad grief and woe,
And we found his drownded body in the Racket flood below.

Young Akey came from Saranac, and this I do explain;
He tried his best to save him, but it was all in vain.
The waters they roared over him, he was forced to let him go,
And away then went poor Tebo for to meet his God, we know.

O, Tebo was an able man, drove many a different stream.
It appeared that very morning that his last hours had came;
He had served his time on earth that he was here for to stay,
He bid goodbye to all the boys, all on the sixth of May.

O, Tebo leaves a widow and five young children small,
All at the mercy of his friends who drove the Racket Fall.
A subscription was made for them, each man his share did pay,
To feed and clothe the orphans he left behind that day.

About four o'clock in the afternoon on the twenty-ninth of May
We found his drownded body, we laid it in the clay.
I hope his soul is in Paradise, with God on high to rest,
While we who mourn for him below will meet him with the blest.

"It is now I bid you all goodbye—my time has come to go
To answer at the Judgment-bar for sins on earth below!"
The past is bad, the future hidden; no earthly tongue can tell
The agony of that poor man when into the water he fell.

In a sense, the lumbering industry of New York has said with Tebo, "My time has come to go". In 1840, New York was the largest timber-producing state in the country; in 1860 we were second; in 1920, twenty-first. The balladry which I have been giving, and some of the stories, are concerned with an era when Albany was the second largest market for the export of lumber in the United States—as it was in 1860; when the lumbercamps were so large and so numerous that the workers thought of themselves as a special profession or guild, with folkways of their own. We still manufacture an enormous amount of paper from pulp, particularly in a dozen towns north of Albany; we still make some of the best furniture, especially at Jamestown (Chautauqua); but the era of the Big Camps and the ballads is pretty well over.

One special type of lumbering lore I have saved till last, partly because it is now least known, partly because it has a unique flavor: the lore of the rafters on the Delaware. So far as I can learn, the first raft on that noble river was made far back in 1764 by a man of Connecticut Yankee stock named Daniel (or David) Skinner. While serving as a sailor in the West Indies he had learned the value of tall pines for masts; consequently his first venture as a raftsman was the floating of six spars, eighty feet in length, for which he received twenty dollars apiece. His feat of running them all the way to Philadelphia from a region where New York and Pennsylvania meet was regarded so highly that he was given the freedom of the City of Brotherly Love and the title of LORD HIGH ADMIRAL OF THE DELAWARE—almost as gaudy as Christopher Columbus's blazon, ADMIRAL OF THE FLEET OF THE OCEAN. Apparently the Yankee knew better than Columbus how to find material value in his title; he gravely collected two bottles of wine from each steersman who ran his river, and one bottle from each "forehand" or subordinate oarsman.

In the century which followed Skinner's first trip, rafting flourished to such an extent that in the peak year of 1875 over three thousand rafts were floated down the Delaware in a single year. The chief season was in the spring, just as the river started to recede from its flooded height; and of course that time of high water was short. If there was a freshet in June, there was another short rafting season. If a June rain started some evening, the raftsman would put out a pail; an inch of water in the pail by morning was the sign of a "suckerfresh"—stranded rafts could be moved on to their destination.

In a raft there might be 100,000 feet of sawn wood or a similar amount of logs; sometimes the logs of hemlock had been stripped for the tanneries. The rafts were made without nails, pinned together with "grubs", pieces of sapling about three feet long. A large raft might be one hundred and fifty feet to two hundred and ten feet in length by forty to fifty feet in width, sometimes with a cabin on it, ten by fifteen feet in size. A hundred bushels of potatoes might be taken along for sale in the Philadelphia market. Food for the rafters themselves was carried along in big grub-boxes, but that supply might be supplemented by other rations when the raft was tied up at night. Steersmen regarded night-running as dangerous; there were sharp turns in the river, swift currents, and great apron-dams to be run. The evenings might be spent at inns along the way, or the rafters might roll up in their blankets and sleep on the raft preparatory to an early start. A "night-cap" was obtainable right on a raft, from the large jug which was placed in the exact center of the structure, at the foot of the "shirt-pole".

During the day, the steersman, who was always the boss of the raft and often its owner, stood in the rear, usually operating a big oar. On the small "colt" rafts there was one large oar in front, worked by as many as three men, for it was very heavy and hard to push. The big rafts had two oars on the front, and either two or (rarely) three aft. The forty-foot oars were set on sixteen-inch blocks and *pushed*, not pulled, breast high with the strength of the mightiest shoulders York State has known. At the top of his clarion lungs the steersman would cry: "Now, boys, pick it up lively. Give her three clips Jersey . . . Now two clips Pennsylvany . . . Holt!" As you went downstream, Pennsylvania was on the right and New Jersey on the left.

It was an exciting life, full of danger to men and property. At a sharp turn, Oven Rocks, a big raft of the Palmer family's lost 130,000 feet of lumber. But if all went well, the raftsmen from Delaware County would be in Philadelphia within two weeks, celebrating on "red-eye".* Then they would probably come back by way of New York City and, after the middle of the nineteenth century, the Erie Railroad, roaring such favorite ditties as "Year of Jubilo" and "Stone-

* In later years the raft was sold oftener at Easton, Pa., or at Trenton, N. J.

blind Jonny, fill up the bowl". One famous rafter of Irish birth, "Boney" Quillan, could make up songs of his own. Conductor Sam Walley of the Erie R. R. knew how to manage Boney and his friends, but some others were not so successful.

I like the story told at Hancock about three famous rafters: "Boney" Quillan, "Rit" Appley, and "Add" Van Loan. They had just completed a trip down the river and were anxious to return home. Finding themselves stranded in a small "depot" on the Erie Railway, they were informed that the last train had left early in the afternoon, they must wait till next day for another. "But we aim to get home," said the rafters. The station-agent paid no attention. "Rit" stepped to the ticket-window, struck his ax deep into the floor, and said, "We want a train out of here mighty quick". "Add" began to bore holes in the floor with his big augur. "Boney" walked outside and began to break off the shrubbery. The telegraph operator swung into action; in almost no time, an engine pulled into that "depot" with a single empty coach to take home the rafters.

At all times, "Rit" was a commanding person. He knew his Bible well enough to speak with authority even to Higher Powers. One dark night he barked his shin and was heard to say in his deep Scotch bass: "By the great Bugaboo! If I was the Almighty and had a moon, I'd hang it out on a night like this." When a Philadelphia storekeeper was trying to sell him an overcoat at a price which shocked his Scotch soul, he rumbled: "By the great Bugaboo! Before I'll pay that much for one of them dad-blasted things, I'll paint myself green and run through the woods."

I don't know the name of that raftsman who stopped at a restaurant on the long trip home. In the seat across from him at table he deposited his carpetbag. When the meal was over, the waiter charged for two lunches, explaining that the bag had occupied a place at table and must therefore pay. Meditatively the rafter looked at his ax, but after a slight hesitation paid the double charge. Then he rapidly stuffed the contents of his bag into his pockets, and began to cram the bag with all the food within reach. "Eat, durn you!" he yelled. "I've paid for yuh—eat!" Then, swinging his ax in glittering arcs, he went out and boarded his train.

"Major" James J. Webb, originally from the Harvard section but later of Walton, had a favorite tale of his rafting, usually told as valuable instruction for youth and quite worthy of a county which produced John Darling. The Major declared that one evening after a hard day's run he tied up his raft, intending to have a good night's rest at a little inn. The supper was hearty and the red-eye satisfactory. The Major retired in great content, only to be wakened shortly by certain crawling inhabitants of his bed who were not paying for their lodging. He knew the species and knew how to take care of the situation. He threw back the covers, lighted match after match, and transferred his unwholesome bedfellows, with the burnt matches, to a convenient receptacle. Early next morning he was awakened by the sound of ethereal music which for some time he was unable to identify or locate. Finally his curiosity got the better of his drowsy musical enjoyment; he arose and walked toward the receptacle. During the night the former denizens of his bed, true sons of the Delaware, had constructed a raft of burnt matches and were now shoving on tiny oars while singing in exquisite harmony, "Pull for the shore, brothers, pull for the shore."

Just what songs the rafters themselves sang it is difficult to learn, though all are agreed that for original ditties "Boney" Quillan was chief troubadour. Mr. Lorin Leonard of Hancock, wise in the ways of the Delaware, sang one song to my friend and student, Fred Mohrman, who first interested me in the rafters. It is a merry description of an accident:

> We sailed around old Butler's,
>   No danger did we fear,
> Until we came to Sawmill Rift,
>   Went plumb against the pier.
>
> There was a man upon the raft,
>   His name it was Big Mose;
> He hopped around among the logs
>   And saved 'most all our clothes.
>
> Chorus: And shove around the grog, boys,
>   The chorus around the room,
>   For we are the boys that fear no noise
>   Although we're far from home.

Beside his talent for composing and singing ballads, "Boney" possessed a trickster's ability to get free drinks and free rides. Mr. Leslie
C. Wood, whose *Rafting on the Delaware River* (1934) is likely
to remain the classic work, tells two stories which I have selected
because I have had both brought to me as exploits known and told
about other folk-heroes; they are true trickster tales of our countryside for which Boney seems the likeliest original inspiration.

After the safe delivery of a raft, "Boney" found himself home-
ward-bound to Fishs Eddy full of spirit and spirits but without the
price of a railroad ticket. Boarding the train blithely, he "passed some
remarks" to those standing on the platform, then drew in his head,
displaying an old slouch hat in which was stuck a piece of paper resembling a ticket. Just before the conductor reached him, "Boney"
stuck his head out of the window and was so engrossed in the view
that he had to be called twice by the ticket-collector before he seemed
to hear. Jerking in his head, he caught the brim of his hat on the edge
of the window, lost his headpiece, and began to roar.

"Stop the train! Stop the train! My ticket's in that hat, and I ain't
got no money to get home on; besides, that's too good a hat to lose.
Stop the train, I say!"

"Here, here!" said the conductor. "You can't pull that rope, it's
a State's prison offence; you might wreck the train and kill us all."

"But my hat! No ticket, no money—I can't walk home, can I?"

"All right, all right! Forget the ticket, but for heaven's sake,
don't pull that bell-rope."

The other rafters tried to hide their mirth; probably the conductor
could guess how he had been tricked, particularly if he recognized
"Boney", but the troubadour was allowed to reach the inn at Fishs
Eddy that night.

Even more woeful was "Boney's" predicament one evening when
he found himself without rum, and, as he well knew, without credit
at the inn. Borrowing a gallon jug, he filled it partly full of water
and marched into the bar with an air of confidence, ordering two
quarts of rum. The bar-tender poured in the two quarts; "Boney"
started for the door.

"Hey, you! Wait a minute! Where's the money for that liquor?"

"I'm busted; you'll have to trust me."

"Sorry, 'Boney'. The boss ordered 'no trust', you know."

Quillan's utmost Irish blandishments and indignation proving of no avail, he said: "All right, if that's the way you treat an honest raftsman. Get that two-quart measure and I'll pour back what you gave me."

Presumably the pouring back was attended by a story, a song, or a masterly exhibition of rafting oaths. At any rate, "Boney" retired with two quarts of liquor to discover how rum tasted mixed in equal parts with water.

They still talk about "Boney" in the Delaware region, remembering that he fought in the Civil War, rafted again for many years, trained horses that nobody else could break, and finally injured his hip while playing with one of the children who regarded him as their favorite. His body died in the home for old soldiers at Bath, N. Y. Rafting on the Delaware was dying too. By 1850 the tall pines were gone; then the hemlocks gave out. "Rit" Appley's old handspike, six feet long and four inches in diameter, was no longer needed. Mighty Oscar Hawley of Downsville, who smashed a lifting machine that could register only one thousand pounds, is no more; he is gone into legend with "Date" Adams of Equinunk, who would carry a barrel of molasses from a box-car into a freight-house. We of a feebler generation are left to dispute whether Admiral Skinner's name was Daniel or David, and to wile from the memories of ancients the tales and songs of "Boney" Quillan. Speaking of songs, Mr. Clarence Cutting of Elizabethtown recites a poem called *Saranac River* which contains the spirit of all our lumbermen:

Ye hardy sons of freedom who round the mountain range,
Come, all you gallant lumbermen, come listen to my song.
On the sunny banks of the Saranac River, where its limpid waters flow,
We'll range the wildwoods over and again a-lumbering go.

And the music of our axes will make the woods resound,
And many a lofty forest pine we'll tumble to the ground;
And then around our good campfire we'll sing while the rude winds blow;
We'll range the wildwoods over and again a-lumbering go.

You may talk about your parties, your pleasures and your plays,
But pity us poor lumber-boys when dashing in our sleighs,

For we don't ask no better pastime than to hunt the buck and doe.
We'll range the wildwoods over and again a-lumbering go.

When our youthful days are over, our pockets getting long,
Each one will take his sweetheart and settle on a farm,
With enough to eat, to drink, to wear—and back to the world we'll go;
We'll tell our wives of the hard pastimes, no more a-lumbering go.

XII: Mountaineers

"THE gods of the mountain are not the gods of the plain." According to tradition, this majestic remark was made by Ethan Allen of Vermont while he sat at his ease in an Albany pub, scornful of the fact that Yorkers had offered a reward for his arrest. Many years later a gentler mountaineer, John Burroughs of Slabsides, uttered a sentence now lettered on a bronze plate adorning one of our hills: "Here the works of man are forgotten." While it is presumptuous to disagree with persons so august, a folklorist must assert his belief that the gods of the mountain were the gods of all our pioneers, and that the folk, looking upon our Catskills and Adirondacks, recall man's works, remembering them in a thousand legends, folkways, and names.

For two centuries we did not even bother to name the Adirondacks. To be sure, many Mohawks hunted there in winter, knew at least five routes to Montreal, and scornfully called the permanent residents "Tree-eaters" (Tatirondaks). The Iroquois knew the mountain lakes called "Tears of the Gods"; they told of the Great White Stag whose ghost drifted near Lake Placid; they trembled at mention of a Great Magic Bear and shivered at the name of Ha-tho, Spirit of Cold.

The traders at Albany were content to buy beaverskins from the Indians and house themselves warm against Ha-tho. In his Geography of 1756 Kitchin was satisfied to name the whole region "Couchsachrage an Indian Beaver Hunting Country".

A few picturesque Indians lived on from the age of Couchsachrage into the era of the White Guides. There was Old Sabael (Sabile, Sebele), an Abenaki born on the Penobscot and present at the battle of Quebec (1759) as a boy of twelve. When the Canadian Abenakis joined Britain in the War of 1812, Sabael left them, preferring to be a lonely hunter and guide in the Adirondacks. He lived to a great age, much admired and trusted by the whites—and for various reasons. He sold the discovery of a valuable iron mine at Keeseville to a white man for a bushel of corn and a dollar. He wore a magic string of beads, powerful against acts of malevolent nature: if there were a storm on the lake, he could escape it by dropping one bead from his canoe; if the thunder rolled, Sabael needed only to hang his beads on a tree; in the forest, he would take them from his pouch to frighten away all the Chepi (ghosts). Of one thing he was not afraid, and that was a wild beast. "Me no 'fraid; government no longer belong to wild beast," he would say, and would recount the legend of how the Wolf told the Lion that regency had passed to Man. Indian Lake is named for him, and you will hear Mt. Colvin called "Sabele".

Another Abenaki guide about whom the people of the Adirondacks still speak is Mitchell Sabattis (St. Baptist, Shabattis), son of old "Captain Peter" Sabbatis, whose eldest son Solomon went to college and turned out badly. Mitchell, on the other hand, who died in 1906 at the age of 105, was reckoned by "Adirondack" Murray and other experienced persons as one of the truly great guides. Incredible tales are told of his woodcraft: of his ability to tell by the sound of a deer's running how badly it was wounded, and to track it in the dark. I like best the story of his gentle advice to a white hunter who had raised his gun to shoot a wild duck. "I wouldn't," said Mitchell, "she has young ones." He married a white woman of Dutch descent and brought up a family of guides. We still honor him in the name of a mountain.

It was not until Mount Marcy was surveyed and named by the

State Geologist in 1837 that we began to hear much about guiding by whites. In that year Professor Ebenezar Emmons made the ascent of the loftiest peak in the Adirondacks (5,344 feet), naming it for a popular Governor; and in a report to the Legislature in 1838 the geologist suggested that *Adirondacks* be made an official designation for the mountain-range. A good many of us wish that a popular writer of that day, Charles F. Hoffman, trained for the law at Albany, had tried to scale Marcy a little earlier. He made his unsuccessful attempt one month after Emmons, and in his *Wild Scenes in the Forest and Prairies* (1839) suggested the strikingly appropriate name Tahawus, "It cleaves the sky". We frequently use the name now, and another suggested by Hoffman from the same Senecan tradition, "Falls of the Hanging Spear".

Upon his historic ascent of Marcy in 1837, Emmons had the services of two guides whose memory is still green. One of them was John Cheney, who was born in New Hampshire, lived in Ticonderoga, and moved to the McIntyre region where he was employed in the iron works. As a hunter he was so skillful and fearless that Hoffman thought that he must be the original of Cooper's Leatherstocking—a claim which must be regretfully denied. Someone asked Cheney how he felt when he suddenly came upon a crouching panther, a single bound in front. "I felt," he said, "as if I should kill him." Only once did Cheney prove careless as a woodsman, when the gun lying in his boat went off and wounded him in the ankle. He was all alone and far from help, but a deer was in view, and, as he said, "I felt that I might need that venison." So he shot the buck, packed some of its meat, cut himself crutches of two notched sticks, and with a bootful of blood made his way to the settlements. He lived to be eighty-seven, enjoying to the last such scenes as he described to Hoffman:

It makes a man feel what it is to have all creation under his feet. There are woods there which it would take a lifetime to hunt over, mountains that seem shouldering each other to boost the one whereon you stand, up and away Heaven knows where. Thousands of little lakes are let in among them so light and clean. Old Champlain, though fifty miles away, glistens below you like a strip of white birch when slicked up by the moon on a frosty night, and the Green Mountains of Vermont beyond it fade and fade away until they disappear as gradually as a cold scent when the dew rises.

The other guide who is known to have led Emmons up Marcy was Elijah Simonds, whom the historian of Elizabethtown calls "the greatest hunter and trapper that the Adirondacks ever produced". Elijah got his first fox when he was only eight years old, his first wolf at ten, and his first bear at eleven; his total bag is estimated at 3,000 fox, 2,000 deer, 150 bears, 12 wolves, and 7 panthers, not to mention uncounted numbers of mink, otter, and marten. Once at Blue Mountain he fought wolves for the possession of the deer he had shot; he explained that in this combat he used only his hatchet because he did not wish to waste ammunition on varmints. If he lacked the poetry and myth-making of certain other guides, his skill and courage will at least place him with such Injun-fighters and trappers as Nick Stoner and Nat Foster.

Possibly that historic first ascent of Marcy was shared by a young man whose fame one day was to surpass that of Cheney and Simonds. This guide, later known as "Old Mountain" Phelps, claimed that he had discovered the peak, and in 1849 he did blaze the first regular trail to its summit. Orson Schofield Phelps (1817-1905), the sage of Keene Valley, owes much of his reputation to a character-sketch published in the *Atlantic Monthly* (1878) by a graduate of Hamilton College, Charles Dudley Warner, whose little book of essays called *In the Wilderness* gives you the Adirondacks in the golden day of the master-guides. According to Warner, Phelps was not a great hunter, nor a very industrious guide; he was not even careful about his personal appearance, though his head had some of the shaggy nobility of Walt Whitman or John Burroughs. "I don't believe in this eternal sozzlin'," he said. "Soap is a thing I haint no kinder use for." What he had was the primitive myth-making that addressed Opalescent River as a pretty girl, that felt on a high peak what he called "heaven up-h'istedness".

He had a peculiar and at times limited vocabulary. He would ask whether you wanted to take "a regular walk or a random scoot"; when he found himself in what seemed an impenetrable thicket, he would say, "Waal, this is a reg'lar random scoot of a rigmarole."

After listening to a sermon that began at the Creation and got no-where, he observed, "It just seemed to me as if he was tryin' to git up a kind of a fix-up." Sometimes his expressions were strikingly just. For example, when Warner wished to make camp at Upper Ausable Pond on the *south* side, so that they might see all day the triple-crested mountain that Phelps and a friend had named the Gothics, the guide preferred to camp on the *north* side so that it would be necessary to row out to see the mountain. "Them Gothics," he said, "ain't the kinder scenery you want to *hog down.*" You can imagine how he felt on that day when he took some young ladies up Marcy, only to have them discuss fashions on the peak. All he would say was, "I was a good mind to come down and leave them there." He might have comforted himself as he did another day when he found a fragile flower in a lonely crevice: he said, "It seems as if the Creator had kept something just to look at Himself."

Probably "Old Mountain" Phelps understood mountains better than he did women, though he is known to have made one sage re-mark about them. At the campfire he terminated a long discussion by his single remark, "Waal, now, when you've said all there is to be said, marriage is mostly for discipline." The philosopher of Keene Valley was happily enough married himself, though his wife, if she tried to read his rambling poems, must have been sorely disciplined. He went on exhibiting his mountains until 1905, when he died at the age of eighty-two. Once when asked plans for the next day he said, "Well, I callerlate, if they rig up the callerlation they callerlate on, we'll go to the Boreas." I hope that, as he callerlated, he is in a place where he can take a random scoot through the mountains, per-haps accompanied by his sturdy son, Ed, who died only five years ago (1934). It is customary to speak of four generations of Adiron-dack guides, but two generations of the Phelps family lived to see all the great era.

Each generation of guides has revealed its contempt for the gods of the plains, worshipped by weaklings subject to "buck-fever". Old John Cheney used to describe the plight of a man who had never seen a moose but who was bound that he would shoot one. Squatting behind a stump, he beheld a great, shaggy creature lunging toward him out of the forest. "There he sot," said Cheney, "shakin' like an aspen, and I heard him say, kinda desp'rate, 'If you'll let me alone, I'll let you alone.' " A novice about to spend a night in an open shelter near Adirondack Loj, timidly asked his guide, Jed Rossman: "Isn't this dangerous? Aren't there wild animals about here?" Jed consoled him by saying, "Why yes, I found two bears in a trap right here, and there was eight more sittin' quietly on their haunches waitin' to get into the trap." The city man can be blamed for anything amiss. Said a native: "The city folks changed the name of Jones Pond to Lucretia, and the fish is got too fussy to take a holt." I remember a young lady calling to an elderly gentlemen who had spent so many summers in the Adirondacks that sometimes he thought like a guide. "Why are you skinning that log, Mr. Waterbury?" she called from her canoe. "So as to get it skun," he replied.

As a rule, the Adirondack guide eschews ridicule of a direct sort in favor of the subtler kind involved in the telling of tall tales. In the golden era the guide was not only a woodsman, hunter, fisherman, oarsman, and cook—with flapjacks as his specialty; he was also quite frequently a master of droll narrative. There was, for example, old Mart Moody of the Tupper Lake Region, who died in 1910 at the age of eighty-six, leaving a reputation for the ability to find anyone lost anywhere in the Adirondacks, and a fame for inexhaustible stories, told with quiet gravity. The advantage of hearing him at his own hearthstone—for which guests were always willing to pay—was that you could get accounts authenticated by his wife. He would turn to her and say: "Now wa'nt that so, Minervy? Wa'nt that so?" Without stopping her work she would reply: "Why, yes, Mart . . . Now what were that you were saying?"

One story was of the time when Mart and his friend Hi were out on the lake shooting ducks. It was one of those enchanting days when you can see into the depths of sky and lake. Suddenly a flock went skimming past. For almost the only time in his life Mart lost his calm, dropping his old-fashioned powderhorn over the side of the guide-boat. Being an excellent diver, Hi volunteered to recover the lost articles, and Mart sheepishly consented to permit the friendly sacrifice. When after a long wait Hi did not appear, Mart peered impatiently into the lucid water. "And what did I see?" Mart would ask. "What did I see? I saw that cuss down there on the bottom of the lake, pouring powder from my horn into his'n."

One day in February, Mart was hunting deer. Creeping around a high and narrow ledge, he slipped into a huge snowdrift. "How was I to get out?" Mart would ask you. "Well, I wondered and thought, and thought and wondered. Finally I had to walk home three miles, git a shovel, and dig myself out. How was that for being frustrated?" *Frustrated* was one of those words that Mart used with sudden effect, but I suppose that he himself was never really anything but triumphant. He would say:

One afternoon last season I was out in the woods when I saw five pa'tridges settin' in a row on the limb of a tree. I didn't have a gun with me; so pulled out my hunting-knife, took aim, and let her go. That danged knife split the limb so nice that all five birds were caught by the toes. That wa'nt all. The knife went skimming across the brook alongside the tree and killed a bear that happened to be loitering on the other side. While I was wadin' across the brook to get the bear, I caught my pants so full of trout that a button busted off, flew forty rod, and killed a fox. I suppose you might call some of that Adirondack luck.

Once Mart actually missed a shot at a deer. In utter disgust he walked to the nearest hardwood tree and proceeded to wrap his gun around its trunk, twisting the barrel into an indifferent letter S. Then with the gun slung over an arm he strolled on until he spied a big buck browsing at the base of a mountain. Forgetting that he had disabled his weapon, Mart fired with customary speed. "Well, yes," he would admit, "I missed the buck; but I didn't do so bad. The shot out of that twisted barrel went three times around the mountain and killed two bears and a woodchuck. I mention the woodchuck to keep the story accurate."

Adirondack luck and splendid timing combined on the day when Mart was in his guide-boat, chopping away at a big tree which had been obscuring his sight of deer. After a faithful description of how he chopped, Mart would say:

After all this careful plannin', the dang tree didn't fall as I had expected; it fell right across the front of the boat, throwin' me and the dog out and turnin' the boat end-for-end in the air. While I was floating in the air, I see the good old boat land in the water, right side up. I give myself a flip, and the next minute I landed right in my proper seat, slick 's a mink. Kind of shaked up, I started rowin' for home. When I got half way, I heard the dog barkin'—I'd clean forgot about him. It sounded 's if it come from the sky. I looked up, and there I saw a little speck about the size of a fly. It come closer and closer and kept gettin' bigger and bigger, until I saw, b'Jeepers, that it was my dog. I thought quick, sculled the oars a little, and the dog landed right smack on the seat he always rides on.

The fact is, boys, that in these mountains you have to think fast, and then it may not do you any good. There was that day on Ampersand Mountain when a couple of bears chased me. I run up a ravine that was just wide enough for one bear; thought I'd fight 'em one at a time. Just as I was ready to turn 'round and take care of them, I see another bear comin' for me from the other end of the ravine. Yep, you have to think fast in the mountains.

Here Mart would knock out his pipe and pretend to make for the door. One of his listeners would be sure to cry: "Hey, Mart! You haven't finished that story. What did you do then?" Mart would pause with his hand on the door. "Do?" he would reply. "I didn't do a dumb thing. The bears et me."

Another of his gloomy stories told of the trouble which he had with his herd of twenty registered Guernsey cows. Morning after morning, he would discover that some intruder had milked them dry. So one night he took his shotgun and went down to the corral close to the lake. He would describe how carefully he hid himself, and how grimly he waited as the hours "drug on". He said:

About midnight I heard a little splash down by the shore, and I peeked out, expectin' to see somebody come out of a boat and milk them cows. Do you know what I saw? Well, I was *frustrated*. A bunch of fish come up out of the water, flipped up to the cows' teets, and sucked them dry. That was too much for me—when a fish will come out of the water to swipe milk. I sold the cows, and if you boys will ketch some of them fish tomorrow mornin', you'll be doin' me a real favor.

After hearing some of Mart's stories one evening, two hunters decided that they would beat the old man at his own game. It was in the days when "jacking" deer at night with a light was still legal;

but even this dubious practice did not avail the two tenderfoot hunters. Next morning they slipped into their seats at breakfast, to be greeted by Mart with the query, "Well, boys, where's the deer?"

"Well, Mart, we had a rather terrifying experience. You know that place down at the foot of the lake where a big hemlock hangs over the water?"

"Eyah, eyah."

"Well, we were paddling along close to shore, where we thought we heard deer browsing among the lily-pads. We slipped along, opened the light, and I drew a bead on a fine buck's neck. But just before I could fire, a wild-cat screamed right over our heads in the trees. We were so confused that neither of us could shoot, and the buck lit out. Did you ever hear of anything like that?"

Mart finished eating a flapjack, laid down his knife, and turned to his wife.

"What did I tell you, Minervy? I was down at that very spot a fortnit ago, and when I was right under that same tree, I seed the biggest dang buck I ever see. I levelled on the feller and was all ready to unhitch, when the blamed cat let out a screech and jumped right onto the bow of my boat. The light fell off my head, but that didn't bother me none; I just reached out and poked the cat into the water. Then I lit up the jack and shot the deer. But I told Minervy at the time and I says, 'Some day that there cat will frustrate some of the boys.' Have another flapjack."

While collecting stories of Mart Moody, one of my students discovered that a great-uncle of her own was the hero of another cycle. Jack Ashwood of Ogdensburg was a mighty hunter whose bullets were as large as a lumberman's fist. With a gun especially made somewhere in Canada, he decided to rid the North Country of vicious bears likely to "frustrate" visitors. Procuring several barrels of honey, on the outskirts of the bear-infested woods he poured a long, straight, generous line of sweetness; then he stood waiting at one end of the line. Soon there was a long, straight row of bears gulping in rhythm, forgetful of everything but the bee-juice. Lifting his mighty gun, Uncle Jack fired once, killing every one of the 144 bears. Since there was a clearing back of the last critter, the hunter always presumed that the bullet kept on going; at any rate, he never did find it. The mighty gun continued its service until that dark day when the biggest moose in North America, with a hoof as large as a dining-room table, stepped on it.

A bear rampant should adorn the heraldry of the Adirondacks; lacking heraldry, we have the favorite ballad of the section, *Allen's Bear Fight Up in Keene*. Anson H. Allen, who claimed kinship with the Vermont hero, Ethan Allen, was a printer and a newspaper editor, appointed to take the census of 1840 in Essex County, New York. It was a man-sized job: the scanty population of 23,634 was scattered over better than a million acres in a county second only to St. Lawrence in area. After listing the eight hundred citizens of Keene Flats, now Keene Valley, the census-taker set out for the village of North Elba along the Biddlecombe road, known for its narrowness as "Tight-Nippin". Perhaps Allen was wearing the famous sky-blue vest which made a rival editor refer to him scornfully as a "Broadway dandy"; at any rate, it was an indomitable figure which faced the bear that day. Soon there was a ballad by an unknown author, immortalizing a combat so heroic that another rival newspaper man was jealously led to question its authenticity, whereupon Allen declared, "To throw suspicions . . . on the bear story is almost unindurable". Personally I have no doubts or suspicions, and am happy to present the spirited account of the ballad-maker:

> Of all the wonders of the day,
> There's none [one] that I can safely say
> Will stand upon the walls [rolls] of fame
> To let all know bold Allen's name.
> The greatest fight that e'er was seen
> Was Allen's bear-fight up in Keene.
>
> In 1840, as I've heard,
> To take the census off he steered
> Through bush and wood for little gain,
> He walked from Keene to Abram's plain.
> But naught of this, it is not well
> His secret motives thus to tell.
>
> As through the wood he trudged his way,
> His mind unruffled as the day,

He heard a deep, convulsive sound
Which shook the earth and trees around;
And looking up with dread amaze,
An old she-bear there met his gaze.

The bear with threatening aspect stood
To prove her title to the wood.
This Allen saw with darkening frown;
He reached and pulled a young tree down,
Then, on his guard with cautious care,
He watched the movements of the bear.

Against the rock with giant strength
He held her out at his arm's length.
"*O God!*" he cried in deep despair,
"*If you don't help me, don't help the bear!*"
'Twas rough and tumble, tit for tat;

The nut-cakes fell from Allen's hat.
Then from his pockets forth he drew
A large jack-knife for her to view;
He raised his arm high in the air,
And, butcher-like, he stabbed the bear.

Let old men talk of courage bold,
Of battles fought in days of old
Ten times as bad; but none, I ween,
Can match a bear-fight up in Keene.

No hunter of our golden age was ever "frustrated" by lack of a gun. Mr. Ernest Wood of Red Creek tells of a man who liked to kill and stuff owls. One day, while working without his rifle he spied a particularly handsome bird on the top of a tree. Moving his ax in the sun so that it glittered, the hunter waited until he had attracted the bird's attention. When the owl finally blinked his big eyes in recognition of the bright object, the man started to walk around and round the tree until, as the story is told, "the danged owl twisted his head clean off".

Another of Mr. Wood's favorite stories deals with blackbirds. The same ardent hunter was crossing a field of buckwheat-stubble when he saw in the far corner a flock feeding on the ground. Before he could get close, the birds took wing; hastily he fired. Not being Mart Moody he missed, aiming just a leetle too low, but he consoled himself when he gathered a bushel-basket full of the blackbirds' toenails, proving by how small a margin they had escaped.

Most summer visitors in the Adirondacks are interested to hear stories about the intense cold of winter, when the temperature actually falls to thirty or forty degrees below zero, Fahrenheit. Ben Snyder used to recall the year when he "went-in" in late autumn, aiming to build himself a little cabin. Several days' tramping from his base of supplies brought him to an ideal spot for winter quarters; but when he had felled his timber, he discovered that he had left the nails at home. There was only one thing to do: he used icicles for nails. They were holding staunchly when he "went-out" in the spring. What was his surprise next autumn to discover that his cabin was still standing: the icicles had not melted.

The second winter was even severer than the first. One January night, Ben started to blow out his candle, only to find that the flame was frozen—had to be picked off and thrown out of the window. The experience gave him an idea. As soon as he could get to the nearest settlement, he invested all his spare cash in candles, took them to his cabin, lit them, broke off the flames, and packed them neatly in boxes. The frozen flames were sold for fresh strawberries, netting a profit of four hundred dollars. Ben's only regret was that the trick could be worked only once. There certainly was an element of luck in the sale, as there was in the case of Ben's favorite hound, who split himself in two on a sapling while running at full speed. Hastily the master slapped the two halves of the dog together. "For a while," said Ben, "I thought I'd ruined the poor dog, because I had slammed him together carelesslike, and two legs were up, two down. But I found that I'd really done him a favor; when he tired runnin' on one pair of legs, he give himself a flip in the air, come down on the other pair, and was fresh as paint."

A recent issue of the *Adirondack Arrow* prints the tale of how Bob Glassbrook, still living, had his great adventure with the "painters" (panthers). When the Adirondack branch of the New York Central was completed, Bob trudged through the woods to have a look at the new railroad. Night fell before the goal was reached; so Bob shot a panther, skinned it, and used its pelt for warmth. Toward morning, the critter's mate, drawn by the odor of blood, approached the spot and crouched on a limb over Bob's head, ready for a vengeful spring. At that fatal moment, the grasshoppers awoke and began to "chant intercessions" for the sleeping hunter. One grasshopper did better: he jumped on the hairtrigger of Bob's gun, which, by Adirondack luck, was leaning against the tree, its muzzle pointed toward the crouching "painter". Bob awoke to thank God for grasshoppers—and Adirondack luck.

As you may judge from the tale just told, the tall story comes easily to the lips of many a living guide. I have never had the pleasure of meeting Mr. Bill Rockwell of North Creek, but one of the men whom he has guided reports Bill's account of a new method of catching deer without waste of ammunition. You put up a wooden fence, on the top rail of which salt is strewn. On the first cold night of the season, you replace the wooden rail with an iron one; so when the buck starts to lick the salt, his tongue is stuck to the rail, and the next morning you can dispose of him as you will. If you prefer rabbits to deer, the thing to do is to paint some stones black and throw them lightly into a snow-bank. When pursued the excited rabbit will think that the black spots are holes; sure as taxes he will make a dive, crack his head on a stone, expire, and save you all the trouble except that of collecting his corpse.

While his estimate of a rabbit's intelligence is not very high, Mr. Rockwell thinks that a real old he-trout of his acquaintance is another matter. In a dry summer this Solomon of the stream decided that his future depended upon getting below a waterfall which he was unable to leap on account of the low level of water above it. So Grandpa Trout wrapped his tail around a tree on one side of the stream, and doggedly pushed his head against a rock on the other, making of his enormous body a splendid new dam. When the water had risen sufficiently, he turned himself loose and went over the fall safely below in a deep pool.

If you go back a century in the search for mountain lore, you can find in books and diaries innumerable accounts of bears, wolves

painters (panthers), and moose. All these critters the pioneer woods-
men faced without fear and exterminated without hesitation; but for
the rattlesnakes which then abounded there was a respect easily explained. The most interesting account of these serpents which I have
found is in the *Letters on the Natural History and Internal Resources
of the State of New York* (1822) by "Hibernicus", who was none
other than the great Governor DeWitt Clinton, whose curiosity in
natural sciences was as great as his tenacity as a statesman. One entire
letter is devoted to the "rattlers", found in great numbers in dens
as far apart as Niagara Falls is from Lake George. At least one
hundred dens were located in the mountains near Lake George. Two
great dens were reported within six miles of Ticonderoga; one at
Rogers Rock, about four miles from the foot of the Lake, and the
other about three miles away on the *east* side. Several persons dug for
a den on a mountain; when they had gone down about fifteen feet,
they were arrested by a great rock under which were two holes, large
enough for a man to enter, "from which ascended volumes of noxious
vapors". On the south side of another mountain west of Lake George
a catcher took in one season 1300 rattlers, but the end of that man
was horrid. It was his custom to carry the snakes in a large basket
covered by a carpet. When, after an absence of several days, he was
found dead and horribly swollen, it was supposed that he might have
been careless in covering his basket. Beside him was a snake cut into
pieces which, it was presumed, he had applied to the wound in his
side.

The Governor mentions other fatalities. One man followed an old
technique in pulling a snake out from under a log by its tail, immediately snapping its head off. Unfortunately, though the man did not
realize it at once, the rattler bit his thumb in the instant of the snapping, and the victim died. Another catcher thought that he had killed
a snake; he cut off about five inches of its head to be buried by a boy
helper. Irritated by the boy's delay, the man seized the head, "which
turned round and bit him so that he died". Further to illustrate the
remarkable vitality of these serpents the Governor says he was told
of a rattler kept eight months in a cage without food and without
apparent diminution of bulk.

With a zest that reminds you of Sir Francis Bacon's, the Governor mingles science with folklore in his account of the rattlesnakes' habits. Usually they select a south-easterly or sunny ravine for their "hybernacula". When they come out in the spring, they are said not to bite anyone until they have tasted water. When they have had a drink, they travel at leisure about eight or ten miles from the den. They couple in August and return to winter quarters in September, "most terrifically furious and ferocious". In general, the migration of springtime is in a westerly direction, and the return is to the same den, but the Governor has heard of a whole den migrating in autumn to another mountain, apparently to obtain a more secure and comfortable residence. The folk say that the rattlers are led by a king who has a carbuncle or other precious stone in his head. Fancy has assigned the rattler an attendant called the "rattlesnake's pilot"—flat-headed, venomous, and colored like its master but without rattles.

It was generally believed that hogs could devour the rattlers with impunity; Diamond Island in Lake George was cleaned out by swine after travelers marooned there had slept in trees for fear of snakes. It was also believed that deer killed them, by "springing on them with collected feet". As for man, who used their oil for sprains and rheumatism and applied their flesh in "consumptions", he might save himself from death by remembering that rattlesnakes like land timbered with white oak, but dislike white-ash leaves and any place timbered with beech and maple. It was said that if you enclose a rattler within a wall partly of white-ash and partly of fire, he will choose to retreat through the flames. (That rattler starved for eight months was furious when stirred up but would not bite at a white-ash stick.) This curious folk-belief was tested by a detachment of the American army in the War of 1812, encamped at Snake Hill, near Niagara. The tents were surrounded by boughs of the ash; but in spite of what the folk had said since the time of Pliny, one soldier shook two rattlers out of his blanket, and several men were killed on parade. It is no wonder that even then man was slaughtering his crawling enemy as fast as possible. The Governor says that Negroes killed 315 rattlers smoked out of a single den at the south end of Canandaigua Lake. Other notorious headquarters of the serpent enemy, beside Lake George, were about the Eighteen Mile Creek in

Genesee County and in the rocks at mountains south of the Mohawk at Nore.

Stranger creatures than rattlers have been seen in our mountains. Again and again the sea-serpent has been reported in Lake Champlain; once at least there *was* a sea-serpent there, manufactured by a nationally famous artist with a sense of humor, loudly applauded by journalists and keepers of hotels. In 1895 another sea-serpent was reported in the very unlikely location of Long Lake. Personally I am much more interested in those numerous creatures of fantasy described by guides, such as the Side-Hill Gouger, or Walloper, which has legs short on one side so that he can manage the steepest hill. Willard Howland of Cranberry Lake had an assortment of these creatures which one of his clients put into an amusing long poem; it tells about the Vociferous Antissmus, the Swamp Auger, the barking Moon Crumbler, and the Woolly Nig—which has five legs and two tails.*

Some of the guides could have schooled Lewis Carroll. Of these lords of fancy the Prince seems to be Herbert Clark. He is the master-guide who has accompanied Bob and George Marshall, sons of the famous New York lawyer, up every one of the forty-six major peaks of the Adirondacks; Herbert Peak is named for him, and Mount Marshall for the brothers whom he guided. Through the year 1919, when he was fifty years old, Clark was the champion oarsman of the Saranacs; Mr. Bob Marshall says that in one day the guide rowed sixty-five miles, twenty-four of them in a heavy freight-boat. According to this mighty man, a rock on Lower Saranac showing a queer dent is the place where Captain Kidd, the pirate, bumped his head; a reach in the Ausable River below the Olympic ski-jump is where the *Merrimac* and the *Monitor* fit their famous battle. Newcomers have been warned by Clark against the ferocious *rugarues*—perhaps related to the *loup-garou* (werewolf) of the French "Canucks". Among the guide's gallery of imaginary characters is the Shiny Slatt, the opposite of Paul Bunyan in that he did everything badly; Jacob Whistle-tricker, compounder of marvelous drugs; Joe McGinnis, who was subject to the Fantod, a disease in which the patient shrinks to the size of a baseball; and Susie Soothingsyrup, a gay lass of colorful

* See *Fearsome Critters* (1939) by H. H. Tryon of Cornwall, N. Y.

accomplishments. Beside his ambition to scale all the major peaks, Herbert Clark has aspired to catch the Grandfather Pickerel of the Adirondacks, to be easily identified by his gold teeth and spectacles.

A book might be written about Paul Smith and other famous inn-keepers of the Adirondacks, most of them members of families of guides, but I have space for mention of only one, the man for whom the great Van Hoevenberg bobsled-run is named. Henry van Hoe-venberg (1849-1918), host at Adirondack Loj, was a Northcountry-man born at Oswego. When he visited the Adirondacks with his fiancée in 1877, he had won fame as an electrician and inventor. The girl died within a year, but he carried on their plan of settling in the mountains. He bought six or seven hundred acres around Heart Lake, including Mount Jo, named for his sweetheart; there he built a great log house three stories high, eighty-five by thirty-six feet, with handsome exterior of giant spruce. He was a small, muscular, bearded man who saw many bitter disappointments but who loved his moun-tains intensely. Old Jed Rossman, a favorite member of Van Hoeven-berg's staff, used to tell stories about Mr. Van, sometimes adding frankly, "Of course, that ain't how it really was". I am glad that before Jed died one of my students from Saranac Lake managed to put down two of these tales from word of mouth.

The first concerns hidden treasure, said to have been taken from the Iroquois by a raiding party of Algonquins, and hidden somewhere in the Adirondacks. (There are numerous stories of this kind: in the Adirondacks the treasure usually belongs to mysterious Spaniards or to a fleeing British or French army; in the mountains below Albany, to Captain Kidd or Claudius Smith.) One day, while walking through the woods, Van Hoevenberg picked up a piece of old parchment on which was written in Algonquin a direction to the famous Indian hoard. (The Algonquins had no written language, but we may sup-pose that they had learned writing from the French Jesuits of Can-ada.) The location was in a cave half-way up Mount Colden; the only time that the cave could be located was in the light of the August full moon, and the observer must sight from the top of Mount McIn-tyre, second highest peak in the Adirondacks, whose other name is Mount Algonquin.

The full moon of the following August found Van Hoevenberg

5,112 feet above sea-level, scanning the face of Colden where, sure enough, he saw something that looked like the opening to a cave. After a stiff piece of mountaineering, he pulled himself up onto a ledge with the aid of a little pine tree growing from a crevice, and advanced into the mouth of a large cave. After he had regained his breath, he summoned courage in this uncanny place and struck a match. There before him were a number of queer old leather trunks, filled, as Jed said, with "wampum and gold and great treasure". Leaning forward eagerly, Van Hoevenberg was stuffing his pockets when he heard a human grunt and turned to find a shadowy figure coming toward him, something that looked like the form of a huge Indian. Just then the match flickered out. The guide and the Indian grappled in the dark. If this was the ghost of an Algonquin guard, it was a spirit substantial enough to be a good wrestler. From this point Van Hoevenberg remembered only dimly a fierce struggle, the sensation of falling, a slowing of the fall as he struck a pine that gave under his weight, and a crash far down the precipice. On his hands and knees the adventurer crawled to Heart Lake, washed his wounds, and was taken to his Lodge. The only evidence for his story was the wampum and gold in his pockets—and two broken legs, three broken ribs, and one broken arm. Jed was not curious as to the disposal of the samples of treasure.

The other story is based upon grim reality—the great forest fire of 1903. Van Hoevenberg had lost ownership of his Lodge in 1895; but after working as postmaster and telegraph operator for the Lake Placid Club, he had been installed in his old quarters as superintendent and host. One day the odor of burning forest warned that fire was near; if the wind shifted, the Lodge was doomed. The route to Placid was cut off; the way to safety lay through Indian Pass. For two of the five miles Van Hoevenberg led his guests silently; then he turned suddenly, muttered that he had forgotten something, and instructed them to continue in the same direction they were following—that he would rejoin them soon. Thinking that he knew the trails better than they, the guests decided to disobey instructions and wait for him where they were.

After a long wait, two of the party decided to hasten back and see whether an accident had occurred. Arriving at the lodge, they hallooed without answer. The danger was now very real, with walls of fire approaching in three directions. One of the party happened to try the handle of Van Hoevenberg's door and found that it was locked. Calling his companion, the man who had made the discovery started to break down the door, when a voice from within warned him to go away or be shot. To prove his intentions, Van Hoevenberg fired twice through the ceiling. Sadly his loyal friends turned and sped toward Indian Pass, leaving the guide to perish in the lodge which meant to him the memory of lost love, the labor and aspiration of a lifetime.

Well, it was a grand story to tell the young 'uns, and up to a point it is true. Alfred L. Donaldson, a New York banker who came to the Adirondacks in 1895 to regain his health, tells the story's end in his *A History of the Adirondacks*: Van Hoevenberg did go back to his lodge, intending to perish in its flames, but when Frank Williams found him and refused to budge without him, he came to a manlier resolution: he would not sacrifice his friend. So the two sped down the trail and escaped from the fire just in time. About a year before his death in 1918, Van Hoevenberg was energetic enough to open an electrical store in the village near the place where, forty years earlier, he had laughed over plans with his fiancée.

Near Lake Placid, at North Elba, is to be found the farm of a more tragic figure in our history, John Brown of Ossawatomie, who in 1859 made his attempt to free the slaves "by the authority of Almighty God". He was a native of Connecticut, not a mountaineer, though he had some of the iron courage of the guides. In 1849 he obtained from Gerrit Smith, the State's leading Abolitionist, the farm now visited every year in May by grateful Negroes. Smith was a graduate of Hamilton College, the son of that wealthy laird for whom Petersboro in Madison County is named. When he found difficulty in disposing of the large tract in Essex County which he had inherited, he decided to cut it up into forty-acre lots to be given to Negroes— a benevolent purpose which did not take into account the fact that the "Tyrol of America" was a cruelly cold home for children of the sun. For a couple of years John Brown gave promise of being a quiet farmer: The Report of the Essex County Agricultural Society for 1850 refers to "a number of very choice and beautiful Devons from the herds of Mr. John Brown, residing in one of our most remote and secluded towns". The neighbors evidently regarded him as an eccentric; some of them later expressed a harsher judgment. For years I have been seeking a satirical ballad about the trial of John Brown, in which, to judge from a fragment which drifted down from the Adirondacks, he was coarsely lampooned. While the little Negro settlement lasted, the occasional visitor must have been amused at the sight of a huddle of log shanties built by the poor colored people, and at their red flag bearing the word TIMBUCTOO.

In 1851 the Brown family moved to Ohio; they returned in 1855, but the father went to Kansas, leaving a son to care for the farm. In 1857 Brown returned, bringing a family tombstone from Connecticut; on a boulder he cut his own plain name, as if aware that his days were numbered. From time to time he would pay visits at North Elba, coming in from Wesport on Lake Champlain. After the last of these visits he left in June of 1859 for his venture at Harper's Ferry. He was executed that December. His friends had to smuggle his body through the City of Brotherly Love, but the coffin reached Essex County and lay one night in the courthouse at Elizabethtown, guarded by six volunteers. Wendell Phillips came from Massachusetts to make the funeral oration at the North Elba Farm. Prayers were said by a clergyman from Vermont who found, upon returning to Rutland, that he was reviled as an anarchist and that six of his wealthiest parishioners were leading a schism from his Unitarian Church. Mrs. Brown sold the farm in 1864; six years later it was bought by a John Brown Association. In 1896 the State of New York took over possession. In 1899 the bones of ten of Brown's followers were brought from the South; and in 1916 another tablet was unveiled.

This is the story as Donaldson was able to discover it, but I have always wanted something more vivid and human. What did the men he had wished to free from slavery think about John Brown of New York? Did any of those shivering refugees survive to tell the tale? My wish was gratified when old "Lime" (Lyman) Eppes of Lake Placid told some of his story to one of my students whom he had known as a lass. I give almost word for word the account brought me by Miss Frances Mihill, whose great-great-grandfather was a member of one of six families living in the North Elba region when old Peter Smith left the tract to his Abolitionist son.

I found, much to my surprise, that "Lym" was born in Troy—he thinks—and his family was the first to come to Placid to claim the land. Lym was two then; that makes him ninety-four now. He had nine brothers and sisters, but they have all died and he laments: "There is nobody to carry on ma name; ye see, I couldn't marry b'cuz they wuz no real colored people here but just some of them city-folks." He seems very proud that he is the only Negro who has "stuck out the snow and the cold up here", but he says, "People don't treat me as though I was colored; they act as though I was just like them, and that's how I want to be."

I asked him what made all the other Negro families leave, and he looked at me chuckling and said: "Well, in the first place, they come here a-planning to farm—come by ox-cart—and their tract of land was all trees. You couldn't grow nothin' 'ceptin' a little wheat and p'tatoes. Why, the deer and the bears and the rabbits was right around the cabin all the time—we was never wantin' for meat. Some families just took one look at the place and turned around and went right back; or after John Brown come, they got him to help 'em into Canada. Mostly they was lazy good-for-nothin's. Ye know, most of them niggers just couldn't git used to the cold. Now me, I never minded it a bit." He laughed and huddled up closer to the wood-stove. He was wearing a heavy mackinaw, a flannel shirt and sweater, heavy boots, and at least two pairs of socks.

It seems that a few families did settle and stay one or two winters; but after John Brown came, the only other Negroes except the Epps family were just stopping on the way through to Canada.

"Underground railroad?" he drawled. "I don't know how they got that name fer it. It was just an old cord'roy road and an ox-cart. But them families was different, y' know: most of them was slaves that come through, but our bunch wa'nt—we was free families. An' then, they wa'nt even grateful to John Brown; why, I remember them complainin' of Miz Brown's table she set."

I asked him if he could remember John Brown. His eyes filled with tears. "I use to sit on his knee and hear him tell about how he was gonna free the colored folks and teach 'em to farm up here. An' then he went away, an' pretty soon word come that he'd been killed an' Miz Brown went down to git his body. He sorta thought he was gonna die, though, 'cuz before he left he wrote a letter to Massachusetts an' told 'em down there to take that stone off his grandfather's grave and send it up here; and he told Miz Brown where he wanted to be buried, him and the Thompson boys. Well, Miz Brown went 'n got him and brung him home, and me 'n ma whole family sung at his funeral. We sung *Blow ye the trumpet, blow*, but I can't remember it all now. Three years ago they let me pull off the curtain that covered his statue when they showed it."

What he really wanted to discuss was how terrible it would be if we didn't get enough snow for the winter sports, and all those city-folks would be disappointed. "Ye know, them city-folks is awful funny— they want the funniest things. Why I had a bedstead of John Brown's here, one of the old-fashioned rope ones; and everybody kep' wantin' some of it, an' I give it away till the hull thing was gone, even the rope. I sorta wanted to keep it, too, but I couldn't refuse it very handy."

Of all the refugees to our Northern Icebox the Negroes may have suffered most, but the French *émigrés* must have felt the added discomforts of those exiled from wealth. In 1788 La Compagnie de New York was founded in France to make settlements in Castorland, a great tract in Jefferson and Lewis Counties which derived its name from the Latin word for beaver, *castor*. Settlement was made at Lyons Falls and Castorville (later Beavertown); then the commissioners sold the remaining land to the Comte LeRay de Chaumont, a pioneer of great ability, first President of the New York State Agriculture Society. As the fortunes of Napoleon waned, de Chaumont sold an estate of 118,000 acres about Diana to Napoleon's brother, Joseph Bonaparte, who lived in New Jersey but built a hunting-lodge and a home called the White House on the Adirondack plateau. In one house constructed at Natural Bridge on the Indian River, there were, it is said, bullet-proof rooms which might have been useful if Joseph had succeeded in bringing over his brother. The story is told in Jefferson County of a noted hunter named Newell being invited to "Bonaparte Clearing". All agog, Mrs. Newell urged her husband to dress in his best and be sure to remember to take off his hat to royalty.

"I tell you, wife," said her Leatherstocking husband, "I am a Massachusetts Yankee, and my people don't take off their hats even to kings."

Later Newell told sheepishly of how he had broken his resolve.

"A hired man showed me and the dog into a room, and almost the next minute here come Bonaparty. He took off his big military cap, made me a bow, and shook hands as friendly as anybody I ever see. I tell ye what, boys, didn't my own coonskin cap come off mighty quick then? Good manners, even from a Yankee, called for it. The idee of such a man takin' off his cap to a coonskin larnt me."

It would be surprising if the numerous émigrés had not left behind such legends of royalty incognito as delighted Huck and Tom Sawyer on their raft. We have our share of such stories, including the traditions of a mysterious Frenchman who built a "castle" (large house) at Muller Hill in Madison County. The loftiest of these wanderers, if you will believe the folk of the North Country, was a certain Eleazer Williams who died at Hogansburg in 1858, leaving many to believe that he was the Lost Dauphin of France, son of Louis XVI and Marie Antoinette. Franklin County preserves as a historical museum the house in which his last years were spent.

Eleazer was the adopted son of an English surgeon named Thomas Williams and his wife Mary, whose mother was a white woman taken on a raid and married to an Indian. Eleazer therefore had knowledge of Indian ways and speech; the Iroquois, who reckon descent through the mother, accepted him as an Indian, and honored his missionary ministration to the Oneidas with whom, in 1821, he moved to Wisconsin. He had previously seen service as scout for the American army and had been wounded in 1814 at the battle of Plattsburg. He returned to New York State about eight years before his death and tried to teach the Indian children in the region of Hogansburg. So much for authentic history.

"They say" that the little Dauphin was so cruelly used by his jailor that he lost all memory of his origin for years until he providentially hit his head on a sharp rock, and thereafter was haunted by the face of the cruel jailor. They say that he married in Wisconsin the daughter of one of Napoleon Bonaparte's marshals. They say that the Prince de Joinville visited him in Wisconsin and tried to induce him to sign a document giving up claims to the throne of France. They say that the French government remained so concerned that it was careful to obtain affidavits to the death of a grandchild of Williams. The Lost Dauphin evidently had enough brains to translate the

Gospels and part of the Episcopal Prayerbook into Mohawk, but I have found no stories that indicate that he was otherwise any more intelligent or amusing than the average half-breed; which is neither here nor there, for the real Lost Dauphin's papa was not very bright.

So far as the mountaineers are concerned, the French who mean much are not the royal and noble émigrés, but guides like "French Louie", and the numerous lumbermen and northern farmers who give color to a Yankee population. Just as the Pennsylvanians like to tell stories about their "Dutch" (Germans), we cherish tales about our "Canucks". Part of the delight is in their speech. Mr. Harry MacDougall, Clerk of Essex County and master raconteur, tells of a Frenchman working with a Yankee who rather unskillfully felled a tree in such a way that its top hit his companion. The "Canuck" sputtered, "My young man, my sonny, if I work for you the past five year, let that be the next time you do that!" Another *habitant*, wishing to memorialize his dead wife and mother for whom "he's feel awful bad", decided to have a tombstone inscription. A neighbor suggested the standard phrase, "Gone but not forgotten". The "Canuck" said to the stonecutter, "You put on, 'Gone and don't you forget it' ".

Some of the tales indicate a shrewdness not unworthy of the North Countryman. A "Canuck" bought a horse from a sharp trader named Melt, demanding from him a receipt. Melt pretended to be surprised at the request. "Well," said the Frenchie, "I die, you die. Saint Pierre say to me, 'You have any deals with Melt? Got ree-ceep?' Suppose I hunt all over hell to find you?"

Sometimes the "Canucks" serve as heroes of tall tales; after all, some say that Paul Bunyan himself was a Frenchie. Another master story-teller of Elizabethtown, Mr. Alec Couchey, tells the following:

Old Papineau Montville come to the United States to skip servin' in the Papineau war up in Canada. One day he was comin' home with his old horse and a *pung*—a Canadian *jumper*. (Tell the Professor that's a single sleigh without seats, used to draw wood; the driver walks behind or stands up on the load.) All of a sudden the horse dropped dead. It was an awful cold night; so he couldn't stop there and wait for someone to come by; so he rolled the horse out of the road and harnessed himself to the pung. He started out, but after a few minutes he happened to think that horses' hides were worth somethin'; so he went back and skinned the horse. The next morning an old peddler come along, and he sold the skin; got four dollars for it. He felt perty good about that, and he kept thinkin' about it while he was doin' the chores.

Well, while he was doin' those chores, he thought he heard somethin' outside the barn. He went out to look, and if there wasn't the old horse without any hide! He'd walked all the way in after bein' skinned. O' course, Papineau felt perty bad to think o' what he'd done to his poor old horse; so he tried to figger out some way to make up for it. All the time he was thinkin', there was the old horse, shiverin' and shakin' till you could 'a' heard his bones rattle.

Well, Papineau finally remembered a cow-moose hide he had. He went and got it and fitted it onto the horse just as tight as he could, and then put the horse into the barn. Well, sir, *that hide grew onto him,* and fitted so well you wouldn't 'a' known but it was his in the first place. The funny part of it was that after that the horse wouldn't eat hay—he had to have brush like a moose; and he never trotted any more—he always run like a moose, and it would have taken two horses to keep up with him.

Old Papineau had a cow too. Gosh she was an immense thing! Had to milk her in a wash-tub. She had a bag bigger'n a bushel-basket. He couldn't keep her though. You see, her teets were so long they wore off as they dragged over the ground; so he couldn't milk her.

The mountaineers are generous in sharing their stories with people from the city; they are also hospitable in welcoming us to their social gatherings. My children look forward to "going-up" to Big Moose in the Adirondacks every summer, partly because they can attend "square dances" over which Barney Lepper presides. During the day, Mr. Lepper is the courteous ticket-agent at the railroad station; in the evening, he is the favorite "prompter", directing the quadrilles all the way from "Join hands and circle left" to "All promenade—you know where and I don't care". The gods of the mountain and the gods of the plain are one when Barney "winds the clock" or orders his dancers to "Swing your Ma, now your Pa; don't forget old Arkansaw". He mingles prose with verse; one of his "second changes" runs:

> Join hands and circle left.
> First couple lead out to the right.

> Join hands and circle four.
> Ladies join your lilly-white hands—
> The gents, the black and tan.
> Ladies bow, gents know how,
> And hippety-hop and around you go.

The Catskills are not a bit behind the Adirondacks in the matter of "square dances"—by which we mean contra-dances as well as quadrilles. One of my students, Beth Osborn, whose *Another Pasture* is a charming novelette with Catskill setting, thinks that the most attractive of dance-calls is *Captain Jinks*. It is a vigorous dance: the lady really does "fly through the air", as the poem suggests:

> First lady swing with Captain Jinks;
> Now with the one that never drinks;
> Now with the one that carries the chinks;
> And now with the dude of the ballroom.

> First gentlemen dance with lady so fair;
> Now with the one with curls in her hair;
> Now with the one that flies in the air,
> And now with the belle of the ballroom.

Another of my "writing gals", Mary Grahn, described the fun she had at a dance held in a barn between Paradox Lake and Schroon Lake in the Adirondacks:

We had one of the best "callers" in the county; somebody said he had corns in his throat, and he could certainly make himself heard above all the noise of the orchestra and sometimes forty and fifty squares. The orchestra was a piano and a violin and the violinist's foot. There were some men there who looked as if they'd come straight out of Hardy, and we always could do the dances when we had one of the real countrymen for partner—their hands were as firm as if upon the plow. The Johnson Pond Breakdown was supposed to wear everybody out, and it did; it was a mental test. It begins:

> Right hands around to the left;
> I guess the other way is best.

There was another awful rough one in which the girls put their arms over the men's shoulders, making two circles, one of men and one of girls, and then the men circled around for God's sake and the girls prayed their arms wouldn't break . . . The barn was beautiful—large and roomy and the general tone a golden brown. A square dance can be heard for miles.

A book called *Good Morning* says, "After a sleep of twenty-five years, old-fashioned dancing is being revived by Mr. and Mrs. Henry Ford". As Lettie Osborn replies, "A great many people have been somnambulists." She brought me from Orange County fifty-nine fiddle-tunes which she has been playing since she was knee-high to a grasshopper: *The White Cockade,* which was my Grandfather Thompson's favorite, *The Delaware Hornpipe, Soldier's Joy, Speed the Plough, Flower of Donnybrook, Emigrants' Reel, Flogging Reel, Devil's Dream,* and many more. Any day when I feel specially dull I can play the records that Mr. George Covell of Chilson made for me of my favorites: *MacDonald's Reel, Mrs. Macleod's Reel* and *Turkey in the Straw,* performed with such flourishes and enormous good nature! At first he wasn't going to play at all; he didn't know how, though he admitted that he owned a couple of fiddles; I had given him a cigar and he rather figgered I was a politician, not likely to appreciate champion fiddlin'. Sometime I want to tell you all this, and about the comical songs that Mr. Joe Searle of Clinton sings as special favor between the "squares" for which he still fiddles and prompts. People keep inviting me politely down to the White Top Folk Festival in Virginia every August, and some summer when I am not teaching I'm going, but I don't have to drive that far to hear ballads and fiddle-tunes. We don't have "hill-billies" in New York State, but we have mountaineers who are some of the best and happiest Americans.

XIII: *Warriors, Colonial and Revolutionary*

THE Pathway of Empire led through fields of battle. Should the red man rule or the white? The dice were loaded, but in New York the white man fought the best organized of Indians. Should France rule or England? The decision was in doubt from the year 1609, when Hudson ascended his river from the south, and from the north Champlain came down to his lake, there to make the fatal blunder of shooting his first Mohawks. From that year until 1759, when Wolfe fell in triumph at Quebec, the Champlain-Lake George region was the Flanders of America. Should Britain rule the United States? In that contest the settlers on the Mohawk and the Schoharie paid the bitterest price, and the battles of Saratoga decided the issue. Should the United States rule the Great Lakes and the West, or was that to be the destiny of Canada?* Perry on Lake Erie and McDonough on Lake Champlain gave the answer in that War of 1812 which is sometimes said to have decided nothing. So a State

* The historian will find some of this paragraph's generalizations deplorably loose: Hudson was exploring for the Dutch, not the English; the importance of Champlain's shot is a popular exaggeration; in 1814 the Canadians were not self-governing.

which contained in its vast waterways the road to Canada and the river to the West was compelled to be a State in arms. When the treaty of Ghent in 1814 brought what we believe to be a perpetual peace between Britain and the United States, the cries of war subsided, but the songs of war still echo.

The oldest of our battle-ballads describes the events of a snowy night in 1690 when a force of French with Indian allies burned the Dutch outpost at Schenectady on the Mohawk. We still call it "the massacre". Angered by a bloody Mohawk raid upon Montreal and eager to eliminate the competition of Dutch and English traders, the Chevalier de Callières Bonnevue had planned to attack Orange (Albany), which he estimated to consist of one hundred and fifty houses, and Manathe (New York) with its two hundred houses. Instead of the two thousand men requested, the expedition mustered about two hundred and ten, nearly half of whom were Indians, the entire party commanded by Canadian Frenchmen, the Sieur Le Moyne de Sainte Hélène and Lieutenant Daillebout de Mantet. In a heroic march of two hundred miles they plunged on through a northern winter, sometimes through forests three to six feet deep in snow, sometimes up to the knees in water. When the restive Indians demanded to know their destination and learned that they were to attack Albany, their fear of cannon made them insist upon turning southwest toward Corlear (Schenectady), which was reached after nightfall of February the eighth.

Meanwhile a political feud was rendering defenceless the doomed village. In the interim following the British revolution of 1688, a New York merchant named Jacob Leisler had put himself at the head of the colony's affairs in the name of the new sovereigns, William and Mary, who, as Protestants, would be more acceptable to all the Dutch than the deposed Stuart. To curry favor with the frontiersmen, it is said, Leisler promised Schenectady the valuable privilege of trading with the Indians—a traffic hitherto monopolized in that region by Albany. At Albany, a committee of safety ("the Convention"), composed of Leisler's political foes, warned their western neighbors regarding a threatened invasion, and even sent a small garrison commanded by Lieut. Enos Talmadge of Connecticut—a guard ridiculed by the majority party at Schenectady. To be sure, the little dorp was defended by a ten-foot palisade of pine logs, but, as the Mohawk allies later said, "The town is not well fortified, the stockades are so short the Indians can jump over them like a dog."

There is a tradition that the infatuated villagers were warned of the approaching attack by Sander (John Alexander) Glen, who, on account of his previous humane treatment of the French and possibly on account of his Scottish name, was spared by the invaders. From his estate across the Mohawk he sent an Indian woman, a vendor of brooms, to warn the village whose political prejudices would not permit him to reside at his town-house. Entering the home of a widow who was regaling the Dutch pastor with chocolate, the Indian committed the sin of shaking off snow upon a freshly scrubbed floor. Driven out by the widow's shrill anger, the messenger departed, her warning unsaid; but legend reports a muttered sentence, "It will be soiled enough before tomorrow". At eleven that night, trusting to the protection of "extream snow above knee deep", the village slept, its open gates guarded only by snowmen erected in ridicule of Talmadge's garrison.

Toward midnight the warwhoop sounded, followed by a ruthless massacre that lasted for two hours and was followed by the burning of the dorp. The French report states that even the chocolate-drinking pastor was killed—by mistake, for it had been hoped that military information might have been wrung from him; that "M. Coudre" (Glen) was put on parole and his town-house left standing together with that of a widow who tended a wounded French officer; that after the first onslaught the lives of fifty to sixty whites and twenty Mohawks were spared. (Although the Mohawks had slaughtered French at Montreal, they were potential customers.) A contemporary Albany account estimates that sixty were killed, including eleven Negroes, and that twenty-seven were carried off toward Canada on the following day, which happened to be the Sabbath. The grim record runs:

Engel the wife of Adam Vroman shot & burnt, her childe the brains dashed out against ye wall . . . Dominie Petrus Tassemaker ye minister kild & burnt in his house . . . Joh. Potman kild, his wife kild & her skalp taken off . . . Women with chyld ript up, children alive thrown into the flames, some their heads dashed agt the doors and windows.

The children of Schenectady are still told of how that same Adam Vroman's life was spared after he had twice wounded a French officer while defending his ravaged home with a spear, and of how the widow Bradt's house was spared when the wounded Frenchman was taken there for succor. But the most heroic incident was the feat of Symon Schermerhorn, whose ride to Albany should be remembered with the better known gallops of the Yankee Paul Revere and the Yorker Phil Sheridan. His was far more heroic. Probably he saw his son and Negro slaves slaughtered before his face; then he took horse to warn Albany and the intervening countryside. Ignoring the severe wound in his thigh, he chose the longer way via Niskayuna and the river road, for six hours shouting his warning to scattered householders until, as legend reports, his horse fell dead at the Albany gate. We are not likely to forget him, or the twenty-five refugees whose limbs were frozen in flight, or the twenty-seven men and boys who departed next morning as captives from their ruined village, many of them never to return.

Five months later, a member of the garrison at Albany composed a ballad about the massacre which survives in the most unlikely places. For example, I have a fragment remembered by an old canaller, and a complete version copied from the log kept between 1849-52 on the bark *Timor* of Sag Harbor, Long Island. I give you Walter Wilie's bouncing metres in what may be their earliest printed form; Watson's *Annals and Occurrences* (1846) states that the song was "preserved in a family of Albany".

A BALLAD

In which is set forth the horrid cruelties practiced by the French and Indians on the 8th of last February. The which I did compose last night, in the space of one hour, and am now writing, the morning of Friday, June 12th, 1690.

W. W.

God prosper long our King and Queen,
    Our lives and safties all,
A sad misfortune once there did
    Schenectady befall.

From forth the woods of Canada
    The Frenchmen tooke their way
The people of Schenectady
    To captivate and slay.

They marched for two and twenty daies,
    All thro' the deepest snow;
And on a dismal winter night
    They strucke the cruel blow.

The lightsome sun that rules the day,
    Had gone down in the West;
And eke the drowsie villagers
    Had sought and found their reste.

They thought they were in safetie all,
    And dreampt not of the foe;
But att midnight they all awoke,
    In wonderment and woe.

For they were in their pleasant Beddes,
    And soundelie sleeping, when
Each Door was sudden open broke
    By six or seven Men.

The Men and Women, younge & olde,
    And eke the Girls and Boys,
All started up in great Affright,
    Att the alarming Noise.

They then were murthered in their Beddes,
    Without shame or remorse;
And soon the Floores and Streets were strew'd
    With many a bleeding corse.

The Village soon began to Blaze,
    Which show'd the horrid sight—
But, O, I scarce can Beare to Tell
    The Mis'ries of that Night.

They threw the Infants in the Fire,
   The Men they did not spare;
But killed All which they could find
   Tho' Aged or tho' Fair.

O Christe! In the still Midnight Air,
   It sounded dismally,
The Women's Prayers and the loud screams,
   Of their great Agony.

Methinks as if I hear them now
   All ringing in my ear;
The shrieks & Groans & Woeful Sighs,
   They utter'd in their Fear.

But some ran off to Albany,
   And told the doleful Tale:
Yett, tho' We gave our chearful Aid,
   It did not much avail.

And We were horribly afraid,
   And shook with Terror, when
They told us that the Frenchman were
   More than a Thousand Men.

The News came on the Sabbath Morn
   Just att the Break of Day,
And with a companie of Horse
   I galloped away.

But soone We found the French were gone
   With all their great Bootye;
And then their Trail We did pursue,
   As was our true Dutye.

The Mohaques joynd our brave Partye,
   And followed in the chase
Till we came upp with the Frenchmen,
   Att a most likelye place.

> Our soldiers fell upon their Reare,
>   And killed twenty-five,
> Our Young Men were so much enrag'd
>   They took scarce One alive.
>
> D'Aillebout them did commande,
>   Which were but Thievish Rogues,
> Else why did they consent and Goe
>   With Bloodye Indian Dogges?
>
> And Here I End the long Ballad
>   The Which you have just redde;
> And wish that it may stay on earth,
>   Long after I am Dead.
>   Walter Wilie.
> Albany, 12th of June, 1690.

The struggle between the French and their Indian allies, on the one hand, and the British, Dutch, and Mohawks on the other, culminated in 1759, the year of Quebec's fall. Three persons in that era have left a mark upon the imagination of the folk: Robert Rogers the Ranger, Campbell of Inverawe, and General Wolfe. Of these Wolfe has left the deepest impression, but our present interest in Rogers, revived by Kenneth Roberts's novel, *Northwest Passage,* justifies first consideration for the Ranger.

Robert Rogers (1731-1795) was born in Massachusetts and grew up on a New Hampshire farm, but his chief exploits for the folklorist concern the campaigns in New York. The roving frontiersman was a Captain in Sir William Johnson's Crown Point expedition of 1755; in the following year he commanded an independent company of Rangers, and in 1758 General Abercrombie made him Major of nine such companies, the scouting force of the British army. He was with Loudon at Halifax in 1757, with Abercrombie at the appalling defeat of Ticonderoga in 1758, with Amherst in 1759 at Crown Point. In other words, he saw active service of great importance throughout all that war in the Champlain region, while his pranks and his daring made him its most colorful figure until the legends connected with his name reached as far as England.

To the people of northern New York the favorite story concerns

a place on the west side of Lake George known as Rogers Slide or
Rogers Rock, immortalized by an exploit of the spring of 1758
when the Ranger escaped death by a characteristic stratagem. Out-
numbered three to one in battle, he had lost by death and capture 108
of 180 men. It was each man for himself, and to some that meant a
grim death. Lieutenant Phillips, for example, surrounded by a yelping horde, surrendered with his eighteen men upon a promise of good
treatment; the treatment consisted in tying them to trees and hacking
them all to death. Finally Rogers found himself alone at the top of
a lofty precipice overlooking Lake George, with certain death before
and behind him. Loosening his pack, he pushed it over the slide to
make a track which resembled the fatal fall of a man. Then putting
his snowshoes on backward he descended to the ice-covered lake
by a roundabout path, reversed his snowshoes, picked up his pack,
and started for Fort William Henry. When the Indians arrived, they
found tracks leading to the edge of the slide, and looking over the
precipice they saw a valiant figure headed southward on the lake.
A brief consultation decided that Rogers was under the protection
of the Great Spirit; the lonely figure was permitted to disappear in
the direction of the British stronghold. Six weeks later, Rogers captured three prisoners almost under the walls of the French forti-
fications at Crown Point.

The only ballad about the Ranger still handed down by the folk
is a Macaulayan *Lay of the Ancient Valley* which was printed as early
as 1851:

> My tale is of a battle,
> God give it worthy rime!
> That fell out in this valley
> All in the golden time:
> Then the stags coursed gaily
> Along our valley's sides;
> The plow had made no furrow then,
> In their track no hunter hides.
>
> Tall waved the pine trees
> On the dark mountain side,
> On Boquet's glittering sheen below

The dead leaves smoothly ride;
For 'twas past the prime of summer,
The woods were red and gold,
The leaves twirl'd round with rustling sound
As fast the year grew old.

Hither came bold Rogers,
As who, none was so bold,
With a small band of heroes,
All brave men of old;
Chased by the yelling Indians,
From Keene, in haste he comes,
He hurries toward the Lake Champlain,
For its shores bear smiling homes.

Scarce had they reached the river,
Which before them glassy glides—
(Noon's sun has still the leafy wilds,
The swift deer sought the shades)—
When from midst the whispering leaves
A storm of flint heads flew,
The forest rung with red men's yells,
Dread sounds for the sturdy few.

Then out spake bold John Rogers,
"There are fearful odds, my men,
(When forest trees bear fruits like these)
Against a band of ten,
But by our children's mothers,
Who wait us at our homes,
If we must pluck this stony fruit
We'll give back as good as comes."

All grasp firm their rifles
(Good aid for bloody work)
And behind the knotty trunks around,
[In] the deathly silence lurk.
For a moment from the river
Comes a gently gurgling sound,

As the eddies in the current
Wheel slowly round and round.

But soon, from out the thicket,
With sly and stealthy tread
Come bands of tall, dark warriors—
Fierce chiefs were at their head.
Sharp, quickly crack then rifles,
From behind the trees around;
E'en red men pale, as the leaden hail
Makes ten chiefs bite the ground.

Then forth like wildcats on them spring
Brave Rogers and his men;
Through teeth and skulls of Indians
Each drives his clubbed gun.
"See," cried Rogers, bold, "the welcome,
Hellhounds! that waits you here,
Well, from to-day, your tribe may say
They've tasted white men's cheer."

Fast through the forest fled they
With a wild and quavering whoop!
Sad remnant of brave warriors,
The Adirondac's hope.
With stouter heart brave Rogers
Hastens toward the lake,
His comrades shout one lusty cheer;
The valley's echoes wake.

Bright shone the autumn's sun
On our wild valley wide;
On Boquet's glittering sheen below
The dead leaves smoothly ride;
Soft run its gentle waters;
While the sedges lowly sigh,
And on its banks, with upturned face,
Those dead men stilly lie.

Rogers had to wait nearly a century for a ballad, but Major Duncan

Campbell of Inverawe, hero of perhaps the most famous ghost story of York State, had to wait longer, for it was not until December of 1887 that *Scribner's Magazine* printed *Ticonderoga* by Robert Louis Stevenson. The story commemorated by the Scottish poet during his residence at Saranac is too long to be reprinted here, but the tale deserves a summary. The Black Watch, Britain's crack regiment of Scottish Highlanders, paid in full measure for the incomprehensible stupidity of the Scottish Commander-in-Chief, General Abercrombie ("Mrs. Nabbycrombie") when, on a fateful July day in 1758 he selected what now seems the only possible method of losing the battle of Ticonderoga to the French General Montcalm. Six times Abercrombie's men charged against breastworks nine feet high, twenty feet thick at the base and ten at the top, not only protected by a trench but "to the distance of a musket-shot" further secured by fallen trees pointed toward the approaching enemy. Through that green hell of leafage plunged the Black Watch until one hundred and eighty men were killed and two hundred and eighty wounded. Of thirty-seven officers only eleven came off unhurt, the wounded including the fey Major of the Regiment, Duncan Campbell, who died at Fort Edward nine days later. The classic version of his tale is found in Parkman's *Montcalm and Wolfe*:

The ancient castle of Inverawe stands by the banks of the Awe, in the midst of the wild and picturesque scenery of the Western Highlands. Late one evening, before the middle of the last century [18th], as the laird, Duncan Campbell, sat alone in the old hall, there was a loud knocking at the gate; and, opening it, he saw a stranger, with torn clothing and kilt smeared with blood, who in a breathless voice begged for asylum. He went on to say that he had killed a man in a fray, and that the pursuers were at his heels. Campbell promised to shelter him. "Swear on your dirk!" said the stranger, and Campbell swore. He then led him to a secret recess in the depths of the castle. Scarcely was he hidden when again there was a loud knocking at the gate, and two armed men appeared. "Your cousin Donald has been murdered, and we are looking for the murderer!" Campbell, remembering his oath, professed to have no knowledge of the fugitive; and the men went on their way. The laird, in great agitation, lay down to rest in a large dark room where at length he fell asleep. Waking suddenly in bewilderment and terror, he saw the ghost of the murdered Donald standing by his bedside, and heard a hollow voice pronounce the words: "Inverawe! Inverawe! blood has been shed. Shield not the murderer." In the morning Campbell went to the hiding place of the guilty man and told him he could harbor him no longer. "You have sworn on your dirk," he replied and the laird of Inverawe, greatly perplexed and troubled, made a compromise between conflicting duties, promised not to betray his guest, led him to the neighboring mountain (Ben Cruachan) and hid him in a cave.

In the next night, as he lay tossing in feverish slumbers, the same stern voice awoke him, the ghost of his cousin Donald stood again at his bedside, and again he heard the same appalling words: "Inverawe! Inverawe! blood has been shed. Shield not the murderer!" At break of day he hastened, in strange agitation, to the cave; but it was empty, the stranger had gone. At night, as he strove in vain to sleep, the vision appeared once more, ghastly pale, but less stern of aspect than before. "Farewell, Inverawe!" it said; "Farewell, till we meet at TICONDEROGA!"

The strange name dwelt in Campbell's memory. He had joined the Black Watch, or Forty-Second Regiment, then employed in keeping order in the turbulent Highlands. In time he became its Major; and, a year or two after the war broke out, he went with it to America. Here, to his horror, he learned that it was ordered to the attack of Ticonderoga. His story was well known among his brother officers. They combined among themselves to disarm his fears; and when they reached the fatal spot they told him on the eve of the battle, "This is not Ticonderoga; we are not there yet; this is Fort George." But in the morning he came to them with haggard looks. "I have seen him! You have deceived me! He came to my tent last night! This is Ticonderoga! I shall die today!" And his prediction was fulfilled.

If Rogers and Campbell had to wait long for their bards, Wolfe was more fortunate. Two old songs about him are still current in York State—the late Mr. Peleg Andrew of Corinth knew both of them—and the more interesting of the pair needs an introductory note. At the Scottish battle of Culloden, in which his regiment lost a third of its men, Major-General James Wolfe (1727-1759) gave proof of that nobility which shines in the ballads. The butcher Duke of Cumberland ordered Wolfe to shoot a wounded Highlander—so runs the story—and Wolfe won royal disfavor by indignantly refusing. There is another story that he wooed a Miss Elizabeth Lawson, but his parents were averse to the match and the lady herself refused him, though it was four years before he gave up hope. After taking part in the successful siege of Louisbourg in 1758, he returned to England and became engaged to Katherine Lowther, sister of the first Earl of Lonsdale. On the night before his death at Quebec, he gave Miss Lowther's miniature to an old school-fellow; evidently this is another tale of premonition. In the great battle of September 13, 1759, when he was wounded for the third time he permitted two grenadiers to assist him to the rear. "Don't grieve for me," he said. "I shall be happy in a few minutes." News of the victory reached him. "Now," said he, "I am contented." Here is the ballad of *Brave Wolfe*.

Cheer up, ye young men all, let nothing fright you;
Though at your love's pursuits, let that delight you;
Don't let your fancy move when come to trial,
Nor let your courage fail at the first denial.

"Bad news has come to town, bad news has carried;
Bad news is whispered round—my love is married.
I'll away to the wars of France where cannon rattle,
Myself I will advance in the front of battle.

"I would go tell my love I'm going to leave her,
Down to the wars of France I'm bound forever;
But whene'er I go to speak, my tongue doth quiver,
So I dare not tell my mind when I am with her.

"Here is a ring of gold, if you'll accept it;
Here, here is a ring of gold, long time I've kept it.
Whene'er you the posy read, think of the giver.
Madam, remember me; I'm done forever."

So then this gallant youth took to the ocean
To free America from its commotion.
We landed at Quebec with all our party,
The city to attact, being brave and hearty.

Brave Wolfe drew up his men in a line most pretty
On the plains of Abraham just before the city.

Not far distant from that place the French did meet us,
With double our number of men resolved to beat us.

Brave Wolfe and Montcalm like brothers talked,
And lovingly between their armies walked,
Till each one took his post as they retired;
Brave Wolfe took his leave and for death prepared.

Till each one took his post as they retired.
So then this numerous host began their fire,
When shot down from his horse fell this brave hero.
We do lament his loss in words of sorrow.

He lifted up his head as he lay dying;
The French their ranks had broke, and the troops were flying.
He lifted up his head while the drums did rattle,
And to his army said, "How goes the battle?"

His aide-de-camp replied: "All in our favor.
Quebec will fall a prize, nothing can save her;
She'll fall into our hands with all her treasure."
So then replies brave Wolfe, "I die with pleasure."

Across the Hudson river from Albany, in the city of Rensselaer, visitors find Fort Crailo, the shrine sacred to the composition of *Yankee Doodle.* The fort was formerly the house of the Van Rensselaers' Upper Manor, where General Abercrombie made his headquarters on the way to the battle of Ticonderoga—as guest of Colonel Johannes Van Rensselaer and his wife, Angelica Livingston. A young surgeon on the General's staff, Dr. Richard Shuckburgh (Shuckbergh, Shakberg, Stackpole), sat on the curb of a well in the back yard while he scribbled (or whistled) a satire on the raw recruits who were enlisting under the stupid General. Sometimes the tune alone is attributed to him. The battle proved who deserved a lampoon, and the song in a later war grated harshly on the ears of Abercrombie's successors, commanders of British forces sent to put down the Revolution.

More than twenty years ago, Dr. Sherman Williams, in *New York's Part in History* (1915), tried to show how decisive our State's rôle

was in the Revolution. Incensed by the emphasis put upon Massachusetts by her historians, he elaborated upon the following facts: Months
before the "Boston Massacre", occurred the "Battle of Golden Hill"
in New York; the first forts captured from the British during the
Revolution were Ticonderoga and Crown Point; the first attempt to
construct a navy was made by Arnold on Lake Champlain; New York
was the only colony which had no breathing spell during the Revolution; its border warfare was the most savage in the history of the
conflict and continued for a year and a half after the surrender of
Cornwallis; though there may have been more Tories in New York
than in any other colony, we furnished more patriot troops than
any other colony except Massachusetts; the most bitterly contested
and bloodiest battle was at Oriskany, where more than a third were
killed or wounded; the most important battle of the war was fought
at Saratoga. In view of these claims it is not surprising that there is
still current enough lore of the Revolution to fill many volumes,
but fortunately the balladry is so small a proportion of the legend
that it can be fairly sampled in a few pages.

Of all the incidents connected with the Saratoga victory, the most
romantic is the death of Jane McCrea, whose body lies near Duncan
Campbell's. Undoubtedly the indignation caused by her murder
aroused the citizens of New England and New York to fill the ranks
of an army which defeated Burgoyne. "Remember Jane McCrea" was
the slogan of the Revolution, just as "Remember Ellsworth" (another
Yorker) was a battle-cry of the Civil War. Inasmuch as the best ballad
about the slain girl and even the stone above her grave do not give
the exact facts, it is fortunate that in 1912 the State Historian, Mr.
James A. Holden, published a careful study which was the result of
several years' research. The account which follows owes most to
Holden's conclusions.

Jane McCrea was the daughter of a Scotch-Irish minister in New
Jersey, descended from an old Highland clan. Upon this parent's
death in 1769, she came to Albany to live with a brother John, a
lawyer and graduate of Princeton who married a girl of the aristo-
cratic Beekman family and then moved north to the frontier settlement of Northumberland, taking Jane with him. When the Revolution came, two of Jane's brothers served with the Tory armies, four

with the Patriots. John McCrea was Colonel of a Saratoga regiment
fighting for independence, served with General Philip Schuyler at
the head of a Committee of Safety, and took part in the expedition
against Quebec. When General Burgoyne invaded New York, he
doubtless had Colonel McCrea's name on the list of those to be
eliminated.

Meanwhile the beautiful and unfortunate Jane had become af-
fianced to David Jones, with whom she had been brought up in New
Jersey. When David's widowed mother moved to a new home about
a mile below Fort Edward, New York, nothing was more natural
than that the children of old neighbors should have fallen in love,
but it could not have been foreseen that Jones would feel in honor
bound to accept a commission as Lieutenant in Peters' corps of Loyal-
ists serving under Burgoyne. As the British army approached, Jane
had the cruel choice of escaping south with her Patriot brother, or
of waiting to see her Loyalist lover. She made the romantic choice.
After visiting David's mother, she went to the home of a Loyalist
"aunt" of hers, a Mrs. MacNeil, who occupied one of the three houses
at the hamlet of Fort Edward. On Sunday morning, July 27, 1777,
Jane was probably hoping for a visit or a messenger from her lover.
Neither she nor Mrs. MacNeil, a cousin of the Scottish General Fraser,
was aware of approaching danger.

The tragedy, however, as Burke and other British statesmen were
to declare, had already been prepared indirectly by Gentleman Johnny
Burgoyne, whose claims to gentrice were as dubious as his talents as
a general. Like most Yorkers who have studied the Revolution, I
find it hard to forget "Sir John Brag's" proclamation issued on June
23d, 1777:

By John Burgoyne, Esq, &c.&c., Lieutenant-General of His Majesty's
Forces in America, Colonel of the Queen's Regiment of Light Dragoons,
Governor of Fort William in North Britain, one of the Representatives
of the Commons of Great Britain in Parliament, and commanding an
Army and Fleet in an Expedition from Canada, &c &c &c . . . I have
but to give stretch to the Indian forces under my direction, and they
amount to thousands, to overtake the hardened enemies of Great Britain
and America . . . If notwithstanding these endeavours and sincere inclination to assist them, the phrenzy of hostility should remain, I trust

I shall stand acquitted in the eye of God and men in denouncing and executing the vengeance of the state against the wilful outcast.—The messengers of justice and wrath await them in the field, and devastation, famine, and every concomitant horror, that a reluctant but indispensable prosecution of military duty must occasion, will bar the way to their return.

The exact details of the "concomitant horror" which destroyed Jane McCrea will never be known. The American General Gates put a blunt charge against Burgoyne:

Miss McCrea, a young lady, lovely to the sight, of virtuous character and amiable disposition, engaged to an officer of your army was with other women and children taken out of a house near Fort Edward, carried into the woods, and there scalped and mangled in a most shocking manner. The miserable fate of Miss McCrea was particularly aggravated by her being dressed to receive her promised husband, but met by her murderers employed by you . . . Upward of one hundred men, women, and children have perished by the hands of the ruffians, to whom it is asserted you have paid the price of blood.

In his characteristic florid style Burgoyne retorted:

I would not be guilty of the acts you presume to impute to me, for the whole Continent of America, though the wealth of worlds was in her bowels, and a paradise upon its surface . . . In regard to Miss McCrea, her fall wanted not the tragic display you have labored to give it, to make it as sincerely abhorred and lamented by me, as it can be by the tenderest of her friends. The fact was no premeditated barbarity. On the contrary, two chiefs who had brought her off, for the purpose of her security, not violence to her person, disputed which should be her guard, and in a fit of savage passion in one, from whose hands she was snatched, the unhappy woman became the victim. Upon the intelligence of the event I obliged the Indians to deliver the murderer into my hands; and though to have punished him by our laws or principles of justice would have been perhaps unprecedented, he certainly should have suffered an ignominious death, had I not been convinced from my circumstances and observations beyond the possibility of a doubt, that a pardon under the terms which I presented, and they accepted, would be more efficacious than an execution.

If any further details are needed in explanation of Jane's murder, we may brush aside the innumerable legends and content ourselves with a brief statement made by one of her nephews. According to his family tradition, Jane was hiding in Mrs. MacNeil's cellar when the Indians arrived. They pulled her out by her long hair—which has so many colors in legend—put her on a horse, and proceeded toward Sandy Hill (Hudson Falls), where they met another party of Indians coming from the murder of a Bains family at Argyle. The second party disapproved taking Jane to the British camp; one of them struck her with a tomahawk and tore off her scalp. This account disposes of the romantic story that she was on the way to her own wedding, and it makes her age twenty-three instead of seventeen, as the stone asserts, but it retains enough of the story to justify all the ballads.

Joel Barlow, one of the so-called Hartford Wits of Connecticut, soon put Jane into his lamentable poem *The Columbiad* under the name of Lucinda, her lover being renamed Heartly; but for proper treatment in a ballad Jane had to wait until a poet appeared whose career and fate were as sad as her own. Henry William Herbert (1807-1858), who wrote under the pen-name of Frank Forrester, was born in London, a kinsman of the Earls of Carnarvon, and a nephew of that Lady Harriet Acland who should have witnessed Jane's wedding. He took honors in Classics at Oxford, migrated to America, and taught in Newark and New York. He committed suicide at a dinner to which he invited his best friends; on his stone was graven the word *Infelicissimus* (unhappiest).

It was not until 1936 that I found the ballad to exist in living memory. Miss Helen Nichols brought a version which her grandmother had dictated slowly from a sickbed, a version which omits the "fancy" description of Herbert's opening and is in other ways distinctly superior to the original. Here it is:

> It was brilliant autumn time
>   When the army of the north
> With its cannon and dragoons
>   And its riflemen came forth.
> Through the country all abroad
>   There was spread a mighty fear

  Of the Indians in the van
   And the Hessians in the rear.

  There was spread a mighty terror,
   And the bravest souls were faint,
  For the Indians were mustered
   In their scalps and their paint;
  And the forest was alive,
   And the tramp of warrior men
  Scared the eagle from his nest
   And the gray wolf from his den.

  For the bold Burgoyne was marching,
   With his thousands marching down,
  To do battle with the people,
   To do battle for the crown.
  But Stark he lay at Bennington
   By the Hoosic's waters bright,
  And Arnold and his forces
   Gathered thick on Bemis height.

  Fort Edward on the Hudson
   It was guarded night and day
  By Van Vechten and his woodmen,
   Right sturdy woodmen they!
  Fort Edward on the Hudson
   It was guarded day and night.
  Oh, but in the early morning
   It saw a bitter sight!

  A bitter sight and fearful,
   And a shameful deed of blood!
  All the plain was cleared around,
   But the slopes were thick with wood;
  And a mighty pine stood there
   On the summit of the hill,
  And a cool spring rose beneath it
   With a low and liquid trill.

  And a little way below,
   All with vine-boughs over-run,

A white-walled cot was sleeping;
  There that shameful deed was done.
Oh, it was a cheery morning,
  In the brilliant autumn time;
The sun shone never brighter
  When the year was in its prime.

But a maiden fair was weeping
  In that cottage day by day;
Tired she was and worn with watching
  For her true love, far away.
He was bearing noble arms,
  Noble arms for England's king!
She was waiting, sad and tearful,
  Near the pine tree, near the spring.

Weary waiting for his coming,
  Yet she feared not, for she knew
That her lover's name would guard her,
  That her lover's heart was true.
True he was, nor did he forget,
  As he marched the wild-woods through,
Her to whom his troth was plighted
  By the Hudson waters blue.

He thought about the madness
  And the fury of the strife;
He thought about the peril
  To that dear and precious life;
So he called an Indian chief
  In his paint and war-array.
Oh, it was a cursed thought,
  And it was a luckless day!

"Go," he said, "and seek my lady
  By Fort Edward, where she stays.
Have her hither to the camp—
  She shall prove a worthy prize."
Then he charged him with a letter,
  A letter to his dear,

Bidding her to follow freely,
  And that she should nothing fear.

Brightly, brightly rose the sun;
  High his heart and full of mirth.
Gray and gloomy closed the night;
  Steamy mists covered the earth.
Then he never ceased to sorrow
  Till his tedious life was o'er,
For that night he thought to see her,
  But he never saw her more.

By the pine tree on the hill
  Armed men were at their post
While the early sun was low,
  Watching for their royal host.
Came a rifle's sudden crack!
  Rose a wild and fearful yell!
Rushed the Indians from the brake!
  Fled the guard, or fought and fell!

Fought and fell, and fiercely over them
  Rose the hideous death-halloo!
One alone was spared of all,
  Wounded he, and pinioned too.
He it was the deed that saw
  As he lay the spring beside.
Had his manly arm been free,
  He had saved her, or had died.

Up the hill he saw them lead her,
  And she followed free from fear,
And her beauty blazed the brighter
  As she deemed her lover near.
He could read the joyous hope
  Sparkling in her sunny eyes.
Lo, the sudden strife! the rage!
  They are battling for the prize!

Guns are brandished, knives are drawn!
   Flashed the death-shot, flew the ball!
By the chief who should have saved her
   Did the lovely victim fall,
Fell, and breathed her lover's name,
   Blessed him with her last sigh;
Happier than he surviving,
   Happier was she to die.

Then the frantic savage seized her
   By the long and flowing hair,
Bared the keen and deadly knife,
   Whirled aloft the tresses fair,
Yelled in triumph and retreated,
   Bearing off that trophy dread.
Think of him who sent them forth!
   Who received it—reeking red!

He received it, cold as stone,
   With a ghastly stupid stare;
Shook not, sighed not, asked not,
   Oh, he knew that yellow hair!
And he never smiled again,
   Nor never did he weep;
And he never spoke her name aloud
   Save when muttering in his sleep.

Yet he did his duty well
   With a chill and dreary heart,
But he never seemed to know it
   Though he played a soldier's part.
Years he lived, for grief kills not,
   But his very life was dead;
Scarcely died he any more
   When the clay was over his head.

Would you farther learn of her?
   Visit then the fatal spot.
There no monument they raised,
   Stories in stone they sculptured not;

But the mighty pine is there—
  Go and you may see it still,
Gray and ghostly, but erect
  On the summit of the hill.

And a little fountain wells out,
  Cool and clear beneath the shade,
Cool and clear as when beside it
  Fell that young and lovely maid.
These shall witness for the tale,
  How on that cruel day
Beauty, innocence, and youth
  Died in hapless Jane McCrea.

If Jane's is the most piteous ballad of the campaigns in York State, the doughtiest is the one sung about John Christian Shell (Schell), hero of Shell's Bush near Fort Dayton. Refusing to take refuge at the Fort, he put his trust in a log residence made like a two-story block-house. The first story had no openings except a massive door and several loopholes; the second projected three feet, with apertures in the overhanging floor to menace an enemy beneath. Attacked by a party of not less than sixty Tories and Indians, Shell, with the aid of his wife and three or four sons, offered a successful defence from two o'clock on a summer afternoon until nightfall. The Tory commander made a hazardous attempt to pry open the door with a crow-bar, but was shot in the leg and dragged into the house as a guarantee against attempts to fire the building. In the breathing-time thus afforded, the beleaguered family raised a Lutheran hymn—perhaps *Ein' feste Burg*. When the attacking party next rushed the house and thrust their guns through the loopholes, Mrs. Shell bent the weapons with blows of an ax. At twilight her husband tried the ruse of yelling to her from the upper story that he saw troops coming to his assistance. The besiegers fled in a panic, taking the young twins captured before the assault. The enemy's loss on the field was eleven (or six) killed and six wounded—good shooting; of twelve wounded who fled toward Canada, nine died on the way.

A story, a story,
  Unto you I will tell,

Concerning a brave hero,
　One Christian Shell.

Who was attacked by the savages
　And Tories, as is said;
But for this attack
　Most dearly they paid.

The sixth day of August,
　He went out to his field,
Determined if the enemy came
　Never to yield.

Two sons he had along with him,
　Resolved were the same.
About the middle of the afternoon
　These invaders they came.

He fled unto his blockhouse
　For to save his life,
Where he had left his arms
　In the care of his wife.

The enemy took prisoners
　Two sons that were twins,
About eight years of age;
　Soon the battle it begins.

They advanced upon him
　And began to fire.
But Christian with his blunderbuss
　Soon made them retire.

He wounded Donald McDonald
　And drew him in the door,
Who gave an account
　There was strength sixty-four.

They fought from two in the afternoon
　Until the closing of the light;

Shell's son was slightly wounded
 Before that it was night.

The old woman she has spoiled
 Five guns, as I have since been told,
With nothing but a chopping ax,
 Which shows that she was bold.

Six there was wounded,
 And eleven there was killed
Of this said party
 Before they quit the field.

The Indians were forty-eight
 And Tories full sixteen,
By [in comparison with] old Shell and his two sons,
 Oh, the like was never seen!

Not like to get assistance
 Nor anybody's help,
They thought for to affright him
 By setting up their YELP.

But God was his assistant
 His buckler and his shield;
He dispersed this cruel enemy
 And made them quit the field.

Come all you Tryon County men
 And never be dismayed,
But trust in the Lord,
 And He will be your aid.

Trust in the Lord with all your might
 And call upon His name,
And He will help you as He did Shell
 To his immortal fame.

If Shell was valiant, his foes were implacable. In the year following (1782), he was working with two sons in a field near Fort Dayton when he was shot by an Indian lurking in the standing wheat. Until help came from the Fort, the worthy sons defended their mortally wounded parent from scalpers; one of them was killed, the other wounded. That's all that I know about the Shells—as stout fellows as we have ever bred.

I used to wonder what songs our Yorkers actually sang in the Revolution, what verses they recited. Part of the answer is found in the Orderly Books of the 4th and 2nd New York Regiments, where lovers of the muses sometimes jotted down their favorite verses. As a sample of their merit—and of their spelling—I begin with a song written down at Fort Schuyler on January 10th, 1781:

Come on my Hearts of Tempered Steale, and Leave your girls and Farms
Your Sports and plays and Hollidays and hark away to arms
   And to conquest we'll all go &c

A Soldier is a Gentleman his honour is his Life
And he that wont Stand by his post will Neer Stand by his Wife

For Love and Honour are the Time [twins] or Els no [so] near all'd
   [allied]
That Neither Can Exist Alone but Flourish Side by Side

The Spring is up the Winter Flies the Trees all green and gay
And all Inviting Honours Call away my boys away

In Shady Tents and Cooling Streams with hearts all firm & free
We'll Chase away the Cares of Life in Songs of Liberty

So Fare you Well you Sweethearts you Smileing girls Adieu
For when the war is Over We'll Kiss it out with you

No Foreign Slaves shall give us Laws, No Brittish Tyrant Reign
Tis Independance made us Free and Freedom We'll Maintain

We'll Charge the Foe from post to post attact their works and Lines
And by some well Laid Stratagem We'll make them all Burgoins

Each hearty Lad shall take his Lass all Beaming Like a Star
And in hur softer arms Forget the Dangers of the war

And when the war is Over We'll set then Down at Ease
We'll plow and sow We'll Reape and Moe & Live Just as we please

The riseing world shall sing of us a thousand years to Come
And tell our Childrens Children the Wonders we have Done

So honest Fellows her's my hand and heart & Very Soul
With all the Joys of Liberty good Fortune and a Bowl

I have given this delightful song of Comradeship as it was written; from this point I shall help the reader by changing spelling and punctuation. The next sample from the Orderly Books is an American version of a song said to have been written upon the occasion of a Scottish soldier's departure in 1775 to serve in America. In the Scottish version he goes to "quell the proud rebels".

> In summer when softly the breezes are blowing
> So sweetly the nightingales sung from each tree;
> By the side of a rock where the rivers are flowing
> I set myself down on the banks of the Dee.
> Flow on, lovely Dee; flow on, thou sweet river;
> Thy banks and pure streams shall be dear to me ever.
> It was there I first gained the affection and favor
> Of Jemy, the glory and pride of the Dee.
>
> But ah, he is gone, and left me amourning,
> To quell the proud Britons, for valiant is he;
> And there is no hopes of his speedy returning
> To wander again on the banks of the Dee.
> He is gone, hapless youth, where the loud roaring billows,
> The kindest and sweetest of all the gay fellows,
> And left me to wander amongst the green willows,
> The loneliest lass on the banks of the Dee.
>
> But time in my prayers perhaps I may see,
> Blest peace may restore my sweet Jemy to me;
> And if e'er he returns, with what care I'll watch o'er him,
> He ne'er shall again leave the banks of the Dee.
> The Dee it shall flow, all its beauty displaying,
> The lambs shall again on each bank be seen playing,

While I and my Jemy are carelessly straying
And tasting again all the sweets of [the] Dee.

Evidently the soldiers of Washington loved *God Save the King*
too well to give up its tune. The Orderly Books have the following
American ditty to that melody, invented long before a Harvard man
penned *America*:

> God save America
> Free from tyrannic sway
>   Till time shall cease.
> Hushed be the din of arms,
> Free from proud war's alarms;
> Followed in all its charms
>   Heaven-born peace.
>
> God save great Washington,
> Fair Freedom's chosen son,
>   Long to command.
> May every enemy
> Far from his presence flee
> And see grim tyranny
>   Bound by his hands.
>
> Thy name, Montgomery,
> Still in each heart shall be,
>   Praised in each breast.
> Tho' on the fatal plain
> Thou wast untimely slain,
> Thy virtue still remains
>   Rescued from death.
>
> Last in our song shall be
> Guardian of Liberty,
>   Lewis the King;
> Terrible god of war,
> Proud in triumphant car,
> Of France and of Navarre,
>   Lewis the king.

The following song in the cavalier strain is certainly the most accomplished verse in the Orderly Books:

> Hark, sweet maid, the trumpet's sound,
>   And Honor calls to war.
> Now Love I leave, perhaps for wounds,
>   And Beauty for a scar.
>
> But ah! surpress the rising sighs,
>   Oh, check the falling tear,
> Lest soft distress from lovely eyes
>   Create a new-born fear.
>
> My life to Fame devoted me
>   Before my fair I knew;
> And if I now desert her cause,
>   Shall I be worthy you?
>
> It is not fame alone invites,
>   Nor fame my bosom warms;
> My country's violated rights
>   Impells my soul to arms.
>   Finis
>   Gen'l Hows Composition
>   the above

Because this lighter touch and courtly air are rather characteristic of something we lost in the eighteenth century, I shall conclude the selections from the Orderly Books with a poem entitled *The Bee.*

> As Cupid midst the roses played,
> Transporting in the damask shade,
> A bee stepped unseen among
> The silken leaves—his finger stung.
>
> His beauteous cheeks with tears were drowned;
> He stormed, he blew the burning wound,
> Then nimbly running through the grove
> Thus plaintive to the Queen of Love:
>
> "I'm killed, Mamma; alas, I die!
> A little serpent winged to fly

That's called the bee on yonder plain
Has stung me, and I die with pain."

Venus smiling thus rejoining:
"My dear, if you such anguish find
From the resentment of a bee,
Think what they feel that's stung by thee."

To conclude the selections from the Revolution, I give a quaint
little song from the Douglass MS., probably written out in the eight-
een-forties. It seems to indicate that the Father of His Country was
known as *Jarge* Washington in York State, if rhyme has reason:

LADY WASHINGTON

"Saw you my hero, saw you my hero, saw you my hero George?
        I have travelled o'er the plain
        And inquired of every swain
        But no tidings can get of my George."—

"I saw not your hero, I saw not your hero, I saw not your hero George,
        But I'm told he's at the van
        Where the battle-path began.—
        I must haste to take care of my men."—

"O'er hills and o'er dales, o'er hills and o'er dales, where the drums they
        sound alarm,
        O ye gods, I give you charge
        To protect my hero George
        And return him safe home to my arms."

XIV: Warriors of the New Nation

IN 1812 greater matters were at stake than the Yorkers could foresee. They realized the constant danger of invasion from Canada—
witness the burning of Buffalo—and the renewed menace of Mohawks on the frontier; they could not foresee that the victories of
Perry on Lake Erie and Macdonough on Lake Champlain would insure the future of the Northwest when the treaty of Ghent found
Britain without strong claims to the Great Lakes. In my own boyhood
in Chautauqua County, before the Great War, we felt that Perry's
triumph ranked with the Gettysburg battle fought by our grand-
fathers. If it was not in New York's waters that the great naval engagement had taken place, our pioneers had lived almost near enough
to hear its guns. We regretted that Oliver Hazard Perry was born in
Rhode Island and lies buried at Newport, but after all, New England
was our back yard. We were told how Midshipman Perry at the age
of fourteen served in the war with Tripoli and was no inexperienced
commander when he reached his headquarters at Erie, Pennsylvania,
a few miles from our county border, on March 23, 1813. We knew
that his second-in-command at the battle, Jesse Duncan Elliott, had
earlier begun the construction of a small fleet, including the *Niagara*

and the *Lawrence*, the latter ship named for that Captain James Lawrence whose command to his sailors on the *Chesapeake* in her fight with the *Shannon* had been, "Don't give up the ship".

When Perry went into battle off Put-in-Bay on September 10, 1813, he had nine sail, mounting fifty-four guns, and manned by five hundred and twelve men. Opposed to him was Captain Barclay with six ships, carrying sixty-three guns, and numbering three hundred and sixty-four men. Perry went into action on his flagship, the *Lawrence*, flying a flag on which was the dying slogan of the man for whom she was named. The battle lasted from 11.45 a. m. until 3 p. m., in most of which time the *Lawrence* bore the brunt of the British fire until eighty-three out of one hundred and three men were killed or wounded. When Perry transferred to the *Niagara*, and after a quarter hour's combat completed his triumph, it was discovered that more than two-thirds of the American casualties had been suffered by the *Lawrence*. In the glow of victory the Yorkers seem to have overlooked Elliott's inaction; we are content to remember Perry's famous message: "We have met the enemy and they are ours: Two ships, two brigs, and one sloop."

In the Grosvenor Library at Buffalo, in an undated old songster called *Songs of the Sea*, there is a jolly ballad entitled *The Battle of Erie—1813*, the alleged composition of a member of Perry's crew on the *Lawrence*:

> Avast, honest Jack! now, before you get mellow,
> Come tip us that stave just, my hearty old fellow,
> 'Bout the young commodore, and his fresh-water crew,
> Who keelhaul'd the Britons, and captured a few.
>
> 'Twas just at sunrise, and a glorious day,
> Our squadron at anchor snug in Put-in-Bay,
> When we saw the bold Britons, and, clear for a bout,
> Instead of put in, by the Lord we put out.
>
> Up went union-jack, never up there before,
> "Don't give up the ship" was the motto it bore;
> And as soon as that motto our gallant men saw,
> They thought of their Lawrence, and shouted huzza!

O! then it would have raised your hat three inches higher
To see how we dash'd in among them like fire!
The *Lawrence* went first, and the rest as they could,
And a long time the brunt of the action she stood.

'Twas peppering work—fire, fury, and smoke,
And groans that from wounded lads, spite of 'em, broke.
The water grew red round our ship as she lay,
Though 'twas never before so till that bloody day.

They fell all around me like spars in a gale;
The shot made a sieve of each rag of a sail;
And out of our crew scarce a dozen remain'd;
But these gallant tars still the battle maintain'd.

'Twas then our cammander—God bless his young heart,
Thought it best from his well-peppered ship to depart,
And bring up the rest, who were tugging behind—
For why—they were sadly in need of a wind.

So to Yarnell he gave the command of his ship,
And set out, like a lark, on this desperate trip,
In a small open yawl, right through their whole fleet,
Who with many a broadside our cockboat did greet.

I steer'd her, and damme if every inch
Of these timbers of mine at each crack didn't flinch;
But our tight little commodore, cool and serene,
To stir ne'er a muscle by any was seen.

Whole volleys of muskets were levelled at him,
But the devil a one ever grazed e'en a limb,
Though he stood up aloft in the stern of the boat
Till the crew pulled him down by the skirt of his coat.

At last, through Heaven's mercy we reach'd t'other ship,
And the wind springing up, we gave her the whip,
And run down their line, boys, through thick and through thin,
And bother'd their crews with a horrible din.

344 BODY, BOOTS AND BRITCHES

Then starboard and larboard, and this way and that,
We banged them and raked them, and laid their masts flat,
Till, one after t'other, they haul'd down their flag,
And an end, for that time, put to Johnny Bull's brag.

The *Detroit*, and *Queen Charlotte*, and *Lady Prevost*,
Not able to fight or run, gave up the ghost:
And not one of them all from our grapplings got free,
Though we'd fifty-four guns, and they just sixty-three.

Smite my limbs! but they all got their bellies full then,
And found what it was, boys, to buckle with men,
Who fight, or what's just the same, think that they fight
For their country's free trade and their own native right.

Now give us a bumper to Elliott and those
Who came up, in good time, to belabour our foes:
To our fresh-water sailors we'll toss off one more,
And a dozen, at least, to our young commodore.

And though Britons may brag of their ruling the ocean,
And that sort of thing, by the Lord, I've a notion,
I'll bet all I'm worth—who takes it—who takes?
Though they're lords of the sea, we'll be lords of the lakes.

Of all the ballads of the War of 1812, the one still strongest in tradition is about James Bird, who served with Perry. Blind Sam Taylor of Westfield, Chautauqua County, who recently died at the County Farm at an advanced age, used to sing it in my boyhood when Sam was a fishpeddler. He said that when he was a young man, seventy years ago, he heard the ballad from a cousin of Bird's, a lady who lived at Kingston, Pennsylvania. According to Sam, after Perry's victory Bird was given a furlough to heal his wound and visit his sweetheart. Unfortunately he overstayed his leave because of bad roads in Western New York, and notices were spread offering a reward for his capture as a deserter. In Westfield he was recognized by a man who, greedy for the reward, offered to give him lodging for the night and to take him in a boat from Barcelona Harbor, a mile from Westfield, to Presque Isle (Erie), where the fleet had headquarters. When the alleged deserter reached Erie, his host of the night before received thirty dollars, and Bird was ordered to immediate execution. Sam said that the officer who ordered the firing squad was in love with Bird's girl. Commodore Perry killed two horses attempting to reach his ships in time to stop the execution, but arrived just as the fatal shot was fired. Bird's enemy at Erie was "so ashamed that he leaned on his sword and died". Nor did the betrayer at Westfield escape: when Bird's mother heard of her son's fate, she put a curse upon the family of the man who had sold her boy for thirty pieces of silver—a curse which has persisted to my own generation.

Here is Blind Sam's version of the ballad, as sung by Bird's cousin:

> Sons of freedom, listen to me,
>   And you daughters too give ear;
> You a sad and mournful story
>   As was ever told shall hear.
>
> How, you know, our troops surrendered
>   And defenceless left the West;
> Soon and quick the troops assembled
>   The invader to resist
>
> Amongst the troops that marched to Erie
>   Were the Kingston volunteers;
> Captain Thomas them commanded
>   To protect our west frontiers.
>
> There was one amongst our number
>   Tall and graceful in his mien;
> Firm his steps, his looks were manly,
>   Scarce a nobler youth was seen.
>
> One sweet kiss he snatched from Mary,
>   Craved his mother's prayer once more,
> Pressed his father's hand and left them
>   For Lake Erie's distant shore.
>
> Soon they came where noble Perry
>   Had assembled all his fleet;

There the gallant Bird enlisted,
 Hoping soon his foe to meet.

Where is Bird? The battle rages.
 Is he in the strife or no?
Hark, the cannon's roar tremendous;
 There he meets the Bastille [hostile] foe.

Ah, behold him, seeing Perry!
 In that self-same ship they fight;
See, his messmates fall around him—
 Nothing can his soul affright.

Lo, behold, a ball has struck him;
 See the crimson current flow.
"Leave the deck," exclaimed brave Perry.
 "No," said Bird, "I will not go.

"Here on deck I took my station;
 Never will Bird his colors fly.
I'll stand by thee, noble Captain,
 Till we conquer or we die."

There he fought, though faint and bleeding,
 Till the Stars and Stripes arose,
Victory having crowned our efforts,
 All triumphant o'er our foes.

Then did Bird receive a pension?
 Was he to his friends restored?
No, nor ever to his bosom
 Clasped that maid his heart adored.

But there came most dismal tidings
 From Lake Erie's distant shore;
Better far had Bird have perished
 'Midst the cannons' dreadful roar.

"Read this letter, dearest parents;
 This will bring sad news to you;

Do not mourn your first beloved,
  Though this brings my last adieu.

"Read this letter, brother, sister—
  It's the last you'll hear from me;
I must suffer for deserting
  From the brig *Niagaree*."

[Lo, he fought so brave at Erie,
  Freely bled and nobly dared.
Let his courage plead for mercy,
  Let his precious life be spared!]

Dark and cloudy was the morning
  Bird was ordered out to die;
Not a heart, not one felt sorry,
  None for Bird to heave a sigh.

See him march and hear his fetters;
  Hark! they clank upon the air.
Firm his steps, his looks were manly,
  And his heart ne'er harbored fear.

See him kneel upon his coffin.
  Sure, his death will do no good.
See him—hark! O God, they've shot him!
  Now his bosom streams with blood.

Farewell, Bird, farewell forever;
  Home and friends you'll see no more.
Now his mangled corpse lies buried
  On Lake Erie's distant shore.

That Bird was not quite so ill-used as the folk believed seems to be
proved by the researches of Mr. Charles B. Galbreath into Naval
records. The lad of twenty had escaped military discipline for mis-
conduct by transferring to the Marines; as a Marine he displayed the
conspicuous bravery which the ballad describes. But when his health
permitted a return to duty he deserted from a guard posted to watch
government stores. When he had been captured and court-martialed,

the President regretfully refused to extend clemency, and in October, 1814, he was one of three deserters executed on board the *Niagara*. The ballad, composed by a Pennsylvania journalist named Charles Miner, follows rather closely Bird's last letter to his parents, in which he makes no excuses but warns others to avoid his fate. It was a gallant, undisciplined, and penitent young man who was made to serve as example to troops which had the frontier's dislike for regimentation.

There is a touching sequel to Bird's own story. In 1825 a weary pioneer named Culver, travelling slowly across New York State, stopped with his family, horse, and oxen at an inn somewhere between Buffalo and Westfield, near Lake Erie. That night Mrs. Culver was hushing her babe with the melancholy ballad of James Bird, when her host and his wife entered the room weeping. They were the parents of the unfortunate youth—and they were hearing the song for the first time. Over and over again the Culvers sang the ballad. Next morning, the Birds refused to accept payment for their hospitality.

Almost exactly a year after Perry's victory, Commodore Thomas Macdonough won another naval triumph that set the bards singing. Macdonough (1783-1825) was born in Delaware, the grandson of a Protestant Irishman from County Kildare, and he was buried in Connecticut, where he had married a wife; but his most famous exploit took place at Plattsburg Bay in the battle of September 11, 1814. Like Perry he had served under Decatur in the Tripolitan War. He was a young man of twenty-nine when he arrived at Lake Champlain in October, 1812, to command the little American fleet. At the battle of Plattsburg he had fourteen ships, with eighty-six guns, and 882 men; his largest vessel, the *Saratoga*, had twenty-six guns. He was opposed by Commodore George Downie with sixteen sail, mounting ninety-two guns, and manned by 937 men; the flagship, the *Confiance*, had thirty-seven guns. While the naval battle was in progress, a British army under Sir George Prevost attacked the American troops commanded by General Alexander Macomb. The Macs won. The British army was repulsed and retreated hastily when Prevost saw the outcome of the naval battle. The lakes were finally free from British menace; citizens of Albany could forget about invasion and continue to boast that theirs is a city which has never been taken by an army.

Undoubtedly the most interesting poem inspired by this victory

was the satirical one entitled *The Noble Lads of Canada*, otherwise
known as *The Battle of Plattsburg*. I first had it from the Cutting
family of Elizabethtown, who collected it from the recitation of
Mrs. Daisy Hathaway and pieced it out from an old clipping of
about 1880 in the *Elizabethtown Post*. Their tradition is that the song
was composed by Miner Lewis of Mooers, Clinton County, near the
Canadian border. "He was chopping wood one day when the words
came to him, and he wrote them down on a smooth chip with a piece
of charcoal." It must have been a large chip.

Come, all ye British heroes, I pray you lend your ears;
Draw up your British forces, and then your volunteers.
We're going to fight the Yankee boys by water and by land,
And we never will return till we conquer, sword in hand,
   We're the noble lads of Canada; come to arms, boys, come.

Oh, now the time has come, my boys, to cross the Yankee's line.
We remember they were rebels once and conquered John Burgoyne.
We'll subdue those mighty rebels and pull their dwellings down,
And we'll have the States inhabited by subjects of the Crown.
   We're the noble lads, etc.

We're as choice a British army as ever crossed the seas;
We'll burn both town and city, and with smoke becloud the skies;
We'll subdue the old Green Mountain boys—their Washington is gone—
And we'll play them *Yankee Doodle*, as the Yankees did Burgoyne.

Now we've reached the Plattsburg banks, my boys, and here we make a
    stand,
Until we take the Yankee fleet Macdonough doth command;
We've the *Growler* and the *Eagle* that from Smith we took away,
And we'll have their noble fleet that lies anchored in the bay.

Now we've reached the Plattsburg fort, my boys, and here we'll have
    some fun;
We soon shall teach those Yankee lads, unless they start and run;
We'll spike all their artillery or turn them on our side,
And then upon the Lake we triumphantly shall ride.

Oh, our fleet has hove in view, boys, the cannons loudly roar.
With death upon our cannon-balls we'll drench their decks with gore;
We've a water-craft sufficient to sink them in an hour,
But our orders are to board and the Yankee flag to lower.

Oh, what bitter groans and sighs we heard on board the fleet!
While Macdonough's cocks are crowing, boys, I fear we shall get beat.
If we lose the cause by sea, my boys, we'll make a quick return,
For if they are true Yankee boys, we all shall be Burgoyned.
   We're the noble lads of Canada; stand at arms, boys, stand.

Now the battle's growing hot, boys; I don't know how 'twill turn,
While Macdonough's boats, on swivels hung, continually do burn;
We see such constant flashing that the smoke beclouds the day,
And our larger boats have struck and the small ones run away.
   We've got too far from Canada; run for life, boys, run.

Oh, Provost (sic) he sighed aloud, and to his officers he said:
"I wish the devil and those Yankees could but sail alongside,
For the tars of France and England can't stand before them well,
For I think they'd flog the devils and send them home to dwell.
   O we've got too far, etc.

"Oh, Vermont is wide awake, and her boys are all alive;
They are as thick around the Lake as bees around a hive,
For the devil and the Yankees no doubt are all combined,
And unless we get to Canada, hard feed we shall find.

"Now prepare for your retreat, my boys; make all the speed you can
The Yankees are surrounding us; we'll surely be Burgoyned.
Behind the hedges and the ditches, the trees and every stump,
You can see the sons of witches and the nimble Yankees jump.

"Now we've reached the Chazy heights, my boys, we'll make a short delay
For to rest our weary limbs and to feed our beasts on hay."
Soon Macdonough's cocks began to crow, was heard at Slack's barn,
And a report through the camp was a general alarm.
   O, we're still too far, etc.

Oh, Provost he sighed aloud and to his officers did say:
"The Yankee troops are hove in sight, and sad will be the day.

Shall we fight like men of courage and do the best we can,
When we know they'll flog us, two to one? I think we'd better run.

"If I ever reach Quebec alive, I'll surely stay at home,
For Macdonough's gained the victory—the devil take Macomb!
I'd rather fight a thousand troops as good as e'er crossed the seas
Than fifty of those Yankee boys, behind the stumps and trees.

"They told us that the Federalists were friendly to the Crown,
They'd join our royal army, and the Democrats pull down;
But they all unite together as a band of brothers joined,
They will fight for Independence till they die upon the ground.

"The old 76s have sallied forth, upon crutches they do lean,
With their rifles levelled on us, with their specs they take good aim,
For there's no retreat to those boys, who'd rather die than run,
And we make no doubt but these are those who conquered John
      Burgoyne,
   When he got too far from Canada, etc.

"Now we've reached the British ground, my boys, we'll have a day of
      rest,
And I wish my soul that I could say 'twould be a day of mirth;
But I've left so many troops behind, it causes me to mourn,
And if I ever fight the Yankees more, I'll surely stay at home.
   Now we've got back to Canada; stay at home, boys, stay."

Here's a health to all the British troops, likewise to George Provost,
And to our respective families and the girls that love us most;
To Macdonough and Macomb and to every Yankee boy
Now fill your tumblers full, for I never was so dry.
   Now we've got back to Canada; stay at home, boys, stay.

Down in Albany the victory of Macdonough was celebrated in a
music-hall song supposedly sung by a Negro—an interesting early
example of dialect which antedates the minstrel show. The *Diamond
Songster* (1817) has this version:

THE SIEGE OF PLATTSBURG

   Back side Albany stan' Lake Champlain,
      One little pond half full a' water,

Plat-te-burg dare too, close pon de main,
　Town small—he grew bigger do hereafter.
　　On Lake Champlain,
　　Uncle Sam set he boat,
　Massa M'Donough, he sail 'em;
　　While Gen'ral M'Comb
　　Make Plat-te-burg he home,
Wid de army, who courage nebber fail 'em.

On 'lebenth day of Sep-tem-ber,
　In eighteen hund'ed and fourteen,
Gubbener Probose, an he British soger,
　Come to Plat-te-burg a tea-party courtin;
　　And he boat come too
　　Arter Uncle Sam boat,
　Massa 'Donough he look sharp out de winder—
　　Den gen'rl M'Comb,
　　An he always a home,
　Catch fire too, jiss like a tinder.

Tang! bang! bang! den de cannons gin t'roar,
　In Plat-te-burg and all 'bout dat quarter;
Gubbener Probose try he hand 'pon de shore,
　While he boat take he luck pon de water—
　　But Massa M'Donough,
　　Knock he boat in the head,
　Break he heart, brake he shin, 'tove he coffin in,
　　As Gen'ral M'Comb,
　　Stat ole Probose home—
To me soul den, I must die a laffin.

Probose scare so, he lef all behime,
　Powder ball, cannon, tea-pot and kittle—
Some say he cotch a colt—trouble in mine,
　Coase he eat so much raw and cole vittle—
　　Uncle Sam berry sorry,
　　To be sure, for he pain;
　Wish he nuss herself up well and harty—
　　For Gen'ral M'Comb,
　　And Massa 'Donough home,
When he notion for a nudder tea-party.

It would be amusing to trace the campaigns of the various Rent Wars, which inspired some mock-heroic balladry; or of the Patriots' War, which nearly involved us again with Canada; or of the Mexican War, with its songs about *Buena Vista*, *The Dying Soldier*, and *The Maid of Monterey*. But it was the Civil War that furnished the heroic background of history for three generations; certainly my Grandfather Kernahan's formidable cavalry sabre and heavy hoss-pistol were as matter-of-course to me as the apple trees and Chautauqua vineyards. Thousands of Yorkers' lives are symbolized by the scythe-tree still standing near the road between Waterloo, New York, and Geneva. When bugles sounded in 1861, James Wyman Johnson, aged twenty-six, hung his scythe in the crotch of a little Balm-of-Gilead tree, saying, "Leave this here till I come back"—and was away to enlist in Company G, 85th New York Volunteers. He died in North Carolina of wounds received on April 20, 1864—a lingering death of more than a month's agony. The scythe is still there, in a tree said to be a hundred feet high. (It doesn't look that high to me.) In 1917 two sons of the same farm enlisted and hung up their scythes on the old tree; but they returned from the wars.

General U. S. Grant's personal-escort bugler, now living in Worcester, New York, remembers how, a lad of fifteen, he was stirred by the singing in school of *Ellsworth's Avengers*—of how the children would chant over and over again:

Down where our patriotic army, near Potomac's side,
Guards the glorious cause of Freedom, gallant Ellsworth died.
Strike, freemen, for your country, sheathe your swords no more
While remains in arms a traitor on Columbia's shore.

> By our hopes of yon bright heaven
> And the land we love,
> By the God who reigns above us,
> We'll avenge his blood.

First to fall the youthful martyr—hapless be thy fate!
Hasten we as thy avengers from thy native state;
Speed we on from town and city, not for wealth or fame,
But because we love the Union and our Ellsworth's name.

After they had sung the chorus, the girls would say: "Why don't you go, boys? We would if we were boys." And Seth Flint, a lad of fifteen, went.

Colonel Ellsworth did for the Civil War what Jane McCrea had done for the Revolution: he aroused the plain folk to battle. Elmer E. Ellsworth (1837-1861) was a Yorker, born at Malta and educated in the schools of Mechanicville, not far from where Jane McCrea had been murdered. Like many an upstate clerk he longed for the city—in this case New York, then Chicago. Out in Illinois he raised and drilled a body called the U. S. Zouave Cadets, whose members were bound to abstain from tobacco, profanity, liquor, and all excesses. Illinois was proud of them; the Governor made Ellsworth a Colonel and Assistant General of the National Guard. The young man was taken into Lincoln's law office at Springfield as a student, and after "old Abe's" election to the Presidency accompanied him to Washington. When the war broke out, he recruited a regiment in New York, chiefly from volunteer firemen, dressed them in the swanky uniform of French Zouaves, and enlisted them as one of the first three-year regiments.

At the occupation of Alexandria, on May 24, 1861, he saw a Confederate flag flying over a hotel called the Marshall House. Going to the roof, he tore down the flag and was descending the stairs with it when he was fatally shot by the inn's proprietor—who instantly paid with his own life. The body of Ellsworth lay in state in the White House, proceeded to New York in a special train, was escorted to Albany, and finally was buried in Mechanicville. The indignation which swept the North found a challenge in Lincoln's call for three hundred thousand volunteers who went to war singing of Ellsworth. To the same gracious and venerable lady who sent me the ballad of Jane McCrea I am indebted for the following song:

COLONEL ELLSWORTH

It was in eighteen hundred sixty-one on the twenty-fourth of May;
The weather was surpassing mild and beautiful the day.
At a place called Alexandria where the rebel flag did wave,
It was there that Colonel Ellsworth came to his untimely grave.

From the city of Chicago in the state of Illinois
He went to New York City—took eleven hundred boys,

Took eleven hundred firemen whose deeds were great and strong;
He picked them out of thousands who desired to go along.

They left their homes and firesides and shook the parting hand,
And started for the Capital, young Ellsworth in command.
They were sent to Alexandria on old Virginia's shore;
'Twas Michigan's First Regiment whose company they bore.

They took and held the city, the steamboats and the cars,
And hauled down the rebel flags, and displayed the Stripes and Stars.
They landed at the city, expecting here a strife.
They took three thousand cavalry without a loss of life.

A rebel flag in the Marshall House was floating in the air.
Young Ellsworth went to take it down and hoist our ensign there.
He unfurled that glorious banner and gave it to the breeze,
And started going down the roof with soldier grace and ease.

He wrapped himself in the rebel flag and started for the street,
Little thinking that that filthy rag would prove his winding sheet.
He started going down the stairs, young Brownell just ahead,
When a ball fired from a rebel gun shot Colonel Ellsworth dead.

His murderer was Jackson, the keeper of the inn,
A traitor of the deepest dye, his heart was black with sin;
But he *paid* the debt of nature—Uncle Sam can never *trust*;
His body, bored by Union lead, lies mouldering in the dust.

Young Brownell shot the traitor, who fell lifeless on the spot.
That's good for you, young Brownell, you ne'er shall be forgot.
And as to Colonel Ellsworth, we'll bid a long farewell;
But in our national history his name shall ever dwell.

What strikes us now about the ballad, aside from its pedestrian quality as verse, is the abuse of an enemy. In the North we no longer talk about rebels—we speak of the Civil War or the War between the States. In 1861, however, few Yorkers felt like being so polite. Even the gentle Quaker Whittier was so carried away by hostile emotion that in *Barbara Frietchie* he imagined a blush of shame coming to the cheek of Stonewall Jackson. "Don't call it the Civil

War," said Mr. Hays, a veteran in Rensselaer County. "Call it the War of the Rebellion, Professor. There wasn't a darn thing about it that was civil."

The least civil feature of the war was the Southern prison. I dare say that Confederates returned with sad tales of the hundreds who died from pneumonia and smallpox at the unfortunately located Northern camp at Elmira, N. Y. Naturally, what Yorkers have handed down in story are the sufferings of their own folks at Libby Prison and elsewhere. The most vivid tale of this kind that I have come upon is an unpublished address of sixty-nine pages delivered in 1901 on *Personal Reminiscences of Prison Life during the War of the Rebellion*, by a leading lawyer of Auburn, the late Mr. Robert L. Drummond. Captured in a rifle-pit after the first battle of Hatcher's Run in October, 1864, he was deprived of overcoat and blanket and jailed in Libby Prison, from whose discomforts he was removed to the horrors of Salisbury, North Carolina.

Into a stockaded open field were herded eight or ten thousand men, without overcoats, hats, or shoes. Inasmuch as the tents would not accommodate half the prisoners, Drummond and four companions dug a hole in the ground with their hands and a piece of broken case-knife. The strongest one lay in this hole next to the wall, the other four packed in tightly on their sides, with half a worn army-blanket to cover the five. They paid $1.50 for one iron spoon, from which all five drank their soup. Sometimes there were no rations for as long as forty-eight hours. Christmas dinner consisted of two unsalted potatoes, "about the size of a partridge egg". They ate rats. In November and December of that year, snow fell several times; midnight was rechristened the "coughing hour". By the thousands they died of cold and hunger, their distress not alleviated by a belief that they were being deliberately starved while a large commissary storehouse in the same town bulged with corn and pork.

From time to time, a Confederate recruiting officer entered the stockade, followed by a handsomely dressed white soldier and a Negro carrying a loaf of bread and a piece of well cooked meat. The Yorkers looked at this symbolic array, then at the buzzards in the sky—and chose the buzzards. The first of the five to die in the pit was reputed to be the tallest soldier from the three counties of

Cayuga, Seneca, and Wayne, a young man who had interrupted his college course to volunteer. Drummond, who was no sentimentalist, says that he held the dying lad and heard him murmur his last words, a quotation from a popular song:

> Come, Mother dear, draw near to me,
> For Mother, I've come home to die.

Two of the five died in the hole. The other three, living skeletons, were paroled on February 22, 1865, when Kilpatrick's cavalry menaced Salisbury. (They had been told that they were all to be mown down by artillery if "Kil" got too near; the cannons were actually set up, pointing inward toward the prisoners.) Of the eighty-six men of the 111th N. Y. Regiment, including Drummond, who had been confined at Salisbury, forty-one had died there within four months. As the paroled skeletons tottered northward, people called to them, "Where are you going?" The Yorkers called back, "To God's Country!"

The most famous naval incident of the Civil War centers around the contest in the spring of 1862 between the *Merrimac* and the *Monitor*. It seemed likely that the ability of the North to blockade the South might be the decisive factor; consequently any new naval invention might turn the tide. The Confederates reconstructed the hull of the sunken U. S. frigate *Merrimac*, equipping her with armor and a steel prow. In the North a company of men headed by Messrs. John F. Winslow and John A. Griswold of Troy, N. Y., associates in patriotic motive, paid royalty to a York State inventor, Theodore R. Timby, for his idea of a revolving gun-turret. Under the direction of the great John Ericsson the "cheese box on a raft" called the *Monitor* was hastily built with iron from northern New York, and on January 30, 1862, was launched at Greenport, Long Island. The construction was rushed in the hope that she might reach Hampton Roads before the Confederate terror of the seas could capitalize on her new features. Before the *Monitor* had time for a trial trip or was accepted by the U. S. Government, she steamed away under the command of Lieut. John L. Worden.

Meanwhile the *Merrimac*, on March 8, 1862, sallied forth from the Roads to revolutionize naval history. Missiles from Northern ships seemed to leave her unharmed as she drove straight at the *Cumberland*, smote with iron prow, and left the wooden sloop sinking. As the water reached her gundeck, the *Cumberland* fired a broadside and went down with flag flying. More than one-half of her crew was lost. The era of wooden navies was over.

At nine o'clock of the night after the battle, the *Monitor* entered Hampton Roads to avenge the *Cumberland's* crew. When battle was joined next day, the *Merrimac* broke her iron prow on the armor of the *Monitor* and limped back to her dock. It was Richmond that must worry now, not Washington. When Norfolk was abandoned by the Confederates on May 9th, they destroyed the *Merrimac*; that December on the 31st, the *Monitor* was lost in a gale off Cape Hatteras.

Something grandly tragic and heroic in the death of wooden navies inspired a ballad which has been a favorite, especially among sailors. Here is the song of *The Cumberland's Crew*, as Blind Sam Taylor liked to recite it:

Shipmates, come gather and join in my ditty
    Of a terrible battle that happened of late.
Let each Union tar shed a tear of sad pity
    When he thinks of the once gallant *Cumberland's* fate.
On the eighth day of March told the terrible story
    And many a tar to the earth bade adieu,
And our flag was wrapped in the mantle of glory
    By the heroic deeds of the *Cumberland's* crew.

On that ill-fated day, about ten in the morning,
    The sky was cloudless and bright shone the sun,
When the drums on the *Cumberland* sounded a warning,
    Telling each seaman to stand by his gun;
For an iron-clad frigate down on her came bearing
    And high in mid-air the Rebel flag flew,
And the pennant of treason she proudly was wearing,
    Determined to conquer the *Cumberland's* crew.

Then up spoke our Captain with stern resolution,
    Saying: "Boys, of this monster we'll not be dismayed;
We are sworn to maintain our beloved Constitution,
    And to die for our country we are not afraid.

We'll fight for the Union, our cause it is glorious,
　　To the Star-spangled Banner we'll ever prove true;
We'll die at our guns or conquer victorious."
　　He was answered by cheers from the *Cumberland's* crew.

Then our noble ship opened her guns' dreadful thunder,
　　Her broadside like hail on those Rebels did pour;
And the people looked on, struck with terror and wonder,
　　To see shells strike her sides and glance harmlessly o'er.
She struck us amidship, our planks she did sever,
　　Her sharp iron prow pierced our noble ship through;
And still as we sank in the dark rolling river,
　　"We die at our guns!" cried the *Cumberland's* crew.

She fought us three hours with stern resolution
　　Till the Rebels by cannon could not be dismayed,
And the flag of Secession had no power to quail them,
　　But blood from her scuppers did crimson the tide.
The Pride of our Navy was never yet daunted,
　　But the dead and wounded her decks they did strew,
Beneath the broad folds on the flag of our Union,
　　Sustained by the blood of the *Cumberland's* crew.

Slowly she sank in Virginia's dark waters.
　　Their voices on earth you will never hear more;
They'll be mourned by Columbia's bright sons and fair daughters.
　　May their blood be revenged on Virginia's bright shore!
In their battle-stained graves they are silently lying,
　　Their names to the earth have forever bid adieu;
But the Star-Spangled Banner above them is flying—
　　It was nailed to the mast by the *Cumberland's* crew.

In Columbia's sweet birthright of Freedom's communion
　　Our flag never floated so proudly before.
May the spirits of those that died for the Union
　　Beneath its proud folds exultingly soar.
Whenever our soldiers assemble in battle,
　　God bless that dear banner, the Red, White, and Blue;
And beneath its broad folds cause tyrants to tremble,
　　Or die at their guns like the *Cumberland's* crew.

As the war went on, the soldiers learned to laugh grimly and even to enjoy satirical songs and ballads. Here is one brought me from the North Country: A Southerner is supposed to be singing:

> Their soldiers reconnoitre like the mischief, Jeff,
>   And appropriate our cattle and our corn.
> They've taken half our niggers and they're bound to free the rest,
>   And I wish they were in Guinea, every one.
> We have got ourselves in trouble with the black men, Jeff,
>   And I think we'd better give it up and run.
>
>   So good-by, Jeff, and good-by, Jeff!
>   I told you so before.
>   There's a nigger in the fence
>   With a little common-sense
>   Tells us we will never figure any more.
>
> Oh, you promised you would meet me at the White House, Jeff,
>   When I left you on the Chickenooga (sic) shore;
> But you're farther from it now than you were, friend Jeff,
>   And your face is never turned toward the door.
> Oh, we'll never see each other at the White House, Jeff,
>   And I think we'd better give it up and run.

After the battle of Gettysburg, in July of 1863, the relief from fear of invasion found expression in the following song:

JEFF DAVIS'S BALL

> Far down in the South there lived Jeff Davis.
> He swindled his friends till they haven't a pound.
> Secession, he thought, would make him a man again,
> Leave him a fortune and plenty of ground.
> He gave a large party to friends and relations
> To stand by his side while his treason they called.
> "But listen—I'll make your eyes glisten!"
> Was the promise they made for Davis's Ball.
>
> He called upon Lee to start up the music,
> And then upon Ewell to lead on the band,
> While Longstreet and Hill could ford the Potomac

And drive all the Yankees from our merry land.
"We'll feast on the best in the Cumberland Valley,
And take enough home to last us a year;
And when we have feasted and made a grand rally,
[We'll] drive to the North those old volunteers."

They all started off in the best of good spirits,
All drinking together to Gettysburg came,
When an accident happened to the great Rebel army,
They routed and ran from the Yankees again.
Says Lee to his army: "We must be mistaken,
They found out our plan, and the road we have lost.
I fear we are whipped, so save your own bacon.
I never would come, had I counted the cost.

"I don't like the tune those Yankees are playing;
Old *Yankee Doodle* they gave us too fine.
We've got a bad thrashing, 'tis no use denying,
The best we've had since Davis's time."
Some took to their heels and fled to the mountains;
A thousand besides on their knees they did fall,
And begged for their lives to save them the trouble
Of leaving their cards for Davis's Ball.

The Yorkers got other fun out of war beside jeering at Jeff Davis.
A lady in Schenectady learned the following song from her older
brothers, who were a little too young to be accepted as soldiers but not
too young to entertain the army-camps:

Our Jimmy has gorn for to live in a tent;
They've grafted him into the Army.
He finally puckered up courage and went,
When they grafted him into the Army.

I told them the child was too young. Alas,
At the Captain's forequarters they said he would pass;
So they trained him up well in an infantry class,
And grafted him into the Army.

Now in my pervisions I see him revealed,
As they grafted him into the Army.

A picket beside the contented field,
They grafted him into the Army.

He looked kinder sickish and begins to cry,
A big volunteer standing right in his eye.
Now what if the duckie should—up and die!
Now they've grafted him into the Army.

During the war there was a considerable number of "Copperheads" in the State. The Democrats had by no means disappeared in the Lincoln administration's era, though New York was pretty strongly Republican, with its distinguished former Governor Seward serving as the chief figure in Lincoln's cabinet. Nor was the Republican party made up entirely of Abolitionists, though it is true that in Gerrit Smith the State had produced an acknowledged leader in that movement. I am on the trail of a ballad about the trial of John Brown, formerly sung in the Adirondack region in ridicule of the man who lies buried there. In Erie County there was even one little village which, after grave deliberation about the merits of the war, seceded from the Union. (Later it furnished a considerable number of soldiers to the Union cause.)

The following poem, which, like the one just given, used to be sung at camps to amuse the soldiers, was learned in Whitehall. In the first stanza there is a punning reference to Vallandingham of Ohio, a leader of the Copperheads.

UNCLE SAM'S FUNERAL

'Twas but a little while ago
That the Copperheads were found
With their great Vallanding-hammers,
A-hammering around;
And they tried to scare us
With their doleful sounds.
   Um-ha, tra, la, la, la, la, la.

Said they, "Oh people dear,
Uncle Sam is dead.
Let us put him in his coffin
And hammer down the lid."

And to work they went
As the word they said.

Uncle Sam, he then arose
Like a great giant, hale and strong,
With his people and his army,
And a glorious, loyal throng;
And the Coppers sneaked
To where they all belong.

So far as the York State soldiers themselves were concerned, the favorite song seems to have been a jigging little tune still current in the eighteen-nineties, when we boys could hear it sung properly by veterans of the G. A. R. In its gayety and lack of sentimentality it seems more like the ballads of the A. E. F. than any other ditty of the Civil War. You remember it—it went about like this:

There was an old soldier, and he had a wooden leg.
He had no tobacco, no tobacco could he beg.
Said another old soldier, "Will you give me a chew?"
Said the first old soldier, "I'll be darned if I do."

Save up your money, and save up your rocks,
And you'll always have tobacco in your old tobacco-box.

America has a wealth of campaign songs; during the Civil War our State had its share. Those interested in politics of that period will like the following ditty used in the campaign of 1860 that elected Lincoln:

THE PEOPLE ARE A-COMING

I hearkened in the East and I hearkened in the West,
And I heard a fifing and a drumming;
And my heart bobbed up in the middle of my breast,
For I knew that the people were a-coming.

Then pull off your coat and roll up your sleeve,
Abe and the people are a-coming!
Oh, pull off your coat and roll up your sleeve,
Lincoln and the people are a-coming, I believe.

I hearkened at the doors of Old Tammany Hall,
    When the leaders at the bar were a-running—
And I heard the poor soft sheels crack agin the wall
    When they found that the people were a-coming!

        Oh, pull off your coat, etc.

I looked in at Mozart, and knocked very loud,
    Where the Wooden-headed guards were a-chumming,
But as soon as I told them that Abe had a crowd,
    Oh, they knew that the people were a-coming!

At Stuyvesant Hall they are rolling on the ball,
    And the rush and the roar are benumbing
To the minions of a dynasty that totters to its fall,
    For they know that the people are a-coming!

There's a panic in the South, and a world of windy talk,
    And the value of the Union they are summing,
But the eaters of their dirt may as well prepare to walk,
    For 'tis certain that the people are a-coming!

There's a rattle in the East and a rattle in the West;
    There's a Yankee Doodle fifing and a drumming;
On the ides of November you'll find out the rest,
    And you'll know that the people are a-coming!

The honest men are waking in our old Empire State,
    In spite of the Democratic gumming
About Seward and Chicago and the smashing of a slate—
    Oh, the people of New York are a-coming!

        Three cheers for "Honest Abe", then, together we'll give—
        Lincoln will be President as sure as you live!

I do not know to what tune that was sung, but *Lincoln and Liberty*
was shouted to the popular melody of *Rosin the Beau*:

        Hurrah for the choice of the nation!
            Our chieftain so brave and so true;

We'll go for the great Reformation—
    For Lincoln and Liberty too!

We'll go for the son of Kentucky—
    The hero of Hoosierdom through;
The pride of the Suckers so lucky—
    For Lincoln and Liberty too!

Our David's good sling is unerring,
    The Slavocrat's giant he slew;
Then shout for the freedom-preferring—
    For Lincoln and Liberty too.

They will find what, by felling and mauling,
    Our rail-maker statesman can do;
For the people are everywhere calling
    For Lincoln and Liberty too.

Then up with our banner so glorious,
    The star-spangled red-white-and-blue;
We'll fight till our flag is victorious,
    For Lincoln and Liberty too!

I once asked one of the last surviving members of the G. A. R. in eastern New York—a fine old gentleman in his nineties who held my class enthralled for more than an hour—whether he remembered the first time that he saw President Lincoln.* "Yes," said Mr. John W. Hays, "it was a special occasion. My regiment was encamped below Arlington. We had thought that we were enlisting for three months, but at the end of that time we were told that we were mistaken—that we'd have to serve two years. They even brought up a regiment with cannon as if to threaten us. We wanted to do right, but we didn't want even the government to cheat us. So then Mr. Seward came to see us and explain things to us, as a New York man, and he brought along Mr. Lincoln. We knew that Seward and Lincoln would know what was right. We stayed." That is my favorite story about Lincoln and New York boys—that and one my Grandfather Kernahan told me: "After I was wounded and got better, they let me ride in a body-guard of cavalry assigned to the President at Washington. He

* For further details about this incident see the Appendix.

liked to take a canter and think things out. He was the greatest man
we ever had, but he was no Phil Sheridan on a horse. He'd get to
thinking, and his big mount would go faster and faster, with the
President bumping up and down. Then all at once he'd seem to make
up his mind about what he was pondering, and he'd pull up suddenly.
We'd be riding single file behind him, and his sudden stop would
make us look like a row of dominoes that you push at one end. After
a while we figured out a kind of signal for the front man to give
when he thought Mr. Lincoln was going to pull up. It was all right
with us, though."

It was all right with us, so far as Lincoln was concerned. The rank
and file knew that he was working for the Union. There is a longish
poem—collected in Chautauqua County from the son of a Civil War
veteran—that expresses what the Yorkers meant in Lincoln's day
when they said that he knew what was right. The best lines are these:

> Oh may this fuss and further strife be like a gal or lover,
> Or like a row 'twixt man and wife, be slicker when it's over.
>
> We will not be scared by any plan that tries to cut in two, sir,
> This land where every man's a man, and every woman too, sir.
>
> Should we, who foes could never lick, [fall] by our own disunion?
> No! We are bound to stick to the Temple of our Union.

XV: Ballad Lovers: Trials and Tragedy

So say they, speak they, tell they the tale: of Jenny Lind, the Swedish Nightingale, and of her American lover, Joseph Burke; of how he sang her the folk-ballads of America AND HID HIS HEART:

> "Of the pains the lover bore
> And the sorrows he outwore
> For the goodness and the grace
> Of his love, so fair of face."

Let the melody of *Aucassin and Nicolette* set the mood while a plain Yorker mumbles the story which he learned from Mr. John Torrance of Batavia, husband of Joseph Burke's niece:

The Burkes were of old from the DeBurgos of France, landed gentry of Ireland, handsome and accomplished in music. In the seventeenth century estates were confiscated, but Joseph Burke's father, Dr. Miles Burke, a son of the Lady Catherine Blake, lived at Lough Corrib House, Galway, inherited musical taste, and, wearing a false beard to hide his youth, passed medical examinations and practiced his calling. His wife was a girl of great beauty, preserved in a portrait belonging to her American descendants. To them was born the boy Joseph, a lad so talented that at the age of four he toured Ireland, performing on violin, 'cello, and piano. "The child prodigy of a century," one London paper remarked. By the time that he was eighteen he had earned eighty thousand dollars which his Irish father, with a love for speculation, lost in a scheme for the colonization of Texas.

America beckoned all the Irish, especially the impecunious gentleman. At New York young Joseph made a hit as concert artist, but you could hardly advertise him as a prodigy any longer; moreover, a gentleman's son should have a profession. So he studied law with Governor Marcy at Albany, playing the organ on Sundays in one of the churches. It was the Governor who advised him to abandon law for a serious career in music; acting under that advice, Joseph Burke sailed to Belgium for study under the great DeBeriot at Brussels. When, at the end of a year, the master had not presented a bill, the anxious lad wondered how his father could possibly meet fees that might be very large indeed. Then DeBeriot informed him that for a pupil of such talent consideration of fees did not exist, and this generous arrangement lasted until Burke returned to America and the romance awaiting him.

The Great Showman, P. T. Barnum, brought the Swedish Nightingale to New York in September of 1850, for what was probably the greatest personal triumph ever granted an artist in this country before the days of the movies. She was thirty, unmarried, glamorous, and for about five years had been recognized as the finest singer on the concert stage. She needed a violinist to play solos while she was resting between groups of songs. Burke was recommended, played one piece to her, and found himself being embraced while the diva's manager offered him a contract for the one hundred and fifty concerts which Miss Lind had promised to give. (She was to have $150,000 for one hundred and fifty concerts, and was to forfeit one thousand dollars for each engagement which she failed to meet.)

It was an exciting but wearying tour which Barnum had arranged. At least twice Jenny Lind slipped away from the crowds to visit Burke's family at Summerville Farm near Batavia. After she had sung sixty concerts, she came to the parting of the ways with the Showman.* The family has been told of how in Charlestown, South Carolina, she refused to sing on Christmas Eve, giving instead a party for her company, with a Christmas tree bearing a gift for each. Finally she left Barnum and made Burke her manager. Apparently she had no reason to regret her move, for again the family tradition states that she took back some $200,000 to England as the result of her two years in America. They were the great years of Burke's life, saddened at their close by the stunning blow of her marriage to Otto Goldschmidt, a pupil of Mendelssohn, nine years her junior, and, like Burke, a member added to her troupe after she reached America. In the midst of the tour a new accompanist was needed; Goldschmidt came over in May, the tour ended in December, the marriage took place in February.

Nobody will ever know why Burke had not told his own love. He used to hint to his niece that he thought of Jenny Lind as above him, a goddess, that he did not like the thought of living in Sweden, that he did not guess his rival's intention. Many years later, on one of his rather frequent visits to the diva's home in England, he innocently told her what she had meant to him, and she replied, "Why didn't you tell me then?" There is also the story of her trying to sing once more to him on his last visit—pathetically trying, stopping, saying, "You see, it is gone, all gone."

The prettiest of the sentimental annals tells of Burke's last years. He abandoned the violin when Jenny Lind sailed away, and earned his living in New York teaching piano to such fashionable ladies as a daughter of Governor Levi P. Morton. Twenty-five years before his death he retired, though he was not entirely forgotten among the musicians—the Philadelphia Orchestra, for which he had played gratis in its early days, kept him on its rolls as an honorary member. Once a year, if he happened to be at Summerville Farm on New Year's Eve, he would take from its wrappings the Cremona that Jenny had given him, tune it carefully, and play a concert to his family in her memory. He always ended with the Swedish Echo Song which her marvelous coloratura had made famous. Then he would dash up-

* See the Appendix for Barnum's version of the affair, which differs from the family legends which I am presenting.

stairs with tears in his eyes, and the family would hear him walking up and down with his memories and his grief. She died before him; he was buried wearing a ring which she had given him.

If I could tell it well, it might be the most charming traditional tale of sentiment in York State. I have tried to outline it, not for its own sake, but chiefly to introduce the irony of Jenny Lind's favorite American ballad. When she was nervous and fatigued, she always asked her lover to sing an American song, preferably one belonging to the folk, and there was a favorite which always brought tears of merriment to her eyes. It is the doleful ballad of *Springfield Mountain* or *The Pizen Sarpent*. Just before his death the late Phillips Barry summarized the debate on the history of this song by stating that Timothy Myrick of Wilbraham (formerly Springfield Mountain) died of snake-bite in Farmington, Connecticut, on August 7, 1761, but that there is no *evidence* that the ballad is of earlier date than the second quarter of the nineteenth century. When Joseph Burke sang it to Jenny Lind, it may have been a recent ballad or a fairly old one; at any rate, Mr. Torrance was able to give me what he believes is the exact text which the Nightingale admired. The name of Curtis instead of Myrick in this version may indicate a Vermont tradition; a family of Curtis is known to have lived in Springfield, Vermont.

On Springfield Mountain there did dwell
A likely youth as I've hearn tell,
A likely youth of twenty-one,
Leftenant Curtis' only son, only son, only son,
Leftenant Curtis' only son.

One Monday morning he did go
Down to the medder for to mow.
He mowed all round; at last he feeled
A cruel sarpint bite his heel, bite his heel, bite his heel,
A cruel sarpint bite his heel.

He sat him down upon the ground,
And with his eyes he looked around
To see if he could someone spy

To take him home where he might die, he might die, he might die,
To take him home where he might die.

He look-ed around but look-ed in vain;
No one was there to ease his pain;
So he made up his mind his time had come,
And he laid his head down on a cold stun, on a cold stun, on a cold stun,
And he laid his head down on a cold stun.

So this young man guv up the ghost
And forth to Abraham's bosom did post,
Up out of the medder where he'd come to mow,
With nobody there to see him go, see him go, see him go,
With nobody there to see him go.

In some versions the hero has a colloquy with his sweetheart after the accident; for example, in this, from Chautauqua County:

> They carried him home to Sally dear,
> Which made her feel so very queer,
>   Rye, terink, terink, a-daddy-ay.

> "O Johnny, dear, why did you go
> Down in the meadow for to mow?"—

> "O Sally dear, O didn't you know
> 'Twas daddy's grass and it must be mown?"

A Jefferson County version has these three stanzas:

> He fell right down upon the ground,
> He shut his eyes and looked around.
>   Rye, tic-a-nac, (3), an-ay-rye-at.

> They took him to his Sally dear;
> It made him feel most awful queer.

> "Why Johnny dear, don't you know,
> 'Twas Daddy's hay you aren't to mow?"

The ballad fascinates "fans" so much, in spite of its crude literary quality, that I am tempted to give one more version which seems to indicate the Myrick story of the eighteenth century, though *Myrick* has been changed to *Murry*.

> On Springfield Mountain there did dwell
> A likely youth, 'twas known full well—
> Leftenant Murry's only son,
> About the age of twenty-one.
>
> On Friday morning he did go
> Down to the meadow for to mow
> A bout or two, and then did feel
> A pesky sarpint bite his heel!
>
> Soon as he felt the deadly wound,
> He threw his scythe upon the ground;
> Straightway for his home was his intent,
> Crying aloud still as he went.
>
> The neighbors round his voice did hear,
>   But none to him did thus appear,
> Thinking for workmen he did call,
>   And so alone this man did fall!
>
> His careful father as he went,
>   Seeking his son was his intent,
> And soon his only son he found
>   Cold as a stone upon the ground!
>
> 'Twas in seventeen hundred and sixty-one
>   That this sad accident was done;
> May this be warning unto all
>   To be prepared when God doth call!

I was reciting this ballad one Commencement when a lady remembered a parody that used to be sung about 1883 by students of the Albany Normal College:

> In Springfield County there did dwell
> A lovely youth—I knew him well:

And Obed Squashbine was his name,
  And Dolly Smyth his charming flame.
    I, toori, oori, oori, ay. (2)

Now Obed he, as you must know,
  Did earn a heap a-shovelling snow;
And when the weather it was good,
  He earned some more a-sawring wood.

One early morn before 'twas light,
  He was sawring wood with all his might.
He hadn't sawred more'n half a cord
  When his three fingers off he sawrd.

Now Obed, when he saw the blood,
  Just like a aspen-leaf he stood,
Then up he picked his fingers quick,
  And ran to Dolly, lickety split.

And when he got to Dolly's door,
  He fell slam-bang right on the floor.
"O Dolly, Dolly, come here quick—
  I've sawred my fingers for a stick!"

Now Dolly forthwith she did run
  To get a doctor for to sew them on;
And Dolly being out of breath
  Straightway fell down and friz to death.

The neighbors then to him did run,
  And said to him, "O come, O come!"
And Obed when he Dolly saw
  Forthwith he died of the lockjaw.

They buried them down in the sand,
  Obed a-holding Dolly's hand.
The weeping friends they stood around,
  And with their tears they soaked the ground.

It is likely that this effort was intended to satirize not only *Spring-*

field Mountain, but also another ballad—about *The Frozen Girl,* otherwise known as *Fair Charlotte*—which is still one of the three or four most popular in Northeastern New York. I used to tell my students the tradition of a blind poet and ballad-singer from Vermont, William L. Carter, carrying *Fair Charlotte* across York State. Alas for romance! Just before his death Mr. Phillips Barry discovered that the song was written by Seba Smith (1792-1868), who was born in Maine but had the felicity to spend his last years on Long Island. It was after he had created the character of a satirical crackerbox philosopher, forerunner of Lowell's Hosea Biglow, that Smith came to New York City and earned a living as a free-lance writer. In 1843 (December 28th, appropriately) he published in a weekly magazine called *The Rover* his ballad, then entitled *A Corpse going to a Ball.* The incident which inspired the verses directly was the death on January 1, 1840, of some unnamed lady who was frozen on the way to a dance; the account is to be found in *The New York Observer* of February 8, 1840. He got his heroine's name from a story published in 1831 about a certain Charlotte J——, found dead in her "bower", all dressed for a ball. So one of our most popular and tenacious ballads was not the work of a blind balladeer without education—which always seemed most unlikely—but of a graduate of Bowdoin College who made a little money by rhyming an incident reported in a newspaper.

The ballad is still current upstate, perhaps because we have severe winters in which mothers have to warn their daughters to dress warmly. The version which I give, however, was not collected recently but is from a copy made in 1872 near Glens Falls. It includes a final stanza which does not usually occur; the folk have added it to Seba Smith's poem:

> Young Charlotte dwelt on the mountain side
>   In a lone and dreary spot;
> No dwellings there in three miles round
>   Except her father's cot.
> But oft on cold and wintry nights
>   Young swains would gather there,
> For her father kept a social board
>   And she was very fair.

Her father liked to see her dressed
  Trim as a city belle,
For she was the only child he had,
  And he loved his daughter well.
At a village inn fifteen miles off
  There's a merry ball tonight;
The weather is exceeding cold,
  But their hearts are warm and light.

'Twas New Year's Eve, the sun went down
  As she looked with an eager eye
Out of the frosty windows forth
  As the merry sleighs passed by.
How restless was her eager eye
  As the well known voice she hears,
And dashing up to the cottage door
  Young Charlie's sleigh appears.

"O daughter dear," her mother said,
  "This blanket round you fold,
For 'tis a dreadful night without,
  And you'll take your death of cold."—
"O no, O no," young Charlotte said,
  And she laughed like a gypsy queen.
"To ride in blankets muffled up
  I never can be seen.

"My silken cloak is quite enough—
  You know 'tis lined throughout;
Besides, I have a silken shawl
  To tie my neck about."
Her gloves and bonnet being on,
  She jumped into the sleigh,
And then they rode o'er the mountain side
  And o'er the hills away.

There's music in the merry bells
  As o'er the hills they go;
Such a squeaking noise the runners made
  As they rode o'er the frosty snow!

With faces muffled silently
  For five long miles they passed,
When in a few and frozen words
  Their silence broke at last.

"Such a dreadful night I never knew
  My lines I scarce can hold!"
Young Charlotte said in a frozen voice,
  "I am exceeding cold."
He cracked his whip, he urged his team
  Much faster than before
Until another five long miles
  In silence they rode o'er.

"How fast," says Charles, "the snow and ice
  Do gather on my brow!"
Young Charlotte said in a feeble voice,
  "I am growing warmer now."
Then o'er the hills and the mountain side
  In the glittering, bright starlight
Until at last they reached the inn,
  And the ballroom was in sight.

They drove to the door, young Charles stepped out,
  He gave his hand to her.
"Why sit you there like a monument
  That hath no power to stir?"
He asked her once, he asked her twice,
  But she answered not a word;
He asked her for her hand again,
  But still she never stirred.

He took her hand in his. O dear!
  'Twas cold and hard as stone.
He tore the mantle from her brow,
  And the bright stars on her shone;
Then quickly to the lighted hall
  Her lifeless body bore.
Young Charlotte was a frozen form
  And words spake nevermore.

He sat himself down by her side,
  And the bitter tears did flow.
He said, "My own intended bride
  I nevermore shall know!"
He put his arm around her waist
  And kissed her marble brow.
His thoughts ran back to where she said,
  "I am growing warmer now."

He bore her back into the sleigh,
  And with her he drove home;
And when they reached her parents' door,
  O how her parents moaned!
They mourned the loss of a daughter dear;
  Young Charles mourned o'er his doom,
Until at length his heart it broke,
  And they slumbered in one tomb.

For the most part, the ballad has few surprises in the way of variants; only once in a while do you find bits of true folk-charm. A lady aged seventy-five dictated a text which she often heard her mother sing when they lived on a farm near Malone. In this version Charlotte lived on a "mounting" side, and the opening picture is pretty:

'Twas New Year's Eve as the sun went down
  And she watched with a rustly sigh.

And there is poetry in these lines:

They rode along the last five miles
  And in the star-pale night.

The dénouement is gruesome:

He lifted the lid from off her face,
  And the pale stars on her shone.

If Joseph Burke had known York State balladry well, he could have found many a "doleful dump" more appropriate than *The Pizen Sarpent.* There is, for example, *Barbara Allan,* the enchanting story of a young man who died in a manner which has appealed to lovers

for centuries, and to such connoisseurs as Pepys and Goldsmith. I like
a version collected in the North Country:

In Scarlet town where I was born, there was a fair maid dwelling,
Made every youth cry Wellaway, and her name was Barbara Allen.*

All in the merry month of May, when the green buds were a-swelling,
Sweet William came from the Western States and courted Barbara Allen.

It was all in the month of June, when all things there were blooming,
Sweet William on his deathbed lay for the love of Barbara Allen.

He sent his servants to the town where Barbara Allen was dwelling.
"My master is sick and sends for you, if your name be Barbara Allen.

"And death is painted on his face and o'er his heart is stealing;
Then hasten away to comfort him, O lovely Barbara Allen."

So slowly, slowly she got up, and slowly she came nigh him,
And all she said when she got there, "Young man, I think you're
    dying."—

"O yes, I'm sick and very sick, and Death is on me dwelling;
No better, no better, I never can be if I can't have Barbara Allen."—

"O don't you remember in yonder town when you were at the tavern,
You drunk a health to the ladies all around and slighted Barbara Allen?"

As she was on the highway home, the birds they kept a-singing;
They sang so clear they seemed to say, "Hard-hearted Barbara Allen."

She looked to the east, she looked to the west, she spied his corpse
    a-coming.
"Lay down, lay down, that corpse of clay, that I may look upon him."

The more she looked, the more she mourned, till she fell to the ground
    a-crying,
Saying, "Take me up and carry me home, for *I* am now a-dying.

"O mother, mother, go make my bed; go make it long and narrow.
Sweet William died for me today, I'll die for him tomorrow."

* Pronounce *dwellin'* and *Allin*.

She was buried in the old churchyard, and he was buried nigh her;
On William's grave there grew a red rose, on Barbara's grew a green
briar.

In another version her scorn is emphasized:

She turned her body round about and spied the corpse a-coming!
"Lay down, lay down, the corpse," she said, "that I may look upon him."

With scornful eyes she then looked down, her cheeks with laughter
swellin',
While all her friends cried out and in, "Unworthy Barbara Allen!"

The last part of another version is interesting in several ways; for
one, the locale seems to be Stonington, Connecticut, from which settlers probably moved to Wyoming County, New York, where the
ballad was set down:

He turned his face unto the wall, he turned his back unto her.
"Adieu, adieu to my friends all, but awoe to Barbara Allen!"

She mounted on her milk-white steed and out of town was going.
She had not rode many a mile before she heard the bells a-tolling.
The bells they tolled all in a row, "O cruel Barbary Allen!"

She looked east, she looked west, and she looked all around her,
And there she saw the lamentable corpse and the barriers (sic) dressed
in mourning.

"Come set you down this clay-cold corpse and let me look upon him,
For once his cheeks they beautifully flowed, and now the color is fading."

Then she trembled like a leaf, and death it stared upon her,
And down she fell as cold as clay, which made all people wonder.

Come now, all you maidens of this town, and listen to my story.
O do not slight nor grieve your love, for 'twill surely blast your glory.

This young man he died for pure love, this damsel followed after;
The richest man in Stonington died for a poor blacksmith's daughter.

A counterpart of *Barbara Allan* is *Lord Lovell*, a ballad so popu-

lar in some parts of the United States that collectors are said to groan
when they hear the name. (I must add that I have never groaned for
this reason.) The story is of a lover who casually left his sweetheart
without declaring his affection, and upon his return found that the lady
had died, presumably of sorrow at his laggard tactics. Here is a
composite of two versions from Essex County:

> Lord Lovell, he stood at the castle gate
>   A-combing his milky white steed,
> When along came Lady Nancibel,
>   A-wishing her lover God-speed, speed, speed,
>   A-wishing her lover God-speed.
>
> "Where are you going?" Lady Nancy she said,
>   "Where are you going?" said she.
> "I'm going, my lady Nancibel,
>   Strange countries for to see, see, see,
>   Strange countries for to see."—
>
> "When will you be back?" Lady Nancy she said,
>   "When will you be back?" said she.
> "In a year or two or three at the most
>   I'll return to My Lady Nancy, -cy, -cy,
>   I'll return to My Lady Nancy."
>
> He had not been gone but a year and one day,
>   Strange countries for to see,
> When a languishing thought came into his mind—
>   Lady Nancibel he must go see, see, see,
>   Lady Nancibel he must go see.
>
> So he rode and he rode with his milk-white steed
>   Till he reached fair London town,
> And there he heard St. Barney's bell
>   And the people all mourning around, -round, -round,
>   And the people all mourning around.
>
> "Is anybody dead?" Lord Lovell he said.
>   "Is anybody dead?" said he.

"A nobleman's daughter," a stranger replied.
"Some call her the Lady Nancy, -cy, -cy,
Some call her the Lady Nancy."

He ordered the coffin to be opened forthwith,
    And the shroud to be folded down,
And he fell to kissing her clay-cold lips,
    Till the tears they came trickling down, down, down,
    Till the tears they came trickling down.

Lady Nancibel died as it might be today,
    Lord Lovell he died on the morrer;
Lady Nancibel died of pure, true love,
    Lord Lovell he died of sorrer, -rer, -rer,
    Lord Lovell he died of sorrer.

And over her grave they planted a rose,
    And over hisen a briar,
And they clim till they reached the church-top,
    Where they couldn't climb any higher, -igher, -igher,
    Where they couldn't climb any higher.

They grew and they grew till they reached church-top,
    And there they couldn't grow any higher,
And they both entwined in a true lover's knot
    Of which all true lovers admire, -ire, -ire,
    Of which all true lovers admire.

There was always the possibility that a wronged lover might return as a ghost. An interminable ballad of the broadside type, *The London Lawyer's Son*, tells how the hero won the love of a lady but before he could be wed was called away to the funeral of a kinsman in Gloucester. In his absence she was wooed by Sir Ralph, a courtier, whose attentions so "puffed her up with shadows vain" that she married him "that night". Meanwhile the lawyer's son "sent fourteen letters or above" without reply. Upon his return, he learned of her wedding, sickened, and died, but not before he had spoken the menacing words, "Alive or dead, I'll to her go". The ballad ends in the following lamentable fashion:

Sometimes his ghastly ghost she see,
And as each night this lady she
Lie sleeping by her husband's side,
And thus the ghost would seem to chide:

"Arise, thou worst of womenkind!
What peace or comfort can you find
If you consider, from of late
You brought me to my ruin-state.

"Pray therefore lodge thou in his arms!
Why doth he thus possess your charms?
Come, follow me, and quit your bed,
For you are mine, alive or dead!"

Then in a flame he seemed to go.
His apparition scared her so
That she fell sick and soon she died,
And as she breathed her last she cried:

"Alas!" says she, "I am going hence
To answer for [my] great offence,
The sin of pride and perjury
Under which guilt I weeping lie.

"Farewell to all my weeping friends.
I'm going to answer for my sins;
It's with a sad, distracted mind.
What mercy can I hope to find—

"Who's wrong [ed] my conscience and my dear!
But as I beg for mercy here,
So let me have it now at last."
This said, from life to death she passed.

So let this now a warning be
To all of a high and low degree,
And let them not for riches' sake
By any means their promise break.

On the other hand, there is a whole cycle of ballads about the betrayed or abandoned girl, of which *Caroline of Edinburgh Town* was popular in York State a century ago:

Come all young men and maidens, attend unto my rhyme.
It's of a young damsel who was scarcely in her prime;
She beat the blushing roses, and admired by all around
Was lovely young Caroline of Edinburgh town.

Young Henry was a Highland man, a-courting to her came;
And when her parents came to know, they did not like the same.
Young Henry was offended and unto her did say;
"Arise, my dearest Caroline, and with me run away."

"We will both go to London, love, and there we'll wed with speed,
And then lovely Caroline shall have happiness indeed."
How enticed by young Henry, she put on her other gown,
And away went young Caroline of Edinburgh town.

Over the hills and lofty mountains together they did roam;
In time arrived in London, far from her happy home.
She said, "My dearest Henry, pray never on me frown,
Or you'll break the [heart] of Caroline of Edinburgh town."

They had not been in London more than half a year
When hard-hearted Henry proved too severe.
Said Henry, "I will go to sea. Your friends did on me frown,
So beg way without delay to Edinburgh town.

"The fleet is fitting out, to Spithead dropping down,
And I will join the fleet to fight for King and Crown.
The gallant tars may feel the scars or in the water drown,
Yet I never will again return to Edinburgh town."

Then many a day she passed away in sorrow and despair;
Her cheeks, though once like roses, were grown like lillies fair.
She cried, "Where is my Henry?" and often did she swown,
Crying, "Sad's the day I ran away from Edinburgh town!"

Oppressed with grief without relief the damsel she did go
Into the woods to eat such fruit as on the bushes grow.
Some strangers they did pity her, and some did on her frown,
And some did say, "What made you stray from Edinburgh town?"

Beneath a lofty spreading oak this maid sat down to cry,
A-watching of the gallant ships as they were passing by.
She gave three shrieks for Henry and plunged her body down,
And away floated Caroline of Edinburgh town.

A note, likewise her bonnet, she left upon the shore,
And in the note a lock of hair with the words, "I am no more;
And fast asleep I'm in the deep; the fish are watching round
Once comely young Caroline of Edinburgh town."

Come all you tender parents, ne'er try to part true love.
You're sure to see in some degree the ruin it will prove.
Likewise, young men and maidens, ne'er on your lover frown;
Think on the fate of Caroline of Edinburgh town.

Another betrayed maid weeps in the pretty song called *The Dawning of the Day*:

It was on one fine morning all in the summer time;
Each bush and tree was dressed in green and alleys in their prime.
Returning homewards from a wake through the fields I took my way,
And there I spied a pretty fair maid at the dawning of the day.

No shoes nor stockings, cap nor cloak, this lovely maid did wear,
And her hair like shining silver-twist lay on her shoulders bare.
With milking pails all in her hand so nobly and so gay
She did appear like Venus bright at the dawning of the day.

Her cheeks were like roses in bloom, her skin like lillies fair,
Her breath was like lavender perfumed with balmy air.
She did appear like Helen fair, or Flora, Queen of May.
This angel bright did me delight at the dawning of the day.

"Where are you going, my pretty maid, where are you going so soon?"
"I'm going milking, Sir," she said, "all in the month of June,

For the pasture I must go to, it is so far away
That I must be there each morning at the dawning of the day."

"You've time enough, my dear," said I, "suppose it was a mile.
Come sit down on this primrose bank and let us chat awhile."—
"Ah no, kind sir—my hurry will admit [of] no delay.
Look round—the morning breaks—'tis the dawning of the day!"—

"O do not be so distant, my only heart's delight,
For I, alas, am wounded all by your beauty bright."—
"O forbear, don't banter me," this lovely maid did say,
"I can't suppose you'd me seduce at the dawning of the day."

As thus she spoke, my arms entwined around her lovely waist;
I sat her on a primrose bank, I there did her embrace.
"Leave off your freedom, Sir," said she, "and let me go on my way,
For the time is come I must be gone; it is the dawning of the day."

But when this lovely damsel came to herself again,
With heavy sighs and downcast eyes she sorely did complain,
And said, "Young man, I'm much afraid you will me betray;
My virgin bloom you got so soon at the dawning of the day."

We rose, shook hands, and departed, and crossed o'er the plain,
And in the course of seven months we there did meet again.
She seemed to me so dropsical as I passed o'er the fay,
And carelessly I passed her at the dawning of the day.

The tears run down her rosy cheeks, and bitterly she cried,
And said, "Young man, I think it's time that I was made your bride.
O make good the damage done, as you before did say,
And don't forget the time we met at the dawning of the day."

I said, "Sweet, lovely damsel, I hope you'll me excuse,
For to join you in wedlock's band indeed I must refuse,
For I've been lately married to a maid near Bantry Bay
By whom I got three hundred pounds at the dawning of the day."

This sudden blunt refusal did not with her agree.
"I think you'll gain no credit, Sir, by thus deluding me,

For I may a warning be to other maidens gay,
And never trust a man alone at the dawning of the day."

The moral of it all is pointed at the close of *The Maid upon the Tide*, a ballad in which a girl drowns herself:

Till fishes fly and seas run dry
A man will ne'er prove true.

Many years ago, the girls in Troy's collar-factories used to sing a song curiously entitled *Wrapped in Red Flannels*:

When I was a-walking one bright summer's morning,
    When I was a-walking one summer in May,
I stopped at the hospital to see my darling,
    All wrapped in red flannel that hot summer's day.

Under her pillow these words she had written,
    Under her pillow these words she did say,
"Never go courting or sporting or gambling;
    It leads to destruction and leads you astray.

"When I am dying, send for my mother,
    Send for my mother, don't let her delay."—
"Woman, dear woman, your daughter is dying,
    And I am the young man who has led her astray."—

"When I am dead, lay me out in white satin,
    Cover my coffin with flowers of May;
Six jolly sportsmen to carry my coffin
    And sing the dead-march as they lay me away."

Now she is dead, and they will all leave her;
    Now she is dead, and they laid her away;
Now she is dead and is highly forgotten
    By the hardy young man who has led her astray.

Like the Southern mountaineers, we have our "lonesome tunes" for those whose sweethearts have proved false. This version of *Green Laurel* comes from Clinton County, near the Canadian border:

Green grows the laurel, damp in the dew.
    Trouble and sorrow since I parted with you!

And at our next meeting I hope to prove true;
We'll change the green laurel for the red, white, and blue.

Once I'd a true-love, but now I have none;
He's gone and left me this wide world to roam;
But since he has left me, contented I'll be,
For he's gone with a girl no better than me.
And at our next meeting I hope to prove true;
We'll change the green laurel for the red, white, and blue.

I don't see why the women they should love men,
I don't see why the men they should love them.
This is my opinion—I'll tell you what I know:
Young men are deceitful wherever you go.
But at our next meeting I hope to prove true;
We'll change the green laurel for the red, white, and blue.

In another version, I found this stanza:

I wrote my love a letter with rosy red lines.
She wrote me an answer twining with vines,
Saying, "Keep your love-letters and I will keep mine;
You write to your sweetheart and I'll write to mine".

At the present time, the most widely known song of this sort in the State is *The Butcher's Boy* or *In Jersey City*. A typical version sung at the State College in Albany is this:

In Jersey City where I did dwell,
There lived a boy I loved so well.
He took my heart away from me,
And now he will not look at me.

He takes strange girls upon his knee
And tells them tales he won't tell me;
And now I know the reason why:
Because they have more gold than I.

Their gold will melt, their silver fly,
And then they'll be as poor as I.
I went upstairs unto my bed
Without a word to mother said.

I took a chair and sat me down,
 With pen and ink I wrote it down,
And on each line I shed a tear,
 Calling back my Willie dear.

When father came from work that night
 And looking for his daughter bright,
He climbed the stairs and the door he broke,
 And found her hanging from a rope.

"O grief, O grief! What have you done?
 Gave up your life for a butcher's son."
He took a knife and he cut her down,
 And on her breast these words he found:

"O dig my grave and dig it deep,
 A marble slab from head to feet
And on my breast a turtle-dove
 To tell the world I died for love.

"I wish, I wish, I wish in vain,
 I wish I were sixteen again.
Sixteen again I'll never be
 Till apples grow on a cherry tree."

There are many variants, of course, even in naming the scene of the tragedy; one of my best versions refers to Georgia Town, describes the suicide as done with "her own bed-rope", and has this additional stanza before the girl goes upstairs:

There is a bird up in a tree;
 Some says he's blind and cannot see.
I wish the Lord had done so with me
 Before I met such company.

Another of the doleful favorites is *The Jealous Lover*, otherwise known as *Luella* or *Ella*, and by other titles. One of the longest and most poetical versions is this, from the North Country:

Down in the valley lonely where the violets fade and bloom
There lies our own Luella in a cold and silent tomb.

She died not broken-hearted or in lingering sickness fell,
But in one moment parted from the home she loved so well.

One night when the moon shone brightly, the stars were shining too,
Beneath her cottage window her treacherous lover drew,
Saying, "Love, come let us wander into the meadows gay,
And undisturbed we'll ponder and name our wedding day".

Deep, deep into the forest he led his love so dear.
Says she, "It's for you only that I have wandered here.
The way is dark and dreary and I'm afraid to stay;
Of rambling I am weary and would retrace my way".—

"Retrace your way nor ever no more these fields you'll roam.
So bid farewell to parents, to friends, and to your home;
For in this forest I have you—from me you cannot fly;
No human heart can save you, Luella, you must die!"

Down on her knees before him she pleaded for her life,
But deep into her bosom he plunged the fatal knife.
"O Edwin, what have I done, that you should take my life?
I always have been loving, and would have been your wife.

"Farewell, my dearest parents; you ne'er will see me more,
Though long you wait my coming at your old cabin door.
Dear Edwin, I forgive you." With her last and dying breath
Her heart it ceased its beating, her eyes were froze in death.

The birds sang in the morning, and mournful was the sound,
'Twas there we found her body lifeless on the ground.
Down in the valley lonely where the violets fade and bloom,
There lies our own Luella in a cold and silent tomb.

In a version current in Little Falls, the motive for the murder
seems to be Emily's refusal to take a walk with Edgar:

> "No, Edgar, I am tired, and do not care to roam;
> No, Edgar, I am weary and would rather stay at home."
> Up sprang her jealous lover, with madness in his eye,
> Up sprang her jealous lover, saying, "Emily, you must die!"

Up to this point you have been reading about tragedies between lover and lover. A numerous group of ballads finds tragic defeat or trial in the opposition of parents (usually the father), brother, sister, or uncle. The conventionally cruel parents appear in the song known at Dolgeville as *Drowsy Sleeper*:

> "Awake, awake, you drowsy sleeper!
>   Awake, awake, and listen to me!"—
> "O who is that at bedroom window,
>   A-weeping there so bitterly?"—

> "It's me—it's me, your own true lover,
>   It's me—it's your own true Willy;
> And now, Mary, rise and ask your mother,
>   If you my wedding-wife can be.
> And if she says no, pray come and tell me,
>   Then I will no longer trouble thee."—

> "O no, O no, I dare not ask her,
>   For she lies in her chair at rest
> With a silver dagger at her side, love,
>   To pierce the one that I love best."—

> "O now, Mary, go and ask your father
>   If you my wedding-wife can be
> And if he says no, pray come and tell me,
>   And I will no longer trouble thee."—

> "O no, O no, I dare not ask him,
>   For he lies in his chair at rest,
> With a silver dagger at his side, love,
>   To pierce the one that I love best.

> "O now, Willy, go and court another."—

> "O I can climb the highest tree, love,
>   Or I can rob the riches' nest,
> Or I can court the fairest maiden,
>   But not the one that I love best."

O then he plunged that silver dagger,
    And he pierced unto his aching heart.
"Sing, farewell, sing farewell, Mother, Father;
    We both must part."

And then she plunged that bloody dagger
    Unto her lilly-white breast,
"Sing farewell, Father, Mother;
    Now we are both at rest."

In another version Willie sends Mary to ask her father's permission, and Mary sends Willie to ask his mother. Similarly, in some of the very old British ballads there are traces of a matriarchal period when a man always asked his mother's advice—sometimes as she was sitting in her stone chair.

In a curious ballad which must be recent, the father has a religious reason for separating the lovers. Here is *The Rabbi's Daughter*:

The Rabbi sat one evening,
    A Bible on his knee,
His daughter Nell beside him
    As he loved her tenderly.
"Come tell me, child, why do you weep and sigh?
    Tell me, is he of Jewish faith or not?
Don't be afraid to trust me, dear.
    Tell me the reason why.

"You are a Rabbi's daughter
    And to him must obey;
Your father you must honor
    Until his dying day.
If you a Christian marry,
    Your father's heart you'll break.
You are a Rabbi's daughter
    And must leave him for my sake."—

"I'm told I must not have you dear,
    Your kind face see no more;
But I shall have no other love,
    Though I may never love."

> Her word came true that very morn,
>   When on a bed of white
> The Rabbi found his only child
>   Who died of love that night.

From Tioga County comes a somewhat blurred ballad of a father whose own hand laid his daughter low; the title is *The London Maid and Boy*:

> There was a rich merchant in London did dwell,
>   He had a fine daughter, a very fine girl.
> Five thousand bright guineas was her portion in gold
>   Until she fell in love with a young soldier bold.
>
> She dressed herself up in a man's suit of clothes,
>   She dressed herself up from the tip of her toes,
> With boots on her feet and a staff in her hand,
>   For to meet her Willie she walked to the Strand.
>
> "O Willy, dear Willy, O Willy!" she cried,
>   "O Willy, dear Willy, I'll save you or die."
>
> Her father espied her as she walked down the Strand;
>   He took her to be Willy, O Willy, the man,
> And out of his mantle a sword that he drew,
>   He pierced her body—was instantly dead.
>
> Finding out his mistake, he fell back in despair,
>   A-wringing his hands and a-tearing his hair,
> Crying, "Old cruel monster, O what have I done?
>   I have slain the flower of fair London town".
>
> Finding out his mistake, then away he did start;
>   He leaned on his sword till he pierced his own heart,
> A-crying for mercy till he drew his last breath,
>   And he closed his eyes in the cold arms of death.

More charming in sound is *Lowlands Low*, collected in the North Country:

Six long years in battle since Edmond had been gone.
He came up to young Emily's door when she was all alone;

He came up to young Emily, his gold all for to show,
Which he had gained all on the main when he plowed the Lowlands Low.

"My father keeps a public house down handy by the stream,
And you go there and enter in and there till morning be.
I will meet you there in the morning. Don't let my father know
Your name it is young Edmond, who plowed the Lowlands Low."

As Emily on her pillow lay, she had an awful dream:
She thought her honest lover, his blood flowed in a stream.
Then she arose and put on her clothes, in search of him did go.
(Although she loved him dearly, he plowed the Lowlands Low.)

"Now I will go down to the riverside to gather lowly greens,
Where once my honored lover, his blood flowed with the stream.
The peril age is over the ocean, and the waves, cast to and fro,
Remind me of young Edmond who plowed the Lowlands Low."

She said, "Father, where's that stranger came here last night to lie?"—
"O he is dead," the father said, "and you no tale shall tell."—
"O Father, cruel Father, you shall die a public show
For the murder of young Edmond who plowed the Lowlands Low."

She went unto the Counsellor, her story she made known,
Her father was quickly taken, his trial soon came on,
The Justice found him guilty, and hanged he was also,
For the murdering of young Edmond who plowed the Lowlands Low.

Most Americans have heard some version of the ancient and imaginative British ballad of *The Twa Sisters*, in which a jealous girl drowns
her prettier sister, the body floats down to the miller, and a harp is
made of the victim's hair. This has been so popular on the radio that
I despaired of getting a really independent, traditional text until this
one was brought from Otsego. It has lost a good deal of its poetry
but has amusing accretions:

> He gave the oldest a golden ring,
>> Bow down, bow down,
> He gave the oldest a golden ring,
>> Bow ye unto me,

He gave to the oldest a golden ring,
And he gave to the youngest—most everything.
　So I will be true, and true to my love;
　　My love will be true to me.

He gave to the youngest a silken hat,
　Bow down, bow down,
He gave to the youngest a silken hat,
　Bow ye unto me,
He gave to the youngest a silken hat.
It made the oldest mad at that.
　So I will be true, etc.

One night as they walked by the river's brim (3)
The oldest pushed the youngest in.

The miller with his hook and line (3)
He caught her by her crinoline.

Next Sunday to church they all did go, (3)
And now they're married I suppose.

I have a curious tragi-comedy which old Mr. James Mack of
Clyde sang to me in his characteristic recitative—somewhat free of
rhythm. A cruel uncle appears, but, as you will see, *The Farmer's
Daughter* was in the end triumphant:

O it's of a farmer's daughter
　So beautiful, I'm told.
Her parents died and left her
　A large amount of gold.

She lived with her uncle,
　The cause of all her woe,
And you soon shall hear [of] this maiden fair.
　How does the story go?

Her uncle had a plow-boy
　That Mary loved quite well,
And in their uncle's garden
　Their tales of love would tell.

There was a wealthy squire
    That often came for her to see,
But still she loved her plow-boy
    On the banks of sweet Dundee.

It was of a bright summer's morning,
    Her uncle went straight away,
He knocked at the maiden's door and said,

"Arise, arise, my pretty fair maid;
    A lady you shall be,
For the Squire is a-waiting
    On the banks of sweet Dundee."—

"O I care not for your squires,
    Your dukes or lords likewise.
My Willie's eyes appears to me
    Like diamonds in the skies."—

"Begone, you erring female!
    You ne'er shall happy be,
For I intend to banish Willie
    On the banks of sweet Dundee."

A press-gang came to Willie
    When he was all alone.
He boldly fought for liberty,
    But there were six to one.

The blood it flowed in torrents.
    "Pray kill me now," says he.
"I'll die for handsome Mary
    On the banks of sweet Dundee."

This maiden fair a-walking,
    Lamenting for her loss,
She met the wealthy squire
    Down in her uncle's grove.

"Stand off, you beastful man!" said she.
"You have sent away the only lad I love
   From the banks of sweet Dundee."

He put his arms around her
   And tried to throw her down.
Two pistols and a sword she saw
   Beneath his morning-gown.

She grasped the weapon from him,
   The sword she used so free,
She fired and shot the squire
   On the banks of sweet Dundee.

Her uncle overheard the noise,
   He hastened to the ground.
"Since you killed the squire,
   I'll give you your death-wound."—

"Stand off then!" cried young Mary,
   "For undaunted I shall be."
She pulled the trigger and slayed her uncle
   On the banks of sweet Dundee.

Then there's a doctor sent for,
   A man of noble skill,
And then there came a lawyer
   For him to sign his will.

He willed his gold to Mary
   Who fought so manfully,
Then he closed his eyes, no more to rise,
   On the banks of sweet Dundee.

(Young Mary and young William
   Are both living yet.)

Mary says to Willie,
   "You're worth your weight in gold."

And Willie says to Mary,
"You're worth more than that, I'm told."

They're both living yet
    On her uncle's farm;
And if they're not dead,
    I suppose they're there today (spoken).

One of the most opportune of escapes from love's trials is told in
the old British ballad of *The Maid Freed from the Gallows*. I have
not found so enchanting a melody as Dean Smith discovered in South
Carolina, but here is a pretty good example of the text, from Eastern
New York, ultimately from Rensselaer County:

"Hangman, hangman, hold the rope!
    Hold it for a while.
I think I see my father coming,
    Coming on the mile.
Father, did you bring me gold,
    Or come to set me free?
Or did you come to see me hang
    Upon that willow tree?"—
"Daughter, I did not bring you gold,
    Nor come to set you free,
But I have come to see you hang
    Upon that willow tree."

In succeeding stanzas she appeals to mother, brother, sister, uncle,
auntie, and cousin, all of whom are equally frank and discouraging
about their intent to see her hung. Finally appears the sweetheart,
who replies to her query:

"Sweetheart, I did not come to see you hung
    Upon that willow tree;
I did not bring you gold,
    But I have come to set you free."

The ballad does not tell how he manages to free her. He was
probably a man of his hands, like the lover in *Bold Soldier*:

'Twas of a bold soldier who just returned from war;
He courted a fair damsel worth money in great store.

Her portion was so large that it scarcely could be told,
And yet she loved the soldier because he was so bold.

"Bold soldier, bold soldier, I'm afraid to marry thee:
My father is so cruel, he'll surely murder me."
He drew his sword and pistol, and hung them by his side,
And said he would be married, whatever might betide.

They went to the church, and returning home again
They met her honored father with several armed men.
"O dear, my dearest jewel!"—"Your beau shall be slain."—
"Fear not," says the soldier, "fear not,"—but all is vain.

Up stepped her honored father and unto her did say:
"O daughter, dear daughter, dear daughter, I pray
If this is your intention, to be young Calvin's wife,
Here in this dark valley I'll end your sweet life."—

"Stop, stop!" says the soldier. "I've no time to battle,
But seeing that I'm just married, I'm fitted for a battle."
He drew his sword and pistol, he caused them for to rattle;
The lady held the horse while the soldier fought the battle.

The first man stepped up to him, he ran him through the main;
The next one stepped up to him, he served him the same.
"Let's run," says the rest, "or we all shall be slain;
To fight this bold soldier we find it all in vain."

"Bold soldier, bold soldier, what makes you fight so bold?
You shall have my daughter, ten thousand pounds in gold."—
"O no," says the lady, "that portion is too small.
Fight on, my bold soldier, and you shall have it all."—

"Bold soldier, bold soldier, if you will spare my life,
You shall have my daughter for your beloved wife."
He took him home unto his house, he made him his heir;
It was not for love, but through cruelty unfair.

Now come, all you rich, fair maidens with money in great store.
Never shun a soldier, although they're sometimes poor,

For they are always jolly—happy, fresh, and free—
And how gallantly they fight for their rights and liberty!

Mr. Jimmie Froggett, sometime of Watertown, later of Broome
County, sang this fierce ballad of escape:

> I went into her mother's house,
>   Inquirin' for my dearie.
> Her mother says she's not within
>   With countenance most severely.
>
> I heard a low, low, fainted voice
>   Just coming from her window.
> "My dear," says she, "I'd go to thee,
>   But locks and bolts doth hinder."
>
> I split the door in pieces four,
>   I made those locks to shatter;
> I took her by her lilly-white hand,
>   And through the room I led her.
>
> Her father and three other men
>   Come soon followin' after.
> They say we shan't return no more
>   But in our blood shall wallow.
>
> I fought those three, three hours or more,
>   I fought those three in bitter,
> For love is pure, I must endure,
>   And she'll be mine forever.

From Northville, in Fulton County, comes this more elaborate ballad on a similar theme, called *The Lady Leroy*:

> I espied a fair couple on old England's shore,
> A-viewing the ocean and the wide billows o'er;
> One being a lady whose beauty shone clear,
> The other a sea-captain persuading his dear.
>
> This young man being grievous, he hung down his head,
> Till at length he took courage and unto her said:

"Your parents are wealthy and angry with me.
If I tarry here longer, my ruin will be."

The young maid was anxious, her heart filled with dread,
But at last she took courage and unto him said,
"I will dress myself up as an American boy
And a fine ship sail to you named the *Lady Leroy*."

She dressed herself up in a suit of men's clothes;
Straightway then unto her old father she goes.
She bought a fine vessel, paid him his demand,
And little did he think 'twas from his own daughter's hand.

Straightway then unto her true lover she goes,
Saying, "Make all things ready; we have not time to lose".
They hoisted their foresail and anchor with joy,
And over the ocean sailed the *Lady Leroy*.

When this news came out for her father to know,
Straightway then unto a sea-captain he goes,
Saying, "We'll hail them, we'll take them, their lives we'll destroy,
For they shall not escape in the *Lady Leroy*!"

They had been sailing a week or ten days,
And the winds from the north-east blew a sweet, pleasant breeze,
When they espied a ship sailing, which filled them with joy,
For they hailed her and found she was the *Lady Leroy*.

"Turn back, O turn back, to old England's shore,
Or showers of grape-shot upon you we'll pour."
Then Mollie's true lover made them this reply:
"Pour on your grape-shot! We'll conquer or die."

Then broadside to broadside those vessels did pour,
And louder than thunder their cannons did roar,
Till Mollie's true lover gained the victory.
Then hail to all lovers—they always get free!

XVI: Ballad Lovers: Comedy

IN OUR Arcadia nearly all the swains were farmers, with just enough soldiers and sailors to play Shakespeare's game of mistaken identity when they returned from distant strands. A century ago, the stout lads and lovely lasses all knew songs about how home-coming wanderers tested faithful maids whose eyes must have been dim indeed—perhaps with tears. The pretty tunes and titles excuse the oft-repeated plot of *Banks of Brandywine*, *The Dark-Eyed Sailor*, *The 'Prentice Boy*, and several other ditties, of which a North Country favorite is called *Mantle So Green*:

> As I went awalking one morning in June
> I viewed the fair meadows and everything green;
> I espied a fair damsel, she appeared like a queen
> With her costly fine robe and her mantle so green.
>
> Said I, "My pretty maiden, if you'll come with me,
> We will join in wedlock and married we'll be."—
> "To the green hills I wandered to shun all men's view,
> For the lad that I love lies at famed Waterloo."—
>
> "As you are not married, tell me your true-love's name;
> I have been there in battle and ought [to] know his name."—

"Draw near to my garment and there you will see
His name is embroidered on my mantle so green."

On the raising her mantle it was there to behold,
His name and his surname in letters of gold—
Young William O'Reilly appeared to my view.
"He was my chief comrade at famed Waterloo.

"We had fought for two nights, and the third day at noon
He received his death-summons on the eighteenth of June.
As he was a-dying, I heard his last cry,
'Were you here, lovely Nancy, contented I'd die'."

I stood in amazement, for the paler she grew;
She fell in my arms with a heart full of woe.
"Through the green hills you've wandered for the last evermore;
Rise up, lovely Nancy, and your love I'll restore!

"Lovely Nancy, lovely Nancy, it was I won your heart;
In your father's garden the day we did part
I clasped you in my arms beneath the old apple tree.
Cheer up, lovely Nancy, and married we'll be."

This couple got married, I've heard people say;
They had dukes to go with them on their wedding day.
"Peace is declared, the war is all o'er;
You're welcome to my arms, lovely Nancy, once more."

Lovely Nancy must have wondered sometimes whether she heard
all of her lover's adventures—whether there might not have been a
Lass of Mohee such as the one remembered throughout the North
Country:

As I sat amusing myself on the grass,
Who should come there beside me but a young Indian lass?
She sat down beside me, taking hold of my hand,
Saying, "You look like a stranger, not one of our band.

"If now my true-love you will consent to be,
I'll teach you the language," said the lass of Mohee.

"No, my fair creature, that never can be,
For I have a sweetheart in my own country,
And I'll never forsake her in her poverty,
For her heart is as dear as the lass of Mohee."

The sun was shining all on the salt sea,
And I went a-roving with this pretty Mohee;
Wooed and we wandered till we came to a grove,
Till we came to a cottage in the cocurnut grove.

This fair young creature be most handsome and kind;
She asked me her pardon by the heavens above;
And I being a stranger, she gave me a home,
Saying, "Think of Mohee when you're roaming alone".

The last time I saw her, she stood on the shore,
And she waved her hand as the ship it sailed o'er,
Saying, "When you get on to the last home you love,
It's think of Mohee . . . and the cocurnut grove".

It's now I'm safely landed on my own native shore,
Where friends and companions gather round me once more.
I look all around me, but not one can I see
That I love half as well as the lass of Mohee.

Sometimes the lady tired of waiting for her sea-borne lover, with
such embarrassing results as are told in *The Sailor and the Tailor*:

There was a rich merchant in Bristol did dwell.
He had a fine daughter; she was courted excell,
And courted she was by a sea-faring man,
A brisk young Tarpolian whose name it was John.

One day this Tarpolian came to let his love know
That he had a long voyage, to the Indies must go;
And if he did live to return back to her,
Then they would be married and live in great cheer.

The sailor was absent for several long years.
At length a young tailor began to draw near,

And soon you shall hear how he acted his skill,
And he won from this fair one a hearty good will.

One day as the sailor was walking the street,
One of his old shipmates by chance he did meet.
"Well met, brother shipmate, and I'll welcome you home;
Just in the right season—I'm sure you will come.

"You know the young lady you once courted grand?
She is going to be married, I well understand;
Tomorrow at Bristol the wedding's to be,
For I was invited by her father, you see."

The sailor took ship, and that very same night
He sailed into Bristol before it was light.
In Bristol's old church yard he amused himself a while,
When he saw them a-coming, which caused him to smile.

He walked right up to her, took her by the hand,
Saying, "You are to be married, I well understand;
And I have come here to block your design,
For I am determined you shall be mine".

"Oh dear!" said the lady. "What shall I do?
I know very well I was promised to you;
And since you were my first love, I'll be your bride,
For there's none in this wide world I fancy beside."

One day as the tailor was walking the street,
One of his old shopmates by chance he did meet.
"Well met, brother shopmate, and how is the bride?"—
"Oh, the sailor has got her," the tailor replied.

Come, all you young men, take a warning, I pray;
I pray you take warning, and take it from me:
Where you have a sweetheart, wed her while you may;
If you don't, some Tarpolian will steal her away.

Sometimes the girl was the one who lost out, as, for example, in the jaunty song called 'Way Down in Maine. The following version was sung by a lady of eighty in Argyle:

Once upon a time I loved a feller,
  'Way down in Maine.
He seed me hum under his umbreller,
  'Way down in Maine.
It rained so hard that I got skeered,
And my new caliker all got teared,
  'Way down in Maine.

Pretty soon we arrived at hum,
  'Way down in Maine.
My mammy was tickled to see me come,
  'Way down in Maine.
She asked my feller into the kitchen
And gave him a lunch, and he pitched in,
  'Way down in Maine.

He took my hand and he squeezed it so,
  'Way down in Maine.
On earth I didn't know what to do,
  'Way down in Maine.
Said he to me, "Don't you like me pretty well?"
Said I, "Get out, now. I shan't tell!"
  'Way down in Maine.

Said he'd be mine, if I'd be his'n,
  'Way down in Maine.
But now I guess he was only a-quizzin',
  'Way down in Maine.
See him again I never will,
But, boys, *I'm in the market still!*
  'Way down in Maine.

One of the embarrassments of courtship is reflected in ballads which
tell about a relative's advice—often not taken. Probably the most
popular is that in which Grandmother gives advice:

My grandmother lives on yonder village green;
  A finer old lady ne'er was seen.
She often cautioned me with care
  Of all false young men to beware.
    Timmy aye, timmy um tum,

Timmy um pah tah.
Of all false young men to beware.

"These false young men, they'll flatter and deceive,
   And so, my dear, you must not believe;
They'll flatter and deceive until you are in their snare,
   And away goes poor old Grandma's care!"

The first to come courting was young Johnny Green,
   A finer young man there never was seen;
But the words of my Grandma ran through my head,
   I could not hear one word he said.

The next to come courting was young Allan Grub.
   'Twas then we met with a joyous love.
With a joyous love I'll never be afraid;
   I'd rather be married than die an old maid.

Says I to myself: "There must be some mistake.
   What a terrible fuss these old folks make!
If the boys and the girls had all been so afraid,
   Grandma herself would have died an old maid."

In at least one case, the advice was countermanded—in the popular
ballad of *The Courtship of Billy Grimes*, of which my best version
comes from Coeymans:

Tomorrow morn I'm sweet sixteen,
   And Billy Grimes the drover
Has popped the question to me, Ma,
   And wants to be my lover.

"Tomorrow morn, he says, Mamma,
   He's coming bright and early
To take a pleasant walk with me
   Across the fields of barley."—

"You shall not go one step, my child;
   There is no use in talking.
You shall not go across the field
   With Billy Grimes a-walking.

"To think of his presumption, too,
  The dirty, ugly drover!
I wonder where your pride has gone,
  To think of such a lover!"

"Old Grimes is dead, you know, Mamma,
  And Billy is so lonely!
Besides, they say, of the Grimes estate
  That Billy is the only

"Surviving heir to all that's left;
  And that, they say, is nearly
A good ten thousand dollars, Ma,
  Besides six hundred yearly."—

"I did not hear, my daughter dear,
  Your last remark quite clearly;
But Billy is a clever lad,
  And no doubt loves you dearly.

"Remember then, tomorrow morn,
  To be up bright and early,
To take a pleasant walk with him
  Across the fields of barley."

The popular old song about *The Quaker's Wooing* shows that the girls did not accept just anyone who offered. I give a version recited by a lady whose parents were early settlers in Philadelphia, New York—a Quaker settlement:

He: Madam, thou art tall and slender,
  Ho, ho, hi, ho, hum;
And I know thy heart is tender,
  Ho, ho, hi, ho, hum!

She: Now I know you are a faker,
  Tralala, lala, lala!
Besides, I never liked a Quaker,
  Tralala, lala, lala!

He: Must I give up my religion?
Then I'll be a Presbyterian.

She: Cheer up, cheer up, loving brother!
If you can't catch one fish, catch another.

He: Here's a ring cost forty shilling,
And thou may'st wear it if thou art willing.

She: I want none of your rings or money;
I want a young man to call me honey.

He: Must I go without one token?
Must I go with my heart broken?

She: You go home and tell your mother
That you soon will find another.

He: Yes, my dear Miss, there's no doubt of it—
As good fish in the sea as ever caught out of it.

Another old man who fared badly appears in a song obtained in
Sullivan County:

There was an old man came over the sea—
    Ha, ha! but I won't have him!—
Came over the sea and came courting me,
    With his old gray beard without shaving.

My mother told me to open the door—
    Ha! ha! but I won't have him!
I opened the door and he came in on the floor,
    With his old gray beard without shaving.

My mother told me to get him a fork.
    I got him the fork and he wanted more pork.
My mother told me to get him some bread.
    I got him the bread and he asked me to wed.

A different version of the ballad makes the situation even clearer:

> There was an old man came over the lea—
>> Ha, ha, ha! but I won't have him!—
> Came over the lea a-courtin' me,
>> With his long gray beard that never was shaven.
>
> My mother she told me to open the door.
> I opened the door and he sat on the floor.
>
> My mother she told me to give him a stool.
> I gave him a stool and he sat like a fool.
>
> My mother she told me to give him some pie.
> I gave him some pie, and he said he was dry.
>
> My mother she told me to give him some beer.
> I gave him some beer, and he called me his dear.
>
> My mother she told me to light him to bed.
> I lit him to bed and he hung down his head.

Even if the wooer were young, he was not sure to please. There was *The Young Man Who Wouldn't Hoe Corn*:

> Come, listen while I sing you a song
>> Concerning a young man who wouldn't grow his corn.
> The reason why I cannot tell,
>> Although this young man I know very well.
>
> He planted his corn in the month of June,
>> And in July it wasn't knee-high;
> And in September there came a frost,
>> And all this young man's corn was lost.
>
> And then he went to his neighbor's door,
>> Where he had often been before;
> And when the courting had begun,
>> She asked him if he'd hoed his corn.

"Nay, fair maiden, it's all in vain,
   It's all in vain for me to try;
I've tried and tried and tried in vain
   But do not think I'll have a single grain."—

"Then why do you come for me to wed,
   If you cannot earn your own corn-bread?
Though single I am and single I'll remain,
   A lazy man I won't maintain."

He bended his head and walked away.
   "Well, fair maiden, you'll rue this day;
You'll rue this day as sure as I am born;
   You've given me the mitten because I wouldn't hoe my corn.

"I won't be bound, I will be free;
   I won't marry a woman who won't marry me.
Neither will I act the foolish part
   And marry a woman who will break my heart."

When the girl was willing, the pigs weren't; so says this ballad from Otsego County:

   I once did love a girl named Sal;
      Each day and night I'd court her.
   She's the farmer's daughter on the hill.
      I tell you, she's a snorter!
   One Sunday noon alone with her
      My love to her revealing,
   The question I was about to pop
      When the pigs set up a squealing.

   The pigs did squeal, they danced a reel,
      The old Tom-turkey gobbled,
   The big Shanghai went cock-a-de-do,
      And the brindled cow was a-sleepin'.

   I went next day to call on her,
      And ask her how she was feeling.
   I found her feeding those little pigs
      To make them stop their squealing.

"The plan's a good one, Sal," said I,
    And a kiss from her was stealing.
The pigs stopped eating, looked at me,
    And then set up a squealing.

I went again last Sunday night
    When the pigs had stopped their squealing.
The old Tom-turkey and the Shanghai
    And the brindle cow was sleeping.
Says I, "Dear Sal, will you be mine?"
    Before her I was kneeling.
Before she'd had time to say Yes or No,
    The pigs set up a squealing.

I got disgusted, left the spot,
    Declared I never would marry;
Before I'd marry a farmer's girl,
    A bachelor I would tarry.
So let her pigs squeal if they choose—
    The truth to you I'm revealing—
For if night or day I pass that way,
    Those darned old pigs are squealing.

A quick-witted girl named Kate—and the ballad-makers love that brisk name as well as Shakespeare did—could escape from even more serious embarrassment; witness *Katie Mora*:

Come all you sly and tricky lads,
    Come listen to my story.
I'll tell you how I fixed my plans
    To 'spoil young Katie Mory.

I went unto her father's house,
    Just like a clever fellow;
I told her the blue grapes were ripe,
    Were charming, plump, and mellow;

And that my sisters wished to meet
    Her down in yonder bower,
There for to gather grapes and plums,
    And spend a social hour.

I waited until she had gone,
   Then wantonly pursued her.
I caught her down in the shady bower
   On purpose to delude her.

"Now I have caught you in this bower—
   My sisters know not the matter—
It's you must die or else comply,
   For I've no time to flatter."

My hand she squeezed, she seemed well pleased.
   "There is one thing I fear, Sir:
My father he hath gone this way—
   Lest he should catch us here, Sir.

"It's you may climb this tree," said she,
   "Till he is out of sight, Sir;
Then I will go along with thee
   Where we will take delight, Sir."

Her counsel then I quickly took—
   I was not the least offended.
My charmer stood at the roots of the tree
   For to see how I ascended.

At every jerk it made such work—
   Stuck hard in my crop, Sir—
The clothes I wore—my shirt I tore
   When in the limbs I had got, Sir.

Then Kate she heeled it from the tree,
   She sung both loud and cheerly:
"You may pick your plums and suck your thumbs,
   For I no longer fear thee.

"You look just like an owl," said she.
   "Your company I shun, Sir.
You may get down as you got up—
   You are welcome to your fun, Sir."

Then Kate she heeled it o'er the plain,
    And left me quite distracted;
I ripped, I swore, my shirt I tore
    For to think how she had acted.

But when I'd thought the matter o'er,
    Her virtues I commended;
And soon I made a wife of her,
    And here my sorrows ended.

She's neat, she's kind, she's to my mind;
    We live in love and fashion.
Blest be the hour she ran away
    And left me in a pashion(sic).

Perhaps the cleverest of ballad-Kates was the one who donned horns. I first had her story from Mr. E. J. Grant, in whose family it had been in oral use without ever being written down—far back to the days of his great-great-grandmother, a redoubtable lady who, during the French and Indian war, carried her flax-wheel across the Mohawk in the dead of winter, leaving blood-tracks in the snow. She had been surprised by Indians and had fled from her cabin before she had time to put on her shoes.

KATE AND HER HORNS

[You that in merriment delight,
Pray listen unto what I write;
So shall your satisfaction find,
It will cure a melancholy mind.]

A maiden fair in Colchester,
And there a clothier courted her
For three months' space, both night and day,
But still this damsel she said, "Nay".

Said she: "Were I to love inclined,
You quickly then would change your mind,
And woo some other damsel fair.
Young men are false, I do declare."

He many protestations made,
And like a loyal lover said
That none but Kate should be his wife,
The joy and comfort of his life.

At last this maiden gave her consent
To marry him; then straight they went
Unto her parents then, and who
Gave both their leave and liking too.

But see the cursed fruit of gold!
It came about as Kate had told:
He left his loyal love behind
To woo the lawyer's daughter kind.

[A lawyer's daughter fair and bright,
Her parents' joy and whole delight,
He was resolved to make his spouse,
Denying all his former vows.]

[And when poor Kate she came to hear
That she must lose her only dear,]
And for the lawyer's daughter's sake,
Some sport of him Kate thought she'd make.

Kate knew when every night he came
From his new love, Nancy by name,
As late as ten o'clock or more.
Kate to a tanner went therefore,

And borrowed there an old cowhide
With spreading horns both long and wide;
And when she'd wrapped herself within,
Her new intrigue she did begin.

Kate to a lonesome field did stray.
At length the clothier came that way,
And he was sore afraid of her,
She looked so like old Lucifer—

A hairy hide, horns on her head
That full three feet asunder spread;
Besides all these, a long black tail.
He tried to run, but his feet did fail.

When with a glum and doleful note
She quickly seized him by the throat,
Saying, "You have deceived poor Kate, I hear,
To woo the lawyer's daughter dear.

"And since you have proved false to her,
You perjured knave of Colchester,
You shall, whether you will or no,
Down to my gloomy regions go".

In fright before the presence grim
He knelt upon his trembling limb,
Saying, "Master Devil, spare me now,
And I'll repay my former vow—

"I'll make poor Kate my lawful bride".—
"See that you do!" the Devil cried.
"If Kate against you should complain,
Soon shall you hear from me again!"

Then home he went, though very late.
He little thought that it was Kate
Who'd thrown him into such a fright;
Therefore next day by morning light—

He went to Kate and married her
For fear of that old Lucifer.
Kate's friends and parents thought it strange
That there was such a sudden change.

Kate never let her parents know,
Nor any other friend or foe,
Until a year she'd married been,
Then told it at her lying-in.

It pleased the women to the heart;
They said she'd fairly done her part.
Her husband laughed as well as they—
'Twas a joyful and a merry day.

In olden days there was another sly lady whose stratagem succeeded merrily. The widely spread ballad of *The Lost Glove* I am
giving in a version that has come down in family tradition from a
Captain of Light Horse at Waterloo.

A wealthy young squire of Falmouth, we hear,
He courted a nobleman's daughter so dear.
All for to be married it was their intent;
All friends and relatives had given their consent.

The day was appointed for the wedding to be,
The farmer was appointed to give the bride away.
As soon as the lady the young man did espy,
It inflamed her heart. "Oh me heart!" she did cry.

She turned herself round, though nothing she said,
But instead of being married, she took to her bed.
The thoughts of the farmer still reign in her mind,
And a way for to have him she quickly did find.

Coat, waistcoat, small clothing this lady put on,
And then went a-hunting with her dog and her gun.
She hunted all round where the farmer did dwell,
Because in her heart that she loved him so well.

Many times she fired, though nothing did kill,
And at length the young farmer came into the field.
And for to discourse him it was her intent;
With her dog and her gun to meet him she went.

"I thought you had been there," the lady she cried,
"To wait on the squire and give him his bride."—
"Oh no," said the farmer. "If the truth I must tell,
I'll not give her away, because I love her too well."

The lady was pleased to hear him so bold.
She gave him a glove that was bordered with gold.
She told him that she found it as she came along,
As she was a-hunting with her dog and her gun.

Then she gave out notice that she had lost her glove.
"To him that will find it I will grant him my love,
To him that will find it and bring it to me,
To him that will find it, I his bride will be."

The farmer was pleasèd to hear of the news.
Straightway to this lady he instantly goes,
Saying, "Here, my dearest lady; I have picked up your glove,
And now will you be pleased to grant me your love?"—

" 'Tis already granted," the lady she cried.
" 'Tis already granted; I will be your bride;
I'll be mistress of my dairy and the milking of my cow
While that jolly young farmer goes whistling after his plow."

Then, after they were married, she told of the fun,
How she hunted the farmer with her dog and her gun,
Saying, "Now that I have him so fast in my snare,
I'll enjoy him forever, I vow and declare".

Another cantrip of love is told in a ballad entitled *The Half-Hitch*, which I owe to the amazing memory of the late Mr. Peleg W. Andrew of Corinth, prince of balladeers:

There was a rich merchant in Plymouth did dwell;
He had a fair daughter, a beautiful girl.
A handsome young man with riches supplied
He courted this lady for to be his bride.

He courted her long and had gained her love,
And the lady intended the young man to prove.
A time she set to him, and then she denied;
She told him right off she would not be his bride.

He vowed and declared that right home he would steer.
By many sad oaths unto her he did swear

He'd wed the first woman that ever he see,
If she was as mean as a beggar could be.

She ordered her servants this man to delay.
Her rings and her jewels she laid them away;
She clothed herself in the worst rags she could find;
She looked like old Cheap-eye before and behind.

Then clapping her hands to the chimney-back
She washed her face over from corner to crack.
Then into the road she flew like a witch
With her petticoats hoisted upon the half-hitch.

This man he came riding, and when he did see her,
He cried, "Oh alas!" for his oaths he did fear.
Her shoes being down at the heel all askew,
He soon overtook her and says, "Who are you?"

Spoken: "I'm a woman, I suppose."

This answer it struck him just like a dead man;
He stumbled, he staggered, he scarcely could stand,
And then he cried, "Oh!" as though he'd been buried,
But soon he says to her, saying, "Are you married?"

Spoken: "No, I ain't."

This answer it struck him quite to the heart;
He wished that he this life might depart.
"Oh, how can I bear to have you?" thought he.
But soon he says to her, "Oh, will you have me?"

Spoken: "Yes, I will."

This answer it suited as well as the rest;
Although they lay heavy and cold in his breast,
By the vows he had made, he must make her his bride;
So soon then he asked her behind him to ride.

Spoken: "Your horse will kick up and throw me off; I know he will."

"Oh no," he said. "My horse he will not."
She fussed 'round a while, on behind him she got.
"My heart it does fail me, I dare not go home;
My parents will say I'm surely undone."

He went to a neighbor with whom he was great;
To them the sad story he dursent relate,
Saying, "Stay here a while; with my neighbor you'll tarry,
And in a few days with you I will marry".

Spoken: "You won't. I know you won't."

He said, "Yes, I will", and right home he did go;
And then to his father and mother also
He told the sad story, and how he had sworn;
But then they said to him, "For that do not mourn.

"Do not break your oath but fetch home your girl,
And we'll snug her up, and she'll do pretty well".
So published they were, and invited the guests.
So then they intended the bride for to dress.

She: "I can be married in my own clothes, I s'pose."

Wedding being over, they sat down to eat.
With her fingers she hauled out the cabbage and meat;
With the pudding she burned her fingers all fags,
She licked them and wiped them along on her rags.

Fiercer than ever she went in again.
Some laughed in private till their sides ached with pain;
And she stood stooping—some called her the bride,
Saying, "Sit yourself down by your true lover's side".

She: "Give me some on a plate, and I will go in the corner and eat it as
I used to at home."

Wedding being over, they frolicked awhile.
Some of them said she would do pretty well.

"We'll invite them to bed and the matter decide."
So then they invited both bridegroom and bride.

She: "Give me a candle and show me the way, and I will go alone."

Some were sorry and were very much grieved;
Others were tickled and very much pleased.
They gave her a candle and what she'd want more;
They showed her the way to the chamber door.

She: "When you hear my old shoes go *klung*, husband, you may come."

She went upstairs and kept stepping about.
His mother said, "What do you think she's about?"
He said, "Dear Mother, do not say a word;
No comfort to me can this world afford."

By and by they heard the old shoes go *klung*.
They gave him a candle and bade him go 'long.
"I choose to go in the dark," then he said,
"For I know very well the way to my bed."

He slewed into bed with his back to his bride.
She rolled and she trembled from side to side;
And as she rolled over, the bedstead would squeal.
He says: "What the deuce ails you? Why don't you lie still?"

She: "I have a sore on my shin. I want a candle to fix it."

He called for a candle to dress his wife's shins.
Behold, she was clothed in the finest of things;
And as he turned over his bride to behold,
Her face it was fairer than pictures of gold!

Taking her in his arms without more ado,
He cried, "O my dear, my dear, is it you?"
Still clasping his arms round her slender waist,
He cried, "It is she!" and they all came in haste.

They went down below, and a frolic they had,
Then all their hearts were merry and glad.
They looked like two flowers, so pleasant and high.
With many fair glasses they wished them much joy.

From the other side of the North Country, at Potsdam, comes *The Buggery Boo*, composed in the somewhat indecorous manner of an older day. The Buggery Boo apparently was what we call the Bogie-Man:

> When I was young and in my prime,
>   I was counted a roving blade;
> When I was young and in my prime,
>   I courted a pretty fair maid.
>
> I courted her a winter's night,
>   A summer day or two,
> And how to win that pretty maid's heart
>   I did not know what to do.
>
> Oh that pretty maid came to my bedside
>   When I was fast asleep;
> Oh that pretty maid came to my bedside
>   And most bitterly did weep.
>
> She wept, she wailed, and tore her hair,
>   And her heart was full of woe,
> When into the bed she quickly fled
>   For fear of the buggery boo.
>
> Now 'twas all the forepart of that night
>   That we did sport and play;
> 'Twas all the latter part of that night
>   That she lie in me arms till day.
>
> The night bein' gone and the day comin' on,
>   That fair maid cried, "Oh, I'm undone!"
> But says I, "Rise up and don't you be alarmed,
>   For the buggery boo am gone."

BODY, BOOTS AND BRITCHES

Now I took that maid and I married her,
 I called her for my wife;
I took that maid and married her.
 Now don't you think 'twas right?

I never chide her of her faults,
 No, damn my eyes if I do!
But every time the little boy cries,
 I think of the buggery boo!

Even when the young man was clever, he was seldom clever
enough. Here is an old song, *The Cambric Shirt,* sung many years
ago in a lumbercamp near Lake George:

Are you going to the fair?
 Flum-alum-a-lee, casa-loma-lee.
Give my heart to a young *girl* there.
 Ca-teedle-o, ca-teedle-o, casa-loma-lee.

Tell her to buy me a cambric shirt
Without one stitch of needle-work.

Tell her to wash it in an old dry well
Where there hasn't one drop of water fell.

Hang it on an old dry thorn
Where the sun ain't shone since Adam was born.—

Are you going to the fair?
Give my heart to a young *man* there.

Tell him to buy me an acre of land
Between salt-sea and salt-sea sand.

Tell him to plow it with a ram's horn,
And sow it with a peppercorn.

Tell him to reap it with a pen-knife,
And draw it in with a yoke of mice.

> And tell him to thresh it with a goose-quill,
> And fan it through an old egg-shell.
>
> When the fool has done his work,
> Tell him to come and get his shirt.

According to a homespun song from Otsego County, *That's So*, it is useless for a man to pretend equality:

> The world gets wiser every day,
>   That's so and that's so;
>
> And woman's bound to have her way,
>   And that's so too.
>
> To contradict will raise a spree,
> But man with her should still agree.
>
> She carries hoops beneath her skirts;
> They show her off where'er she flirts.
>
> She wears her bonnet very small,
> And flounces deep if she is tall.—
>
> Now woman—we will let them pass,
> For men are biggest fools at last.
>
> 'Tis of the gents with shawl I sing,
> With big moustache and all such things.
>
> He talks of freedom and of right,
> But we can show him how to fight.

In the most delightful story of the North Country ever written—and of course I mean *Eben Holden*—Mr. Bacheller has a pretty ballad which shows that love is sometimes returned graciously and without any tricks. I give a version which is almost word for word the same as that printed by Mr. Bacheller, though the man in Lawrenceville who sang and whistled *Going to Salem* said he had no idea where he learned it:

I was goin' to Salem one bright summer day
　　When I met a fair maiden a-goin' my way.
　　Oh my fallow, faddeling-fallow, faddel away!

An' many a time I had seen her before,
　　But I never dare tell 'er the love that I bore.

"Oh where are you goin', my purty fair maid?"—
　　"Oh, Sir, I am goin' t' Salem," she said.—

"Oh why are ye goin' so far in a day?
　　Fer warm is the weather and long is the way."—

"Oh Sir, I've forgotten, I hev, I declare,
　　But it's nothin' to eat and it's nothin' to wear."—

"Oho! then I have it, ye purty young miss:
　　I'll bet it is only three words an' a kiss.

"Young woman, young woman, Oh how will it dew
　　If I go see your lover and bring 'em to you?"—

"It's a very long journey," says she, "I am told,
　　An' before ye got back they would surely be cold."—

"I hev 'em right with me, I vum and I vow;
　　An' if you don't object, I'll deliver 'em now."

She laid her fair head all onto my breast,
　　And ye wouldn't know more if I tole ye the rest.*

For a final picture of rustic bliss there is a song which, though
not in the old ballad tradition, comes from the days before the Civil
War:

　　　　　　Sitting in the corner
　　　　　　　On a Sunday eve,
　　　　　　With a taper finger
　　　　　　　Resting on your sleeve;

* Mr. Bacheller writes: "You are welcome to use the ballad. . . . I heard a man
sing and whistle it 50 years ago but I composed the words for Uncle Eb."

Starlight eyes casting
  On your face their light—
Bless me, this is pleasant,
  Sparking Sunday night!

How your heart is thumping
  'Gainst your Sunday vest!
How wickedly 'tis working
  On this day of rest!
Hours seem but minutes
  As they take their flight.
Bless me, ain't it pleasant
  Sparking Sunday night!

Dad and Mom are sleeping
  On their peaceful bed,
Dreaming of the things
  The folks in meeting said.
"Love ye one another,"
  Ministers recite.
Bless me, don't we do it,
  Sparking Sunday night!

One arm with gentle pressure
  Lingers 'round her waist.
You squeeze her dimpled hand,
  Her parting lips you taste.
She freely slaps your face
  But more in love than spite.
O thunder, ain't it pleasant
  Sparking Sunday night!

But hark, the clock is striking.
  It is two o'clock, I snum!
As sure as I'm a sinner,
  The time to go has come.
You ask with spiteful accent
  If that old clock is right,
And wonder if it ever
  Sparked on a Sunday night.

One, two, three sweet kisses,
  Four, five, six you hook.
Bethinking that, you robber,
  Give back those you took.
Then as home you hurry.
  From the fair one's sight,
[How] you wish each day was
  [Sparking] Sunday night.

XVII: Murderers

A<small>T DAWN</small> of June 17, 1825, the roads into the village of Buffalo were crowded; the whole Niagara frontier was coming to see the three Thayers hanged by the neck until dead. As Judge Reuben H. Walworth of the 4th Circuit—later the famous Chancellor—came stepping stately from his lodging, he met York State's greatest orator, Red Jacket of the Senecas, striding away from the village. "Aren't you going to the hanging?" asked the Judge, evidently piqued to learn that so distinguished a contemporary was unappreciative of the entertainment provided by the Judge's own Court. "Fools enough there now," grumbled Red Jacket. "The place to see men die is battle."

At nine o'clock the militia formed for parade, wearing new uniforms with crossed shoulder belts, shakoes gay with blue pompons. They were preceded by the Buffalo Village Band, making a first public appearance. At ten, the military came to rest before the old stone jail, a building of two stories surrounded by a high wooden palisade—one of the few structures which had survived the burning of Buffalo by the British twelve years before. At noon the soldiers formed a hollow square to receive the procession which emerged from the jail: the Sheriff, judges, members of the bar, clergy, officers of the village, invited guests, mourners, a cart bearing three coffins, and finally the three prisoners wearing white shrouds and caps. To the beat of muffled drums they marched to a gallows erected on Court Street, about fifty yards east of Morgan.

During prayers the boys knelt at seats provided (briefly) for them, and their fortitude held out well during the "short discourse" which followed. Then, with only two or three minutes left to live, they "seemed to lose command of their feelings" and asked a surgeon standing near to bleed them to mitigate their sufferings. He dissuaded them and encouraged them to meet their fate. They shook hands with those on the platform, bade farewell to each other, and "in a few interrupted accents commended themselves to their God". There followed the swift consummation for which thirty thousand spectators had waited. A year which saw the opening of the Erie Canal and the visit of LaFayette had provided a third great show for the "western" village.

The Thayer case might be entitled "Murder on the Frontier, or the Death of the Wandering Usurer"; it illustrates, with primitive background, that frequent cause for homicide in all societies, the Greed for Gold. Only such specialists in the art of murder as William Roughead and Alexander Woollcott would enjoy all the details preserved in two ballads, four pamphlets, and various newspaper accounts. Only as much need be told as will serve for preface to the more entertaining of the ballads, an illiterate masterpiece vended on the streets for a penny. You need to know that at the time of their execution the three Thayers were only twenty-one, twenty-three and twenty-five years of age; that they had migrated with their father, "whose moral sentiments were of the loosest kind", from Massachusetts to the hamlet of Boston, New York, near Buffalo; that they "prided themselves on notoriety", wore bonnets instead of hats or caps, spent their evenings in shooting out candles or frequenting a tavern, and scandalized their neighbors further by calling their oxen by Holy Names.

Their victim was an Englishman named John Love, who had served on the American frigate *Constitution*, had wandered across

York State to engage in the "carrying trade" on Lake Erie, and had spent his winters in rural retirement, "trading and trafficking with his money". Here enters Usury. Two years before the murder, he had lent the Thayers about sixty dollars; by renewing notes often and by charging interest exorbitant even on the frontier, he had increased the debt to two hundred and fifty dollars, a sum which the thriftless farmers were totally unable to pay. Finally the Thayers agreed that Israel and Nelson should put their property into the hands of Isaac, the youngest, and that he should "confess judgment" to the usurer, whereupon Love should levy upon the entire property. Later, Nelson Thayer explained the crime which he had proposed by declaring that "Love obtained almost all the property for small favors . . . and then threatened to take it from them and send them to State's Prison besides".

Upon that lonely frontier the death of a wandering usurer might have gone unpunished if the Thayers had so far conquered their own greed as to be content with saving their land. What they did, however, was to sell their victim's "pumpkin and milk colored colt". With stupidity even more insolent, Isaac Thayer went about trying to collect debts due to Love, presenting a forged power-of-attorney. Rather a grim soul, young Isaac. Passing a rope-factory on his way to jail, he inquired: "Do you suppose they have got a hemp one there? I should hate dam'dly to be hanged with a flax rope!" He could not guess that his worthy father, who had taken no active part in the murder, was soon to aid searchers for Love's body by asking, "Have they looked on the hill?" The Thayers were all pretty stupid. The only male member of the family who arouses any compassion is young Isaac, at whose house the crime was committed. Though he had wielded neither rifle nor pork-cleaver, the weapons used by his brothers, he was so haunted by bloody memory that he used to get a boy of eleven out of bed to accompany him to the barn when he gave the horses their evening meal.

As I said, two ballads about the crime were hawked through the streets of Buffalo. One of them, a comparatively literate and very pious performance of twenty-seven stanzas, need not detain us beyond a quotation of its opening lines:

> Again the murderers' ruthless hand
> Has stained with blood our happy land;
> Again the hapless victim dies
> To lust of gain a sacrifice.

With these lines as motto, you are prepared for whatever enjoyment may be found in the other ballad, *A Song of the Time*:

> In England sevrel years a go
> the seen was plesent fair and gay
> John Love on bord of a Ship he entred
> and Sald in to a merica
>
> Love was a man very persevering
> in making trades with all he see
> He soon in gaged to be a Sailor
> to sail up and down on lake Erie
>
> he then went in to the Southern countries
> to trade for furs and other skins
> but the cruel French and savage Indias
> come very near of killing him
>
> But God did spare him a little longer
> he got his loding and come down the lake
> he went in to the town of Boston
> whare he made the grate mistake
>
> with Nelson Thair he made his station
> thrue the sumer thare to stay
> Nelson had two brothers Isaac and Israel
> Love lent money for thare debts to pay
>
> Love lent them quite a sum of money
> he did befriend them every way
> but the cruel cretres tha coulden be quiet
> till tha had taken his sweet life a way
>
> One day as tha ware all three to geher
> this dredful murder tha did contrive
> tha agreed to kill Love and keep it secret
> and then to live and spend thare lives

On the fifteenth evening of last december
in eighteen hundred and twent four
thain vited Love to come home with them
and tha killed and murdered him on their floor

First Isaac with his gun he shot him
He left his gun and went away
then Nelson with his ax he chopt him
till he had no life that he could perceve

After tha had killed him and most mortly brused him
tha drawed him our [out] whare tha killd their hogs
tha then caried him of apease from the house
and deposited him down by a log

the next day tha were so very bold
tha had Love's horse ariding round
som askd the reason of Love being absent
tha sed he had clrd and left the town

tha sed he had forgd in the town of Erie
the sherief was in persuit of him
he left his place and run a way
and left his debts to colect by them

tha went and forgd a pour of turney
to collect loves notes whe tha ware due
tha tore and stormd to git thare pay
and sevel nabors tha did sue

after tha had run to ahie degree
in killing Love and in forgery
tha soon were taken and put in prison
whare tha remaind for thare creulty

tha ware bound in irons in the dark dungon
for to ramin for a little time
tha ware all condemd by the grand Jury
for this most foul and dredful crime

then the Judge pronounced thare dredful sentence
with grate candidness to behold
you must all be hangd untill your ded
and lord have mursey on your Souls

Murder for greed lurked everywhere on the frontier, not only
for such a stray usurer as Love, but more frequently for the drovers
and peddlers who roamed its lonely roads. Owners of cattle traced
to Smoky Tavern in Schenectady men who had disappeared with
valuable herds. Investigation at the inn revealed bloodstains and goods
belonging to a lost drover. Finally, behind the great fireplace, there
was discovered a little door; when it was opened, the bodies of *three*
drovers dropped out. The great-grandmother who told this incident
added that "pails of blood had been poured out in the back yard of
the inn".

As for the peddlers, probably there is not a county upstate which
hasn't at least one story about their perils. At Dresden on Lake
Champlain there is an empty old inn which was a favorite resort of
boatmen at the time of our second war with Britain. Late one night,
a peddler arrived and, passing a party of guzzling boatmen, went
immediately to a room upstairs. At three o'clock in the morning,
half a dozen revellers dragged the peddler down to the well-head in
the cellar, murdered him, and cast his body into the well. From that
date, the patronage of the tavern fell off; it was widely known that
on moonlit nights the ghost of the peddler floated from the well,
flopped across the lake—screeching all the way—and disappeared at
the foot of Red Rock. As lately as 1937 I had a report of this darting
ghost.

The most horrid ballad about the death of a peddler is a printed
broadside which I found in Chautauqua County in the collection
of Mr. Roscoe Martin, who does not know where the murder occurred. A vague and cautious footnote states: "It is a Report, & that
not accurately copied; whether true, or not, I cannot say." I fear that
essentially it is true; I know of a similar case in Oneida County. The
title is *A MOST TRAGICAL ACCOUNT of a Woman's Murdering a Peddler, & Then Burning to death her Own Child.* Don't say
that you weren't warned.

People and Friends of every name,
   Attend to what I write;
Such horrid deeds my heart doth pain
   As ne'er beheld the light.

A mother casts her darling child
   Into the burning flame!
To screen her guilty soul, defil'd
   With murder and with shame!

But more of this you soon shall Know
   As you the story Read;
O can you not one tear bestow
   For such a barb'rous deed.

A Pedler traveling on his way
   As evening did advance,
He call'd if he the night might stay,
   Within a Farmer's house.

As he Retir'd to his Repose,
   This wicked thought did Rise,
To search the pedler's pack & clothes,
   His goods and merchandize.

& finding much that pleas'd them well,
   They shortly did agree
To Kill the man—O sad to tell!
   And steal his property.

But here we note, as we proceed,
   The husband did decline
To perpetrate the horrid deed,
   Or Form the base design.

Therefore his wife she did Repair
   Unto the Pedlers cot,
The Fatal Knife she had prepar'd
   And there she cut his throat!

And then to hide the wicked deed,
    When she'd the murder done,
It seems the husband he agree'd
    That it should not be known.

And then with speed they did prepare
    A grave to hide the man;
And thus with secrecy and care
    Conceal'd the cruel plan.

But Providence would them detect,
    Therefore it was in Vain;
And in a way you'd not expect
    The secret was made plain.

The mother from the pedler's pack
    Did make the little girl
A beauteous handkerchief and Frock
    Which she did wear to school.

The mistress she admir'd the same,
    And of it wish'd to buy;
She ask'd the girl from whence it came,
    The child made this Reply:

She said her Mother had a store
    Of articles like these,
And others she had many more,
    That might the Madam please.

The Mistress by the child did send
    To see if she could trade,
Nor knew what mischief would await
    The errand that she made.

The mother she quite ang'ry grew
    Against the little girl;
Because by her the neighbors knew
    That she had goods to sell.

She to her husband then did say,
    The child will bring us out;
Therefore her life we'll take away,
    And this will end the doubt.

They did devise the barb'rous plan,
    That he should dig her grave;
And she would send her to him then
    To bury her alive!

So when he had the grave prepar'd
    The child was sent with speed;
But then he thought he could not bare
    To do the cruel deed.

At this the Mother's anger flew—
    She would Revenged be;
She said she'd try what she could do,
    O what a wretch was she!

She het the oven blazing hot,
    And then in angry Fraim
Her infants cries she heeded not,
    But plung'd it in the flame!

But soon a neighbor chanc'd to come,
    The scent did fill the house;
He Kindly ask'd what had been done,
    Or what might be the case.

The woman answer'd so abrupt,
    He did some crime suspect;
And in the oven then he look'd,
    Which did the crime detect.

But O may all a warning take
    From this base tragidy;
And Know that life, and soul's at stake,
    If they from *Virtue* flee.

In a second group of murders on the frontier, Indians were involved. Sometimes they were punished without benefit of court. At Wales, near Buffalo, there stood what was known as the tomahawk tree. According to legend, an Indian showed what he alleged to be the skin of a white child, declaring that he was going to have a tobacco-pouch made of it. This may have been a drunken boast, but a certain Truman Allen followed him, killed him, and stuck a tomahawk in a tree *in terrorem.*

Perhaps the most puzzling of these Indian cases was that of Tommy Jimmy, who in 1821, upon instructions from the Senecas, executed an alleged witch named Kauquatau. Although there was some doubt as to whether the Indian could be tried by any tribunal except one of his own nation, he was brought before a white man's Court of Oyer and Terminer and defended by the great orator Red Jacket. When asked by the prosecutor whether he believed in God, Red Jacket said, "More truly than one who could ask me such a question". The high point of the trial was reached when Red Jacket reminded the whites of such incidents as the Salem trials for witchcraft: "Do you denounce us as fools and bigots because we still believe what you yourselves believed two centuries ago? Your black-coats thundered this doctrine from the pulpit, your judges pronounced it from the bench, and sanctioned it with formalities of law; and would you now punish our unfortunate brother for adhering to the faith of his fathers and of yours?" The orator's question, and the doubts regarding jurisdiction, confounded the wisest. The case was removed by a writ of *certiori* to the State Supreme Court, where, by consent of the Attorney General, without judgment being rendered the prisoner was discharged.

You will ask whether, after the Revolution, any Indians dedicated themselves in racial hatred to the destruction of white men, as such whites as Quick, Murphy, and Foster did to the murder of Indians. A long poem preserved in broadside at the Seneca Falls Museum tells of an Indian who had the desire, if not the opportunity, for such wholesale slaughter. The title is: *Poetry on the Death of/ EZEKIEL CRANE/ and Execution of/ INDIAN JOHN/ Composed by Jason Smith/ And sung by him at a concourse of young persons convened at a house near the/ spot where the tragic scene was enacted: June,*

1818. If the young persons were kept in convention through the singing of the entire poem, they heard some 280 lines; I can spare the
reader.

The scene of the case of the berserk Indian is Junius, later Tyre,
N. Y. On December 12, 1803, Indian John and a white man named
George Phadoc were hunting together when, as the Indian is made
to say:

> "A great big bunch came in my breast,
> And rising, got into my head—
> Then me would kill all white men dead."

Putting the idea into action, he fired at Phadoc just as the white came
to the door with venison. The ball, shot apparently haphazard through
the door, hit the venison and grazed Phadoc's coat near his armpit.
Seizing his rifle, Phadoc escaped up Black Brook to the home of
the poet's father. We are not told that any measures were taken
against John, but evidently his murderous ambition was not satisfied.
In 1818, Ezekiel Crane and a friend were viewing some land in that
neighborhood. Coming to John's cabin-door, Ezekiel was struck in the
shoulder by a ball fired in the same savage and haphazard fashion.
With the aid of his friend the wounded man escaped but died five
days later, leaving a widow and five children. After the funeral, a
meeting of white men was joined by three Senecas who evidently
wished to redeem the good name of their nation. The party surrounded John's cabin. Here let the Muse have sway:

> "More shoot, more shoot," is all his cry—
> The war whoop raise, the war song sing,
> Which made those echoing valleys ring:
> The assailants brave, though to their heart
> The life blood thrills with sudden start.
>
> His tawny brethren loudly sung,
> In Indian style and Indian tongue—
> That he might think no white men near,
> And thus divert him of his fear.
> Up to the cabin door they walked,
> And to the assassin friendly talked:
> A league with you we make, say they—

All white men we will quickly slay.
Deceive him thus, and thus beguile,
'Till quite deluded by their wile.

By chance or fraud secure his arms—
Then to the white men gave the alarm;
Just at the word they all rushed in—
A furious fray doth now begin—
Most furious grew, when brought to see
He was betrayed by treachery.
Just like a demon incarnate,
Destruction, death, and sudden fate;
They seize and bear him to the ground,
And fast with thongs his hands were bound.

Now well secured, the Indian[s] said;
"You ugly man, you must be dead.
You much bad Indian, we do hear—
You ran away when you came here.
Much long ago you kill your squaw—
Your hand be like a panther's claw:
Nay, badder still are you than they—
They only catch and kill their prey;
But you kill Indian, white men too—
We glad the white men have got you."

The murderer was tried, found guilty, and sentenced to be hanged
and his body dissected. Thousands saw his death-cart, heard his death-
song. The poem ends with an attempt at Indian folklore, with a
modest Author's Note to the effect that he is describing at the close
"the Indian's idea of the place where bad Indians go":

His death song rings with cheerful glee—
"Me scare away Chepi,"* said he.

They reach, at length, the fatal spot;
With busy hands they knit the knot.
The cart moves on—from thence he's hurled,
And launched into the unknown world.
Nor parting screams, nor fish, nor bird,

* [spirits]

> Nor songs, nor mirthful shouts are heard,
> Nor deer, nor bear, nor foxes roam—
> A dreary waste his final home.
> There he must lead another life,
> Without a battle axe or knife.

Whatever the merit of this poem, it fails to establish any clearer reason for the murders than a blind hatred for whites and a savagery which did not spare members of John's own race. There is more of dignity in the murders committed by the Antone family in Broome and Madison Counties; these killings illustrate a primitive feeling for justice not unlike the Highland code of vengeance. Abram Antone was the son of a dignified and respected chief who presided over a small reservation in Broome County. The land of this little colony did not escape the cupidity of certain white men, one of whom induced young Abram to sign a paper, supposedly a promise to pay a pile of beaver-skins as tall as the rifle coveted by the chief's son. When the duped lad discovered that what he had signed was a deed to the reservation, he swore vengeance against the trickster and, it is said, finally killed him. Apparently he was not prosecuted, but white neighbors shook their heads over the savagery which led him to knock his own father into a blazing fire for rebuking the son's inebriety.

When Abram moved to Madison County, he was at first admired for alleged services to the Patriots in the Revolution; but about the year 1800, at a house-raising, he damaged his reputation by shooting another Indian whom he charged with defrauding him of his government-allowance. Though his tribesmen accepted a peace-ransom of money—as our Anglo-Saxon ancestors might have done—sinister stories began to circulate about the evil temper of a man for whom youth could no longer be alleged as an excuse. (He was born about 1750.) It was rumored that in one of his rages he had thrust a crying child into hot coals. During a short residence in Canada, it was whispered, he had fatally knifed a white man who had insulted him with a lashing.

Abram's character was further blackened in 1814 when his beautiful daughter Mary, alias Polly, was hanged at Peterboro for the murder of another Indian girl. The defendant summarized her case

and her code when she said: "She got away with my man and deserved to die." Legend reports that Sheriff Elijah Pratt, who conducted the execution, escaped the vengeance of Antone by migrating
to a western state. The principal witness for the prosecution, a half-
breed named John Jacobs, did not fare so well. He too removed
from the neighborhood but foolishly accepted Abram's message of
amnesty, returned to a farm near Middleport, and fell before the
knife of an avenging father.

For some time, the old man escaped arrest by posses of Indians
and whites, but was finally captured by a stratagem well known to
our Injun-killers. A man named Curtis induced him, through pride
in his markmanship, to shoot at a target; when Antone's rifle was
emptied, officers overpowered him and took him to the Morrisville
jail, where he is said to have answered the exhortations of pious
Christians by the simple declaration, "I believe in the God of my
fathers". At his trial an attempt to deny the jurisdiction of New York
State was over-ruled. Two or three tribes petitioned for him; it was
noted, however, that his own people, the Oneidas, were silent. He
seems to have been puzzled by the whole proceeding. After all, this was
not his first murder; he stated indignantly that the claims of justice
had been fulfilled when he paid $270 as peace-ransom to the proper
Indian authorities. Dissatisfaction with the court's sentence he expressed in curt, Indian fashion: "No good way to hang like a dog."
Before a huge crowd and amid the wails of Indian women he was
"turned off" in September, 1823; his title of Terror of Madison
County passed to a band of Yankee horse-thieves. Mr. D. H. Teed,
who has written the completest account of the case, supplies an
ironic after-word: Curtis, who had betrayed old Abram, moved to
Ohio, where he was murdered by Indians.

A desire on my part to present in truthful fashion the folklore of
our frontier has compelled the inclusion of a few Indian murderers.
Justice demands that I call your attention to the fact that if you
scrutinize our history after the Revolution, you will find the record
of the Red Men clean compared with that of those savage Injun-
killers to whom I have devoted an entire chapter. Mention of justice
recalls an unforgettable anecdote about Red Jacket. After watching
the trial of an Indian, he pointed to the coat-of-arms of the State.

"What him call?"

"Liberty."

"Ugh! What *him* call?"

"Justice."

"Where—him—live—now?"

As you have seen, *greed* and *pride* have taken their toll in York State. The case of Mary Antone reminds us that here (as everywhere) a third motive has not been lacking—what is vaguely called *love*, what might better be called envy, jealousy, and hate. Murdered wives, husbands, and lovers are recalled in many a ballad or folktale, sometimes of local fame, at least once of national renown. For example, in our northeastern counties and in Vermont you may still hear the doleful ballad of *The Murdered Wife: or, The Case of Henry G. Green, of Berlin, Rensselaer County, N. Y.*, which might also be called, *The Strolling Player, or, The Bride of a Week*. Let me give a summary of the facts behind the ballad.

On Sunday, February 10, 1845, a few days before the date previously announced for their nuptials, Green was married at Stephentown to pretty Mary Ann Wyatt, who had been an actress in a wandering troupe which presented *The Reformed Drunkard*. On Tuesday, when the supposedly happy couple returned to the groom's house at Berlin, N. Y., Mary was in perfect health. On Wednesday, Green's mother told him of rumors—almost certainly false—regarding the actress, whose profession was still regarded with disfavor in the "deeply rutted villages". On Thursday, Green organized a sleighride attended by several friends of the groom including Alzina Godfrey, who is said to have declared at the party that she had expected to be the bride. It seems likely that Alzina's charms—social, financial, and sentimental—made her former lover resent his captivity to another; at any rate, on Friday he obtained from a physician some opium pills for a "slight indisposition" of his wife. An overdose of this medicine would have served the groom's purpose if Mary had not had a fit of vomiting which rid her of the poison. Green then secured in less formal fashion some arsenic. On Monday, the eighth day after her marriage, Mary Ann died.

The trial for murder opened at Troy, the County-Seat, on July 7th,

and lasted for what was then regarded as a long session of twelve
days. Though the hanging on September 10th was a "private" one
to which only fifty carefully selected spectators were admitted, for
twenty-four hours before the execution crowds flocked from afar
until two or three thousand were jammed into the interesting
proximity of the jail. At 3:40 P. M. the murderer-bridegroom
mounted the scaffold to join the fifty fortunates in singing *Rock of
Ages*; thereafter his power to entertain was limited to a confession,
published five days after the execution, and to a printed broadside-
ballad in twenty-four stanzas, probably first sold before Green was
hanged.

The following version was handed down from a member of the
sleighride party who remembered the "other girl" as Priscilla
Brownell, instead of Alzina Godfrey, and reported that she said:
"Why did you marry Mary? I would have married you in the end."

Come listen to my tragedy, young people young and old;
I'll tell to you a story that will make your blood run cold,
Concerning a young lady, Miss Wyatt was her name,
Who was murdered by her husband, and he hung for the same.

This lady she was beautiful, not of a high degree.
Young Henry Green was wealthy, as you shall plainly see.
He said, "My dearest Mary, if you will be my wife,
I'll guard you at my peril throughout this gloomy life".

She said, "My dearest Henry, I fear that ne'er can be:
It's you have rich relations, I'm not as rich as thee;
And when your parents came to know, they would spurn me from their
        door,
They'd rather you would wed someone had wealth laid up in store."

He said, "My dearest Mary, why thus torment me so?
For if you longer me deny, I vow I'll take my life,
For I no longer wish to live unless you are my wife."

Believing all he said was true, she thus became his wife.
Oh little did she think, poor girl, or e'er did she expect
He'd take away the life of one he'd just sworn to protect!

They had been married scarce a week when she was taken ill,
Or was it e'er expected he meant his wife to kill.
Great doctors they were sent for, and none of them could say;
Soon it was proclaimed by them she must go to her grave.

Her brother, hearing of the same, straight unto her did go,
Saying, "Sister dear, you're dying; the doctors tell me so";
Saying, "Sister dear, you're dying, your life is at an end.
Say, have you not been murdered by the one you think your friend?"—

"It's as I'm on my bed of death and know that I must die,
I'm going to my Maker, the truth shall not deny.
I know that Henry poisoned me, but, brother, for him send,
For I do love him now as well as when he was my friend."

When Henry got the tidings, he went his wife to see.
She said, "My dearest Henry, have I e'er deceived thee?"
Three times she said, "Dear Henry!" then sank into death's swoon.
He gazed on in indifference, and in silence left the room.

An inquest on her body held according to the law,
And soon it was proclaimed by them that arsenic was the cause.
Green was apprehended, lodged down in Troy jail,
There to await his trial—the courts could not give bail.

On the day of his trial, he was brought on the stand
To answer for the blackest crime committed on our land.
Judge Parker read the sentence, He 'peared to me unmoved;
He said he was not guilty, although it had been proved.

He said he was not guilty, and he did her friends defy;
He pled that he was innocent, although condemned to die.

Green's stupid crime recalls a more recent mountain-murder which
the genius of Theodore Dreiser has celebrated. His *An American
Tragedy*, you recall, is based upon the killing at Big Moose in the
Adirondacks of Grace Brown by Chester Gillette, a dazed young
Yorker who decided too late that he wished to marry another girl.
The following ballad about the case is a version sung at Gloversville

by a former woodsman. When a student of mine asked the singer how he could remember all his ballads, the reply was, "How do you remember your way home?"

THE BALLAD OF GRACE BROWN AND CHESTER GILLETTE

The dreams of the happy is finished,
The scores are brought in at last;
A jury has brought in its verdict,
The sentence on Gillette is passed.

Two mothers are weeping and praying;
One praying that justice be done,
The other one asking for mercy,
Asking God to save her dear son.

All eyes are turned on the drama,
A-watching the press night and day,
A-reading those sweet pleading letters,
Wondering what Gillette would say.

He is now in State's Auburn dark prison
Where he soon will give up his young life,
Which might have been filled with sweet sunshine
Had he taken Grace Brown for his wife.

But Cupid was too strong for Gillette,
It was playing too strong with his heart,
For the one that had loved him so dearly,
Yet from her he wanted to part.

'Twas on a hot, sultry day in the summer
When the flowers were all aglow,
They started out on their vacation
For the lakes and the mountains to roam.

Did she think when he gathered those flowers
That grew on the shores of the lake
That the hand[s] that plucked those sweet lilies
Her own sweet life they would take?

They were seen on the clear, crystal waters
Of the beautiful Big Moose Lake,
And nobody thought he'd be guilty
Of the life of that poor girl to take.

It happened along in the evening,
Just at the close of the day,
With the one that had loved him so dearly
They drifted along on South Bay.

They were out of the view of the people
Where no one could hear her last call,
And nobody knows how it happened,
But Gillette and God knows it all.

Having described some types of murder remembered by the folk,
I must add that to me the jurors, the sheriffs, the crowds at public
executions—all the folkways revealed—are at least as interesting as
the criminals. The perils and codes of the frontier are implicit in
nearly all the cases which I have reported, but I should like to add
one more scene similar to that with which this chapter opened. To
omit it would be to lose caste in the land of my fathers; it is the first
and last public execution in the county of Chautauqua. Though it
occurred on May 15, 1835, my cousin "Hugh Willie" Thompson,
for fifty years editor of the State's oldest Republican newspaper, talks
about it as though it occurred last year.

The murder was a crude, brutal one. In April, of 1834, in the
township of Pomfret, one Joseph Damon killed his wife with a poker.
After more than a year of legal skirmishing, his execution was set
for the date already mentioned. Some idea of the careful preparation
for the great event can be gathered from the following stately communication written by a local Dogberry to a lakeland Verges:

Lieutenant Stephen Williams *Sir* by order from William Sexton High
Sheriff of the County of Chautauqua you are hereby Commanded to
be and appear with your respective Company at Mayville on the 15th
day of this month at 7. aclock forenoon of that day Completely armed
and equipt according to the Law for the purpose of being a part of the
guard to attend the Execution of J. Damond you will parade near the
Jail Get good music and keep them still untill the Square is formed

keep your men Still and allow none in the Company only Such as is well armed, you must parade without any Ceremoneal as there will be a great Croud and it will be very different from parade days

    fail not under the penalty of the Law

    Given under my hand at Mayville the first Day of May 1835

                 William D. Bond

                 Col 207th Regt.

As the Colonel had predicted, a "croud" of some ten or fifteen thousand attended the ceremonies—perhaps a quarter of the County's population, and it is a spacious County. The place of the hanging has occasioned disputes in later years; for the sake of Chautauquans only, I am about to give the exact location as authenticated in the sworn statements collected by Mr. John J. Thompson of the Mayville Museum: If you take the road running from the Courthouse toward Sherman, you will pass an open field then owned by Donald McKenzie, who did so much to open the American Northwest. The said field lies some five hundred feet west from the highway, at the second ravine of the hill, on a declivity not far from the school. If you cannot find the spot, don't blame the Thompson family. East of that field was another owned by a Mr. Tinkham, who is said to have made a tidy sum renting camping space for the night before the execution, at ten cents for each individual.

The clergy always claimed a prominent place at these exercises. At Damon's request, Elder Sawyer preached at the gallows from *Proverbs*, XI, 19: "So he that pursueth evil, pursueth it to his own death." The condemned had the further satisfaction of making a speech regarding his own case, declaring that he was "unconscious" when he wielded the poker. With the possible exception of the Colonel, the Sheriff was the only person present who appeared nervous. As the drop fell and the prisoner ducked through the trap, the fastening for the rope gave way, and Damon hit the ground with a thud. The delicate question now arose as to whether he had not been hanged—whether he should be permitted to depart at once without further molestation from the law. Certainly the crowd had enjoyed all that could reasonably be expected. Anxiously the Sheriff put the case before a competent Judge who pointed out that the sentence always reads, "Hanged by the neck until dead". Somewhat disappointed Damon ascended the scaffold once more, to be "turned off" with a stouter rope.

Ancient British songs remembered in the State prove that the frontier's interest in murders was not an American phenomenon. My collection of "Child ballads", so called from the name of a Harvard professor who made the most important edition of British examples, includes a number which I like to call Penknife Ballads. In the late middle ages the penknife seems to have been as formidable a weapon as a Harlem razor, particularly useful in cases of "malice domestic".

From Mrs. Frances Ramsay of Lake George, who has enriched my collection with many a letter, comes a version of *The Cruel Mother* (Child, 20), known to her as *Down by the Greenwood Side*. She says: "The older girls of the neighboring families and their mothers sometimes sang it. We small fry were not supposed to hear it. We sometimes overheard, but did not put cotton into our ears." By overhearing she has preserved in a York State tradition one of the oldest British ballads:

> There was a lady, she lived in York,
>   All along the lonely-ay.
> She fell in love with her father's clerk,
>   Down by the greenwood side-ee.
>
> While walking through her father's corn,
>   All along the lonely-ay,
> She had two pretty babies born,
>   Down by the greenwood side-ee.
>
> She had nothing to wrap them in,
> Only one poor apron thin.
>
> She had a penknife long and sharp;
> With that she pierced their tender hearts.
>
> She flung them into the raging foam,
> Saying, "Take your turn in the fair maid's home".
>
> While walking near her father's hall
> She saw two pretty boys playing ball.

"O dear children, if you were mine,
I would dress you in silk so fine."—

"O dear mother, we were thine;
You did not dress us in silk so fine.

"You had a penknife long and sharp;
With that you pierced our tender heart.

"You flung us into the raging foam,
Saying, 'Take your turn in the fair maid's home'."—

"O dear children, can you tell
If my poor soul's for heaven or hell?"—

"Seven years a hawk in the wood,
Seven years a fish in the flood,

"Seven years attending the bell,
Seven years a keeper in hell!"—

"[I'd] like very well to be hawk in the wood,
Like very well to be fish in the flood,

"Like very well to be tending the bell,
But God keep my soul from being keeper in hell!"

XVIII: Place-Names

OLD Matthew Arnold, full of high seriousness and that combination of self-appreciation and despair for others which makes him so charming, meditated his essay on *Civilisation in the United States*. Partly to irritate the English, he confesses that our American social and political problem seems to be solved with remarkable success; our institutions do work well and happily; we are singularly free from the distinction of classes, singularly homogeneous; we see clear and think straight. Although in America "all luxuries are dear except oysters and ice", the bulk of the population is better paid and better fed. We have dispensed with ridiculous titles, and our women have great charm of natural manner—a "free and happy manner". Yet in spite of these triumphs and advantages our civilization is not interesting because we lack distinction and beauty. "In the long-settled States east of the Alleghanies the landscape in general is not interesting." As for our place-names:

The mere nomenclature of the country acts upon a cultivated person like the incessant pricking of pins. What people in whom the sense for beauty and fitness was quick could have invented, or could tolerate, the hideous names ending in *ville*, the Briggsvilles, Higginsvilles, Jackson-

449

villes, rife from Maine to Florida; the jumble of unnatural and inappro-
priate names everywhere? On the line from Albany to Buffalo you
have, in one part, half the names in the classical dictionary to designate
the stations; it is said that the folly is due to a surveyor who, when
the country was laid out, happened to possess a classical dictionary;
but a people with any artist-sense would have put down that surveyor.
The Americans meekly retain his names; and indeed his strange
Marcellus or Syracuse is perhaps not much worse than their congenital
Briggsville.

So much as to beauty.

It would be easy to retort that a man incapable of finding beauty
of landscape on the Hudson River can hardly be taken seriously as
possessing what he calls so barbarously the "artist-sense". It will
be wiser to observe that Arnold lacked, even more, a knowledge of
American history and an appreciation of American humor—or of any
other sort of humor. For sheer beauty of sound we are ready to have
our Indian names compared with the loveliest words found in Mexico
and the Scottish Highlands; but beauty was not our sole or chief
aim in nomenclature. What we desired even more was an expression
of veneration for heroes of war and frontier, and a perpetuation of
some jokes that are quite as typical as heroism.

How does a frontiersman select a place-name? Take an example
from Yates County, settled after the Revolution. In one community,
settlers from Pennsylvania and New England Yankees could not
agree upon a name. Outsiders suggested Pandemonium, but that was
not kindly taken. Finally a jovial miller-farmer suggested as a compromise Pang Yang. The *New York Gazetteer* for 1813 calls the
place Pennyan or Penn-Yank; a second edition of this book explains
that the name is a sort of "fantastical compound for the land of
whiskey and the land of pumpkin pie". I, for one, am unwilling to
abandon that joke.

If legend be trustworthy, Troy got its name from a similar dispute
between its oldest settlers, who wished to name the town for a Dutch
pioneer, and a group from New England who, slightly in the majority, agreed on a classical name "to beat the Dutch". Utica was
earlier known as Fort Schuyler—named for a powerful Dutch
family and commander. When the members of the little Oneida

County settlement met at historic Bagg's Tavern and smithy, it was agreed to accept whatever name came on the lucky slip drawn from a hat. Everyone had the privilege of contributing one name to the hat; it happened that lawyer Erastus Clark had written *Utica* on the slip which was finally drawn. Out in Tioga County a similar ceremony was conducted. One young man couldn't think of any name except that of his mother-in-law—you may speculate on the reason; he wrote *Barton*, saying that he would "give the old lady a chance anyhow". The name is still Barton.

In Allegany County, citizens were sitting on the steps of a general store, discussing a name for their hamlet, when some boys passed with a basket of nuts. That is said to be the origin of *Almond*. In another hamlet of the same county, the hill-dwellers had frequent combats with the valley-folk; the place was named Fighting Corners. Gradually the zest in battle waned; the name was changed to Friendship. In the neighboring county of Cattaraugus, a settlement was called Jugville from the jugs wherewith lumbermen comforted themselves. For some reason the joke grew stale, and a meeting was held to select another name. Every suggestion was met with cries of "No! O no!" Whereupon the town's humorist suggested Onoville, and his motion was carried with acclaim. In Cayuga County the townships of Conquest and Victory express the satisfaction of groups who wished to be cut off from earlier, larger divisions; Victory, for example, was once a part of Cato. The township of Hopewell in Ontario County has the same story; the people hoped that they would be separated from Gorham township. These triumphant names have a somewhat more rational derivation than Sardinia (Erie), said to have been named by General Nott after his favorite psalmtune. I prefer Elma in that county, said to have been named after a grand old tree. In general, Erie County illustrates the miscellany that suited the frontier: For example, the story goes that the town of Erie wanted a change in name, but, failing to agree, the citizens referred the matter to Fillmore, their assemblyman. He, in turn, followed the suggestion of his wife, who had been reading Byron; the name became Newstead for the poet's castle of Newstead Abbey. In the same county Lodi was named for Napoleon's bridge, and Alden, known to scoffers as "Grannytown", was called after a gentleman's mother-in-law.

Sometimes ridicule led to a change of name. Down in Ulster County admirers of Burns called their hamlet Lang Syne. In front of the village store, which was also the postoffice, there was a long board which read:

LANG SYNE POSTOFFICE, JOHN LOUNSBURY, POSTMASTER

Scoffers on the stage-coaches always laughed at a witticism of one traveler who renamed the hamlet Long Sign. A joke is all very well when made at home, but not when shouted twice a day by outlanders. The village fathers petitioned to have the name changed to Stone Ridge. When you look at the face of Washington on dollar bills— often, I trust—you see a reproduction of the portrait made by a man from that hamlet, the once famous Vanderlyn.* Lang Syne is no more, but we still have Burns in Allegany County and Afton in Chenango County, though the bard might not be pleased to learn that the name of his gently-flowing river was chosen partly because it began with A and the people of Afton wanted to get ahead of their neighbors of Bainbridge, if only alphabetically.

Even the names of fairly large cities were chosen casually. Once in a while a meeting made an appropriate if slightly sentimental choice, as when Auburn was named for Goldsmith's "loveliest village of the plain". But Glens Falls is also a beautiful little city, and what is its story? We are told that it was once named for a landholder named Wing, who—according to one story, to pay a debt of honor— let Colonel Glen of Schenectady rename it if he would give a large and moist supper for a group of friends. Nobody feels sure about the name of the city of Tarrytown, though many like to believe that farmers used to tarry there at an old inn on the present Post Road. Washington Irving has helped along this interpretation:

This name was given, we are told, in former days, by the good house- wives of the adjacent country, from the inveterate propensity of their husbands to linger about the village tavern on market days.

I should like to accept this casual naming, but science demands that I add the weighty opinion of President Ernest Griffin of the West-

* Here I am following local tradition. Examples of Vanderlyn's art are to be seen in the Kingston Museum.

chester Historical Society that the name derives from *tarwe*, a Dutch word for wheat.

As we shall see later in treating the Indian names, the folk are always willing to venture what the scientist calls a folk-etymology. The city of Olean was obviously named by Major Hoops for some relative of the Latin word for oil, *oleum;* but the children are told that a fat squaw named Oily Ann used to wash her clothes there in a place where the Allegheny River was oily. In the early days of that county (Cattaraugus), a considerable part of the county was named Ischua and of course was an object of jealousy to Oleanders, who still tell a little folktale which explains the rival's name. A drunken traveler stopped at a cluster of houses north of Olean and inquired, "Ish a way to Olean?" Hence Ischua, named by a drunk.

I have always thought that the Federal postoffice must have had many a headache over these casually and humorously chosen names. The point is illustrated in two anecdotes which Mr. Woodford Patterson, Secretary of Cornell University, told me. His old home was at Newark Valley. The settlers there asked for the name Westfield; the Post Office Department replied that Chautauqua County had a Westfield. Finally the people let the Congregational minister have the naming, and he chose Newark Valley because he came from Newark, New Jersey. Mr. Patterson has been told about the experience of Trumansburg (Tompkins), named for a hero of the Revolution named Treman, granted lands there in the Military Tract. His townsfolk understood that the place was to be named for their leader, but the Post Office Department sent an official document in which the name was spelled with *u*, and refused to make a correction.

Bearing in mind this rather casual and humorous tradition in nomenclature, we may now proceed to a more orderly view, beginning with what are certainly our most beautiful names, those inherited from the Indians. At the annual convention of our New York Historical Association in 1937 we had the pleasure of welcoming a young Canadian archivist who made an arresting statement to me in conversation. "Ontario and New York," said he, "are alike in a thousand ways. To me the most interesting difference is your attitude toward the Indians. To us an Indian is just a Red Man, no object of special admiration; but you celebrate his history, represent his people at your historical pageants, respect his achievements, name your counties, cities, and rivers for him—are proud of him. I am constantly made aware of the fact that this is the land of the Iroquois."

At the time when Mr. Talman made this remark, our State Historian, Dr. Flick, was writing for the great ten-volume history which he edited, a chapter on *New York Place Names* (1937)—by all odds the best short study of the subject. He finds that about five hundred Indian names have survived in the state, including the names of twenty of our sixty-two counties and twelve of our sixty cities. The county names have for many of us the thrill of a Homeric catalogue, the touching quality which a Scot finds in his old ballads. They are: Allegany, Cattaraugus, Cayuga, Chautauqua, Chemung, Chenango, Erie, Genesee, Niagara, Oneida, Onondaga, Ontario, Oswego, Otsego, Saratoga, Schenectady, Schoharie, Seneca, Tioga, and Wyoming. Four of the Six Nations are represented there: Cayuga, Oneida, Onondaga, and Seneca; Erie is the name of an Iroquoian nation never taken into the inner council but finally utterly defeated by the Senecas. Of the other two nations of the Longhouse, the Mohawks are remembered in the name of a noble river as well as in the names of four small places including the considerable village of Mohawk in Herkimer County; the Tuscaroras, welcomed to the Great Council at a late date by the other Five Nations, have given names to hamlets in Broome and Livingston Counties. Delaware County and River bear the name given by white men to the Lenape Algonkians; our loftiest mountains are named for the Adirondacks ("tree-eaters"); and Long Island preserves the names of several Algonkian Mohican tribes—the Canarsies, Setaukets, Patchogues, Shinnecocks, Montauks, Manhassetts, Cutchogues, and Rockaways. Our two Great Lakes are the Erie and Ontario, and the Finger Lakes are named Skaneateles, Owasco, Cayuga, Seneca, Keuka, and Canandaigua. The cities include—among those with a population greater than 25,000—Schenectady, Niagara Falls, Poughkeepsie; the smaller cities include Lackawanna, Cohoes, Oswego, Irondequoit, Ossining, Saratoga Springs, Tonawanda, Oneonta, Mamaroneck, Oneida, Mineola, Saranac Lake, Canandaigua, Patchogue, Seneca Falls, Tuckahoe, Cheektowaga, Nyack, Mount Kisco, Hoosick Falls, and Owego. Beside the Mohawk and the Delaware, our great rivers include the Allegheny and the Susquehanna and many others with Indian names. We named canals Erie, Chenango, Chemung, Oswego; even railroads took such names as Erie and Lackawanna.

While my Canadian acquaintance was commenting upon our Indian names, I was hoping that he would not ask me to explain their meaning. My plan was to side-track his inquiry by explaining that you can distinguish between names of the Iroquois and those of other tribes by remembering that the Six Nations can talk with the pipe in their teeth—they haven't the labial consonants, p, b, v, f. Consequently, when you see a name like Paumanack (Paumonock), which Walt Whitman liked to use for his native Long Island, or Yaphank— known to many a soldier—you guess that you are dealing with an Algonkian word from Long Island or the Hudson River region. I fear that this scrap of learning would not have satiated any scholar, and I should soon have been admitting that in most cases our Indian names are of very doubtful etymology, partly because of the many dialects involved, partly because the Indians did not have a written language, partly because white men have difficulty hearing such sounds as we now spell *nh*, partly because there were no trained linguists among our early Yorkers, partly because the few remaining Indians now live on reservations where they have no occasion to use many place-names.

To be sure, the white man has not hesitated to invent funny folk-etymologies. For example, in Jefferson County they say that the river Oswegatchie derives its name from an occasion when an Indian pulled his drowning steed out of the water with the exclamation, " 'Oss, we got ye!" In Tioga County you may be told that the pretty name Owego is the exclamation of sadly departing aborigines after Sullivan's raid upon their homes. There are a number of more or less learned derivations for Schenectady, but the folk will refer you to the story of a captive begging for stay of execution, only to receive the curt reply from his Indian captor, "Skin neck t'day!" The Genegantslet Creek in Chenango County has inspired a number of guesses. One legend says that an Indian girl was drowned there; her lover, when asked why he returned so often to the stream, replied sadly, "Jenny gone sleep". Another version has it that a woman fell in while crossing on a log, whereupon her imperturbable spouse observed, "Jenny gone a slick". One long and romantic version recounts the wooing of a maiden by a member of a hostile tribe to whom her father, a chief, gave a flat denial. The disappointed girl jumped madly into the drink, while an old woman ran screaming to the chief, "Jenny gone slick!" A more far-fetched derivation from the same county is that of Canasawacta, another creek: a Revolutionary soldier fell in, causing his illiterate officer to exclaim, "Canst thee walk the creek?" Others will tell you that a blind Indian used to say, when he found himself on familiar banks there, "Can see to walk".

Our doubts might all be resolved if we had the courage of a town in Greene County. Does the name Coxsackie mean "the hoot of an owl", or "the cry of wild geese", or has it some other less plangent significance such as "place of cut banks"? Our great authority, Dr. Beauchamp, thought that "owl-hoot" was "as well sustained as any". The matter is settled now: the school paper is called *The Hoot-Owl*, and the students have used owl and Indian on the school-rings. The flaw in such decisions is that people will be tempted to accept the prettiest interpretation or even invent one. At Saranac you will be told that the upper lake there has an Indian name meaning "Lake of the Silver Sky", the lower one a name meaning "Lake of the Clustered Stars". According to the famous Indian guide Sabattis (St. Baptist), the word Saranac means "entrance of a river into a lake"; but after careful study Dr. Beauchamp said, "No meaning has been definitely assigned to this name". As for the two pretty lakes, Beauchamp says: "The guide-books say the Indians called Upper Saranac lake 'The Lake of the Silver Sky'. What an improvement on *sky of brass*. Unluckily the Indian word is not given."

With a few exceptions these Indian names are more beautiful in sound than in meaning; they were not intended to be poetical but usually merely to designate a location. If you don't know the significance, be bold and state that the word means "meeting of waters" or "headquarters". Some meanings are so general that they were applied to more than one place. I remember being puzzled when a Canadian Mohawk, visiting me in Albany, insisted that the proper name for my town is Schenectady, which he defined as "beyond or at the gate"—the eastern marches of the Mohawk nation. Later I found in Beauchamp's book that Ska-neh-ta-de, "beyond the openings", was given by the great early anthropologist Morgan as the Iroquois

name for Albany, later transferred to the present Schenectady when
the Mohawks moved. Beauchamp decided on "beyond the pines or
openings" or "on the other side" of the pine plains. Major J. W.
MacMurray favors "without the door" and explains that the name
of the present city was S'Guan-ho-ha, "the door", changing when their
chief village was moved west to S'Guan-hac-ta-tie, "without the door".

This kind of fussing is dull enough to the layman. I am glad that
Tahawus really means "he splits the sky", and that a good many people use it in preference to Mt. Marcy, the English name given to
honor a Governor. There are other poetical meanings that even the
cautious Beauchamp admitted: Caneadea ("Where the heavens rest
on the earth"), Utsyanthia ("beautiful spring"), Genesee and Geneseo
("beautiful valley"), Honeoye Lake ("finger lying"), Chittenango
("where the sun shines out"), Sauquoit ("smooth pebbles in a
stream"), Ontario ("very pretty lake"), Niskayuna ("field covered
with corn"), Patchogue ("where they gamble and dance—make
merry"), Kerhonkson ("place of wild geese"). I am glad that Kenoza
Lake, where I first fished with my father, is named for the pickerel;
and that Chautauqua Lake, where I fish with my brother, may mean
"fish taken out"—the fish, according to legend, being that noble and
valorous critter the Muskallunge. I was pleased in 1938 to learn from
my friend Harry Bush, learned antiquary and Mayor of Canajoharie,
that he had been taking seriously the name of his city, "the pot that
washes itself". The old glacial pot in the Canajoharie Creek had long
been filled with silt; so men were put at work until the city could
celebrate the restoration of its venerable name to the realms of truth.
The pot is now washing itself like anything.

In spite of the scholars, you are entitled to one or two dubious
derivations. Go on thinking that Ontiora (Onteora) means "mountains of the sky"; it is a grand name for the Catskills even if Beauchamp did suspect an earlier scholar, Schoolcraft, of having invented
it about a century ago. (It *is* odd that this should be the only Iroquoian
name in Greene County, but the Mohawks could certainly see the
mountains from afar.) Go on thinking that Horicon (Horican) means
"silver waters" and that James Fenimore Cooper was right in be-
stowing it upon Lake George, even if it was a tribal name of Indians
west of the lake, its meaning doubtful to Beauchamp. And by all

means assert that Niagara means "thunder of waters", even if Beauchamp is right in declaring that the lovely word means just "neck" between two Great Lakes. There are at least thirty-nine early spellings for Niagara anyway, and people who cannot spell perhaps cannot hear correctly. The amiable and learned Sir Thomas Browne confessed in his *Religio Medici* that his "greener studies" had been "polluted with two or three heresies". Mine are Ontiora, Horicon, and Niagara.

A heretic is inevitably foolish. It is the sheerest presumption for a man who speaks no Indian language to present a list of Indian names with possible meanings; yet I am so often assailed with questions that I feel sure that such a list will be welcomed. In general I follow Beauchamp (B), with occasional use of Tooker (T), an authority on Long Island place-names; Ruttenber (R), who made a long study of the Delawares (Lenape) and Hudson River tribes; and Dr. Erl Bates of Cornell. I omit names upon which comment has already been made.

Agawam, "place abounding in fish"
Allegany, Allegheny, "fair river"
Amagansett, "place of the well" (T), or "near the fishing place"
Ashokan, "to cross the creek", or "blackbird"
Callicoon, "turkey"
Canadice, "long lake"
Canandaigua, "town set off" or "place selected for settlement" (Morgan)
Canarsie, "at the boundary"
Canasseraga, "among the milkweeds (or slippery elms)"
Canastota, "pine tree standing alone", or "group of pines standing still" or "frame of a house"
Canisteo, "board on the water"
Canopus, named from a chief or tribe
Cattaraugus, "stinking shore"
Cayuga, "where they haul boats out"
Cayuta, "log in the water" or "lake", or "prickly ash", or "mosquito"
Erie, "cat", a Huron name for the nation
Esopus, "river". The Esopus Indians lived on the west bank of the Hudson.
Garoga, "creek on this side" (of the wilderness beyond Indian settlement)
Geneganstlet, "at the sulphur spring or marshy place"

Gowanda, "almost surrounded by hills or cliffs"

Gowanus, "he sleeps", or "he rests"—named for an individual

Hackensack, "lowland"

Hoosick, "place of stones" (R)

Irondequoit, "a bay"

Ischua, "floating nettles"

Jamaica, "beaver" (T) unless it was borrowed from the W. Indies, where
   it meant "land of wood and water"

Katonah, "great mountain"

Kayaderosseras, Kaydeross, "lake country"

Keuka, "boats drawn out", for a portage

Kill Buck, English name of a Delaware chief

Kisco, "land on edge of a creek"

Lackawack, "at the forks"

Mahopac, "large inland lake" (R), or "snake lake"

Mamakating, name of a chief, or "red or bloody place"

Mamaroneck, "he assembles the people" (T)—name of a chief

Manhansett, "island land", old name for Shelter Island (T)

Manhasset, name of a tribe (T)

Manhattan, "hilly island", I fear, though I should like to accept the idea
   of the missionary Heckewelder, "place of general intoxication"

Maqua, "bear", a name for the Mohawks

Matteawan, "good or charmed furs"

Minisink, "land from which the water is gone", or "place of islands"

Mohawk, perhaps "to eat living things", an Algonkian name used by
   the foes of the Mohawks. The *Jesuit Relations* gives evidence that
   the nation did indulge in ceremonial cannibalism. The Dutch called
   this warlike nation Maquas ("bears").

Mohegan, "wolf", name of a nation, more properly a Connecticut nation.
   The Mohicans were a confederacy on the upper Hudson; Arthur
   Parker and other authorities now use the spelling Mahikans. These
   Indians were east of the Iroquois. Parker says that in the lore of
   the forest area the wolf symbolizes the east; the moose, the north;
   the panther, the south; and the bison, the west.

Monsey, name of the Minsis, Delaware subdivision, perhaps "Wolf tribe"

Montauk, "fort country" (T) or "island country" or "small cedars in a
   swamp" (Bates)

Moose, Big Moose, name of the animal, "he trims or cuts smooth";
   symbol of the north

Nanuet, name of a chief

Neversink, "place abounding in birds" (R), or "highlands between water" (Schoolcraft)

Nunda, "hilly", or "potato ground"

Nyack, "a point"

Oneida, "standing stone", or "people of the stone". In 1850 their most sacred stone was moved to the Forest Hill Cemetery at Utica; legend connects it with the resting place of two brothers who founded the tribe and tells of it moving unassisted with the nation. Evidently they had other sacred stones; e.g., the one now to be seen at Nichols Pond.

Oneonta, "stony place". According to one romantic legend, Oneonta was a daughter of chief Schenevus. "Place of overhanging rocks" likely.

Onondaga, "people of the mountain or great hill", or "people of the hills" (Bates). Since the sixteenth century this nation has had the headquarters of the Six Nations, south of the present city of Syracuse.

Oriskany, "nettles"

Osceola, name of a Seminole chief from the South, "black drink"

Ossining, "stone upon stone". Bates suggests "cairn of a great chief".

Oswegatchie, "black water flowing out" or "black river"

Oswego, "flowing out", or "small water flowing into large"

Otego, "have fire here"

Otisco, "waters much dried away"

Otsego, "place of the rock", perhaps at the lake's outlet

Otselic, "plum creek", or "capful"

Owasco, "lake of the floating bridge", or "bridge on the inlet"

Owego, "where the valley widens"

Paumanack, "land of tribute"

Piseco, named for an old hermit chief. Bates gives meaning of "fish lake with low banks"

Pocanteco, "at the clear stream" (T)

Podunk, "a clean place", though the white man uses it to mean an insignificant hamlet anywhere

Pokeomoonshine, perhaps a corruption from Algon. Pohqui-moosi, "where the rocks are smoothly broken off"

Poughkeepsie, "reed-covered lodge by the little water place" (Miss H. W. Reynolds)

Ramapo, "river which empties into a number of round ponds" (R)

Rockaway, "sandy place" (T)

Sacandaga, "swamp, drowned lands", or "where the cedars grow in waters" (Bates)

Sagamore, Algon. title of a principal chief

Sag Harbor, shortened from Sagaponack, "place where ground-nuts grow" (T)

Saratoga, Beauchamp was doubtful; Bates gives "place of springs"

Schaghticoke, "landslide", or "two streams meeting"

Schenevus, "first hoeing of corn", or "where the corn is hoed early", also the name of a chief

Schodack, "fire" of the council

Schoharie, "floodwood", or "driftwood"

Seneca, has given trouble because it seems to be connected with an Algon. word, "to eat", which might refer to "eating 'em alive" in war or to such early ceremonial cannibalism as has been mentioned in connection with the Mohawks. Bates seems to me right in his theory that the name refers to the Senecan myth of the great snake at Canandaigua Lake who *ate* all the Senecas except a young man and maiden. The Council name of the nation is "Great Hill People".

Sewanhacky, "land of loose or scattered shell beads", applied to all Long Island but more accurately to the eastern half. The Long Island Indians made wampum.

Shawangunk, "southern rocks" or "white rock" (Schoolcraft). Other guesses include "place of minks" and "place of wild onions".

Shinnecock, "where loose wampum is got", or "level land". A few of this tribe still live on Long Island.

Sing Sing, "place of stones"

Skaneateles, "long lake", though there was an attempt to make it mean "beautiful maiden" or "tall virgin", and there is not wanting a legend of a disappointed lover whose tears created the lake.

Sodus, "shiny knife", or "sun glistens on knife here" (Bates)

Susquehanna, "muddy river" (Heckewelder, who should have known), or "river of booty", or "long winding waters" (Bates)

Syosset, "settlement on bay protected by islands"

Tagh-ka-nick, Taconic, "great, woody mountain" (T), or "water enough", or "forest wilderness", or "fall of timber". In other words, doubtful.

Tappan, name of a tribe, "cold river or spring"

Taughannock Falls, named for a chief who lived there. The Falls are higher than Niagara.

Ticonderoga, "place of sounding waters", says Bates, who got this mean-

ing from eight Mohawks at the St. Regis reservation. This fits fairly
well with Morgan's suggestion, "noisy", and with the French name
for their fort there, Carillon. Mr. C. C. King, Jr. recently published
a history of Lake George in which he quotes "old documents and
maps", one of which has "Cheonderoga—Indian for Between-two-
lakes, improperly Ticonderago". This would make a clear meaning.

Tioga, "at the forks" of the Chemung and Susquehanna, or "waters
between the hills" (Bates)

Tioughnioga, "meeting of roads and waters", or "flowers on its banks"

Tomhannock, "flooded river"

Tonawanda, "swift water", or "at the rapids"

Tuscarora, "shirt wearers" who came from North Carolina and were
accepted as the sixth nation of the Iroquoian confederation

Unadilla, "place of meeting", or "meeting of waters" at the forks

Wappinger, "east-land", name given tribe who lived east of the Iroquois

Watchogue, "hilly land"

Wawarsing, "a winding about"

Winona, "first-born girl", a Western Indian name used in York State.
I know a very nice little Seneca girl named Winona Blue-Eye.

Wyoming, "great plains", or "bottom lands", a name borrowed from
Pennsylvania

Yaphank, "river-bank" (T), or "place to set traps" (Bates), or "traps".
Some members of the A. E. F. will make an easy choice among these.

Thanks largely to Washington Irving, we still think of colonial
New York as Dutch, though the people from Holland were in
political control only about fifty-five years and occupied only the west
end of Long Island, the Hudson, the lower Mohawk, and Manhattan and Staten Islands. Consequently only about fourteen per cent
of the seven thousand place-names studied by Dr. Flick are Dutch.
My friends from other States and countries usually are able to guess
that *wyck* in numerous names means *town*, but *kil* usually puzzles
them and almost invariably *clove*. The word *kil*, meaning *creek*, and
clove (*kloof*), meaning gap, ravine, pass in mountain, or gulley, are
found combined in Kaaterskill Clove—"wildcat-creek-gap". As you
come up the west bank of the Hudson, such names as Catskill and
Bear Mountain remind you of that era, not long ago, when York
State was a wilderness inhabited only by uncounted wild beasts and
a few Indians.

The names of our *kills* afford constant reminders of forgotten facts in colonial history. The most important creek in Albany County is the Normanskill; about the year 1630 a certain Albert Andriessen Bradt, "the Norman", settled at its mouth. He was not a Norman in our sense of the word but a native of Frederickstad, Norway—which reminds us that the patroon Van Rensselaer populated his vast estate with many colonists who were not Dutch. Across the Hudson River, in Rensselaer County, you find the Poestenkill, named for the patroon's cowherd (*poest*), a certain Jan Barentse Wemp (died 1663), founder of a not undistinguished family. If you proceed north into Washington County, you find the beautiful Battenkill, really a river, which was probably named for Bartholomew Hoogeboom; his Dutch nickname should have been Mees or Meus for Bartholomeus, but his English-speaking neighbors called him Bat. Cobleskill in Schoharie County, settled by Palatines and Dutch, probably preserves another nickname, 'Cobus for Jacobus. Walkill in Ulster County is probably Walloon-Kill from early settlers; *Waal* is the Dutch singular, *Walen* the plural. Krum kill (Albany) uses the Dutch word *krom* or *kromme*, "crooked". Moordener kill (Rensselaer) is the creek of a "murderer" (*moordenaer* or *moordenaar*). The legend is that Muitzes kill in the same county commemorates the distress of a Dutch woman who lost her *hat* crying, "Di muitz is in de Kil". Our great authority on all Dutch matters, Archivist A. J. F. Van Laer, thinks that this name may be derived from *muts*, "a woman's lace cap", but more probably *Muitzes* is a corruption of *muizen*, "mice". The Quaken kill (Rensselaer) probably got its name from *quacken* or *kwakken*, meaning "herons". Binne kill (Schenectady) is defined as "inner river", and the same county has a diminutive (*killetje*) in Adams Killetye, named probably for a certain Adam Mull who had the misfortune to be taken prisoner by the Indians. There are dozens of other *kills*, many named for individuals. After the English had taken over the Hudson Valley, they evidently liked the word so well that we have such creeks as Bear Kill, Fishkill, Otter Kill, Owl Kill, Pine Kill, Saw Kill, Stony Kill, and so on, some of them doubtless previously named by the Dutch.

A number of other Dutch combining syllables turn up in our names.

The word *wyck* meant a district, ward of a city, or neighborhood.*
Kingston was once Wiltwyck; the first half of the word may mean
wild game or the wild Indians; so the name meant a district where
there was much game or where there were Indians—probably not,
as is often said, a *refuge* from the Indians. Albany was Rensselaerwyck,
the district of the great patroon.

The word *bush* in several names refers to woods, not bushes.
Greenbush is *het greene bosch*; the *greene* is deceptive, because it
means "pine"; the name therefore means, "the pine woods". A *hook*
(*hoek*) is a point; Kinderhook is "Children's Point", and of course
there are various stories to explain the name, including one pretty
tale that Indian children from this point watched the white wings of
Hudson's ship ascending his river. A *rack* is a reach, a straight stretch
in the river; so Claverack originally referred to a stretch in the river
where there were clover meadows or where there were three or four
meadows that reminded you of a clover. At any rate, the name is old:
Mr. Van Laer showed me *Kleve-rack* in the 1630 edition of Joh. de
Laet's *Nieuwe Wereldt*. He also produced a patent-map of 1681
showing the meadows there, but alas, there were five and not the
three clover-leaves I hoped to see, and they were all in a row.

A *dael* (pronounced *dahl*) is a valley; Rosendale (Rosendael) is
"the valley of roses". A *dorp* is a village; the name is applied specially to Hurley and also, curiously, to Schenectady, a city of about
a hundred thousand people who, though they include engineers and
skilled workman from many nations, are proud of their town's Dutch
origins. The hamlet of Boght (Albany) preserves the Dutch word for
a bend in a river—here the Mohawk. More puzzling is *vly* or *vleye*,
not found in Dutch dictionaries but often used in old deeds; probably
it is a contraction of *valey* (*valei* now), meaning a valley or marshy
land. A *vliet* is a stream, a flowing; so the name of the city of Watervliet is what the grammarians and rhetoricians call a pleonasm—the
stream could hardly be of anything except water. A *cripplebush* is a
creupel bosch, a stunted growth of trees or thicket. A *berg* is a mountain, but Holland is so flat that any hill looked mountainous to our
Dutch forefathers.

* *Wyck* (from Latin *vicus*, village) is the same as English *wick* in bailiwick, or
wich in Greenwich.

After you have seen the few explanations I have given, you can have fun puzzling out our old Dutch names. I found Mr. Van Laer chuckling over a record which undoubtedly explains the odd-looking name of Parda Hook, a point south of Albany, just a mile below Van Wie's Point. This record shows that in 1643 a group of wedding guests was going down the river on the ice from Albany when a mare belonging to a certain Cryn (Quiryn Cornelisz) and a stallion belonging to Lawyer van der Donck broke through the ice and were drowned. Poor Cryn believes that the lawyer collected 150 guilders from the wedding guests, but he, a laboring man, has had no recompence! There's your Parda Hook: *Paerde hoeck* is Horse Point. I hope that Cryn collected from someone.

There are plenty of other amusing Dutch names, but I can mention only a few. Don't let anyone tell you except in fun that Tinbrook (Orange) comes from a family name meaning Thin Breeches. Ten Broeck is a very old name in Friesland, but it means "at the marsh"; *Ten* is a contraction of *Te den*, "at the". Ten Eyck, the name of an Albany hotel famous in political life, and also of an honored Dutch family, means "at the oak". Mr. Van Laer has an interesting comment here:

The name Ten Eyck may have been a nickname for a man whose house stood near a large oak tree. More likely, however, the name is derived from a sign on which was painted an oak tree. The first Ten Eycks in this country were tanners and shoemakers, and their ancestors in Holland may likewise have been tanners. As oak bark is commonly used for tanning purposes, an oak tree would have been an appropriate sign for a tannery.

Some of the deviltry in Dutch names is old and some is the product of Washington Irving and other wags. Hell Gate (Helle Gat) is an old name, and so is Spuyten Duyvel, but the folktale about a Dutch Leander who swam to his girl "in spite of the devil" doesn't impress the scientific etymologists—*Spuyten* could mean "spouting" but not "in spite of". The Devil's Dance-Chamber (De Duyvel's Dans Kamer), near Newburgh on the Hudson, has legendary fame from the seventeenth century. At the point jutting out into the river to form the head of Newburgh Bay a Dutchman beheld a strange ceremonial dance of Indians. At the culminating moment the devil appeared in the shape of a beast; legend further states that if the shape was that of a harmless animal the omen was good, but if that of a ravenous beast, evil was sure to follow. This spot was so much feared by the Dutch that none of them would approach it:

> For none that visit the Indian's den
> Return again to the haunts of men.
> The knife is their doom; oh sad is their lot;
> Beware! Beware of the blood-stained spot.

Poor Hans Hansen and his bride Katrina, returning from New York to Albany, beached their boat at this *danskamer*. They had not proceeded more than a few feet when the spirits of Indians caught them and led them to death by torture at the stake.

In Rockland County, west of Tappan on the shore of what was once a beaver pond, is a knoll in a tract now called the Green Woods. That knoll was long called Wilder Mans Kerk-hoff (Indian's or Wild Man's Church), another relic of Indian rites. It is said that the last of the Tappan Indians lived there. Speaking of Tappan, there is the Tappan Zee in the Hudson. The Dutch word Zee means ocean, sea, or lake; in this case it means a widening in the river. This is the scene of the well known legend of Rombout Van Dam. He rowed from his home at Spuyten Duyvel the length of the Tappan Zee to attend a frolic; full of Dutch courage, he broke the Sabbath by starting back after midnight on Saturday. He swore that he would not land till he reached Spuyten Duyvel; he hasn't reached there yet, but the devil may have provided other quarters unless those are right who have seen him rowing on the Zee. He has company there sometimes, for the Storm Ship scuds before a wind as it did in the seventeenth century when it passed Nieuw Amsterdam, running against a full tide and headed north. As someone has said, she is a "barometric craft": if you see her, you may be sure of a storm shortly to arrive. I wonder whether Major André saw her. He was hanged near Tappan.

Six of our counties have names showing the Dutch influence: Orange, Nassau, Rensselaer, Cortland, Schuyler, and Bronx—though Jonas Bronck was really a Dane. (In 1644, Kieft told Father Jogues that there were "men of eighteen different languages" in Manhattan; the population was only about 2500.) There are a number of cities with Dutch names. Brooklyn was named for the Dutch village of Breukelen. Yonkers bears the courtesy-title of Sheriff Adriaen Van der Donck; a Jonker was a man of "good family", not necessarily a nobleman—we had no Dutch noblemen among the settlers. The title is somewhat like that of 'Squire so freely bestowed in the Yankee villages. (As a matter of fact, in the Middle Ages there *was* a noble family in Gelderland called Van der Donck, with which the Sheriff may have enjoyed claiming relationship.) Rensselaer was named for the patroons; Watervliet has been explained. Nieuw Amsterdam became New York; later the city which we know as Buffalo was called New Amsterdam because it was part of the Holland Land Company's domain, but the settlers preferred the name of a good American critter, long associated with a creek in that neighborhood. However, we do have a city of Amsterdam in Montgomery County, and a Rotterdam Junction in Schenectady County. It might be supposed that Albany's old name of Beverwyck, preserved in a park and a brew, represents merely the fact that beaver-pelts were the source of our early wealth; we still have on the city's coat-of-arms the figure of a beaver. It happens that Beverwyck is also an old place-name in Holland.

Some of the villages also have Dutch names; for example, Haverstraw and Saugerties ("the little sawyer's"). There are townships in eighteen counties bearing such names as Guilderland (Gelderland). There are even vestiges of Dutch royalty. For a time the Hudson River was named Mauritius for Prince Maurice (d.1625), Prince of Orange and Count of Nassau. For a short time after 1673 Albany was called Willemstadt in honor of William III of Orange, and the city preserves in the name of a famous club the memory of Fort Orange.

When the western part of the State was opened at the close of the Revolution, the Holland Land Company gave us a mint of new Dutch names. The beautiful village of Cazenovia (Madison) is named for one of its agents, Theophilus Cazenove, and you find there a hotel named for Colonel John Lincklaen, another agent who is further commemorated in the township of Lincklaen in Chenango

County. The company's headquarters in western New York was appropriately named Batavia (Genesee).

Next to the Indian and Dutch names, the visitor is always most attracted by those "shaken out of the classical pepperpot"—some two hundred of them in all. The explanation given to Matthew Arnold still has currency but needs reservation. It is true that in 1789-90 the Surveyor-General of New York, Simeon De Witt, supervised the survey of a Military Tract which embraced all of four counties and parts of four more, laid out in townships six miles square and offered to the veterans of our Revolution. De Witt was incensed when city slickers in New York began to ridicule his "classical spree". Two popular scribblers, Drake and Halleck, hailed him in a pretty bad Ode as "God-father of the christened West!" They assured the Surveyor-General that only one touch was needed to "consummate the grand design":

> Select a town—and christen it
> With thy unrivall'd name, De Witt!
>   Soon shall the glorious bantling bless us
> With a fair progeny of Fools,
> To fill our colleges and schools
>   With tutors, regents and professors.

Poor De Witt asserted that he "knew nothing of these obnoxious names, till they were officially communicated to him" by land commissioners who had already approved them. Our State Historian, Dr. Flick, is reasonably certain that the names were added to the maps by Robert Harpur, Deputy Secretary of State, acting under direct orders from the Land Commission.

There is a second qualification to be made in the ancient charge against Simeon De Witt. It is quite true that the classical names are most numerous in the Military Tract—Onondaga County alone has twenty-four of them; but how do you account for a hundred classical names in counties outside the tract? And why didn't the citizens repudiate the choices of the Land Commission? The fact is, as Professor Alexander Drummond of Ithaca observed, that Yorkers felt themselves akin to those dwelling in the ancient democracies; we were repeating their noble experiment under fairer auspices. Recently I edited the letters written by Governor De Witt Clinton, builder of the Erie Canal, to his undergraduate son at Hamilton College. It is plain that "Magnus Apollo", as his foes called him, thought of himself as a Roman; surrounded by a yelping pack of enemies, he comforts himself and instructs his son by quotations from Horace and Cicero. No matter how unlettered we may be nowadays, anyone passing through Central New York, with its pillared houses and sonorous Latin names, hears not only the muffled drums of the Senecas but the distant tramp of Mediterranean legions. Christopher Morley was right when he wrote of a trip from Utica to the Finger Lakes, "Some Hellenist surveyor must once have swept over the land with a Greek theodolite, sprinkling lovely place-names from the classics".

So we have our cities of Troy, Utica, Rome, Syracuse, and Ithaca. Ithaca and Syracuse are the seats of great universities; Troy has the oldest engineering college in America; Utica and Rome have for neighbors two sturdy "classical" colleges, Hamilton and Colgate. There are thirty villages with classical names, including Aurora, Homer, Ilion, Ovid, and Tully (Marcus *Tullius* Cicero). There are fifty-seven townships with such names as Brutus, Cato, Cicero, Pompey, Ulysses, and Virgil. Even in the Hudson River region you find a Corinth and an Athens.

Greece and Rome did not circumscribe our love of antiquity. We have Egypt, Carthage, Phoenicia, Babylon, and Tyre. The Bible is well represented in such names as Bethany, Bethel, Beulah, Canaan, Carmel, Ephratah, Goshen, Jericho, Jerusalem, Gilead, Lebanon, Gilboa (pronounced pretty frequently "Gilboy"), Mount Sinai, Pisgah, Nineveh, and so on; we even have a Sodom!

In the same post-Revolutionary period which saw the rainfall of classical names, we borrowed from European and Asiatic capitals and other famous foreign cities. The ten towns of St. Lawrence County were named Cambray, Hague, Potsdam, De Kalb, Louisville, Canton, Lisbon, Madrid, Stockholm, and—the one American name—Oswegatchie. This was rather silly, of course, though I can't help thinking that it may have been frontier humor rather than affectation. It is funny to see how the counties in the ice-box of northern New York chose names of warm places; I have been snowed in at Mexico (Oswego) with the comforting thought that I was in the same county with Palermo. Sometimes you feel that European names are appropriate; Geneva, at the northern end of Seneca Lake, has a fair seat that does remind you of the Swiss city's on Lac Leman; it has also an air of distinction and one street which seems to me unsurpassed in the quiet elegance of its houses. Usually, however, the choice must have had some such proud inspiration—when not humorous—as that which prompted John Wilkinson, reading an Oxford Prize poem, to exclaim that his salty little village so resembled ancient Syracuse that it should borrow its name. Bless his soul, it was time to come to some decision: the town had previously been known as South Salina, Bogardus' Corners, Cossit's Corners, Milan, and Corinth. At any rate, the name was honestly chosen. There is a legend that Ohio in Schenectady County was given its name in order that swindlers could sell lots to people who thought they were getting land in the state of Ohio. (This tale I tell with hesitation, and reject with confidence.)

While these dignities were being bestowed, the settlers remembered Britain's great writers. We have an Addison (Steuben), a Burns (Allegany), a Dryden (Tompkins), a Port Byron (Cayuga), a Milton (Saratoga), and even an Ossian (Livingston), not to mention a Waverly (Franklin), and an Afton (Chenango). Speaking of Scottish writers, we have a few Scottish place-names, though not so many as you might expect: Cameron, Campbell, Scotia, Scotch Bush, Broadalbin, Perth, Argyle, Coila, Edinburg (yes, without the final *h*), Athol, and such places as New Scotland and Scotchtown; all of these indicate Scottish pioneers. There are very few Irish names: there is Sullivan County, named for a Revolutionary General; Allegany County has a Belfast; Schuyler County has a Tyrone; Tioga has an Erin; Saratoga has a Galway; Ulster County was named for one of the titles of the Prince who became James II of England. (Albany was named from his Scottish title.) As I have said, Auburn was named for Goldsmith's deserted village. Avoca (Steuben) is said to have been suggested by Tom Moore's "Sweet vale of Avoca". On the whole, the Irish and Scots have meant more to York State than the place-names would indicate; they arrived a little too late.

The French, who claimed two-thirds of the present state from 1609 till 1763, left their mark. Two Counties—St. Lawrence and

Orleans—have French names. A few others survive from early times: Boquet, Celeron, Montcalm, Chateaugay, Chazy, Raquette, St. Regis. Raquette, name of a lake and considerable river, was the French word for *snowshoe*, known to the Jesuits. One theory is that Indians hunted there on snowshoes. A romantic legend says that in May, 1776, Sir John Johnson, the Tory, fled with three hundred followers from the great estates of his family in the Mohawk region. The season was so late that they started on snowshoes which they abandoned at Raquette Lake because of the spring thaw. The lake, says this story, was named for the heap of *raquettes* left piled on the shore of South Inlet. I am afraid that this is an example of discovering a name a century after it had been adopted. I prefer the honest folk-etymology of the guides in that region who are quite confident that the river was named for its racket (noise). (The Indians did call it Tanawadeh, "swift water" or "noisy water".)

Fortunately, Lake Champlain has preserved the name of the great French Governor and explorer whose fatal shot at a party of Mohawks, fired in 1609, is somewhat romantically said to have decided that Britain should triumph over France in America. Certainly the Mohawks never forgave. The lovely lake south of Champlain was named Lac St. Sacrement (1646) when St. Isaac Jogues arrived there on the eve of Corpus Christi; but this tribute to the Blessed Sacrament was cancelled during the French and Indian Wars when the Irish Sir William Johnson renamed the lake for his German-English master, King George II. Schroon Lake may be named for Françoise d'Aubigné, Madame Scarron. There is some reason to believe that she was born here, daughter of a refugee Huguenot. When her parents were killed by the Indians, the child was brought up by priests of a mission; she was later adopted by the Scarron family, and finally married to the crippled poet, Paul Scarron (1610-50). The young widow is known better to fame as Madame de Maintenon, Marquise and "Consort" of Louis XIV. If you don't like this story about a Royal Mistress, perhaps you might prefer a lengendary Algonquin Indian Princess named Scaroon who drowned herself in this lake rather than fall captive to the Iroquois. If this won't do, there have been two Indian words suggested, sounding somewhat like Schroon, one meaning "largest lake" and another signifying "it is left behind".

We shall still have in Niagara County a memorial to the Marquise's royal lover in Lewiston and Royalton. We still talk in western New York of the Sieur de la Salle's little wooden vessel of fifty tons, *Le Griffon*, named for the two heraldic beasts on Frontenac's coat-of-arms; on an August day of 1679 she sailed away from the Niagara frontier, from Squaw Island and up Lake Erie, never to return. She is the ghost ship of the Great Lakes. Until recently the Catholic French history of our State was almost as ghostly, remembered by such vestiges as the old Portage (canoe-carry) between Lakes Erie and Chautauqua. At present, however, there is renewed interest, particularly in the French Jesuit missionaries. A shrine at Auriesville (Montgomery) recalls the heroism of St. Isaac Jogues and his companions; the researches of the Reverend A. M. Stewart of Rochester, a Protestant, are awakening us to the importance of the Catholic French in the history of our western frontier.

When it comes to be a consideration of the Protestant French in *eastern* New York, the study is complicated by the fact that many of the supposedly Dutch settlers were French-speaking Walloons from the Low Country, often married into Dutch families inextricably. Even the so-called Palatine Germans who came in large numbers during the eighteenth century included French who had taken refuge for a time in Germany—such as the Nellis family for whom Nelliston on the Mohawk is named. Old Governor Peter Minuit himself had a French name, and many of the patrician names of old New York—such as De Lancey and L'Hommedieu—remind us of the French strain. The thirty families who arrived on the *New Netherland* in 1624 were mostly Walloons, speaking French but hating the Bourbons. The Huguenots could never forget the fall of La Rochelle in 1628; many years later, in 1688-9, they founded in Westchester County, again with thirty families, what is now the city of New Rochelle. Even more interesting is the founding of New Paltz* in Ulster County by a dozen Huguenot families who bought land there in 1677 and until after the close of the Revolution maintained an *imperium in imperio*, a government by twelve heads of families, chosen annually, called the Dusine. Stout fellows were Colonel Dubois, Abram Hasbrouck, the Beviers, and the rest, as their beau-

* Dutch *Palts*, German *Pfaltz*, for *Palatinate*.

tiful stone houses still testify, not to mention their very able descendants.

The French part in our Revolution is commemorated by such place-names as LaFayette and Fayetteville in Onondaga County, and Fayette in Seneca. Dr. Flick reminds us that hundreds of French refugees from Canada and Nova Scotia came to our state in 1776 and later; two hundred and fifty-two were assigned land in the Refugee Tract in Clinton County. The name Luzerne commemorates not the lovely Swiss city but the Chevalier de la Luzerne, from 1779 till 1783 Minister of France to the United States.

A fascinating book could be written about the French refugees, royalists, and republicans, who took flight to New York State. Up in Jefferson County you find a number of French names connected with a single family of Franklin's friend, Le Ray de Chaumont: Leraysville, Chaumont, Theresa (for his daughter), Cape Vincent and Alexandria Bay (for two sons), Juhelville (for his mother-in-law), and Plessis for his dog! As I have said in another chapter, a good many people in the North Country still believe that a mysterious Eleazar Williams, missionary among the Oneida Indians, was the "Lost Dauphin" of France; unfortunately, we have no place named for him. However, we do have Muller Hill near Georgetown (Madison), home of the mysterious person calling himself Lewis Anathe Muller, who came to York State in 1810, built an expensive house, and hurried back to France when news arrived of Napoleon's abdication. He has been given a number of noble and royal names in legend, including that of the Duc du Barry whom Napoleon hated. By the way, Lake Bonaparte (Lewis) and King's Falls commemorate Joseph Bonaparte, who did come to York State; and famous battles of Napoleon Bonaparte, who did not visit us, are found in Austerlitz, Borodino, Lodi, Marengo, and Waterloo.

There are many other French names, but I mention only a recent experience with Gallic nomenclature. About fifty years ago, an attorney descended from the house of Valois built himself a "castle" at North Hector (Schuyler), filled it with what were said to be heirlooms of French royalty, and bargained with the village fathers that if they would change the name of North Hector to Valois he would erect a bandstand and defray the expenses of starting a band. The change was made. Arthur Valois returned to France some years ago; his "castle" burned down, and parts of the bandstand recently were used to make a chicken-coop, but his name persists.

Our own Revolution left its mark upon our place-names. Tryon County became Montgomery, and Charlotte County became Washington. Of the fifty-two new counties added after the war, nineteen were named for Revolutionary soldiers and statesmen, nine of whom were Yorkers: Clinton, Cortlandt, Hamilton, Herkimer, Lewis, Livingston, Montgomery, Schuyler, and Steuben. Virginia was represented by Washington, Jefferson, Madison, and Monroe—all of whom were Presidents anyway; Pennsylvania gave us Franklin and Wayne; New England contributed the names of Generals Greene, Warren, Sullivan, and Putnam. Of the remaining counties, three had Dutch associations—Rensselaer, Nassau, and Bronx; three honored State executives who helped to set up the counties—Broome, Tompkins, and Yates; two were of French origin—St. Lawrence and Orleans; two had English origins—Essex and Delaware; one was named for Fulton, who built the Hudson steamboat; one is a descriptive name, Rockland. The other twenty, in spite of memories of border warfare against the redman, were given Indian names. This is not the whole story: there is not a county without names reminiscent of the Revolution; even the extreme western county of Chautauqua, where the first permanent settlement was not made until 1802, has five townships named for signers of the Declaration of Independence—Clymer, Ellery, Gerry, Sherman, and Stockton.

The War of 1812 gave us a few more heroic names, such as Mc-Donough and Bainbridge in Chenango County, named for Commodores, as well as Perry (Wyoming) and Decatur (Otsego); the naval heroes came into their own. The wartime governor had Tompkinsville on Staten Island named for him, and its streets (some of them, at least) named for his children. Of the Generals, Porter and Mooers left their mark upon the map. The Mexican War elevated General Winfield Scott; there is a township of Winfield, not to mention several villages using his second name; there are also Cherubusco, Monterey, Buena Vista, Taylor, and Rough and Ready. For heroes of the Civil War we named Lincoln, Grant, Seward, Sherman, Sheridan, and a few other places. Since that time, war-heroes have had to be content with being honored in the names of streets and squares and parks.

The English place-names are not very interesting. Even before the English took over New Amsterdam in 1664, there were in eastern Long Island and Westchester such names as Southampton, East Hampton, Chester, and Rye. In 1683 the province was divided into ten counties. Two of them, Westchester and Suffolk, were given names made on the models of English counties; the other eight honored members of the Royal Family—Kings, Queens, Richmond, New York, Dutchess (whose old spelling we retain), Orange, Ulster, and Albany. We didn't bother to change these after the Revolution, though we did get rid of four county names originating in the decade before the war: Cumberland, Gloucester, Charlotte, and Tryon. The last was named for a Royal Governor whose reputation is still a stench; Cherry Valley of the massacre was in that large county.

When New England invaded at the close of the Revolution, its land-hungry people brought hundreds of English names, sometimes adding thoughtfully the word *New* to their memories of Massachusetts and Connecticut in such names as New Hartford, New Salem, New Windsor. When in Delaware County you come upon Roxbury and Stamford, you scarcely need to inquire whether the Connecticut Yankees were prominent in founding the villages; that example will serve for hundreds of cases. As Professor Kittredge of Harvard observed to me, New York was to New England the first West. For years he looked for trace of a member of his family about whom nothing was known except that he had "gone West"; finally the stray was located in Central New York. Nay, I remember a gracious lady at Cambridge, Massachussetts, telling me that she had once been west, and when I asked her how far, she said, "Albany". (Dean Briggs of Harvard, one of God's good men, always pronounced my county's name Tshatauqua, which did not irritate me so much as it did the lads from Illinois when he said Tshicago.)

The Germans, who arrived in no great numbers before the Palatines of the eighteenth century, have given us only four per cent of our names. The settlements on the Hudson gave us Newburgh, Rhinebeck, Rhinecliff; in Schoharie County you find such a name as Blenheim. Some Schoharie names are closer to Dutch than to German—the population was mixed. For example, the curious place-name Breakabeen is a corruption of Dutch *Brekabeen* (horse-tail or scouring-rush, *Equisetum Limosum L.*) rather than a derivative of the German form, *Brechebein*. In the Mohawk Valley you have such names as Palatine, German Flats, and Manheim. The services of Baron Steuben—whose name we pronounce Stew-ben' or Stoo-ben'*— are commemorated in names for a county, a creek, a township, and two villages; and General Herkimer has a county, a town, and a village. It is sometimes said that Germans named the Helderberg Mountains, but the present form of the name is Dutch; the German form, Helleberg, does occur. We have both a Berlin and a New Berlin, but we accent the name on the first syllable. The German Swiss gave us the Bernes in Albany County, a Zurich in Wayne, a Mount Rigi in Columbia, and an Interlaken in Seneca, though I am not sure how far these names represent any considerable Swiss population.

Matthew Arnold's objection to the Briggsvilles and Higginsvilles has a certain validity, though Rochester, Jamestown, Binghamton, and scores of other places followed a generous impulse in selecting a pioneer's name. In one case, at least, nobody could wish for a change: the village of James Fenimore Cooper, settled by his father, a colorful judge, wrassler, and laird, should always remain Cooperstown. What a quaint lot of names we might have had if western New York had followed the example of Jamestown in selecting the *first* name of its great man—in this case James Prendergast—and had used the Biblical "given names" of such early settlers as Didymous Kinney, Apollos Hitchcock, Zattu Cushing, Epaphras Mattison, Elizur Webster, and Noadiah Hubbard!

We did manage to get a handsome lot of women's names, drawn from all walks of life. Joseph Bonaparte called his town in Lewis County, Diana, whereas Elmira was named for the little daughter of an inn-keeper. Bath (Steuben) and Henrietta (Monroe) were named for Henrietta Laura, Countess of Bath, daughter of Sir William Pulteney, whose great tract in western New York was opened by

---

* Mr. Van Laer suggests that the accentuation of the General's name may be traced to the French officers who served with him; he often wrote the name *de Steuben*, in the French manner.

"Charles the Great" Williamson, a Scot. Bath was started with ceremonies worthy of a countess. By July of 1796 guests from as far away as Virginia began to arrive to see the opening of the race-course in September, when the finest horses were to compete for a prize of a thousand pounds. The Southerners properly bet their shirts and slaves on Virginia Nell, owned by Williamson. When she lost to a New Jersey mare named Silk Stockings, some of the Southern sportsmen are said to have decided not to return home. Festivities lasted until October, while the value of land increased from two shillings to four dollars an acre. Williamson must have sighed with relief; in America's first great advertising campaign he had spent a half million dollars.

Other lairds named places for their ladies. The county seat of Essex is called Elizabethtown for the wife of the pioneer William Gilliland, whose own name appears in Willsboro. There was a Bessboro, too, for his daughter, but that name has been changed to Westport. The pretty name of Angelica (Allegany) honors the mother of Judge Church; she was a daughter of that great gentleman, General Philip Schuyler. William Constable of Constableville (Lewis) probably did best by his gals: Harrietstown (Franklin) is named for the daughter who married James Duane of Duanesburg (Schenectady), and similar honors are paid to four other daughters —Anna, Emily, Jane, and Everetta. We mustn't forget Dosoris on Long Island, named for the dowry (Latin *dos uxoris*) which a fortunate early settler was able to obtain. There may be a tragic story in some of the names, too; it is said that Fowler's Lake became Sylvia when Mr. Fowler's beautiful daughter wept for a rejected lover who drowned himself there.

By this time you may be a little weary of historic and romantic names; you may be saying, as a friend of mine did recently: "All very interesting, but I like best your crazy names like Painted Post and Paradox Lake—let's hear about them." Well, even the crazy names can be explained. Painted Post commemorates, said a white eye-witness, the burial of a chief for whom a post was erected, painted with his blood; the chief was no less a person than "Captain" Montour, son of the ferocious half-breed "Queen", Catherine Montour. Red Jacket admitted that the post marked the burial of a chief, but stated that it was painted with berry-juice and refused to tell the chief's name. I get from students all sorts of variants on this story; sometimes the deceased is a slaughtered white man.

Paradox Lake really is paradoxical. It is only slightly higher than Schroon River into which it normally flows through a quarter-mile brook. In a spring freshet the river rushes up the brook into the lake. I thought I had found a really daft name for a body of water when I came upon a pond in Essex County named Grisly Ocean; but my learned friend Dr. Alexander explained that Grisly is probably a corruption for Griswold and Ocean is just an amiable exaggeration in a county of tall tales. I cherish Grisly Ocean none the less, and the name for an Essex road and valley, Stony Lonesome. Often roads have delightful names: near Candor (Tioga) you find two called Lovely Vale and Honey-Pot. Or a dirt road may lead past such an assortment of tiny hamlets as Pinchgut, Irishtown, and Dogtown, between Schroon Lake and Olmsteadville in Essex.

It is time to write down the queer names of our hamlets before sissies get them all changed. On Long Island, Skunk's Misery is now Malverne, Cow Neck has become Manhasset. In Otsego County, Toots Huddle is Fall Brook, Sodom Point is now South Hartwick (named for a missionary), and Bulldog is Gilbertsville. We should even preserve the uncomplimentary nicknames conferred upon one village by a rival; for example, the fight to obtain the county seat of Allegany led to such feeling between the sweetly named villages of Belmont and Angelica, that even today the older people of Angelica (which at least retained the county fair) refer to Belmont as Pilfersville.

If you wanted a rich collection of daft names, about all you would need to do would be to wheel up and down Orange County where, by the way, there is a Thompson Ridge. If you didn't have enough of such names as Spanktown, Shin Hollow, and Purgatory Swamp ("easy to git in, hard to git out"), you could find more in the county histories; you would learn, for instance, how Goosetown in a fit of patriotic fervor had its name changed to La Grange, the paternal estate of General the Marquis de Lafayette. In case you prefer to sit at home and read, here are a few names from my notebook, selected from various counties:

Bangall, Bare Market, Bull Pout, Cakeout (a road), Comfort,

Dead, Devil's Nose, Doodletown, Dumpling, Eden and Paradise, Endwell, Gallows, Graphite, Grindstone, High Up, Hogtown, Horseheads, Index, Johnny Cake Corners, Lazy, Ligonee ("up to his leg an' knee in the swamp"), Little Rest, Looneyville, Mertensia ("furrin name for the bluebell"), Moan, Modern Times, Nobodys, Peanutville, Satan's Kingdom, Sheepskin Corners, Snufftown, Surprise, Tug Hill, Vinegar, and Whiskey Hollow. Sometime I hope to see Cat Hollow (Delaware) where, to get even with a boarder who shot pussy, the critter's mistress served a cat stew. Frequently I pass through Esperance (French for "Hope"), and I like Liberty, but I seem to keep away from Integrity, Amity, Freedom, Sociability, Harmony, and several other villages whose virtues I need to cultivate.

I don't blame Dean Briggs for mispronouncing our place-names, about which we are "plain wilful". I had left the Dean's gracious presence at Harvard before I knew that Valatie near Albany is pronounced Valayshia. (This name is derived from the Dutch Valletje, "Little Falls".) We are being highschooled out of our convictions, but the true Yorker pronounces Athens and Cairo with a long *a* as in *late*; Corinth with accent on the second syllable; Ovid, with a long *o* as in *note*; Medina with a long *i* as in *line*; Rheims and Greenwich with a long *e* as in *need*; Canton and Berlin with accent on the first syllable. In a number of names *ch* has the French sound of *sh*: in Chateaugay (Shatty-gee), Chautauqua, Chazy (preferred accent on second syllable), Chemung, Chenango; but you find the *ch* of *chin* in Cheektowaga, Chippewa, and Chittenango. We pronounce *sch* as *sk* in Schaghticoke (Shattycook or Skattycoke), Schenectady, Schenevus, Schodack, Schoharie, Schroon Lake, Schuylerville, all of which are either Dutch or Dutch spellings of Indian names—Schroon may ultimately be French. We do not pronounce the Dutch *uy* as the people of the Netherlands do; we use the sound of long *i* as in *dice* for such names as Spuyten Duyvel, and for such Dutch families as Schuyler, Huyck, and Pruyn. The accent falls on the second syllable in Ashokan, Chemung, Chenango, Chautauqua, Chazy, Mamaroneck, Menands, Oswego, Oriskany, Otsego, Otselic (long *e*), Patchogue (*o* like *aw*), Pyrites (3 sylls.), Schenectady, Schoharie (*har* like *hair*), Taughannock, Tioga (*i* and *o* long). The accent falls on the third syllable in Cassadaga (the accented syllable with *a* as in *date*), Catteraugus, Cincinnatus (long *a*), Dannemora, Geneseo and Genesee, Mineola (*e* and *o* long), Monticello (*c* like an *s*), Oneonta (first *o* long, second as in *on*), Onondaga (accented syllable like *aw*), Sacandaga (another *aw*), Skaneateles (accented *a* as in *ant*, but lots of people say Skinny-attles), and Tonawanda (all four vowels pronounced *ah*). The accent is on the first syllable in Bolivar, Coeymans (Kweemans), Esperance, Honeyoye (Honey-oy), Islip (long *i* as in *ice*), Leyden (long *i*), Lima (long *i*), Matteawan (silent *e*), Saugerties (*au* like *aw*), Shawangunk (Shong-gum). There are few examples of accent on the fourth syllable: Canajoharie (*har* like *hair*), Oliverea, and Ticonderoga. Compared with the attritions and blurring in English and Scottish names, our nomenclature still is crisp and clean.

History and humor: these I have tried to give you in accounting for our names. I hope that you have also found some of the beauty which a Yorker enjoys; but, beautiful or not, more names will be made for the sake of history and humor. It was only recently that Dr. Julian Boyd renamed worthily the streets of old Ticonderoga, which heard the drums and tramplings of all our early wars. First Street became Algonkin; Second Street, Father Jogues Place; Third Street, Iroquois; Exchange Street became Montcalm; and so it went, dull names giving place to those of historical significance and beauty —Champlain Avenue, The Portage, Amherst Avenue, Burgoyne Road, Lord Howe Street.* The children of "Ti" are lucky. The fun goes on too. An item in a recent newspaper says that the hamlet of Blanchardville (Fulton) is about to build a log church in twelve hours and assume a new name—PROGRESS.

* Dr. Boyd was assisted by Mr. LaFayette Perry.

XIX: *Proverbs*

WE YORKERS used to bring up our children on the Bible and folk-proverbs. We still use the proverbs. After I had made that remark in a lecture, two sisters went home and wrote down in one evening sayings which they had learned from their father. One sister had three hundred and fifty, the other two hundred and ninety. Then Miss Nelle Schmidt of Oneida County decided to make a book of proverbs and did it—in ninety-three typed pages, of which fifteen were an essay composed in proverbs entitled "Central New York Speaks Its Piece". This piece was so ingeniously done that Carl Sandburg called it "a kind of prose poem", and traded a signed poem of his own for a copy of the Oneida County saws that he liked best.

You are not to suppose, of course, that any large proportion of these originated in York State. I remember chuckling over one of Miss Schmidt's epigrams expressing scorn for pretense, "I wasn't brought up in the woods to be scared by owls". I looked it up in the *Oxford Dictionary of English Proverbs* (1935) and didn't find it. Then I tried it on my barber; Schuyler was brought up in the country near Albany "quite a while ago" and is a walking dictionary of proverbs. He said sure he had heard it back on the farm. I began to think of this proverb as an example of York State wit—even quoted it as one of the best examples, though always with an admission that I might be wrong about its origin. Then one day a student at Cornell showed me the exact words of my York State prize in *A Complete Collection of Polite Ingenious Conversation*, written by Jonathan Swift two centuries ago to satirize those who quote old saws in lieu of original wit.

While I am not making any statement about the origin of the proverbs which I am about to quote, their age or provenience, I am taking care to give them exactly as I have heard them or as they have been heard by my students. Thousands more are known to practically everyone in America; hundreds of additional epigrams now rare I could have culled from such old almanacs as the set published by Phinney of Cooperstown. What I now present is a selection from the most interesting proverbs now current. Even after a long study and regretful elimination of hundreds, I have still so many that this chapter is bound to seem tedious to anyone who tries to read it through at a sitting. Nobody acquainted with the form will make such an attempt.

For the present purpose no former classification seems very valid. I shall therefore try a new one, and commence by saying that our York State proverbs seem to fall into two classes: proverbs of wisdom and proverbs of poetry. There is some meaning in that classification, for a good many proverbs are enjoyed chiefly because they give shrewd comment on the conduct of men, whereas others are valuable chiefly as imaginative comparison or other description that rises above the commonplace rather to delight than to instruct. You will see, however, that the proverbial wisdom is often expressed in poetical form, and that the innumerable proverbial comparisons and descriptions imply wisdom.

Quite naturally, students are interested in the proverbial wisdom which concerns *love* and *marriage*. "Love and a cough cannot be hid", or "Love and smoke cannot be hidden". "Love goes where it is sent", and it is sent delightfully:

> Always to court and never to wed
> Is the happiest life that ever was led.

A good many already know that

> Every Jack has his Jill;
> If one won't, another will.

The parents may hold that it is wise to "marry your sons when you will, your daughters when you can", but upstate the girls still receive a good deal of proverbial advice. "Love in a tub and the bottom will fall out" means that if you marry on love only, you may not find your state unsatisfactory. It is still desirable that the girl be a good housekeeper, for

> Where the cobwebs grow
> The beaux don't go.

Too often we have a case of "dimple outside, devil inside", or of "street angel, house devil".

There are grandmothers to warn a girl, as one was warned long ago at Sidney, against the peril of trying to keep two beaux interested: "Two are too many: one will break loose, and the other will let go." Or Missie is told that "man gets and forgets, woman gives and forgives". She may even be warned against a certain lad by the words, "Who marries him will keep the apron to her eye". If the wooer is too old, too rich or too poor, of another race, the advice comes, "Like blood, like gold, and like age". I like best the advice of a Chenango County mother to her son's intended bride: "You must take two bears to live with you—Bear and Forbear".

As for the lad, he may be told that "matrimony is not a word but a sentence", or that "it is better to be half hanged than ill wed". Some gaffer may remind him that "gold is tested with fire, a woman with gold, and a man with woman". If he knows his proverbs, he may retort that "faults are thicker where love is thin". At any rate, it is unlikely that the young people will let proverbial wisdom stand in the way. Not long ago one of my graduate students brought me two apparently modern proverbs of which she could approve: "Pity is achin' to love", and "A ring on the finger is worth two on the 'phone". In June she married a pleasant young Doctor of Philosophy who has reason to applaud her choice of proverbs. I felt no need to quote at the ceremony my favorite of certain marriage-maxims current in Jefferson County: "Never speak loudly to one another unless the house is on fire."

It must be confessed that when the wooing is o'er and the maid wed, the proverbs turn cynical. Sometimes it is because "the gray mare is the better hoss"; sometimes because "an old man marrying a young girl is like buying a book for someone else to read"; sometimes because "no roof can cover two families". The neighbors will observe: "If marriages arè made in heaven, you had but few friends there"; or, "A deaf husband and a blind wife are always a happy couple". In the old days people said:

> A woman, a dog, and a walnut tree,
> The more you beat 'em, the better they be.

Indeed, that ungallant proverb is still current in Jefferson County. If the couple quarrel openly, the neighbors say, "They'll never comb gray hair together".

The comfort is that "it will all be the same after you're twice married". Of course, "Once bitten, twice shy", and "You can't marry a widow, for the widow marries you". It is encouraging to a second wife to remember that she is bound to be more leniently judged than her predecessor—"The second wife always sits on the right knee". Anyway, "What can happen once can happen twice", and "Sorrow for a husband is like a pain in the elbow—sharp and short". In other words, "Onions can make heirs and widows weep". Whatever may be said about matrimony, there is always the proverbial loyalty of daughters:

> My son's my son till he gets himself a wife;
> My daughter's my daughter all her life.

In any relationship, "He laughs best whose laugh lasts"—a modern improvement on the older saw.

To most Americans a mention of the word *proverb* recalls immediately the shrewd advice of Benjamin Franklin—not so much his observations on love and marriage as his sayings about *industry* and *thrift* and on *work* in general. In York State we say, "God sends every bird its food, but He does not throw it into the nest", or, "The world is your cow, but you have to do the milking". Especially on the farm,

"They must hunger in frost that will not work in heat". The good farmer knows that "dirty hands make clean money", and that—

> He that by the plow would thrive
> Himself must either hold or drive.

In fact, "You have to hoe a row of corn with a man to know him". If he is really industrious, you may say of him as they do in Otsego County, "That young man will make his living on any four-corners". He is of the sort that proves, "Deeds are fruits, words are but leaves". Until recently he knew that "at a workingman's house hunger looks in but does not enter". He knew that "there was ne'er a five pound note but there was a ten pound road for it", and that "a bag full of flour and a purse full of money are the best relations in the world".

The typical Yorker has always felt contempt for those who were "able to work but not willin'", though we sometimes shrug our shoulders and observe, "The Lord provides for the lame and the lazy". It is more likely that such people will be "living on wind pudding and air sauce"; we say, "A young man idle and an old man needy", and "A man who watches the clock generally remains one of the hands", and "*Can't* is a tramp that sits by the roadside and begs". The lazy man is ineffectual, he "works all day in a peck measure"; he is not likely to "use his head to save his heels". He doesn't heed the old advice: "Mend the first break, kill the first snake, and conquer everything you undertake." He may "put a lot of church work into it", but all this show amounts to little. He doesn't even take care of his tools, for

> Lazy fools
> Drop their tools.

He has one ambition:

> Lazy folks work the best
> When the sun is in the west.

If you accuse him of being indolent, he is likely to use the proverb which the good worker never quotes except with a smile of apology: "It's a poor job that can't afford one boss."

Of the lazy man we have a saying which conceals a folktale: "He

wants his corn shelled." I give you the story as recorded by Miss
Judith B. Rogers of Genesee County:

There was once an old man who was so lazy that he was horribly poor,
but for a long time his neighbors made contributions to his support and
kept him alive. Finally they decided that he was so worthless that he
would have to be taken off and buried. Just as they had him loaded into
the carriage, a stranger came up and asked what was happening. When
he heard what it was all about, he was sorry for the old man and volunteered to contribute a bushel of corn to keep him from burial. Hearing
the offer, the old man stuck his head out of the carriage and said, "Is the
corn shelled?"

"No," was the reply.

"Drive on," he said, "drive on."

Just as they contrast the industrious man with the lazy, so our
proverbs set the thrifty man above the spendthrift; but observe that
thrift is praised not because "money is flat and meant to be piled" but
because it leads to that noble independence which Robert Burns
praised and desired. From Ireland can be traced one proverb which
says:

> For age and want save while you may;
> No morning sun lasts the whole day.

Or, as another saying brought over from England goes, "Make spare
of plenty, and you'll always have a plenty". In one of the oldest townships of Oneida County they say, "He who has four and spends five
has no need of a purse". After all, thrift is only wise planning:
"Measure your cloth ten times; you can cut but once."

While we are willing to permit a man to "pare the cheese pretty
close to the rind" when his thrift is not ignoble, we realize that "you
can save at the tap and lose at the bung". Many a miser would "ruin
a Barlow knife worth a shilling to skin a flint worth sixpence", or,
as a Scotch proverb found near Albany says, there are men who would
"skin a louse for the tallow o't". After all, "Your wooden overcoat
won't have any pockets".

Too often the thrift of the man injures the health of his wife. In
Essex County they say:

> Man works from sun to sun,
> But women's work is never done.

A proverb that summarizes woman's work is still heard: "Well, I must wash, iron, bake, and make a shirt for Will." Perhaps the ladies are fond of such sayings partly because a number of proverbs describe the *unthrifty* wife; for example: "A woman can throw out on a spoon more than her husband can bring in on a shovel", and "Silks and satins put out the kitchen fire".

There seem to have been two infallible tests for a thrifty house-wife: Does she make her own candles? Does she wash clothes on Monday?

> Wife, make thine own candle,
> Spare penny to handle.

> Provide for thy tallow ere frost cometh in,
> And make thine own candles ere winter begin.

> Who washes on Monday has all week to dry,
> Who washes on Tuesday is not so much awry,
> Who washes on Wednesday is not so much to blame,
> Who washes on Thursday washes for shame,
> Who washes on Friday washes in need,
> Who washes on Saturday is lazy indeed.

A slattern is an abomination in the proverbs; we say scornfully:

> An apple, an egg, and a nut
> Anyone can eat after a slut.

To be sure, a woman should not be too finical, especially about clothes:

> Fond of dress is sure a very curse;
> Ere fancy you consult, consult your purse.

When a husband quotes something of that sort, he may be boorish enough to refuse aid in bringing in wood, saying, "There's no use keeping a dog and barking yourself"—a Scotch proverb not always used so ungallantly. The woman may retort that "it is a poor house that can't support one lady", or that she has earned help and support because "he that rides the mule shoes her", and you should "never ring a pig that has to root for a living". Maybe her mate is critical because he can't see what she will finally accomplish: "Never show a fool a half-done job." But I am sure that in most families these brusque remarks are never heard.

Children are taught industry, thrift, and patient workmanshop in many a proverb:

Little strokes fell great oaks.
Reach for the high apples first; you can get the low ones any time.
A short horse is soon curried. (That wasn't much of a job.)
        Haste makes waste,
        Waste makes want,
        Want makes a poor man a beggar.
One boy is a boy, two boys are half a boy, three boys are no boy at all.
        (Be content to do your work alone.)

Yet for all these proverbs, we realize a child's limitations and say, "Don't send a boy on a man's errand"—though we use the phrase often when we do not literally mean a boy but have in mind inadequate effort or some other metaphorical meaning.

There is a last side to this treatment of work and thrift—the horror of debt. "Debt is the worst kind of poverty." If you pay your debts and remember that "short reckonings make long friends", you should never have to say, "Poor Trust is dead; Bad Pay killed him". Then you won't complain, even though you "have to work the life out of you to keep the life in you"; but you can smile and say:

        Those who have money have trouble about it,
        Those who have none have trouble without it.

The Biblical book of *Proverbs* has a good deal to say about fools in contrast to wise men, a subject not entirely neglected in York State. We may therefore call these epigrams about *folly* a third type of the proverb of wisdom. Mr. Sandburg liked one of these so well that he included it in his book entitled *The People, Yes*: "He doesn't know enough to pound sand in a rat-hole." Similar are the following:

He doesn't know enough to pull in his head when he shuts the window.
He hasn't the brains God gave an owl.
He has snow on the roof.
He doesn't know twice around a broomstick.

He can't see a hole through a ladder.
He is so dumb he can't crawl through a knothole backwards.
He has brass enough to make a five-pail kittle and sap enough in his head
  to fill it.
He doesn't know enough to suck alum and drool.

The trouble is that "experience is a dear school, yet fools will learn in no other". They do not heed the warning, "Let not your tongue cut your throat"; they do not realize that "he who gives advice is a bigger fool than he who takes it". They do not realize that "silence is the virtue of fools".

Even for fools the proverbs can find something good to say. To be sure, one saw has it that "a fool says *I can't*, a wise man says *I'll try*"; but another proverb says:

> The wise man said it couldn't be done,
> And the fool came and did it.

While they exclaim in the North Country, "A drunk man will sober up, but damn a fool", a friendlier proverb reminds us, "Better a kindly fool than a proud wise man", and the best of all sayings about fools is this: "If all fools wore white caps, we should all look like geese".

If you like that jovial saying, you will enjoy a fourth type of wisdom, the proverbs of *comfort* and *courage*, among which I like:

> In the end
> Things will mend

> What cannot be cured
> Must be endured.

Everything may be except a ditch without a bank.
He that is born to be drowned will ne'er be hanged.
If you can get over a dog's head, you can get over his tail.
It's all down hill after the Equator. (This comes from the Navy.)
It's just as 'tis, and 'taint no 'tis-er.
Sicker cats than that have been cured.
The ways of men are narrow, but the gates of heaven are wide.
There's many a chill, but few are frozen.

Whatever's allotted cannot be blotted.
Who has loved most, he best can love again.

There is irony in some other sayings:

A creaking gate never breaks.
Don't cry over spilt milk; there's enough water in it already.
Hearts don't break; they bend and wither.
If all the troubles were hung on bushes, we would take our own and run.
One sorrow drowns another: yesterday my husband died, and today I
    lost my needle.
Pity is a poor plaster.
There's no help for misfortune but to marry again.

More often the proverbs are full of sturdy courage. "A good
soldier never shines the heels of his shoes"—that is, he never looks
back. Even for age there is comfort:

> An old dog for a hard road.
> A stout heart for a stiff brae (hill). (Scotch)
> It's the life of an old hat to cock it.

A fifth kind of wisdom is found in the numerous proverbs of *caution*
or *warning*:

A wedge from itself splits the oak tree. (That is, a man is his own most
    dangerous enemy.)
Mud thrown is ground lost.
Don't write—and fear no man.

If thou wishest to be wise,
    Keep this truth before thine eyes:
What thou sayest and how, beware,
    Of whom, to whom, when and where.

Said first and thought after
Brings many to disaster.

To whom thy secret thou dost tell
To him thy freedom thou dost sell.

There are four good mothers
Who have four bad daughters:

Truth hath Hatred,
Prosperity hath Pride,
Security hath Peril,
And Familiarity hath Contempt.

A dog that will bring a bone will carry a bone. (Said of the danger of
    telling anything to a gossip who is regaling you.)
A liar needs a good memory.
Bacchus has drowned more than Neptune.
Eavesdroppers never hear any good of themselves.
Give neither salt nor counsel till asked for it.
He who lies with dogs, arises with fleas.
If you want to put your foot into a family row, stick your nose in first.
Never bid the devil good morning until you see him.
People that talk to *themselves* have money in the bank.
Proud looks make foul work on fair faces.
Stretch your arm no longer than your sleeve will reach.
Sue a beggar and catch a louse.
Tell everybody your business, and the devil will do it for you.
The crying cat always gets the scratch. (Scotch)
There's a slippery step at every man's door.
Those who live in the Bye and Bye soon come to the house of Never.

A sixth kind of wisdom is found in various proverbs of *ironical* and
even *cynical observation*, of which Robert Frost has selected one for
a famous poem: "Good fences make good neighbors." A number of
these concern the Biblical truth that one does not gather figs from
thistles, or perhaps we might say the eugenic theory that you can't
expect too much from a poor heritage. One of my graduate students
from Allegany County was commenting on the fact that a neighbor's
child, while attractive in appearance, was what the Bible would call
froward. "Well," was the response, "she didn't lick it up off the
ground." As a Rensselaer County farmer remarked, "If you breed a
pa'tridge, you'll git a pa'tridge". Another way of setting that truth
forth is, "Plant the crab-tree where you will, it will never bear pip-
pins", or "Nits make lice", or "An apple never falls far from the
tree". There is, however, a crumb of proverbial comfort: sometimes
a child is better than his parents, in which case he is called "an eel
in a snake's den"; sometimes the youngest child is an improvement

upon the older ones, in which case we say that "the shakings of the bag is the finest meal".

We are also somewhat cynical about the law, though many farmers still enjoy a "lawing". We say, "The law catches flies but lets hornets go free", or "Laws are like cobwebs where the small flies are caught and the big ones break through". On the whole, however, we are not suspicious of any race or profession, but rather dubious regarding human improvement. We say:

> If you are not handsome at twenty,
> > not strong at thirty,
> > not rich at forty,
> > not wise at fifty—
> You never will be.

And here are some other examples of ironical wisdom:

A man does not look behind the door unless he has stood there himself.
A new broom sweeps clean, but the old one finds the corners.
Better a lean lintie on the hand than a fat finch on the wand. (Scotch)
Far-off cows wear long horns. (The distance lends enchantment.)
Fast bind, fast find. (Shylock approved of this text.)
Honey draws more flies than vinegar.
Hope is a good breakfast but a bad supper.
If each before his own door swept, the village would be clean.
In a calm sea every man's a pilot.
Many a man wears a sailor hat who never owned a rowboat.
Rich men's tables have few crumbs.
The jests of the rich are ever successful.
There is more than one way to kill a cat besides soaking him in butter.
There is small choice in rotten apples.
Vows made in storms are forgotten in calms.
When drums speak out, laws hold their tongues.
Who wants to beat a dog soon finds a stick.
You can never tell the depth of the well from the length of the handle on the pump.
You can't judge a horse by its harness.

Give a pig when it grunts and a child when it cries,
And you will have a fine pig and a bad child.

These old landmarks of wisdom, which I have tried to illustrate in six types, are constantly inspiring modern parodies, amendations, and plain "wise-cracks", of which a few samples will suffice:

Charity begins at home and usually stays there.
Early to bed and early to rise,
   Work like hell—and *advertise!*
Every dog has his day and the cats their nights.
It's better to be neat and tidy than to be tight and needy.
She was pure as the snow but she drifted.
Spring is the time when a young man's fancy turns to what a young
     woman has been thinking all winter.

I think that the wittiest example of this sort that I have heard recently came from a musician, who observed bitterly that the saxophone is an ill wind that nobody blows good.

Up to this point, samples have been given of what I called the proverbs of wisdom; it is time to consider the other main type, the proverbs of poetry, which, as I said, "are enjoyed chiefly as imaginative comparison or other description that rises above the commonplace rather to delight than to instruct". The source of delight is not always in sound—alliteration and assonance—nor in picture, polished form, or fanciful thought; because we are Americans, the pleasure sometimes arises from turns of humor. No one acquainted with the poetical gifts of Sandburg, Frost, Christopher Morley, and Grant Wood will be surprised at the blend of humor with poetry.

Simplest of this type are the innumerable *proverbial comparisons*, usually based upon an adjective or adverb. For example:

Behind like a cow's tail
Big as life and twice as natural
Black as a stack of black cats in the dark
Blacker than a black cat's belly
Blue as a whetstone
Broad as a Dutch barn
Busy as a cat on a tin roof
Busy as a fiddler's elbow
Busy as a fish-peddler in Lent
Busy as a one-armed paper-hanger with the seven-year itch

Ca'am as a pan of skim-milk
Cheerful as a coroner's inquest
Close as a fist
Cold 's a corncrib
Colder 'n a dead puppy's nose
Common as pig's tracks
Contrary as a mule in a mud-puddle
Cranky as a sore-headed bear
Crazy as a shitepoke (green heron)
So crooked he could hide behind a cork-screw
So crooked he couldn't sleep in a round-house
Crummy (lousy) as a pet coon
Cut off like a worm in the ground
Cute 's a pig's ear

Dark as a stack of black cats
Dark 's a cow's belly
Dirty as dishwater
Dirty as mice
Drier 'n a covered bridge
So dry he's spitting cotton
Dumb as a beetle
So Dutch he has sauerkraut hanging out of his ears

Easy as shooting fish in a barrel

Fascinating as a loose tooth
Flat as a flounder
Free from money as a frog is of feathers
Friendly as a pup

Good as the wheat
Green as Kelly's necktie

Handy as a pocket in a shirt (sometimes ironical)
Handy as a cow with a musket, as a hog with a fiddle
Happy as a clam in high water
Happy 's a skunk in a hen-roost
Hard as lignum vitae
Hard as the hammers of hell

High as Gilderoy's kite
Homelier than a basket of knot-holes
Hot as Dutch love
Hotter 'n hell's half-acre
Hotter 'n the hobs of hell
Hotter 'n Hannah (Perhaps Hannah is the sun, as among Southern
    Negroes.)
Hotter 'n seventeen French wagons (Great War?)
Hungrier 'n a fiddler's bitch

Independent as a hog on ice
Irish as Paddy's pig

Four ounces lighter 'n a chip (straw) hat
Limber as an eel
Long as a country block
Long 's a yard of pump-water
Longer than an Irishman's dream
Longer than the moral law
Looser than a string of suckers
Looser than a wagon-tire in dry weather
So low you can chin yourself on the curb
Lower than the worms of the earth

Meaner than pusley (purslane)
Merry as a wedding bell, as a grig (cricket)

Neglected as the bones at a banquet
Nervous as a bridegroom
Nervous as a cat with wet feet
Noisy as Coxey's army

Odd as Paddy's daddy
Old as my unpaid bills
Older 'n God
Out and gone like Riley's eye

Plain as a pipestem
Poor as a parson

Poor as Job's turkey—couldn't raise more'n three feathers and had to
    lean against the barn to gobble
Poor as poverty's back-kitchen
Popular as a skunk at a lawn-party

Quicker 'n a cat can lick her ear

Rougher than a hetchel (hatchel, used in dressing flax)
Rotten as a turkey-buzzard's neck

Safe as a thief in a mill (perhaps a reference to old joke that millers are
    all thieves)
Shaped like an old apple-tree
Short and sweet, like a donkey's gallop
Shy as a colt
Slick 's a mink
Slick 's a seal
So slow you can watch the snails whizz by
Slow as a buck-maggot
Slower 'n West Injie molasses
Slower than death to a snail
Soft as pap
Sour enough to make a pig squeal
Stiff as Paddy dead nine days
Stiffer 'n a mackerel
Steady as a clock
Straight as a cob
Strong enough to work by the day (said usually of coffee or tea)
Suspicious as a juryman

Tall as a Shanghai
Talkative as a Galway fish-woman
Thick as Susan's straw-tick
So thin you have to shake the sheets to find her
Tight as a blonde's belt
Tight as bark to a tree
Tight as wax
Tight enough to hold kerosene
Tough as bull beef at a penny a pound

Tough as a halter
Tougher 'n a catamount

Unlucky as a fifth calf (because the mother cow has only four filling-
    stations)

Wide-awake as a marigold

Yellow as saffron

In other cases the proverb is developed from a verb:

Cling like a pup to a root
Cling like a wet kitten to a hot
    brick
Dance like a poppet (old word for
    doll)
Feel like the last run of shad
Feel like a penny with a hole in it
Feel like a skunk in hell with his
    back broke
Feels like being nibbled to death
    by ducks
Fits like a duck's foot in the mud
Fits like a fist in a nigger's eye
Fits like a saddle on a sow
Go on with your poppy-show!
    (puppet-show, nonsense)
Go sidewise like a hog going to war
Go stiddy by jerks, like the Paddy
    went to heaven
Hang on like death to a sick nigger
Jump around like a flea in a mitten
Look as if you had limburger
    cheese on your upper lip

Looks as though the devil had had
    a vendue (auction) and hadn't
    half sold out
Look as though a fly would slip up
    on you
Laugh as though you'd swallowed
    a feather-duster
Lie like a rug
Look like a jug-handle, all on one
    side
Look like a singed cat (who is
    better than he looks)
Make more noise than a boatload
    of calves (on the Hudson)
Mill around like a herd of cows
Say something plunk and plain
Shiver like a dog on a briar
Stick like death to a nigger
Surround them like Paddy did the
    seven Injins
Walk like a furrow-hopper
Watch like a hawk
Work like a lamb's tail in the dark

Occasionally the proverb is built on a noun:

Belly like a poisoned pup
Disposition like a cross-cut saw
Disposition like a rotten egg
Drag like a mop (a gait)

Eyes like burnt holes in a blanket
Face long enough to eat oats out
    of a churn
Gait like a pair of bars

Mouth that runs like a whip-poor-   More neck (impudence) than a
    Will's tail   canal-hoss
Neck like the great Atlantic cable

The use of humorous and vigorous *metaphor* is common. My colleague Dr. Adam Walker tells of an expression current in St. Lawrence County in his boyhood. Neighbors assisted turn-about in harvesting and usually went home for the evening meal, but one member of a community largely made up of Scots always stayed, defending himself with the remark, "Where I scratch, there I peck". Some idea of the range of such metaphorical proverbs can be gained from the following samples:

He's climbing Fool's Hill in a hurry: (showing the erratic conduct of an
    adolescent).
He's sick abed on two chairs with his feet in the woodbox: (not seriously
    ill; sometimes means shamming illness).

One is deep in the mud as the other in the mire.
Your eyes are too near your bladder: (usually said to a tearful child).
That buttonhole would suck eggs: (it gapes, ill made).
He wasn't behind the door when feet were handed out (got his share,
    has big feet).
He's breeding a scab on his nose: (looking for an argument).
Body, boots, and britches: (the whole thing).
He's throwing his hat over the windmill: (making a wild attempt).
He's a woodpile relation: (kindred is pretty well mixed up).
He's a backyard relation: (their cat came over into our yard once).
We are swinging on the same gate: (agreeing).
He's sawing it off: (snoring).
That's teroo's hair and turtle's quills: (short, dry, poor grass).
I'm waiting for the cork to bob: (something to turn up).
He's poor potatoes and few in a hill.
Don't stir up a hurrah's nest over it: (like mare's nest).
Let's see what kind of trees it takes to make shingles: (make a plan).
He's hung the fiddle at the door: (merry without, morose within).
My stomach thinks my throat is cut.

You can never tell from where you sit
Just where the balcony's going to spit.

He's the knot out of a knothole, the scum offa nothin'.

Many of our descriptive phrases show the American fondness for *exaggeration*:

That horse is old enough to have been born in Adam's stable.

If he fell into a well, he'd come up with a gold watch and chain.

It rained so hard that the water stood ten feet out of the well.

It was so dry that fishes kicked up an awful dust getting upstream.

I'm so hungry my tongue has slivers in it from dragging on the floor.

Don't make me mad, or I'll jump down your throat and swing on your tonsils. (probably recent)

You're so low you'd have to stand on stilts to scratch a snake's back; or, You can chin yourself on a curb; or, You can walk under a snake's belly with a high hat on.

If that isn't so, I'll eat the greaser. (The salt pork used to grease the pancake-griddle.)

She's so nosy she can hear the grass grow.

I could eat a horse and chase its rider.

He's melting away to a ton; or, small compared to a barn; or, falling away to a cartload.

I'll hit you so hard you'll starve to death bouncing.

I'm so busy I wouldn't have time to curse a cat without getting a mouthful of fur.

All the way from hell to breakfast; or, hell to Harlem.

He's scared skinny.

He's so feeble he couldn't pull the shad off a gridiron.

I've been looking all over God's creation and a part of Pond Gut (local name of a lake in Dutchess County).

I'm so poor that if steamboats were selling at ten cents apiece, I couldn't buy a gangplank.

He doesn't know B from bull's foot.

I wouldn't trust him any farther than I can throw the meetin'-house, or, a bull by the tail.

I'm just walking around to save funeral expenses.

She could talk a tin ear on a brass pot.

He's tearing the airth right out of the ground.

He's so thin he has to stand twice in the same place to make a good shadow.

I wouldn't trust him to carry meat to a bear and bring the plate back.

Occasionally but seldom we use phrases that are examples of *euphemism* or even *understatement*. Instead of saying you are ready to die or commit suicide, you say that you are "ready to make a hole in the river". Instead of saying a man is an habitual drinker, you say that he has "fourteen drops every fifteen minutes". If his conduct is indecorous, you observe that he has been "smelling of the bar-cloth", though this phrase is sometimes used by practiced drinkers in scorn for the inexperienced.

There are *retorts* and *proverbs for special occasions*. If someone asks where you are going, the retort is, "Going to random—want to come along?" If asked what you are doing, you may say, "Peeling pertaters with a buzz-saw", or, "Making a handle to a hen's nest". (Both of these examples are from Dutchess County, where, if a man acts angry, you say to him, "Jump up and bite, and see what you'll hang to".) Other examples of these tart phrases for various special occasions are:

Pigs *may* whistle, but they have an ill mouth for it. (An expression of doubt over another's ability.)

I'd hate to be hanging since she was forty.

You'd take a worm from a blind hen's mouth.

It's just gone down the street with a shawl on its head; or, It's down cellar in a teacup. (When you are asked where something is.)

What's your hurry? You didn't come for fire, did you? (Goes back to the days before matches, when children might be sent to a neighboring house for fire.—Chenango County.)

Thanks killed a cat. (When someone thanks without paying. This refers to a story of a good-natured and unpaid miller's retort when asked where his cat was.)

Was it with his teeth he bit you? (When you hear a tall tale.)

What a long tail our cat has! (When someone boasts, especially about his family.)

God speed scut! (When you are glad to see something or someone go.—Irish.)

As I was saying when the hearse came around the corner. (After an interruption, usually by way of rebuke.)

Did you know Dan Crandall's dead? (Example of a local reference. When anyone in Greenwich tells stale news, this phrase is used. Mr. Crandall has been dead a long time.)

There'll be more than one kind of hair on the floor. (A threat to a belligerent person.)

Next week at two o'clock. (Indefinite time given in tart reply.)

Who is he? Joe Tweetman from Pea-leg Point.
Honest men are all in bed, and rogues are on the way.
We hear ducks from Jersey. (Expression of disbelief.)
Castles are falling, dunghills are rising.
You look like ten cents worth of God-help-us.
Hell's tapped with a two-inch augur and no pitcher ready.
There's a puff for Mitchell! (Boastful prize-fighter defeated by John
    L. Sullivan.)

When you buy the land, you buy the stones;
When you buy the meat, you buy the bones. (Retort of an itinerant
    butcher in Oneida County.)

Fine weather for young ducks and stage drivers. (Retort when some-
    body calls a rainy day fine weather.)
You can't teach your granny to lap 'lasses.
A dog of my age would be no pup. (To avoid telling your age.)

Not all proverbial sayings of this sort are tart. In old-fashioned
apology you may avoid the banal reference to pot-luck by saying,
"You'll have to take monkey-fare today—catch as catch can"; or, more
poetically, "Welcome is the best dish on the table". If anyone has
the misfortune to eructate at the table (or elsewhere), there is an
old proverb that turns off the accident with a smile, "An empty house
is better than a bad tenant". If one trouble follows another, you
say, "Get up, Jack, and let Jim sit down".

There is a special type of proverb, usually for an occasion, called
the Wellerism, because it involves a comparison such as Mr. Sam
Weller of *Pickwick Papers* used to enjoy making. You remember?—
" 'Fine weather for them as is well wropped up,' as the polar bear
said while he was a-trying of his skates." That is a sample of Sam's
efforts. The favorite Wellerism in York State undoubtedly is, " 'Every
man to his taste,' as the Irishman said when he kissed the cow"—there
are several variants. Here are other Wellerisms:

"Neat but not gaudy," as the devil said when he painted his tail green.
"I'll take your part," as the dog said when he stole the cat's dinner.
"What next?" as the toad said when his tail dropped off.
"O Lord, how you made me jump!" as the grasshopper said when he was
    created.

"Well, well!" as the monkey said when he came up in the bucket.

"Great cry and little wool," quoth the devil when he sheared his hogs.

"Mair whistle than woo'," quo' the souter (cobbler) when he sheared the sow. (Scotch form)

"The young girls are crazy," as the old woman said when she jumped over the straw.

"That's neither here nor there," as the steeplejack said when his foot slipped.

"This is the end of my tale (tail)," as the monkey said when he backed into the lawn-mower.

"I go through my work," said the needle to the boy. "But not till you are hard pressed," said the idle boy to the needle.

This last example shows a shading off into another form: the quotation of some witty remark which is less retort than proverbial wisdom or simplicity—such as two which Miss Nettie Sessions collected in Oneida County:

The old woman said: "Zigzagg goes the scythe and down falls the grass, but knitting strains every bone in my body." (In other words, a man's work is easier than a woman's.)

The old woman said: "I know my boys didn't drink anything when they went out last night, because they were so dry in the morning." (The ungodly will explain.)

Part of the fun of collecting proverbs arrives when you *cannot* explain a phrase or word. For example, in Oneida County they say, "In spite of hell and Dr. Foster". I am not quite content with Miss Nelle Schmidt's learned explanation that Dr. Foster may be Dr. Faustus, who sold his soul to the devil. Then there is the phrase, "As crazy as Dick's hatband". If you inquire about its meaning, you will be told that "it went nine time around and stopped in the middle", or that "it went half-way round and then tied in a bow-knot". But who was Dick? Was he only a humorous shade, *nominis umbra,* or was he a real person? Some folklorists think that he was Richard Cromwell, the ineffectual son of the great Lord Protector, Oliver Cromwell. I am not so well satisfied with that explanation as with one concerning the expression, "We'll have potatoes and pints". Miss Schmidt has heard that in Ireland the people were sometimes so destitute that they had nothing to eat but potatoes. If they managed to get a little piece of pork, they would suspend it over the center of the table, or set it in a dish, and then they would *pint* their potatoes at it instead of eating it. The explanation is at least as amusing as the proverb.

Perhaps some upstater who knows horses could explain an old rhyme for which I have never heard any explanation whatever:

> One white foot, buy him;
> Two white feet, try him;
> Three white feet, deny him;
> Four white feet and a white nose—
> Take off his hide and feed him to the crows.

One other proverb about the critters remains a puzzle to me. I can understand that a love for alliteration might explain a phrase such as "odder than Job's off-ox", but what is the sense of "homelier than God's off-ox"? Presumably, if there is any difference in oxen, the off-ox is the stronger and more reliable of the pair—you drive oxen from the left (nigh) side. Perhaps we need a special commission to explain some of our proverbs from a farmer's point of view; certainly most of these old saws are the creation of an agricultural people.

Now and again you come upon puzzling *single words* in proverbs. For example, there is a phrase from Otsego County which uses a word that could be explained at Oxford: "If he doesn't do right, give him *gowdy*." Presumably this is the English word *gaudy*, derived from Latin *gaudium* (joy); a *gaudy*, says the *Oxford Concise Dictionary*, is "a grand entertainment, especially annual college dinner to old members". It is not so easy to explain a word used in Erie county to mean wasting time by puttering, *feustering*. Of course, every section has its own expressions, not necessarily proverbs. The word *strainy*, meaning difficult to converse with, I have only from Ontario County, in the Honeoye Valley, where farmers say *in good rig*, when they mean that an animal is in good condition; *pretty good hickory* when they mean at good speed ("He came down the road pretty good hickory"); and *out of fix* when they mean *impatient, angry*. In the South Bay region of Long Island, killing a bird that your hunting companion has missed is called *wiping the eye*. There are even phrases and words whose use seems to be limited to a single family; for example, in one Orange County household a spanking has the euphemistic name of a *spanking tea*, and if the evening meal is to be omitted on Sunday, the mother says, "We'll have *skip* for supper". And there is the grandmother who says scornfully, if someone makes a good cake with poor icing, "That is putting the beggar on the gentleman". Doubtless that last phrase has been in the family for a long time, just as the Coffin family of Dutchess County has retained through a century and a half the words and proverbs of the whaling days on Nantucket. (See the chapter on the Whalers.)

I might double the length of this chapter by quoting proverbs collected from Jewish, Russian, German, Dutch, Bulgarian, Polish, Italian, and other stocks which have been transplanted rather recently to York State, but that must wait for another book. What I have done is to suggest the wisdom and poetry of that Yankee-Irish-Scottish tradition which inspires all our culture. Its humorous tang has been emphasized, perhaps at the expense of its occasional tug at our softer emotions. To me there is more than humor in the proverbial question of our inland lakes, "What shall we do—or go fishing?" I do not know when I heard first an old Scottish proverb which creates for me in five words a tenderness and a hope. What the proverb is saying is simple if taken literally: we all come home at evening; but it hints at that reconciliation and that compassionate humanity which it is so hard to achieve in youth and so precious to attain in age: "The e'ening brings a'hame."

When I think of our proverbs, I like to recall a Yorker who recently went home in the late e'ening, the truly Honorable Elihu Root. Great and patient statesman as he was, he loved the ways and speech of his Yankee ancestors; he strengthened his spirit in the hills of Oneida County under ancient trees that frame an old gray college. When others were so in haste to recast the world that they despaired of civilization, he would quote a saw which he had learned in Clinton when a boy and kept as the motto of his life: "Leg over leg, the dog went to Dover." With the help of our proverbs we may yet get to Dover.

XX: *Appendix: Who Told You?*

BEFORE I try to answer that question, let me make some suggestions for more fun. You like maps, or you will. The State Historian, Dr. Flick, and P. M. Paine have a map of the History of New York State with canals, trails, turnpikes, and other matters of interest clearly indicated. About the best of the pictorial maps is one called *Indian Episodes of New York*, the material compiled by A. C. Parker and Mrs. W. Henricks and published by the Rochester Museum, of which Mr. Parker is the Director—he is also the most distinguished scholar on the affairs of the Iroquois. An interesting booklet goes with this map. There is a series of "Romance Maps" of different sections of the State, the first being of the Niagara Frontier, the material compiled by Mrs. J. W. Wickser. Others include maps of the Northern Gateway (C. Eleanor Hall, Port Henry); of the North Country (James G. Riggs, Oswego); with a separate explanatory sheet; of the Hudson River Valley (Marguerite H. Parrish); and of the Finger Lakes Region (Mrs. Walter Henricks and Sidney E. Ayres, Penn Yan). These maps can all be obtained at the State Historical Museums in Ticonderoga and Cooperstown.

We are proud of the ten-volume History recently brought to completion (1937) under the editorship of Dr. A. C. Flick. An older History of the State edited by Dr. James Sullivan still is useful for its brief histories of each county. A beautifully illustrated volume and—whether you are a farmer or not—a most entertaining book is Dr. U. P. Hedrick's *A History of Agriculture in the State of New York*, 1933; it has chapters on such subjects as Turnpikes, Country Life a Hundred Years Ago, Waterways, Railways, and Country Food and Drink. It tells what sort of people inhabited New York State in the times whose folklore I have collected. The best literary trip around the State is *Pathway of Empire*, 1935, by Edward Hungerford, Vice President of the N. Y. Central R. R. This introduces you to localities in logical fashion, as I wished to do and found impossible under the final plan. It is one of the best geographies I know, but it is a good deal beside. You don't need to be told about Carl Carmer's books; they tie up our past with our present, and they are written with high spirits.

If you are looking for other American folksongs, I recommend three collections: Sandburg, Carl, *The American Songbag*, 1927, with tunes and accompaniments; Lomax, John A. and Alan, *American Ballads and Folk Songs*, 1934, with tunes; Pound, Louise, *American Ballads and Songs*, 1922, a smaller collection, without music. For the Lomax book I furnished a Bibliography of nine pages, and I am preparing a similar list for another Lomax volume soon to appear.

There should be an annotated list of New York's county histories. Under my direction a number of dissertations on the folklore of individual counties have been written. Of these I have used oftenest for the present book the following: Margaret T. Flanagan on Allegany County, State College, 1939; Lou Ella E. Gridley on Chenango County, State College, 1938; Winifred C. Maloney on Erie County chiefly, Cornell, 1939; Janice C. Neal on Otsego County, State College, 1938; Ruth A. Sickles on Columbia County, State College, 1938. I hope that ultimately each county will have been explored with equal thoroughness; I have some material from each of the sixty-two counties. I shall be glad to suggest topics and bibliographies to any groups or individuals who will undertake collecting New York folklore which is likely to prove of value.

Among the many librarians who made my researches pleasant I should like to mention with special gratitude Dr. Shearer of the Grosvenor Library at Buffalo, and Miss Jacobsen and Miss Lyon of the State Library at Albany.

In the weary task of tabulation, revision and correction I have received assistance from several people, among whom I mention with special gratitude Mrs. Agnes Underwood, who has filed and indexed my collection, and Professor A. M. Drummond of Cornell, whose encouragement of the folk-drama in the State seems to me of great importance. In spite of all that I can do, assisted by many friends, there are probably errors in the summaries which follow. The acknowledgments are as detailed as space will allow. Whatever their faults of omission may be, they will at least furnish the beginning of a bibliography which will lead to a fuller enjoyment of the American past and, I hope, a new confidence in what Burke called "the unbought grace of life".

Chapter I. Preliminary Chirk

Stories about the Risley shawl and the Sprague piano retold with permission of Miss Ellen E. Adams, from her *Tales of Early Fredonia*, 1931.

Chapter II. Pirates

For the facts about Captain Kidd see Brooks, G. (ed.), *Trial of Captain Kidd*, 1930; Seitz, D. C., *The Tryal of Captain William Kidd*, 1936; Jameson, J. F., *Privateering and Piracy in the Colonial Period: Illustrative Documents*, 1923; Monoghan, F., "An Examination of the Reputation of Captain Kidd", in *N. Y. History*, XIV, 250 ff. (1933). The interpretation of Kidd as an injured man will be found in such works as Paine, R. D., *Book of Buried Treasure*, 1911; Dalton, C., *The Real Captain Kidd*, 1911; Milligan, C., *Captain William Kidd, Gentleman or Buccaneer?* 1932. Standard works on piracy are P. Gosse's *The Pirates' Who's Who*, 1924, and *The History of Piracy*, 1932. For piracy on Long Island see Overton, J., *Long Island's Story*, 1929, Chapter IV. For the episode at Gardiner's Island see Gardiner, J. T., *The Gardiners of Gardiner's Island*, 1927.

Ballads: *Captain Kidd*, from *The Forget Me Not Songster*, n.d., c. 1848; *Captain Ward* and *The Bold Pirates*, from the Douglass MS.; *Elder Bardee*, from P. W. Andrew, Corinth; *The Flying Cloud*, from Hugh Norton, from Frank Van Vranken, Gloversville; *The Brave Lafitte*, from an anonymous songster found by Constance McCoy at her grandmother's, Spencertown; *Three Pirates Came to London Town*, from Nelle A. Schmidt, Utica.

Tales: Marion Snedecor, Bayport, information about buried treasure from Commodore L. R. Hand, Riverhead; story of the treasure-map, from her uncle; account of the divining rod from Shaw, E. R., *Legends of Fire Island and the South Shore*, 1895.

Chapter III. Injun-Fighters

Indian atrocities: The story of Boyd and the Torture-Tree will be found in Seaver, J. E., *A Narrative of the Life of Mrs. Mary Jemison*, 1824, which had a 22nd ed. in 1925; also in Wilkinson, J. B., *The Annals of Binghamton*, 1872; in Stone, W. L., *Life of Joseph Brant*, 1838, vol. II; Turner, O., *Pioneer History of the Holland Purchase of Western*

New York, 1849. For St. Isaac Jogues see Birch, J. J., *The Saint of the Wilderness*, 1936. Regarding rewards for scalps see O'Callaghan, E. B., *Docs. Relating to the Colonial Hist. of N. Y.*, vols. VI and VII (1855).

Tom Quick: Quinlan, J. E., *Life and Adventures of Tom Quick, Indian Slayer*, 1852, reprinted in 1891, and *History of Sullivan County*, 1873; Smith, P. H., *Legends of the Shawangunk*, 1887; Crumb, F. W., *Tom Quick, Early American*, 1936, which has a short bibliography; Allerton, J. M., *Hawk's Nest*, 1892, historical romance in which Tom appears.

Tim Murphy: The chief early source is an anonymous *Life and Adventures of Timothy Murphy*, 1839, 1863, 1912, written by a law student named Sigsby. See also Simms, J. R., *History of Schoharie County, and Border Wars of New York*, 1845; Stone, W. L., *Ballads and Poems Relating to the Burgoyne Campaign*, 1893; Gardner, E. E., *Folklore from the Schoharie Hills, New York*, 1937. Three stories from Dean M. G. Nelson, State College, Albany; account of the legendary first wife's murder from Mrs. E. Ribley, who got the story in Stamford; other tales from students include those in the Neal dissertation.

Nat Foster: The two principal sources are Simms, J. R., *Trappers of New York*, 1850, 1935, and Byron-Curtiss, A. L., *The Life and Adventures of Nat Foster*, 1897.

Nick Stoner: Simms, J. R., *Trappers of New York*, 1850, 1935; a paper by C. Durey printed in the souvenir program prepared for the dedication of the Stoner monument at Caroga Park on August 21, 1929; novel by R. W. Chambers, *The Little Red Foot*, 1921, not used for my account.

CHAPTER IV. SONS OF ROBIN HOOD

Claudius Smith: Ruttenber, E. M., and Clark, L. H., *History of Orange County*, 1881; Stickney, C. E., *A History of the Minisink Region*, 1867, Chapt. XIV; Quinlan, J. E., *History of Sullivan County*, 1873; Green, F. B., *The History of Rockland County*, 1886; Eager, S. W., *An Outline History of Orange County*, 1846-7; stories collected in Orange County by Clarice L. Fitch, Evelyn R. O'Brien, and Marjorie Crist (who heard the "Shoot and be damned" story).

The Loomis Gang: Mr. George W. Walter of Utica has generously gone through my account, making corrections and additions. Mr. Thomas L. Hall of Hamilton, Historian of Madison County, furnished valuable aid through a student, Miss Helen Finen. Mr. Dapson's article will be found in *New York History* for July, 1938. The earliest newspaper account seems to be that in the New York *Weekly Sun* for May 21, 1879, by Amos Cummings; this was followed in June of the same year by stories in the *Cazenovia Republican*, reprinted by the *Hamilton Republican*, Nov. 14, 1929-Jan. 23, 1930.

The Prison Association's report will be found in the *Twentieth Annual Report* of its executive committee, transmitted to the Legislature on February 2, 1865; there is a copy in the State Law Library. The same report says: "102 indictments were found in the county of Albany; of these only 11 were tried and five convicted; 20 confessed their guilt; the remainder of the persons indicted were allowed to go out on bail. One hundred and three bail bonds were estreated, amounting to $30,000; but not a dollar of this amount has been collected; nor, indeed, has an item of forfeited bail been paid into the county treasury in ten years."

Helen Finen had from Mr. Hall the account of Grove's hunting, of Wash at the tavern, of the neighbor and her cows, of the kidnapped child, of Plum and the *know*. From her grandfather she had the story of the horse sold to its owner. From Erasmus Throop she had the story of the girl dressed as Wash, of the horse that recognized his master and whinnied, of the neighbor who lent money to Plum, one version of the killing of Wash (corrected by comparison with versions from Messrs. Hall and Walter), the stories of hanging Plum by his thumbs and the hanging of Grove by the neck.

Caroline Bishopp had from Charles Watson of Clinton stories of the "Wagert" horse, of the Muffs, of the exchanged shoes, and of the methods of disguising horses; from her grand-uncle, Hubert Root of Deansboro, the story of the counterfeit money and the boots. Adelaide Schmid got the story of the bees from a Mrs. Brown of Camden whose father-in-law had a bee-farm near Woodstock; from W. P. Doyle of Rome she got the story of his grandfather's warning to Wash and its consequences.

Kathleen Kenny had from John J. Bennett of Utica, formerly a next-door neighbor to Plum, the stories of alleged shoplifting, of brothers exchanging shoes, of the turkey eggs, of the hired man tried at Deansboro, of the "planted" watch, of the confederate sent to try his friendship, and of the horses blinded by smoke.

From Clarice Fitch comes the letter from her grandfather, Charles Fitch, formerly of Brookfield, now of Manhasset. From Prof. R. G. Scholes of Middlebury comes the information about his grandfather meeting "the one with the crooked neck" in Canada. From Mrs. Marjorie Loomis—whose husband is not related to the gang—comes the story about how Plum tightened his neck-muscles.

I have numerous variants of the tales given, and a considerable number of other stories. There have been other famous gangs; see, for example, Charles Brutcher's *Joshua: A Man of the Finger Lake Region*, 1927, about the so-called "Rockwell gang".

CHAPTER V. UNCANNY CRITTERS

For Indian stories of the supernatural see Cornplanter, Jesse, *Legends of the Longhouse*, Lippincott, 1938. The author lives on the Tonawanda Reservation and is deeply learned in the lore of the Senecas. The tale of Manaho I had from Ruth Bedell, who learned it from Roy B. Kelley, who was told it by his grandfather in Schenevus; in other versions this is one of the well known stories of lovers' leaps. The tale of Nawisga was collected by Ruth C. Wright of Schenectady from "Old Norm". The legend of Diamond Rock was brought by M. E. Stoddard, who had it from Raymond Robinson of Lansingburg, who guides in the Raquette region.

Witches: For the attitude of the Dutch toward witchcraft see Howland, A. C. (ed.) *Material Toward a History of Witchcraft Collected by H. C. Lea*, III, 1217 (1939). The tale of Baas will be found in an anonymous article in *Harper's New Monthly Magazine* for 1880, p. 532. Witch Kanniff: Green, F. B., *The History of Rockland County*, 1886. Ludlowville witch: Article by M. C. Townley in Ithaca *Democrat*, May 5, 1904. The Halls: O'Callaghan, E. B., *Doc. Hist. of State of N. Y.*, IV, 133-8 (1851). Goody Garlick: Taylor, J. M., *The Witchcraft Delusion in Colonial Connecticut*, 1908; Gardiner, D., *Chronicles of the Town of East Hampton*, 1871. Harrison: Taylor, also Riddell, W. R., "Witchcraft in Old New York", in *Journal Am. Inst. Criminal Law and Criminology*, XIX, 252 (1928-9). Riddell cites the cases of Aquandero and Buckinjehillish. Aunty Greenleaf: Marion Snedecor from Mortimer Corwin, formerly of Bellport; see also Wilson, R. R., *Historic Long Island*, 1902. The Stamford cats: Mrs. E. Ribley from Mrs. Daisy Willis, Stamford. Rensselaer County witch: Dolores Leffler of Rensselaer, from her father; her great-grandfather lived in Steam Mill near Berlin. Mohawk Valley witches: M. Wetterau of Fort Plain. Recipe for making witch: Ruth C. Wright, Schenectady. The Thomas witch: Margaret Mattison, Fort Ann.

The devil: On Long Island: Overton, J., *Long Island's Story*, 1929; Furman, G., *Antiquities of Long Island*, 1875. In Rensselaer County card-game, from A. C. Knapp, Albany; in Columbia County, from Ruth

A. Sickles, from Major A. Callan, Valatie; in Gloversville, from Hugh Norton.

Curses: The Troy monster, from Mary A. C. Halpin. The Cattaraugus claws, from Maloney thesis, from a Mr. Schultz of the County—name of place withheld. The French mendicant, Aurore Granger, Cohoes, from French-Canadian grandparents.

Loup-garou and chasse-galerie: Pearl Hamelin of Utica, whose family comes from Clinton County, neighborhood of Mooers. See also Beaugrand, M., *La Chasse-Galerie*, 1900.

Washington Irving's lore: Pochmann, H. A., "Irving's German Sources in *The Sketch Book*", in *Studies in Philology*, XXVII, 477 (1930); Sprenger, R., *Über die Quelle von Washington Irvings Rip Van Winkle*, Northeim, 1901; Beatty, E. F., *Washington Irving and the Sources of the Hudson River Legends*, Columbia University, unpublished Master's dissertation, 1923.

Ghosts: C. F. Wilde, *Ghost Legends of the Hudson Valley*, N. Y. State College, unpublished Master's dissertation, 1937; some of it has appeared in newspapers. His version of the legend of Forbes Manor he had from Kenneth McFarland of Rensselaer. Ruth Bedell's study of the Horseman of Leeds led her to the belief that the best versions are to be found in Mrs. J. Van V. Vedder's *Historic Catskill*, 1922, and R. L. De Lisser's *Picturesque Catskills*, 1894. For the Cooperstown ghost see Cooper, J. F., *The Legends and Traditions of a Northern County*, 1920, 1921, 1936; in the section called *Ghosts—Ours and Others* are to be found some of the best ghost-stories of the State.

Chapter VI. Heroes of Tall Tales

This is the chapter on which I have left the scaffolding; therefore some notes may be omitted.

Paul Bunyan: Agnes S. Holsapple lives in Albany; Mrs. Burke lives in Slingerlands. John Darling: Mildred M. Tyler of Cochecton Center made that village her headquarters when collecting. Mr. Lieb's editorial is dated March 21, 1935. The Greenfields: Janet Lewis was assisted in her search by Frank Hardmyer and Joseph Ouellette. Margaret Mattison of Fort Ann had information from E. P. Murray of Great Meadow.

Cap'n Tuthill of Sayville told his stories to Marion Snedecor and Ruth Freeman. Aunt Kitty's story: told to Ann B. Service. Mr. Merrihew's tale: told to Betty Hayford. Myndert Crounse had his story from his mother. Whispering Somes: Josephine Cypher from Mrs. B. F. Sharpe, the historian of Greenwich. Essex County miser: E. E. Cutting from Clarence Cutting, Elizabethtown. Big John Kingston: Ray Belanger of Schenectady, formerly of St. Lawrence County. Oneida County cat: Caroline Bishopp from Hubert Root, Deansboro. Cornelius Cole: D. Nelson, from Ben and Ward White, Frewsburg; Cole lived near that town and told the stories on himself. The Meacham cheese: Johnson, C., *History of Oswego County*, 1877; see also Landon, H. F., *The North Country*, 1932.

Chapter VII. Tricksters and Retorts

Hoss-traders: For David Harum and the Cardiff Giant see Wolner, L. J., *Literary Sketches of the Village of Homer*, State College Master's dissertation, 1936, some of it published in newspapers; also Vance, A. T., *The Real David Harum*, which I did not use. Bailey: B. Hayford from Ernest Griffin, Tarrytown. Deacon Turner: Harriet Harkness from Mrs. C. Colwell, now of Cato. Father Spencer: Johnson, C., *Centennial History of Erie County*, 1876. Otsego County Quaker: Janice Neal from Anna Manning, Oneonta. *Napoleon*, from the Ford family, Slingerlands. *Ballad of the Deacon's Ox:* Hugh Norton, from Frank Van Vranken, Gloversville. Schoharie County trader: B. Hayford from Mrs. Emma Houck, Slingerlands.

Tales of roads and turnpikes: Doc Higby: Eager, S. W., *An Outline Hist. of Orange County*, 1846-7. Oneida County Tolls: Caroline Bishopp, Clinton, from C. C. Bishopp. Judge Sterling: Abdy, E. S., *Journal of a . . . Tour in the U. S.*, I, 265 (1835); the incident was recorded in 1833. Chenango County tolls: L. E. E. Gridley, from R. and H. H. Lyon, Bainbridge.

The Kennebec Bite: Douglas MS. Wit Cook: from Thomas G. Cook, Ticonderoga. Sophronie: M. M. Pappa, from Mrs. Francis Burns, formerly of Watertown. Chenango County miller: Gridley thesis, from Mrs. Jasper Cheney and her father, Norwich-Whitestone Road.

Lawyers: Counsellor Root: Ketcham, W., *Hist. of Buffalo*, vol. II, 1864-5, and Johnson, C., *Centennial Hist. of Erie County*, 1876, both indebted to an address by H. W. Rogers on *Wits of the Buffalo Bar*. Justice Thompson: Gridley thesis, from J. H. Turner, Norwich. Justice in Erie County: Johnson, op. cit. Columbia County: Sickles thesis, from Bradbury, A. R., *A Hist. of the City of Hudson*, 1908. Rasters Hopkins: Neal thesis, from Mrs. V. Johnson, Edmeston. Chautauqua County:

Dow, C. M., *The Lawyers and Petifoggers of Chaut. County,* an address, a copy in the Mayville Museum. Schoharie Court: Deming, P., *Tompkins and Other Folks,* 1885.

Churches: Sessions: from Nettie L. Sessions of Whitesboro. Sarah Wells: Eager, S. W., *An Outline Hist. of Orange County,* 1846-7. Goodwill Church: Moffat, A. S., *Orange County,* 1928, from a letter of Wm. Graham, formerly of Montgomery, previously contributed to the *Westminster Bulletin.* Charlie of Roseboom: Neal thesis, from F. E. Neal, Oneonta. Sharpe (name changed): Neal thesis, from A. G. Shaw, Oneonta. Quaker's balky horse: Neal thesis, from Anna Manning, Oneonta. Delaware County members: H. Harkness from her father, formerly of Kortright Center. Spraker: scrapbook of Miss C. F. Dewey, Batavia. Westchester County minister: B. Hayford, from E. Griffin, Tarrytown. Jakway: H. Harkness, from Hugh Hunter, Cato.

Wars: Aunt Sally Gee: from E. R. O'Brien, Cornwall, also Eager, S. W., *Hist. of Orange County,* 1846-7. Goodwife Osborne: Marion Snedecor, Bayport; Halsey, W. D., *Sketches from Local History,* 1935, for further information. George Washington: B. Hayford from E. Griffin, Tarrytown; letter owned by Miss Van Courtland, Croton. War of 1812: C. P. Turner, *The Pioneer Period of Western New York,* 188-. Red Jacket and the Colonel, and story of muddy road: Johnson, C. *Cent. Hist. of Erie County,* 1876. Orleans County: J. B. Achilles, Albion; on banks, *Orleans American and Weekly News,* Oct. 7, 1937.

Lovers: Westchester County: B. Hayford from E. Griffin, Tarrytown. Warwick girl: E. O'Brien, Cornwall; also Eager, S. W., *An Outline Hist. of Orange County,* 1846-7. Oneonta husband: Eliz. A. Mahon. Downsville husband: Lois C. Odwell. Horicon widow: Thos. G. Cook, Ticonderoga.

Indians: Weiser: biography by C. Z. Weiser, 2nd ed., 1897. Ellicott: Johnson, C., op. cit. General Lincoln: *The Christian Almanac for the Western District,* 1830. Onondaga chief: Clark, J. V. H., *Onondaga,* vol. I, 1849. The Brants: Stone, W. L., *Life of J. Brant,* 1838,—I, 387 and II, 496. Rochester millyard and Capt. Pratt, Johnson, C., op. cit. King Tandy, and the Indian woman's retort: Beth Ford, from W. J. Wheeler, Little Valley, and Mrs. J. Champlin, Salamanca.

CHAPTER VIII. WHALERS

I am specially indebted to Mrs. J. E. Rattray and her father, Captain E. J. Edwards, both of East Hampton, not only for permission to use

information found in their book, *Whale Off!* (1932), but also for correct-
ing the manuscript of this chapter. While Captain Edwards explained
things to me, he stood in the very boat in which he had killed whales
with his father, the late Captain Joshua, and his uncle, Captain Gabe
Edwards. Mrs. Rattray has two other books with sections about whaling:
Three Centuries in East Hampton, 1937, and *Montauk*, 1938.

The best place to see relics of Long Island whaling is in the museum at
Sag Harbor. Miss Sally E. Logan of that town collected material for me,
including songs, *Sally Brown* and *Come, all ye bold seamen*; she also
interviewed Captain Gabe at Amagansett.

In East Hampton you will find the remarkable collection of books,
articles, and manuscripts about Long Island presented to the village
library by Mr. and Mrs. Morton Pennypacker, who gave me valuable
material and advice. I used there the logs of the *Nimrod*, *Timor*, and
Tuscarora; the story of the *Octavia* I found in an article by H. L. Osborn,
printed in the Sag Harbor *Express* for July 30, 1903. The Collection has
a wealth of all sorts of material except whaling songs.

Marion Snedecor got *The Sailors' Alphabet* and *'Round Cape Horn*
from Mr. Mortimer Corwin of Albany, formerly of Bellport; the second
of these has often been printed. The Log of the *Caleb Eaton* I am permitted to use through the courtesy of Mrs. Flora White and Edith Cutting of Elizabethtown. The information about whaling from Hudson is
borrowed from the Sickles dissertation on Columbia County; see also
Miller, S. B., *Historical Sketches of Hudson*, 1862, and Ellis, P., *History
of Columbia County*, 1878, and Carmer, C., *The Hudson*, 1939. The
expressions of the Coffin family are from Doris Coffin of Stanfordville.

For other accounts of Long Island whaling see: Sleight, H. D., *The
Whale Fishery on Long Island*, 1931; Overton, J., *Long Island's Story*,
1929; Halsey, W. D., *Sketches from Local History*, 1935; Harris, J. A.,
The Whaling Vessels and Whaling Industry of Cold Spring Harbor,
[1914]; Adams, J. T., *History of the Town of Southampton*, Chapt. XI,
1918; Andrews, R. C., *Whale Hunting with Gun and Camera*, Chapt.
XXI, 1916. Dr. E. P. Hohman's *The American Whaleman*, 1928, is a
scholarly work stressing economic factors.

I still hope to get many more songs. Meanwhile I recommend J. Colcord's *Song of American Sailormen*, 1938, and A. H. Verrill's *The Real
Story of the Whaler*, 1916, Chapter VIII.

CHAPTER IX. PLAIN SAILORS

Blind Sam Taylor lived for many years at Westfield and died on the Chautauqua County Farm in May, 1937. I describe as one *two* visits which I paid him in September, 1935. His word raynick may be the Boer *rooinek*, red-neck, which, I have been told, was first used in South Africa in disparagement of British troops. The *Albion* was wrecked on April 22, 1822.

Other songs: *As I Was A-Walking* and *Blow, Boys, Blow*, from Eleanor Cleland, Mannsville, now of Scotia. *Handsome Harry* and *The Ghost of Polly Rock*: Constance McCoy, from an old songster whose title-page and cover are lost. *Green Beds;* first version from Ruth M. Tanner, Gloversville, from her mother, who learned it from *her* mother; second version from James Mack, Clyde. *The Sailor Boy:* Josephine Cypher, Greenwich, from her grandmother, who learned it from *her* mother; the first line is supplied from the version of P. W. Andrew, Corinth. *Jack Riley:* from Ruth M. Tanner, Gloversville. *The Murmaid,* from Douglass MS. *The Sailor and His Bride:* Eleanor R. Jones, as known by Capt. Hiram Beldin of Lake Champlain, by courtesy of Mrs. Laurel Dodge, Hudson Falls. *A Yankee Ship:* from *The American Vocalist,* n.d., in the Grosvenor Library, Buffalo. For other songs of American sailors, see the volume by Miss Colcord listed under Chapter VIII.

CHAPTER X. CANAWLERS

For historical background see N. E. Whitford's *History of the Canal System of the State of New York,* 1906, and his *History of the Barge Canal of N. Y. State,* 1922. An admirable little study is F. P. Kimball's *New York—The Canal State,* 1937, which shows the value of the canal at the present time. He quotes part of *The Song of the Wolverines* from S. Farmer's *History of Detroit and Michigan,* 1884. Mention should be made of a thesis by J. Winden at the University of Wisconsin, *The Influence of the Erie Canal upon the Population Along Its Course,* 1900. Mrs. D. Bobbé's *DeWitt Clinton,* 1933, tells about the builder of the canal. The romance of the canal is best described in the stories of W. D. Edmonds: *Rome Haul,* 1929, and *Erie Water,* 1933, and *Mostly Canallers,* 1934; the last a volume of short tales.

Songs: *Paddy on the Canal:* broadside in the Grosvenor Library, Buffalo. *The Boatman's Boy:* Mrs. A. H. Shearer, Buffalo, from Mrs. Broadbeck of Tonawanda. *The Raging Canal,* from *The American*

Vocalist, 1853, in Grosvenor Library. From the collection of A. M. Walsh, Buffalo, I am permitted to use the following: *Boatin' on a Bull-Head,* from Alex. Stearns, Syracuse; *Lay Me on the Horse-Bridge,* from Capt. Jake Oatman and Capt. Wesley Thomas; *Black Rock Pork,* from Capt. W. Thomas. From a collection made at Port Byron by Lois E. Rowley come these: *Hash Is Fried* and *Canalman's Farewell* from Capt. J. Wimett; *So Pull In Your Towline,* from R. E. Ray; *Here Lies the Bones,* from Myrtle Ray. *Attend, All Ye Drivers* was sent me by Mrs. W. W. Hay of S. Glens Falls, as recited some forty years ago by Uncle Walter Rozelle, Fort Edward. *Low Bridge, Everybody Down:* by T. S. Allen, used with the permission of the publishers, the F. B. Haviland Publishing Co. *E-ri-e:* from Carl Sandburg's *American Songbag,* 1927, used with the permission of Harcourt, Brace & Co. From Lomax, John A. and Alan, *American Ballads and Folk Songs,* 1934, the songs *I've Traveled* (from D. Gillispie and "Kip" Conway), and *You Yacht on the Hudson* (from R. G. Sumners), used with permission of the Lomaxes and the Macmillan Co. *A Life on the Raging Canal:* from *The Boquet Melodist,* n.d., in Grosvenor Library. Songs of the Sidecut listed below. *Drop a Tear* from *Rome Haul* is used with the permission of Little, Brown and Co.; its first two lines are from Sandburg's *American Songbag.*

Joel Barlow's *Vision of Columbus* was published in 1787. Hubbard's description of the Irish: Wager, D. E., *Our Country and Its People,* 1896. Story of Colt: Jones, Pomroy, *Annals and Recollections of Oneida County,* 1851. Stories from Waterloo: Catherine Morgan, from her grandfather, George Denniston. Stories collected by Ruth Dillon: tales of Tommy Collins, Waterford; the fight at Mechanicville, from George Leland. Tales and songs of Cohoes: Frances Gildea, from her grandfather, once a raft-boy.

The Sidecut (Watervliet): The account of Paddy Ryan the Champion was given me by his daughter, Mrs. Nelly M. Asher of Green Island, and her son; she has a collection of newspaper clippings and a copy of the broadside ballad from which I quote. For other information about the Sidecut I am indebted to Nan Emery and Myndert Crounse, who consulted Mr. Emery in Troy and several people in Watervliet, including "Footy" Gilboy, John Mace, Leonard Mitchell, and Michael Conroy. Mr. Emery furnished the song about *The Edison Machine.* I am indebted to my friend, Mr. D. A. Tomlinson of Watervliet, who introduced me to Mrs. Asher and to Mr. Charles Dann, aged eighty-two, a respected citizen of Watervliet who assured me that the city's vice has

been grossly exaggerated. Certainly the section on Second Avenue between 23d and 25th Streets is now decent enough. The Troy *Record* for
October 26, 1935, printed an entertaining article on the gaudier side of
the old Sidecut.

Stories of Ed. Scouten and the Charley-Jack fight: from Oviatt Mc-
Connell, Buffalo newspaperman. Stories of the canal-boys: Eaton,
Deacon M., *Five Years on the Erie Canal,* 1845. The packet-boats and
passengers: Harlow, A. F., *Old Towpaths,* 1926; stories from Chapt. 32
used with kind permission of the Appleton-Century Co.; a delightful
book.

CHAPTER XI. LUMBERMEN AND RAFTERS

For historical background and some good pictures see W. F. Fox's
"History of the Lumber Industry in the State of New York", in the Sixth
Annual Report of the Forest, Fish and Game Commission, for 1900,—
published in 1901. Then there is J. E. Defebaugh's monumental *History
of the Lumber Industry of America* in 2 volumes, 2nd edition, 1906.

For acquaintance with Uncle John Nichols of Stratford, I am indebted
to Eleanor Waterbury, now Mrs. L. Franz, of Dolgeville. To Edith E.
Cutting of Elizabethtown I owe the following songs: *Lumberman's
Alphabet* (first version), from Charles and Clarence Cutting; *On Monday
Morning,* from John Cutting; *The Dance at Clintonville,* from Mrs. Etta
Brewster, Peasleyville; also for the stories of the shrunken harness, from
Clarence Cutting; the mosquitoes, from Alec Couchey; Jim (name
changed) and the phosphorus, from Leon O. Cutting. G. R. Plumb
brought me the following material from George Colon of Saranac Lake:
Lumbermen's Alphabet, second version, learned from Eddie Locklin;
Blue Mt. Lake, said to have been composed by a lumberjack named Oat
Bets; *The Lumberman's Lament,* which has twenty-eight stanzas, in
some of which Mr. Colon's father appears. The *Lumberman's Song*
which mentions Newcomb was obtained by Gertrude A. Jenks from her
grandmother, Mrs. Alice Jenks of Schroon Lake, who thinks that the
song was composed by a lumberjack about the year 1870.

Frances Studebaker got from George Colvin, Osceola: ballad of *Mill
Stream Camp,* composed in 1926 by Joe Twiss, Nate Bristol, and others
—I have fifteen stanzas; and the story of the bank-beaver. Fighting
bedbugs: Frances Mihill, Lake Placid, from A. Gordon Wilson. From
E. J. Grant, now of Glens Falls, come stories of Tug Hill, Old Charlie,

and the hazing. Ruth Tanner, Gloversville, got the story of Martin Kelly from her father. Emily Bain, Edmeston, brought from Ralph Potter, Hartwick, stories of Otsego lumbering. Mildred Kornmeyer brought the story of the peaveys from Lewis Grant, Boonville; the tale of Charlie's parrot from Frank Breen, Boonville. *Old Dan Tucker:* Mildred Tyler, Cochecton Center, from her father. *Frank Farrow:* Mary Bida from Mrs. L. H. De Forest, Sidney.

Rafting: The best account is Leslie C. Wood's *Rafting on the Delaware River*, 1934, to which I am indebted. I also got information from Mr. E. F. Weeks, born in 1858 and brought up in Deposit. Fred Mohrman of Hancock got information from Editor H. W. Wagner, Pierre De Nio, Lorin Leonard, and F. J. Littell. Stories of Appley: Lois Odwell, Downsville, from her father. From Mr. Wood the stories of Webb and Boney; from Mohrman the story of the rafters at the station. In 1928, a raft was run from Tyler's Switch, above Hancock, to Portland, Penn. In 1929, articles on rafting were published in the Hancock *Herald*.

CHAPTER XII. MOUNTAINEERS

This chapter has been read for corrections by Dr. John M. Sayles of Star Lake and Albany.

A. L. Donaldson's *A History of the Adirondacks*, 2 vols., 1921, is entertaining and has a good bibliography; R. M. L. Carson's *Peaks and People of the Adirondacks*, 1928, is full of information. I have the permission of the Adirondack Mountain Club to use information appearing in an admirable series about the guides, published in *High Spots*, the Club's periodical: articles by G. O. Webster with accounts of Sabael (Jan., '37), Sabbatis (April, '35), Cheney (Jan., '35), and Simonds (Jan., '35); articles by R. M. L. Carson about Sabael (July, '31), Emmons (July, '37), Cheney (Jan., '34); articles by R. V. Riley about Sabbatis (Oct., '34), Hoffman (Sept., '30), and Cheney (June, '30); article by H. W. Hicks about Rossman (Jan., '33); article about Herbert Clark (Oct., '33) by Bob Marshall.

Stories about Mart Moody: Mrs. Marjorie A. Cameron, from Seaver Miller, Saranac; G. R. Plumb, from George Colon, Saranac Lake; Ruth Freeman, from Joseph Downie, now of Albany. Jack Ashwood: Ruth Freeman, from Ida Ashwood, Syracuse, and from her grandfather; she also got stories of Ernest Wood. Ben Snyder: Leo Scott, from his mother, who heard Ben tell the tales at Carlisle. Bob Glassbrook: *Adirondack*

Arrow, anniversary ed., winter of 1938-9. Bill Rockwell: Bessie Stapleton, from her brother. Willard Howland: Hugh Flick, Albany. Van Hoevenberg: Mrs. M. A. Cameron, from Jed Rossman, Adir.Loj. Newell and Bonaparte: Mary M. Pappa, from a paper by Alta M. Ralph. *Allen's Bear Fight:* see excellent article by Dr. Edward Alexander in *High Spots,* January, 1939. Dance calls: Osborn, Eliz., "Country Dance Calls from the Catskill Mts.", in *American Speech,* III, 142-3 (1927). Corrections on Moody: P. H. McCarthy, Jr., Tupper Lake.

CHAPTER XIII. WARRIORS, COLONIAL AND REVOLUTIONARY

This chapter and the following have been read by Mr. Hugh M. Flick, Acting Director of the State Division of Archives and History.

The Schenectady Massacre: ballad in Watson, J. F., *Annals and Occurrences of N. Y. City and State, in the Olden Time,* 1846; for historical background see Munsell, Joel, *The Annals of Albany,* 2nd ed., 1871, vols. II and IV, also Schenectady county and city histories by Howells (1886), Yates (1902), and others.

A Lay of Our Ancient Valley, by Samuel Hand of Elizabethtown. See Brown, G. L., *Pleasant Valley,* 1905, where it is copied from the Elizabethtown *Post* of Oct. 17, 1851. The author is said to have been eighteen when he wrote the ballad. Edith Cutting got another version at Elizabethtown from the memory of Charles Jenkins.

Campbell of Inverawe: account from Parkman, Francis, *Montcalm and Wolfe,* 1884. See Richards, F. B., *The Black Watch at Ticonderoga,* n.d., reprinted as a book from Vol. X, *Proc. N. Y. State Hist. Ass'n.*

Brave Wolfe: from P. W. Andrew, Corinth, who knew another about Wolfe in 5 stanzas beginning, "King George and Louis could not agree".

Jane McCrea: ballad from Helen Nichols, Castleton, from her grandmother, Mrs. Ida Nichols. The original poem in Stone, W. L., *Ballads and Poems Relating to the Burgoyne Campaign,* 1893. Best account of Jane in Holden, J. A., *Influence of the Death of J. McC. on the Burgoyne Campaign,* 1912.

Ballad of Shell: from Campbell, W. W., *Annals of Tryon County,* in Appendix of 1924 ed. The songs from Orderly Books were checked from the MSS. in the State Library; they are excellently edited in Lauber, A. W., *Orderly Books of the Fourth N. Y. Regt., 1778-1780; The Second N. Y. Regt., 1780-83,* 1932. *Lady Washington:* in Douglass MS.

CHAPTER XIV. WARRIORS OF THE NEW NATION

War of 1812: *The Battle of Erie—1813,* from *Songs of the Sea,* n.d. Another account of the battle collected from memory is "Ye tars of Columbia". *James Bird:* I am indebted to Miss E. W. Piehl and Mrs. D. H. Curtis of Westfield for important information. See articles by C. B. Galbreath in the *Ohio Archaeological and Historical Quarterly* for October, 1911, and January, 1917; also an article by A. B. Culver in the Westfield *Republican* for Dec. 29, 1897. *The Noble Lads of Canada:* Edith Cutting's reconstruction has four stanzas not in a version sent me by Virginia Mason of Peru, from a copy that has come down through the Lewis family; Miss Mason's story is that the ballad was written on a peeled stump. The *Growler* and the *Eagle* had been captured by the British from the command of the American Lieut. Sydney Smith, and had been renamed the *Finch* and the *Chub.* One of the first British shots at the battle of Plattsburg smashed a coop on Macdonough's flagship, releasing a gamecock who flew to the mizzen and crowed—a good omen.

The Civil War:—*Ellsworth Avengers:* Janice Neal, from Seth Flint, Worcester, N. Y. Second stanza from a MS collection bought at Delanson. *Colonel Ellsworth:* Helen Nichols, Castleton, from her grandmother. The Drummond address: a copy is on deposit in the N. Y. State Library, Albany; for comparison with a Northern prison see Holmes, C. W., *The Elmira Prison Camp,* 1912. *The Cumberland's Crew:* from Blind Sam Taylor, Westfield. *Good-by, Jeff:* from Vivian Salisbury, Pulaski. *Jeff Davis's Ball:* from P. W. Andrew, Corinth. *Grafted into the Army* and *Uncle Sam's Funeral*: Iva E. Saxe, from Mrs. Robinson, Schenectady, who learned the second at Whitehall. Erie County secession: at hamlet of Town Line, in townships of Alden and Lancaster; on the vote, 80 were for Secession, 40 for the Union. *The People Are A-Coming* and *Lincoln and Liberty*: from *The Republican Campaign Songster of 1860,* edited by W. H. Burleigh, given me by Harry Woolf, Darien Center. Mr. Hays and Lincoln: this happened to the 14th N. Y. Volunteer Infantry in August, 1861, when they were encamped across the river from Georgetown, below Arlington. They had answered Lincoln's call for 75,000 volunteers for a service of three months; the State had enlisted them for two years and had turned them over to the Federal Government. They served bravely; Chancellorsville was their last battle before the two years expired. *O May This Fuss:* David Nelson from P. D. Morrison of Frewsburg, as dictated by his father, a veteran. It begins, "I am Yankee Doodle, Uncle Sam, of Freedom's mighty farm", and runs to thirty lines, of which I have rearranged a few as samples. Let me recommend Neeser, R. W., *American Naval Songs and Ballads,* 1938.

CHAPTER XV. BALLAD LOVERS: TRIALS AND TRAGEDY

The story of Jenny Lind needs to be checked with P. T. Barnum's *Struggles and Triumphs,* 1871, and with such a study as C. Wagenknecht's *Jenny Lind,* 1931. The diva was thirty years old when she arrived in New York on September 1, 1850; Goldschmidt arrived in May, 1851, and married her in February, 1852; her last American appearance was in New York on May 24, 1852. Barnum says that he really ceased to be her manager after the 93d concert, on June 9, 1851; she had given notice that she would terminate their arrangement after the hundredth. As for the Charleston episode—he says that they were in that city ten days and gave two concerts; they were waiting for the ship to Havana. He mentions the Christmas party, and also one on New Year's Eve when she stopped Burke's playing of the piano fifteen minutes before midnight in order that she might usher in the year properly, in meditative silence. Barnum is spiteful about the intrigues of her "secretary", whom he does not name. There is a letter of hers to Burke in 1853 (Wagenknecht, 140) in which she praises her husband, probably answering rumors that she was unhappy with him. She died in 1887.

Springfield Mountain: Chaut. County version, David Nelson, Frewsburg; Jefferson County, Mrs. A. H. Shearer from Wm. Nims, Chaumont; "Murry" version, Prof. Martha Pritchard who found words stuck in an old songster (1874) and traced them to G. A. Pritchard, originally from Bangor, Maine. The parody is from Mrs. G. V. Dillenbach, Slingerlands. Barry's article in *Bulletin of the Folk-Song Society of the Northeast,* No. 12, 1937. *The Frozen Girl:* first version from Eliz. Strong, from a copy made in 1872 for a sister of Mrs. Claflin of Hartman Hill; other version, Nelle Schmidt from Mrs. Rhoades, who learned it from her mother, Lucinda Dustin, on a farm near Malone. For Barry's article see preceding note.

Barbara Allan: first two versions from Vivian Salisbury, Pulaski, from Violet White and from Mrs. A. Hurd's scrapbook; third version, Douglass MS. *Lord Lovell:* first six stanzas and tenth, Edith Cutting from Mrs. Marcia W. Benedict, Lewis; stanzas 7-9, Mrs. L. L. Banker, Lewis. Next three from Douglass MS.: *The London Lawyer's Son, Caroline*

of Edinburgh Town, The Dawning of the Day. From Ruth C. Wright,
The Maid upon the Tide and *The Maid Freed from the Gallows*, from
her mother, from *her* mother, Mrs. F. Meiniker, Rensselaer. Wm.
Swackhamer brought *Wrapped in Red Flannels* from his mother, and
Drowsy Sleeper, second version, from Mrs. A. Saulpaugh, Troy.

Green Laurel: first version, Eleanor Cleland, from Lucy Smith, from
her mother, Mooers; second, N. M. Reynolds, Lansingburg, from Mrs.
White. *The Butcher's Boy:* first, Bettina Hanna, from Helen Hicks;
second, Rita Boire, from Mrs. T. Collins, Treadwells Mills. *The Jealous
Lover:* first, Vivian Salisbury, Pulaski, from her father; second, Eileen
Santry, from Mrs. Lee, Little Falls. *Drowsy Sleeper:* first, Eleanor
Waterbury Franz, from Jennie Decker, Dolgeville. *The Rabbi's Daughter:* Josephine M. Reilly, from Mrs. L. Broderick, Albany. *The London
Maid and Boy:* Martha Lopke, from Mrs. B. Dunham, Apalachin, who
learned it in Candor. *Lowlands Low:* Ruth Tanner, Gloversville, from
her mother, from *her* mother. *Twa Sisters:* Thelma Shatzel, from her
father, originally of Edmeston. *The Farmer's Daughter,* James Mack,
Clyde. *Bold Soldier:* V. Salisbury, Pulaski, from her father, from his
father. *I Went into Her Mother's House:* Sam Spector, from J. Froggett,
Binghamton. *The Lady Leroy:* Ina Young, from Mrs. May Shepard,
Northville.

Chapter XVI. Ballad Lovers: Comedy

Mantle So Green: V. Salisbury, Pulaski, from her father. *Lass of
Mohee:* G. W. Keenan, from Mrs. W. Sherman, Hague; *Mohee* was
Maui, Hawaii. *The Sailor and the Tailor:* Edith Cutting, from Mrs. Etta
Brewster, Peasleyville. *'Way Down in Maine:* Eileen MacDougall, from
Mrs. Eliz. M., Argyle; slight changes from version of Nettie Sessions,
from Mrs. L. Genter, Whitestown. *Grandmother's Advice:* from Janet
Dibble, Lynbrook. *The Courtship of Billy Grimes:* Mrs. J. Finch, from
Mrs. G. D. Kelley, Coeymans. *The Quaker's Wooing:* Betty Smith, from
Miss Clark, Spragueville. *With His Old Gray Beard:* first, Mildred
Tyler, from her father, Cochecton Center, who remembers it sung to
the rhythm of flails at threshing; second, Eleanor Cleland, Scotia, from
her grandmother. *The Young Man Who Wouldn't Hoe Corn:* Gladys
Rifenburg, from Mrs. H. C. Bennett, Troy, from her grandmother. *The
Pigs Did Squeal:* Thelma Shatzel, from Mrs. E. B. Holdridge, S. Edmes-
ton. *Katie Mora* and *Sparking Sunday Night:* Douglass MS. *Kate and*

Her Horns: E. J. Grant, GlensFalls; lines in brackets from Douglass MS. *The Lost Glove:* Constance McCoy, from Esther Mousley, from her father, Rev. Wm. M., of Hall, who had it from his grandfather, second son of Sir Thos. Mousley, a Captain at Waterloo; two lines in brackets from Douglass MS. *The Half-Hitch:* P. W. Andrew, Corinth. *The Buggery Boo:* from a gentleman at Potsdam. *The Cambric Shirt:* Louise Pitkin, Schroon Lake, from Morris Wilson, who learned it in a lumbercamp near Lake George. *That's So:* from a MS collection bought at Delanson. *Going to Salem:* Ray Belanger, from Walter Sawyer, Lawrenceville; the words used with permission of Irving Bacheller.

CHAPTER XVII. MURDERERS

The Three Thayers: ballads from the Museum of the Buffalo Historical Society. I have used a dissertation by Winifred C. Maloney, made under my direction at Cornell, *A Study of Folklore in Two Regions of New York State,* 1939. In the State Law Library are four pamphlets on the case, two dated 1825, two without date but probably of the same year. There is an article by N. Wilgus in the first volume of the *Pubs. of the Buffalo Hist. Soc.,* 1879. Miss Maloney used these and also contemporary newspapers.

The three drovers: R. Bain, Jr., Schenectady, from his great-grandmother. Peddler of Dresden: Eleanor R. Jones, Hudson Falls. Ballad about peddler: broadside kindly lent by Roscoe Martin, Forestville. Tomahawk Tree and Tommy Jimmy: Johnson, C., *Centennial History of Erie County,* 1876. Indian John ballad: broadside in Museum of the Seneca Falls Historical Society, used by courtesy of Miss Caroline Foote Lester. Antone family: the Broome County phase in Wilkinson, J. B., *The Annals of Binghamton,* 1872; Madison County incidents, Hammond, Mrs. L. M., *Hist. of Madison County,* 1872; also Teed, D. H., *The A. Murders in M. County,* 1935, reprinted from Syracuse newspaper. Red Jacket: W. L. Stone's biography, 1866 ed. *The Murdered Wife:* J. Cypher, Greenwich, from her grandmother, who learned it from her mother, who attended the sleighride. This has had the best study ever made of a New York ballad: Jones, L. C., "The Berlin Murder Case in Folklore and Ballad", in *New York History,* April, 1936, vol. XVII. Brown and Gillette ballad: Hugh Norton, from Frank Van Vranken, Gloversville. The murder was committed on July 11, 1906. Damon case:

Material at Mayville Museum, courtesy of the curator, J. J. Thompson.
The Cruel Mother (Child, 20): Mrs. Frances Ramsay, Lake George.

CHAPTER XVIII. PLACE-NAMES

This chapter has been read for me by Archivist A. J. F. Van Laer, who
was of great assistance also in my study of Dutch names. The best brief
discussion is the chapter on New York Place-Names in Volume X of
the *History of the State of New York*, 1937; Dr. Alexander C. Flick, the
general editor, wrote this chapter himself and furnished a useful bibliography. As authorities on Indian names I have used: Beauchamp, W. M.,
Aboriginal Place Names in New York, which is Bulletin 108 of the
State Museum, 1907; Tooker, W. W., *Indian Place Names on Long
Island and Islands Adjacent,* 1914; Ruttenber, E. M., *Indian Geographic
Names,* Vol. VI of the Proceedings of the N. Y. Hist. Soc., 1906; Bates,
Erl A., two articles in *Cornell Rural School Leaflets,* for Sept., 1930,
and Sept., 1928. I regret that the great number of names about which I
have written makes it impossible to list all those who assisted. If you
are amused by the pronunciation of names, see Holt, A. H., *American
Place Names,* 1938. I am dubious about some pronunciations myself;
for example, I doubt whether there can be said to exist a "standard"
pronunciation of *Onondaga*—certainly not at Syracuse, the big city of
the County.

CHAPTER XIX. PROVERBS

Here again I must regret that it is impossible to name the hundreds
of people who have contributed. The two largest and most interesting
collections were made by Nelle Schmidt in Oneida County, and by Doris
Coffin in Dutchess County. The Ontario County expressions were collected near Livonia by Marjorie Thomas. I find that I get more com-
munications from a radio audience regarding proverbs than I receive
when talking about any other subject. One well known stock-man wrote:
"Those sayings are a hundred per cent true. Bring the kids up on them."

INDEX

In this index will be found the titles of songs in *italics*, names of folk-heroes and heroines, and a few other significant names and topics. Limitation of space forbids listing any places except counties. The author hopes that a later edition may have a more complete index; meanwhile he provides two blank pages for the reader to use in making his own.

Abercrombie, General, 317, 321, 324
Albany County, 11, 102, 119, 148, 228, 229, 277, 368, 372, 387, 456, 463, 464, 467
Albany Jail, The, 229
Alexander, E. P., 478
Allegany County, 198, 451, 477, 491
Allen, Anson H., 293
Allen, Ethan, 284, 293
Allen's Bear Fight, 293
Almanacs, 152, 482
Andrew, P. W., 15, 138, 140, 153, 417
Animals, imaginary, 299
Antone family, 439
Appley, "Rit", 279, 282
As I rode Out, 153
Ashwood, Jack, 292
Attend, All Ye Drivers, 248

Baas the Baker, 102
Bacheller, Irving, 18, 423, 424
Bailey, Hachaliah, 157
Banks of the Dee, 337
Barbara Allan, 377
Barlow, Joel, 220
Barnum, P. T., 156, 368
Bates, Erl, 458
Battle of Erie, The, 342
Bears, 291-3
Beauchamp, W. M., 456-62
Bee, The, 339
Beldin, Capt. Hiram, 217
Bird, James, 206, 344

Black Rock Pork, 243
Blow, Boys, Blow, 209
Blow the Man Down, 209
Blue Mountain Lake, 267
Boatin' on a Bull-Head, 241
Boatman's Boy, The, 238
Bogardus, Ross, 143
Bold Pirates, The, 38
Bold Soldier, 397
Bonaparte, Joseph, 305
Boyd, Lieut., 46
Brant, Joseph, 178
Brant, Molly, 178
Brave Laffitte, The, 41
Brave Wolfe, 323
Broome County, 399, 439
Brown, John, of Ossawatomie, 302
Buggery Boo, The, 421
Bull, Sarah and William, 169
Bunyan, Paul, 129, 299
Burgoyne, Gen. John, 326-7
Burke, Joseph, 367
Burroughs, John, 284
Butcher's Boy, The, 387

Call, Joe, 142
Cambric Shirt, The, 422
Campbell, Duncan, 321
Canalman's Farewell, 246
Cape Horn, 196
Captain Kidd, 23
Captain Ward, 33
Cardiff Giant, 155

Carmer, Carl, 12, 17, 250
Caroline of Edinburgh Town, 383
Catholic missionaries, 472
Catskills, 284, 309
Cattaraugus County, 115, 180, 453
Cayuga County, 158, 171, 245, 247, 356, 451
Chapin, Cyrenius, 172
Chasse-galerie, 117
Chaumont, Comte Le Ray de, 305, 473
Chautauqua County, 9-11, 150, 167-8, 201, 277, 342, 344, 358, 366, 371, 432, 445, 457, 472, 474, 476
Chemung County, 356, 476
Chenango County, 81, 89, 162, 165, 167, 452, 455, 456, 467, 474, 483, 500
Cheney, John, 286, 288
Child ballads, 33, 37, 216, 377, 379, 393, 397, 447; 38, 163, 417, 422
Churches and churchmen, 158, 168, 169-70
Clark, Herbert, 299
Clinton County, 116, 144, 268, 348, 386, 473
Clinton, De Witt, 221, 297, 469
Coast of Peru, The, 194
Coffin family, 14, 190, 197
Cole, Cornelius, 150
Colgate University, 170, 469
Collins, Thomas, 226
Colon, George, 267
Colonel Ellsworth, 354
Columbia County, 41, 114, 119, 167, 197, 464, 479
Colvin, George, 273
Come, All Ye Bold Seamen, 194
Come, All You Old-timers, 267
Come On, My Hearts, 336
Connecticut, 105, 106, 107, 113, 220
Cook, "Wit", 165
Cooper, J. F., 18, 45, 64, 69, 286, 476
Copperheads, 362
Corey, Cal, 145
Cornell University, 12, 15
Cornplanter, Jesse, 102, 510
Cortland County, 155, 469
Courtship of Billy Grimes, 406
Cruel Mother, The, 447
Cumberland's Crew, The, 260, 358
Curses, 114

Damon, Joseph, 445
Dance at Clintonville, The, 264

Dancing, 308-10
Darling, John, 132, 250
Dauphin, the lost, 306, 473
Dawning of the Day, The, 384
Deacon's Ox, The, 159
Delaware County, 57, 60, 81, 109, 171, 176, 277, 475
Derby Ram, The, 153
Devil lore, 113, 115, 139
De Witt, Simeon, 468
Dickens, Charles, 451-2, 501
Douglass Ms., 14, 33, 216, 218, 340, 379, 424, 507, 512, 515, 521, 522, 523
Down by the Greenwood Side, 447
Down Bed, The, 211
Drowsy Sleeper, 390
Drummond, A. M., 12, 468, 506
Dutch, The, 102, 104, 143, 149, 462-8, 479
Dutchess County, 14, 19, 190, 199, 499, 500, 504

Eaton, Deacon M., 237
Edison Machine, The, 234
Edmonds, W. D., 18, 222, 250, 268
Edwards family, 182, 187, 188
Elder Bardee, 37
Ellicott, Joseph, 178
Ellsworth Avengers, 353
Emigrés, French, 305
Emmons, Ebenezar, 286
Epps, Lyman, 303-4
E- ri- e, 250
Erie County, 158, 166, 167, 172, 173, 178, 179, 221, 236, 237, 243, 362, 427, 436, 451, 467, 503
Essex County, 13, 142, 149, 165, 262, 263, 265, 268, 271, 272, 282, 293, 299, 302, 307, 380, 471, 477, 478, 480

Fair Charlotte, 374
Farmer's Daughter, The, 394
Fiddlers, 310
Flick, A. C., 454, 505
Flying Cloud, The, 39
Foster, Nat, 62
Frank Farrow, 275
Franklin County, 299, 300, 306, 377, 456
French-Canadians, 115, 130, 144, 272, 275, 299, 307
French names, 470, 471
Frost, Robert, 269, 491, 493

Frozen Girl, The, 374
Fulton County, 63, 68, 69, 114, 141, 159, 255, 390, 399, 443, 480

Gardiner, Lion, 184
Garlick, Goody, 106, 184
Gee, Aunt Sally, 171
Genesee County, 299, 367, 368, 457, 468, 488
Germans, 109, 119, 475
Ghost of Polly Rock, The, 210
Ghosts, 120, 126
Gillette, Chester, 443
Glassbrook, Bob, 295
God Save America, 338
Going to Salem, 423
Good-by, Jeff, 360
Grace Brown and Chester Gillette, 443
Grafted into the Army, 361
Grandmother's Advice, 405
Grant, Charlie, 269
Green Beds, 211
Green, H. G., 441
Greene County, 120, 158, 456
Greenfield, Bill and Abner, 136
Green Laurel, 386
Greenleaf, Aunty, 108
Griffon, 472

Half-Hitch, The, 417
Hall, Ralph and Mary, 105
Hamelin family, 116
Hamilton College, 11, 287, 302, 469, 504
Hamilton County, 271, 471
Handsome Harry, 209
Hard, Walter, 18, 269
Hark, Sweet Maid, 339
Harrison, Katharine, 107
Harum, David, 155, 181
Harvard University, 475, 479
Hash Is Fried, 245
Haunted Houses, 121
Hedrick, U. P., 17, 505
Hendrick, King, 177
Hendricks, Mrs. W., 505
Henry, Frank C., 16
Herkimer County, 64, 65, 67, 273, 308, 389, 390, 443, 476
Higbey, "Doc", 162
Hoffman, C. F., 286
Hopkins, "Rasters", 167
Horsemen, spectre, 119, 120

Horses and horse-traders, 155, 157, 158, 159, 161, 171, 180
Howland, Willard, 299
Hungerford, Edward, 17, 505

Indians, Chapter III, 101, 108, 113, 123-7, 156, 177-80, 183, 221, 284, 300, 312, 326, 436, 453
Indian John, 436
Ireland and the Irish, 17, 57, 222-3, 264, 279, 367, 470, 502
Irving, Washington, 21, 22, 45, 118, 128, 511
I've Travelled All Around, 244
I Went into Her Mother's House, 399

Jam on Gerry's Rock, The, 259
James Bird, 206, 344
Jane McCrea, 328
Jealous Lover, The, 388
Jeff Davis's Ball, 360
Jefferson County, 165, 209, 305, 371, 399, 407, 455, 473, 484
Jogues, St. Isaac, 471
Johnson, Sir John, 58, 177, 471
Johnson, Sir William, 48, 317, 471

Kanniff, "Naut", 104
Kate and Her Horns, 413
Katie Mora, 411
Kelly, Martin, 271
Kennebec Bite, The, 163
Kidd, Capt. William, 21 ff.
Kings County, 467
Kingston, Big John, 149
Kittredge, G. L., 12, 475

Lady Leroy, The, 399
Lady Washington, 340
Lafayette, Marquis de, 9, 428
Laffitte, pirate, 41
Lake George, 297, 298, 422
Lass of Mohee, The, 402
Lawyers and judges, 166-8
Lay Me on the Hoss-bridge, 246-7
Lay of the Ancient Valley, 318
Lewis County, 273, 305, 473, 477; see also Tug Hill
Life on the Raging Canal, A, 254
Lincoln, Abraham, 354, 363-6
Lincoln and Liberty, 364
Lind, Jenny, 367
Livingston County, 46

Livingston, Robert, 27
Logs, 192-3
Lomax, John and Alan, 12, 13, 18, 506, 516
London Lawyer's Son, The, 381
London Maid and Boy, The, 392
Long Island (Nassau and Suffolk Counties), 21 ff., 73, 77, 105, 108, 113, 147, 148, 172, Chapter VIII, 314, 357, 374, 455, 475, 478, 503
Loomis Gang, 81-100
Loper, James, 184
Lord Lovell, 379
Lost Glove, The, 416
Loup-garou, 115
Low Bridge, 249
Lowlands Low, 392
Lumberjacks' Dance, The, 263
Lumbermen's Alphabet, 262
Lumbermen's Song (from Newcomb), 265

Macdonough, Commodore Thomas, 348
Mack, James, 213, 394
Madison County, 81, 83, 84, 302, 306, 439, 467, 473
Maid Free from the Gallows, The, 397
Maid upon the Tide, The, 386
Manaho, legend of, 123
Mantle So Green, 401
Martineau, Harriet, 252
McCrea, Jane, 325
   ballad of, 328
Meacham, Col. T. S., 151
Melville, Herman, 183, 184
Mermaids, The, 216
Monitor, The, 357
Monroe County, 152, 179, 476
Montgomery County, 63, 64, 112, 457, 467, 474
Montour, "Queen" Catherine, 477
Montville, "Old Papineau", 308
Moody, Mart, 289
Morgan, Daniel, 57
Morley, Christopher, 16, 219, 469, 493
Most Tragical Account, A, 432
Mulford, "Fish-Hook", 185-6
Mulford, Prentice, 191
Munchausen, Baron, 129, 134
Murdered Wife, The, 441
Murphy, Tim, 51, 57 ff.
Myths, 125-6

Napoleon, 161
Nawisga, legend of, 125
Negroes, 18, 302, 303, 351
Never Tickle a Mule, 227
Newell, Hunter, 306
New Jersey, 57
Niagara County, 298, 458, 472
Nichols, Uncle John, 255
Noble Lads of Canada, The, 348

O May This Fuss, 366
Old Dan Tucker, 274
Oneida County, 43, 81, 85, 150, 162, 168, 176, 222, 336, 450, 460, 481, 501, 502, 504
Onondaga County, 155, 156, 225, 241, 460, 468, 470
Ontario County, 124, 451, 470, 503
Orange County, 53, 72, 162, 169, 171, 175, 310, 465, 478
Orleans County, 174, 471
Osborne, Goodwife, 172
Oswego County, 81, 82, 151, 469
Otsego County, 47, 57, 81, 123, 126, 145, 152, 158, 167, 170, 171, 176, 271, 353, 393, 410, 423, 478, 503

Paddy on the Canal, 223
Paddy Ryan's Victory, 232
Parker, A. C., 459, 505
Peddlers, 432
Pennsylvania, 57, 67, 342, 344, 450, 473
People Are A-Coming, The, 363
Perry, Commodore O. H., 342 ff.
Phelps, "Old Mountain", 287
Philadelphia, 277, 278
Pigs Did Squeal, The, 410
Pizen Sarpent, The, 370
Poetry on the Death of E. Crane, 436
Pound, Ezra, 11, 12, 85
Pound, Louise, 506
Prison camps, 356
Putnam County, 127

Quakers, 158, 171, 197
Quaker's Wooing, The, 407
Quick, Tom, 48 ff.
Quillan, "Boney", 279-82

Rabbi's Daughter, The, 391
Raging Canal, The, 238
Railroads, 278, 279, 281, 295

Red Jacket, 46, 173, 177, 178, 427, 436, 440
Rensselaer County, 110, 113, 114, 121, 125, 324, 356, 357, 386, 397, 441, 463, 464, 491
Riley, Jack (George Reily), 216
Roberts, Kenneth, 18
Rockland County, 73, 104, 466
Rockwell, Bill, 296
Rogers, Ranger Robert, 317
Root, Counsellor John, 166
Root, Elihu, 504
Rossman, Jed, 289
'Round Cape Horn, 195
Ruttenber, E. M., 458
Ryan, Paddy, 230-34

Sabael, 285
Sabbatis, Mitchell, 285, 456
Sailor and His Bride, The, 217
Sailor and the Tailor, The, 403
Sailor Boy, The, 214
Sailors' Alphabet, The, 194
St. Lawrence County, 64, 131, 149, 299, 421, 423, 469, 470, 498
Sally Brown, 193
Sandburg, Carl, 19, 249, 250, 488, 493, 506
Saranac River, 282
Saratoga County, 15, 57, 63, 68, 136, 144, 153, 226, 227, 354, 417
Schenectady County, 112, 125, 312, 432, 452, 455, 457, 463, 464, 470
Schenectady, The Burning of, 193, 314
Schermerhorn, Symon, 314
Schoharie County, 57, 81, 110, 161, 168, 463, 475
Schuyler County, 473
Scotland and Scots, 26, 36, 118, 137, 143, 279, 470, 486, 498, 504
Scouten, Capt. Ed., 236
Scythe-tree, 353
Seneca County, 158, 224, 353, 436, 461
Sessions, "Black", 168
Shanty-Boy, The, 256
Shanty-Girl, The, 258
Shell, J. C. (ballad of), 323
Sidecut, 229, 234
Siege of Plattsburg, The, 352
Simonds, Elijah, 287
Skinner, "Admiral", 277
Slang, of lumbermen, 267; of whalers, 199

Smith, Claudius, 72 ff.
Smith, Seba, 374
Snakes, 297
Snyder, Ben, 295
Somes, "Whispering", 149
Song of the Time, A, 430
So Pull in Your Towline, 246
Sparking Sunday Night, 424
Springfield Mountain, 370
Steuben, Baron, 476
Steuben County, 180, 476, 477
Stevenson, R. L., 321
Stoner, Nick, 68
Stryker, M. W., 12
Sullivan County, 49, 80, 81, 132, 274, 280, 408
Sullivan, J. L., 233
Swiss, 476

Tall Tales, Chapter VI, 191, 200, 268 ff., 289, 299
Tandy, "King", 180
Taylor, "Blind Sam", 201-9
Tebo (Thibault), 275
That's So, 423
Thayers, The Three, 427
There Was an Old Soldier, 363
Thomas, Richard, 113
Three Pirates, 43
Tioga County, 392, 451, 453, 455, 462, 478
Tollgates, 162
Tompkins County, 75, 104, 453, 468
Tooker, W. W., 458
Treasure, hidden, 21, 300
Tricksters, Chapter VII, 272, 281
Tug Hill, 267, 269, 273
Twa Sisters, The, 393

Ulster County, 56, 93, 148, 452, 463, 464, 467, 472
Uncle Sam's Funeral, 362

Van Dam, Rombout, 466
Van Hoevenberg, Henry, 300
Van Laer, A. J. F., 463, 464
Van Loan, "Add", 279
Vermont, 18, 85, 143, 284, 303
Vroman, Adam, 313
Vroman, Colonel 59

Walloons 472
Ward, Captain, 33

Warner, C. D., 287
Warren County, 113, 141, 165, 296, 374, 452
Washington County, 113, 149, 326, 362, 404, 432, 463, 500
Washington, George, 172, 340
'Way Down in Maine, 404
Wayne County, 153, 213, 294, 394
Webb, Major, 279
Weiser, Conrad, 177-8
We Sailed Around, 280
Westchester County, 105, 107, 119, 157, 171, 172, 175, 452, 467, 472
Westcott, E. N., 155
Wilkinson, Jemima, 178
Williams, Eleazar, 306-7, 473
Williamson, Charles, 477

Wimett, Capt. J., 245-6
Witches, 103-13
With His Old Gray Beard, 408
Wolfe, Gen. James, 322
Wood, Ernest, 294
Wood, Grant, 493
Woollcott, Alexander, 12, 17, 428
Wrapped in Red Flannels, 386
Wreck of the "Albion", The, 204
Wyoming County, 14, 379, 462

Yankee Doodle, 324
Yankee Ship, A, 219
Yates County, 450
Young Man Who Wouldn't Hoe Corn, The, 409
You Yacht on the Hudson, 246

A CATALOG OF SELECTED
DOVER BOOKS
IN ALL FIELDS OF INTEREST

A CATALOG OF SELECTED DOVER
BOOKS IN ALL FIELDS OF INTEREST

DRAWINGS OF REMBRANDT, edited by Seymour Slive. Updated Lippmann, Hofstede de Groot edition, with definitive scholarly apparatus. All portraits, biblical sketches, landscapes, nudes. Oriental figures, classical studies, together with selection of work by followers. 550 illustrations. Total of 630pp. 9⅛ × 12¼.
21485-0, 21486-9 Pa., Two-vol. set $25.00

GHOST AND HORROR STORIES OF AMBROSE BIERCE, Ambrose Bierce. 24 tales vividly imagined, strangely prophetic, and decades ahead of their time in technical skill: "The Damned Thing," "An Inhabitant of Carcosa," "The Eyes of the Panther," "Moxon's Master," and 20 more. 199pp. 5⅜ × 8½. 20767-6 Pa. $3.95

ETHICAL WRITINGS OF MAIMONIDES, Maimonides. Most significant ethical works of great medieval sage, newly translated for utmost precision, readability. Laws Concerning Character Traits, Eight Chapters, more. 192pp. 5⅜ × 8½.
24522-5 Pa. $4.50

THE EXPLORATION OF THE COLORADO RIVER AND ITS CANYONS, J. W. Powell. Full text of Powell's 1,000-mile expedition down the fabled Colorado in 1869. Superb account of terrain, geology, vegetation, Indians, famine, mutiny, treacherous rapids, mighty canyons, during exploration of last unknown part of continental U.S. 400pp. 5⅜ × 8½. 20094-9 Pa. $6.95

HISTORY OF PHILOSOPHY, Julián Marías. Clearest one-volume history on the market. Every major philosopher and dozens of others, to Existentialism and later. 505pp. 5⅜ × 8½. 21739-6 Pa. $8.50

ALL ABOUT LIGHTNING, Martin A. Uman. Highly readable non-technical survey of nature and causes of lightning, thunderstorms, ball lightning, St. Elmo's Fire, much more. Illustrated. 192pp. 5⅜ × 8½. 25237-X Pa. $5.95

SAILING ALONE AROUND THE WORLD, Captain Joshua Slocum. First man to sail around the world, alone, in small boat. One of great feats of seamanship told in delightful manner. 67 illustrations. 294pp. 5⅜ × 8½. 20326-3 Pa. $4.95

LETTERS AND NOTES ON THE MANNERS, CUSTOMS AND CONDITIONS OF THE NORTH AMERICAN INDIANS, George Catlin. Classic account of life among Plains Indians: ceremonies, hunt, warfare, etc. 312 plates. 572pp. of text. 6⅛ × 9¼. 22118-0, 22119-9 Pa. Two-vol. set $15.90

ALASKA: The Harriman Expedition, 1899, John Burroughs, John Muir, et al. Informative, engrossing accounts of two-month, 9,000-mile expedition. Native peoples, wildlife, forests, geography, salmon industry, glaciers, more. Profusely illustrated. 240 black-and-white line drawings. 124 black-and-white photographs. 3 maps. Index. 576pp. 5⅜ × 8½. 25109-8 Pa. $11.95

THE BOOK OF BEASTS: Being a Translation from a Latin Bestiary of the Twelfth
Century, T. H. White. Wonderful catalog real and fanciful beasts: manticore,
griffin, phoenix, amphivius, jaculus, many more. White's witty erudite commentary on scientific, historical aspects. Fascinating glimpse of medieval mind.
Illustrated. 296pp. 5⅜ × 8¼. (Available in U.S. only)   24609-4 Pa. $5.95

FRANK LLOYD WRIGHT: ARCHITECTURE AND NATURE With 160
Illustrations, Donald Hoffmann. Profusely illustrated study of influence of
nature—especially prairie—on Wright's designs for Fallingwater, Robie House,
Guggenheim Museum, other masterpieces. 96pp. 9¼ × 10¾.   25098-9 Pa. $7.95

FRANK LLOYD WRIGHT'S FALLINGWATER, Donald Hoffmann. Wright's
famous waterfall house: planning and construction of organic idea. History of site,
owners, Wright's personal involvement. Photographs of various stages of building.
Preface by Edgar Kaufmann, Jr. 100 illustrations. 112pp. 9¼ × 10.
                                                               23671-4 Pa. $7.95

YEARS WITH FRANK LLOYD WRIGHT: Apprentice to Genius, Edgar Tafel.
Insightful memoir by a former apprentice presents a revealing portrait of Wright
the man, the inspired teacher, the greatest American architect. 372 black-and-white
illustrations. Preface. Index. vi + 228pp. 8¼ × 11.   24801-1 Pa. $9.95

THE STORY OF KING ARTHUR AND HIS KNIGHTS, Howard Pyle.
Enchanting version of King Arthur fable has delighted generations with imaginative narratives of exciting adventures and unforgettable illustrations by the author.
41 illustrations. xviii + 313pp. 6⅛ × 9¼.   21445-1 Pa. $5.95

THE GODS OF THE EGYPTIANS, E. A. Wallis Budge. Thorough coverage of
numerous gods of ancient Egypt by foremost Egyptologist. Information on
evolution of cults, rites and gods; the cult of Osiris; the Book of the Dead and its
rites; the sacred animals and birds; Heaven and Hell; and more. 956pp. 6⅛ × 9¼.
                                               22055-9, 22056-7 Pa., Two-vol. set $21.90

A THEOLOGICO-POLITICAL TREATISE, Benedict Spinoza. Also contains
unfinished *Political Treatise*. Great classic on religious liberty, theory of government on common consent. R. Elwes translation. Total of 421pp. 5⅜ × 8½.
                                                               20249-6 Pa. $6.95

INCIDENTS OF TRAVEL IN CENTRAL AMERICA, CHIAPAS, AND YU-
CATAN, John L. Stephens. Almost single-handed discovery of Maya culture;
exploration of ruined cities, monuments, temples; customs of Indians. 115
drawings. 892pp. 5⅜ × 8½.   22404-X, 22405-8 Pa., Two-vol. set $15.90

LOS CAPRICHOS, Francisco Goya. 80 plates of wild, grotesque monsters and
caricatures. Prado manuscript included. 183pp. 6⅛ × 9⅜.   22384-1 Pa. $4.95

AUTOBIOGRAPHY: The Story of My Experiments with Truth, Mohandas K.
Gandhi. Not hagiography, but Gandhi in his own words. Boyhood, legal studies,
purification, the growth of the Satyagraha (nonviolent protest) movement. Critical,
inspiring work of the man who freed India. 480pp. 5⅜ × 8½. (Available in U.S. only)
                                                               24593-4 Pa. $6.95

ILLUSTRATED DICTIONARY OF HISTORIC ARCHITECTURE, edited by Cyril M. Harris. Extraordinary compendium of clear, concise definitions for over 5,000 important architectural terms complemented by over 2,000 line drawings. Covers full spectrum of architecture from ancient ruins to 20th-century Modernism. Preface. 592pp. 7½ × 9⅜. 24444-X Pa. $14.95

THE NIGHT BEFORE CHRISTMAS, Clement Moore. Full text, and woodcuts from original 1848 book. Also critical, historical material. 19 illustrations. 40pp. 4⅝ × 6. 22797-9 Pa. $2.50

THE LESSON OF JAPANESE ARCHITECTURE: 165 Photographs, Jiro Harada. Memorable gallery of 165 photographs taken in the 1930's of exquisite Japanese homes of the well-to-do and historic buildings. 13 line diagrams. 192pp. 8⅜ × 11¼. 24778-3 Pa. $8.95

THE AUTOBIOGRAPHY OF CHARLES DARWIN AND SELECTED LETTERS, edited by Francis Darwin. The fascinating life of eccentric genius composed of an intimate memoir by Darwin (intended for his children); commentary by his son, Francis; hundreds of fragments from notebooks, journals, papers; and letters to and from Lyell, Hooker, Huxley, Wallace and Henslow. xi + 365pp. 5⅜ × 8. 20479-0 Pa. $5.95

WONDERS OF THE SKY: Observing Rainbows, Comets, Eclipses, the Stars and Other Phenomena, Fred Schaaf. Charming, easy-to-read poetic guide to all manner of celestial events visible to the naked eye. Mock suns, glories, Belt of Venus, more. Illustrated. 299pp. 5¼ × 8¼. 24402-4 Pa. $7.95

BURNHAM'S CELESTIAL HANDBOOK, Robert Burnham, Jr. Thorough guide to the stars beyond our solar system. Exhaustive treatment. Alphabetical by constellation: Andromeda to Cetus in Vol. 1; Chamaeleon to Orion in Vol. 2; and Pavo to Vulpecula in Vol. 3. Hundreds of illustrations. Index in Vol. 3. 2,000pp. 6⅛ × 9¼. 23567-X, 23568-8, 23673-0 Pa., Three-vol. set $37.85

STAR NAMES: Their Lore and Meaning, Richard Hinckley Allen. Fascinating history of names various cultures have given to constellations and literary and folkloristic uses that have been made of stars. Indexes to subjects. Arabic and Greek names. Biblical references. Bibliography. 563pp. 5⅜ × 8½. 21079-0 Pa. $7.95

THIRTY YEARS THAT SHOOK PHYSICS: The Story of Quantum Theory, George Gamow. Lucid, accessible introduction to influential theory of energy and matter. Careful explanations of Dirac's anti-particles, Bohr's model of the atom, much more. 12 plates. Numerous drawings. 240pp. 5⅜ × 8½. 24895-X Pa. $4.95

CHINESE DOMESTIC FURNITURE IN PHOTOGRAPHS AND MEASURED DRAWINGS, Gustav Ecke. A rare volume, now affordably priced for antique collectors, furniture buffs and art historians. Detailed review of styles ranging from early Shang to late Ming. Unabridged republication. 161 black-and-white drawings, photos. Total of 224pp. 8⅜ × 11¼. (Available in U.S. only) 25171-3 Pa. $12.95

VINCENT VAN GOGH: A Biography, Julius Meier-Graefe. Dynamic, penetrating study of artist's life, relationship with brother, Theo, painting techniques, travels, more. Readable, engrossing. 160pp. 5⅜ × 8½. (Available in U.S. only) 25253-1 Pa. $3.95

HOW TO WRITE, Gertrude Stein. Gertrude Stein claimed anyone could understand her unconventional writing—here are clues to help. Fascinating improvisations, language experiments, explanations illuminate Stein's craft and the art of writing. Total of 414pp. 4⅜ × 6⅜. 23144-5 Pa. $5.95

ADVENTURES AT SEA IN THE GREAT AGE OF SAIL: Five Firsthand Narratives, edited by Elliot Snow. Rare true accounts of exploration, whaling, shipwreck, fierce natives, trade, shipboard life, more. 33 illustrations. Introduction. 353pp. 5⅜ × 8½. 25177-2 Pa. $7.95

THE HERBAL OR GENERAL HISTORY OF PLANTS, John Gerard. Classic descriptions of about 2,850 plants—with over 2,700 illustrations—includes Latin and English names, physical descriptions, varieties, time and place of growth, more. 2,706 illustrations. xlv + 1,678pp. 8½ × 12¼. 23147-X Cloth. $75.00

DOROTHY AND THE WIZARD IN OZ, L. Frank Baum. Dorothy and the Wizard visit the center of the Earth, where people are vegetables, glass houses grow and Oz characters reappear. Classic sequel to *Wizard of Oz*. 256pp. 5⅜ × 8. 24714-7 Pa. $4.95

SONGS OF EXPERIENCE: Facsimile Reproduction with 26 Plates in Full Color, William Blake. This facsimile of Blake's original "Illuminated Book" reproduces 26 full-color plates from a rare 1826 edition. Includes "The Tyger," "London," "Holy Thursday," and other immortal poems. 26 color plates. Printed text of poems. 48pp. 5¼ × 7. 24636-1 Pa. $3.50

SONGS OF INNOCENCE, William Blake. The first and most popular of Blake's famous "Illuminated Books," in a facsimile edition reproducing all 31 brightly colored plates. Additional printed text of each poem. 64pp. 5¼ × 7. 22764-2 Pa. $3.50

PRECIOUS STONES, Max Bauer. Classic, thorough study of diamonds, rubies, emeralds, garnets, etc.: physical character, occurrence, properties, use, similar topics. 20 plates, 8 in color. 94 figures. 659pp. 6⅛ × 9¼. 21910-0, 21911-9 Pa., Two-vol. set $15.90

ENCYCLOPEDIA OF VICTORIAN NEEDLEWORK, S. F. A. Caulfeild and Blanche Saward. Full, precise descriptions of stitches, techniques for dozens of needlecrafts—most exhaustive reference of its kind. Over 800 figures. Total of 679pp. 8⅛ × 11. Two volumes. Vol. 1 22800-2 Pa. $11.95
Vol. 2 22801-0 Pa. $11.95

THE MARVELOUS LAND OF OZ, L. Frank Baum. Second Oz book, the Scarecrow and Tin Woodman are back with hero named Tip, Oz magic. 136 illustrations. 287pp. 5⅜ × 8½. 20692-0 Pa. $5.95

WILD FOWL DECOYS, Joel Barber. Basic book on the subject, by foremost authority and collector. Reveals history of decoy making and rigging, place in American culture, different kinds of decoys, how to make them, and how to use them. 140 plates. 156pp. 7⅞ × 10¾. 20011-6 Pa. $8.95

HISTORY OF LACE, Mrs. Bury Palliser. Definitive, profusely illustrated chronicle of lace from earliest times to late 19th century. Laces of Italy, Greece, England, France, Belgium, etc. Landmark of needlework scholarship. 266 illustrations. 672pp. 6⅛ × 9¼. 24742-2 Pa. $14.95

ILLUSTRATED GUIDE TO SHAKER FURNITURE, Robert Meader. All furniture and appurtenances, with much on unknown local styles. 235 photos. 146pp. 9 × 12. 22819-3 Pa. $7.95

WHALE SHIPS AND WHALING: A Pictorial Survey, George Francis Dow. Over 200 vintage engravings, drawings, photographs of barks, brigs, cutters, other vessels. Also harpoons, lances, whaling guns, many other artifacts. Comprehensive text by foremost authority. 207 black-and-white illustrations. 288pp. 6 × 9. 24808-9 Pa. $8.95

THE BERTRAMS, Anthony Trollope. Powerful portrayal of blind self-will and thwarted ambition includes one of Trollope's most heartrending love stories. 497pp. 5⅜ × 8½. 25119-5 Pa. $8.95

ADVENTURES WITH A HAND LENS, Richard Headstrom. Clearly written guide to observing and studying flowers and grasses, fish scales, moth and insect wings, egg cases, buds, feathers, seeds, leaf scars, moss, molds, ferns, common crystals, etc.—all with an ordinary, inexpensive magnifying glass. 209 exact line drawings aid in your discoveries. 220pp. 5⅜ × 8½. 23330-8 Pa. $4.50

RODIN ON ART AND ARTISTS, Auguste Rodin. Great sculptor's candid, wide-ranging comments on meaning of art; great artists; relation of sculpture to poetry, painting, music; philosophy of life, more. 76 superb black-and-white illustrations of Rodin's sculpture, drawings and prints. 119pp. 8⅜ × 11¼. 24487-3 Pa. $6.95

FIFTY CLASSIC FRENCH FILMS, 1912–1982: A Pictorial Record, Anthony Slide. Memorable stills from Grand Illusion, Beauty and the Beast, Hiroshima, Mon Amour, many more. Credits, plot synopses, reviews, etc. 160pp. 8¼ × 11. 25256-6 Pa. $11.95

THE PRINCIPLES OF PSYCHOLOGY, William James. Famous long course complete, unabridged. Stream of thought, time perception, memory, experimental methods; great work decades ahead of its time. 94 figures. 1,391pp. 5⅜ × 8½. 20381-6, 20382-4 Pa., Two-vol. set $19.90

BODIES IN A BOOKSHOP, R. T. Campbell. Challenging mystery of blackmail and murder with ingenious plot and superbly drawn characters. In the best tradition of British suspense fiction. 192pp. 5⅜ × 8½. 24720-1 Pa. $3.95

CALLAS: PORTRAIT OF A PRIMA DONNA, George Jellinek. Renowned commentator on the musical scene chronicles incredible career and life of the most controversial, fascinating, influential operatic personality of our time. 64 black-and-white photographs. 416pp. 5⅜ × 8¼. 25047-4 Pa. $7.95

GEOMETRY, RELATIVITY AND THE FOURTH DIMENSION, Rudolph Rucker. Exposition of fourth dimension, concepts of relativity as Flatland characters continue adventures. Popular, easily followed yet accurate, profound. 141 illustrations. 133pp. 5⅜ × 8½. 23400-2 Pa. $3.50

HOUSEHOLD STORIES BY THE BROTHERS GRIMM, with pictures by Walter Crane. 53 classic stories—Rumpelstiltskin, Rapunzel, Hansel and Gretel, the Fisherman and his Wife, Snow White, Tom Thumb, Sleeping Beauty, Cinderella, and so much more—lavishly illustrated with original 19th century drawings. 114 illustrations. x + 269pp. 5⅜ × 8½. 21080-4 Pa. $4.50

CATALOG OF DOVER BOOKS

AMERICAN CLIPPER SHIPS: 1833–1858, Octavius T. Howe & Frederick C. Matthews. Fully-illustrated, encyclopedic review of 352 clipper ships from the period of America's greatest maritime supremacy. Introduction. 109 halftones. 5 black-and-white line illustrations. Index. Total of 928pp. 5⅜ × 8½.
25115-2, 25116-0 Pa., Two-vol. set $17.90

TOWARDS A NEW ARCHITECTURE, Le Corbusier. Pioneering manifesto by great architect, near legendary founder of "International School." Technical and aesthetic theories, views on industry, economics, relation of form to function, "mass-production spirit," much more. Profusely illustrated. Unabridged translation of 13th French edition. Introduction by Frederick Etchells. 320pp. 6⅛ × 9¼. (Available in U.S. only)
25023-7 Pa. $8.95

THE BOOK OF KELLS, edited by Blanche Cirker. Inexpensive collection of 32 full-color, full-page plates from the greatest illuminated manuscript of the Middle Ages, painstakingly reproduced from rare facsimile edition. Publisher's Note. Captions. 32pp. 9⅜ × 12¼.
24345-1 Pa. $4.95

BEST SCIENCE FICTION STORIES OF H. G. WELLS, H. G. Wells. Full novel The Invisible Man, plus 17 short stories: "The Crystal Egg," "Aepyornis Island," "The Strange Orchid," etc. 303pp. 5⅜ × 8½. (Available in U.S. only)
21531-8 Pa. $4.95

AMERICAN SAILING SHIPS: Their Plans and History, Charles G. Davis. Photos, construction details of schooners, frigates, clippers, other sailcraft of 18th to early 20th centuries—plus entertaining discourse on design, rigging, nautical lore, much more. 137 black-and-white illustrations. 240pp. 6⅛ × 9¼.
24658-2 Pa. $5.95

ENTERTAINING MATHEMATICAL PUZZLES, Martin Gardner. Selection of author's favorite conundrums involving arithmetic, money, speed, etc., with lively commentary. Complete solutions. 112pp. 5⅜ × 8½.
25211-6 Pa. $2.95

THE WILL TO BELIEVE, HUMAN IMMORTALITY, William James. Two books bound together. Effect of irrational on logical, and arguments for human immortality. 402pp. 5⅜ × 8½.
20291-7 Pa. $7.50

THE HAUNTED MONASTERY and THE CHINESE MAZE MURDERS, Robert Van Gulik. 2 full novels by Van Gulik continue adventures of Judge Dee and his companions. An evil Taoist monastery, seemingly supernatural events; overgrown topiary maze that hides strange crimes. Set in 7th-century China. 27 illustrations. 328pp. 5⅜ × 8½.
23502-5 Pa. $5.95

CELEBRATED CASES OF JUDGE DEE (DEE GOONG AN), translated by Robert Van Gulik. Authentic 18th-century Chinese detective novel; Dee and associates solve three interlocked cases. Led to Van Gulik's own stories with same characters. Extensive introduction. 9 illustrations. 237pp. 5⅜ × 8½.
23337-5 Pa. $4.95

Prices subject to change without notice.
Available at your book dealer or write for free catalog to Dept. GI, Dover Publications, Inc., 31 East 2nd St., Mineola, N.Y. 11501. Dover publishes more than 175 books each year on science, elementary and advanced mathematics, biology, music, art, literary history, social sciences and other areas.